THE FOUNDATIONS OF EUROPEAN TRANSNATIONAL PRIVATE LAW

This collection identifies and assesses the place and role of EU private law, beyond the EU marketplace, but within the transnational market. It explores the current and potential implications of the external reach of European private law at both a substantive and normative level. Contributions from a team of experts relate the external dimension of European regulatory private law to two discussion points: its concrete contribution to different sectors of transnational markets; and its relevance to contemporary legal conceptions of transnational law and ordering. This allows the book to set out the role of European private law in the global political economy.

The Future of Private Law

Series Editors

Marija Bartl, Anna Beckers, Simon Deakin, Daniel Markovits and Hans-W Micklitz

A new wave of scholarship is remaking and invigorating private law. Legal regimes that were long understood as invisible systems of technical rules governing purely private relations are being reconsidered in their social, economic, and political context. This scholarly trend interacts with three major developments in 20th century private law. First, private law itself has undergone a series of fundamental transformation. Openly public and political values were inserted into private law regimes both before and immediately after 1945, only to be rejected in favour of a purported re-privatisation of law and society alike in the heyday of neoliberalism. Neoliberalism itself is now subject to increasingly intense critique, under the mounting pressure of multiple social and environmental crises. Second, private law has had to respond to fundamental transformations in the global economy, which have simultaneously placed inherited legal orders under economic and political pressure, and denaturalized previously unquestioned doctrinal arrangements. And, third, private law has been challenged by the call for and recognition of legal pluralism as a constitutive feature of legal systems.

Legislatures and courts, responding to these forces, have relied on private law to achieve openly moral ends, such as social justice, gender and ethnic equality, and more recently, sustainability, climate change and intergenerational justice, as well as adaptation to a digitalized economy and society. Scholars have similarly begun to observe the regulatory character of private law, its connection to public values, and even its 'constitutionalisation'. These developments blur the boundaries between what has been perceived as the 'classical' private law of the nineteenth century and the new regulatory private law of the twentieth. Along the way, they are redefining the relation between private law, societal values, and political objectives. Even 'classical', formal, or, as it is sometimes labelled, 'neutral' private law, is becoming inflected with political objectives. The possibility that the basic concepts that traditional private law scholarship deploys could themselves be related to hegemonies based on race, gender, or class, or the outcome of colonial imaginaries and interests, only reinforces the importance of unmasking the supposedly neutral or technical quality of private law. All these developments suggest that private law will in the future become even more clearly interwoven with normative objectives and societal claims. The question of which values will infuse private law therefore becomes unavoidable.

Changes in the economic regime that private law governs – both domestically and at a global scale – are reinforcing the need for new approaches. Within countries, private actors (including civil society organisations, trade and industry groups, and even individual firms) have gained the power to influence law-making and legal enforcement, and to create their own regulatory orders. Private forms of rule-making and administration have therefore become a part of private law, both by constraining the state from making effective law, and by empowering non-state actors to use law as a tool for promoting private interests. Moreover, across countries, a liberal commercial order that once purported to separate international economic law from domestic private law has been displaced by a transnational commercial regime that openly confers on private law a central role in global economic arrangements. Digital technologies, and the new forms of regulation that they enable – including in particular data- and code-driven regimes that fuse legal regulation with technical infrastructure and interfaces – further reinforce these trends. These new forms of digital governance threaten the state's traditional monopoly over legal regulation, while breaking down the legal categories through which private law has traditionally constrained state over-reach. In short: non-state actors have increasingly used private law for their own increasingly political ends, and states have sought to shape nominally private economic arrangements in order to promote national economic and geopolitical interests. Critical legal scholarship is beginning to expose the ways in which these developments within private law are not simply failing to address inequalities of resources and power, but actively perpetuating them.

Such developments are not entirely new, but they were previously confined to the borders of private law. Now, under new conditions, they appear in a vivid and insistent light. Together, these developments demand a new orientation from private law and place private law scholarship at the centre of the broader development of legal thought. The objective of this series is to publish books that answer this call.

This objective requires the series to embrace a broad understanding of private law, which combines the traditional core of private law with regulatory private law and its interaction with international economic law and legal pluralism. Substantively, the series stresses the need to think through the future of private law and to understand anew its pillars, modules, and institutions, including its most fundamental conceptions of the person, contract, tort, and property. The series will also pay close regard to legal process, by attending to interactions among the several national private law orders and between domestic and transnational law. To this end it will aim to analyse the relationships among different levels of legislation and between law, private regulation and technology. It will also pay close attention to the way private law is made to work in practice through a variety of public and private enforcement mechanisms, on the part not just of the executive and judiciary, but via non-state actors.

Methodologically, the series is committed to exploring the breadth and depth of the challenges private law is facing from the perspective of multiple disciplines. We expect the series to reflect the growing debate about exactly what doctrinal method consists of, as part of which a comparison of legal methods with those of other disciplines is becoming increasingly necessary. Thus not just the paradigms of other disciplines in the human and social sciences, but the methods they typically employ, ranging from statistical and other quantitative approaches to the ethnographies used in fieldwork and the hermeneutic techniques employed in the analysis of texts, will be of interest. Contributions from scholars engaged in critical analysis of inequalities and power relations, associated with race, gender and class among other categories, are among those we particularly welcome, as are contributions from legal researchers engaging with the data sciences across a broad range of applications, including but not limited to those associated with artificial intelligence. Our hope for the series is that it will expand the boundaries of private law scholarship as conventionally understood, while retaining the coherence necessary for private law as both discipline and practice.

The Foundations of European Transnational Private Law

Edited by
Anna Beckers
Hans-W Micklitz
Rodrigo Vallejo
and
Pia Letto-Vanamo

• HART •
OXFORD • LONDON • NEW YORK • NEW DELHI • SYDNEY

HART PUBLISHING

Bloomsbury Publishing Plc

Kemp House, Chawley Park, Cumnor Hill, Oxford, OX2 9PH, UK

1385 Broadway, New York, NY 10018, USA

29 Earlsfort Terrace, Dublin 2, Ireland

HART PUBLISHING, the Hart/Stag logo, BLOOMSBURY and the Diana logo are trademarks of Bloomsbury Publishing Plc

First published in Great Britain 2024

A catalogue record for this book is available from the British Library.

A catalogue record for this book is available from the Library of Congress.

Library of Congress Control Number: 2024931657

ISBN: HB: 978-1-50996-292-1
ePDF: 978-1-50996-294-5
ePub: 978-1-50996-293-8

Typeset by Compuscript Ltd, Shannon

Table of Contents

List of Contributors

Anna Beckers, Professor of Private Law and Social Theory, Faculty of Law, Maastricht University.

Anna Chadwick, Senior Lecturer, School of Law, University of Glasgow.

Klaas Hendrik Eller, Assistant Professor, Faculty of Law, University of Amsterdam.

Pia Letto-Vanamo, Professor emerita, Faculty of Law, University of Helsinki.

Ulla Liukkunen, Professor of Labour Law and Private International Law, Faculty of Law, University of Helsinki.

Antonio Marcacci, Senior Compliance Expert at an EU Global Systemically Important Bank and Lecturer (*Lehrbeauftragter*) at Leipzig University and at Passau University, Germany.

Mislav Mataija, Member of the Legal Service, European Commission.

Hans-W Micklitz, Professor of Economic Law, Robert Schuman Centre, European University Institute.

Mathias Möschel, Associate Professor, Department of Legal Studies, Central European University (CEU, Vienna).

Katerina Pantazatou, Associate Professor in Tax Law, Faculty of Law, Economics and Finance, University of Luxembourg.

Mikko Rajavuori, Assistant Professor, Faculty of Law, University of Turku and University of Eastern Finland.

Jaakko Salminen, Associate Senior Lecturer, Department of Law, Lund University and Assistant Professor, Copenhagen Business School.

Vibe Ulfbeck, Professor in Private Law, Faculty of Law, Centre of Private Governance (CEPRI), University of Copenhagen.

Rodrigo Vallejo, Assistant Professor, Faculty of Law, University of Amsterdam, and Marie Curie Fellow, Centre for Private Governance, University of Copenhagen.

1

European Transnational Private Law – Considerations for a Research Agenda

ANNA BECKERS, HANS-W MICKLITZ, RODRIGO VALLEJO, PIA LETTO-VANAMO*

I. BY WAY OF PREFACE

This book represents an end and a new beginning.

A. Ending the External Dimension of EU Private Law

The book is an end in that it represents the closure of the research project on the 'External Dimension of EU Private Law' funded by the Finland Distinguished Professor Programme (FiDiPro) of the Academy of Finland and hosted at the Faculty of Law of the University of Helsinki, 2015–2021. This research project investigated the role of European (regulatory) private law in different parts of the world beyond the EU internal market with an emphasis on the under-researched Global South. It was conceived as a complement to an earlier project on European regulatory private law,[1] which aimed to shape the foundations of EU private law after the failure of initiatives to establish an EU Civil Code and an EU Constitution. The project on European regulatory private law was inward-looking, focusing on the transformative power of EU lawmaking (by the Court, the Commission, and the EU agencies) in interaction with the private-law orders of its Member States.[2]

* Anna Beckers, Professor of Private Law and Social Theory, Faculty of Law, Maastricht University; Hans-W Micklitz, Professor of Economic Law, Robert Schuman Centre, European University Institute; Rodrigo Vallejo, Assistant Professor, Faculty of Law, University of Amsterdam, and Marie Curie Fellow, Centre for Private Governance, University of Copenhagen; Pia Letto-Vanamo, Professor emerita, Faculty of Law, University of Helsinki.

[1] ERC Advanced Grant 2011–2016 [grant agreement: 269722], located at the European University Institute.

[2] For a representative account of the research design and main conclusions of the project, see HW Micklitz, 'The Visible Hand of European Regulatory Private Law – The Transformation of European Private Law from Autonomy to Functionalism in Competition and Regulation' (2009) 28 *Yearbook*

The FiDiPro project was conceived of as a complementary outward-looking project. It focused on the ways European (regulatory) private law interacts with those of foreign countries or regions. To analyse these interactions, the project involved several perspectives. It took a top-down perspective to investigate the substance, the form, and the impact of European (regulatory) private law in those foreign countries or regions. It also took a bottom-up view of diverse types of regulated market and modes of private ordering that underpinned these same interactions. It finally looked horizontally across different fields of EU (regulatory) private law in their projections beyond the EU internal market. Based in one of the border countries within the EU, as it is in Finland, the FiDiPro project sought in this way to scrutinise the role of European (regulatory) private law beyond EU frontiers.[3]

The core findings of the project have already been reported. Publications focus on regulated industries, such as energy,[4] telecommunications,[5] and finance.[6] This sectoral ambition was also paralleled with a focus on relatively eccentric yet ubiquitous sources of rulemaking in contemporary private law – standards, contracts, and codes – in this way extending attention on the role of European private law beyond the gravitation that case law has usually had within traditional private law studies.[7] An additional strand of research took a more geographical perspective, focusing on the impact of EU (regulatory) private law in different regions of the world. These included specialised studies on the role of EU consumer law in Asia,[8]

of European Law 3–60; HW Micklitz, *The Politics of Justice in European Private Law: Social Justice, Access Justice, Societal Justice* (Cambridge, Cambridge University Press, 2018). For varied accounts on the European Regulatory Private Law project, see also the special issue on the project published in the 22 (5) edition of the *European Law Journal* (2016), available at https://onlinelibrary.wiley.com/toc/14680386/2016/22/5. For an overall description and other research outputs in the project, see in general: https://cordis.europa.eu/project/id/269722.

[3] For an earlier framing of this FiDiPro research endeavour, see HW Micklitz, 'The Internal versus the External Dimension of European Private Law: A Conceptual Design and a Research Agenda' in M Cremona and HW Micklitz (eds), *Private Law in the External Relations of the EU* (Oxford, Oxford University Press, 2016).

[4] L de Almeida, 'Market Access, Harmonization, and Governance in Network Industries: The European Union and the World Trade Organization compared' in E Brousseau, JM Glachant and J Sgard (eds), *Oxford Handbook of Institutions of International Economic Governance and Market Regulation* (Oxford, Oxford University Press, 2021); 'Standardization of Standard Contracts: Fairness in EU Energy Exchanges' in HW Micklitz and M Cantero Gamito (eds), *The Role of the EU Transnational Legal Ordering: Standards, Contracts, and Codes* (Cheltenham, Edward Elgar Publishing, 2020).

[5] M Cantero Gamito, 'Europeanization through Standardization: ICT and Telecommunications' (2018) 37 *Yearbook of European Law* 395–423; 'The External Dimension of the EU Digital Single Market. Geo-Blocking and Open Internet' in T Pihlajarinne, J Vesala, and O Honkkila (eds), *Online Distribution of Content in the EU* (Cheltenham, Edward Elgar Publishing, 2019); 'Latin America' and 'Access to Justice' in M Durovic, G Howells, A Janssen and HW Micklitz (eds), *Consumer Protection in Asia* (Oxford, Hart Publishing, 2022).

[6] T Juutilainen, 'EU Securitisation Regulation: Legal Ordering in Symbiosis with Transnational Bodies' in Cantero Gamito and Micklitz (n 4); S van Erp, J Uitdehaag, P Athanassiou, T Juutilainen and D Philippe, *ELI Principles on the Use of Digital Assets as Security*. Report of the European Law Institute (Vienna, European Law Institute, 2022), available at www.europeanlawinstitute.eu/projects-publications/completed-projects-old/use-of-digital-assets-as-security.

[7] Cantero Gamito and Micklitz (n 4); L de Almeida, M Cantero Gamito and HW Micklitz, 'Institutional and Normative Cooperation in Private Law, Beyond the Hague Conference Towards Standard Setting Organizations' in J Odermatt and R Wessel (eds), *Research Handbook on the European Union and International Organisations* (Cheltenham, Edward Elgar Publishing, 2019).

[8] Durovic, Howells, Janssen and Micklitz (n 5).

Africa,[9] and South America, each accompanied by a conference held on each continent – in Hong Kong, Cape Town, and Porto Alegre.[10] The project covered interactions among these various regions and international institutions in consumer law, connecting them to the development of transnational law.[11] A final strand of research took up the role of case law by looking into the impact of Court of Justice of the European Union (CJEU) judgments on the courts in neighbouring countries, in the Eurasian Economic Union, Continental Europe, Post-Soviet States, the Middle East, as well as East and North Africa.[12] This range of research outputs is a testimony of the diverse and vibrant terrain covered throughout these analyses of the external dimensions of European (regulatory) private law.

B. Beginning European Transnational Private Law

While consolidating the findings and closing the project, it proved necessary to give a new conceptual and theoretical frame to the diverse and technical observations in terms of where EU private law played a role outside the EU. This is where this book is also a new beginning. Reporting on the findings, the book proposes, at its core, to understand the external dimension of EU private law through the prism of an evolving *European transnational private law*.

This conceptual direction is the result of the FiDiPro project's two closing conferences that we held (virtually and in hybrid fashion) at the University of Helsinki in September 2020 and 2021, jointly organised by the four editors of the book. These conferences brought together a combination of established and upcoming scholars from diverse backgrounds who usually do not share the same venues, ranging from jurisprudence, history, and socio-legal scholarship, as well as several legal fields traditionally associated with either private law (for instance, financial law or international commercial law) or public law (for example, tax law, trade law, or EU external relations law), all united under the umbrella of investigating the relation between European private law and global markets and orders. We sought in this way to transcend established cleavages and disciplinary silos within contemporary legal studies – between and among not only European and international, global, or comparative legal research, but also diverse areas of legal specialisation and theoretical strands.

The overall ambition was to enable this kind of cross-sectional exchange to tackle a double-edged challenge. On the one hand, the challenge consisted of the need to

[9] HW Micklitz, T Naude and C Twigg-Flesner (eds), 'Special Issue on Consumer Law and Policy in Africa' (2018) 41 *Journal of Consumer Policy* 303–471.

[10] M Barata, L Bernstein, C Lima Marques and HW Micklitz (eds), 'Special Issue Consumer Law in South America' (2022) 45 *Journal of Consumer Policy* 1–147.

[11] HW Micklitz, A Mathios, LA Reisch, J Thøgersen and C Twigg Flesner (eds), 'Celebrating 40 Years of the Journal of Consumer Policy: The Future of Consumer Law and Policy – Internationalisation, Digitalisation and Sustainability' (2020) 43 *Journal of Consumer Policy* 1–248, elaborated on by HW Micklitz in chapter 8 of this book.

[12] A Reich and HW Micklitz, *The Impact of the European Court of Justice on Neighbouring Countries* (Oxford, Oxford University Press, 2020).

know better what is going on in the various fields of European private law by means of specialised research about private law in different sectors of the global economy. On the other hand, the challenge was also to find an appropriate conceptual framework that can productively encompass different ways of identifying, understanding, and assessing the place of European private law and the role that it is playing or could play in the (re-)configuration of foreign or transnational markets as well as reflecting upon its material, cultural, or normative implications. In other words, the challenge was to elaborate a framework that can strengthen the analytical link between theory and practice but without necessarily hampering theoretical and methodological positioning and experimentation. This is particularly relevant regarding an object of study such as the foreign reach of European private law, which situates itself at the crossroads of countless domains within and beyond legal studies and thereby resists disciplinary categorisation. It is out of those conversations that the concept of European transnational private law emerged as a productive way to address these challenges.

This introductory chapter expounds on why and how this is the case by elaborating on each of its components. As we move along these components, the emphasis is placed on the ways in which this notion relates to multiple strands of research concerning the role of the EU in global governance, as well as some of the latest approaches in global and comparative-law studies discussing Eurocentrism and colonialisation, which can productively be integrated into an emerging realm of European transnational private law. Along the way, we also underscore some of the prospects that the notion of European transnational private law conveys as a research agenda within and beyond this volume. Under this rubric we thus aim to inaugurate a dynamic interdisciplinary dialogue that integrates doctrinal analysis with theory, history, as well as practical or empirical insights on the place and role of EU private law in the changing landscapes of the global political economy. The title 'foundations' is a deliberate choice. We thereby seek to emulate a similar volume on the internal dimension of European private law that was published nearly a decade ago[13] and the title emphasises the preliminary and exploratory character of a concept that requires further shaping.

This introductory chapter starts by discussing the different components of the notion, that is, European law (section II) transnational law (section III) and private law (section IV). It then continues by discussing how the relation between European and private law is conceived in this book (section V) and then concludes with the methodological dimension of the project (section VI).

II. EUROPEAN

Studying European private law is a difficult endeavour, as the field itself is a moving target. It can relate to the self-standing rules on EU private law that the FiDiPro project

[13] R Brownsword, HW Micklitz, L Niglia and S Weatherill (eds), *The Foundations of European Private Law* (Oxford, Hart Publishing, 2011).

has been investigating under the umbrella of a self-sufficient regulatory private law.[14] EU regulatory private law then refers to the EU as the central political and legislative actor and a notion of private law that intersects with market regulation. But as every EU private-law scholar recognises, the field of private law in the EU, including its regulatory connotation, rests significantly on the private law of the Member States. Investigating the EU without the European is not possible. EU integration is unthinkable without a shared (European) understanding of law and its role in economic and societal life.

Yet, the analysis of the national level of conceiving private law expands our understanding of this European dimension of private law in many ways. Beyond merely representing sites of implementation of EU rules and being viewed comparatively from the perspective of different 'legal families' and traditions, European private law has a heritage of its own. In fact, one may conceive of private law as we understand and research it as having a distinctly European origin. Despite current approaches with the aim of de-Europeanising legal scholarship, private law is not free from the conceptual heritage of nineteenth- and twentieth-century European scholarship. Furthermore, the main monuments of nation-building, namely (European) private law codifications, have until today been central parts of legal communication with a global dimension. With increasing international trade and communication, not least with European colonialism and the considerable growth of academia, (ideas of) codes have circulated – both from and to Europe – and been translated into each national reality.

However, a wider, global perspective has demonstrated that the internationalisation of law and legal scholarship has been leading to what has been called the 'Europeanisation of the world'. As a consequence, studies of the reception of European law and references to expert cultures and elite networks have until today dominated legal history and private-law scholarship, for instance in Africa, Latin America, and Asia.[15] Therefore, with the move from an EU to a European perspective on private law we want to pay due respect to the fact that the concept of private law in and of itself originates in Europe but not necessarily in the EU.

III. TRANSNATIONAL (LAW)

What, then, has prompted the shift from the 'external dimension' to transnational law and ordering? In investigating the 'reach' or 'moving' of European and EU private law, the target has initially been understood relatively broadly; the project had been looking at other countries or regions of the world and their adaption of EU concepts as well as international private and public organisations. But one result of the FiDiPro research has also been the insight that the expansion of European private law has

[14] For the concept, Micklitz, 'The Visible Hand of European Regulatory Private Law' (n 2), specified in HW Micklitz, G Comparato and Y Svetiev, 'The Regulatory Character of European Private Law' in CH Twigg-Flesner (ed), *Research Handbook on EU Consumer and Contract Law* (Cheltenham, Edward Elgar Publishing, 2016).

[15] See P Letto-Vanamo, in chapter 5 of this book.

been significantly related to processes of (legal) ordering that are shaped and imagined by epistemic communities.

The paradigm of transnational law is increasingly capturing the imagination or re-imagination within law and legal thought nowadays. Driven by widespread and fast-evolving modes of normative ordering that have emerged in the context of cross-national commercial, political, and cultural activities, this ascendancy is manifested in an exponential range of publications on the topic in all genres of legal scholarship.[16] Yet transnational law is not only a scholarly or pedagogic endeavour. Even more importantly, it has started to permeate the legal consciousness of all those participating in these perceived transnational legal orders, inciting concomitant claims to legal/political authority, responsibility, and contestation.[17]

These developments have proceeded alongside ongoing transformation of the international economic and political order from multilateralism to segmented coalitions, which go hand in hand with the internal transformation of the nation state,[18] adding a new layer of complexity to the phenomenon and the scholarly debate. In addition, from the perspective of private law, processes of financialisation, digitalisation, and the rise of global value chains have propelled a new discussion on the role and function of different areas of private law. These phenomena have started a debate on the extent to which legal categories and legal institutions, contract in particular,[19] but also torts,[20] fit these new forms of global economic organisation. The result is not only a de-territorialisation of private law in the functional use of contracts and contract law by private actors along the value chain across borders, but also fundamental changes within core legal distinctions which the notion of transnational law intends to capture. This is apparent in the vanishing of the product/process divide that governs international economic law and old, taken-for-granted principles in contract law, such as privity of contract. This all sits uneasily on the legal concept of extraterritoriality, the predominant understandings of economic

[16] These certainly include specialised essays and monographs, but also – and most notably – signature textbooks or 'cases and materials', as well as prominent handbooks. See, eg, MW Reimann, JC Hathaway, TL Dickinson and JH Samuels, *Transnational Law, Cases and Materials*, 1st edn (St Paul/MN, West, 2013); AC Aman and CJ Greenhouse, *Transnational Law: Cases and Problems in an Interconnected World* (Durham/NC, Carolina Academic Press, 2017); and, for an overview of its diverse epistemic ramifications, P Zumbansen (ed), *The Oxford Handbook of Transnational Law* (Oxford, Oxford University Press, 2021).

[17] P Zumbansen, 'Transnational Law, Evolving' in JM Smits (ed), *Elgar Encyclopedia of Comparative Law*, 2nd edn (Cheltenham, Edward Elgar Publishing, 2012); TC Halliday and G Shaffer (eds), *Transnational Legal Orders* (Cambridge, Cambridge University Press, 2015); J Black, '"Says Who?" Liquid Authority and Interpretive Control in Transnational Regulatory Regimes' (2017) 9 *International Theory* 286–310; and H Lindahl, *Authority and the Globalisation of Inclusion and Exclusion* (Cambridge, Cambridge University Press, 2018): all offering rich accounts of these developments based on several concrete examples.

[18] R Michaels and N Jansen, 'Private Law beyond the State? Europeanization, Globalization, Privatization' (2006) 54 *The American Journal of Comparative Law* 843–90; HW Micklitz and D Patterson, 'From the Nation State to the Market State: The Evolution of EU Private Law' in B van Vooren, S Blockmans a nd J Wouters (eds), *The EU's Role in Global Governance: The Legal Dimension* (Oxford, Oxford University Press, 2013).

[19] A Beckers, *Enforcing Corporate Social Responsibility Codes: On Global Self-Regulation and National Private Law* (Oxford, Hart Publishing, 2015).

[20] R Condon, *Network Responsibility: European Tort Law in the Society of Networks* (Cambridge, Cambridge University Press, 2022).

organisation and, indeed, with the very concept of boundaries in transnational regulatory terrains.[21]

This focus on transnational legal problems has innovatively challenged traditional doctrines of legal sources by illuminating the extent to which several legal situations and positions are purportedly governed by modes of rulemaking or adjudication that transcend the frontiers of any single state. This insight underpins the emblematic definition of transnational law advanced by Jessup as encompassing 'all law which regulates actions or events that transcend national frontiers', including public and private international law as well as 'other rules which do not wholly fit into such standard categories'.[22] In this sense, the notion of transnational law has become disruptive. It undermines several pillars that had traditionally sustained modern legal imaginaries, such as assumptions of hierarchy, territoriality, universalisation, and what counts as 'law' through the inclusion of private regulation. It also breaks the taboo regarding the ultimate legal and political authority of the nation state by highlighting how several states perform as agents rather than as principals within broader modes of transnational legal orderings.[23]

This has several advantages. The concept of transnational law has contributed to opening up modern legal imaginaries to a range of undercurrents and countercurrents that have long been populating modern law and legal thought, including those of legal pluralism, law-in-action, law-in-context, and other strands of legal theory and socio-legal studies broadly conceived.[24] The concept has indeed become a venue for prominent theoretical innovation and methodological experimentation for studying law and dynamics of legal change in a post-national context, which are driven by concurrent modes of purported legal ordering happening without, above, below, within, beside, between, or beyond states.[25] In this sense, the concept of transnational

[21] See, in general, M Renner, *Zwingendes transnationales Recht: zur Struktur der Wirtschaftsverfassung jenseits des Staates* (Baden-Baden, Nomos, 2010); GP Calliess and P Zumbansen, *Rough Consensus and Running Code: A Theory of Transnational Private Law* (Oxford, Hart Publishing, 2010); and R Brownsword, RAJ van Gestel and HW Micklitz (eds), *Contract and Regulation: A Handbook on New Methods of Law Making in Private Law* (Cheltenham, Edward Elgar Publishing, 2017).

[22] PC Jessup, *Transnational Law* (New Haven, Yale University Press, 1956) 3.

[23] P Glenn, 'A Transnational Concept of Law' in P Cane and MV Tushnet (eds), *The Oxford Handbook of Legal Studies* (Oxford, Oxford University Press 2005); R Cotterrell, 'What Is Transnational Law?' (2012) 37 *Law & Social Inquiry* 500. See also G Handl, J Zekoll and P Zumbansen, *Beyond Territoriality: Transnational Legal Authority in an Age of Globalization* (Leiden, Martinus Nijhoff Publishers, 2012); and HM Watt, 'Private International Law beyond the Schism' (2011) 2 *Transnational Legal Theory* 347–437.

[24] S Engle Merry, 'New Legal Realism and the Ethnography of Transnational Law' (2006) 31 *Law & Social Inquiry* 975–95; P Zumbansen, 'Sociological Jurisprudence 2.0: Updating Law's Inter-Disciplinarity in a Global Context' in R Buchanan and P Zumbansen (eds), *Law in Transition: Human Rights, Development and Transitional Justice* (Oxford, Hart Publishing, 2014); and R Cotterrell and M Del Mar (eds), *Authority in Transnational Legal Theory: Theorising Across Disciplines* (Cheltenham, Edward Elgar Publishing, 2016).

[25] For some landmark contributions, see G Teubner, 'Global Bukowina: Legal Pluralism in the World Society' in G Teubner (ed), *Global Law Without a State* (Dartmouth, Aldershot, 1997); B de Sousa Santos, *Toward a New Legal Common Sense: Law, Globalization, and Emancipation* (Cambridge, Cambridge University Press, 2002); R Wai, 'The Interlegality of Transnational Private Law Transdisciplinary Conflict of Laws' (2008) 71 *Law and Contemporary Problems* 107–27; R Michaels, 'Transnationalizing Comparative Law' (2016) 23 *Maastricht Journal of European and Comparative Law* 352–58; and N Krisch, 'Framing Entangled Legalities beyond the State' in N Krisch (ed), *Entangled Legalities Beyond the State* (Cambridge, Cambridge University Press, 2021).

law is productive in terms of transcending entrenched heuristics and cleavages that have been driving modern legal thinking, such as the public/private, national/international, hard/soft, or law/non-law distinctions. More incisively, the concept has also prompted salient modes of historiographical revisionism that have challenged the alleged centrality of the nation state in lawmaking processes even during modern times. In this way the concept of transnational law has revitalised some of the old wars of faith regarding where the authority of law stems from, whether on political will, transcendental reason, or social practices.[26] Thus the concept of transnational law has nowadays become in itself an 'essentially contested concept'.[27]

Jessup of course acutely anticipated such tensions. In a relatively overlooked excerpt, he stated that:

> Although every generation is confronted with novel complexities, it is a truism that the developments which these decades are witnessing require that old concepts be constantly re-examined with a mind unfettered by blind acceptance of traditional classifications and labels. It is to ease the transmission of thought in its approach to legal problems which transcend national frontiers that the term 'transnational' has recently come to be used more and more widely.[28]

Drawing upon this seminal status and sustained scepticism raised by the concept of transnational law that was originally foregrounded by Jessup, throughout this volume and our overall research agenda on European transnational private law we propose to reflexively turn Jessup's own predicament about this notion of transnational law to itself. This entails an invitation to use and scrutinise the very notion of 'transnational law' as a productive way to imagine or re-imagine current and future developments of European private law. Thus, by seeking to overcome established cleavages and disciplinary silos within contemporary legal studies, our project on European transnational private law – in the reflexive spirit of Jessup – precisely seeks to prompt a way for the very place and role of European private law in shaping transnational markets and orders to 'be constantly re-examined with a mind unfettered by blind acceptance of traditional classifications and labels'. Through the research agenda on European transnational private law that we inaugurate in this book, we therefore seek to encourage interdisciplinary and transdisciplinary analysis and interrogation, as Jessup himself concluded, on 'the interrelationships between the multiple factors which contribute to the unending processes of legal evolution' in European private law.[29]

IV. PRIVATE LAW

By investigating private law at the intersection of the European and the transnational, we also suggest a specific focus on the legal areas and the conceptual apparatus for

[26] For an overview, see G Shaffer, 'Theorizing Transnational Legal Ordering' (2016) 12 *Annual Review of Law and Social Science* 231–65; N Jansen, *The Making of Legal Authority: Non-Legislative Codifications in Historical and Comparative Perspective* (Oxford, Oxford University Press, 2010).

[27] WB Gallie, 'Essentially Contested Concepts' (1955) 56 *Proceedings of the Aristotelian Society* 167–98.

[28] PC Jessup, 'The Concept of Transnational Law: An Introduction' (1963) 3 *Columbia Journal of Transnational Law* 1–24, esp 1.

[29] ibid 2.

our research project. The book contains two central conceptual chapters that outline the different ways in which to conceive of private law for the purposes of our project,[30] but it is nonetheless worth providing some more background and substance to the concepts as they shape the conceptual understanding of our research project. The focus on private law has been a stable factor; it was characteristic of the FiDiPro project on the external dimension as well as a characterising feature of our subsequent work on developing the concept of European transnational private law. And yet, the concept has been undergoing some transformation along the way.

A. Regulatory Private Law

Starting from the premise of private law as the core rules that constitute the economic institutions of – amongst others – property, contract, tort, and personhood, it became clear early on that such a 'traditional' understanding could be a useful starting point, but it would not get us sufficiently far in understanding private law beyond the nation state.

Already on the level of the EU, it is insufficient to equate private law with the perspective of a European civil code of which the Draft Common Frame of Reference[31] or the Common European Sales Law[32] are understood as building blocks. The Draft Common Frame of Reference suffered from serious shortcomings, such as missing rules on *relational contracts*,[33] where the parties engage in long-term commitments in contrast to one-shot transactions;[34] on *network contracts*, which play a dominant rule in the energy, telecommunications, transport and financial services sectors,[35] and on *contract governance*, which cuts across relational and network contracts.[36] The same holds true of the many open questions with regard to the so-called optional model on which the Common European Sales Law was based.[37] As is well-known, the two projects failed, as did academic proposals to build a European Civil Code from bottom-up rather than top-down.[38]

[30] See HW Micklitz in chapter 3 and A Beckers in chapter 2 of this book.

[31] C Von Bar, E Clive and H Schulte-Nölke, *Principles, Definitions and Model Rules of European Private Law*, 9 volumes (Köln, Otto Schmidt, 2009).

[32] COM (2011) 635 final 11 October 2011.

[33] S Macaulay, 'Non-Contractual Relations in Business: A Preliminary Study' (1963) 28 *American Sociological Review* 55–67.

[34] C Joerges (ed), *Das Recht des Franchising: Konzeptionelle, rechtsvergleichende und europarechtliche Analysen* (Baden-Baden, Nomos, 1991) 153.

[35] G Teubner, *Networks as Connected Contracts* (Oxford, Hart Publishing, 2008); F Cafaggi, 'Contractual Networks and the Small Business Act' (2008) 4 *European Review of Contract Law* 493–570; M Amstutz and G Teubner (eds), *Networks: Legal Issues of Multilateral Co-Operation* (London, Hart Publishing, 2009).

[36] F Cafaggi and H Muir Watt (eds), *Making European Private Law* (Cheltenham, Edward Elgar Publishing, 2008); S Grundmann, F Moslein, and K Riesenhuber (eds) *Contract Governance – Dimensions in Law and Interdisciplinary Research* (Oxford, Oxford University Press, 2015).

[37] Special issue in (2013) 50 (1–2) *Common Market Law Review*.

[38] H Collins, *The European Civil Code: The Way Forward* (Cambridge, Cambridge University Press, 2008); W van Gerven, J Lever and P Larouche, *Cases, Materials and Text on National, Supranational and International Tort Law* (Oxford, Hart Publishing, 2001); D Schieck, L Waddington and M Bell, *Cases, Materials and Text on National, Supranational and International Non-Discrimination Law* (Oxford, Hart Publishing, 2007); HW Micklitz, J Stuyck and E Terryn, *Cases, Materials and Text on Consumer Law*

European private law – this is the lesson to be learnt – should be conceived of as a genuine legal order which remains largely distinct from the national private law orders – an order which is autonomous in its 'own right' and self-standing.[39] This private law is understood as economic law,[40] covering not only contract and tort – systematically speaking, the European civil law continental codifications – but also public and private regulation of the economy. At the forefront is regulation of services, such as telecommunications, postal services, energy, transport, and financial services. In that respect, the new path of private law on a European level consisted of a regulatory private law that is inherently linked to the European Union understood as a market state.[41]

The Treaty of Rome did not affect national private law orders. It presupposes their existence and their functionality in governing private economic transactions across national borders. The 1968 Brussels Convention on Jurisdiction and the 1980 Rome Convention on the Applicable Law were based on traditional mechanisms of international lawmaking, meant to complement the European Economic Community as it then was. Savigny's international private law provided the conceptual answer to building national private law orders as a means and technique to decide on jurisdiction and applicable law in cross-border transactions. In the new millennium the original Conventions from 1968 and 1980 were transformed into EU regulations: the Brussels Convention into Regulation 44/2001/EC on jurisdiction, the Rome Convention into Regulation 593/2008/EC on contract law and Regulation 423/2007/EC on tort law. In a constant stream of judgments, the Court of Justice of the European Union (CJEU) has given shape to the Brussels Convention/Regulation on Jurisdiction, but not to the Rome Regulations I and II. The development of European private law took another path. It developed through constitutionalisation and through secondary regulation.

The constitutionalisation of European private law through the CJEU occurs via economic freedoms and fundamental rights. Private law is submitted to EU – and European – constitutional values. Largely unnoticed, the CJEU has used the economic freedoms and competition to develop an autonomous understanding of the key concepts underpinning private law. Plenty of cases affect the concepts of contract, of property, unjust enrichment, tort, state liability, prescription periods, and procedural rules.[42] The second strand of constitutionalisation goes back to the

(Oxford, Hart Publishing, 2010); A Hartkamp, C Sieburgh and W Devrou, *Cases, Materials and Text on European Law and Private Law* (Oxford, Hart Publishing, 2017); JM Smits, *Private Law 2.0: On the Role of Private Actors in a Post-National Society* (Chicago, Eleven International Publishing, 2011).

[39] The interaction between European private law and the national private law orders is a topic in itself to be studied in G Comparato, HW Micklitz and Y Svetiev *Private Law and Regulation* (Oxford, Hart Publishing, forthcoming).

[40] HD Assmann, G Brüggemeier, D Hart and C Joerges, *Wirtschaftsrecht als Kritik des Privatrechts* (Königstein/Ts. Athenäum, 1980).

[41] A Afilalo and D Patterson, 'Statecraft and the Foundations of European Union Law' in J Dickson and P Eleftheriadis (eds), *Philosophical Foundations of European Union Law* (Oxford, Oxford University Press, 2012).

[42] E Steindorff, *EG Vertrag und Privatrecht* (Baden-Baden, Nomos, 1996); C Schmid, *Die Instrumentalisierung des Privatrechts durch die Europäische Union* (Baden-Baden, Nomos, 2010); AS Hartkamp, *European Law and National Private Law* (Alphen aan den Rijn, Kluwer Law International, 2012); AS Hartkamp, et al

Charter of Fundamental Rights, which was made legally binding in the Treaty of Lisbon. The case law of the CJEU illustrates the impact of fundamental rights on economic freedoms and on secondary EU law. In labour law, social security, migration law and even in consumer law there is a certain tendency to apply the Charter in a non-economic non-market-driven context. Tendencies to overstep the boundaries of the internal market rationale are sometimes interpreted as a move to genuine European statehood.[43] However, in the core of private law relations, contract and tort, private law – 'traditional private law' – the instrumental market-driven use of economic freedoms and fundamental rights clearly dominates.

By far the most visible Europeanisation of private law matters has happened through secondary EU law, first through directives which had to be implemented and later ever more often through directly applicable regulations. It all started with the two unanimously agreed consumer policy programmes in 1976 and 1981. In the late 1960s the Member States had begun to react to the rise of the consumer society by adopting laws on consumer credit, on consumer safety, and on unfair terms. The decline of the welfare state goes along with the rise of the EU to boost the development of consumer law as a means of completing the internal market in the aftermath of adoption of Single European Act.[44] For nearly 25 years – until the adoption of Directive 99/44/EC on Consumer Sales in 1999[45] – building a European consumer contract law remained largely unnoticed. It remained a domain for consumer lawyers around the globe, disconnected from traditional private law scholarship. After the adoption of the Consumer Sales Directive, the European scene changed dramatically. Academics and politicians began to realise that the Europeanisation of consumer law had led to a growing body of rules which steadily and ever more intrusively affected national private law orders – much more than the Brussels and the Rome Conventions.[46] Closely connected to consumer law are attempts by the EU to harmonise labour law and in particular non-discrimination law. Two phenomena stand out. First and foremost is anti-discrimination law, which started in employment law and social security, but which entered into the private law domain to the dismay of some sections of legal academia, but largely supported by politics. Today, non-discrimination is a common European value which cuts across all areas of law.[47]

The third, and more covert, path of European regulatory private law comprises: (1) network markets and network law; (2) commercial practices, intellectual property

The Influence of EU Private Law on National Private Law (Alphen aan den Rijn, Kluwer Law International, 2014); HW Micklitz and C Sieburgh (eds), *Primary EU Law and Private Law Concepts* (Antwerp, Intersentia, 2017).

[43] See the (critical) contributions by Collins, Commandé, Ciacchi, Cherednychenko, Got and Mak in HW Micklitz (ed), *Constitutionalisation of European Private Law* (Oxford, Oxford University Press, 2014).

[44] S Weatherill, *EU Consumer Law and Policy* (Cheltenham, Edward Elgar Publishing, 2005); HW Micklitz, *Politics of Justice in European Private Law* (Cambridge, Cambridge University Press, 2018) 222.

[45] Directive 1999/44/EC of the European Parliament and of the Council of 25 May 1999 on certain aspects of the sale of consumer goods and associated guarantees [1999] OJ L171/12.

[46] See HW Micklitz in chapter 8 of this book.

[47] On the rise of non-discrimination law, see HW Micklitz (n 44) 201; on the relevance of non-discrimination in a sociological perspective, see R Münch, *European Governmentality, The Liberal Drift of Multilevel Governance* (London, Routledge, 2010) 28 et seq.

rights, and contract law; (3) competition law, state aid, and public procurement; and (4) health, food safety, and regulation of services. These four areas of European private law create new principles, new modes of concluding contracts, new remedies, new forms of contractual standard-setting, and new liability standards. The overview aims to demonstrate the vast areas of regulatory private law which are shaped by the EU and which are downgraded in analysis of European private law. It is here that the clash between the traditional concept of private law and modern market state concepts is most visible.

This concept of EU regulatory private law, namely as EU law intervening in private law relationships, has shaped this project significantly. It has been a core conceptual basis for the project of the external dimension, and it continues to influence the conception of European transnational private law. One can see this in the decisions of sectors and contributions that examine European private law through the lens of specific markets and the intersection between market regulation and private law.

B. Transnational Private Law and Private Regulation

Besides, the inquiry into European regulatory private law, whether horizontal like consumer law or sector-related like that of regulated industries, leads us also into new forms of rule/lawmaking and of new devices for enforcement. A common regulatory technique in European private law is co-regulation. Secondary law sets the statutory frame, which is then completed by rules which are either developed by private bodies (comitology, for example European and national standards bodies) or by European and national enforcement authorities (the Lamfalussy procedure). Whether and to what extent these rules affect private law is mainly a matter of empirical research.[48] The open method of co-ordination used to attract much more attention despite how ubiquitous these co-regulatory processes still are.[49] A strong governance dimension is evident in that these new processes of lawmaking and rulemaking are developed outside the scope of legal procedures – whether they are quasi-constitutional, quasi-administrative, or entirely self-organised.

These new forms result from the ever-increasing importance of European regulation, which typically mixes national with European regulatory approaches. The key players are national and European agencies as well as the European Commission, which intervene in lawmaking and law enforcement, often in a grey legal zone. This refers to boundary shifts in the division of competences between the EU and the Member States, typically in formally non-binding rules that nevertheless enjoy a wide de facto reach. These new forms of governance oscillate between lawmaking

[48] Cafaggi and Muir-Watt (n 36); F Cafaggi and H Muir-Watt (eds), *The Regulatory Function of European Private Law* (Cheltenham, Edward Elgar, 2009).

[49] J Zeitlin and P Pochet (eds), *The Open Method of Coordination in Action: The European Employment and Social Inclusion Strategies* (Brussels, PIE-Peter Lang, 2005); S Smismans, *Civil Society and Legitimate European Governance* (Cheltenham, Edward Elgar Publishing, 2006); FC Sabel and J Zeitlin 'Learning from Difference. The New Architecture of Experimentalist Governance in the EU (2008) 14 *European Law Journal* 271–327; CF Sabel and J Zeitlin, 'Experimentalism in the EU: Common Ground and Persistent Differences' (2012) 6 *Regulation & Governance* 410–26.

and law enforcement and are not limited to market regulation, but spill over into the relationship between private parties. Sometimes national and European actors intervene jointly in ongoing contractual relations. The rise of these new modes of governance presupposes the existence of a dense net of national and European agencies, which reach out to all relevant parts of the market.

Technical standards have also acquired a very special significance. Here state and private actors closely co-operate, typically in a constant exchange across national and European regulatory levels. This form of co-regulation is supplemented by constantly growing due-diligence obligations. The law on financial services is the forerunner in a development where the EU imposes on companies ever more sophisticated obligations which have to be implemented through internal or external compliance mechanisms and supervised and monitored by national and European enforcement authorities. In the Digital Services Act,[50] the EU regulator went one step further in promoting, as one form of compliance, elaboration of codes of conduct in which companies are encouraged to involve stakeholder organisations. Functionally, European technical standards and state-induced codes of conduct take on the role of a non-existent European contract law in business to business (b2b) relationships.[51] They form a regulatory underground, which is accomplished through the supervisory superstructure. In that sense b2b relations are sandwiched between EU regulation both from above and from below.[52]

A considerable part of regulatory private law, new forms of private lawmaking and enforcement in the EU have evolved as a self-standing dimension of transnational law. As is visible in several contributions, the focus on these new forms of private regulation prompts a shift in perspective: from the EU as a regulator intervening in private relationships to private actors setting their own regulations. A concept of transnational private law so conceived can trace not only formal rules, but also incorporate self-regulation, technical standards, contracts or the travelling of concepts via intellectual circles in academic projects.

V. RELATING EUROPEAN AND TRANSNATIONAL

Having clarified the concepts, we turn to the question of relation: How does our book, in the chapters and our conceptual foundations, relate the European and the transnational to one another? Is European private law something other than transnational private law or does one represent a part of the other? The book, with its diverse contributions, does not offer one single answer to this; instead, the contributions themselves yield different results in terms of what the relation between the two can be. The following analytical accounts of this relation suggest some directions as to how these relationships can be conceived and how our book relates to this question.

[50] Art 43 of Regulation (EU) 2022/2065 of the European Parliament and of the Council of 19 October 2022 on a Single Market for Digital Services and amending Directive 2000/31/EC (Digital Services Act) [2022] OJ L277/1.

[51] HW Micklitz, 'Soft Law, Technical Standards and European Private Law' in M Eliantonio, E Korkea-aho and U Mörth (eds), *Research Handbook of Soft Law* (Cheltenham, Edward Elgar Publishing, 2023).

[52] HW Micklitz in chapter 3 of this book.

A. European Law as Transnational Law

One dominant approach has been to understand EU law as an example or even as a paradigmatic case of transnational law. From this view, EU law would qualify as a particular type of transnational legal ordering and can be productively conceived and studied as such.[53] This approach boasts a long heritage within EU legal studies. Its articulation can be traced to the enduring debate over the nature of the EU as a polity and its legal ordering. In particular, it can be traced to those that conceive the EU as neither a federal state nor an international organisation, but as a *sui generis* entity with its own and – in many ways distinctive – legal configuration as well as scientific and political appeal.[54] Certainly, this categorisation comes with many internal qualifications, disputes, and divergent positions.[55] Nevertheless, the concept of transnational law has proven jurisprudentially productive, in all its plasticity, to structure and channel these enduring debates.[56]

In our book, this understanding features in the historical analysis by Pia Letto-Vanamo, which relates current global or transnational legal vocabulary first and foremost to Europe.[57] It is also visible in the jurisprudential contribution by Rodrigo Vallejo, who discusses the European legal process in relation to the broader idea of transnational legal processes.[58] Instead of merely assimilating or distinguishing EU law from transnational law, our project conceptually conceives EU law as already immersed in broader modes of transnational legal ordering that transcends EU frontiers. In this view EU law is conceived as just a node within these larger and far-reaching arrays of networks that compose transnational legal orderings across the globe. These orderings are driven by a wide range of actors as well as recursive and multipolar processes of more/less formalised instances of rulemaking, monitoring, and enforcement, as well as political contestation at any stage of policy processes. This view thus aligns with some prominent articulations of transnational law as

[53] See, eg, for some salient articulations of this simile, KH Ladeur, 'European Law as Transnational Law – Europe Has to Be Conceived as an Hierarchical Network and Not as a Superstate' (2009) 10 *German Law Journal* 1357–89; and M Maduro, K Tuori and S Sankari, *Transnational Law: Rethinking European Law and Legal Thinking* (Cambridge, Cambridge University Press, 2014).

[54] A *locus classicus* of the latter is JHH Weiler, 'In Defence of the Status Quo: Europe's Constitutional Sonderweg' in JHH Weiler and M Wind (eds), *European Constitutionalism Beyond the State* (Cambridge, Cambridge University Press, 2003). See also, more recently, J Habermas, *The Crisis of the European Union: A Response* (Hoboken, John Wiley & Sons, 2014). On the scientific appeal of EU law, see HW Micklitz, 'A European Advantage in Legal Scholarship?' in R van Gestel, HW Micklitz and EL Rubin (eds), *Rethinking Legal Scholarship: A Transatlantic Dialogue* (Cambridge, Cambridge University Press, 2017).

[55] Some of which may be found in G de De Búrca and JHH Weiler, *The Worlds of European Constitutionalism* (Cambridge, Cambridge University Press, 2011); Dickson and Eleftheriadis (n 41); M Poiares Maduro and M Wind (eds), *The Transformation of Europe: Twenty-Five Years On* (Cambridge, Cambridge University Press, 2017).

[56] For some further instantiations and variations, see PF Kjaer, *Between Governing and Governance: On the Emergence, Function and Form of Europe's Post-Nation al Constellation* (Oxford, Hart Publishing, 2010); A Vauchez and B de Witte (eds), *Lawyering Europe: European Law as a Transnational Social Field* (Oxford, Hart Publishing, 2013); S Sankari and K Tuori (eds), *The Many Constitutions of Europe* (London, Routledge, 2016); Jiří Přibáň (ed), *Self-Constitution of European Society: Beyond EU Politics, Law and Governance* (London, Routledge, 2016).

[57] See P Letto-Vanamo in chapter 5 of this book.

[58] See R Vallejo in chapter 4 of this book.

rendering a kind of method to productively navigate the increasing legal complexity of our interdependent worlds.[59]

In the analysis of sectors, we can see this transnational character of EU law, in solidly concrete form, in the field of finance and taxation. In these areas, as Anna Chadwick[60] and Katerina Pantazatou[61] show, the EU has been largely aligning to transnational paradigms of regulation; the EU has been downloading a significant degree of what has evolved on a transnational level. And, as Vibe Ulfbeck shows, in the field of climate change we also see in litigation and regulation how the European states are embedded within a wider transnational trend in terms of relying on tort law and regulation through corporate group and supply-chain obligations.[62] A prominent field of European transnational private law is European consumer law, where the EU has turned into a major regulatory power, quite often indirectly in countries through adaptation of national laws via amendments to the legal order of the former colonial power.[63]

B. European Law vs Transnational Law

A second perspective would be to distinguish EU law sharply from transnational law. In this view, EU law would stand separate from transnational legal orderings that populate the fluid realm of global governance. This approach has lately gained momentum in addition to ample analytical traction within EU law and EU legal scholarship as a basis for examining how EU law interacts (or should interact) with these diverse sets of transnational legal orderings.[64] This momentum has been boosted by a series of political agendas advanced by the Commission and the Council regarding global issues, as well as polemic ECJ judgments concerning these relationships based on established doctrine on the so-called *autonomy of EU law*. One illustration comes from the landmark *Kadi* judgment and its impact in the reconfiguration of the transnational counterterrorism regime.[65] A second illustration comes from the more recent *Achmea* judgment concerning the relationship of EU law and transnational investment law that has been paralleled by a political agenda

[59] Along these lines, see TC Halliday and G Shaffer, 'Transnational Legal Orders' in TC Halliday and G Shaffer (eds), *Transnational Legal Orders* (Cambridge, Cambridge University Press, 2015); P Zumbansen, 'Defining the Space of Transnational Law: Legal Theory, Global Governance, and Legal Pluralism' (2012) 21 *Transnational Law & Contemporary Problems* 305–36. See also K Tuori, *Properties of Law: Modern Law and After* (Cambridge, Cambridge University Press, 2021).

[60] See A Chadwick in chapter 9 of this book.

[61] See K Pantazatou in chapter 12 of this book.

[62] See V Ulfbeck in chapter 13 of this book.

[63] See HW Micklitz in chapters 3 and 8 of this book.

[64] A seminal study in this regard is M Avbelj, *The European Union under Transnational Law: A Pluralist Appraisal* (Oxford, Hart Publishing, 2018).

[65] Joined Cases C-402/05 P and C-415/05 P *Yassin Abdullah Kadi and Al Barakaat International Foundation v Council of the European Union and Commission of the European Communities* [2008] ECLI:EU:C:2008:461. For a specialised study, see K Istrefi, *European Judicial Responses to Security Council Resolutions: A Consequentialist Assessment* (Leiden, Brill Publishers, 2018). On this transnational regime, see also, more broadly, G Sullivan, *The Law of the List: UN Counterterrorism Sanctions and the Politics of Global Security Law* (Cambridge, Cambridge University Press, 2020).

strongly advanced by the EU by way of establishing a permanent world investment court to replace the ad-hoc arbitration panels that are currently driving the regime.[66]

In our book, this perspective also takes its place. This is particularly the case because of our reliance on and connection to previous works that look on the EU as a global regulatory actor and that investigate the European extension of law and extraterritorial effect of EU law. Seminal work by Anu Bradford and Joanne Scott has broken new ground in our understanding of the impact of EU law beyond its proper territory. Throughout the book we have taken their findings as a point of reference, and we asked the contributors to link their research to Bradford and Scott. At the same time, however, Bradford and Scott's research includes neither traditional private law nor regulatory private law but, rather, focuses on the law of external relations more broadly under inclusion of data protection, food, and competition law.[67] What we have learned from this salient research during the last decade is that EU law holds a significant place and fulfils a significant role among this diverse range of transnational nodes. This explains why, throughout this volume on European transnational private law, we have made the conscious choice of taking a distinctively European perspective in examining the place and role of European private law within these transnational legal configurations. In terms of research design, this entails figuratively positioning the EU at the centre of these complex networks so as to render it our protagonist within our object of study.

This is highly visible in the conceptual apparatus with its understanding of the concept of private law as an essentially European concept and regulatory private law as one closely entangled with the EU and its effects on European private law. We can see this in the contributions centring on the European construction of regulated industries and the external dimension of EU consumer law by Hans-W Micklitz. Similarly, the contribution by Anna Beckers shows how, specifically, the concept of regulatory private law can be assigned a European origin that has increasing effects beyond borders. Moreover, in the sectoral contributions, we see a distinct European-ness vis-à-vis transnational law appearing in the labour law analysis related to European Works Councils by Ulla Liukkunen[68] and transnational securities regulation as investigated by Antonio Marcacci.[69] It also features prominently in the analysis of trade

[66] Case C-284/16 *Slovak Republic v Achmea BV* [2018] ECLI:EU:C:2018:158. This has prompted a huge amount of literature analysing these tensions between EU law and transnational arbitration within and beyond the investment regime. See, eg, J Berger, *International Investment Protection within Europe: The EU's Assertion of Control* (London, Routledge, 2020); C Baltag and A Stanič (eds), *The Future of Investment Treaty Arbitration in the EU: Substance, Process and Policy* (Alphen aan den Rijn, Kluwer Law International, 2020); and K von Papp, *EU Law and International Arbitration: Managing Distrust Through* Dialogue (Oxford, Hart Publishing, 2021). See also, more generally, JR Mata Dona and N Lavranos (eds), *International Arbitration and EU Law* (Cheltenham, Edward Elgar Publishing, 2021).

[67] A Bradford, 'The Brussels Effect' (2012) 107 *Northwestern University Law Review* 1, where she developed the theory and the book, A Bradford, *The Brussels Effect – How the European Union Rules the World* (Oxford, Oxford University Press, 2019); J Scott, 'The New EU "Extraterritoriality"' (2014) 51 *CMLR* 1343–80; J Scott, 'Extraterritoriality and Territorial Extension in EU Law' (2014) 62 *American Journal of Comparative Law* 87–125; M Cremona and J Scott (eds), *EU Law beyond EU Borders: The Extraterritorial Reach of EU Law* (Oxford, Oxford University Press, 2019). See also, E Fahey, *The Global Reach of EU Law* (London, Routledge, 2016).

[68] See U Liukkunen in chapter 6 of this book.

[69] See A Marcacci in chapter 10 of this book.

law by Mislav Mataija,[70] who shows the distinct place that the EU takes in structuring global trade relationships. For his part, Mathias Möschel shares the distinctiveness of European conceptions in anti-discrimination law as a starting point, but reminds us that such distinctiveness can also be absent on the transnational level.[71]

C. Transnational Law as European Law

To these rather classic understandings of the relation between European law and transnational law, more recent debates have added another perspective: transnational law and ordering as European and as originating in Europe. This understanding very much relates to blind spots in past debates that have arguably failed to acknowledge the strong European influence on the evolution and conceptual apparatus of transnational law. In the current debate, this 'Europeanness' of transnational law very much links to the post-colonial dimension, as the concept of transnational law has been used to explain – and thereby more or less implicitly legitimise – foreign modes of ruling and distributive disparities by those actors that already hold asymmetrical powers within our global political economies.[72] This debate has gained considerable momentum in recent years and focuses on the meaning of colonialism and post-colonialism,[73] on Eurocentrism and EU-centrism, on the Europeanness of 'law', culminating very recently in the debate on who is allowed to speak and write on post-colonialism.[74] A related, second strand, approaches the topic from other critical perspectives, such as gender[75] or race theory.[76]

[70] See M Mataija in chapter 11 of this book.

[71] See M Möschel in chapter 7 of this book.

[72] See, eg, EW Said, *Orientalism* (New York, Vintage Books Edition, 1978); A Anghie, *Imperialism, Sovereignty and the Making of International Law* (Cambridge, Cambridge University Press, 2007) 223–35; AC Cutler and Thomas Dietz (eds), *The Politics of Private Transnational Governance by Contract* (London, Routledge, 2017); P Singh, 'The Private Life of Transnational Law: Reading Jessup from the Post-Colony' in P Zumbansen (ed), *The Many Lives of Transnational Law: Critical Engagements with Jessup's Bold Proposal* (Cambridge, Cambridge University Press, 2020).

[73] A Behm, C Fryar, E Hunter, E Leake, S Lin Lewis and S Miller-Davenport, 'Decolonizing History: Enquiry and Practice' (2020) 89 *History Workshop Journal* 169–91.

[74] KK Patel, 'The Latence of the European Colonial Past' (2022) 1 *European Law Open* 1059–62; M Brown, 'A Reply by the Author' (2022) 1 *European Law Open* 1063–66 and the review by P Dann, I Feichtner and J von Bernstorff (eds), *(Post)Koloniale Rechtswissenschaft: Geschichte und Gegenwart des Kolonialismus in der deutschen Rechtswissenschaft* (Mohr Siebeck, 2022); C Barskanmaz, 'Die Autorenauswahl des Bandes (Post)koloniale Rechtswissenschaft ist ein Akt Symbolischer Gewalt' ('The Authors' Choice in the Volume (Post)Colonial Jurisprudence is an Act of Symbolic Violence') *Frankfurter Allgemeine Zeitung* (16 March 2023) and the reply by A Kemmerer, E Anfang 'ist gesetzt (Post)Koloniale Rechtswissenchaft' ('A Beginning has been Made') *Frankfurter Allgemeine Zeitung* (17 March 2023).

[75] R Ziadah and B Bhandar (eds), *Revolutionary Feminisms: Conversations on Collective Action and Radical Thought* (New York, Verso, 2020); S Tamale, *Decolonization and Afro-Feminism: An Afro-Feminist-Legal Critique* (Wakefield/Québec, Daraja Press, 2020); and AK Joseph-Gabriel, *Reimagining Liberation: How Black Women Transformed Citizenship in the French Empire* (Champaign/IL, University of Illinois Press, 2019). See also, N Bourbonnais, 'Gender and Decolonisation' (*Geneva Graduate Institute*, October 2021), available at https://globalchallenges.ch/issue/10/gender-and-decolonisation/.

[76] K Crenshaw, N Gotanda, G Peller and K Thomas (eds), *Critical Race Theory. The Key Writings that Formed the Movement* (New York, New York Press, 1995); R Delgada and J Stefanic, *Critical Race Theory. An Introduction* (New York, New York University Press, 2017); R diAngelo, *What Does it Mean to be*

Another critical strand focuses on the post-social connotations of transnational law, closely connected to the rise of neo-liberalism in whatever shape. The concept of transnational law in this view would be undermining the imaginaries of the social that have underpinned most struggles for economic redistribution and political revindication. The concept of transnational law would in this way be eroding modern pathways to social justice by assimilating the claims of disadvantaged groups to those of mere interest groups. Along the way, transnational legal thinking transforms the political achievements of social democracy into a mere stakeholder democracy, thereby subjecting the political process to entrenched modes of marketisation or 'market capture'.[77] The EU and its law are usually assigned a prominent role in this trend, specifically due to its '(internal) market rationality'.[78] The various strands have led to reactions by 'Eurocentrists', which cover a broad range of counter-critique from highlighting their quasi-religious character of race theories[79] to the moral relativism of post-colonial theories, to which radical universalism is offered as an enlightened alternative.[80] In these post-colonial and post-social connotations, the concept of transnational law has also responded with some conceptual changes and a more critical orientation.[81]

The fierce controversies surrounding the European-ness of concepts require positioning through a book that explicitly problematises the relation between the transnational and the European. In our book, we recognise that the evolution of the notion 'European transnational private law' that we pursue is from a European perspective, both in authorship and in conceptual orientation. We do indicate on occasions that an external perspective exists and that the concepts we identify are open to contestation.[82] Indeed, several of the sector-specific and issue-specific contributions prominently address this critical issue of possible European economic and

White?: Developing White Racial Literacy. Counterpoints (New York, Peter Lang, 2012); R diAngelo, *Nice Racism: How Progressive White People Perpetuate Racial Harm* (Boston, Beacon Press, 2021).

[77] A Somek, 'The Social Question in a Transnational Context' in Zumbansen (n 16); and E Christodoulidis, *The Redress of Law: Globalisation, Constitutionalism and Market Capture* (Cambridge, Cambridge University Press, 2021). For a case study in this vein, see also AJ Cohen and A Lang, 'Ethical Markets and Economic Development: How the Fair Trade Movement Created a Neoliberal "Social"' in R Buchanan, L Eslava and S Pahuja (eds), *Oxford Handbook of International Law and Development* (Oxford, Oxford University Press, 2023).

[78] M Bartl, 'Internal Market Rationality, Private Law and the Direction of the Union: Resuscitating the Market as the Object of the Political' (2015) 21 *European Law Journal* 572–98.

[79] S Schröter, *Global Gescheitert? Der Westen zwischen Anmaßung und Selbsthass* (Freiburg, Herder, 2022) 88.

[80] O Boehm, 'Radical Universalism. Beyond Identity' *Süddeutsche Zeitung* (15 September 2022), available at www.sueddeutsche.de/kultur/omri-boehm-radikaler-universalismus-identitaetspolitik-1.5657989, as well as the contributions in O Liav and R Koopmans (eds), *Majorities, Minority Rights, and the Future of Nationhood* (Cambridge, Cambridge University Press, 2023).

[81] P Zumbansen, 'Can Transnational Law Be Critical? Reflections on a Contested Idea, Field and Method' in E Christodoulidis, R Dukes and M Goldoni (eds), *Research Handbook on Critical Legal Theory* (Cheltenham, Edward Elgar Publishing, 2019).

[82] See HW Micklitz in chapter 8 of this book emphasising the possible reading of colonialism and imperialism of external EU consumer law; A Beckers in chapter 2, ending her contribution by highlighting the current contestation of European expansion of private regulation; R Vallejo in chapter 4, on the geopolitical setting and post-colonial encounters that impinge on developments of European transnational private law; and P Letto-Vanamo in chapter 5, referencing global legal history as a necessary theoretical frame to understand the travelling of normative concepts.

colonial domination.[83] But although our hints may offer a direction for further debate, a comprehensive analysis from a non-EU perspective remains to be written. It is our hope that the book inspires such further research.

VI. METHOD: STUDYING EUROPEAN TRANSNATIONAL PRIVATE LAW

This open invitation to further research brings us to the final question on method: How to study the notion of European Transnational Private Law? In reality, the methodological question presents itself in a twofold manner. First, a methodological quest lies behind our project: How have we, methodologically, developed the concept of European transnational private law? What have been its theoretical and methodological building blocks? What, consequently, are its assumptions and limitations? And what would be viewed differently if other choices were made?

Second, the very concept of European transnational private law as such poses a methodological question: How can we further study European transnational private law? How can this concept be fruitful for further analysis in terms of the methodological implications? And how do we engage in what social scientists would qualify as 'theory-testing', as an inquiry on the validity and boundary of the theoretical concept that we develop in this book?

A. Developing European Transnational Private Law

The starting point of our project was an idea of understanding the recursive dynamics between the European and the transnational that we observed throughout the project. Indeed, observation of different sectors and fields, of discussions during the conferences with experts from inside and outside the EU, provided the starting point for the conceptual work. In this regard, the project has developed very much in the sense that Richard Swedberg understands as the methodological work of theorising that should be based on observation of the social facts.[84] As Swedberg describes it:

> At the early stage of the research process the emphasis is on getting a good empirical sense of the phenomenon you want to study, in order to theorise it in a preliminary way. What is at issue is not to study it in the rigorous way that is necessary once the research design has been constructed and the main study is carried out. But again, without any data at all, it is impossible to theorize well.[85]

[83] Examples include A Chadwick in chapter 9 of this book, who addresses the market critique by embedding the analysis of EU financial regulation within the framework of global political economy and argues that it is ultimately also EU law that is on the global market, as well as chapter 14 by J Salminen, M Rajavuori and KH Eller, who highlight how the EU's regulatory piggybacking on Global Value Chains for sustainability can be read as an extension of internal market discipline to global production with huge repercussions on the Global South.

[84] R Swedberg, *The Art of Social Theory* (Princeton, Princeton University Press, 2014) chapter 2.

[85] ibid 29.

In our case, this has been, at a deeply concrete level, a list of fields and topics that we needed to have covered in order to understand the phenomenon of the external dimension of European private law. For the first Helsinki conference in 2020, we delineated the different theoretical and doctrinal origins from which we needed experts, with a focus on public law and EU external relations, private law, and private international law, legal theory, and transnational legal studies and historiography of legal globalisations and post-colonial legacies.[86] For all areas, we invited what we called 'sector-level' experts that could provide empirical evidence from the different fields and senior-level experts that could help us with working on the main lines.

Moving ahead with the insights we gained, we organised a second conference in 2021 in which the goal was to gather evidence from a wide range of sectors: private law and codifications, private international law, social rights, labour law, non-discrimination, and consumer law. In addition, we excavated three central, sector-crossing areas on which the EU is regulating, sustainability/Green Deal, digitalisation, and the European Health Union. Finally, we wanted to include the global economic law dimension related to investment, development, trade, finance, and taxation. This, we thought, would help us move forward with the conceptual apparatus, as indeed it largely did.

But – and this brings us to the somewhat shaky terrain in methodology – choices are not always one's own and determinations on the decision for a direction may also be influenced by the highly practical imperative of possibility. With such a large-scale project, we ran into the practical problem – familiar to many – of invitations to contribute that were declined, selective perspectives because of the choice of experts and the somewhat erratic process of publication where coincidence and also other factors determine what ends up being represented in the book. We were fortunate enough to receive wide-ranging support from different scholars, who provided discussion papers and contributions for the conference that we could rely on for our process of theorising and conceptual advancement.[87] But still, relying on expertise in the fields covered and experts' theoretical orientation provides at least some direction. This all helped enable our context of discovery.[88] It turned out to be a painful – but fortunate – coincidence that the material we collected and the contributions we received depict a diverse image on the role of the EU. This made theorising immensely challenging, but helped us to not be satisfied with easy answers that would fit in our frame.

[86] See the Workshop programme of the 2020 conference.

[87] This refers to the discussion papers of the 2020 conference by M Everson, 'Reconstituting the Private – The Example of Capital Markets and Corporate Governance'; J Kleinheisterkamp and M Pénades Fons, 'Commercial Law and International Arbitration'; H Lindahl, 'Terrestrializing (European) Private Law'; H Muir Watt, 'The Political Economy of EU Private Regulatory Law from the Perspective of Normativity'; S Sankari and S Frerichs, 'Consumer Choice and Sustainability'; T Wilhelmsson, 'External Dimension of European Regulatory Private Law – a Perspectivist Perspective' as well as the contributions for our 2021 conference by L Burgers, 'Rights of Nature v Rights of Future Generations'; J Mähönen, 'External Dimensions of EU Sustainable Finance'; T Juutilainen, 'Digital Assets – European Transnational Law?'; M Hesselink, 'Reconstituting the Code of Capital: Could a Progressive European Code of Private Law Help us Reduce Inequality and Regain Democratic Control?'; and M Rizzi, 'The Transnational Dimension of EU Regulation of Implants – a View from Down Under'.

[88] H Reichenbach, *Experience and Prediction* (Chicago, University of Chicago Press, 1938) 6ff.

Nevertheless, methodologically, we are aware that our concept and how we have filled it with substance along the way has evolved from material that suffered from some inherent limitations, the most important being: (1) the influence of our own conceptions that in turn influenced what we considered as (EU) private law;[89] (2) the absence of certain sectors and topics;[90] (3) the perspective that the authors presented to us;[91] and (4) the largely European and overall Western perspective that the book takes.[92] These gaps should not lead to dismissing the concept that we propose, but indicate our own awareness of the context and input that helped us build this concept.

It is our hope that, with this methodological openness, we allow further research on the concept of European transnational private law that may expand upon its relevance or, conversely, limit it to certain sectors or policy issues.

B. How to Study European Transnational Private Law

This brings us to the second methodological dimension of our concept: How can we further study European transnational private law? To that end, our book offers methodological inspiration: We can research the relation between European private law and transnational law strictly speaking legally, by what legal scholars would call the dogmatic or doctrinal method.[93] This may lead us to close analysis of the legal rules in the EU in terms of how they define and extend European territory and how they legally reconstruct transnational law, including private regulation. We also fulfil the role of empirical – in particular qualitative empirical – research whenever research in the field tackles the activities of private actors, such as corporate counsel, global value chains, technical standardisation bodies[94] and the norms (for instance, standards, contracts, codes[95]) that they produce as well as the broader social understandings that support these norms in their formulation and implementation. These are the 'unusual places' in which European private law is unfolding or may yet unfold.[96]

[89] The context was preceding projects on European regulatory private law, which led us to centre a regulatory private law concept.

[90] This applies specifically to the topic of digitalisation (including data protection, platform regulation, and Artificial Intelligence) on which the EU is regulating intensively, but where we – despite making several efforts – did not manage to obtain a separate contribution in this book.

[91] Examples are the lead firm-centric perspective on Global Value Chains of J Salminen, M Rajavuori and K Eller, in this book, in chapter 14, or the specific reading of transnational finance through the lens of political economy by A Chadwick, in chapter 9 of this book.

[92] See the elaborations above in section V.C.

[93] J Smits, 'What is Legal Doctrine? On the Aims and Methods of Legal Dogmatic Research' in R van Gestel, HW Micklitz and E Rubin (eds), *Re-Thinking Legal Scholarship* (Cambridge, Cambridge University Press, 2017); R van Gestel, HW Micklitz, 'Why Methods Matter in European Legal Scholarship' (2014) 20 *European Law Journal* 292–316.

[94] See M Möschel in chapter 7 of this book, J Salminen, M Rajavuori and KH Eller in chapter 14 and HW Micklitz in chapter 3.

[95] Cantero Gamito and Micklitz (n 7).

[96] N Affolder, 'Looking for Law in Unusual Places: Cross-Border Diffusion of Environmental Norms' (2018) 7 *Transnational Environmental Law* 425–49. See also, more generally, A Beckers, 'EU Law's Dark Private Legal Space: Researching Private Regulators and the Importance of Legal Doctrine' (2022) 18 *European Constitutional Law Review* 657–81.

Previous research on the Brussels effect and the EU as a global actor also teaches us the importance of including the field of international relations and geopolitics for any research that looks into how and why European norms with an impact on private law doctrines, relations, or institutions are taken on board. In this respect, the question of normative evaluation in our book only features as a side element. As noted, some contributions take a normative stance on the phenomenon we see,[97] while others highlight the significance of researching deontological visions and pragmatic compromises sought by participants in the relevant practices as a sign of evolving normative conventions rather than evaluating those practices from a merely external, ready-made normative parameter.[98] We also had these normative inroads featured during the conference[99] and in previous publications.[100] Yet a thorough normative perspective on our concept, on its critical, emancipatory potential or hegemonic character, is something that can only be properly developed on the basis of further research concerning the role of European private law across different sectors of the economy and possible theoretical frameworks underpinning those roles.

VII. ACKNOWLEDGEMENTS: IN PRAISE OF TEAMWORK

We hope that our book may provide a starting point for further discussion amongst (EU) private lawyers on the relation between the European and the transnational and that our concept of European transnational private law helps as a conceptual apparatus in this endeavour. In developing the concept, the four editors stand for its visible part, both in receiving compliments and taking critique 'on the chin'. Yet, behind the concept has been a huge network of actors and institutions that have lent their personal, professional, and institutional knowledge. Without this vast network, we would never have been able to come up with such an ambitious concept.

First and foremost, we would like to mention the postdocs in the FiDiPro project team, namely Lucila de Almeida, Marta Cantero Gamito, and Teemu Juutilainen. Pia Letto-Vanamo provided endless support for the FiDiPro project for over five years, first as the former Dean of the Law Faculty of Helsinki, later as an editor of and contributor to this book. The participants at the 2020 and 2021 Helsinki conferences related to this volume turned into an invaluable source of inspiration. In alphabetical order – in addition to the contributors to this book – these are Laura Burgers, Damian Chalmers, Peter Drahos, Antoine Duval, Michelle Everson,

[97] Specifically, A Chadwick in chapter 9 of this book and J Salminen, M Rajavuori and KH Eller in chapter 14.

[98] See R Vallejo in chapter 4 of this book.

[99] This refers particularly to contributions and discussion papers by Martijn Hesselink, Antoine Duval, and Laura Burgers at our 2021 conference and by Isabel Feichtner Horatia Muir Watt, Ralf Michaels, and Hans Lindahl at our 2020 conference who all emphasised the need to normatively and critically embed the findings on the role of the EU.

[100] HW Micklitz, 'The Role of the EU in the External Reach of Regulatory Private Law – Gentle Civilizer or Neoliberal Hegemon? An Epilogue' in Cantero Gamito and Micklitz (n 7).

Isabel Feichtner, Sabine Frerichs, Martijn Hesselink, Poul Kjaer, Jan Kleinheisterkamp, Hans Lindahl, Jukka Mähönen, Ralf Michaels, Horatia Muir Watt, André Nunes Chaib, Heikki Pihlajamäki, Manuel Penades Fons, Marco Rizzi, Ralf Rogowski, Suvi Sankari, Robert Wai, Thomas Wilhelmsson, and Jan Wouters. The book could not have been finalised without the helping hand of Simona Ciccarini and Hilma Mäkitalo in collecting material and supporting us with editorial assistance, let alone Christopher Goddard, who with endless patience corrected the non-native contributions.

Last but not least, we would like to thank the Academy of Finland, which enabled our research on the external dimension of European private law through a generous grant and the Faculty of Law of the University of Helsinki and Dean Johanna Niemi, who supported funding of formatting and corrections until the very end.

Part I

Bases

Private Law

2

Three Concepts of European Private Law and the Transnational

ANNA BECKERS*

I. SETTING: EU PRIVATE LAW WITHIN THE BROADER TRANSNATIONAL LAW DEBATE

THE IDEA OF the Foundations of a European Transnational Private Law is distinct in two ways. First, building on vastly evolving scholarly interest in the EU as a global regulatory and policy actor, it seeks to direct said debate to the private law dimension. What, if any, is the role of European *private* law in any perceived global reach, extraterritorial effect or territorial extension of EU law that others, notably Anu Bradford and Joanne Scott, have observed? Second, with the distinctly chosen terminology of a European *transnational* private law, we aim to animate discussions on transnational legal thought within EU private-law discourse. The question of the global is thus not one about the external relations of the EU with other countries or international organisations, or what Rodrigo Vallejo describes as the international relations paradigm.[1] Instead, we relate EU law to the broader transnational law debate that broadens our understanding of what can qualify as law, namely private, public, or hybrid.[2]

* Professor of Private Law and Social Theory, Faculty of Law, Maastricht University. This chapter stands as an intellectual engagement with the FiDiPro project and has benefitted enormously from the comments by Pia Letto-Vanamo, Hans-W Micklitz and Rodrigo Vallejo. Research on the second part of this contribution (section IV and V) is related to the project *CHAINLAW: Responsive Law for Global Value Chains* [ERC-2022-STG, Grant Agreement No.101076292], funded by the European Research Council.

[1] See R Vallejo in chapter 4 of this book.

[2] In this context, we draw on the original understanding of PC Jessup, *Transnational Law* (New Haven, Yale University Press, 1956). For the importance of Jessup for our project, see the introductory chapter of this book by A Beckers, HW Micklitz, R Vallejo and P Letto-Vanamo. And again, the contribution by R Vallejo, in chapter 4; for a practical application of Jessup in the context of labour law, see U Liukkunen in chapter 6 of this book.

A. From the Transnational to the Private

This approach raises important questions: How do we define transnational law and, relatedly, transnational legal thought to which we link European and EU private law? Theoretically, Rodrigo Vallejo takes on this challenge by proposing the transnational legal process tradition as a theoretical inroad. Complementarily, Pia Letto-Vanamo's chapter analyses this transnationalisation of legal thought as originating from Europe from a historical perspective. Then, how do we understand the connection between transnational law and European private law and what perspective do we take? This question we take up collectively in the introductory chapter. And, finally, what concept of private law undergirds our project? What is the object that is exported, transplanted, and integrated into transnational law and legal thought? This third set of questions is the one that this contribution will tackle.

Reviewing the contributions to this book certainly begs the question what is *private* about our sector-specific and issue-specific analyses. This is a fair point as the contributions we have collected focus heavily on the topics and sectors 'around private law', but rarely private law rules themselves. Some centre the EU's role in global finance,[3] trade,[4] and taxation,[5] whereas others discuss issue-specific regulatory objectives, such as non-discrimination,[6] climate change and sustainability,[7] labour standards,[8] consumer protection,[9] and regulated markets.[10] Treating such analyses as part of private law places our analysis in the specific regulatory tradition of private law. It treats regulatory objectives related to the market as an influential component of the legal constitution of private relations. Such understanding builds on an influential strand in EU private-law discourse, namely the concept of European regulatory private law,[11] and regulatory understandings of private law as debated on a national level.[12]

With our ambition of developing the foundations of a new concept of private law, we will need to think more broadly, however. European transnational private law can certainly not mean equating European regulatory private law with private law in general and to then give it a transnational touch. What, then, are the different ways of 'thinking private law' and what is its influence on the transnational level? How can we think of the 'p',[13] the private in European transnational private law?

[3] See the contributions by A Chadwick in chapter 9 of this book and A Marcacci in chapter 10.
[4] See M Mataija in chapter 11 of this book.
[5] See K Pantazatou in chapter 12 of this book.
[6] See M Möschel in chapter 7 of this book.
[7] See V Ulfbeck in chapter 13 of this book and J Salminen, M Rajavuori and KH Eller in chapter 14.
[8] See U Liukkunen in chapter 6 of this book.
[9] See HW Micklitz in chapter 8 of this book.
[10] See HW Micklitz in chapter 3 of this book.
[11] Fundamentally HW Micklitz, 'The Visible Hand of European Regulatory Private Law – The Transformation of European Private Law from Autonomy to Functionalism in Competition and Regulation' (2009) 28 *Yearbook of European Law* 3–59. See further the contributions in R Brownsword, R Van Gestel and HW Micklitz (eds), *Contract and Regulation: A Handbook on New Methods of Law Making in Private Law* (Cheltenham, Edward Elgar Publishing, 2017).
[12] From a common-law perspective, see H Collins, *Regulating Contracts* (Oxford, Oxford University Press, 1999); in German law, see A Hellgart, *Regulierung durch Privatrecht* (Tübingen, Mohr Siebeck, 2016).
[13] The lower-case 'p' is deliberate; it takes inspiration from N Walker's distinction between big-C and small-c constitutionalism to apply it to the idea of private law, see N Walker, 'Big "C" or Small "c"?'

B. Method, Perspectives and Definitions

This chapter takes on this monumental task, but with several – methodological, conceptual and definitional – strings attached. First, the concept of private law is built heuristically by relying, in the first place, on the insights and voices that we received on the path of working on this project. I thus build on the contributions to this book, but also on discussions from the two conferences that we organised[14] and the papers, even the preliminary and sketchy ones and the skeletons, that we were fortunate enough to receive from experts in the various fields even if some of them, for various reasons, did not end up in this book.[15] To this, I expand on some categories and aspects that we deem important for presenting a broader perspective on private law that are missing in this book. This applies mainly to the elaborations on private international law and EU regulatory private law in the field of digital markets. Second, I postulate looking at private law through three conceptions: formal and positivist law, material and regulatory law, and societal and reflexive law. This, inevitably, ends up being a *tour de force* that animates different understandings of private law with the aim of linking the European to the transnational. In that regard, this contribution wants to take perspectivism seriously:[16] It places the different concepts of private law within particular traditions and modes of legal thought to then discuss what, from this perspective, European private law's relation with the transnational level looks like. Third, this contribution relies on two, certainly contestable, definitions to delineate the object of study: When referring to European and EU law, I consciously distinguish between European private law, on the one hand, and EU private law on the other. When using the terminology of European private law, I refer to a mode of thinking of private law that has been prevalent in Europe and, relatedly, the private law of the European states. EU private law, in contrast, refers to the body of private law rules that institutionally originate from the EU itself. So, it comes as no surprise that 'European' is the term mostly used in my first perspective on private law, while 'EU private law' is mostly relied upon when discussing the second, regulatory, perspective on private law. When relating European and EU private law to the transnational and discussing exportation, transplantation, and translation, I generally use the – admittedly on occasions clumsy – concept of 'transnational reach'. This means

(2006) 12 *European Law Journal* 12–14. The private in this contribution is developed out of smaller, issue-specific areas rather than as an all-encompassing process leading to a comprehensive European transnational private-law system. An attempt to achieve a Big-P process has been made, for instance, by MW Hesselink, 'Reconstituting the Code of Capital: Could a Progressive European Code of Private Law Help us Reduce Inequality and Regain Democratic Control?' (2022) 1 *European Law Open* 316–43.

[14] 'Exploring European Private Law in the (Re-)Shaping of Global Markets and Orders', 7–8 September 2020, University of Helsinki; 'Tracing the Nature, Place, and Effects of European Private Law in (Re-)-shaping Global Markets and Orders', 16–17 September 2021, FiDiPro Project, University of Helsinki.

[15] This refers to short draft papers developed for our 2020 conference by M Everson, 'Reconstituting the Private – The Example of Capital Markets and Corporate Governance'; J Kleinheisterkamp and M Pénades Fons, 'Commercial Law and International Arbitration'; H Lindahl, 'Terrestrializing (European) Private Law'; H Muir Watt, 'The Political Economy of EU Private Regulatory Law from the Perspective of Normativity'; S Sankari and S Frerichs, 'Consumer Choice and Sustainability'; T Wilhelmsson, 'External Dimension of European Regulatory Private Law – a Perspectivist Perspective' and the contributions for our 2021 conference by L Burgers, A Duval, J Mähönen, T Juutilainen, M Hesselink, and M Rizzi.

[16] On the urge to consider perspectivism in the project, see Wilhelmsson (n 15): 'In such an assessment, the chosen perspective clearly must affect the outcome.'

that I contrast EU/European and transnational.[17] In this context, I further rely on Rodrigo Vallejo's argument that our project moves from the concept of international to transnational relations through which we place a stronger emphasis on the role of private actors and hybrid modes of lawmaking.

C. Argument and Course of Analysis

As an analytical lens, this contribution then approaches private law through three different private law concepts that – for want of a better term – I refer to as 'formal positivist', 'regulatory', and 'societal' conceptions of private law. With formal conceptions (see section III), I refer to what is commonly called the body of 'classic' rules on private law, that is, the legal rules governing and stabilising the socio-economic institutions of property, contract, tort, (corporate) legal persons, and localisation of disputes through private international law. But this formalist conception is not only a particular body of rules, but is also connected to a particular perspective on private law. In Europe, it is connected to a period of evolution of modern positivist law and an understanding of private law as law having the objective to govern private society with due respect to its (presumed) private interests. Hence, formal private law also refers to a particular period in time when this mode of private-law thinking was dominant.

The second perspective, regulatory private law (section IV), refers to private law that is heavily and openly intertwined with public law and public objectives. I count as part of this mode of thinking the debates surrounding the constitutionalisation of private law[18] and the vanishing public/private divide in the EU.[19] Viewed through this regulatory private law perspective, one can identify a significant transnational relevance of EU private law. An EU Transnational Private Law that builds on a regulatory private law perspective will find a significant transnational reach whenever a public interest of the EU arises. It will identify the markets that the EU seeks to enter and shape with private law rules, the policy areas where it seeks to be a 'global leader', and the areas in which it has identified a capacity to do so. Through this regulatory lens, one can identify a much stronger influence of the EU. This is the case in those areas in which the EU sees itself as strongly advanced – for instance, consumer law[20] – and where it relies on a strategy of 'Europeanising' successful international

[17] By contrasting EU/European and transnational, I deliberately depart from the perspective that would qualify EU and European private law as a mode of transnational law as well. While I do not mean this to be a disagreement with other contributions, for instance, P Letto-Vanamo, in chapter 5, and her suggestion that transnational private legal thinking is also happening within Europe, the distinction is useful in this contribution for conceptual reasons.

[18] O Cherednychenko, Fundamental Rights, Contract Law and the Protection of the Weaker Party. A Comparative Analysis of the Constitutionalisation of Contract Law, with Emphasis on Risky Financial Transactions (Munich, Sellier – European Law Publishers, 2007); C Mak, Fundamental Rights in European Contract Law. A Comparison of the Impact of Fundamental Rights on Contractual Relationships in Germany, the Netherlands, Italy and England (Alphen aan den Rijn, Wolters Kluwer International, 2008).

[19] H Schepel, 'Constitutionalising the Market, Marketising the Constitution, and to Tell the Difference: On the Horizontal Application of the Free Movement Provisions in EU law' (2012) 18 *European Law Journal* 177–200.

[20] See HW Micklitz in chapter 8 of this book.

regulatory frameworks for particular markets for its own purposes – for instance, financial markets, taxation.[21] It is also visible in the strategic areas that the EU has been recently focussing on, namely sustainability and climate change, digitalisation, and the Health Union.[22] In this context, the EU has been not only regulating markets, but also extending the impact on private law and the core institutions of contract, tort, property, and company law.

The third, societal, perspective on private law views private law as shaped not only by the state through lawmaking, but also by non-state actors and reliance on them in the system of legal rules (section V).[23] This very much places private law in the tradition of proceduralisation,[24] of a post-regulatory, reflexive,[25] and responsive law[26] and puts the emphasis on societal capacity to regulate that private law needs to consider. It is also a perspective that has been strong in transnational legal thought with its focus on private ordering,[27] transnational private regimes,[28] and the idea of 'looking for law in unusual places'.[29] From an EU perspective, one may find this reliance on private actors even as part of my second category, that is, as part of regulatory private law, as instrumentalising private actors for creating and enforcing EU law.[30] From the perspective of transnational legal thought, however, I suggest that it merits its own category. In our book, we have manifold evidence of these private actors on the transnational scene, be it globally operating companies, global production networks and standardisation organisations, or transnational academic communities. The European dimension comes into play when looking distinctly at their European origin and whether they transport to the transnational level a particular European-centric mode of regulating. This dimension of export, which markedly takes place in the offices of corporate counsel, in private expert committee hearings, or the confidential space of transnational contractual negotiations, appears to be in the process of becoming a building block of European transnational private law. Private actors serve as the basis for exporting standardisation, for creating sustainability standards and

[21] Although it is also explained, in particular in the contributions in this book by A Chadwick and K Pantazatou in chapters 9 and 12 respectively, that this EU regulatory private law is itself often influenced by global developments in the respective sector. Hence, the EU also 'downloads' a significant amount of global (partially soft-law) rules, translates them into binding rules within the EU which then – regularly also via private law – enjoy global reach.

[22] See section IV.B, where I focus on sustainability and digitalisation as two core areas of regulatory private law.

[23] For more in-depth reflections on a societal private law and how it relates to socio-economic institutions, see A Beckers, 'A Societal Private Law' (2022) 1 *European Law Open* 380–89.

[24] R Wiethölter, 'Proceduralisation of the Category of Law' in C Joerges and DM Trubek (eds), *Critical Legal Thought. An American-German Debate* (Baden-Baden, Nomos, 1989).

[25] G Teubner, 'Substantive and Reflexive Elements in Modern Law' (1983) 17 *Law and Society Review* 239–86.

[26] P Nonet and P Selznick, *Law and Society in Transition: Toward Responsive Law* (New York / Hagerstown / San Francisco / London, Harper Torchbooks, 1978); M Grünberger, 'Responsive Rechtsdogmatik – Eine Skizze' (2019) 219 *Archiv für die civilistische Praxis* 924–42.

[27] T Dietz, Global Order Beyond Law: How Information and Communication Technologies Facilitate Relational Contracting in International Trade (Oxford, Hart Publishing, 2014).

[28] G Teubner, 'Global Bukowina: Legal Pluralism in the World Society' in G Teubner (ed), *Global Law Without A State* (Aldershot, Dartmouth Gower, 1997).

[29] N Affolder, 'Looking for Law in Unusual Places: Cross-Border Diffusion of Environmental Norms' (2018) 7 *Transnational Environmental Law* 425–49.

[30] See below, a more extensive explanation in section V on European and transnational perspectives.

non-discrimination. European transnational private law then involves not only, and maybe not even primarily, a transfer of EU rules, but transfer, translation and production via private actors and their own rules. It is – in the terminology of Robert Wai's conception of transnational private law as a contestation between private (ordering) and private (law)[31] – the creation of European transnational law through private ordering rather than through private law. But even this is not the end of the story: We also encounter here a new EU dimension of societal private law. The EU comes increasingly into play when we look at how the EU is increasingly piggybacking and instrumentalising private actors with a view to exporting its own values and policy objectives.

II. PERSPECTIVES: FORMALIST, REGULATORY, SOCIETAL PRIVATE LAW

Private law does not equate to private law. Throughout time and in different parts of the world, the concept of private law has been changing, both as part of the academic discourse and in the lawmaking discourse. If we look for European and EU private law and its transnational reach, what private law do we then look for? We cannot claim to encompass all possible readings of private law. This is why I develop here three analytical categories of 'thinking private law': formalist, regulatory, and societal. Why these three categories? Because they appear in other works that had the aim of categorising modes of private-law thinking[32] and they relate to different historical periods in Europe.[33] The categories can be related to the *trias* of formalism, materialisation, and proceduralisation[34] and the intellectual history of freedom of contract, regulation, and reflexivity.[35] They also feature, albeit in a slightly different manner, in Kennedy's legal consciousness that has globalised with the terms 'classical legal thought', 'the social' and 'neoformalism'.[36]

Quite handily, though not intended, the three categories can also be related to the different areas that we investigate in our book. I suggest that the formalist conception can be found in the European historical understanding of modern (private) law that relied on the idea of positivism coupled with the idea that such positivist law should govern private society and its interests. Regulatory private law is strongly linked with

[31] R Wai, 'Private v Private: Transnational Private Law and Contestation in Global Economic Governance' in H Muir Watt and DP Fernández Arroyo (eds), *Private International Law and Global Governance* (Cambridge, Cambridge University Press, 2014).

[32] These categories roughly resemble those used by R Michaels and N Jansen, 'Private Law beyond the State? Europeanisation, Globalisation, Privatisation' (2006) 54 *American Journal of Comparative Law*, 846ff., although these authors do provide further sub-distinctions.

[33] F Wieacker, *A History of Private Law in Europe with Particular Reference to Germany* (T Weir (trans), Oxford, Oxford University Press/Clarendon Press, 1995 [1959]).

[34] R Wiethölter, 'Materialisation and Proceduralisation in Modern Law' in G Teubner (ed), *Dilemmas of Law in the Welfare State* (Berlin/New York, de Gruyter, 1986).

[35] On freedom of contract and regulation, see HW Micklitz, 'On the Intellectual History of Freedom of Contract and Regulation' (2015) 4 *Penn State Journal of Law & International Affairs* 2–32; on reflexivity in contrast to regulation, see G Teubner, 'Substantive and Reflexive Elements in Modern Law' (1983) 17 *Law & Society Review* 239–86.

[36] D Kennedy, 'Three Globalisations of Law and Legal Thought: 1850–2000' in DM Trubek and A Santos (eds), *The New Law and Economic Development. A Critical Appraisal* (Cambridge, Cambridge University Press, 2006).

the rise of the EU and its own private law; societal private law builds on the idea of a global society and takes note of non-state law and order. The categories can be disputed; they certainly lack some nuances, and they carry a European heritage in thinking about private law. But, given their recurrence in different theoretical concepts, they do provide a useful starting point to make visible how complex European transnational private law can be, depending on the perspective that one takes.

A. Formalised Private Law: Modernity, Positivism, Private Relations

Formalist private law refers to the idea that private law consists of a set of rules that apply to private (economic) institutions; private law thus encompasses the law of contracts and torts, property, the person, commercial law, and legal personhood. It also includes rules on localisation of disputes and the governing law, that is, private international law and, here, can link to the formalist conception that seeks to determine the rules governing a dispute and localisation according to private interests, what in private international law has been coined by Savigny.[37] In the formalised understanding, this becomes linked to an argument that these rules need to be oriented to private relations and their interests (as opposed to public interests). It is a perspective on private law that has recently come under much scrutiny and attracted critique.[38] But what is more, this formalist understanding of private law has also arisen from a particular historical period. The conception of private law as the law governing private relations with a focus on their (perceived) needs, is strongly linked to the period of codifying and positivising private law. Formalised private law has become dominant in the context of the evolution of modern positivist law and the importance of the state. So understood, formalised private law presents itself as areas of law that link private law closely to the state and positivist law, but then rests upon the public/private divide within the law itself. Consequently, within the system of legal rules, one can distinguish those that serve the private and those that serve the public. As such, this understanding of classical private law is very much a Continental European understanding; it already juxtaposes, for instance, to the common law understanding that treats laws generally as public laws.[39]

When investigating transnational reach through this perspective of private law (section III), different roads appear that we will take. Formal private law can be traced to the adoption of state-centric private law rules, such as civil codes, or in a particular mode of thinking of private law that orients private-law rules on private relations. The analysis of the role of Europe and the EU will look into historical research on

[37] FC v Savigny, *Private International Law. A Treatise on the Conflict of Laws and the Limits of Their Operation in Respect to Time and Place* (W Guthrie (trans), London, Stevens & Sons 1869); R Michaels, 'Globalising Savigny? The State in Savigny's Private International Law and the Challenge of Europeanisation and Globalisation' (2005) 74 *Duke Law School Legal Studies Research Paper Series* 1–29 calls this the privatisation of private international law that contrasts with earlier approaches grounded in questions of sovereignty.

[38] See, most prominently, the recent critique by K Pistor, *The Code of Capital: How the Law Creates Wealth and Inequality* (New Haven, Princeton University Press, 2019).

[39] Michaels and Jansen (n 32) 846.

how this mode of thinking as originating from Europe may indeed have become transnationally relevant. This often happened within the context of colonialisation. As to the EU, this formal perspective will direct us to EU private law harmonisation projects, in particular those projects related to a European civil code or European common core and harmonisation of private international laws.

B. Regulatory Private Law: Instrumentalism, Materialisation, Regulation

The second perspective for looking at private law is to understand it as closely interconnected or even equating it with regulatory legal intervention in private relations. This not only refers to the idea that 'all law is public law', but also includes infiltration of private relations with regulatory objectives and the impact that regulatory laws have on – originally laissez-faire – private law. In different national contexts, this understanding of private law as part of regulation has been highly influential. It can be dated back to the legal realism movement in the USA[40] and in Scandinavia[41] that has become quite influential in common law systems.[42] It has also been present in Continental discourses as an alternative proposal as far back as in the codification periods, with Otto von Gierke's 'social role of private law' being a particularly prominent early voice.[43] The idea of the 'materialisation' of private law, the influx of social and welfare issues into private law, and the perceived constitutionalisation of private law has subsequently been driving private law discourse in different European countries. What this regulatory concept has in common with the formalist perspective outlined above is its positivist and state-centric character. Both the early formalist conceptions and newer ideas on regulatory intervention build on the state as the central actor for private lawmaking. Yet the important difference between the two is their normative orientation. Regulatory private law relates the rules on private law not only to private relations and their assumed market interests; instead, it treats private law as part of the regulatory agenda and as an instrument to foster specific values. It comes as no surprise that regulatory private law is a perspective on private law that has a distinct origin within the EU itself.[44] With its competence-based system and reliance on internal market competence for legislating private law, regulatory objectives have always been key for the development of EU private law.[45] One may say that the category of regulatory private law is strongly occupied by the EU. It is the EU that intervenes in the market for the sake of protection, market-making, and exclusion. Consequently, European transnational private law viewed through regulatory

[40] MJ Horwitz, 'The History of the Public/Private Distinction' (1982) 130 *University of Pennsylvania Law Review* 1423–29.

[41] A Ross, *On Law and Justice* (J v H Holtermann (trans), Oxford, Oxford University Press, 2019 [1958]).

[42] M Reimann, 'The American Advantage in Global Lawyering' (2014) 78 *Rabels Zeitschrift für ausländisches und internationales Privatrecht* 1–36, at 13ff.

[43] OV Gierke, *Die soziale Aufgabe des Privatrechts: Vortrag gehalten am 5. April 1889 in der juristischen Gesellschaft zu Wien* (E McGaughey (trans), Berlin, Verlag Julius von Springer, 1889), translated as OV Gierke, 'The Social Role of Private Law' (2018) 19 *German Law Journal* 1017–1116.

[44] Micklitz (n 11) 28.

[45] See very pointedly on the basis of specifically market regulation and contract law, M Durovic, *European Law on Unfair Commercial Practices and Contract Law* (Oxford, Hart Publishing, 2016); for product regulation and tort law, see R Condon, *Network Responsibility. European Tort Law nad the Society of Networks* (Cambridge, Cambridge University Press, 2022).

private law has to be looked for in sector-specific regulation, in economic law, with its global reach and its impact upon private law categories.

C. Societal Private Law: Private and Societal Structures

Both formalist and regulatory private law share as a common denominator a state-centric and positivist character. This contrasts them with a third perspective of private law that takes not only the state, but also societal actors, as the makers of private law. Societal private law, which I coin here as a third perspective, shifts from the distinction between state and society to considering them both as part of private law. One starting point of this understanding is to recognise the laws, norms, or ordering mechanisms that private parties develop. In a nutshell, the field of contract law builds as much on law as it does on contract as a legal source. This understanding of private law has been influential in socio-legal research where the claim was made to recognise the agreement and not solely the doctrines of private law.[46] It is also an insight already central for the legal process school that Rodrigo Vallejo extensively reviews and considers as a relevant theoretical foundation for our project.[47] It further comes as no surprise that this private lawmaking, this conception of private ordering as part of law, has found its way into different national debates on private law.[48]

At the same time, this perspective on private actors and society as part of private law has received particular prominence in the evolution of transnational legal thought and the concept of transnational law,[49] regularly also portrayed as global law without a state.[50] While societal private law is not only a transnational category (it had also been existing within national private law discourse early on), it has become particularly visible in debates on transnational law when the state is in decline. Consequently, it is in particular in transnational private law discourse that scholars became interested in the legal relevance of model contract clauses,[51] standard contract terms,[52] contracts,[53] corporate policies,[54] or standards.[55]

[46] S Macaulay, 'The Real and the Paper Deal: Empirical Pictures of Relationships, Complexity and the Urge for Transparent Simple Rules' (2003) 66 *MLR* 44–79.

[47] R Vallejo in chapter 4 of this book, referring here to the work of Hart and Sacks.

[48] See, on different national contexts, DV Snyder, 'Private Lawmaking' (2003) 64 *Ohio State Law Journal* 371–449; C Bumke and A Röthel (eds), *Privates Recht* (Tübingen, Mohr Siebeck, 2012).

[49] G-P Calliess and P Zumbansen, *Rough Consensus and Running Code. A Theory of Transnational Law* (Oxford, Hart Publishing, 2010); G-P Calliess and M Renner, 'Between Law and Social Norms: The Evolution of Global Governance' (2009) 22 *Ratio Juris* 260–80.

[50] G Teubner, 'Global Bukovina: Legal Pluralism in the World-Society' in G Teubner (ed), *Global Law Without A State* (London, Dartmouth Publishing, 1996); Wai (n 31).

[51] Insightfully on the development of financial market capitalism, specifically the International Swaps and Derivative Association Master Agreement, see J Horst, 'Lex Financiaria: Das transnationale Finanzmarktrecht der International Swaps and Derivatives Association' (2015) 53 *Archiv des Völkerrechts* 461–500.

[52] D Wielsch, 'Global Law's Toolbox: How Standards Form Contracts' in H Eidenmüller (ed), *Regulatory Competition in Contract Law and Dispute Resolution* (Munich/Oxford, CH Beck/Hart/Nomos, 2013).

[53] F Cafaggi, 'The Regulatory Functions of Transnational Commercial Contracts: New Architectures' (2013) 36 *Fordham International Law Journal* 557–1618.

[54] LC Backer, 'Economic Globalisation and the Rise of Efficient Systems of Global Private Law Making: Wal-Mart as Global Legislator' (2007) 39 *Connecticut Law Review* 1739–84.

[55] H Schepel, The Constitution of Private Governance. Product Standards in the Regulation of Integrating Markets (Oxford, Hart Publishing, 2005).

When viewing private law through the lens of private lawmaking, the analysis will shift towards analysing, on the one hand, the activities of these private actors on a global scale. From a European perspective, this would mean looking specifically into how European private actors export or impact the transnational level with their own European concepts.[56] As regards the role of the EU, the analysis aims to focus on the rules and policies that the EU is using to rely on and instrumentalise private actors' activities as part of the EU lawmaking process and how these have transnational reach.[57] With this perspective, we are approaching European transnational private law from the societal standpoint and identify the informal structures through which the EU engages in global reach.

With these three perspectives on private law – formalist, regulatory, societal – let me then move on to the journey of exploring the terrain of private law through those same perspectives. I promise a rough journey that, more than once, will ask me to question my own categories of private law.

III. FORMAL PERSPECTIVES: EUROPEAN AND EU TRANSNATIONAL PRIVATE (INTERNATIONAL) LAW

Starting with the perspective of modern positivised private law oriented to private relations, I suggest following three pathways appearing for analysis of the transnational reach of private law:

- The historical road (subsection A) can take us to European expansion of this state-centred private law conception. It will take us to a road where we see the conception of modern positive private law, grounded in the heritage of Roman law, as a European project[58] and the different paths in which it has gained influence outside European territory. Yet this perspective on expansion cannot be fully grasped without also looking at current counter-developments in academic scholarship that seek to contextualise and de-centre this formal understanding and provide different historical perspectives.
- Another, somewhat narrower EU-centric, street (subsection B) takes us to the field of harmonising and codifying private law and private international law in the EU and its transnational reach.
- And, in this context of analysing private international law's transnational reach, we find, almost as a backdoor, a small alley (subsection C) that takes us to the EU's contribution to formalist private international law. This alley turns into a road, later on, when bridged in the second part where the focus is on the regulatory private law perspective.

[56] For a plea in this direction and some considerations on how to do this methodologically, see A Beckers, 'EU Law's Dark Private Legal Space: Researching Private Regulators and the Importance of Legal Doctrine' (2022) 18 *European Constitutional Law Review* 657–81.

[57] For a powerful and detailed analysis with a view to private regulation in the legal profession, sports and standardisation within the EU, see M Mataija, *Private Regulation and the Internal Market: Sports, Legal Services, and Standard Setting in EU Economic Law* (Oxford, Oxford University Press, 2016).

[58] See extensively on this, P Letto-Vanamo in chapter 5 of this book.

A. Europeanisation: Colonial Transfers and their Contestations

When looking at the formal mode of private law, we see a private law that has been predominantly associated with the modern positivist understanding of law. Private law has been strongly associated with the state. As emphasised by others, state-centric positivist law is a conceptual language that originates from Europe.[59] It is an understanding that is even difficult to translate into the EU context[60] let alone to use it outside the European context. For our transnational reach of European private law so understood, it is of utmost importance to see this modern perspective on private law as intertwined with the period of colonialism. This suggests that we may find the transnational reach of European concepts in the 'export' of such private-law thinking via colonial lines. Hence, when analysing 'expansion' or 'transnational reach', one inevitably ends up investigating how the state-centric modern conception of private-law thinking was enabled, fostered, and set by Europeans. Thinking about the world through the lens of modern positivist private law could even be understood as a European invention.

Several historical research projects have been investigating how European private law concepts have been shaping the law of colonies and beyond to transplant a particular European mode that was understood as progressive and modern. One interesting example is the detailed analysis by Bonilla Maldonado on the Ethiopian Civil Code. While Ethiopia has not been a colony and thus not subject to the imposition of foreign law, its own government has been taking the initiative to model its civil code based on French conceptual language on the ground of aiming to be progressive.[61] When it comes to explicit colonial transfers, we may mention a large-scale research project on commercial law in the context of colonialism that has been identifying commercial and company law – core fields of private law – as objects of transfer and with the underlying idea of fostering the economic prosperity of homeland manufacturers and entrepreneurs.[62] Export of private law concepts, this seems to suggest, has followed the idea of expanding the reach of European state power through private actors and, in that context, organising private law to serve the private interests of European companies and merchants. Yet, albeit this being a common strategy, research into the colonial expansion of commercial law for different contexts and countries also shows how concrete strategies have partly differed depending on the specific context. In some cases, a transfer of private law rules took

[59] K Tuori, 'Transnational Law: On Legal Hybrids and Perspectivism' in M Maduro, K Tuori and S Sankari (eds), *Transnational Law: Rethinking European Law and Legal Thinking* (Cambridge, Cambridge University Press, 2014) 12ff; for the field of political theory, see O Eberl, *Naturzustand und Barbarei: Begründung und Kritik staatlicher Ordnung im Zeichen des Kolonialismus* (Hamburg, Hamburger Edition, 2022).

[60] See, for an attempt to develop a common conceptual and doctrinal language through a European commentary, N Jansen, 'Making Doctrine for European Law' in R Van Gestel, HW Micklitz and E Rubin (eds), *Rethinking Legal Scholarship: A Transatlantic Dialogue* (Cambridge, Cambridge University Press, 2017).

[61] D Bonilla Maldonado, *Legal Barbarians: Identity, Modern Comparative Law and the Global South* (Cambridge, Cambridge University Press, 2021) 117ff.

[62] S Dauchy, A Cordes, D De Ruysscher and H Pihlajamäki, 'Introduction – Colonial Adventures: Commercial Law and Practice in the Making' in S Dauchy, H Pihlajamäki, A Cordes and D De Ruysscher (eds), *Colonial Adventures: Commercial Law and Practice in the Making* (Boston, Brill Publishers, 2020).

place, specifically company law, to the colonies,[63] either without changes or with significant adaptations to local circumstances in the colony to ensure more effective exploitation.[64] Expansion could take place via civil codes and their extension to private relations in the colonies, in others it took place via administrative law and the state-business nexus in commercial activity led it to being recognised as private law.[65] In a detailed analysis of the expansion of German law, Zollmann shows that transfer could also take place through ordinary jurisprudence and an extension that we would, now, discuss as part of private international law, and an expansionist reading of it. By analysing the jurisprudence of the *Reichsgericht*, he identifies that the extension of private law to the colonies happened through an extension of the competence of the German courts to colonial disputes, yet these disputes concerned disputes between the colonisers, tort law disputes on strict liability or family matters for which the competence remained with the *Reichsgericht*.[66] This strategy of extending the private law jurisprudence of the highest courts in the country to colonial disputes was quite common.[67]

Yet, despite the value of tracing different modes of export of European concepts, there is an obvious criticism to this perspective. The history of private law transfers is, again, written from a European perspective and puts the emphasis on the expansion of the European state. It is not only as such a history of domination through private law leading to elimination of non-European ideas and rulemaking and even to racialisation.[68] It is also a research perspective that takes European concepts as a basis and as the central perspective in order to identify how rules and concepts have been travelling. The perspective of the dominated and colonised, their conceptual apparatus and epistemologies, remains a blind spot in this research. The perspective of modern positivist private law expanding through codification and 'colonial transfers' identifies particular movements of European expansion that are, and rightly so, subject to critique as to what history they write. Analysing the state-centric conception of private law leaves significant blind spots. In her contribution to this book, Pia Letto-Vanamo emphasises the value of several independent research projects that seek to engage with a different history about the globalisation of (private) legal ideas that is developed from a different conceptual apparatus. Within Europe, one major trigger is the project on decolonial comparative law[69] and its aim

[63] For this based on a case study on South-East Asia, see P Mahy, 'Company Law Transplants and Change in Colonial Southeast Asia' in Dauchy et al (n 62).

[64] This is shown for Australia with a view to adapting company law with the intention to exploit natural resources through mining: P Lipton, 'The Transplant and Adaption of Company Law in Colonial Victoria 1850–1900' in Dauchy et al (n 62).

[65] This appears to have been specifically the case in the German colonies: J Zollmann, '"Neither the state nor the individual goes to the colony in order to make a bad business": State and Private Enterprise in the Making of Commercial Law in the German Colonies' in Dauchy et al (n 62).

[66] J Zollmann, 'Bausteine einer kolonialen Geschichte des Privatrechts: Das Reichsgericht und die deutschen Kolonien 1888–1920' (2016) 5 *Rechtskultur – Zeitschrift für europäische Rechtsgeschichte* 14.

[67] This has been highlighted by P Letto-Vanamo in her comments to this contribution.

[68] This history has been particularly written with a view to the role of property laws in the colonial context, see most prominently and critically B Bhandar, *Colonial Lives of Property: Law, Land, and Racial Regimes of Ownership* (Durham/NC, Duke University Press, 2018).

[69] L Salaymeh and R Michaels, 'Decolonial Comparative Law: A Conceptual Beginning' (2022) 86 *Rabels Zeitschrift für ausländisches und internationales Privatrecht* 166–88.

to coin a decolonial comparative legal history, including aspects that would belong to the field of private law.[70] The other major research project 'Historical Regimes of Normativity' seeks to decentre law as a concept from the European tradition of law and place the focus on the concept of regimes of normativity.[71] With this shift in conceptual framing, the idea is to adopt a broader understanding of what qualifies as law and hereby identify movements that evolve below and beyond the radar of modern European private law. In addition, by analysing the translation of normative knowledge, rather than export, transfer, transplantation or globalisation of a mode of thought, the focus is placed much more strongly on local conditions impacting upon what, when, and where a specific understanding of normativity gains wider (global) relevance.[72] This research can provide a wider perspective on how to conceive of the globalisation of European private-law thinking beyond our familiar categories of codification and private-law institutions. With a perspective on a modern positivist and formal concept of private law, such translations may be difficult to capture. Yet, as emphasised by Rodrigo Vallejo in his contribution, if we conceive of our project in a process tradition, it may, in the same spirit, open up a broader conceptual framework for thinking about transnational private legal processes.[73] In this context, the understanding will have to shift to the third perspective on societal private law that will be discussed below, the travel of legal ideas and communities rather than state-centric rulemaking.[74] And this, of course, may equally include marginalisation and contestation of European ideas. The importance of contestation is a point that will accompany us further in this chapter.[75]

B. EU Private Law: Harmonising Procedure Over Substance

So far, we have analysed a particular modern positivist form of the European concept of private law and where and to what forms of transnational reach it can take us. Yet, with our notion of the 'European', we also need to include a reading of our project that refers to the EU and its formalised private law. But what, then, can be said about the EU as an actor in terms of shaping private law on a global level? In providing the answer, a distinction will have to be drawn as to whether one tackles the substantive or the procedural dimension of EU private law, namely whether one centres codification and common core projects regarding a European civil code or, instead, looks at harmonised procedural rules on private international law.

[70] See the workshop organised as part of this project: 'Decolonial Comparative Legal History: Indigenous and Global South Law Prior to Colonialism', 9–10 September 2022, available at www.mpipriv.de/1546693/dcl2_program.pdf.

[71] See the description, available at www.lhlt.mpg.de/department2.

[72] T Duve, 'Legal History as a History of the Translation of Knowledge of Normativity' (2022) 2022 *MPILHLT Research Paper Series* 1, 7ff.

[73] See the contribution by R Vallejo in chapter 4 of this book.

[74] See below, section V.A.

[75] See last point, section V.C.

i. Substance: Political Failures and Academic Travels Over Harmonised Private Law

When it comes to private law in substance, the most obvious and initial answer would be that, simply, no EU private law could have a transnational reach as private law.[76] Yet the situation seems to be more complex. When looking at the formalisation of EU private law through a European civil code, there does indeed seem to be nothing in terms of a common codified project that could be exported. The EU had a period aimed at developing large-scale unification projects on private law. Such initiatives started as far back as the 1980s, the European institutions intended this and thereby considered the relevance of this project on a global level.[77] The heydays of developing EU private law based on the common core of national laws were in the 2000s with the large-scale, academic-driven projects of the Draft Common Frame of Reference (DCFR),[78] the Principles of European Contract[79] and Tort[80] Law (PECL), and the concept of European Property law.[81] These remained academic efforts that were not translated into substantive policy or legislation. The large, globally relevant unification projects that followed a formalist aim organised around rule-based or principle-based codification took place at the level of the International Institute for the Unification of Private Law (UNIDROIT) and the UN Convention on Contracts for the International Sale of Goods (CISG).[82] A similar fate was meant to be for the idea of a Common European Sales Law (CESL),[83] a unification project that took the form of an optional instrument. Recent policy developments within the EU in the field of private law suggest that, instead of comprehensive codification work on private law principles, private-law questions are dealt with much more instrumentally and as connected to EU regulatory objectives.[84]

However, while formally unsuccessful, a heritage is carried on with these academic attempts to develop a written framework of the common core of private law in Europe. Indeed, it is this mode of thinking that one may identify as European-driven with transnational reach. As an academic endeavour, the idea of developing common principles has been taken up in other parts of the world. Initiatives similar

[76] This also has been a major point made by Kleinheisterkamp and Penades Fons in their contribution to the conference (n 15): 'The grandiose dreams of a single legal framework of private law for the Internal Market by mimicry of the milestones of uniform commercial law, the UNIDROIT Principles and the CISG, thus have to be put to rest (at least for this generation)'.

[77] European Parliament Resolution of 26 May 1989 on action to bring into line the private law of the Member States [1989] OJ C158/400, requesting that 'a start be made on the necessary preparatory work on drawing up a common European Code of Private Law', based in part on the consideration that 'a modernised, common system of private law is a means of directly or indirectly broadening the Community's links with countries outside itself, with particular reference to the Latin-American countries'.

[78] C Von Bar, E Clive and H Schulte-Nölke, Principles, *Definitions and Model Rules of European Private Law*, 9 volumes (Köln, Otto Schmidt, 2009).

[79] The Research Group on the Existing EC Private Law (Acquis Group), *Principles of the Existing EC Contract Law (Acquis Principles)*, Contract I (2007); Contract II (2009).

[80] European Group on Tort Law, *Principles of European Tort Law* (2005).

[81] S van Erp and B Akkermans, 'European Union Property Law' in C Twigg-Flesner (ed), *The Cambridge Companion to European Union Private Law* (Cambridge, Cambridge University Press, 2015).

[82] This point has equally been emphasised by Kleinheisterkamp and Penades Fons (n 15).

[83] European Commission, Proposal for a Regulation of the European Parliament and of the Council on a Common European Sales Law, COM (2011) 635.

[84] On this more extensively, see below, section IV.B in relation to the regulatory objectives in digitalisation and sustainability.

to the DCFR and PECL have taken place in Asia,[85] though their success remains uncertain.[86] Similarly, unification projects have been conducted (but not carried further) in Africa.[87] In South America, a recent academic endeavour towards a common core of South American contract law can be said to have been successful, at least if success is defined as development of a common document.[88] Hence, we do see ideas and modes of thinking about private law as comprehensive, formalised and codified rules in the EU being carried on in other parts of the world as well.

Moreover, in the EU itself, the idea of developing comprehensive private law principles, and possibly codifying them in a document, has been revitalised. A current bold and far-reaching proposal in this direction has been made by Martijn Hesselink with the idea of a Progressive European Civil Code. Such a Civil Code, to him, should be principle-based, informed by normative ideals of justice and equality, and explicitly include a transnational dimension.[89] Another, very different, perspective has been put forward by Jürgen Basedow in his latest opus. His claim has been to revitalise the idea of EU private law by identifying EU common private-law principles, relying on stronger maximum harmonisation in the EU and combining this with clear, formalist principles of private international law to regulate the external dimension of those principles with other countries.[90]

But as much as these are ideas worth discussing, there still remains little evidence and support that would allow us to consider that any such renewed codification efforts, even if based on principles, would be more successful than previous endeavours. When synthesising EU efforts towards private-law codification and its potential for global reach, one rather appears to see a history unfinished. As an intellectual idea of codifying private law, it has been and continues to be attractive within academic circles. But as a perspective that focuses on private law as positivist and focussing on comprehensive codification of existing rules of private law, transnational reach nevertheless remains negligible.

ii. Procedure: Harmonising Private International Law and its Transnational Reach

When shifting to the procedural dimension of EU private law, my answer will, however, be very different: In relation to private international law with its core rules on jurisdiction and enforcement in civil matters and conflict of laws, EU harmonisation has enjoyed success with – inevitably for the field of private international law – strong transnational reach. The Brussels I (now Brussels I bis), Rome I, and Rome II

[85] For an overview, see S Han, 'Principles of Asian Contract Law: An Endeavour of Regional Harmonisation of Contract Law in East Asia' (2013) 58 *Villanova Law Review* 589–99.

[86] For a detailed critique on the central assumptions underlying this unification project, see A Grebieniow, 'Principles of Asian Contract Law at the Crossroads of Standardisation and Legal Pluralism' (2021) *First View Asian Journal of Law and Society* 1–33.

[87] J Monsenepwo, 'Vereinheitlichung des Wirtschaftsrechts in Afrika durch die OHADA' (2021) 84 *Rabels Zeitschrift für ausländisches und internationales Privatrecht* 97–124.

[88] R Momberg and S Vogenauer, 'The Principles of Latin American Contract Law: Text, Translation, and Introduction' (2018) 23 *Uniform Law Review* 144–70.

[89] Hesselink (n 13) 338ff.

[90] J Basedow, *EU Private Law: Anatomy of a Growing Legal Order* (Anwerp/Cambridge, Intersentia, 2021) passim, but summarised at 728ff ('The Future – Some Propositions').

Regulations[91] provide a core EU-centralised mechanism for allocating cross-border private disputes to the courts and substantive legal systems to the Member States.[92] The success of harmonisation of private international law has also been building on the difficulties and failures of harmonising EU law in substance. That such a comprehensive effort has been successful can thus partly be explained by precisely the above-described political reluctance towards harmonisation in substance. Concentrating the rules that allocate private disputes centrally within the EU to Member State systems has turned out to be a fruitful compromise between the irreconcilable positions of aiming to achieve full private law harmonisation and those seeing fragmentation as a desirable outcome.[93]

In general, the EU rules on both jurisdiction and conflict of laws follow a formalist approach that allocates disputes to the competent courts and determines the law applicable based on proximity to the private dispute in question but interprets (regulatory) public policy exceptions rather narrowly. Harmonised regulations on jurisdiction, applicable law, and enforcement in civil matters has not only led to a huge debate within the EU and in respect of the relation between the national private international law of the Member States and the private international law of the EU.[94] Harmonised regulations are also analysed as to their relation to outside the EU that they carry with the specific form of allocation of disputes and the applicable law. In this regard, several dimensions of transnational reach can be discussed: The regulations can be discussed against the background of being themselves influenced by global frameworks and competition with the Hague Conference as the international organisation that drives the rules on private international law. This has been analysed by others.[95] In addition, one can look into how the rules of the Brussels I bis Regulation and the Rome Regulations and the respective interpretations by the Court of Justice of the European Union (CJEU) have or have not fostered a movement attracting disputes into EU territory. This is what the following analysis will focus on.

[91] Regulation (EU) No 1215/2012 of the European Parliament and of the Council of 12 December 2012 on jurisdiction and the recognition and enforcement of judgments in civil and commercial matters (recast) ('Brussels I bis') [2012] OJ L351/1; Regulation (EC) No 593/2008 of the European Parliament and of the Council of 17 June 2008 on the law applicable to contractual obligations ('Rome I') [2008] OJ L177/6; Regulation (EC) No 864/2007 of the European Parliament and of the Council of 11 July 2007 on the law applicable to non-contractual obligations ('Rome II') [2007] OJ L199/40.

[92] Pointedly on this change from coordination to allocation in private international law, see R Michaels, 'Towards a Private International Law for Regulatory Conflicts?' (2016) 59 *Japanese Yearbook of International Law* 175–201, at 181: 'For the first time, conflicts rules were no longer based within domestic legal systems, but instead were hierarchically superior to national laws. As a consequence, their function changed from one of decentralised coordination to one of centralised allocation.'

[93] For the argument of focusing on procedure rather than substance in harmonisation, see H Koch, 'Private International Law: A "Soft" Alternative to the Harmonisation of Private Law?' (1995) 3 *European Review of Private Law* 329–42; J Taupitz, 'Privatrechtsvereinheitlichung durch die EG: Sachrechts- oder Kollisionsrechtsvereinheitlichung?' (1993) 48 *Juristenzeitung* 533–39.

[94] On which extensively, see J Von Hein, E-M Kieninger and G Rühl, 'Introduction' in J Von Hein, E-M Kieninger and G Rühl (eds), *How European is European Private International Law: Sources, Court Practice, Academic Discourse* (Antwerp/Cambridge, Intersentia, 2019) 14, who find, on the one hand, that 'legislative measures adopted by the European legislature have already led to a considerable amount of uniformity in the field of European Private International Law and International Civil Procedure', but that considerable differences remain as well.

[95] L De Almeida, M Cantero Gamito and HW Micklitz, 'Institutional and Normative Cooperation in Private Law' in RA Wessel and J Odermatt (eds), *Research Handbook on the European Union and International Organisations* (Cheltenham, Edward Elgar Publishing, 2019).

a. Jurisdiction in Brussels I: Attracting and Rejecting Disputes to 'European Legal Space' and the Concept of 'Red Lines'

In relation to the Brussels regime on jurisdiction, three tendencies in that regime are relevant for an analysis as to its transnational reach. The first tendency is that the Brussels regime remains a formalist one that – also following the jurisprudence of the CJEU – does not provide courts with discretion to decline jurisdiction in favour of non-EU space.[96] This has followed the idea of 'attributing general jurisdiction to the European legal space'[97] in cases where proximity (via the defendant's domicile) to the EU exists. In cases of proximity to the dispute being because of the defendants, the EU seems to have a tendency to also attract them into its space. Yet, interestingly enough, the CJEU has been considering that this does not apply to the reverse situation, that is, about establishing jurisdiction against non-EU defendants, even if there is a possible basis within the Brussels regime. This is the second tendency worth discussing. For disputes over non-EU defendants, the CJEU has confirmed that the Brussels Regulation only applies to EU defendants but not for jurisdiction over non-EU defendants.[98] This means that disputes involving non-EU defendants are not centralised within the EU as part of 'European legal space'; they remain decentrally coordinated through the private international law of the countries that have been seised in the matter. Because of significant differences between the rules on jurisdiction within the EU Member States, this leads to a wide spectrum of 'convenient' fora that attract foreign disputes (such as the Netherlands) and those that are less attractive.[99] These two tendencies in the Brussels regime thus suggest an almost schizophrenic tendency, as fostered by the CJEU. When it comes to EU defendants, central allocation to EU courts is deterministic even if transnational elements characterise the dispute; for non-EU defendants, the opposite is true and attraction to the EU depends on the national jurisdictional rules of the Member States. This leads to fragmentation among particular Member States in terms of whether their rules draw global private conflicts into the EU. A key actor in fostering this differential attraction of transnational disputes has been the CJEU, which enjoys – also due to some historical specifics – long-standing competence to rule on jurisdictional questions in European legal space.[100]

Besides, the construction of the Brussels regime on jurisdiction has a very specific construction in itself that opens up the space for transnational private dispute

[96] C-281/02 *Andrew Owusu v N.B. Jackson* ECLI:EU:C:2005:120, ECR 2005 I-01383.

[97] C Chalas and R Fentiman, 'Judicial Discretion (from Bhopal to Brexit): Owusu v Jackson' in H Muir Watt, L Bíziková, A Brandao De Oliveira and DP Fernández Arroyo (eds), *Global Private International Law: Adjudication without Frontiers* (Cheltenham, Edward Elgar, 2019) 42ff.

[98] See Case C-645/11 *Land Berlin v Sapir and others* ECLI:EU:C:2013:228 (in relation to Art 8 Brussels Regulation).

[99] See, for a close analysis of the Netherlands as a 'forum conveniens' for transnational disputes for collective redress, also because of their jurisdictional rules, the workshop held on 5 February 2021, reported on here: https://eapil.org/2021/02/16/the-netherlands-a-forum-conveniens-for-collective-redress/. A large study on differences in the Member States has been conducted by T Lutzi, E Piovesani and D Zgrabljic Rotar (eds), *Jurisdiction over Non-EU Defendants: Should the Brussels Ia-Regulation be Extended?* (Oxford, Hart Publishing, 2023).

[100] This is different from the Rome Regulations, where this jurisdiction has only recently been established and thus a less strong role has been given to the CJEU. See, on this aspect and more in detail, the introductory chapter of this book by A Beckers, HW Micklitz, R Vallejo and P Letto-Vanamo, section IV.A.

settlement. The Brussels regime recognises the choice of the parties in terms of jurisdiction. However, by excluding (transnational) arbitration[101] and thus relying on international frameworks,[102] the EU rules allow the parties' autonomous departure from the EU in resolving their disputes and refrains from intervention. In relation to jurisdiction, the private autonomy of the disputing parties becomes an important trigger for the departure of private disputes from European legal space and is a tool used frequently.[103] Hence, the autonomy of private parties appears to prevail. Yet, while allowing such departure, the EU – through the CJEU – simultaneously engages in a process that I will call drawing 'red lines'. Rather than engaging in the direction of attracting disputes, the EU – here through the judiciary and specifically the CJEU – takes an approach to gain hindsight control over party choice for a transnational forum. This has been most visible in relation to the control of arbitration awards, where the Court has constantly expanded notions of public policy from the internationally accepted minimalist approach to one informed by the effectiveness of EU law in the post-award phase in enforcement proceedings.[104] But direct control of party choice, the arbitration agreement, is a mechanism that can also be used.[105]

This development suggests that the EU appears to enter rather formalist rules on jurisdiction with a regulatory perspective. Allowing allocation of disputes to the transnational space and to outside the EU is accepted; private agreements and the post-dispute phase are used to infiltrate regulatory objectives. That this trend towards a regulatory private international law[106] related to jurisdiction continues in a much broader manner in issue-specific and sector-specific rulemaking processes will be shown later when approaching transnational reach through a perspective on regulatory private law.[107]

b. Choice of Law: Global Allocation and Public Policy

Next to jurisdiction and enforcement, the other large area of (European) private international law is the field of conflict of laws. Similar to jurisdiction and enforcement, this area has been harmonised through the Rome I Regulation on the law applicable

[101] Brussels I bis (n 91) Rec (12).

[102] The New York Arbitration Convention on the Recognition and Enforcement of Foreign Arbitral Awards, New York, 10 June 1958.

[103] JF Coyle and CR Drahozal, 'An Empirical Study of Dispute Resolution Clauses in International Supply Contracts' (2019) 52 *Vanderbilt Journal of Transnational Law* 323–86 (England, Switzerland, USA). For similar observations, see S Vogenauer and C Hodges, *Civil Justice Systems in Europe: Implications for Choice of Forum and Choice of Contract Law* (Oxford, Hart Publishing, 2016).

[104] M Penades Fons, 'The Effectiveness of EU Law and Private Arbitration' (2020) 57 *CMLR* 1096 with a view to the decisions by the CJEU in Joint cases C-430/93 and C-431/93 *Jeroen van Schijndel and Nicolaas Cornelis van Veen v Stichting Pensioenfonds voor Fysiotherapeuten*, ECLI:EU:C:1995:441, ECR 1995 I-04705; C-126/97 *Eco Swiss China Time Ltd v Benetton International NV* ECLI:EU:C:1999:269, ECR 1999 I-03055; C-168/05 *Elisa María Mostaza Claro v Centro Móvil Milenium SL* ECLI:EU:C:2006:675, ECR 2006 I-10421; C-185/07 *Allianz SpA and Generali Assicurazioni Generali SpA v West Tankers Inc* ECLI:EU:C:2009:69, ECR 2009 I-00663; C-284/16 *Slowakische Republik (Slovak Republic) v Achmea BV* ECLI:EU:C:2018:158.

[105] J Kleinheisterkamp, 'From Contract to Status: The Myth of Transnational Public Policy' (early draft), LSE 2014.

[106] For the concept, see Michaels (n 92).

[107] See below, the private international law considerations in digitalisation and sustainability, section IV.B.

to contractual relations and Rome II on the applicable law related to non-contractual relations. Again similar to jurisdiction and enforcement, the EU regulations essentially codify a formalist perspective on conflict of laws that determines the law applicable on the basis of criteria of proximity to a private dispute. There is no imposing of European policy considerations in the first approximation of determining the applicable law. Yet some important contrasts exist between the rules on jurisdiction and conflict of laws that are relevant for placing EU rules in a global setting.

First of all, choice-of-law rules do not distinguish between intra-European constellations and constellations in which the EU and its external relations are concerned.[108] This is different from the rules on jurisdiction, where the EU rules generally apply to intra-EU disputes and disputes involving a foreign defendant are to be handled by national rules on jurisdiction. This – in principle – general application essentially renders the EU rules on conflict of laws geographically unlimited. This, in turn, is only constrained by the (above-discussed) jurisdictional rules, as it is only European courts that apply these choice-of-law rules when being called upon in a dispute. Therefore, the EU Rome Regulations are able to draw foreign law into the EU courts when the jurisdictional rules lead to the competence of a court in the EU. EU conflict-of-law rules appear, in this regard, to be indifferent as to whether this is about the law of another Member State or a foreign law.

The second difference between the European rules on conflict of laws and the rules on jurisdiction relates to their different treatment of transnational rules. The Brussels I bis Regulation refrains from regulating allocation of disputes to transnational dispute settlement fora, specifically arbitration,[109] which essentially implies the stepping back of the EU in favour of allowing parties to choose international dispute settlement. In contrast, the Rome Regulations explicitly deal with transnational, non-state, frameworks, though not as a law chosen by the parties, but within the choice for a national legal system. While the Rome Regulations do not consider a transnational legal framework as the applicable law – as the applicable law always has to be the law of a country[110] – the Rome I Regulation – for contractual relations – allows the parties to refer to non-state law in their contract.[111] The Rome II Regulation includes in the consideration the applicable law rules on safety and conduct, which can also be non-state technical rules.[112] Both rules suggest a more positive and active acceptance of transnational non-state law as part of a dispute, but only in the context of a chosen nationally applicable law. They are rather considered supportively as rules on conduct (in Rome II) or as part of the agreed contractual terms (Rome I) that only apply when they do not conflict with the applicable national law.

This results in the Rome Regulations becoming a formalist allocation of the law applicable depending on the proximity to a private dispute combined with a possibility to consider transnational rules as support. Yet, similar to the rules on jurisdiction,

[108] S Francq, 'The External Dimension of Rome I and Rome II' in M Cremona and HW Micklitz (eds), *Private Law in the External Relations of the EU* (Oxford, Oxford University Press, 2016).

[109] See above (n 101).

[110] MA Petsche, 'The Application of Transnational Law (Lex Mercatoria) by Domestic Courts' (2014) 10 *Journal of Private Internationall Law* 489–515, at 493ff.

[111] Rome I Regulation (n 91) Rec (13).

[112] Rome II Regulation (n 91) Art 17.

in conflict of laws one also finds rulings by the CJEU that suggest infiltration with regulatory objectives. In conflict-of-laws rules, we do not have a sufficient number of rulings from the CJEU to develop a solid argument on how the Europeanisation of disputes takes place.[113] One development that we can see, however, is hindsight intervention by the CJEU in private choices for the purpose of regulatory objectives. Above, we have seen that in the rules on jurisdiction, this drawing of 'red lines' occurs in the post-award phase when foreign court decisions or arbitral awards are subject to enforcement within the EU. In this context, the EU draws the boundaries in which foreign and arbitral decisions can be taken into the EU. In conflict-of-law rules, a similar approach is taken, but here mediated in mirroring rules on applying 'overriding mandatory provisions' of the EU and rejecting foreign norms due to the 'public policy' of the forum.[114] Ever since the early decision by the CJEU in *Ingmar*,[115] the concept of overriding mandatory provisions and public policy have come to serve as an entry point for the EU to contest application of foreign law that goes against its own regulatory objectives. Originally conceptualised as narrowly confined exceptions, they, together with some other smaller provisions in the Regulations, have become used to 'mirror substantive EU policies' within conflict of laws.[116] Much of these seem to be related to competition law, consumer protection, and weaker party protection, which also have been core topics in drawing 'red lines' on the jurisdictional stage. The concept of overriding mandatory provision has – as will be discussed below in the discussion on regulatory private law – expanded to more areas (such as sustainability or digitalisation). In this context, intervention has also shifted from being driven by the CJEU to explicit integration into newer EU policies and legislative frameworks.[117]

C. Conclusion

This last section has taken a bird's eye view of the potential expansion of European and EU private law to transnational space when viewed through the perspective of modern positive private law. This perspective opened the door to investigation of rather diverse forms of transnational reach. Historically, the concept of European private law, as comprehensive and state-centred rules on private relations, was an idea that was strongly coined in European space. To what extent this perspective on formalist European private law in a transnational setting has led to a blind spot towards other non-European concepts of lawmaking is currently being debated among legal historians with several research projects seeking to widen the scope. Moving from a European to an EU perspective, one can see this European imprint on formal and positive private law vanishing with failed harmonisation efforts in

[113] This also has historical reasons as to lack of ECJ competence over earlier conflict-of-law conventions (n 100).

[114] This refers to Rome II (n 91) Arts 16 and 26 and Rome I (n 91) Arts 9 and 21.

[115] C-381/98 *Ingmar GB Ltd v Eaton Leonard Technologies* ECLI:EU:C:2000:605, ECR 2000 I-09305.

[116] Francq (n 108) 85ff, who also refers to other provisions in Rome I and Rome II that fulfil this purpose.

[117] See below, section IV.B.ii on the Proposal for a Corporate Sustainability Due Diligence Directive (CSDDD).

relation to private law. What remains here is an academic endeavour that has inspired similar academic projects in other countries. At the same time, the procedural harmonisation of private law through core private international law frameworks has opened up European legal space to acceptance of transnational disputes and deference to transnational frameworks. In EU private international law, we do see a clear transnational reach or dimension in the ambiguous, partly contradictory, way in which the EU (through the CJEU) attracts or rejects transnational disputes to European space. At the same time, this field is being invaded from the margins (meaning narrowly confined provisions that allow inclusion of public policy). Relying on specific regulatory objectives, the EU increasingly draws its red lines in terms of what autonomous choice by the parties can be. With this regulatory intervention, a bridge is formed to regulatory perspectives on private law, which the next section will turn to.

IV. REGULATORY PERSPECTIVES ON EU TRANSNATIONAL PRIVATE LAW

While the last section emphasised the lack of positivist EU private law oriented to the interest of private parties that has a global reach, the picture looks very different when we approach private law through a regulatory lens. Regulatory private law is a terrain that the EU has been occupying quite centrally. The public/private divide in EU law has not been present in a similarly clear-cut manner as in national legal discourse.[118] One important factor is certainly the fact that legislation of private law in the EU is based on competences related to the functioning of the internal market, that is, a regulatory objective, and an expansive reading of that competence by the CJEU.[119]

This suggests that EU law significantly shapes the rules of private law. However, it does not intervene by building comprehensive rules that govern private relations. Instead, intervention comes from the EU through market regulation that, however, impacts upon core private-law concepts. EU law intervenes in private-law concepts, quite often implicitly and not necessarily in a directional manner; the aim is often to foster regulatory objectives that are linked to the objective of market-making and, recently, 'European values' through regulatory law, but thereby indirectly link to core rules on private law. This regulatory terrain in private law has been occupied by the EU from its very start, one perhaps might even dare to say that it has been the core private law idea without a preceding era of coining 'classical' or formalist private law.[120] The question arising for our endeavour in terms of European

[118] G Low and E Muir, 'Editorial: The Privatisation of European Law and Constitutionalisation of Private Law: Two Sides of the Same Coin' (2013) 21 *European Review of Private Law* 1159; HW Micklitz, 'Rethinking the Public/Private Divide' in Maduro, Tuori and Sankari (n 59); and N Reich, 'The Public/Private Divide in European Law' in HW Micklitz and F Cafaggi (eds), *European Private Law After the Common Frame of Reference* (Cheltenham, Edward Elgar Publishing, 2010).

[119] S Weatherill, *Contract Law of the Internal Market* (Cambridge/Antwerp, Intersentia, 2016); *cf* on this point also D Leczykiewicz and S Weatherill (eds), *The Involvement of EU Law in Private Law Relationships* (Oxford, Hart Publishing, 2013).

[120] HW Micklitz, 'The Constitutional Transformation of Private Law Pillars Through the CJEU' in H Collins (ed), *European Contract Law and the Charter on Fundamental Rights* (Antwerp, Intersentia, 2017) at 58ff.

Transnational Private Law as regulatory private law is then: What is the transnational relevance, the link to the foreign, that exists or will exist in this EU-driven regulatory private law? Where does regulatory private law travel to outside the EU? There are different places where one can look for paths. Based on the contributions in this book and the wider research conducted within this project, I suggest a closer look at two dimensions. First, one may look at this relevance horizontally to identify how such regulatory EU rules and understandings are transferred to other countries. This perspective is quite comparable to what was discussed in our first section as part of the European colonial transfer.[121] It invites a perspective that looks into formal adoption of similar approaches in other countries and to modes of thinking in other countries that resemble this regulatory understanding. This perspective is also very similar to what Anu Bradford has coined as the *de jure* effect. Second, one may also look at the transnational reach of regulatory private law through EU rules on market regulation and their own extension to transnational space. This uses Joanne Scott's terminology, but it relates territorial extension to private law categories that are impacted by expansionist EU regulatory law. This latter path is also similar to what I have analysed above in the context of private international law.

A. *De jure* Effect of Regulatory Private Law: Sector-Specific Differences

One possible way to analyse the transnational reach of European regulatory private law is to look for horizontal transfers from the EU to other countries through legislation, court references, or even a specific type of legal thought within academic circles that organises law as a regulatory undertaking. Do other countries and regions use and themselves implement the EU's regulatory private law concepts? There may very well not be a uniform answer to this. It is very likely that there are sector-specific or issue-specific differences as to whether the EU's understanding proves to be horizontally exported, although in this context there are also likely transformations happening. It may be worth a look back at our research on European transnational private law and its preceding research project on the external dimension of European regulatory private law, because here there have already been investigations on such effects. In this regard, we already see quite significant differences depending on the regulatory objective that is pursued. For the field of consumer protection, Micklitz points out that EU regulatory private law can be – and is in fact – exported to other countries that have been adopting similar legislation or courts in other countries referencing the CJEU's perspective on consumer protection.[122] In contrast, Möschel shows us in this book that one searches in vain for such export in the field of anti-discrimination. The concept of anti-discrimination and its impact on private law appears to remain limited geographically to the EU.[123] One may only speculate about the reasons: Could anti-discrimination perhaps be a too sensitive and

[121] See above section III.A.

[122] See HW Micklitz in chapter 8 of this book, building on earlier research on consumer law in Asia, Africa, and South America, referenced in the chapter.

[123] See M Möschel in chapter 7 of this book.

culturally specific field for it to be successfully exported? And could, in contrast, the success story of consumer protection within the EU, strong regulatory intervention in core areas of private law, have led to strong consideration in the EU? And what is the role of the EU itself in fostering export of its own vision? A strong consumption market in the EU linked to a high level of consumer protection certainly benefits from similar initiatives outside the EU, whereas the stakes are different for the field of anti-discrimination. Looking at horizontal transfers in the field of regulatory private law in various areas from a comparative perspective may ultimately shed light on how priority-setting and the importance of regulatory objectives influence the transnational reach of EU law.

B. Territorial Extension of Regulatory Private Law

Next to horizontal transfer, this chapter will also provide a perspective of the potential transnational reach of regulatory private law that relies on the concept of territorial extension in EU law itself.[124] As documented by Joanne Scott (who coined this concept), EU market regulation in various fields and sectors extends in application beyond the EU. By relying merely on a territorial trigger, most often market access, the EU extends its reach to include the global operations of market actors. Scott explains this with the example of aircraft regulation, which uses entry into European airspace as a trigger for regulation, but then relies on the worldwide safety record and performance in the country of origin for substantive regulation.[125] One can find many other such types of regulation. Yet the concept of territorial extension largely focuses on regulation rather than on the field of private law, as portrayed in the first section. But translating this very idea into private-law thinking, one can see another inroad for a regulatory private law dimension with transnational reach: Transnational reach of EU regulatory private law can occur directly through the EU when the EU – as it currently does in quite a few areas – follows up on regulation with mirroring private-law directives that perpetuate this global extension. Or such extension can happen on the national private-law level that is impacted by EU regulation. In this second perspective, a twofold step is necessary for such private law concepts to achieve transnational reach: First, we do need to link national private-law concepts as infiltrated by regulatory objectives fostered by the EU, a development exemplified in this collection by Ulfbeck with the example of tort law and EU climate-change policies.[126] And then, those regulatorily infiltrated private law concepts themselves need to be territorially expanded via related private international law that pays respect to the regulatory nature. There thus needs to be a combination between regulatory private law and regulatory private international law.[127]

The following analysis will complement the analysis by Ulfbeck on climate change and tort law by looking into two core regulatory areas that also impact upon

[124] J Scott, 'Extraterritoriality and Territorial Extension of EU Law' (2014) 62 *American Journal of Comparative Law* 87–125.

[125] J Scott, 'The New EU "Extraterritoriality"' (2014) 51 *CMLR* 1343–80, at 1343ff.

[126] See V Ulfbeck in chapter 13 of this book.

[127] On this concept of a regulatory private international law, see Michaels (n 92).

private law concepts: digitalisation – specifically regulation of Artificial Intelligence (AI) – and sustainability centring on corporate due diligence. Both areas are highly interesting because they represent core priority areas of the EU (digitalisation and sustainability), they both link – in different ways – regulatory objectives with a core private law concept (civil liability), and they show the interrelation between both EU law and national law and between private law and private international law.

EU law itself does not have a uniform system of liability apart from harmonisation in the field of product,[128] environmental[129] and food safety liability.[130] In addition, some regulations as well as CJEU rulings require infringements of EU law to be connected to national civil liability rules. This has been stated explicitly in the field of competition law[131] but has also prominently shaped the field of product regulation, specifically medical devices.[132] In the past, much of this linking between market regulation and liability has been developed by the courts, the CJEU or national courts. But recently, the question of civil liability has also become directly influential in the legislative process of sector-specific or issue-specific regulation with a territorial extension.

i. Digitalisation: The Example of the AI Act and Product Liability

There is a current, quite heated, debate surrounding regulation of technologies (via product regulation) and technology actors (via actor-based regulation). Following her widely noted claim on the Brussels effect by which the EU becomes a regulatory superpower, Bradford[133] has also been suggesting that the EU has been rising to the status of a regulatory superpower specifically in the digital realm.[134] This discussion has included regulation of AI that the EU has engaged in with the 2021 AI Act and the 2022 Proposals on Revision of the Product Liability Directive.[135] The AI Act as the regulatory area indeed focuses on the 'classical' territorial trigger of

[128] Council Directive 85/374/EEC of 25 July 1985 on the approximation of the laws, regulations and administrative provisions of the Member States concerning liability for defective products ('Product Liability Directive') [1985] OJ L210/28.

[129] Directive 2004/35/CE of the European Parliament and of the Council of 21 April 2004 on environmental liability with regard to the prevention and remedying of environmental damage [2004] OJ L143/47.

[130] For an early construction of EU liability rules in food law, see Micklitz (n 11) 28.

[131] See the fundamental rulings in C-453/99 *Courage Ltd* v *Bernard Crehan* ECLI:EU:C:2001:465, ECR 2001 I-06297; Joined Cases C-295/04 to C-298/04 *Vincenzo Manfredi v Lloyd Adriatico Assicurazioni* ECLI:EU:C:2006:461, ECR 2006 I-06619, paras 61, 62; see also Directive 2014/104/EU of the European Parliament and of the Council of 26 November 2014 on certain rules governing actions for damages under national law for infringements of the competition law provisions of the Member States and of the European Union Text with EEA relevance [2014] OJ L349/57.

[132] C-219/15 *Schmitt* v *TÜV Rheinland* ECLI:EU:C:2017:128 for a detailed analysis of how the ruling links the medical device rules to tort law; Condon (n 45) 170ff.

[133] A Bradford, The Brussels Effect: How the European Union Rules the World (Oxford, Oxford University Press, 2019).

[134] A Bradford, 'Europe's Digital Constitutionalism', Working Paper, 2023.

[135] On the discussion of the Brussels effect of the AI Act, see M Hildebrandt, 'Global Competition and Convergence of AI Law' in J Smits, J Husa, C Valcke and M Barreto Torres De Mendonca Narciso (eds), *Elgar Encyclopedia of Comparative Law*, 3rd edn (Cheltenham, Edward Elgar, 2023) MS 12ff; C Wendehorst, *AI Liability in Europe: Anticipating the EU AI Liability Directive* (London, Ada Lovelace Institute, Expert Explainer, 2022) 8ff.

access to the internal market to make EU regulation also applicable to actors located outside the EU.[136]

To this, the EU Commission has recently also added a genuine EU private-law dimension. In that context, the Commission has published two proposals for directives that concern revision of the Product Liability Directive and establish procedural rules related to liability for AI.[137] The AI Act as the regulatory framework and the liability directives have to be read in conjunction as the public-law and private-law side of EU regulation of AI.[138] The AI Act sets the basis in terms of duties of operators and manufacturers of risky AI systems, including developing systems of enforcement while the liability directives focus on the private rights of those harmed when the rules are breached and cause damage. As far as the core of liability is concerned, the EU relies on two proposals; revision of the General Product Liability Directive that now changes the concept of defect and the definition and extent of liable actors and, in addition, a specific AI liability directive that links liability for AI to duties under the AI Act and contains some procedural rules that seek to improve the situation for those suffering damage by autonomous technology.

Once global actors intending to access the internal market become obliged under the AI Act due to the territorial trigger, that obligatory position will be expanded to the civil-law dimension of damage proceedings in the Member States. In the proposed AI liability directive, this is limited to procedural aspects, such as a change in the burden-of-proof and disclosure rules. Yet, with the simultaneously proposed revision of the General Product Liability Directive that reach is going even further. Relying on the earlier tendency of the CJEU to expand the range of liable actors through the concept of the manufacturer,[139] the proposed directive now deviates from the dominance of the manufacturer as a liable subject to enumerate the potential range of actors involved in the (global) production process and considers them all as potential economic operators that may face substantive liability for a defective product.[140] The Proposal determines that civil liability claims can be addressed to an actor that is established in the EU, but makes this actor responsible for breach of duties of actors that happen outside the territory of the EU. The regulatory reach of the AI Act thus becomes a relevant factor in civil liability proceedings. In addition, the debate on global regulation of AI in the EU has triggered a wider debate that also covers private international law. In particular, it has led to suggestions to extend jurisdiction and rules on the applicable law to allow other non-EU actors to be included in private-law proceedings in the EU, or to rely on expansive readings

[136] Proposal for an AI Act (Proposal for a Regulation of the European Parliament and of the Council Laying Down Harmonised Rules on Artificial Intelligence (Artificial Intelligence Act) and Amending Certain Union Legislative Acts), COM(2021) 206 final) Art 2.

[137] Proposal for a Directive of the European Parliament and of the Council on liability for defective products, COM (2022) 495; Proposal for a Directive of the European Parliament and of the Council on adapting non-contractual civil liability rules to artificial intelligence, COM (2022) 496.

[138] P Hacker, 'The EU AI Liability Directives: Critique of a Half-Hearted Approach and Lessons for the Future' (2023) 51 First View *Computer Law & Security Review* 1–42.

[139] See C-264/21 *Keskinäinen Vakuutusyhtiö Fennia v Koninklijke Philips NV* ECLI:EU:C:2022:536, para 38; C-127/04 *Declan O'Byrne v Sanofi Pasteur MSD Ltd and Sanofi Pasteur Sam* ECLI:EU:C:2006:93, ECR 2006 I-01313; C-358/08 *Aventis Pasteur SA v OB* ECLI:EU:C:2009:744, ECR 2009 I-11305.

[140] Proposal for a Revision of the Product Liability Directive, Art 7.

of the current regulatory inroads into private international law, such as jurisdiction and applicable law in consumer law or product liability cases.[141] While much of this is still an academic debate, there are indications that EU regulatory private law's extraterritorial dimension is evolving in close proximity to the debate on private international law. Interestingly, this development of regulatory private international law does not occur again as a comprehensive codification exercise and, concretely, a great reform of the existing Brussels and Rome Regulations; instead, it evolves in a piecemeal fashion, always closely related to the regulatory silo in which it is embedded.[142] The debates on European regulation of AI and private international consequences are differently organised depending on the regulatory issue involved. We will see this when now contrasting the debate in the field of AI – that is largely organised around product liability and specific regulatory inroads in private international law – with the field of sustainability.

ii. Sustainability: Corporate Due Diligence and Civil Liability

In the field of sustainability regulation, one clear development is towards territorial extension that works with the concept of corporate sustainability due diligence. The Corporate Sustainability Due Diligence Directive Proposal[143] is an attempt by the European Union to impose sustainability requirements on large corporations in relation to their global operations. It contains obligations that are mirrored in other regulations that impose similar obligations on importers and economic operators in relation to specific sustainability issues.[144] The Due Diligence Directive Proposal qualifies as a contribution to European economic law that contains market-based regulation and introduces a regime of administrative supervision and enforcement. Moreover, with its focus on large non-EU corporations that operate in the EU and have a significant turnover in the internal market, the Directive also has an extraterritorial

[141] Generally, B Cappiello, *AI-Systems and Non-Contractual Liability: A European Private International Law Analysis* (Turin, Giappichelli, 2022); see also for private international law considerations with a particular view to self-driving cars and sector-specific traffic regulation, T Kadner Graziano, *Cross-Border Traffic Incidents in the EU – The Potential Impact of Driverless Cars* (Brussels, Study for the Juri Committee, 2016). Critically, on including private international law in the regulation of AI (based on the European Parliament's proposal), J von Hein, 'Forward to the Past: A Critical Evaluation of the European Approach to Artificial Intelligence in Private International Law' in S Voeneky, P Kellmeyer, O Müller and W Burgard (eds), *The Cambridge Handbook of Responsible Artificial Intelligence – Interdisciplinary Perspectives* (Cambridge, Cambridge University Press, 2022).

[142] This may also have to do with the difficult experience of harmonising conflict of laws with the Rome Regulations earlier.

[143] COM (2022) 71 final (Due Diligence Directive Proposal).

[144] For the issue of conflict minerals: Regulation (EU) 2017/821 of the European Parliament and of the Council of 17 May 2017 laying down supply chain due diligence obligations for Union importers of tin, tantalum and tungsten, their ores, and gold originating from conflict-affected and high-risk areas [2017] OJ L130/1; for the issue of deforestation: Art 4 (2) Deforestation Regulation (Regulation (EU) 2023/1115 of the European Parliament and of the Council of 31 May 2023 on the making available on the Union market and the export from the Union of certain commodities and products associated with deforestation and forest degradation and repealing Regulation (EU) No 995/2010 [2023] OJ L150/206); for batteries: Art 47 ff Batteries Regulation (Regulation (EU) 2023/1542 of the European Parliament and of the Council of 12 July 2023 concerning batteries and waste batteries, amending Directive 2008/98/EC and Regulation (EU) 2019/1020 and repealing Directive 2006/66/EC [2023] OJ L191/1).

extension.[145] At the same time, the proposed Directive is one of the few that aims to create a direct link to private law by determining breach of obligations as relevant for civil liability.[146]

This private-law link is interesting for many reasons. First of all, quite in contrast to many other directives in the field of market regulation, it is astonishing that the Directive contains a link to civil liability and thus links market regulation and tort law. Secondly, the Directive – in contrast to the field of digitalisation and AI – does not work with a separate European liability framework, but instead establishes a link to national private liability systems. It thus connects EU market regulation that itself extends beyond the internal market by covering non-EU companies with a liability consequence that is doctrinally worked out on national law. In this way, it is able to draw globally operating companies located outside the EU within reach of national liability regimes in the EU. Liability is then not determined solely on the basis of the general rules on negligence that characterise national legal systems; it is influenced by the obligations that the EU has set for operators that access the internal market. Breach of EU market regulation rules links to civil liability. In the case of the Due Diligence Directive, the global reach is very strong because the liability provision ultimately aims at providing a remedy for those affected by breach of due diligence obligations, which can also themselves be typically located outside the EU. In this respect, the Proposal for the Directive intervenes – quite similar again to the Product Liability Directive revision – not only in the substantive liability rules of the Member States, but also establishing procedural rules of liability that relate to disclosure and burden of proof in civil proceedings.[147] And, finally, the EU Due Diligence Directive shows very clearly how the inclusion of private-law concepts in the EU Directive follows up with a parallel debate on the private international law dimension and its regulatory transformation. Initially, the first draft of the Directive contained a proposal that would revolutionise the rules on private international law themselves by adding new rules on jurisdiction and the applicable law in sustainability and human rights cases. The original idea was to create significant choice for those damaged by breach of the EU due diligence obligation in terms of forum and applicable law, and to add a *forum necessitatis* that provides courts with discretion to accept cases.[148] Although this proposal was not successful, a regulatory path continued at least in relation to the applicable law by considering EU regulatory obligations as an overriding mandatory provision under the Rome II Regulation.[149] This suggests a true extension of the concept of regulatory private law to private international law. Rather than changing the general rules that orient jurisdiction and applicable law in relation to proximity to a dispute, the path taken is to consider

[145] Due Diligence Directive Proposal, Art 2(2) (n 143).

[146] ibid Art 22.

[147] ibid Art 22(2) on burden of proof and assumption of compliance.

[148] See the initial proposal by European Parliament Resolution of 10 March 2021 with recommendations to the Commission on corporate due diligence and corporate accountability (2020/2129(INL)) that contained rules on choice of law and jurisdiction as an amendment to the Brussels (recast) and Rome II Regulation.

[149] Due Diligence Directive Proposal, Art 22(5) (n 143).

breach of EU regulation by foreign actors in civil proceedings even if these occurred outside the EU and would lead to application of foreign law.[150]

In both cases – digitalisation and sustainability – one can observe a tendency to change private law concepts, specifically civil liability, to draw disputes with global relevance and the regulatory interest of the EU, and link them to the core private-law concepts of tort. Tort is used in a regulatory manner by the EU and is used to remedy global regulatory problems.[151] This occurs on two levels: On the EU level, private law gains renewed attention as a component of the legislative process of EU regulatory frameworks that have a global reach. Private law is here conceived of as linking to substantive private-law rules, the procedural dimension in terms of civil proceedings as well as integrating regulatory developments within private international law that allow drawing civil proceedings into the EU courts based on regulatory concerns. In this context, technical standards play an important role. They provide the yardstick for measuring compliance and are also relied upon to determine private liability.[152]

C. Conclusion

When approaching European Transnational Private Law through the lens of regulatory private law, we thus encounter a different situation compared to the formalist private law perspective. In regulatory private law, the EU has occupied the terrain very well, both autonomously and in relation to influencing Member-State private law systems. This dominance of the EU in regulatory private law does impact what we see in relation to global reach. Horizontally, we can see indications that regulatory private law is becoming a concept that can be adopted by other countries, though we may see sector-specific and issue-specific differences. At the same time, we also see regulatory private law expanding through the legislation of the EU itself. By means of linking market regulation that already has a global reach to private law concepts, we can see how the EU expands its global regulatory ambition to private-law disputes and how it instrumentalises Member States' private laws for its regulatory objectives. Once regulatory objectives are pursued by the EU beyond the EU itself and once this occurs combined with a linking between regulation and private law (as discussed above in terms of civil liability), private law concepts themselves become subject to

[150] That this expansionist tendency in private international law is not necessarily a positive development and can lead to marginalisation of non-EU legal systems and a trend towards delocalising justice had been emphasised by Antoine Duval in his contribution to our conference, Duval, 'Delocalized Justice and the Spectre of Neocolonialism' (n 15) and, with lesser focus on the EU, by A Duval and M Plagis, 'Delocalized Justice: The Delocalisation of Corporate Accountability for Human Rights Violations Originating in Africa', Blog symposium on Afronomics, 4 October 2021, available at www.afronomicslaw.org/category/analysis/delocalized-justice-delocalisation-corporate-accountability-human-rights.

[151] See the similar conclusion by V Ulfbeck in chapter 13 of this book, in relation to climate change.

[152] See more extensively on European technical standards in sustainability and digitalisation, HW Micklitz in chapter 3 of this book. In this context, however, we see differences in how technical standards are integrated between different regulations, see for the rules on digitalisation and the differences between the Digital Services and Markets Act on the one hand and the AI Act on the other, N Helberger, HW Micklitz and P Rott, *The Regulatory Gap: Consumer Protection in the Digital Economy – Addendum to the Report 'Structural Asymmetries in Digital Consumer Markets'* (Brussels, BEUC, 2021) 17ff, paras 48–50.

that global regulatory reach. By highlighting the parallel evolving discussion within private international law on adjusting the rules on jurisdiction and applicable law to this novel regulatory reality, we also see a similarly expansive tendency. Proposals are made to change jurisdictional rules for these private law disputes with a regulatory interest to draw them into the competence of Member State courts and to expand the conflict-of-law rules to allow the EU regulatory rules to become applicable.

That tendency was documented in this contribution in relation to the question of corporate sustainability and digitalisation, specifically regulation of AI and, in other contributions, with a view to climate change. At the same time, the hope is that this analysis offers a frame for further research on what European regulatory transnational private law may look like in other areas and in relation to other private-law concepts.[153]

V. SOCIETAL PERSPECTIVES: TRANSNATIONAL EU PRIVATE LAW

Both classical and regulatory private law are analytical perspectives that link private law very strongly to the state. In the classical formalist understanding, private law appears as codified rules that relate to private relations, that constitute the 'private law society' and that, traditionally, are oriented to private interests. In the regulatory understanding, the instrumental – including constitutional – perspective on private law comes to the fore. In both cases, it is the state that constitutes and regulates through private-law rules.

Yet, when thinking of transnational private law, a third and highly important category of private law needs to be introduced. Private law can also be detached from the state and be related to private and societal rulemaking by non-state actors. Such inclusion of non-state law exists in national private law discourses and is closely linked to understandings of proceduralisation,[154] private governance[155] and polycontextuality.[156] This understanding has been influential in the economic analysis of private law that also distinguishes – not between public and private law, but between public (law) and private regulation.[157] And in the debate on transnational law, this understanding of private actors as lawmakers and regulators has even been constitutive.[158] As Rodrigo Vallejo's foundational contribution shows, this procedural understanding, grounded in the idea of transnational legal processes, can be an immensely fruitful conceptual framework for developing European Transnational

[153] Other private law concepts may focus on contract in the light of regulation of unfair trading practices that apply outside the EU, eg, through the Unfair Trading Practices Regulation or the Business to Platform-Rules and the Digital Markets and Digital Services Acts or the concept of personhood in light of the EU's regulatory interventions in the field of taxation. All of these, however, merit their own detailed analysis.

[154] See above (n 24).

[155] Schepel (n 55).

[156] G Teubner, 'After Privatisation? The Many Autonomies of Private Law' (1999) 51 *Current Legal Problems* 393–424, at 395ff.

[157] F Cafaggi and A Renda, 'Public and Private Regulation: Mapping the Labyrinth' (2012) *Dovenschmidt Quarterly* 16.

[158] Calliess and Zumbansen (n 49).

Private Law when we approach the concept of European Transnational Private Law from a transnational perspective.[159]

From an EU perspective, one may argue that the difference between regulatory private law and private regulation is not that sharp and that, as a consequence, the procedural perspective on private law does not merit its own perspectivisation. After all, in EU law, reliance on private actors for its regulatory objectives has been important from the start.[160] EU law has been constituted to foresee a role for private actors and their own lawmaking and, with the better regulation agenda, self-regulation and co-regulation became part of the EU's toolbox to foster its objectives.[161] In the discussion on regulatory private law, I have indeed omitted the dimension of private regulation. In aiming to foster sustainability and digitalisation, the EU is not only turning to private law, but also to private actors and their self-regulatory capacity. Notified bodies, standardisation for digital technology, as well as corporations and societal 'stakeholders' in sustainability due diligence characterise regulatory initiatives as much as does the shift to the rules on tort and contract. Hence, from the EU aspect, this perspective on private regulation might even form part of EU private law; yet, nevertheless, the transnational perspective would emphasise the difference. Private law and its constitution and regulation of the market and non-state law and private lawmaking are two entirely distinct categories.[162] From a transnational private-law viewpoint, reliance on private actors and their regulation merits its own perspective. From this transnational perspective, one can again identify two possible inroads for analysing European Transnational Private Law: One can first look at the way in which EU private regulators act transnationally and thus how private regulation that has developed in the EU enjoys global reach. Second, the perspective can be placed on EU law, its reliance on and responsiveness to global private regulation, and thus how EU law contributes to transnational private legal processes.

In spelling out these dimensions, I have the benefit of being able to rely significantly on the contributions in this book. Interestingly, all contributions in this book have put significant emphasis on this global reach of EU private law in relation to private actors. Regardless of whether the topic was finance, climate change, non-discrimination, or collective labour law, fostering private actors' regulatory capacity through the EU, or the autonomous influence by EU-based private actors were, in different ways, all taken up as part of the sector-specific European transnational private law. This tells us something about the importance of private lawmaking in relation to the EU's transnational reach. Hence, in this last part, my aim is to order the insights from the book and to categorise them analytically. I propose to distinguish between two levels of analysis in terms of the global reach of private actors' regulatory engagement: On the one hand, EU private regulators and, on the other hand, the level of EU private law that links to private regulation.

[159] See R Vallejo in chapter 4 of this book.

[160] I thank Hans Micklitz for this comment on the chapter.

[161] EU Commission Communication, 'European Governance – A White Paper', 25 July 2001, COM (2001) 428 final.

[162] See R Wai, 'The Interlegality of Transnational Private Law' (2008) 71 *Law and Contemporary Problems* 107–28; Wai (n 31).

A. Societal (Non-State) Actors as Exports

In many contributions to this book, the role of private (non-state) actors as subjects features quite prominently. It even looks as if this informal role filled by private actors has been a largely neglected aspect of how EU and European law travels. In the field of labour law, we see Liukkunen's text as a detailed analysis with not only the legal framework but also the practices and autonomy of European Works Councils in the field of global labour governance within multinational corporations.[163] Based on earlier research about the global regulatory efforts of transnational corporations and contracting, Möschel has taken us on a journey where corporate counsel and legal departments become engaged in drafting European-inspired anti-discrimination policies.[164] And in the two previous sections where I discussed formal and regulatory private law perspectives, the role of private, non-state actors already came to the fore. When analysing the formal perspective on private law, it became clear that many transfers of private law rules were actually not taking place via formal fora. Attempts to comprehensively codify the rules on private law and to engage in a systematic way of thinking about private law have been successful where the transfer has happened via academic and epistemic communities, not via formal lawmaking and state-exchange.[165] In her contribution, Pia Letto-Vanamo emphasises this strong role of academic communities to translate particular modes of thinking into other parts of the world. Moreover, in the field of private international law, it is largely party autonomy, but not the formal rules themselves, that trigger the inclusion of transnational rules and dispute resolution fora into disputes between European parties. Similarly, the analysis of the regulatory private law perspective has illustrated a high degree of transnational reach via technical standards. This, as Hans-W Micklitz also analyses in his chapter, places standardisation organisations in a position to influence global standard-setting. And, finally – and we will come back to this in the next section – different contributions also emphasise the role of European companies and 'lead firms' in exporting 'European values' through corporate policies, contracting, and informal governance mechanisms.[166]

B. Societal EU Private Law: Constituting and Piggybacking on Transnational Regulators

When reversing the perspective and looking at EU law and how it links to private regulators, we do see a connection in terms of why EU private actors may engage so heavily in global regulation. The fact is that EU law is not detached from private regulation; it is heavily engaged by means of (1) constituting a permissive environment

[163] See U Liukkunen in chapter 6 of this book.
[164] See M Möschel in chapter 7 of this book.
[165] See section III.A on the idea of 'normative knowledge' and section III.B in relation to academic codification projects.
[166] In particular the contributions by J Salminen, M Rajavuori and KH Eller in chapter 14 of this book and V Ulfbeck in chapter 13.

for private actors to regulate and (2) actively piggybacking on transnational private regulators. Let me discuss both of them:

In the first place, there are different occasions where the EU fosters the regulatory capacity of private actors by granting them autonomy to pursue their interests and by constituting the market environment in which they operate. Liukkunen explains that transnational labour governance is strongly fostered by the principle of party autonomy in private international law and its related EU regulation.[167] In her contribution to this book, she explains how this relates to the role of European Works Councils in influencing global contractualised labour governance.[168] Developing the concept of EU law on the (financial) market, Chadwick takes a similar path. She points out how the EU has created a permissive environment through private international law and capital mobility that empowers private actors to choose which regulatory environment they aim to be subjected to and thus levels them up to governing global financial space.[169]

These sector-specific observations can well be related to the broader conceptual critical discussions that are taking place at the moment around the constitutive role of private law for global markets. Whether it be concepts of the constitutive role of legal institutions for financial capitalism,[170] the law of political economy,[171] or the invisible hand of law in fostering private regulation,[172] a debate has started that turns to the invisible role of law in fostering the market and its autonomy. In this context, the EU has also been pointed out as being particularly prone to creating such a permissive environment upon which the market and its self-regulatory capacity thrives.[173] Mataija has also shown that trade law has contributed to this permissive environment in which the focus is on private regulators and their capacities.

Yet, and what is more, our book shows that for several sectors, the EU has not only participated in the constitution of global markets that are left to their own regulatory dynamics and thus has been fostering global private regulation. Private actors and their global regulatory potential are increasingly and actively instrumentalised by the EU to foster its policy objectives and extend those objectives globally. Indeed, we are witnessing piggybacking on private regulators for the purpose of expanding the reach of EU law.

On the one hand, this is visible in the EU's reliance on global private regulation as models for its own regulatory frameworks, a 'downloading' of transnational law. For

[167] U Liukkunen, 'Employment and Private International Law' (2020) *Elgar Research Reviews in Law* 2020.

[168] See U Liukkunen in chapter 6 of this book, section VII.

[169] A Chadwick in chapter 9 of this book, concluding section.

[170] S Deakin, D Gindis, G Hodgson, K Huang and K Pistor, 'Legal Institutionalism: Capitalism and the Constitutive Role of Law' (2017) 45 *Journal of Comparative Economics* 188–201.

[171] PF Kjaer, 'The Law of Political Economy: An Introduction' in PF Kjaer (ed), *The Law of Political Economy: Transformation in the Function of Law* (Cambridge, Cambridge University Press, 2020); I Kampourakis, 'Bound by the Economic Constitution: Notes for "Law and Political Economy" in Europe' (2021) 1 *Journal of Law and Political Economy* 301–32.

[172] J Bakan, 'The Invisible Hand of Law: Private Regulation and the Rule of Law' (2015) 48 *Cornell International Law Journal* 279–300.

[173] E Christodoulidis, *The Redress of Law* (Cambridge, Cambridge University Press, 2021) shows this with the example of European labour law.

instance, in the field of financial markets, as Chadwick shows, the EU has been relying on international – including private, regulatory frameworks – to model its own rules. One of the aims was surely that the EU's own rules would be suitable for transnational markets and allow EU law to operate successfully on the global level. But, as Pantazatou shows, a translation of global frameworks is also taking place in the field of taxation (although this downloading has been coming more from the international realm of the Organisation for Economic Co-operation and Development (OECD) than from private actors).[174] In both cases, one can see that a driver for downloading international frameworks has been to attract private actors, but also to implicitly pursue the EU's strategic and normative policy objectives. In taxation, this is most visible in the EU's shift from gaining revenue to the 'ethical' dimension of fighting tax avoidance. In the context of taxation, one can identify that the purpose of downloading international frameworks has, however, shifted as well. From gaining widespread acceptance when EU law is on the market, the aim is also to 'Europeanise' international frameworks to foster the EU's own policy objectives.[175]

On the other hand, the EU has recently started to levy transnational regulators for its own instrumental objectives. In this book, that development is most visible in relation to corporate regulation through tort law,[176] in trade law,[177] as well as in the use of global value chains. The contribution by Salminen, Rajavuori and Eller has been coining this interaction between the EU and transnational levels in relation to global value chains as the EU's reliance on transnational regulators as 'regulatory proxies' and the idea of an 'extension through law'.[178] This phrase refers to the EU's strategy of 'us[ing] a rather specific political substratum ("sustainability", "human rights", "security of supply") to move from a territorially defined vision of the Internal Market to a vision of global embeddedness through myriads of production networks'.[179] An earlier publication, and related to this project, by Cantero Gamito and Micklitz has shown a similar trend in relation to standardisation and contracts.[180] While in relation to sustainability, the EU relies significantly on global value chains and EU corporations as regulatory proxies, the field of regulated markets as well as the objectives of leading digitalisation has been fostering a trend of relying on standardisation.[181]

Reliance on private actors and their self-regulation is an old idea that, with the trend towards self-regulation and co-regulation, has been exerting a significant

[174] See K Pantazatou in chapter 12 of this book. Similarly for securities regulation, see A Marcacci in chapter 10 of this book.

[175] The clearest example here is the use by the EU Commission of international frameworks in taxation by the OECD, but to give them an autonomous meaning in the context of EU proceedings on state aid.

[176] On which, in relation to climate change objectives, see V Ulfbeck in chapter 13 of this book.

[177] See M Mataija in chapter 11 of this book.

[178] See J Salminen, M Rajavuori and KH Eller in chapter 14 of this book.

[179] ibid, at 39. See for similar observations HW Micklitz in chapter 3 of this book.

[180] M Cantero Gamito and H Micklitz (eds), *The Role of the EU in Transnational Legal Ordering: Standards, Contracts and Codes* (Cheltenham, Edward Elgar, 2019) and HW Micklitz in chapter 3 of this book.

[181] On the relevance of the standardisation organisations in the AI Act, see M Veale and F Zuiderveen Borgesius, 'Demystifying the Draft EU Artificial Intelligence Act' (2021) 22 *Computer Law Review International* 97–112, at 104ff; for regulated markets: HW Micklitz in chapter 3 of this book.

influence on the creation and enforcement of EU law.[182] Indeed, as we have seen, from the EU's position, reliance on private actors and their regulatory activities may just be seen as part of private law, but in regulatory form. Yet, the use of private regulators by the EU to engage in global markets means an expansion of the EU's vision of private regulation in the transnational arena. While, from the transnational perspective, private regulation has been portrayed regularly as non-state ordering as detached from public ordering, the EU's expansion to the transnational arena illustrates the interconnection between the private and public dimensions of transnational law. But at the same time this also leads to a different kind of foreign reach. First and foremost, while piggybacking on transnational regulation can be underpinned by the idea of disciplining private actors to EU objectives, reliance on the transnational also leads to a situation where private actors become more active in shaping the concepts that they are subjected to. From a theoretical perspective, this also seems an inevitable consequence. If the EU orients its legislation on responsiveness to private actors and uses reflexive modes of regulation to activate private regulatory capacity, the regulatory objectives are necessarily translated by the private actors themselves. This tendency has been exposed in the transnational literature,[183] but, in the EU, still seems to be an underdeveloped concern. For the field of anti-discrimination law, Möschel's analysis sheds light on how – absent specific regulation on the matter – private actors develop their own perspective on the topic and select what documents and frameworks to seek guidance on. Rather than orienting themselves on the EU legal setting in which they are embedded, EU companies integrate anti-discrimination into the human rights and international labour-centric perspective. Möschel indicates that the involvement of specific departments in companies and other actors, with their cultural background and organisational setting, may be influential in how specific concepts are understood.[184]

Again, it remains to be seen how, for the different sectors and issues involved, piggybacking on private actors and regulation by those actors for exporting the European vision is stronger and for which areas it is weaker.

C. Conclusion: Societal Global Presence and Absence

Creating a permissive market environment through law for transnational regulators and piggybacking on transnational regulators for policy objectives together shape – it should be noted – a particular form of transnational regulation through the EU. The previous analysis discussed the way in which the EU relies on private companies, standard-setters, and contracting modes to export its visions. Yet what is discussed also begs the question: what is absent? In the here-portrayed global reach of EU law

[182] Extensively on private actors within the institutional context of the EU and their involvement in lawmaking, see Mataija (n 57); recently, with a consideration of the methodological consequences for legal research on EU law, see Beckers (n 56).

[183] See, eg, AC Cutler and T Dietz (eds), *The Politics of Transnational Governance by Contract* (London, Routledge, 2017).

[184] See M Möschel in chapter 7 of this book.

through private regulators, what is lacking is the wider societal perspective and its regulatory potential. From a transnational perspective, there are manifold discussions around the contested transnational governance terrain. One can identify this in particular in the debate on global production and value chains.[185] Rather than being solely created by powerful actors, transnational private regulation itself becomes a struggle, an arena of conflict where different actors aim to foster their own interests and put their regulation in place. However, when looking at the EU perspective on these matters, this conflicting understanding of transnational regulation is absent. Actors outside the EU as well as societal actors outside the market have been largely ignored in the EU's reliance on transnational regulators,[186] though with the notable exception of technical standardisation.[187] Some even go further by criticising the neo-colonial perspective of the EU that now appears not only in the EU's ignoring the export of private law as a Western concept,[188] but also in the EU's selective reliance on EU actors as makers of transnational regulation rather than those affected.[189] Undoubtedly, EU regulation is responsive to a particular vision of the private and society that, in its transnational reach, is focused on European society.

VI. EUROPEAN AND EU PRIVATE LAW GLOBALLY: *QUO VADIS*?

This chapter has completed a long journey through the potential and actual transnational reach of European and EU private law. It has made an attempt at showing the traces of where to look for European and EU private law in a global setting. However, rather than providing a direct answer to whether and how European and EU private law appears on the transnational scene or showing clear trajectories, this contribution could only reveal directions and a trajectory if we conceive of private law from different perspectives. The answer as to where to trace private law and what private law can be traced depends heavily on what perspective we take: formal, regulatory, or societal. Each of these perspectives opens up different paths that we can explore but none of them leaves us with a sole and single answer. When being asked to draw

[185] DL Levy, 'Political Contestation in Global Production Networks' (2008) 33 *Academy of Management Review* 943–63; J Bair and F Palpacuer, 'CSR Beyond the Corporation: Contested Governance in Global Value Chains' (2015) 15 *Global Networks: A Journal of Transnational Affairs* S1–S19; C Scheper and CA Vestena, 'Die Pandemie offenbart die Defizite des transnationalen Menschenrechtsschutzes: Ein Plädoyer für eine Konfliktperspektive auf globale Lieferketten' (2020) *Zeitschrift für Friedens- und Konfliktforschung* 429–41.

[186] See, J Salminen, M Rajavuori and KH Eller in chapter 14 of this book, section IV.

[187] Regulation No 1025/2012 of the European Parliament and of the Council of 25 October 2012 on European standardisation [2012] OJ L316/12 Art 5.

[188] See above, section III.A.

[189] Most pointedly this criticism has been raised by C Omari Lichuma, 'Centering Europe and Othering the Rest' *Völkerrechtsblog* (16 January 2023), available at https://voelkerrechtsblog.org/de/centering-europe-and-othering-the-rest/ in relation to EU legislative attempts. The argument is more extensively developed in relation to comparable German legislation in C Omari Lichuma, '(Laws) Made in the "First World": A TWAIL Critique of the Use of Domestic Legislation to Extraterritorially Regulate Global Value Chains' (2021) 81 *Zeitschrift für ausländisches öffentliches Recht und Völkerrecht* 497–532. *cf* also on a similar argument with respect to French law on regulating global supply chains, D Bose, 'Decentring Narratives around Business and Human Rights Instruments: An Example of the French Devoir de Vigilance Law' (2023) 8 *Business and Human Rights Journal* 18–42.

the broad lines of how European and EU private law have travelled, one may perhaps not see those lines immediately. But one may see a formal terrain of private law rules that seems not to be strongly coined by the EU in terms of substance, but more in terms of procedure. And one may see how such procedural rules are infiltrated by societal private law through reliance on party autonomy and the opportunity for private actors to choose transnational rules as well as by regulatory private law whenever the CJEU draws 'red lines' on private activity. One may see further a regulatory private law terrain that is well occupied by the EU and has led to strong transnational reach, both in policy processes and in territorial extension of private law itself. And one may see a crucial – but largely invisible – terrain of societal private law in which non-state actors from the EU influence global regulatory and epistemic processes of private law-making. If there were a question on what path to further differentiate and research, it seems to me that the societal perspective is worth pursuing.

And a second, rather implicit, conclusion can be drawn from the concepts and perspectives offered in this contribution: A choice has been made to offer a European perspective on private law and trace its impact on constellations outside of the EU. On different occasions, it has been mentioned that the categories may not fit an analysis that looks at European expansion from the outside or those categories may be contested from this perspective. For the research agenda on European transnational private law, this means that a complementary analysis is needed from the perspective of those affected, together with a related discussion on what European transnational private law means from the outside. Yet this complete story of private law concepts emerging outside Europe and the perspective of those affected has still to be written, but this needs to be done by others.

Markets

3

European Law of Regulated Industries and Transnational Private Law

HANS-W MICKLITZ*

I. CLAIM, ARGUMENT, METHODS

THIS CHAPTER FOCUSES on the global reach of European private law in regulated markets – banking and finance, energy, electronic communication and transport – but excludes pensions and insurance. It rolls out a new field of research, thereby building on previous research on European private law *within* the European Union (EU): on its regulatory nature and its interaction with technical standardisation. The concept of European regulatory private law here asserted opens space beyond a classic bilateral understanding of private law relations. It integrates the executive, independent agencies and private collective identities such as standardisation bodies. Private law relations – as was the major finding with regard to their role in the internal market[1] – are sandwiched between administrative supervisory regulation from above and technical standards from below. Market regulation at either end serves as a substitute for the missing competence to regulate b2b relations, which triggers questions as to the accountability and legitimacy of European

* Professor of Economic Law, Robert Schuman Centre, European University Institute. I would like to express my gratitude to Simona Ciccarini for her long lasting and careful assistance in the background research. My deep thanks go to the Finland Distinguished Professor Programme which generously financed my sojourn at the University of Helsinki and to Dean Pia Letto-Vanamo who provided me with all the support one could dream of as a guest scholar, to my esteemed colleague Takis Tridimas and to all those young scholars with whom I collaborated in the ERC and the Fidipro Project over the last decade and who provided critical comments: Lucila de Almeida, Anna Maria Barata, Anna Beckers, Marta Cantero Gamito, Guido Comparato, Teemu Juutilainen, Roseta Karova, Pia Letto-Vanamo, Antonio Marcacci, Federico della Negra, Elena Sedano, Yane Svetiev, Barend van Leeuwen, and Rodrigo Vallejo. The final responsibility remains mine alone.

[1] HW Micklitz, *Politics of Justice in European Private Law* (Cambridge, Cambridge University Press, 2018); HW Micklitz, 'Soft Law, Technical Standards and European Private Law' in E Korkea-aho (ed), *Handbook of Soft Law* (Cheltenham, Edward Elgar Publishing, 2022); H Schepels, 'The Constitution of Private Governance: Product Standards in the Regulation of Integrating Markets (Oxford, Hart Publishing, 2005).

regulatory private law. The overall argument remains functional, though, and not content-based. The meat – private law relations – can and could only be identified through empirical research on administrative practices of supervisory agencies which govern the regulated markets and on the impact of technical standards on contract and tort.[2]

The search for the global reach of European (regulatory) private law formed the core of a project financed by the Academy of Finland.[3] Theoretically the project is connected to Anu Bradford's 'Brussels effect' and Joanne Scott's 'external extension' of EU law.[4] This chapter extends the two strands of European private law beyond EU legal borders. The EU, in the result, is turning the law of regulated markets inside out, from the internal market to the EU's external economic relations. The extent of the success of externalisation depends decisively on the degree of integration the EU achieves in the respective markets and on the existence or non-existence of international treaties in the respective sectors. The particular approach as to how the EU designs the rules affects the external reach. The emerging picture is therefore differentiated. Where the law on regulated markets bears values beyond the market – such as health and safety, sustainability or fundamental rights – the EU opens space for societal justice through administrative co-operation and technical standardisation. The depth and breadth of *internal* integration hits the mark. Seen from above, administrative regulation and administrative actors, the European and national supervisory agencies, are key. Where administrative cooperation *within* the EU is well established, the EU succeeds in carrying its ideas, ideologies and values of surveillance and monitoring to the outside world. Private law relations are gradually becoming the subject of administrative regulation and enforcement. The situation is different with regard to technical standards, regulation from below. Here, the EU can rely on institutional and regulatory structures over 100 years old that have enabled the Western industrialised countries to play a leading role in the production and distribution of industrially manufactured products around the world.[5] The EU is using its long-standing experience to de-territorialise European standards and even to upload them with non-economic policy issues. Private law is located in between administrative regulation and technical standardisation mostly in the form of contract law. The metaphor of the sandwich proves also to be powerful in the EU's external relationships. The only way to catch the reality of b2b relations in external relations

[2] B Van Leeuwen Barend, *European Standardisation of Services and its Impact on Private Law: Paradoxes of Convergence* (London, Hart Publishing, 2017); H Schepel and J Falke, *Legal Aspects of Standardisation in the Member States of the EC and EFTA*, Vol 1, Comparative Report (Office for Official Publications of the European Communities, 2000); J Falke and H Schepel (eds), Legal Aspects of Standardisation in the Member States of the EC and EFTA, Country Reports, Vol 2; J Falke, *Legal Aspects of Standardisation in the Member States of the EC and EFTA*, Country Report Germany (in German) Vol 3 (Office for Official Publications of the European Communities, 2000).

[3] HW Micklitz and M Cremona (eds), *Private Law in the External Dimension of the EU* (Oxford, Oxford University Press, 2016); on the role of the European Commission, see M Cantero Gamito and HW Micklitz (eds), *The Role of the EU in Transnational Legal Ordering: Standards, Contracts and Codes* (Cheltenham, Edward Elgar Publishing, 2020).

[4] Explained in the introductory chapter of this book.

[5] R Michaels, 'Make A Buy – A Public Market for Legal Transplants' in H Eidenmüller (ed), *Regulatory Competition in Contract Law and Dispute Resolution* (London, Bloomsbury Publishing, 2013) 27–42.

is to look beyond classic categories of international private law.[6] A caveat is needed, though. This chapter deals neither with the role of private parties and their market power in general nor the role of private parties in the ongoing privatisation of law enforcement through compliance or self-certification and third-party certification. Such an analysis deserves a separate chapter.[7]

A. Methodology

The following analysis is limited to the European perspective, to the search for EU rules in regulated markets in the EU regulations and directives that deal with the interaction between EU and non-EU countries, of the scope and reach of the rules, on interinstitutional agreements and on the role and function of technical standardisation within regulated markets and their connection to private law relations. The rules investigated on the external dimension of banking, energy, telecoms and transport are vast and even a reprint of the titles covers over 30 pages, of which some two-thirds deal with standardisation. The study covers the period 2010–2020. However, with regard to energy the data had to be updated due to regulatory activities in the aftermath of the war in Ukraine.

In order to filter the material, I used catchwords such as: 'third country'; 'international relations'; 'extra-EU'; 'non-EU'; 'standards'; 'international standards'; and 'European standards'. This allowed me to extract rules on both strands – external administrative regulation and technical standardisation and to identify the law in the books. Technical standards, however, are not publicly available, they are copyright protected and have to be bought in order to be studied. It seems as if the European Court of Justice (ECJ) is ready to seriously question the access barriers, which would bring some light into the black hole.[8] In order to get an idea of the *practical* effects, I analysed publicly available reports of European agencies as well as the three European standardisation bodies, where possible back to 2010. No ECJ case law deals with the external dimension of regulated markets regulation and the role of technical standardisation. That is why the chapter does not claim to contrast theory and practice. Despite these limits, the chapter manages to demonstrate the strategic use of European private law in regulated markets to open new markets for European industry and to stretch European values enshrined in these rules beyond EU territory.

B. How the Argument Goes

The analysis starts with a deep examination of trade statistics, the import and export of the four services and their relevance for the internal market. This explains the

[6] L de Almeida M Cantero Gamito and HW Micklitz, 'Institutional and Normative Cooperation in Private Law, Beyond the Hague Conference Towards Standard Setting Organisations' in J Odermatt and R Wessel (eds), *Research Handbook on the European Union and International Organisations* (Cheltenham, Edward Elgar Publishing, 2019) 386–409.

[7] With regard to banking and finance, see A Marcacci, *The Uncomfortable Position of the Compliance Function under the EU Law of Investment Services*, to be published in the *Journal of Banking Regulation*.

[8] Case C-160/20 *Stichting Rookpreventie Jeugd and Others* ECLI:EU:C:2022:101 at 48 and 52.

policy which stands behind the four sectors, why the EU has engaged in multilateral agreements on the energy, aviation and transport community occasionally on the basis of Article 218 of the Treaty on the Functioning of the EU (TFEU), but first and foremost why Article 114 TFEU is of utmost importance for understanding the potential external effects of the European approach to regulated markets. The rest of the chapter is broken down into two parts – first, regulation of regulated markets in and beyond the EU, followed by standardisation of regulated markets in and beyond the EU. Both parts follow a similar structure: a brief recap builds the bridge to previous research, the external dimension dominates analysis, first in the books – the rules on regulated markets and the rules on standardisation of regulated markets – then the law in action – the administrative practice of European agencies and European standardisation bodies. The interim conclusion should help illustrate the link to private law relations. The overall conclusion aims at combining the two strands – regulation from above and regulation from below with regard to their external reach in private law relations. Private law stands in between and is characterised through a dense set of rules wrapped around the core of the contract. Its atypical nature facilitates its export via administrative regulations and technical standards.

II. EXTERNAL TRADE AND THE EU COMPETENCE ORDER

A. EU External Trade

The current exchange rates of products exported from the EU and imported into the EU are taken from the Eurostat website.[9] The website distinguishes between goods and services, such as transport, banking and finance, energy and telecommunications. The data allow an understanding of the dependence and interdependence of the EU with the outside world and shed light on why the EU is economically and politically forced to engage in building legal ties with regions and countries. A look into the trade agreements the EU has concluded with its trading partners complement the picture.

Setting aside energy, which until 2022 was governed by a certain though decreasing dependence on Russian imports, EU import/export rates demonstrate reliance on established trading partners in the Western world: the United States (USA), the United Kingdom (UK), Norway and Switzerland. The notable exception is China, in the telecommunications sector and in maritime transport. The current situation within the four regulated markets may be characterised as sensitive: an investment agreement with China is pending, the EU–UK Trade and Cooperation Agreement (TCA) has to be filled with life, the relationship between Switzerland and the EU is in limbo,[10] the energy market is in turmoil. The EU and the Member States have built up a stable regional energy community, aviation community and transport community with South East European (SEE) Countries (the Western

[9] Eurostat website at https://ec.europa.eu/eurostat/statistics-explained/index.php?title=Main_Page.

[10] R Ibbetson, 'Switzerland Walks Away from EU Cooperation Deal Talks' *Mailonline* (26 May 2021), available at https://rotf.lol/dailym.

Balkans).[11] The following data that break down the different types of services in terms of export vs import are taken from Eurostat.[12]

i. Banking and Finance

In 2017 the EU imported six per cent and exported 9.5 per cent financial services. The EU is a net lender in direct investment.

> Based upon Eurostat estimations, EU aggregated net assets in direct investment outside the EU amounted to EUR 1 422.6 billion in 2020 (EUR 1 845.7 billion in 2019). A positive net position in direct investment resulted from considerably higher values of external assets (EUR 10 757.4 billion) compared to figures for external liabilities (EUR 9 334.8 billion).[13]

As for investments, the main trading partners are the USA (2017 and 2018) and Switzerland.[14] From 2010 to 2018, export of financial services increased: exports of 59.7 billion and imports of 26.3 in 2010 and in 2018 exports of 82.5 and imports of 50.4.[15]

In August 2021 the USA and the European Central Bank (ECB) drafted a Memorandum of Understanding (MoU) covering 'consultation, cooperation and the exchange of information related to the supervision and oversight of certain cross-border over-the-counter derivatives entities in connection with the use of substituted compliance by such entities'.[16] In December 2020 the EU concluded negotiations for a Comprehensive Agreement on Investment (CAI) with China, which is awaiting ratification. Investment protection agreements with Singapore and Vietnam are equally pending. The agreement between the EU and Switzerland on automatic exchange of financial information[17] has run into problems because Switzerland has left the EU trade agreement. The EU–UK intend to adopt a 'Joint Declaration on Financial Services Regulatory Cooperation or memorandum of understanding'.[18] Moreover, there is an MoU between the ECB and the UK's Prudential Regulation Authority, which was signed in 2020, but it only entered into force on 1 January 2021.[19]

[11] R Karova, 'The Energy Community in its Second Decade: Where Does it Stand and Where is it Heading?' in L de Almeida, M Cantero Gamito, M Durovic and KP Purnhagen (eds), *The Transformation of Economic Law, Essays in Hour of HW Micklitz*, (London, Hart Publishing, 2019) 271; on the legal nature, see R Karova, 'The Application of the EU Constitutional Principles in the Energy Community; Reaping the Full Benefits of the Regional Integration' (2015) 3 *European Networks Law and Regulation Quarterly* 2, 176–86.

[12] 'File: Value of Extra-EU Trade in Selected Services, EU-28, 2010 and 2018 (billion EUR) 0219.png' (*Eurostat, Statistics Explained*) (europa.eu), available at https://rotf.lol/stathistics.

[13] 'International Investment Position Statistics' (*Eurostat, Statistics Explained*) (europa.eu), available at https://ec.europa.eu/eurostat/statistics-explained/index.php?title=International_investment_position_statistics.

[14] 'Foreign Direct Investments – Stocks' – (*Eurostat Statistics Explained*) (europa.eu), available at https://rotf.lol/2y73s5cf.

[15] Eurostat File (n 12).

[16] Memorandum of Understanding between the United States Securities and Exchange Commission and the European Central Bank, 2021, see www.bankingsupervision.europa.eu/press/pr/date/2021/html/ssm.pr210816~e2e5b73eb1.en.html.

[17] GEN at https://rotf.lol/consiluimeu.

[18] 'What Happened to the UK-EU Joint Declaration on Financial Services Regulatory Cooperation?' (*Eversheds Sutherland*, 5 August 2021), available at https://rotf.lol/eversheds.

[19] Joint Declaration UK-EU, available at https://rotf.lol/UKmous.

ii. Energy

In 2019, the main imported energy product was petroleum products (including crude oil, the main component), accounting for almost two-thirds of energy imports into the EU, followed by gas (27 per cent) and solid fossil fuels (six per cent). At that time, Russia was the main EU supplier of crude oil, natural gas and solid fossil fuels: In 2019, almost two-thirds of extra-EU crude oil imports came from Russia (27 per cent), Iraq (nine per cent), Nigeria and Saudi Arabia (both eight per cent) and Kazakhstan and Norway (both seven per cent). A similar analysis shows that almost three-quarters of the EU's imports of natural gas came from Russia (41 per cent), Norway (16 per cent), Algeria (8 per cent) and Qatar (5 per cent), while over three-quarters of solid fuel (mostly coal) imports originated from Russia (47 per cent), the USA (18 per cent) and Australia (14 per cent).[20] The decrease in primary energy production in the EU over recent decades led to increased imports of primary energy and energy products. The quantity of imported natural gas more than doubled over the period 1990–2019. This makes natural gas the second largest imported energy product, with record import levels in 2019, 19.3 per cent higher than in 2009. Crude oil again ranked first in terms of quantities imported, with 513 Megatons in 2019, only 1.2 per cent less than 10 years previously.[21]

The war in Ukraine has led to a dramatic change, first in promotion of non-fossil fuels and second in reduction of gas imports from Russia, which had dropped by 80 per cent (as of September 2022). Europe's alternatives to Russian energy involve: extra storage, extra Liquid Natural Gas (LNG) and lower energy demand.[22] Since the prices of all resources have soared (US$ 250 for a barrel of oil) the EU is preparing to reduce demand for oil by 20 per cent and by 50 per cent for coal in this decade,[23] a 15 per cent reduction in natural gas demand and a mandatory five per cent reduction in electricity during peak hours. All these efforts match the aim of using renewable energy sources.

The EU and the Russian Federation had agreed on a 'Roadmap: EU-Russia Energy Cooperation until 2050',[24] which is now obsolete. The relationship between Norway and the EU is laid down in the EEA Agreement,[25] through which Norway is part of the EU's internal energy market, which at present includes 30 countries with a total population of some 500 million. The agreement entered into force on 1 January 1994.[26] The energy community set up in 2006 is meant to extend EU internal energy market rules and principles to countries in South East Europe, the Black Sea region

[20] 'Where Does our Energy Come From?' (*Eurostat*), available at https://ec.europa.eu/eurostat/web/interactive-publications/energy-2023.

[21] 'Energy Statistics – An Overview' (*Eurostat Statistics Explained*) (europa.eu), available at https://rotf.lol/enerstathistics.

[22] 'World Energy Outlook 2022' (*OECDiLibrary*) 33, available at www.oecd-ilibrary.org/energy/world-energy-outlook-2022_3a469970-en.

[23] ibid 9–20; 30–40; 60–90; 241.

[24] 'Russia: EU–Russia Cooperation on Energy Issues' (*European Commission*), available at https://rotf.lol/russiaenergy.

[25] Annex IV, Energy, list provided for Art 24 EEA Agreement, ANNEX IV, available at efta.int.

[26] The EEA Agreement and Norwegian energy policy – Energifakta Norge.

and beyond on the basis of a legally binding framework.[27] The most significant importer of energy is Switzerland: Switzerland and the EU started energy collaboration in 2007. Switzerland does not automatically implement the EU energy acquis. There is collaboration but no agreement with the EU, even if the energy market is strongly connected. The EU–UK (TCA) consists in a free trade agreement signed on 30 December 2020 between the EU, the European Atomic Energy community (Euratom), and the UK. There is to be regulatory and technical cooperation, as a reconfirmation of the Paris Agreement climate goals.[28]

iii. Telecommunication (Electronic Communication)

Relative to its population, the EU's fixed broadband subscription was 34 for every 100 inhabitants in 2018. The EU remains behind South Korea, Canada and the UK. If we consider telecommunication from the production point of view (services, devices, infrastructure): in 2020, 20 per cent of high-tech products were imported from China, whereas 18 per cent of exports go to the USA.[29] Some 50 per cent of export percentage (in billions, telecommunication exports) goes to the USA and China as main trading partners.[30]

The pending CAI Agreement on Investments[31] deals with telecommunication/cloud services: China agreed to lift the investment ban for cloud services and will now be open to EU investors, subject to a 50 per cent equity cap – a significant improvement in comparison to the current situation. The Agreement includes rules to ensure that equity caps imposed for value-added telecom services will not be applied to other services such as financial, logistics, medical and the like if offered online. The US–EU Mutual Recognition Agreement (MRA) and US–EEA European Free Trade Association (EFTA) states MRAs are meant to streamline conformity assessment procedures between the USA and EU Member States.[32] The EU MRA is a bilateral, multi-sector agreement, including matters such as telecommunication and electromagnetic compatibility (EMC). Sectors include telecoms, EMC, pharmaceuticals, good manufacturing practices, electrical safety, medical devices, and recreational crafts. The US Federal Communications Commission (FCC) is the regulatory authority for EMC and telecoms.[33] The UK–EU relationship in the telecommunication sector forms part of the TCA.[34]

[27] For details, see 'Legal Frameworks' (*Energy Community*, July 2022), available at https://www.energy-community.org/legal/acquis/LFs.html.

[28] Euratom-UK agreement EUR-Lex – L:2021:150:TOC – EN – EUR-Lex (europa.eu). The EU-UK Trade and Cooperation Agreement | European Commission (europa.eu).

[29] 'File: EU Total Sold Production of High-Tech Products by Sector, 2010-2020.png' (*Eurostat Statistics Explained*) (europa.eu).

[30] 'Production and International Trade in High-Tech Products' (*Eurostat Statistics Explained*) (europa.eu).

[31] 'CAI Agreements EU – China Comprehensive Agreement on Investment (CAI): List of Sections – Trade' (*European Commission*) (europa.eu).

[32] Federal Communication Commission (FCC), 'EU MRA Equipment Authorisation – EU MRA' (fcc.gov).

[33] ibid.

[34] Official Journal of the European Union Publications Office (europa.eu).

iv. Transport

Between 2010 and 2019 the EU exported more than it imported. The EU exported 17 per cent to the USA, 15 per cent to the UK and imported from the USA (14 per cent) and UK (12 per cent). Breaking the analysis down into the different means of transport shows a more sophisticated picture. In maritime transport, EU exports to the USA amounted to 15.5 per cent and to the UK 7.5 per cent, whereas EU imports came to 11.8 per cent from the USA and 8.4 per cent from China.[35] In air transport, overall exports are significant compared to imports: exports UK 20.4 per cent and USA 23.5 per cent, imports 6.3 per cent from the USA and 14.7 per cent from the UK. Other modes of transport[36] besides sea and air can be disaggregated to space transport, rail transport, road transport, inland waterway transport, pipeline transport, electricity transmission and other supporting and auxiliary transport services – that is, all other transport services that cannot be allocated to any of the components of transport services previously described. Imports and exports remained equal from 2010 to 2019. In 2019, the UK was the main trading partner in exports with 27.5 per cent; Switzerland accounted for second place with 23.4 per cent and Russia third with 9.5 per cent. With regard to imports, the main partner was again the UK with 19.9 per cent; the USA second with 11.8 per cent (the overall percentage in 2017 was exports at 16.1 per cent and imports at 16 per cent).[37]

The USA and EU Air Transport Agreement[38] contains rules for co-operation on safety, security, the environment/climate, competition policy, as well as creating a favourable framework to develop business. The Air Transport Agreement ensures recognition of equal market access for any EU carrier and so 'provides legal certainty for the transatlantic market in light of the requirements of the European Court's Open Skies Judgments'.[39] The EU–UK TCA includes air transport. The Agreement provides for continued and sustainable air, road, rail and maritime connectivity, though market access falls below what the Single Market offers. It includes provisions to ensure that competition between EU and UK operators takes place on a level playing field, so that passenger rights, workers' rights and transport safety are not undermined.[40]

The 2004 EU–US Maritime Transport Agreement is the result of a five-year co-operative effort that recognises the importance of facilitating US–EC trade in marine equipment and through bilateral co-operation on international marine equipment regulations.[41] The EU–China Maritime Agreement,[42] in force since 2008, aims to improve the conditions under which maritime cargo transport operations are carried out. The maritime agreement is based on the principles of freedom

[35] 'File: Main Trading Partners of the EU in Sea Transport Services, 2019.png' (*Eurostat Statistics Explained*) (europa.eu).

[36] 'EU International Trade in Transport Services' (*Eurostat Statistics Explained*) (europa.eu).

[37] 'International Trade in Services Statistics – Background' (*Eurostat Statistics Explained*) (europa.eu).

[38] See the Agreement 114872.pdf (state.gov).

[39] Fact sheet, EU–US Transport Agreement.

[40] EU–UK free trade agreement. The EU–UK Trade and Cooperation Agreement, European Commission (europa.eu).

[41] US-EU-Short-Sea-MOC-2011.pdf (dot.gov) Mutual Recognition Agreements (uscg.mil).

[42] European Commission, China-EU Maritime Agreement [2008] OJ L046/25.

'to provide maritime transport services, free access to cargoes and cross trades, unrestricted access to and non-discriminatory treatment in the use of ports and auxiliary services as well as regarding commercial presence'.[43] In 1999 the EU and Switzerland stipulated the 'Overland Transport Agreement', which[44] applies to the carriage of goods and passengers, opening the railway transport market between the European Union and Switzerland.[45]

Of particular importance are the aviation community and the transport community which were built after the model of the energy community. The European Common Aviation Area (ECAA) Treaty is signed between the European Community and its Member States with the SEE countries as well as Norway and Iceland. The Treaty establishing the Transport Community (TCT) was signed between the EU and the SEE countries and is similar to the Energy Community Treaty. It remains to be seen whether these three treaties read together form a kind of substitute for EU membership of SEE countries.[46]

B. Competence Order

When the then European Economic Community entered the field of supranational regulation, the various sectors of the economy were already heavily populated with building international organisations and with multilateral and bilateral treaties. It would be a different matter to look into the institutional linkages between the International Organisations (IOs) and the EU as well as contrasting EU rules on regulated markets with the international treaties in the field. The gradual development of a common commercial policy – or more broadly the law of EU external relations – can be reconstructed as a conflict over competences between, on the one hand, the EU, which is trying to get a foot in the door in order to co-ordinate if not harmonise the different existing bilateral and multilateral commitments of the Member States, and, on the other, the Member States themselves, which fought hard to defend their role and place and – be it as a minimum – through joint competences.[47]

A closer look into the four fields under investigation reveals a more nuanced picture. Whilst litigation between the EU and the Member States in banking, finance, energy and telecoms is rather limited, transport has turned into a true battlefield. The reason behind this might be that common market-building began with freedom of trade for goods, a field where international treaties were abundant. Over time and with the support of the ECJ, the EU gained major competences in air travel and railways, with particular emphasis on safety, security and interoperability. Banking

[43] European Commission, 'EU-China Maritime Transport Agreement Enters into Force' (Press Release, 28 February 2008), available at https://ec.europa.eu/commission/presscorner/detail/en/IP_08_349.

[44] The Overland agreement final version is available at www.eda.admin.ch/europa/en/home/bilateraler-weg/bilaterale-abkommen-1/landverkehr.html.

[45] Confederazione Svizzera, European policy – the Overall agreement.

[46] For a comparison between the three treaties, see Korova, 'The Energy Community in its Second Decade' (n 11) 287.

[47] M Cremona, 'External Relations of the European Union: The Constitutional Framework for International Action' in P Craig and G De Bùrca (eds), *The Evolution of EU Law*, 3rd edn (Oxford, Oxford University Press, 2021) 431–79.

and finance – not least after Lehman Brothers – have become a prominent field of international regulation, quite often and to a growing degree via soft law.[48]

The same – though to a lesser degree – is true for energy. Litigation on distribution of competences is increasing,[49] though probably as a result of the growing powers of the competent European regulatory agency. Liberalisation and privatisation of the telecoms market through the EU is understood as a success story. Technology triggered the need to go beyond EU territory. Currently the EU is trying to shape a regulatory framework for the digital economy, which heavily affects the outside world. Any attempt to build a European market – this is a lesson to be learned from 65 years of European integration – has to be made compatible with existing and emerging international rules and treaties. There might be clashes but also leeway to develop genuine European rules, where the international legal framework remains incomplete and where geopolitics change the regulatory environment, such as the fight against climate change.[50]

The body of law to be analysed is by and large based on Article 114 TFEU, subject to special competences with regard to banking (prudential supervision) – ECB – Article 127(6) TFEU and in energy Article 195 TFEU. However, in response to the current energy crisis, the EU mobilised Article 122 TFEU to ensure security of supply.[51] None of the rules under investigation are based on the Common Commercial Policy (Article 206 TFEU) or International Agreements (Article 218 TFEU). This simple finding tells a crucial message: the global reach of European private law in regulated markets, if there is one, is to be achieved through extension of internal market competence. The rules fly under the radar of international treaties. Notable exceptions are the EEA, the EU–Swiss Agreement and, in particular, the energy, aviation and transport community, where the EU extends the rules of the Internal Market to Switzerland, Norway and the Western Balkans. Here the law of the regulated market is part of international treaties. Outside and beyond, reference to Articles 113 and 206 TFEU would immediately catapult any EU regulatory initiative into the limelight of national, regional and international politics. The EU's strategy is to use internal rules on regulating the four markets in order to engage with the external dimension of EU law on regulated markets. The EU and the Member States are the key actors in terms of international treaties. However, below international treaties or in the realm of international treaties, European agencies stand out, through the development of soft rules on co-ordinating supervision as well as through involvement in elaborating technical standards. It is in the grey zone between law and non-law where the impact on private law relations materialises.

[48] A Marcacci, *Transnational Securities Regulation, How it Works, Who Shapes It* (Berlin, Springer, 2022).

[49] A de Hauteclocque and L Hancher, 'An Overview of Recent Energy Case Law of the CJEU' (*Florence School of Regulation, European University Institute*), available at https://rotf.lol/euievent.

[50] T Juutilainen, 'EU Securitisation Regulation: Legal Ordering in Symbiosis with Transnational Law' in Cantero Gamito and Micklitz (n 3) 180–99.

[51] Council Regulation (EU) 2022/1854 on an emergency intervention to address high energy prices [2022] OJ L261 I/1; Council Regulation (EU) 2022/1369 on coordinated demand reduction measures for gas [2022] OJ L206/1.; Proposal for Council Regulation enhancing solidarity through better coordination of gas purchases, exchanges of gas across borders and reliable price benchmarks COM (2022) 549 final, 18 October 2022.

The rules investigated highlight the intermingling of administrative law and technical standards with private relations, spread over the vast array of EU regulations and EU directives. The field is not easily accessible, certainly not for non-specialists. Disclosing the private law nature of this 'mixture' requires pulling the bits and pieces together and defining a common analytical frame for a field of law which looks rather arbitrary and repetitive. So far, Directive 2018/1972 on the European Electronic Communication Code[52] is the sole effort by the EU legislature to develop a kind of system that explicitly addresses private law issues. There is no counterpart in any of the other fields, although Regulation 1227/2011 REMIT[53] and NEON (National Energy Ombudsmen Network)[54] could be understood as a functional equivalent in energy.

III. REGULATION OF REGULATED MARKETS IN AND BEYOND THE EU

The regulatory approach of the EU in shaping networked services markets places the European agencies at centre stage. That is why their competences in external relations form the starting point for analysis. The competence rules in regulations which establish the agencies are then further specified in sector-related rules on supervision and monitoring, as well as in product and contract regulation. Read together, they demonstrate that extending European enforcement culture through international commitments and agreements paves the way for a top-down approach where the EU designs the rules which administrative authorities can use to monitor and supervise private – mainly contractual – relations. Whether and to what extent the regulatory philosophy behind this approach affects private law practice will be analysed through information drawn from reports and websites of the European agencies. A short recap of the law of regulated markets *within* the EU and their impact on private law serves as a starter in order to illustrate the background from which analysis of the EU's global reach begins.

A. Recap of EU Regulated Markets and Private Law

After the adoption of the Single European Act, the EU started to liberalise and privatise former state monopolies in sectors such as telecommunications, energy and transport. Hand in hand followed liberalisation of the market for insurance and financial services. The European Commission aimed to open up markets for competitors to enhance cross-border services. These markets are regulated from cradle to grave, from the making of harmonised European rules and standards to enforcement through harmonised supervision standards and dispute settlement procedures.

[52] Directive (EU) 2018/1972 of the European Parliament and of the Council of 11 December 2018 establishing the European Electronic Communications Code (Recast) [2018] OJ L321/36.
[53] Regulation (EU) No 1227/2011 of the European Parliament and of the Council of 25 October 2011 on wholesale energy market integrity and transparency [2011] OJ L326/1.
[54] See National Energy Ombudsmen Network, available at https://neon-ombudsman.org/.

The first step took the shape of institution-building: liberalisation (and privatisation) went hand in hand with the establishment of regulatory agencies, first at the national level, later at the European level.[55] Each sector has its own agency. In banking and finance are three European agencies: the European Insurance and Occupational Pensions Authority (EOIPA), European Banking Authority (EBA) and European Securities and Markets Authority (ESMA).[56] In transport the European agencies are built around the means of transport, European Union Aviation Safety Agency (EASA) (air), European Union Agency for Railways (EAR) (rail) and European Securities and Markets Authority (EMSA) (water). Only in energy European Union Agency for the Cooperation of Energy Regulators (ACER) and in electronic communication Body of European Regulators for Electronic Communications (BEREC Office) is there but one European agency. The European agencies differ considerably in status, degree of independence and regulatory powers. Banking and finance is special in that the European agencies may adopt de-facto binding rules and even take regulatory action against financial institutions located in the EU.[57] ACER has gradually gained incremental regulatory powers in resolving disputes between national regulatory agencies in cross-border conflicts between Member States, in defining binding guidelines for network codes and potentially in taking emergency action in the aftermath of the current energy crisis.[58] Within the European Energy Community ACER has recently been empowered to adopt individual decisions in case of referral by or lack of agreement between National Regulatory Authorities where both contracting parties and EU Member States are concerned.[59] In telecoms and transport the European agencies are co-ordination bodies where national regulatory agencies are getting together under the auspices of the European Commission to exchange information, co-ordinate their activities and/or consult the European Commission in preparation of administrative guidelines.[60]

[55] F Gilardi, 'The Institutional Foundations of Regulatory Capitalism: The Diffusion of Independent Regulatory Agencies in Western Europe' (2005) 598 *The Annals of the American Academy of Political and Social Science* 84–101. In this sense Europe is also part of broader global patterns: see J Jordana, D Levi-Faur and X Fernándes i Marín, 'The Global Diffusion of Regulatory Agencies Channels of Transfer and Stages of Diffusion' (2011) 44 *Comparative Political Studies* 1343–69.

[56] On the history, see R Veil, *European Capital Markets Law*, 3rd edn (Oxford, Hart Publishing, 2022).

[57] As to ESMA under Directive 2014/65/EU of the European Parliament and of the Council of 15 May 2014 on markets in financial instruments and amending Directive 2002/92/EC and Directive 2011/61/EU (recast) ('MiFID II') [2014] OJ L173/349, see A Marcacci, *Regulating Investor Protection under EU Law, The Unbridgeable Gaps with the U.S. and the Way Forward* (London, Palgrave, 2018). On regulatory powers: H Marjosola, 'Bridging the Constitutional Gap in EU Executive Rule-Making: The Court of Justice Approves Legislative Conferral of Intervention Powers to European Securities Markets Authority: Court of Justice of the European Union (Grand Chamber) Judgment of 22 January 2014, Case C-270/12, *UK v. Parliament and Council* (Grand Chamber)' (2014) *European Constitutional Law Review* 10, 500–27.

[58] L de Almeida, 'Market Access, Harmonisation, and Governance in Network Industries: The European Union and the World Trade Organisation Compared' in E Brousseau, J M Glachant and J Sgard (eds), *The Oxford Handbook of Institutions of International Economic Governance and Market Regulation* (New York, Oxford University Press, 2021).

[59] By incorporation of the new electricity acquis in the Energy Community on the basis of Titles II and III of the Energy Community Treaty through Ministerial Council Decision 2022/03/MC-EnC adopted on 15 December 2022, complemented by Procedural Act 2022/01/MC-EnC on Regional Energy Market Integration.

[60] M Everson and E Vos, 'European Union Agencies' in M Riddervold, J Trondal and A Newsome (eds), *The Palgrave Handbook of EU Crises* (Springer Nature Switzerland AG, 2021) 315–37, part of Palgrave Studies in European Union Politics, https://doi.org/10.1007/978-3-030-51791-5_17.

The second step aims at establishing a regulatory framework for the particular market. Scholarly attention has long concentrated on the public administrative dimension of the EU's liberalisation and privatisation policy. The European Research Council (ERC) project on European regulatory private law filled the gap through a sector-related research series,[61] using socio-legal research, though to a different degree, ranging from full reconstruction of a series of ECJ cases up to field-related interviews. Rulemaking – this is one of the lessons – unites the formal and the informal authority of the law.[62] Formal, in that the EU remains the legislator which sets the frame for institutional design through building regulatory agencies, through procedural rules to be followed by public and private actors in rulemaking and dispute resolution, and through guidance on the substance of the rules. New modes of governance in the form of co-regulation and co-enforcement suggest speaking of relative rather than formal or informal authority.[63]

Implementation of secondary EU law into national legal systems has yielded 'strange' scenarios: administrative private law enforcement, administrative enforcement of collective actions, administrative complaint management and administrative settlement of conflicts. At the level of rulemaking a tendency could be observed to delegate ever more politically sensitive issues to standardisation bodies, still in the realm of co-regulation. National courts have intervened only in situations of severe conflict, when the regulatory approach – jointly promoted by the EU legislator, the national legislator, the competent administrative authorities and business organisations and actors – meets strong and organised resistance on the part of those who have not been involved in making and implementing the rules.[64] The more regulatory power the European agencies gain, the more likely it is that regulatory action is challenged before the courts.[65] A similar phenomenon can be observed in standardisation, where national courts are referring to Luxemburg cases which question the technicality of technical standards and seek an answer as to their legal nature.[66]

Regulated markets *within* the EU may be characterised through a vanishing public-private divide, an intermingling of public and private regulation through standardisation, of public and private regulators, and public and private enforcement.

[61] L de Almeida, *Integration through Self-Standing European Private Law: Insights from the Internal Point of View to Harmonisation in Energy Market*, PhD thesis (Florence, European University Institute, 2017); M Cantero Gamito, *The Private Law Dimension of the EU Regulatory Framework for Electronic Communications: Evidence of the Self-Sufficiency of European Regulatory Private Law*, PhD thesis (Florence, European University Institute, 2015); F Della Negra, *MiFID II and Private Law: Enforcing EU Conduct of Business Rules* (Oxford, Hart Publishing, 2018); G Comparato, *The Financialisation of the Citizen* (Oxford, Bloomsbury Publishing, 2018); Y Svetiev, *Experimentalist Competition Law and the Regulation of Markets* (Oxford, Hart Publishing, 2020).

[62] N Jansen, *The Making of Legal Authority: Non-Legislative Codifications in Historical and Comparative Perspective* (Oxford, Oxford University Press, 2010).

[63] I Venske and J Mendes, 'The Idea of Relative Authority in European and International Law' (2018) 16 *International Journal of Constitutional Law* 1, 75–100; I Venske and J Mendes, *Allocating Authority Who Should Do What in European and International Law?* (Oxford, Hart Publishing, 2018).

[64] Illustrative of the conflict on the increase of gas prices in the city of Hamburg, see https://rotf.lol/energie; P Derleder, 'Der Stopp der Gaspreiserhöhungen durch die Zivilrechtsprechung. Vorstellung und Analyse eines wundersamen Eingriffs' (2010) *Kritische Jutis* 292–316.

[65] de Hauteclocque and Hancher (n 49) report one single case T-735/18 *Aquind v ACER* ECLI:EU:T:2020:542; on appeal before the Court of Justice C-46/21 P.

[66] C-613/14 *James Elliott Construction* ECLI:EU:C:2016:821.

Private law is turning into an amalgam of private/public lawmaking and private/public law enforcement. Banking and finance are setting the tone. Here the development is most advanced.[67] Vallejo coined the term 'private administrative law'[68] for the kind of interaction and intermingling which governs the four regulated markets, while Marcacci speaks of 'transnational privatised regulatory law'.[69]

B. International Commitments and Agreements of the European Agencies

Direct exchange between administrative agencies from EU and non-EU countries is common practice today. No detour is needed via diplomatic avenues, via politics and foreign ministries.[70] The constituting regulations – based on Article 114 TFEU – grant European agencies powers to elaborate and adopt non-binding co-operation agreements with non-EU agencies within their mandate. However, the degree of autonomy varies considerably and depends by and large on whether the existence of an international treaty for engaging in international commitments is conditional or not. If there are international treaties, European agencies are obliged to operate within that regulatory frame. If not, the agencies' autonomy varies, depending on the competences left to the European Commission and potentially on those of the Member States in sector-related rules. Full autonomy – meaning that agencies are empowered to conclude agreements alone – are the exception to the rule.

The ECB, ESMA and EBA seem to be neither dependent on the existence of international treaties nor on a particular mandate of the European Commission or the Member States – nor both. Article 8 International Relations, Regulation 1022/2013,[71] Single Supervisory Mechanism (SSM), Article 33 International Commitments including Equivalence of Regulation 1095/2010[72] establishing ESMA and Article 33 International Relations Regulation 1093/2010[73] establishing EBA grant the three agencies the power and the authority to engage in international co-operation mechanisms, provided these are non-binding and subject to various specifications in the constitutive documents or in additional secondary EU rules adopted to govern the financial market.

[67] K Pistor, *Code of Capital How the Law Creates Wealth and Poverty* (Princeton, Princeton University Press, 2021).

[68] R Vallejo Garreton, *The Idea of a Private Administrative Law*, PhD thesis (Florence, European University Institute, 2021), available at https://cadmus.eui.eu/handle/1814/71519.

[69] Marcacci (n 48), who borrows the concept from the tradition of Italian Administrative Law, in particular the 'privatisation of public employment', which means the use of private law means to govern public employment relationships without altering the public spirit of the civil service.

[70] U Beck, *Risikogesellschaft Auf dem Weg in eine andere Moderne* (Frankfurt, Suhrkamp, 1986), in English, *Risk Society: Towards a New Modernity* (New York, AGE Publishing, 1992) where he speaks of 'Weltinnenpolitik' – global domestic policy.

[71] Regulation (EU) No 1022/2013 of the European Parliament and of the Council of 22 October 2013 amending Regulation (EU) No 1093/2010 establishing a European Supervisory Authority (European Banking Authority) as regards the conferral of specific tasks on the European Central Bank pursuant to Council Regulation (EU) No 1024/2013 [2013] OJ L287/5.

[72] Regulation (EU) No 1095/2010 of the European Parliament and of the Council of 24 November 2010 establishing a European Supervisory Authority (European Securities and Markets Authority). [2010] OJ L331/84.

[73] Regulation (EU) No 1093/2010 of the European Parliament and of the Council of 24 November 2010 establishing a European Supervisory Authority (European Banking Authority) [2010] OJ L331/12.

In theory, however, it might also be possible that international treaties upgrade the role and function of the European financial agencies. In practice, their role and function are hard to identify, due to the leeway that non-binding international commitments are opening. A case in point is ESMA's role within the International Organisation of Securities (IOSCO).[74]

Article 43 Regulation 2019/942[75] establishing ACER ties the involvement of third countries to the existence of international treaties concluded between the EU, the Member States and third countries. A case in point is the Treaty on the Establishment of the Energy Community in the Western Balkans. The Treaty sets out the regulatory framework under which ACER may operate. International non-binding agreements are therefore bound to the procedure laid down in the Treaty. Article 43 Regulation 2019/942 is not self-standing. Article 35 Regulation 2018/1971[76] establishing BEREC empowers the European agency – BEREC Office – to conclude non-binding working arrangements, inter alia with the competent authorities of third countries and with international organisations, subject to prior approval by the Commission. The European Commission holds the final power to supervise and control BEREC Office external activities.

The transport sector is far from being homogenous; the competences of the European agencies depend on the sector. Article 90 Regulation 2018/1139,[77] establishing EASA draws a twofold distinction: of its own motion EASA may engage in ad hoc agreements or in non-binding working arrangements to be coordinated with the European Commission; within the scope of International Civil Aviation Organisation (ICAO) and the European aviation community EASA has been explicitly mandated. Article 44 Regulation 2016/796[78] establishing EAR and Article 17 Regulation 1406/2002[79] establishing EMSA tie their competences to the existence of an international treaty, such as the European transport community. The reasons behind the patchwork of arrangements might be sought inter alia in the type of EU competence, the intensity of EU legislation in each area; the dominance and influence of professional associations, and industry (financial regulation) and political sensitivity.

The broad variety of regulations and directives has not prevented identification of key parameters, which are suggested as relevant for a deeper understanding of how extending EU rules beyond the internal market operates. These can be broken down

[74] See under section IV.C.iv.

[75] Regulation (EU) 2019/942 of the European Parliament and of the Council of 5 June 2019 establishing a European Union Agency for the Cooperation of Energy Regulators (recast) [2019] OJ L158/22.

[76] Regulation (EU) 2018/1971 of the European Parliament and of the Council of 11 December 2018 establishing the Body of European Regulators for Electronic Communications (BEREC) and the Agency for Support for BEREC (BEREC Office), amending Regulation (EU) 2015/2120 and repealing Regulation (EC) No 1211/2009 (Text with EEA relevance) [2018] OJ L321/1.

[77] Regulation (EU) 2018/1139 of the European Parliament and of the Council of 4 July 2018 on common rules in the field of civil aviation and establishing a European Union Aviation Safety Agency [2018] OJ L212/1.

[78] Regulation (EU) 2016/796 of the European Parliament and of the Council of 11 May 2016 on the European Union Agency for Railways and repealing Regulation (EC) No 881/2004 (Text with EEA relevance) [2016] OJ L138/1.

[79] Regulation (EC) No 1406/2002 of the European Parliament and of the Council of 27 June 2002 establishing a European Maritime Safety Agency (Text with EEA relevance) [2002] OJ L208/1.

into procedural rules that aim at establishing a kind of homogeneity in the design of sector-related agencies and substantive rules which concretise the powers they have to exercise in supervising and monitoring private law relations.

i. Equivalence, Non-Discrimination, Participation

Equivalence is the catchword which dominates not only the regulations establishing the EU agencies but also and in particular sector-related directives and regulations. Equivalence requires the existence of a similar body of rules in non-EU countries, based on similar rules governing the markets and similar rules on supervising and monitoring the markets or – if the rules are not similar – similarity in terms of effects.

The energy, aviation and railway rules (here on safety) require the 'independence' of the non-EU agency, while the telecom rules specify the potential content of the agreement. The whole set of EU rules share a common spirit, an inside-out philosophy, to shield the level of market integration and social regulation achieved to the benefit of European companies and European citizens through extending the internal market rationale to the outside world. The policy objective may be financial stability and investor protection, security of supply in energy, or safety/security in transport. All of them require safeguards in case of upcoming or potential risks. The European agencies play a key role in preparing the ground through appropriate advice to the European Commission, which takes the final decision on whether there is equivalence or not.

The benchmark for equivalence is not EU law alone, though. The European agencies and the European Commission 'should have regard' (Recital 80 SSM and Recital 41 MIFID II) to international political commitments such as the G-20 or international technical standards elaborated by the International Organisation for Standardisation/ International Electrotechnical Commission (ISO/IEC) or IOSCO by, at least, taking them into account. In the field of transport, the EU sticks to international conventions as far as they exist. EU rules are meant to fill gaps (Article 59 Regulation 2018/1139[80] on establishing EASA) but they will not apply when they are in conflict with third country rules and international standards. If the benchmark for equivalence is not EU law alone, the potential influence of the EU (and its agencies) in defining equivalence internationally becomes crucial. The formal decision remains in the hands of the European Commission and can be withheld for any reason. Brexit demonstrates how the equivalence mechanism has been instrumentalised for political purposes.[81]

Equivalence and non-discrimination go together. Overall, and with very few exceptions, EU rules do not exclude countries from becoming a party to an international agreement. One of these exceptions is the list of jurisdictions suspected of strategic deficiencies in their national anti-money laundering and countering

[80] Regulation (EU) 2018/1139 of the European Parliament and of the Council of 4 July 2018 on common rules in the field of civil aviation and establishing a European Union Aviation Safety Agency [2018] OJ L212/1.

[81] House of Lords, 'The UK–EU Relationship in Financial Services', June 2022, available at https://rotf.lol/ukparliament.

the financing of terrorism regimes (Article 9 Directive 2015/849[82] or Article 5(2) Regulation 2020/1503[83] on crowdfunding). There is a blacklist which requires and enhances due diligence with regard to countries such as Iran, Iraq, and Monte Carlo. The same technique applies when imposing an operating ban on air carriers.

In the absence of internationally binding treaties, the benchmark for the equivalence test are EU rules, such as the energy, aviation and transport community. Non-EU countries may participate in supervision and enforcement by the European agencies provided they can demonstrate compliance with EU rules or the equivalent. Access for non-EU based companies to the internal market is conditional on their acceptance of EU rules/equivalence. If they do, they may benefit from the building of a 'common supervisory culture' (Article 29 Regulation 1093/2010 on EBA, Article 53(1) Regulation 2016/1011[84] on indices), to be developed by the European agencies with their counterparts in non-EU countries. The EU rules are inspired by the belief that it is possible to build trust around peoples who share a joint interest in ensuring the workability and the functionality of the particular market sector. The workshops organised in the telecoms and energy sector with the participation of the European agencies, national agencies, stakeholders, business, consumers and law firms demonstrate a kind of 'comradeship', which means the EU has promoted a 'common supervisory culture'.[85]

More ambitious forms of co-operation such as 'participation of third countries' require international treaties, in line with Article 216 TFEU, Article 75 Regulation 195/2010 ESMA, Article 75 Regulation 1093/2010 EBA, Article 43 (2) Regulation 2019/942 ACER, and Article 35 (2) Regulation 2018/1971 BEREC. Here the equivalence test is built into the broader context of how EU rules on the relevant markets are to be merged with the rules of the contracting partners, now laid down in international treaties. The European agencies are required to report on non-binding international agreements. However, it is not easy to get a full picture of the type of agreements that the European agencies have concluded. Their websites do not follow a common pattern. Only ESMA and EBA list all guidelines, recommendations and opinions on the equivalence of non-EU countries as well as memoranda concluded with third countries – mainly with the UK, the USA and South-Eastern Europe – in an easily accessible way.[86]

[82] Directive (EU) 2015/849 of the European Parliament and of the Council of 20 May 2015 on the prevention of the use of the financial system for the purposes of money laundering or terrorist financing [2015] OJ L141/73.

[83] Regulation (EU) 2020/1503 of the European Parliament and of the Council of 7 October 2020 on European crowdfunding service providers for business, and amending Regulation (EU) 2017/1129 and Directive (EU) 2019/1937 (Text with EEA relevance) [2020] OJ L347/1.

[84] Regulation (EU) 2016/1011 of the European Parliament and of the Council of 8 June 2016 on indices used as benchmarks in financial instruments and financial contracts or to measure the performance of investment funds and amending Directives 2008/48/EC and 2014/17/EU and Regulation (EU) No 596/2014 (Text with EEA relevance) [2016] OJ L171/1.

[85] The results of the ERC workshops were included in the PhDs of de Almeida and Cantero Gamito (n 61) as well as the contributions in *The Public and the Private – European Regulatory Private Law and Financial Services* 10, *European Review of Contract Law* 4, 473–595 with contributions from HW Micklitz, O Cherednychenko, Y Svetiev/A Ottow, H Marjasola, and F della Negra.

[86] See ESMA at www.esma.europa.eu/about-esma/international-cooperation#title-paragrah-7:~:text=ESMA%20RECOGNITION%20DECISIONS-,List%20of%20equivalence%20decisions%2C%20MoUs%2C%20and%20ESMA%20recognition%20decisions,-LATEST%20PUBLICATIONS.

ii. Guidance on Substance

The seven regulations establishing the seven European agencies in the four sectors provide basic information on the potential content of international non-binding agreements, either through a limited mandate such as safety in the transport sector or through concrete requirements. Overall, however, sector-related directives and regulations contain much more specific guidance. What looks bewildering from the outside, in fact follows the rationale of the degree of market integration achieved and the degree to which the EU is dependent on export and import.

In banking and finance, Article 19 Regulation 2015/2365[87] on trade repositories[88] deserves a mention, in energy it is support for building the Southern Gas Corridor (SGC) (transmission of gas from the Caspian Basin, Central Asia, the Middle East and the Eastern Mediterranean Basin to the Union to enhance diversification of gas supply), the electricity highways around the Northern and Baltic Seas, the call for renewable generation of energy in South East Europe and North Africa (Regulation 2022/869[89]) and last but not least comprehensive rules in the European energy community. In electronic communication, net neutrality (Regulation 2015/2120[90]) deserves to be highlighted. In transport, guidance focuses on safety, security and interoperability through establishment of the European aviation community, which includes Iceland and Norway (Decision 2006/682), the Cooperation Agreement on Aerial Navigation Safety with Africa and Madagascar (Decision 2018/1603) and the Single European Sky Regulation 549/2004[91] with neighbouring countries (Article 7). The European transport community sets standards for co-operation between the EU and the Western Balkans. Particular attention is given to the interoperability of the Baltic railway with continental Europe, including Russia (Directive 2016/797).[92]

C. Regulatory Tools and Private Law

In line with the research design on the role of private law in regulated markets, the question to be investigated is whether and to what extent sector-related rules

[87] Regulation (EU) 2015/2365 of the European Parliament and of the Council of 25 November 2015 on transparency of securities financing transactions and of reuse and amending Regulation (EU) No 648/2012 (Text with EEA relevance) [2005] OJ L337/1.

[88] Trade repositories 15.01.2020 in Deutsche Bundesbank Eurosystem, available at https://rotf.lol/bbank.

[89] Regulation (EU) 2022/869 of the European Parliament and of the Council of 30 May 2022 on guidelines for trans-European energy infrastructure, amending Regulations (EC) No 715/2009, (EU) 2019/942 and (EU) 2019/943 and Directives 2009/73/EC and (EU) 2019/944, and repealing Regulation (EU) No 347/2013 [2022] OJ L152/45.

[90] Regulation (EU) 2015/2120 of the European Parliament and of the Council of 25 November 2015 laying down measures concerning open internet access and amending Directive 2002/22/EC on universal service and users' rights relating to electronic communications networks and services and Regulation (EU) No 531/2012 on roaming on public mobile communications networks within the Union (Text with EEA relevance) [2015] OJ L310/1.

[91] Regulation (EC) No 549/2004 of the European Parliament and of the Council of 10 March 2004 laying down the framework for the creation of the single European sky (the framework Regulation) (Text with EEA relevance) – Statement by the Member States on military issues related to the single European sky [2004] OJ L96/6.

[92] Directive (EU) 2016/797 of the European Parliament and the Council of 11 May 2016 on the interoperability of the rail system within the European Union (recast) (Text with EEA relevance) [2016] OJ L138/44.

complement the seven constitutive regulations on establishing the European agencies, first with regard to exchange of administrative practice, potentially also on monitoring of contracts, and secondly with regard to possible yardsticks against which supervised private transactions can be measured.

i. Information Exchange and Confidentiality

The various types of non-binding international commitments/agreements first and foremost build on information exchange between national agencies, European agencies, and the European Commission. To anticipate the result, many rules contain some concrete indications, which can also be interpreted as meaning that there is indeed scope for a qualified exchange of information on contractual practices. The approach in the banking sector is paradigmatic.

Both Regulation 1093/2010 and Regulation 1095/2010 (Recast 2019/75) encourage ESMA and EBA to develop guidelines on 'the regulatory regime' and 'the supervisory approach' (both in Article 33(4). Such wording, which looks more like a policy statement than a legal requirement, comes close to a 'carte blanche'. More concrete requirements can be found in Article 75 and 76 Regulation 648/2012[93] EMIR on trade repositories, Article 4(72) Regulation 575/2013[94] on credit risks, Article 97(5) and 98 Regulation 2014/59[95] on recovery and resolution, Article 19 Regulation 2015/2365[96] (transparency), Article 47(2) Regulation 600/2014[97] on financial instruments, Article 38(2) Regulation 236/2012[98] (short selling), and Article 20 Directive 2015/2366[99] on payment services. A similar approach is to be reported from the energy sector. Decision 2017/684[100] regulates information exchange with regard to binding and non-binding intergovernmental agreements in some detail. Again, electronic communication stands apart. The only provision referring to information exchange with non-EU countries, non-EU agencies and international

[93] Regulation (EU) No 648/2012 of the European Parliament and of the Council of 4 July 2012 on OTC derivatives, central counterparties and trade repositories (Text with EEA relevance) [2012] OJ L201/1.

[94] Regulation (EU) No 575/2013 of the European Parliament and of the Council of 26 June 2013 on prudential requirements for credit institutions and investment firms and amending Regulation (EU) No 648/2012 (Text with EEA relevance) [2013] OJ L176/1.

[95] Directive 2014/59/EU of the European Parliament and of the Council of 15 May 2014 establishing a framework for the recovery and resolution of credit institutions and investment firms [2013] OJ L173/190.

[96] Regulation (EU) 2015/2365 of the European Parliament and of the Council of 25 November 2015 on transparency of securities financing transactions and of reuse and amending Regulation (EU) No 648/2012 (Text with EEA relevance) [2015] OJ L337/1.

[97] Regulation (EU) No 600/2014 of the European Parliament and of the Council of 15 May 2014 on markets in financial instruments and amending Regulation (EU) No 648/2012 (Text with EEA relevance) [2014] OJ L173/84.

[98] Regulation (EU) No 236/2012 of the European Parliament and of the Council of 14 March 2012 on short selling and certain aspects of credit default swaps (Text with EEA relevance) [2012] OJ L86/1.

[99] Directive (EU) 2015/2366 of the European Parliament and of the Council of 25 November 2015 on payment services in the internal market, amending Directives 2002/65/EC, 2009/110/EC and 2013/36/EU and Regulation (EU) No 1093/2010, and repealing Directive 2007/64/EC (Text with EEA relevance) [2015] OJ L 337/35.

[100] Decision (EU) 2017/684 of the European Parliament and of the Council of 5 April 2017 on establishing an information exchange mechanism with regard to intergovernmental agreements and non-binding instruments between Member States and third countries in the field of energy, and repealing Decision No 994/2012/EU (Text with EEA relevance) [2017] OJ L99/1.

organisations is enshrined in Article 119 Directive 2018/1972. The European Commission is required to share such information with Member States' authorities and with BEREC Office. This seems to contradict the role and function that Article 35 Regulation 2018/1971 grants BEREC Office. In transport there are particular rules on exchange of information on road safety-related traffic offences (Directive 2015/413[101]), aircraft accidents (Regulation 996/2010[102]) and railway accidents (Directive 2016/798[103]). The degree to which European agencies are involved depends on the concrete regulatory powers in sector-related secondary EU law. EASA 'participates' in the investigation of aircraft accidents, but does not lead the inquiry.

Information exchange on markets and even more on market participants and their behaviour in the market immediately raises issues of confidentiality, of where to draw the line between confidential and non-confidential information, and of whether disclosure of information to the public at large infringes trade secrets. There is no common denominator in terms of the rules on what type of information can be exchanged and what type of information is excluded. The distinction between confidential and non-confidential surfaces in the shape of major sector-related secondary EU rules, but all that can be found is a reference to EU law on trade secrets.[104] If exchange of confidential information is rendered possible, it is bound to a whole set of context-related requirements, such as Article 98 Directive 2014/59 (Recovery and Resolution), Article 33(4) Regulation 1060/2008[105] (Credit Rating) or Article 88(1) Regulation 2014/65 MIFID II. Decision 2017/684[106] guarantees that information on particular energy agreements can be treated as confidential, if required.

ii. Contract Regulation and Product Regulation

EU rules on regulated markets aim at building and shaping the *market* for banking and finance, energy, electronic communications and transport. Usually, they do not deal directly with private law relations. If they do, they are mostly limited to b2c relations, such as in energy or electronic communication, although the 'c' stands not only for consumers but also for customers (for example, Article 98 Directive 2018/1972).

[101] Directive (EU) 2015/413 of the European Parliament and of the Council of 11 March 2015 facilitating cross-border exchange of information on road-safety-related traffic offences (Text with EEA relevance) [2015] OJ L68/9.

[102] Regulation (EU) No 996/2010 of the European Parliament and of the Council of 20 October 2010 on the investigation and prevention of accidents and incidents in civil aviation and repealing Directive 94/56/ EC (Text with EEA relevance) [2010] OJ L295/35.

[103] Directive (EU) 2016/798 of the European Parliament and of the Council of 11 May 2016 on railway safety (recast) (Text with EEA relevance) [2016] OJ L138/102.

[104] Directive (EU) 2016/943 on trade secrets [2016] OJ L157/1 and Regulation (EC) No 1049/2001 regarding public access to European Parliament, Council and Commission documents [2001] OJ L145/44.

[105] Commission Regulation (EC) No 1060/2008 of 7 October 2008 replacing Annexes I, III, IV, VI, VII, XI and XV to Directive 2007/46/EC of the European Parliament and of the Council establishing a framework for the approval of motor vehicles and their trailers, and of systems, components and separate technical units intended for such vehicles (Framework Directive) (Text with EEA relevance) [2008] OJ L292/1.

[106] Decision (EU) 2017/684 of the European Parliament and of the Council of 5 April 2017 on establishing an information exchange mechanism with regard to intergovernmental agreements and non-binding instruments between Member States and third countries in the field of energy, and repealing Decision No 994/2012/EU (Text with EEA relevance) [2017] OJ L99/1.

Typically, the EU regulates private relations indirectly, through EU rules which address agencies but affect private parties and which do not fit into the public versus private law distinction. Uncertainty on the nature of EU rules cuts across the four sectors and is widely discussed in legal doctrine.[107]

Typical examples are rules which aim at influencing the behaviour of companies, such as 'know your product' and 'know your customer' rules, due diligence rules, indeed all sorts of EU rules which define legal requirements on products and services themselves. These rules are sometimes closer to, sometimes further away from, private law. Take as an example Regulation 2016/1011 on indices and benchmarks. Recital 1 nicely expresses the accompaniment of prudential supervision and private law relations: 'The pricing of many financial instruments' (admitted to trading on a MiFID Trading Venue 'and financial contracts' (consumer credit and mortgage credit, to be accomplished through investment funds AIF Directive 2011/61[108] and UCTS Directive 2009/65[109]) 'depends on the accuracy and integrity of benchmarks (LIBOR and EURIBOR)'. Accuracy and integrity clouds what in private law language is termed defectiveness or conformity of products and services.

Regulation 1227/2011 on wholesale energy markets prohibits 'abusive practices', again a legal concept widespread in private law. Any scholarly attempt which tries to pull the EU rules into either one of the two directions – public or private – fails to understand their twofold legal nature. Scholars unfamiliar with the complexity of the regulated markets may look at Regulation 2020/1503 on crowdfunding. This rather recent regulation contains in a nutshell all the ingredients of the EU approach that are characteristic of European regulatory private law: the existence of competent agencies with prudential and regulatory powers, legal obligations imposed on the project owners without clarifying whether they are private or public in nature and, last but not least, even rules on dispute settlement and the like, the usual cradle-to-grave thinking. In the transport sector there are fewer rules on the proper behaviour of market participants. The Single European Sky Regulation 550/2004[110] and the Single Rail Area Directive 2012/34[111] specify the supervision requirements of the national authorities and clarify the advisory task in rulemaking and the co-ordinating task in supervising the European agencies, (Regulation 2018/1139 and 2016/796), but provide less guidance on substance in comparison to Regulation 2020/1503 on crowdfunding or similar rules in the banking and finance sector.

[107] S Grundmann, *Europäisches Schuldvertragsrecht* (Berlin, De Gruyter New York, 1999); J Basedow, *EU Private Law, Anatomy of a Growing Legal Order* (Cambridge, Intersentia, 2021); T Tridimas, 'Financial Regulation and Private Law Remedies: An EU Law Perspective' in O Cherednychenko and M Andenas (eds), *Financial Regulation and Civil Liability in European Law* (Cheltenham, Elgar Publishing, 2020) 47.

[108] Directive 2011/61/EU of the European Parliament and of the Council of 8 June 2011 on Alternative Investment Fund Managers and amending Directives 2003/41/EC and 2009/65/EC and Regulations (EC) No 1060/2009 and (EU) No 1095/2010 (Text with EEA relevance) [2011] OJ L174/1.

[109] Directive 2009/65/EC of the European Parliament and of the Council of 13 July 2009 on the coordination of laws, regulations and administrative provisions relating to undertakings for collective investment in transferable securities (UCITS) (recast) (Text with EEA relevance) [2009] OJ L302/32.

[110] Regulation (EC) No 550/2004 of the European Parliament and of the Council of 10 March 2004 on the provision of air navigation services in the single European sky (the service provision Regulation) (Text with EEA relevance) [2004] OJ L96/10.

[111] Directive 2012/34/EU of the European Parliament and of the Council of 21 November 2012 establishing a single European railway area (recast) (Text with EEA relevance) [2012] OJ L343/32.

The particular approach on how the EU designs the rules on regulated markets affects the EU's external reach. This message cannot be repeated often enough. Squeezed into the private/public divide, the EU legislator has to choose between two options in extending the law on regulated markets beyond EU territory, either by relying on European international private law or by simply stretching the law of the regulated markets beyond EU territory.[112] The EU leaves the proper legal classification to the Member States, in the end to the ECJ. The non-decision tilts the balance towards the regulatory side. Global reach materialises first and foremost through communication channels in administrative bodies enshrined in non-binding international commitments and occasionally bound to legally binding rules on how the exchange operates and what kind of criteria should be applied in assessing private law relations of market participants, but also through educational training, twinning programmes, and technical assistance.

D. External Administrative Practice of European Agencies

The analytic distinction between the key role of 'international non-binding co-operation agreements' between EU/non-EU agencies and 'private law regulatory tools' have guided evaluation of publicly available administrative reports and websites of the seven European agencies from 2010 on, each from the date of their inauguration. Based on the findings of the research project on regulatory private law *within* the EU, the hypothesis is that the supervision authorities use administrative powers – prominently, the contractual tool of commitment decisions – to force those under regulation to change contractual arrangements, which not only affects the counterparty but also third parties.[113] In a perfect world, reports from the European agencies would not only provide information on the degree to which they use the powers they have been granted to engage with supervisory authorities from third countries, but in addition they would also provide, if not evidence, then at least an idea of the kind of problems that triggered administrative enforcement of private law. To anticipate the result: the high hopes and the enormous investment of time in reading hundreds of pages, did not pay off. What remains, though, is the justified assumption that deeper research would increase the probability that the overall hypothesis is correct.

i. Opportunities and Limits of Reports and Websites

Annual reports suffer from two restrictions in that EU law draws a distinction between reports that have to be made public, but where the scope is limited through

[112] Attempts to transfer international private law to administrative law failed, see K Neumeyer, *Internationales Verwaltungsrecht* (München/Berlin, Verlag Schweitser, 1910).

[113] A Ottow and Y Svetiev, 'Financial Supervision in the Interstices between Public and Private Law' (2014) *European Review of Contract Law* 10, 496–544; Y Svetiev, 'Settling or Learning: Commitment Decisions as a Competition Enforcement Paradigm' (2014) *Yearbook of European Law* 33, 466–500; G Comparato, *The Rationale of Financial Inclusion in the Changing European Private Law* (2015) *European Review of Contract Law* 11, 22–45; WM Weidemaier, M Gulati and A Gelpern, 'When Governments Write Contracts: Policy and Expertise in Sovereign Debt Markets' in G Mallard and J Sgard (eds), *Contractual Knowledge:*

confidentiality requirements under Regulation 1049/2001,[114] and those which have to be kept confidential right from the beginning. The information provided through the websites of the seven agencies is directly connected to the mandate. Both EBA and ESMA are mandated in their founding regulations to set up a European rulebook. Their websites allow for an interactive search of the rules which EBA – European Rulebook[115]/ESMA – Interactive Single Rulebook (IRBS)[116] developed and which the Commission approved through implementing regulations. The websites illustrate article by article whether the agencies have adopted regulatory technical standards (RTS) and implementing technical standards (ITS), guidelines, recommendations or additional reports. Both websites contain a rubric on supervision. EBA reports are on an annual basis on 'supervision convergence' via a publicly accessible report. However, there is no interactive register to connect the legal basis to the guidelines and working programmes related to rulemaking and supervision, let alone their co-operation with ACER and BEREC Office, for instance.

ESMA distinguishes between direct 'supervision' and 'convergence' in national supervision. 'Supervision' is broken down into 'supervision' and 'enforcement'. Supervision refers to rating agencies and trade repositories, where ESMA holds supervisory powers. Clicking on 'trade repositories' informs the reader how ESMA exercises its supervisory tasks – through a risk-based approach – and the way supervision is exercised as well as the applicable RTS and ITS. The website equally informs potential addressees on the criteria ESMA asks for in the registration process and provides a list of registered companies. 'Enforcement' leads to regulatory action that ESMA has taken since its existence, in particular the fines ESMA has imposed on companies which have breached the law. ESMA's regulatory decisions are publicly accessible. 'Convergence' deals with supervisory convergence, the kind of rules, procedures and programmes ESMA has effectuated and what has been achieved so far. However, in contrast to EBA there is no annual progress report on supervision convergence.

With this proviso in mind, the reports show a relatively clear picture of the way in which the European agencies engage with the outside world. One might bring the overall findings under the formula of *in foro interno, in foro externo*.[117] The EU rules which govern the four markets under investigation (banking, energy, telecoms and transport) determine the design, shape and impact of their external reach. This also means that the ever-deeper integration of the four markets since the early 2010s correlates with an increase not necessarily of external powers but a much more intensive use of external powers to shape external reach through all sorts of international 'hard' and 'soft' commitments. Put differently, the existence of co-ordinated supervision between EU and non-EU agencies presupposes a high degree of harmonised supervision standards, methods, and techniques within the EU. This does not

One Hundred Years of Legal Experimentation in Global Markets (Cambridge, Cambridge University Press, 2016) 92–117.

[114] Regulation (EC) No 1049/2001 of the European Parliament and of the Council of 30 May 2001 regarding public access to European Parliament, Council and Commission documents [2001] OJ L145/43.

[115] EBA, Single Rulebook, available at https://rotf.lol/rulebookeu.

[116] ESMA, Interactive Single Rulebook, available at https://rotf.lol/esmarb.

[117] P Pescatore, 'External Relations in the Case-Law of the Court of Justice of the European Communities' (1976) 16 *CML Rev* 615–45.

exclude the possibility that EU supervision rules target a particular policy, provided the EU's internal rules are properly developed. The analytical categories 'international agreements/arrangements/working arrangements' do not matter. However, concrete information on the behaviour of market participants and how potential infringements of contractual practices have been corrected and by what means is missing. Management of particular crisis situations provide limited insights.

ii. Sector-Related Findings

The *financial* sector is characterised by a large number of MoU concluded by the ECB with non-EU central banks and an ever-growing number of co-operation agreements concluded by EBA and ESMA in their field of competence. Already in 2015 Directive 2013/35[118] on Capital Requirement (CRD) and Regulation 575/2013[119] on Capital Requirements (CRR) triggered the need to identify areas in which co-operation with third countries needs to be intensified. Therefore EBA started the initiative to provide consistency in treatment of third countries across Member States: 'in order to facilitate the consistent participation of third country supervisory authorities in supervisory colleges EBA, on its own initiative (*sic, HWM*), issued a recommendation on the equivalence of the confidentiality regime of 29 non-EU supervisory authorities from 13 countries'.[120] The European Commission asked EBA for technical advice on the equivalence of the legal and supervisory regimes in regard to the memoranda of co-operation with the authorities of Macedonia, Albania and Montenegro. The applied methodology links equivalence and co-operation. The more co-operation agreements there are, the more European supervisory agencies become involved in monitoring and supervising concrete commercial practices beyond EU territory.

The bank supervisory[121] and bank resolution colleges[122] were established worldwide in the aftermath of the financial crisis through the Basel Committee and under the SSM within Europe. The supervisory college comprises 'home' and 'host' supervisors. The underlying objective is to help college members, also supervisory authorities from third countries, to develop a better understanding of risk profiles and vulnerabilities, to share information and to strengthen co-ordinated supervision. These colleges play a major role in practice in light of the fact that European banks maintain subsidiaries in more than 100 non-EU countries and that six major banks headquartered outside the EU operate significant subsidiaries in the EU. Here, the ECB is host supervisor.

[118] Directive 2013/36/EU of the European Parliament and of the Council of 26 June 2013 on access to the activity of credit institutions and the prudential supervision of credit institutions and investment firms, amending Directive 2002/87/EC and repealing Directives 2006/48/EC and 2006/49/EC (Text with EEA relevance) [2013] OJ L176/338.

[119] Regulation (EU) No 575/2013 of the European Parliament and of the Council of 26 June 2013 on prudential requirements for credit institutions and investment firms and amending Regulation (EU) No 648/2012 (Text with EEA relevance) [2013] OJ L176/1.

[120] EBA Annual Report 2015.

[121] ECB, 'What Are Supervisory Colleges?' (last updated 12 December 2018), available at https://rotf.lol/supervisocoll.

[122] See the Single Resolution Board website at www.srb.europa.eu/en/content/cooperation.

Central Counterparty Clearing Houses (CCP) were to a large extent located in the UK and thereby able to operate *within* the EU under EMIR. After Brexit, the European agencies were forced to find a solution. Brexit worked as a game changer. The solution found the UK turned into a kind of benchmark for all non-EU supervisory authorities. Within the SSM regime, Brexit changed the interaction between the ECB and EBA. EBA moved away from crafting rules to prudential supervision and came ever closer to managing concrete supervisory practices with due regard to private law relations. ESMA seems closest to supervising contracts through the register of trade repositories, which was promoted by G-20 in order to avoid the uncontrolled rise of derivatives. Co-operation agreements between ESMA and its non-EU counterparts centre around the question of gaining access to the register. The reports do not disclose whether the authorities are managing the contracts and in what way they require amendments, though.

There is no information on contracts with international bodies involved in private lawmaking, such as the United Nations Commission on International Trade Law (UNCITRAL) in sales and commercial law, or the Hague Conference in international private law rules. ESMA, however, drafted an administrative arrangement with IOSCO for the transfer of personal data between EU securities markets regulators and third country regulators.[123]

The rather sophisticated design of the external reach of European supervision standards in banking and finance has no counterpart in energy, telecoms and transport. Supervision of the three latter markets is only foreseen with regard to particular market practices or policy fields. As a result of the Third Energy Package and REMIT (Article 7 Regulation 1227/2011), ACER and Member States' national authorities are obliged to mutually co-operate in supervising the monitoring of insider information and market manipulation.[124] The REMIT implementing regulation requires market participants to inform ACER of market transactions in the wholesale market. These data are processed by an artificial intelligence (AI) system called ARIA and feed national regulators with information about potential market manipulation. ACER monitors the internal market but lacks enforcement power beyond dispute resolution among Member-State agencies. As to co-operation with non-EU authorities, the energy community deserves mention. Inclusion of market participants from the Western Balkans in ARIA will facilitate supervision. Brexit worked as a game changer in the energy sector, too, not least through co-operation between ACER and ESMA in control of market abuse in wholesale markets. Qualifying wholesale energy products as financial instruments ties the two European agencies together. In addition, there is a well-developed net of co-operation agreements between EU transmission system operators and non-EU operators in electricity and gas.

Reports from the remaining European agencies, BEREC Office and EAR (rail), EASA (air) and EMSA (maritime) demonstrate perfunctory activities only. BEREC Office reports a growing interest by non-EU countries and their agencies in the EU regulatory framework, triggered through roaming regulation. Bilateral co-operation

[123] Marcacci (n 57).

[124] See ACER website at www.acer.europa.eu/remit/market-surveillance/detect.

agreements exist with India, Central and Southern America and Canada, but with no concrete guidance on supervision. EAR co-operates with ISO, which has led to establishment of a new unit on 'strategy, international relations and innovation'. EASA focuses on air traffic safety and security issues. In this particular policy field EASA is becoming ever stronger, not only in the EU but also in ICAO and in IATA. EASA established SAFA (Safety Assessment of Foreign Aircraft) and BASA (Bilateral Agreements on Safety Measures). Thereby EASA is well connected to the rest of the world. SAFA and BASA aim at developing 'risk assessment principles.' Regulation 2018/1139 granted EASA more competences and new tools to face changes in a sector marked by steady growth, unprecedented technological developments, environmental pressures and new threats such as cybersecurity. However, it would be too early to interpret extensive activities as a form of coordinated supervision. The current rules might prepare the ground for managing risks, though. EMSA focuses on its competence in training and monitoring seafarers. The Convention on Standards of Training, Certification and Watch-keeping for Seafarers Convention (STCW) provides the benchmark against which EU and non-EU flagged vessels are measured. EMSA is heavily involved in inspection oversight, currently preparing a Convention on the Maritime Labour Convention with an impact on labour law.

E. Interim Conclusion

The many winding roads through the laws of the regulated markets and their extension to the outside world through treaties, through competences granted to agencies and through the bulk of sector-related or problem-specific rules shows that the upper half of the sandwich has clear contours. The EU is using the European agencies as spearheads in expanding its influence. Recognition of equivalence between EU and non-EU institutions is key. Equivalence presupposes two things: the existence of market regulations comparable to those of the EU and the existence of supervisory authorities with similar competences. Once the EU has paved the way for intensifying co-operation through formal approval of equivalence, the European agencies can unfold activities that have only one goal, namely, to bring the non-EU institutions involved into line with the European regulatory philosophy. Here, non-binding international agreements allow for opening up space to develop a common enforcement culture, one which is governed by a spirit of mutual trust.

Banking and finance show how far development has already progressed, a development which goes back to a long history of close international co-operation among central banks and prudential regulators within the Basle Club. Here, the autonomy of the agencies is greatest, here they have regulatory powers with which they can intervene in contractual relations not directly but indirectly through monitoring and supervision: banking and finance function as a forerunner. The Ukraine crisis demonstrates how the EU is trying to seize the opportunity to expand ACER's regulatory competences, with massive implications for contractual relations. It is not difficult to predict that emergency measures will leave deep traces in the distribution of responsibilities. Once ACER receives more competences within the internal market, it will also use those competences externally. A similar development cannot be reported from telecoms (electronic communication) and transport. It is somewhat surprising that the telecom sector is lagging behind. However, the gap will probably be closed through the currently pending set of rules with which the EU is about to regulate the digital economy. The transport sector shows some parallels which point in the direction that banking and finance have set. Whilst there is a relatively clear development in enhancing co-operation between EU and non-EU agencies in supervision and enforcement, the subject matter is very much limited to health and safety issues.

IV. STANDARDISATION OF REGULATED MARKETS WITHIN AND BEYOND THE EU

The second main section of the chapter changes the perspective of administrative agency practices squeezing from above to the bottom-up perspective of technical standards, or squeezing from below. Many of the EU directives and regulations that purport to have extraterritorial effect explicitly contemplate a role for technical standardisation. In order to understand the significance of technical norms for private law relations, it is necessary to delve deeply into a completely different world, one dominated by other actors and by a different language. The key actors are technical experts, usually located in the business environment, that dispose of the necessary knowledge and skills which the four sectors are asking for. At the beginning of the industrial age, they organised themselves into national, international and later European standardisation bodies. The EU integrated these bodies – European Standardisation Organisations (ESOs) – into its regulatory approach on completing the internal market. But the development did not stop there and again banking and finance is taking the lead. Technical – meaning financial – expertise is not outsourced to institutionalised European standardisation bodies, but supervised and monitored by the European agencies themselves. In banking and finance the EU is not a standard giver but a standard taker elaborated at the international level.

After a short recap of the role and function of technical standards in the EU legal order and their relevance for private law relations, the bulk of EU directives and regulations in the four sectors is screened so as to demonstrate how, where and when technical standards are establishing a solid regulatory underground, the lower layer of the sandwich which narrows down the space of private law relations. The chapter will guide the reader through a complex underworld of rules composed not of hundreds but of thousands of pages, which still lack one crucial element – access to the content of technical standards themselves which concretise the abundant legal requirements. The next step is to turn to the outside perspective, to the ways in which ESOs are engaging in international commitments with the rest of the world and how the activities of the Comité Européen de la Normalisation Électrotechnique (CEN)/Comité Européen de la Normalisation Électrotechnique (CENELEC) and European Telecommunication Standards Institute (ETSI) are unfolding in energy, telecoms and transport. Banking and finance deserve to be treated separately. One of the most important actors in the development of standards is undoubtedly IOSCO, a body to which the EU is seeking access via ESMA.

A. Recap on Regulation Through Standardisation in the EU

The leading industrial states established national standardisation bodies, the UK and USA in 1901, Germany in 1917, France in 1926.[125] They promoted the foundation of international counterparts, ISO in 1947 and the IEC in 1901. Their European counterparts were set up after the foundation of the EU, CEN in 1961, CENELEC in 1978, ETSI in 1988 under the initiative of the European Commission. Over time, technical standardisation went beyond mere measuring techniques to approach the composition of products and the production process.[126] The transformation of technical standards from mere measuring, into quality and process standards is well documented and led to sophisticated categorisations.[127]

In 1969 the EU set up its first programme to eliminate technical standards as 'non-tariff barriers to trade' through the elaboration of EU law directives.[128] The EU legislature could not handle the technicality, though, and in 1985, prior to the Single European Act, the European Commission developed the so-called New Approach, inspired by the Low Voltage Directive 73/23 (today 2014/35).[129] In 2012 the EU turned the New Approach into the New Legislative Framework (NLF),[130] currently under revision.[131]

The 'General Guidelines for Co-operation' between the European Commission and the European Standardisation Bodies – CEN, CENELEC and later ETSI – enable the European Commission to mandate elaboration of a standard in exchange for taking over parts of the costs.[132] These so-called 'harmonised standards' are published in the Official Journal after approval by the European Commission (Articles 2(1)(c), 10(5)(6) Regulation (EU) No 1025/2012,[133] as amended through

[125] British Standard Institute, National Bureau of Standards (today, the National Institute of Standards and Technology), Deutsches Institute für Normung, Association Française de Normalisation.

[126] T Büthe and W Mattli, *The New Global Rules, The Privatisation of Regulation in the World Economy* (Princeton, Princeton University Press, 2011); JL Contreras (ed), *Cambridge Handbook on Technical Standardisation, Further Intersections of Public and Private Law* (Cambridge, Cambridge University Press, 2019).

[127] P Marburger, *Die Regeln der Technik im Recht* (Tübingen, Mohr Siebeck, 1979).

[128] JC Falke, HW Micklitz and G Brüggemeier, 'European Product Safety, Internal Market Policy and the New Approach to Technical Harmonisation and Standards' (1997) 10 *EUI Working Paper Law* 14 (with a new foreword reprinted in 6 *Hanse Law Review* (2010) 109–14.

[129] Directive 2014/35/EU of the European Parliament and the Council of 26 February 2014 on the harmonisation of the laws of the Member States relating to the making available on the market of electrical equipment designed for use within certain voltage limits (recast) (Text with EEA relevance) [2014] OJ L96/357.

[130] 'Resolution on a New Approach to technical harmonisation and standards' [1985] OJ C 136/1; on the New Legislative Framework, see https://single-market-economy.ec.europa.eu/single-market/goods/new-legislative-framework_en.

[131] Evaluation of NLF available at https://rotf.lol/evaluationeu.

[132] General Guidelines for the Cooperation between CEN, CENELEC and ETSI and the European Commission and the European Free Trade Association [2003] OJ C91/7–11.

[133] Regulation (EU) No 1025/2012 of the European Parliament and the Council of 25 October 2012 on European standardisation, amending Council Directives 89/686/EEC and 93/15/EEC and Directives 94/9/EC, 94/25/EC, 95/16/EC, 97/23/EC, 98/34/EC, 2004/22/EC, 2007/23/EC, 2009/23/EC and 2009/105/EC of the European Parliament and of the Council and repealing Council Decision 87/95/EEC and Decision No 1673/2006/EC of the European Parliament and of the Council (Text with EEA relevance) [2012] OJ L316/12.

EU Regulation 2022/2480,[134] are part of EU law.[135] The website of the European Commission[136] states the areas in which harmonised standards have been elaborated, the subject matter and the respective EN number. Harmonised European standards have to be distinguished from stand-alone 'voluntary industry standards', which are entirely industry-financed and not mandated.

The 1985 New Approach established the still valid interaction between *binding* secondary EU law and complementary *non-binding* technical standards (European harmonised and industry standards). EU legislation is limited to formulating 'binding general requirements' which are concretised through technical standards. Manufacturers remain free to choose a different technical option, as long as it complies with the 'binding general requirements'.[137] Manufacturers have to ensure that their products meet technical requirements and to document compliance through the CE label. The EU may require – via secondary EU law – the involvement of third parties, so-called accredited certification bodies, which substitute self-certification. The Low Voltage Directive triggered the General Agreement of Tariffs and Trade (GATT)/World Trade Organisation (WTO)/Technical Barriers to Trade (TBT) Agreement pursuing a similar approach.

The 'law of standards' came visibly closer to private law through the Service Directive (Directive 2006/123/EC[138]). In services, technical specifications easily transgress legal boundaries in formulating legal rights and obligations which determine the scope and the content of services to be performed.[139] However, the European Commission did not really succeed in pushing the technical standardisation of services either in b2b or in b2c relations, mainly those which do not fall under the mutual recognition mechanism of the Service Directive. Some 70 per cent of EU gross income results from services, but only two per cent of all EU standards deal with services.[140] In its Roadmap for a new Standardisation Strategy,[141] the European Commission is returning to services – in particular to social policy, education, sport and health – where the competence of the EU is limited.

There is one crucial exception though – namely, the field of banking and finance. Here the EU adapted the New Approach to the particular needs of the sector, through the so-called Lamfalussy procedure.[142] The developers of technical specifications in the field of banking and finance are not the European standardisation bodies but technical experts in charge of preparing draft technical specifications under the

[134] Regulation (EU) 2022/2480 amending Regulation (EU) No 1025/2012 as regards decisions of European standardisation organisations concerning European standards and European standardisation deliverables [2022] OJ L323/1.

[135] *James Elliott Construction* (n 66).

[136] For more information see https://rotf.lol/internalmasme.

[137] On the de facto binding effect, see Case C-171/11 Fra.bo [2012] ECLI:EU:C:2012:453.

[138] Directive 2006/123/EC on services in the internal market [2006] OJ L376/36–68; HW Micklitz, *Services Standards: Defining the Core Elements and Their Minimum Requirements*, study commissioned by ANEC, 2007, available at www.anec.eu/attachments/ANEC-R&T-2006-SERV-004final.pdf.

[139] Van Leeuwen Barend (n 2).

[140] Figures referenced in the Roadmap for a European Standardisation Strategy (May 2021), available at https://ec.europa.eu/info/law/better-regulation/have-your-say/initiatives/13099-Standardisation-strategy_en.

[141] ibid.

[142] European Commission, 'Regulatory Process in Financial Services', available at https://rotf.lol/financeeu.

auspices of three European banking institutions – the EOIPA, EBA and ESMA – which have to undergo an approval procedure as laid down in Articles 290 and 291 TFEU depending on whether they are regulatory or implementing standards.[143]

B. Standardisation of EU Regulated Markets within the EU

In order to understand the key role of technical standards in the external reach, it is necessary to clarify their place and function within internal market-building as well as its potential impact on private law relations with each of the regulated markets identified above. As the analysis shows, banking and finance is setting a high benchmark which is not (yet) achieved in energy, telecoms and transport. Whilst it is common sense that banking and finance works as a forerunner, it is far from clear whether a similar role can ever be attributed to standardisation in other fields. The reasons lie in the different nature of private law relations as well as the business environment in which standardisation operates.

i. Banking and Finance

Banking and finance operate under RTS and ITS. Both are published in the Official Journal. RTS and ITS will concretise legal requirements and will 'not imply strategic decisions and policy choices', for example Article 10(1) on RTS and Article 15(1) ITS Regulation 1093/2010. What they are in fact doing is exactly the opposite. They frame the contractual environment, if not the contract itself.

The most advanced examples result from recent attempts at greening finance[144] through Regulation 2015/760[145] (Long-Term Investment Funds) and Regulation 2019/2088[146] (Sustainability-Related Disclosure). In sustainable finance EBA, EIOPA and ESMA are required to jointly draft the RTS and ITS. Regulation 2015/760 lays down rules on eligible investments, on redemption policy and the life of European long-term investment funds (ELTIFS), on disposal of ELTIF Assets and on cost disclosure. Article 18(7) paragraph 3 in combination with Recital 53 demonstrates the regulatory philosophy: ESMA will develop draft regulatory technical standards specifying the circumstances in which the life of an ELTIF is considered sufficient to cover the life-cycle of each of the individual assets of the ELTIF. Regulation 2019/2088 contains obligations on the transparency of adverse sustainability impact – at the entity level and at the financial product level – on environmental and social characteristics in pre-contractual

[143] A Heritier, C Moury and K Granat, 'The Contest for Power in Delegated Rulemaking' in CF Bergstrom and D Ritleg (eds), *Rulemaking by the European Commission: The New System for Delegation of Powers* (Oxford, Oxford University Press, 2016) 105–29.

[144] ESMA, sustainable finance at https://rotf.lol/sustfin, A Marcacci, 'Global Finance and the Anthropocene: Regulatory Shifts and Prospective Effects' (2023) 34 *European Business Law Review* 4, 619–64.

[145] Regulation (EU) 2015/760 of the European Parliament and of the Council of 29 April 2015 on European long-term investment funds (Text with EEA relevance) [2015] OJ L123/98.

[146] Regulation (EU) 2019/2088 of the European Parliament and of the Council of 27 November 2019 on sustainability-related disclosures in the financial services sector (Text with EEA relevance) [2019] OJ L317/1.

disclosures, on transparency of websites, periodic reports and marketing communication. Each of the obligations can be specified through RTS and ITS. Reading the respective articles in connection with the RTS and ITS is a necessary condition to understand how detailed the legal requirements imposed on development of technical standards are.

Lawyers have to apply the whole art of hair-splitting dogmatics in order to define the boundaries between public law – market regulation in the hands of the EU – and private law – the law of contracts in the hands of the Member States. The examples only refer to secondary EU law and not yet to the RTS or ITS. In October 2021, the European agencies presented their draft, which was approved by the European Commission on 6 April 2022[147] and is now pending before the European Parliament and the Council, see Article 290 TFEU and Article 13 Regulation 1093-1094-1095/2010 EBA, ESMA and EIPOA. The proposed RTS strongly promote development of templates for the supply of information, similar to development of information leaflets in consumer law.

ii. Energy

Under Article 3(2) of Implementing Directive 1348/2014 (REMIT), ACER has to draw up a list of standard contracts on each wholesale energy product to facilitate reporting.[148] Thereby ACER gains a detailed overview of standard contracts, which in turn enables the agency – at least in theory – to inform providers of standard contracts of prospective revisions so as to comply with EU law.

In energy, two types of technical standards dominate the regulatory approach – on the one hand voluntary industry standards, on the other harmonised European standards, 'European standards', 'agreed' technical standards and 'established' technical standards. Harmonised technical standards are defined in the NLF, while the other three categories are context-bound, each establishing a particular approval procedure. Article 2(11) Directive 2010/31[149] on energy performance of buildings defines 'European standards', not to be conflated with *harmonised* European standards. European standards are approved by private standard bodies. 'Agreed' and 'established' technical standards refer to co-regulation. Their elaboration is outsourced to Technical System Operators (TSOs), which can be public or private. These standards require approval by public authorities, either national or European depending on the context.

'*Agreed*' European standards cover electricity transmission system operations, network codes, on-demand connection, guidelines on electricity balancing, network codes on harmonised transmission tariff structures for gas and on grid connection of high voltage systems. '*Established*' technical standards deal with network codes

[147] JP Gomez, 'The Commission Finally Adopts the Final Version of RTS for the SFDR' (*Societe Generale*, 10 May 2022), available at https://rotf.lol/ycydufpb.

[148] ACER, 'Guidance on the List of Standard Contracts' (8 October 2015), available at https://rotf.lol/acereu.

[149] Directive 2010/31/EU of the European Parliament and of the Council of 19 May 2010 on the energy performance of buildings (recast) [2010] OJ L153/13.

for grid connection of generators, on-demand connection and on-grid high voltage connection. The rules can be broken down into compatibility and measuring techniques and policy requirements, such as safety, security of supply or climate change. In real life, the distinction between mere technicalities and value-loaded policies is hard to draw. The EU legislature tends to involve standardisation bodies in non-technical requirements, through the non-discrimination principle, through rules on security of supply, through the 2022 emergency measures and more recently through the integration of sustainability, such as the mushrooming rules on 'petrol and diesel fuels', 'renewable energy', and 'ecodesign'.

The EU rules tend to favour international standards over European ones, but tie the applicability of international standards to compliance with EU law. The two directives – Directive 2015/863[150] on petrol and diesel fuel and Directive 2018/2001[151] on renewable energy – are paradigmatic. International standards or national standards may be taken into account if there are no European standards. The European Commission is granted the power to ensure compliance with European standards, provided these 'meet adequate standards of reliability, transparency and independent auditing and provided adequate assurances that no materials have been intentionally modified or discarded' are given. Directive 2009/125[152] on ecodesign, currently under revision,[153] builds on 'harmonised European standards'. Implementing measures concretise 'generic ecodesign requirements' with regard to products, information, and manufacturers.

The European Commission has adopted a long list of implementing measures on a broad range of products which are complemented through 'harmonised European standards'. The parameters of the Directive, the implementing measures and the harmonised European standards to which the implementing measures refer can be aligned with Article 8 Directive 2019/771[154] on consumer sales in b2c contracts[155] and with the United Nations Convention on Contracts for the International Sale of Goods (CISG) Opinion on the role of technical standards in b2b contracts.[156] The Ecodesign Directive is a perfect example of how EU law interferes in contracts through a three-layer approach, at the end of which there are (or should be) 'harmonised standards'.

[150] Commission Delegated Directive (EU) 2015/863 of 31 March 2015 amending Annex II to Directive 2011/65/EU of the European Parliament and of the Council as regards the list of restricted substances (Text with EEA relevance) [2015] OJ L137/10.

[151] Directive (EU) 2018/2001 of the European Parliament and of the Council of 11 December 2018 on the promotion of the use of energy from renewable sources (recast) (Text with EEA relevance.) [2018] OJ L328/82.

[152] Directive 2009/125/EC of the European Parliament and of the Council of 21 October 2009 establishing a framework for the setting of ecodesign requirements for energy-related products (recast) (Text with EEA relevance) [2009] OJ L285/10.

[153] European Commission, proposal for ecodesign requirements for sustainable products, available at https://rotf.lol/energyclimate.

[154] Directive (EU) 2019/771 of the European Parliament and of the Council of 20 May 2019 on certain aspects concerning contracts for the sale of goods, amending Regulation (EU) 2017/2394 and Directive 2009/22/EC, and repealing Directive 1999/44/EC (Text with EEA relevance.) [2019] OJ L136/28.

[155] HW Micklitz, V Mehnert, L Specht-Riemenschneider and P Kenning, *Recht auf Reparatur* (Veröffentlichungen des Sachverständigenrats für Verbraucherfragen, 2022).

[156] CISG-AC Opinion No 19, Standards and Conformity of the Goods under Article 35 CISG, available at https://cisgac.com/wp-content/uploads/2023/02/CISG_Advisory_Council_Opinion_No_19b.pdf.

iii. Telecoms

Article 39 Directive 2018/1972 (Electronic Communications Code) defines the role and function of technical standards in the telecoms market. The reference point are voluntary standards which the European Commission publishes and updates. In case there are no standards, the European Commission can give the ESOs a mandate to draft a harmonised European standard following consultation with the Committee established by Directive (EU) 2015/1535.[157] The European Commission is equally empowered to make technical standards compulsory via an implementing act. International standards will serve as a reference point in case there are no European standards. The Code guarantees access to the 11600 emergency number for missing children and disabled people and to the Europe-wide emergency number 112. The law imposes access; the technical details are laid down in standards.

Directive 2014/53[158] on the market for radio equipment formulates essential binding legal requirements which are then concretised through harmonised European standards. The Directive complements the Electronic Communication Code. Article 21 concretises the essential requirements, by obliging the manufacturer to provide technical documentation which is specified in all details in the Annex. Just to give an example on how this works in practice: The Commission Delegated Regulation (EU) 2022/30[159] supplements Directive 2014/53/EU with regard to application of essential requirements. Harmonised European standards are 'accessible' in the Official Journal by way of a summary. The summary does not generate legal effects and does not help in getting to know the 'contractual' details.

iv. Transport

The methodology applied pointed to nearly 500 pages of EU documents dealing with 'standards' as a catchword, amounting to 132 regulations and directives. They could be grouped around interoperability, market management through statistics, collection of information (inter alia on accidents), market design, international relations and labour, safety, security, and the environment.

The transport sector documents perhaps much more visibly than the other three sectors the manifold meaning of 'standards' and 'standardisation'. Everything can be standardised: substance, procedure, conformity requirements, testing, inspection, statistics and information collection. Standards are neither necessarily 'private' nor are they necessarily 'technical'. Standards may be 'legal rules' to which the legislator refers or 'standards' may be a synonym for setting a benchmark or a yardstick,

[157] Directive (EU) 2015/1535 of the European Parliament and of the Council of 9 September 2015 laying down a procedure for the provision of information in the field of technical regulations and of rules on Information Society services (codification) (Text with EEA relevance) [2015] OJ L241/1.

[158] Directive 2014/53/EU of the European Parliament and of the Council of 16 April 2014 on the harmonisation of the laws of the Member States relating to the making available on the market of radio equipment and repealing Directive 1999/5/EC (Text with EEA relevance) [2014] OJ L153/62.

[159] Commission Delegated Regulation (EU) 2022/30 of 29 October 2021 supplementing Directive 2014/53/EU of the European Parliament and of the Council with regard to the application of the essential requirements referred to in Article 3(3), points (d), (e) and (f), of that Directive (Text with EEA relevance) [2022] OJ L7/6.

which could again be public or private (standard working hours). Standards can be connected to references where the legislator aims to define common private and/or public rules for inspection activities by public authorities or to shape private and/or public professional qualifications of drivers, seafarers, and so on. The number of hits decreases considerably when the search is reduced to 'technical standards', to 'harmonised standards', 'agreed standards', 'established standards', 'recognised standards' or 'open standards' and increases when 'international standards' or 'European standards' are taken into account. The confusion is complete when the respective EU law defines standards, thereby blurring the lines between voluntary private and mandatory public standards or adds a qualification such as 'relevant', 'established' or 'recognised'. Thereby the EU seems to multiply the purposes that can be pursued through standards as alternatives to legal rules or regulatory interventions.

Looking beyond the bewildering use of 'standards', it seems that a simple reference to 'standards' does not necessarily disclose its legal or non-legal, its public or its private character. An analysis one by one demonstrated that nearly all of the 132 pieces of EU law are related in one way or the other to the technical side of standardising transport regulation, in enhancing market-building, such as open skies, through ensuring the interoperability of exchange mechanisms needed to organise transport across borders, or at the substantive level through laying down 'technical requirements' on particular transport devices (their production, repair and maintenance), such as type approval mechanisms, or at the educational level with regard to professional qualifications of the personnel which bear the responsibility for ensuring safe traffic or at the supervisory level of public authorities through extensive rules on administrative procedures. All these efforts sail under the flag of 'standards' or 'standardisation'.

In a more systematic perspective, the EU approach to technical standards can be condensed in the following way, with variations according to the means of transport: wherever possible, the EU seizes the opportunity to develop and establish European standards under due consideration of international standards, typically to ensure interoperability of technologies or measuring techniques. Technical specifications – often in annexes – are used as a kind of entry card into standardising administrative supervision requirements. The EU is in a stronger starting position if standardisation connects to policy fields such as safety, security, and sustainability. The EU is keen to occupy new policy fields through standardisation. EU transport rules refer five times to 'harmonised European standards', all dealing with either safety or environmental issues. The EU wants to be perceived as an international forerunner as in promotion of multimodal transport systems.[160]

The vast volume of rules only rarely indicates a direct link to contracts. Indirect references are characteristic, such as service quality standards, standards on marine equipment and standards on deployment of Intelligent Transport Systems in road transport. Interfaces with other modes of transport are to be concretised through technical 'European' standards, focusing primarily on the optimal use of road, traffic and travel data, continuity of traffic and freight management Intelligent Transport

[160] E Eftestol-Wilhelmsson, S Sankari and A Bask, *Sustainable and Efficient Transport: Incentives for Promoting a Green Transport Market* (London, Elgar Publishing, 2019).

Systems services, road safety and security applications, linking a vehicle with the transport infrastructure.

C. Standardisation of EU Regulated Markets Beyond the EU

The CEN/CENELEC reports demonstrate the deep links and interconnectedness with the world, strongly driven by the interests of the respective industries which can be closely connected to trade statistics. The ETSI reports serve as an example of how the activities unfold in three of the four sectors under review: energy, electronic communication, and transport. They provide extensive information on international co-operation and concrete transnational projects, but they remain rather silent on their relevance. The reports do not provide insights into whether and to what extent the legislative intentions laid down in essential requirements and annexes to directives and regulations have been concretised in European (harmonised) standards, but they highlight how the ESOs are stretching their influence and thereby the content of the technical standards which are designed to serve internal market building purposes beyond EU territory.

i. International Commitments/Agreements of the ESOs

CEN/CENELEC are private bodies established under Belgian law as associations. ETSI was established under French law. Whether or not they engage in international commitments, agreements or MoU is their decision alone, at least as long as they use their freedom of contract to elaborate voluntary industry standards. Neither Regulation 1025/2015 (NLF) nor the Co-operation Agreement between CEN, CENELEC/ETSI and the European Commission interfere in their freedom. However, both the Regulation and the Co-operation Agreement encourage ESOs to engage in international co-operation, in particular with ISO/IEC but more generally with third countries and their organisations. EU funding does not exclude investments in international co-operation. Articles 28 and 29 Regulation 1025/2012 do not distinguish between voluntary standards and harmonised European standards. Neither publicly accessible data, nor reports of the ESOs or the progress report of the European Commission on the implementation of Regulation 1025/2012[161] disclose the degree to which harmonised European standards may involve non-EU institutions.

ii. CEN and CENELEC

In 1991 CEN and ISO signed the Vienna Agreement[162] and CENELEC and IEC the Frankfurt Agreement.[163] The standard formula is the following: 'Wherever appropriate, priority is given to cooperation with ISO provided that international

[161] Report on implementation of Regulation (EU) No 1025/2012 from 2016 to 2020 COM/2022/30 final, available at https://rotf.lol/europeaeu.

[162] Vienna Agreement ISO-CEN, available at https://rotf.lol/viennaagr.

[163] For more information on the Frankfurt Agreement, see www.cencenelec.eu/about-cenelec/cenelec-and-iec-cooperation/.

standards meet European legislative and market requirements and that non-European global players implement these standards'. The Vienna Agreement is supplemented by jointly developed guidelines.[164] The rhetoric is full of language that underpins the importance of standards in order to create markets, support global competitiveness, overcome technical barriers to trade, and foster market access. Standards are claimed to lift research and innovation outcomes and take them right ahead of the curve into the work of making markets before they exist, ahead of their material existence.

CEN and CENELEC have established partnerships with key regional and national standardisation bodies outside Europe. These partnerships vary according to the interests and co-operation needs of each partner. Companion Standardisation Body (CSB) status counts for national standards bodies that want direct access to the European Standards catalogue, to the network of standards-developing bodies and to participate in technical work. The CSB is complemented via a whole series of MoU concluded with regional standardisation organisations around the world: CEN-CENELEC-ETSI with the Association for Standardisation in the Mercado Común del Sur (AMN-MERCOSUR); with EASC (Euro-Asian Interstate Council for Standardisation, Metrology and Certification); with GSO (Standardisation Organisation of the Cooperation Council for the Arab Gulf States); with COPANT (Pan American Standards Commission); CEN-CENELEC with EEC (Eurasian Economic Commission); with AFSEC (African Electrotechnical Standardisation Commission); with AIDMO (Arab Industrial Development and Mining Organisation) and SARSO (the South Asian Regional Standards Organisation); CEN with ARSO (African Organisation for Standardisation); with SADCSTAN (Southern African Development Community Cooperation in Standardisation); and with AIDMO (Arab Industrial Development and Mining Organisation). The Memoranda are available on the Internet. Language is telling. The ESOs copy the language of the New Approach, thereby giving themselves a semi-official outlook. Co-operation Agreements exist with Canada, China, India, Korea, Japan, Russia, India and the USA.[165] The ESOs (CEN, CENELEC and ETSI) and the American National Standards Institute (ANSI) have established a long-standing dialogue, spanning over 25 years. ANSI is the ISO Member Organisation representing the USA. It also hosts the secretariat of the IEC National Committee of the USA (USNC).

CEN and CENELEC are joining forces in two projects that maintain standardisation experts in India and China. The standards bodies of countries that are candidates for EU membership are eligible for affiliate status in order to align with the European standardisation system. CEN and CENELEC put strong emphasis on the

[164] See Vienna Agreement, available at https://boss.cen.eu/media/CEN/ref/va_guidelines_implementation.pdf.

[165] Co-operation agreement between CEN, CENELEC and the Japanese Industrial Standards Committee, available at https://rotf.lol/cenjapan; Co-operation agreement between CEN, CENELEC and KATS (Korean Agency for Technology and Standards), available at https://rotf.lol/cenkats; Co-operation Agreement between CEN, CENELEC and the Russian Federal Agency on Technical and metrology Regulation, available at https://rotf.lol/cenruss; Co-operation with Administration Standardisation of China, available at https://rotf.lol/chinacoop; Co-operation with Canada, available at https://rotf.lol/canadacoop; Co-operation with ANSI, available at https://rotf.lol/parthnerUSA.

global outreach of European standardisation,[166] sometimes in connection with the ISO and IEC, for instance with China-Japan, India, Africa and the Gulf.[167]

iii. ETSI

ETSI is omnipresent in energy, electronic communication and transport. It looks as if the constantly rising importance of the digital economy has pushed ETSI into an ever more prominent role. Reports are full of details, which can be grouped roughly around three major categories: a) partnership agreements in the widest sense; b) transnational projects on particular topics; and c) more focused activities coming closer to private law issues.

During the period under investigation – 2010–2020 – the number of partnership agreements grew constantly. Co-operation with China and India has been extended and deepened, through concrete projects but also in the organisation of joint seminars.[168] Worth mentioning are the MoU with the Broadband India Forum, the International Marine Electronics Association, the Center for Internet Security, the Digital Mobile Radio Association, the Federation of Electrical, Electronic and Communication Industries and Open Pan European Public Procurement Online (OpenPEPPOL). Since 2009 ETSI has been involved in the 3GGP (Third Generation Partnership Project) concerning development of communication systems. The programme was established to develop globally applicable specifications for third generation mobile telecommunications (the International Telecommunication Union's (ITU's) IMT-2000 family). 3GPP is responsible for the maintenance and evolution of specifications for the enormously successful Global System for Mobile communication (GSM™), which was defined by ETSI, and for transitional technologies, including the General Packet Radio Service (GPRS), Enhanced Data for GSM Evolution (EDGE) and High Speed Packet Access (HSPA). The move to 4 GGP and now 5 GGP has kept the project alive. Within the Generation Partnership programme, five regional standardisation organisations in Asia and North America are coming together, plus business organisations as well as a large number of telecom companies. Other projects concern satellite and language communication across business sectors, energy efficiency for ICT, smart cities, development of specifications for Digital Enhanced Cordless Telecommunications (DECT), and international standards for distress messages to fill a gap in maritime standardisation. Few projects suggest a strong focus on private transactions. Worth mentioning is 'Design for All', which aims at ensuring access for everybody including the elderly and the handicapped to devices, systems and services.

iv. IOSCO and ESMA

The picture would be incomplete without mentioning IOSCO.[169] This is a non-institution with no particular legal status, which brings together the world's securities

[166] For more information on CENELEC global outreach, see https://rotf.lol/globalcen.
[167] For more information on Adoption of European Deliverables, see https://rotf.lol/imagest.
[168] M Cantero, *Telecommunication Policy Standards as Governance: the Escalation of China in AI Governance through Standardisation*, Telecommunications Policy 47 (2023) 102673.
[169] Marcacci (n 48) deals extensively with the role, function and work of IOSCO.

regulators. On its website, IOSCO states that it 'is recognised as the global standard setter for the securities sector'.[170] IOSCO is developing non-binding rules with a huge impact on financial markets. The argument goes that MiFID I and II should be understood as having transformed non-binding international soft law into binding EU law. IOSCO is equally involved in the development of supervision standards, where it overlaps with EBA.

Full members are national regulatory agencies, *associate* members are supranational governmental regulators, subnational governmental regulators, intergovernmental international organisations and international standard-setting bodies, *affiliated* members are self-regulatory organisations, securities exchanges, financial market infrastructures, international bodies other than governmental organisations with an appropriate interest in securities regulation, investor protection funds and compensation funds, and other bodies with an appropriate interest in securities regulation. Both the European Commission and ESMA are Associate Members, but not EBA. ESMA is the only IOSCO Associate Member that is currently a member of the IOSCO Board, although with observer status.[171]

ESMA has gained more weight within IOSCO and more leverage vis-à-vis its US counterparts due to post-2008 EU law. Within the IOSCO perimeter, however, ESMA is (still) a lame duck due to its limited sectoral supervisory and enforcement powers. The strong push for a European capital market enabled the EU to increase its influence on the elaboration of substantive and procedural (supervisory) standards. Lately IOSCO has engaged in what can be defined as 'Conflicts of Securities Regulation'. As neither 'The 2006 Hague Securities Convention' nor the 'Geneva Convention' found strong support from signatory states,[172] IOSCO seems to be looking for new pathways to bring international private law rules and IOSCO standards closer together in the resolution of disputes.

D. Standardisation in the EU Framework on the Digital Economy

The steadily growing importance of ETSI indicates where the wind is blowing. Digitisation is gaining pace and again it is the EU that jumps on the bandwagon to steer it with more integration – through law and through technical standards. Strongly interlinked to the Roadmap – indeed, one of the reasons for the Roadmap – is the ongoing attempt by the European Commission to lay down an overall framework on the digital economy and digital society (sic) through the Data Governance Act (DGA), The Digital Market Act (DMA),[173] the Digital Services Act (DSA),[174] the envisaged Artificial Intelligence Act (AIA),[175] the Data Act (DA)[176] and the

[170] See IOSCO website at www.iosco.org/about/?subsection=about_iosco.
[171] Marcacci (n 48) ch 22, 33 at 46.
[172] Hague Convention – Mauritius, Switzerland, US; Geneva Convention – Bangladesh.
[173] Regulation (EU) 2022/1925 on contestable and fair markets in the digital sector [2022] OJ L265/1.
[174] Regulation (EU) 2022/2065 on a Single Market For Digital Services [2022] OJ L277/1.
[175] See www.europarl.europa.eu/news/en/headlines/society/20230601STO93804/eu-ai-act-first-regulation-on-artificial-intelligence.
[176] See Regulation (EU) 2023/2854 on harmonized rules on fair access to and use of data (2023) OJL series 22.12.2023.

Act on Cyber Security (ACS).[177] The framework mirrors the New Approach rationale; broadly worded legally binding general requirements will have to be specified and concretised through harmonised European standards and voluntary industry standards.[178] Thereby the EU Commission aims at gaining influence through regulation of technical standards which affect internet giants in the USA and in China. The EU is transferring all its experience gained and developed in regulating the old industries into a regulatory framework that by definition is meant to address the digital economy and digital society far beyond Europe. What becomes gradually visible in the four sectors under investigation is now turning into a much broader and further reaching move towards a New Approach type of thinking which is meant to govern the digital economy as a whole.

The ESOs will be entrusted with ever more public policy issues, first physical safety, now mental health and respect for fundamental rights.[179] A clear divide exists between the DGA and DSA on the one hand and the AIA on the other. Within the DGA and DSA the European Commission relies on 'voluntary industry standards', in the AIA on 'harmonised European standards'. The regulatory technique implies that, within the scope of the AIA, the European Commission gains a triple role: as instigator, it may make a request; as financier, it may influence choice; as compliance authority, it has to check whether the mandated standards respect the general requirements laid down, in particular for high-risk products.[180]

E. Interim Conclusions

The missing knowledge on the content of the technical standards looks like a disadvantage. Nevertheless, the analysis provides key insights into the use of technical standards as an instrument of market regulation to indirectly shape contractual relations through an ever denser net of rules.

First of all, there is multi-level regulation: binding general requirements, often supplemented by increasingly detailed recitals, then extensive annexes, which contain specifications down to the smallest detail, and finally the technical standards themselves, which are accessible at least when adopted in the form of an implementing act. European technical standards have to be fitted into the corresponding international

[177] Regulation (EU) 2019/881 on information and communications technology cybersecurity certification and repealing Regulation (EU) No 526/2013 (Act on Cyber Security) (Text with EEA relevance) OJ L151/15.

[178] HW Micklitz, N Helberger and P Rott, *EU Consumer Protection 2.0: The Regulatory Gap: Consumer Protection in the Digital Economy*: Addendum to the report 'Structural Asymmetries in Digital Consumer Markets' (2021) available at https://rotf.lol/beuceuconsumer.

[179] K Vieweg, 'Technische Normung und Wirtschaftsrecht – Zu den ethischen Anforderungen beim Einsatz künstlicher Intelligenz' in *Festschrift für Werner E. Ebke zum* 70. Geburtstag, Hrsg B P Paal, D Poelsig, O Fehrenbacher, C H Beck (2021) 1025; M Ebers, 'Standardising AI – The Case of the European Commission's Proposal for an Artificial Intelligence Act' in LA DiMatteo, M Cannarsa and C Poncibò (eds), *The Cambridge Handbook of Artificial Intelligence: Global Perspectives on Law and Ethics* (Cambridge, Cambridge University Press, 2022).

[180] For a comprehensive analysis, see HW Micklitz, 'The Role of Standards in Future in EU Digital Policy Legislation' (BEUC, 14 July 2023), available at www.beuc.eu/sites/default/files/publications/BEUC-X-2023-096_The_Role_of_Standards_in_Future_EU_Digital_Policy_Legislation.pdf.

legal framework. International technical standards – this is the rhetoric throughout the material – will take precedence, as long as they do not contradict EU law, specifically EU law on regulated markets. Insofar as gaps open up in the international legal framework, the EU actively uses these opportunities to promote the development of European standards. New technological developments or structural changes in geopolitics, which are not yet subject to international treaties or regulatory initiatives, immediately call the EU into action. This can be seen in the promotion of climate protection in all four sectors or the development of a legal framework for the digital economy. Typically, the EU tries to exert its influence through harmonised European standards. The regulatory mechanism puts the European Commission into a comfortable position; it can steer the process by initiating and financing the process and the Commission can supervise and control the results in the approval procedure. Harmonised European standards form part of EU law, which enhances the weight of their external effects.

The analysis of the four markets shows all too clearly how technical standards are placed like a wreath under, before and behind contract law. Under, in that technical standards define the reference point for quality, safety and environmental standards; in front and behind, because pre-contractual and post-contractual regulations are by and large excluded in a classic understanding of contract law. Technical standards dealing with pre-contractual information obligations or post-contractual conflict management fall under the concept of market regulation and are typically discussed outside contract law in specific fields, such as commercial practices or after sales services and dispute resolution. The strategic use of technical standards to achieve specific political goals, such as climate protection, reduces the importance of classic private law and thereby raises legitimacy concerns. Without touching the hot potato, the EU can de facto and de jure shape private law with the help of technical standards. Here we are back to the understanding of European private law as European *regulatory* private law, which starts from a much broader understanding.

V. MAJOR FINDINGS, OPEN QUESTIONS AND LOOSE ENDS

A. Reverse External Effect

Through the interplay of market integration and social regulation, the EU has built up a huge apparatus in the law of regulated markets. This apparatus is primarily addressed to establishing the internal market – in the EU context this is the market with a social face. Once market integration achieves a certain level of consistency, the EU takes precautionary measures to shield the internal market against intrusion from the outside. This is a kind of a reverse external effect which materialises mainly in two different strands, first through the prominence of European regulatory agencies, which tie co-operation to 'equivalence', equivalence of the substantive, the procedural and the institutional rules, predominantly through extension of EU regulatory culture via all sorts of soft agreements, and secondly – but even less visibly – through strong promotion of technical standards, which may carry political purposes, such as safety and environmental protection. Here the EU projects the power it has built over a century to the outside world with the help of ESOs as their long arm. Private law is in between and is characterised through a dense set of rules wrapped around the core of the contract. Its atypical nature facilitates its export via administrative regulations and technical standards.

B. Private Law

The analysis confirms the pioneering role of banking and finance, internally and externally. In all other areas, the European Standardisation Organisations compensate for the power deficits of the relevant agencies: ACER in energy, BEREC Office in telecoms and the EASA, ERA in transport. If one wants to recognise a strategy in regulations and directives, one may assume that the EU is reducing the importance of classic private law by expanding administrative supervision from above while at the same time accelerating elaboration of technical standards from below. This is at least true if one links private law with autonomy and freedom of contract. The 'regulatory' in European regulatory private law is gaining the upper hand and thereby downgrades de jure the role and function of individual parties, if not in reality then at least in the regulatory approach. In contrast to consumer law in the internal market, there is no CJEU in the position of re-establishing or at least counterbalancing market (private) regulation against freedom of contract and private autonomy beyond EU territory.[181] This chapter does not engage with privatisation of enforcement through compliance, self- and third-party certification, where public administrative enforcement is reduced to monitoring and surveillance and where EU law falls short of guaranteeing protection to the victims of insufficient compliance and certification.[182] Nor has it dealt with dispute resolution and arbitration, which are crucial in resolving conflicts in b2b relations. Here a gap is waiting to be filled. In European private law beyond EU territory, all these semi-voluntary forms have a prominent role to play. They lead to an increase of private responsibilities in the making and enforcement of market regulation.

C. Function

The law of regulated markets is and remains functional, related to the four sectors and the internal market, which it seeks to shape first internally and then to protect externally. Private law relations are reduced to fulfilling a particular function. They are instrumentalised and transformed into market regulation. Its functional character suggests that the content of private law relations does not matter so much as long as the EU legal framework ensures that private law relations fulfil the function assigned to them. Market regulation is not concerned with the rights and obligations of individual companies on whatever side of private law relations. Market regulation

[181] C Leone, '*The Missing Stone in the Cathedral of Unfair Terms in Employment Contracts and Coexisting Rationalities in European Private Law*, PhD thesis (University of Amsterdam, 2020).

[182] P Rott (ed), *Certification – Trust, Accountability, Liability* (Springer, 2019).

understands private law relations as a collective tool, which does not leave much room for differentiation. The competence deficit in the EU legal order promotes such an approach. The unifying element in the law of regulated markets is the functional understanding and use of market regulation. This regulatory function is fulfilled in a strikingly clear way by double market regulation from above and from below. In this respect, the frequently expressed criticism that European private law is market-functional and not value-based seems justified.[183]

D. Substance

However, such an understanding sets aside the social dimension in EU market regulation, the internal market with a social face, the interaction between market integration and social regulation. The mandate to guarantee a high level of consumer protection has enabled the EU to adopt social regulation to the benefit of European citizens and all non-EU citizens who have a residence permit. Therefore, whenever the European agencies tie 'equivalence' to internal market rules, they push social standards on protection of the customer beyond its borders. The situation is different for b2b relations. Here, EU private law is thin, if one sets aside the measures to protect SMEs in the law of regulated markets.[184] Market regulation from above and from below, this is the overall result serving as a substitute for missing competence. This implies that values, if there are any, have to be carried through rules that determine the benchmark of supervision or through technical standards themselves. Thereby health, safety, environmental protection and sustainability find their way into private law relations. Less obvious are the values that functional law carries by way of a piggy-back procedure. Equivalence, non-discrimination and interoperability are not value-free. They transport a highly particular understanding of how markets should be organised and what private law relations – which keep the markets alive – should look like. In that sense the functional law of the regulated market has an impact on b2b private law relations, too. However, there is more. Technical standards usually enshrine value judgements in one form or the other. The fairy tale of 'neutrality' or 'mere technicality' is misleading. Technology, too, is subject to the political economy of market economies.

E. Form

The field of regulated markets looks messy and is hardly accessible to non-specialists in the four sectors of the economy. One might feel tempted to call for clearance, for systematisation, for coherence and maybe even for a banking, energy and transport

[183] Esp M Hesselink, 'EU Private Law Injustices' (2022) *Yearbook of European Law* (41), first published online 28 September 2022.

[184] L de Almeida, V Cappelli, N Klausmann, and H van Soest, *Peer-to-Peer Trading and Energy Community in the Electricity Market Analysing the Literature on Law and Regulation and Looking Ahead to Future Challenges* (April 2021), available at https://library.wur.nl/WebQuery/wurpubs/fulltext/558791.

code which mirrors the electronic communication code. Whilst such code thinking might undoubtedly be helpful and might enable (not only) the outside world to better study the external effects as far as realised through law (not soft law), it does not, however, solve the much deeper problem of the direction European regulatory private law is taking, internally and externally. One might also take the findings upside down and understand the messy field as an integral part of the new private law, the one which governs the twenty-first century. This would equally require study of the interaction between European transnational (regulatory) private law and classic international private law. The law of the regulated markets, in particular the law on banking and finance, works like a forerunner and a source of detection and inspiration.

F. Method

How to handle the collection of black boxes, the lack of 'content', of 'substance', of 'values' of 'administrative practices', of technical standards? The three crucial places where the influence of EU law on private law should materialise in practice remain to some extent empty – this is true with regard to administrative enforcement of private law, with regard to lack of access to copyright-protected technical standards, and with regard to compliance, certification and dispute resolution. The identification of black boxes triggers a kind of reflex – a call for further research, for better empiricism, for evaluating the administrative practice of the European agencies, of the European standardisation bodies, for looking behind all the co-operation agreements, the supervisory colleges and the agreements between European and non-European standards bodies, for raising funds so as to be able to interview public and private regulators and to buy access to technical standards and analyse them jointly with competent experts working in the four fields. Important as it may be, this call, if it is one, should not obscure the structural reason behind the triple black box. This chapter is a first attempt to offer an answer, despite all these limitations, an answer which calls for a broader understanding of private law. Including the regulatory dimension is the only way forward to get to grips with the way in which private law is developing.

G. Civil Society

The structural semi-empirical analysis of the law on regulated markets is far from complete. There are loose ends which need to be addressed as they require further investigation. Ongoing research should focus on private actors in terms of business, consumer, and civil society organisations. In *Politics of Justice in European Private Law* I introduced 'societal justice' as a category which allows European citizens to actively participate in building a European society – beyond the market. To my dismay, I have not exhausted the potential that the law of the regulated market offers, internally and externally. This chapter has opened a window, though very much seen through EU regulatory lenses, without investigating private and societal actors.

Shifting the focus towards societal actors opens new insights, in the upper and lower layers of the sandwich in light of potential participation by civil society in administrative supervision, in development and execution of international commitments, in compliance and certification, and – last but not least – in elaborating technical standards. In the near future, I will turn my research to the role that civil society organisations are playing and could play in the making of technical standards, which are relevant not only for the EU – but for the rest of the world – I am referring to technical standards in the European Framework on the digital economy (and society).[185]

[185] HW Micklitz, The Role of Technical Standards in Future EU Digital Policy Legislation, 2023 https://www.beud.eu.

Legal Theory

4

The Jurisprudence of Process and European Transnational Private Law

RODRIGO VALLEJO*

> 'In the world where the United States projects hard power through its military and engagement in trade wars, and China economic power through its loans and investments, the EU exerts power through the most potent tool for global influence it has – regulation.'[1]

> 'Not every question of group concern can be decided by officials, and certainly not every such question in the first instance. Every society necessarily assigns many kinds of questions to private decision, and then backs up the private decision, if it has been duly made, when and if it is challenged before officials. ... In a genuine sense, these procedures of private decision, too, become institutionalized. An understanding of how they work is vital to an understanding of the institutional system as a whole'.[2]

* Assistant Professor, Faculty of Law, University of Amsterdam, and Marie Curie Fellow, Centre for Private Governance, University of Copenhagen. All websites were last visited during June 2023. The research that led to section III of this chapter was developed during my post-doctoral fellowship at Helsinki Law School as part of the FiDiPro project on the External Dimension of European Private Law. The research that led to sections I, II and IV has been developed as part of a MSCA Fellowship funded by the European Union at the Centre of Private Governance of Copenhagen Law School (Horizon-MSCA-2021-PF-01; Project Number: 101068203). Views and opinions expressed are, however, those of the author only and do not necessarily reflect those of the European Union or the European Research Executive Agency (REA) as granting authority. Neither the European Union nor the granting authority can be held responsible for them.

[1] A Bradford, *The Brussels Effect: How the European Union Rules the World* (Oxford, Oxford University Press, 2020) 24.

[2] HM Hart and AM Sacks, *The Legal Process: Basic Problems in the Making and Application of Law* [1958] (Washington, Foundation Press, 1994) 7.

I. EXCAVATING FOUNDATIONS: PROCESS AND PROCEDURALISATION IN THE EXTERNAL DIMENSION OF EU LAW

EU LAW HAS nowadays achieved a noticeable external dimension. Since the publication of seminal studies by Anu Bradford and Joanne Scott in the early 2010s,[3] this phenomenon has been extensively documented by a wide-ranging set of scholarly work in different areas of EU law.[4] This interest has been paralleled by salient reports from influential media and non-governmental organisations (NGOs), which signals a growing drive within public opinion to grasp and scrutinise the ventures of EU law beyond EU frontiers.[5] This drive is especially welcome at a time when the EU has most forcefully entered the complex geopolitical power play by seeking to 'promote European interests and values on the global stage' through building 'a stronger Europe in the world' and fostering 'our European way of life' as one of its 'strategic priorities'.[6] Despite their polemic overtones, these are the ambitions that are now officially guiding the political actions and regulatory programmes of EU institutions within and beyond the internal market in several socio-economic realms.[7] The EU is thus currently experiencing a salient 'geopolitical awakening'.[8]

[3] See mainly A Bradford, 'The Brussels Effect' (2012) 107 *Northwestern University Law Review* 1; J Scott, 'Extraterritoriality and Territorial Extension in EU Law' (2014) 62 *The American Journal of Comparative Law* 87; and J Scott, 'The New EU Extraterritoriality' (2014) 51 *CML Rev* 1343.

[4] See, eg, and with further references, E Fahey, *The Global Reach of EU Law* (Oxfordshire, Taylor & Francis, 2016); L Ankersmit, *Free Trade, Fair Trade, and Green Trade in and with the EU: Process-based Measures within the EU Legal Order* (Cambridge, Cambridge University Press, 2017); M Cremona and J Scott (eds), *EU Law Beyond EU Borders: The Extraterritorial Reach of EU Law* (Oxford, Oxford University Press, 2019); HCH Hofmann, E Vos and M Chamon (eds), *The External Dimension of EU Agencies and Bodies: Law and Policy* (Cheltenham, Edward Elgar Publishing, 2019); I Hadjiyianni, *The EU As a Global Regulator for Environmental Protection: A Legitimacy Perspective* (London, Bloomsbury Publishing Plc, 2019); T Giegerich (ed), *The European Union as Protector and Promoter of Equality* (Berlin, Springer Nature, 2020); N Cunha Rodrigues (ed), *Extraterritoriality of EU Economic Law: The Application of EU Economic Law Outside the Territory of the EU* (Berlin, Springer Nature, 2021); MC Eritja (ed), *The European Union and Global Environmental Protection: Transforming Influence into Action* (Oxfordshire, Routledge, 2020); and E Fahey and I Mancini (eds), *Understanding the EU as a Good Global Actor: Ambitions, Values and Metrics* (Cheltenham, Edward Elgar Publishing, 2022).

[5] See, eg, 'EU Deforestation Law Triggers Ire of its Trading Partners' *Financial Times* (6 February 2023), available at www.ft.com/content/c2f2eea9-1eb5-478f-ac53-5666776c0a35, noting how 'the law is particularly galling for the two South-East Asian Countries' whose agricultural economies are significantly dependent upon the production of palm-oil that is directly targeted by the legislation and how 'Brazil, Argentina, Ghana, Nigeria, and Canada – all exporters of Agricultural commodities – also regard Brussels's move as a protectionist measure.' See also, more generally, 'Whose Paying the Bill?: (Negative) Impacts of EU Policies and Practices in the World' (*SDG Watch Europe*, 2019), available at https://sdgwatcheurope.org/who-is-paying-the-bill/, documenting inconsistencies between the EU's embrace of the Sustainable Development Goals and the foreign effects of its policies in several socio-economic realms, such as fisheries, land-use, finance, and chemicals.

[6] See European Union, 'European Union Priorities 2019–2024', available at https://european-union.europa.eu/priorities-and-actions/european-union-priorities-2019-2024_en.

[7] See, European Commission, 'A Stronger Europe in the World', available at https://commission.europa.eu/strategy-and-policy/priorities-2019-2024/stronger-europe-world_en; and European Commission, 'Promoting our European Way of Life', available at https://commission.europa.eu/strategy-and-policy/priorities-2019-2024/promoting-our-european-way-life_en signalling several socio-economic realms as the focus of these political priorities and concurrent policy programmes, including health, migration, security, and trade.

[8] L van Middelaar, 'Europe's Geopolitical Awakening' (2021) 8 *Groupe d'études géopolitiques*, available at https://geopolitique.eu/en/2021/04/15/europes-geopolitical-awakening/.

While the existing literature regarding the external dimension of EU law is by now diverse in its substantive focus and geographical reach, the several contributions to this volume represent a valuable addition to this overarching scholarly effort. There are several reasons for this. Some of these contributions are novel in terms of the entities or sectors that are studied, such as European Works Councils (Liukkunen, chapter 6), taxation (Pantazatou, chapter 12), and regulated industries (Micklitz, chapter 3). Others are novel due to the theoretical and methodological approaches used, such as chapter 9 from Chadwick that uses political economy as a framework to critically review the place and role of EU law within contemporary developments in transnational finance, or chapter 14 by Salminen, Rajavuori, and Eller that shows how the EU is drawing upon global value chains to export its internal market discipline through a reconstructive account of recent EU legislative and regulatory developments in the field. The study developed by Letto-Vanamo in chapter 5 on how European law travels through epistemic communities adds new layers to these two planes of novelty by expounding on the historical and sociological dimensions of the phenomenon.

Finally, other chapters stand out due to their provocative outlook. One example is chapter 7 from Möschel that shows the limited external effect of EU non-discrimination law and discusses some of the possible explanations. This is also the case of chapter 11 from Mataija that shows how the EU is leveraging international trade law to discipline foreign production and commercialisation processes. A final example is chapter 13 from Ulfbeck that discusses how European tort law doctrines are evolving to foster regulatory change towards climate neutrality in foreign market relations. Each of the case studies in this volume can thus be read as enhancing this overall scholarly endeavour regarding the foreign sway of EU law by either exploring new terrain and approaches or by adding relevant nuances to existing sectoral accounts.

Any research project of this diversity and ambition faces a crucial challenge. The risk is that the book becomes a mere *collage* of varied and interesting journeys into different domains of EU law beyond the frontiers of the internal market. This would transform the book into a sort of travel guide for whoever would like to further embark on and deepen each of these foreign adventures of EU law. The challenge is thus to bring this range of exciting journeys into a common vocabulary to make them amenable for comparison, and thus reciprocal enrichment. In other words, we need a conceptual framework.

Two provisos are in order here. The first is that, to prevent the malaises of so-called *Begriffsjurisprudenz*, this conceptual framework should be sufficiently open and nuanced to encompass what is happening in practice throughout a wide range of EU legal-policy fields beyond the internal market. This includes tracing the different modalities through which EU private law is travelling abroad, the role of law in shaping those modalities, as well as its material and cultural consequences. I call this the anti-mystification proviso. The second proviso is the Janus-face of the previous one: concepts in law and legal studies are not mere labels that aim to describe something that exists independent of their descriptions. Unless merely nominal, legal concepts partially produce the reality that they aim to describe by institutionalising a set of socio-political practices according to certain immanent aims or dispositions that are meant to purposively guide those practices. I call this the performative dimension of legal concepts.

While avoiding mystification, any productive mode of legal conceptualisation inevitably involves a performative dimension. To say it *à la* Habermas, in other words, legal concepts and institutions usually place themselves in 'between facts and norms'.[9] Eighty years before Habermas, this insight was perhaps best articulated by Felix Frankfurter, when addressing a similarly challenging scenario of how to make sense in legal terms of widespread regulatory practices:

> … the way in which law reflects social forces partly helps to shape them. This is where scholarship comes in, or whatever one may call the systematic process of rational inquiry. … mere empiric unfolding, piling precedent upon precedent, is bound eventually to beget a bewildering and unpersuasive mass of unrelated instances. A philosophy is needed. But if particulars without a binding philosophy are the easy prey of distortion or misunderstanding, abstract generalities are like paper flowers, pretty but lifeless.[10]

In this vein, our choice of how to conceptualise the phenomenon of EU law beyond EU frontiers has not been random. As explained in our introductory chapter of this volume, the notion of transnational law renders itself useful to identify, understand, and assess the place and role of EU private law throughout a vast array of legal regimes or policy domains beyond the frontiers of the internal market. This is mainly due to its capacity to pluralistically trace the diverse actors, norms, and processes involved in those regimes and to bridge established distinctions between the private/public, national/international, or law/non-law. With its pluralistic framework, transnational law thus offers a distinctive analytical ductility that has been mainly attributed to its methodological nature, rather than conceiving it as some kind of theory or substantive field.[11]

Yet what are the assumptions and normative dispositions regarding socio-political power and legal authority underlying this method? Why are we to engage with this phenomenon by tracing actors, norms, and processes but not in some other ways? How can we assess the suitability and desirability of these transnational interactions informing the intrepid voyages of EU private law beyond the frontiers of the internal market? In other words, what justifies this methodological approach? These are all foundational questions that cannot be avoided under the veneer of simply following some kind of method – regardless of how scientific, descriptive, or objective it purports to be.[12] In line with the foundational ambitions of the book, and as a complement to the chapters from the other co-editors in the volume, the object of

[9] J Habermas, *Between Facts and Norms: Contributions to a Discourse Theory of Law and Democracy* [1992] (Cambridge, The MIT Press, 1996).

[10] F Frankfurter, 'The Final Report of the Attorney General's Committee on Administrative Procedure. Foreword' (1941) 41 *Columbia Law Review* 585, 586.

[11] For a discussion, see P Zumbansen, 'Defining the Space of Transnational Law: Legal Theory, Global Governance, and Legal Pluralism' (2012) 21 *Transnational Law & Contemporary Problems* 305.

[12] M Bartl and JC Lawrence (eds), *The Politics of European Legal Research: Behind the Method* (Cheltenham, Edward Elgar Publishing, 2022). See also, PW Kahn, 'Freedom and Method' in R van Gestel, HW Micklitz, EL Rubin (eds), *Rethinking Legal Scholarship: A Transatlantic Dialogue* (Cambridge, Cambridge University Press, 2017).

this chapter is thus to 'excavate foundations' for this research agenda on European transnational private law by focusing on its jurisprudential or legal theory facets.[13]

The working hypothesis guiding the chapter is that the emphasis on 'process' that has been informing this method has significant potential to illuminate these foundational questions. The emphasis on 'process' or 'proceduralisation' is nowadays ubiquitous in contemporary legal theory and practice. Much of contemporary lawyering and legal studies are indeed driven analytically and normatively by the need to enhance the procedural qualities of rulemaking and their operationalisation within national or transnational policies.[14] For the purposes of this volume, most importantly, these studies include some of the most salient scholarly analysis of the external dimension of EU law[15] as well as its relevant practices.[16] To the extent that these external effects of the EU, and its overall 'geo-political awakening', have been given the significance of potentially renovating or invigorating the EU's own *raison d'être*, process and proceduralisation have thus become integral to this pathway for reinvigoration.[17]

[13] M Loughlin, 'Excavating Foundations' in MA Wilkinson, MW Dowdle (eds), *Questioning the Foundations of Public Law* (London, Bloomsbury Publishing, 2018): noting how 'the common challenge' in the search for foundations of legal institutions 'is to devise a conceptual scheme through which the constitution of political authority can be explained'. Throughout this chapter, I use the terms 'legal theory', 'philosophy of law', and 'jurisprudence' as synonyms and thus interchangeably.

[14] See, eg, F Bignami and D Zaring (eds), *Comparative Law and Regulation: Understanding the Global Regulatory Process* (Cheltenham, Edward Elgar Publishing, 2016); TC Halliday and G Shaffer (eds), *Transnational Legal Orders* (Cambridge, Cambridge University Press, 2015); and J Waldron, 'The Rule of Law and the Importance of Procedure' in JE Fleming (ed), *Nomos: Getting to the Rule of Law* (New York, NYU Press, 2011). See also, in general, R Weithölter, 'Proceduralization of the Category of Law' (2011) 12 *German Law Journal* 465.

[15] M Cremona and J Scott, 'Introduction – EU Law Beyond EU Borders' in M Cremona, J Scott (eds), *EU Law Beyond EU Borders: The Extraterritorial Reach of EU Law* (Oxford, Oxford University Press, 2019) 20: concluding that '… it is the present authors' contention that the Commission ought to be required to pay close attention to the possible impacts of EU measures on third countries, and to develop a transparent framework for assessing trade-offs between competing interests in third countries, and between interests inside and outside the EU'. In the same vein, see also Bradford (n 1) 262–63: outlining the type of economic, political, and distributional costs that the foreign reach of EU law through the so-called 'Brussels Effect' generates and expounding how an 'effective implementation of the Commission's Better Regulation Agenda' and 'the greater incorporation of foreign stakeholders' views as part of the impact assessment process … could mitigate some of the criticisms associated with regulatory imperialism'.

[16] These practices do not only come from the EU itself. One recent example is the letter that ambassadors from 17 southern countries across all continents, including Nigeria, Bolivia, and Indonesia, sent to EU authorities on 7 September 2023 concerning the external effects of the EU Regulation on Deforestation-Free Products (2023), available at https://twitter.com/VidigalGeraldo/status/1700190159549981105. Apart from questioning the regulatory effectiveness and distributive effects of the referred regulation, as a basis for its 'repairment' or 'mitigation', these countries called upon the EU to enhance the procedural qualities of its policymaking in the field by engaging 'in a more meaningful and open dialogue with producing countries than what has been undertaken so far'.

[17] G De Burca, 'Europe's Raison d'Etre' in D Kochenov, F Amtenbrink (eds), *The European Union's Shaping of the International Legal Order* (Cambridge, Cambridge University Press, 2013); G De Burca, 'EU External Relations: The Governance Mode of Foreign Policy' in B Van Vooren, S Blockmans and J.Wouters (eds), *The EU's Role in Global Governance: The Legal Dimension* (Oxford, Oxford University Press 2013). See also, Middelaar (n 8): noting that 'this new period of [European] history', far from being 'a struggle between democracy and autocracy', is a 'post-pax Americana' that entails an 'age of encounters with other great powers, other civilizations' and 'demands pluralistic thinking'.

Yet this emphasis on process is neither new nor unique to contemporary developments in transnational law or the law of global governance. It corresponds to an established tradition in modern legal theory that dates back at least to the 1950s, if not earlier. This chapter interconnects this emphasis on process in the studies of the external dimension of EU law and contemporary legal thinking with the broader jurisprudential tradition of process in modern law and legal thought to reflect upon its foundations. The research question informing this chapter is whether and to what extent this 'jurisprudence of process' can contribute to illuminating some of these foundational queries regarding the notion of European transnational private law.

The exploration proceeds in three steps. The next section outlines the 'jurisprudence of process' as a tradition of modern legal theory and its relationship with European law. For these purposes, the section traces the origins of this tradition to distinctive strands of post-war jurisprudence that emerged within the national, international, and transnational contexts during the 1940s and1950s. It also explains how this 'jurisprudence of process' became propelled into EU law and legal thought by influential modes of juristic thinking and concurrent practices, while underscoring the relevant jurisprudential continuities between these national, international, and transnational realms of law and legal thought. This is achieved by characterising this 'jurisprudence of process' as a post-formalist and post-realist approach to modern law and legal thought centred around inter-institutional dynamics of lawmaking and implementation, and by identifying five shared analytical cornerstones that sustain it as a jurisprudential tradition. These analytical cornerstones and its overall characterisation make the jurisprudence of process a productive framework to channel current and future studies on European transnational private law, yet with relevant blind spots or limits that are key to keep in sight.

Section III draws upon this jurisprudential framework to intervene in contemporary studies on the foreign reach of EU law. The section builds on the seminal work by Bradford and Scott, and the insights offered by the different chapters of this volume as well as other complementary studies on the phenomenon. This is done so as to discuss how the notion of European transnational private law grounded on the tradition of process jurisprudence can contribute to expanding and refining the parameters that have been driving this range of contemporary studies on the foreign reach of EU law. Alongside tracing some relationships, (dis-)continuities, and gaps within the literature, this section also identifies some of those limits or blind spots of the jurisprudence of process tradition as applied to the foreign reach of EU private law. This forms the basis for the concluding section that reflects upon these continuities and how to overcome those limits. In that way, the present chapter seeks to sketch a jurisprudential baseline for the prospective development of a research agenda on European transnational private law that can contribute to the relentless search for a renewed *raison d'être* for the EU beyond its frontiers.

II. THE JURISPRUDENCE OF PROCESS AND EUROPEAN LAW

The 'jurisprudence of process' is a relatively overlooked strand within modern law and legal thought. It is a strand of jurisprudence that is largely absent from the canon of contemporary philosophy of law or legal theory.[18] It is also an account generally absent from the private law canon.[19] This absence is surprising, to say the least, given how ubiquitous the appeals to process and proceduralisation have become in contemporary legal reasoning and developments, including the realm of private law.[20] This gap possibly explains why it has been recently diagnosed, as part of the advancement of a 'new private law theory', that 'the potential for a procedural legitimation of private law is still largely unexplored' and that this is especially relevant for contemporary modes of transnational private lawmaking that 'can no longer build on the symbolic legitimacy of nation state institutions'.[21]

This suggests a puzzle concerning how and why this widespread turn to process and proceduralisation in the external dimension of EU law and contemporary legal thinking can contribute to ground the sprawling phenomenon of transnational private law and thereby inform a research agenda from an EU perspective as the present volume inaugurates. At least one piece of this puzzle can be uncovered through a recollective engagement with the historiographical origins of this process tradition of modern jurisprudence, which has a much longer lineage within Western legal thinking.[22] Based on the reconstruction of this jurisprudential tradition that I've elaborated at length elsewhere, the present section explains what is the 'jurisprudence of process' by outlining the basic tenets and how it relates to European law by expounding on its pivotal place and role in the development of EU law and legal thought.[23]

On this basis, the present section advances three key building-blocks of the overall argument. First, this section elaborates on why the 'jurisprudence of process' deserves to be recognised as a distinctive strand of jurisprudence in the canon of contemporary philosophy of law or legal theory. It also shows that the 'jurisprudence of process' should not be reduced to mere standards of due process or natural justice in

[18] For some notable exceptions that confirm the rule, see, eg, N Duxbury, *Patterns of American Jurisprudence* (Oxford, Clarendon Press, 1995) chs 3–4; and A Bianchi, *International Law Theories: An Inquiry into Different Ways of Thinking* (Oxford, Oxford University Press, 2016) chapter 5.

[19] See, eg, for two recent accounts of this canon H Dagan and BC Zipursky, *Research Handbook on Private Law Theory* (Cheltenham, Edward Elgar Publishing, 2020); and AS Gold, JCP Goldberg, DB Kelly, E Sherwin and HE Smith (eds), *The Oxford Handbook of the New Private Law* (Oxford, Oxford University Press, 2020).

[20] GP Calliess and P Zumbansen, *Rough Consensus and Running Code: A Theory of Transnational Private Law* (London, Hart Publishing, 2010); F Cafaggi and HM Watt (eds), *Making European Private Law: Governance Design* (Cheltenham, Edward Elgar Publishing, 2010); R Wai, 'Transnational Private Law and Private Ordering in a Contested Global Society' (2005) 46 *Harvard International Law Journal* 471.

[21] M Renner, 'Formalism, Substantive and Procedural Justice' in S Grundmann, HW Micklitz, M Renner (eds), *New Private Law Theory: A Pluralist Approach* (Cambridge, Cambridge University Press, 2021) 204.

[22] I use the term 'tradition' not in the antimodern sense of a fixed and static set of uses or norms that are typically invoked for reactionary purposes. I use it in the modern hermeneutic sense of some immanent commitments informing a certain strand of thought, which dynamically unfold in history, self-actualising themselves to adapt to renewed socio-cultural circumstances through varied and contending modes of reflexive discourse, as the liberal tradition or the socialist tradition in political thought. On the 'recollective' approach for such a study of ideas in history, I draw methodological inspiration from R Brandom, *Reason in Philosophy: Animating Ideas* (Harvard, Harvard University Press, 2009) 23. I thank my colleague Laura Burgers for alerting me of this ambivalence in the use of the term 'tradition' and the importance of clarifying it.

[23] R Vallejo, 'The Jurisprudence of Process as the Structure of EU Legal Thought and the Crisis of Europe' (draft, on file with the author).

the exercise of legal or political authority, as it is usually done in many contemporary appeals to process or proceduralisation whether in the name of 'legitimacy', 'constitutionalism', 'the rule of law', or 'good governance'. This section rather shows that the jurisprudence of process encompasses a much wider set of analytical/methodological tools and normative commitments to understand and assess contemporary legal developments. In this sense, this recollective engagement with the 'jurisprudence of process' can be read as a mode of immanent critique of those reductive accounts of process and proceduralisation in the external dimension of EU law and contemporary legal thinking more generally. Finally, the section indicates the ways in which the 'jurisprudence of process' has become an integral part of the European legal heritage in special and innovative ways and thereby it is culturally suitable to inform studies of European transnational private law.

From a historiographical perspective, the 'jurisprudence of process' tradition is usually given a specific origin. At least in its seminal formulation, this tradition is generally associated with the renowned teaching materials on *The Legal Process: Basic Problems in the Making and Application of Law* by Henry Hart and Albert Sacks.[24] Albeit not published until the 1990s, the seminal place of these materials is justified not only by the innovative account of law elaborated in these materials and its wide application across several legal fields. Their seminal place is also justified by the huge impact that they had in shaping legal thinking, education, and practice within and beyond the USA since the 1950s.[25] But the focus and relevance of this jurisprudential tradition is not circumscribed to the national realm that informed the scholarly work by Hart and Sacks. One can find equally seminal contributions to the configuration of a 'jurisprudence of process' in the pioneering scholarship by Myers McDougal and Harold Lasswell at the international level and by Philip Jessup at the transnational one as well.[26]

McDougal and Lasswell (Yale Law School) and Jessup (Columbia Law School) were contemporaneous to Hart and Sacks (Harvard Law School) as representatives of post-war jurisprudence. Despite their diverse (even rival) academic affiliations, the different focus and emphases informing their scholarship, and the difficulties of causally proving reciprocal influences, a systematic reading of their scholarship reveals significant continuities or similarities in their respective ways they conceive law and analyse legal developments. From a recollective standpoint, therefore, one can productively conceive their scholarship as pivotal contributions for the development of a distinctive mode of post-war philosophy of law or legal theory to be referred to as the 'jurisprudence of process' tradition, which encompasses the

[24] Hart and Sacks (n 2).

[25] D Kennedy, 'Henry M Hart Jr and Albert M Sacks' in D Kennedy and WW Fisher III (eds), *The Canon of American Legal Thought* (Princeton University Press, 2006) 243, 249: noting that '[a]lthough the Hart and Sacks teaching materials were published only posthumously, in 1994, the course for which they were prepared was taught to a generation of law students at dozens of law schools' and how these 'legal process ideas have been [subsequently] picked up by scholars, judges, and advocates of the left and the right'.

[26] See, in general, HD Lasswell and MS McDougal, *Jurisprudence for a Free Society: Studies in Law, Science, and Policy* (Leiden, Martinus Nijhoff Publishers, 1992); and PC Jessup, *Transnational Law* (New Haven, Yale University Press, 1956).

national (Hart and Sacks), international (McDougal and Lasswell), and transnational (Jessup) levels.[27]

What are these continuities that give the 'jurisprudence of process' theoretical cohesion and distinctiveness? Within the canon of modern jurisprudence, law has been typically conceived as a set of abstract and general norms, whether those norms proceed from the will of the sovereign (legal positivism), transcendental reason (natural law), or the circumstantial motivations of judges and other political authorities (legal realism). What makes the 'jurisprudence of process' distinctive and innovative is one basic proposition that defies and seeks to surmount this established account of law. This proposition is that, instead of a set of abstract and general norms, law is better conceived as a process of authoritative modes of decision-making, whereby the concept of 'law' and legal developments are not reduced only to decisions from the legislator (that is, 'statutory law') or courts and tribunals (that is, 'case law') as typically conceived. Integral to this proposition is the observation that these legal processes rather consist of a myriad of actors and institutions with lawmaking capacities, including the legislator, the government/administration, courts, yet also ubiquitous modes of 'private ordering' developed by individuals and a range of civil society institutions. Moreover, these are also regarded as interactive and dynamic lawmaking processes among these varied actors, involving concomitant instances of rulemaking, implementation, monitoring, enforcement, and dispute resolution that operate in sequential, overlapping, or recursive ways and always remain in some significant sense open-ended.[28]

This proposition entails a jurisprudential breakthrough that cannot be overstated. On the one hand, it overcomes the classicist account of law as a sphere that is meant to be insulated from socio-political dynamics by a set of abstract rules that can be neutrally applied to concrete cases through methods of logical deduction. With its emphasis on the inter-institutional, dynamic, and open-ended nature of lawmaking processes, the jurisprudence of process marks a transition from the categorical style of thinking that characterised classical legal thought. This entails a transition towards questions of institutional competence and interaction within lawmaking

[27] Vallejo (n 23). My characterisation of the 'jurisprudence of process' as a post-war philosophy of law or legal theory does not entail overlooking the intellectual influences from the pre-war period that contributed to forge that tradition. For a specialised study of these pre-war influences, see respectively WN Eskridge and PP Frickey, 'A Historical and Critical Introduction to the Legal Process' in Hart and Sacks (n 2); and R Derrig, 'International Law, Science and Psychology in the New Haven School' in R Schäfer and A Petters (eds), *Politics and the Histories of International Law – The Quest for Knowledge and Justice* (Leiden, Brill Nijhoff, 2021).

[28] MS McDougal, 'Law as a Process of Decision: A Policy-Oriented Approach to Legal Study' (1956) 1 *Natural Law Forum* 53, 56: 'what we as law students are, in sum, concerned with is not a mere body of rules but a whole process of decision, and a process of decision taking place within the context of, and as a response to, a larger community process'; and Hart and Sacks (n 2) 5, 161–80: 'The answers to questions such as these [concerning what the law *is*] call always for a perceptive understanding of the role which the particular processes of decision involved play in the total complex of decisional processes which make up the institutional system as a whole.' In the same vein, see Jessup (n 26) 3, 8–9, 11–15. For an updated account of this insight at the national and international levels, often referred to as the 'new legal process,' see WN Eskridge Jr , 'Dynamic Statutory Interpretation' (1986) 135 *University of Pennsylvania Law Review* 1479; and MW Reisman, 'International Lawmaking: A Process of Communication' (1981) 75 *Proceedings of the Annual Meeting (American Society of International Law)* 101.

processes associated with the rise of 'the social' in modern legal thought, expressed through concurrent doctrines of discretion, deference, and modes of weighing among competing public interests or values.[29]

On the other hand, the jurisprudence of process also sought to overcome the rule-scepticism that informed much of the legal realist movement and its anti-formalist implications, by highlighting how and why legal rules matter in these processes of authoritative decision-making. Against the view that conceived law as a mere epiphenomenon of existing power relations, the legal process stressed how socio-political power and authority usually stand in a dialectical dynamic that is ultimately recognised and institutionalised by legal means throughout this range of decision-making processes at the national and international levels.[30] The legal process tradition thus sought to overcome the tension between formalist and realist approaches to modern jurisprudence by productively transcending them through building upon several of their respective insights. For these reasons, the legal process tradition is widely regarded a post-formalist and post-realist strand of modern legal theory.[31]

One illustration of the innovative account of law introduced by the jurisprudence of process comes from the contemporary law of climate change. Within growing socio-political concerns over exponential levels of global warming, much of the lawyerly attention has been focused on certain specific legal developments. Whether it is the 'Green Deal' legislative package advanced by the European Union or widespread modes of climate change litigation against governments and transnational corporations, most legal discussion focuses upon statutory law or case law outputs as a proxy for what is the contemporary 'law of climate change'. Think of the growing expectation that the prospect of an advisory opinion from the International Court of Justice on the 'Obligations of States in Respect of Climate Change' under international law is generating as a reaffirmation or a potential source of transformation with respect to current legal developments.[32]

Yet, from a jurisprudence of process perspective the law of climate change cannot be reduced to any of these specific legal decisions or developments, whether they come from courts or legislators. According to the jurisprudence of process, the 'law of climate change' is better represented by the totality of modes of authoritative

[29] For a reconstruction of these modes of legal thought, see in general D Kennedy, 'Two Globalizations of Law & Legal Thought: 1850-1968' (2003) 36 *Suffolk University Law Review* 631.

[30] The point is perhaps most eloquently articulated with respect to international law by MS McDougal and HD Lasswell, 'The Identification and Appraisal of Diverse Systems of Public Order' (1959) 53 *The American Journal of International Law* 1, 3: 'The processes of law have as their proper office the synthetizing and stabilizing of creative efforts towards a new order by the procedures and structures of authority, thereby consolidating gains and providing guidance for the next steps along the path towards a universal system. By pretending in one mood that international law is a contemporary and presumably well-constructed edifice [of merely formal rules] while insinuating in another that it is a pretentious and dubious fantasy, the true dimensions of the task are concealed.'

[31] N Duxbury, 'Postrealism and the Legal Process' in D Patterson (ed), *A Companion to Philosophy of Law and Legal Theory* (Hoboken, John Wiley & Sons, 2010).

[32] See, International Court of Justice, 'The General Assembly of the United Nations Requests an Advisory Opinion from the Court on the Obligations of States in Respect of Climate Change' (Press Release, 19 April 2023), available at www.icj-cij.org/sites/default/files/case-related/187/187-20230419-PRE-01-00-EN.pdf.

decision-making concerning the problem of climate change – whether official or unofficial, hard or soft law – including the decisions of other competent authorities, such as administrative agencies, international organisations, and concurrent modes of private ordering that develop as a result or alongside these official decisions at every stage of the policy process at the national, international, or transnational levels. The 'law of climate change' is thus not the result of some latest legal decision or policy programme that must be only understood retrospectively. It is rather the open-ended result of a dynamic, interactive process of authoritative decision-making among several types of governmental and civil society institutions within and beyond the state that needs to be understood both retrospectively and prospectively as part of continuing hermeneutic spirals through which renewed norms or understandings may emerge.[33]

The instantiation of this basic proposition in several types of private relations already signals the prominent place and role held by ubiquitous modes of socio-economic ordering among individuals or civil society institutions within this jurisprudential framework. Moreover, as the epigraph from the seminal textbook by Hart and Sacks highlights, private law, as the general framework of these modes of socio-economic ordering, is assigned an integral place and role within this jurisprudential framework.[34] In fact, due to the integral place and role of private law within its jurisprudential framework, the legal process has been regarded as distinctively reintegrating within the canon of modern legal thought 'a kind of private- or common-law sensibility to a new public-law world' that was taking shape at the time.[35] This makes the process tradition *prima facie* a suitable jurisprudential framework for a research agenda on transnational private law.

As a post-formalist and post-realist approach to modern law and legal thought, the referred basic proposition informing the 'jurisprudence of process' is complemented by at least five shared corollaries informing the scholarship of Hart and Sacks, McDougal and Lasswell, and Jessup that merge key formalist and realist insights in renewed and productive ways. These corollaries represent the basic analytical pillars or cornerstones of the jurisprudence of process tradition. Given that law is better conceived as a dynamic and open-ended process of authoritative decision-making rather than a set of merely abstract norms, the first cornerstone is that an

[33] For an earlier application of the jurisprudence of process to the field of international environmental law, see RM Bratspies, 'Rethinking Decisionmaking in International Environmental Law: A Process-Oriented Inquiry into Sustainable Development' (2007) 32 *Yale Journal of International Law* 363. See also, D Bodansky, 'Climate Change: Transnational Legal Order or Disorder?' in T Halliday and G Shaffer (eds), *Transnational Legal Orders* (New York, Cambridge University Press, 2015).

[34] As Hart and Sacks further explain: 'There are elements of a chicken-and-egg relationship between private decisions and official decisions in the flow of social living which defy any facile description of the process. Two broad conclusions, however, seem warranted: 1) The structure of official institutions is immensely significant in shaping the general character and direction of private activity, since it determines both the permissible range of private decision and the conditions under which the decisions are made: 2) Within this general framework, the mass of private decisions are the primary motive force which determine the direction of the society from day to day. It is useful to think of the working apparatus of official procedures, taken as a whole, as engaged in a continuous review of these private decisions, and in continuous revision of the terms and conditions under which similar decisions will be made in the future.' In a similar vein, see McDougal (n 28) 56–58; and McDougal and Lasswell (n 30) 8.

[35] Kennedy (n 25) 247.

appropriate entry-point to grasp and understand the nature and significance of law is a pragmatic focus on concrete 'problems' rather than first principles.[36] What is theoretically distinctive and methodologically innovative about this pragmatic approach? And more importantly for the purposes of this research agenda, how and why can this approach be relevant for the study of the external dimension of EU private law through a transnational lens? As eloquently remarked by Friedrich Kratochwil for the context of contemporary legal thinking (and as a teaser of what this chapter elaborates in section III):

> Beginning with the analysis of a 'problem,' rather than with the blueprint of higher order principles has some advantages. Since there is no actual blueprint from which institutions diverge but only a set of feasible, but problematic alternatives, attention is not restricted to this divergence, but to the more complicated issues of comparing and choosing between feasible alternatives, which makes the analytical enterprise more 'useful.' … [This requires] a *conscious reflection on the very criteria we use* when we judge different alternatives, a problem that blueprint analysis tends to marginalise. In addition, the appropriate methodological tools are no longer those of building grand theories, but of identifying 'cases,' of keeping one's eyes open for surprises, rather than clearing the ground right at the beginning and dispensing with ambiguities through clear-cut definitions and 'operationalisations' of the key terms.[37]

The second cornerstone informing the jurisprudence of process represents the Janus face of these pragmatist commitments. This cornerstone is the need to embrace a socio-legal approach regarding the sources of law and legal developments that underscores the interplay between law and concurrent socio-economic processes.[38] From this socio-legal purview and pragmatic focus stems the third cornerstone: the importance of analysing legal developments 'in context'. This is done by tracing the range of considerations that inform legal decisions, as well as the drivers that explain concurrent patterns of institutional reproduction or change.[39] As section III also further elaborates, these last two cornerstones of process jurisprudence are key to contemporary studies of transnational private law.[40]

[36] The textbook by Hart and Sacks is particularly illustrative in these respects, as the whole analytical construction is based on the discussion of 9 concrete 'problems' associated with representative 'cases', such as 'problem 1 – the case of spoiled cantaloupes', 'problem 3 – the case of the jittery landlady', or 'problem 6 – the case of the absent veteran', *cf*, Likewise, see Jessup's table of contents in *Transnational Law* (n 26) and 11: 'To the understanding of transnational legal problems we then address ourselves.' Regarding the pragmatist commitments informing New Haven School at Yale, see the revisionist study by R Derrig, 'Educating American Lawyers: The New Haven School's Jurisprudence of Personal Character' (2020) 31 *European Journal of International Law* 829.

[37] F Kratochwil, *The Status of Law in World Society: Meditations on the Role and Rule of Law* (Cambridge, Cambridge University Press, 2014) 288.

[38] Hart and Sacks (n 2) 2–4 (on the normative dimension of 'civil associations'), 161–63 (on 'private lawmaking'), 167–68 (on 'local institutions'), 174–80 (on 'lawyer-made law'); McDougal and Lasswell (n 30) 15–22; Jessup, (n 26) 3, 6, 8–9, 11–15.

[39] See, eg, MS McDougal, 'The Impact of International Law upon National Law: A Policy-Oriented Perspective' (1959) 4 *South Dakota Law Review* 25; and Jessup (n 26) 32–34, 46–51, 58.

[40] Calliess and Zumbansen (n 20) xiii: stressing 'the elusiveness of settling on a definite model of law through which one could distinguish in a clear-cut way between law and non-law' and explaining that 'the attempt to make this very distinction always occurs in a particular context, with a particular set of stakes, interests, and conditions [, which requires] the "application" of legal theory to these different contexts from the perspective of asking "what is at stake?" and "for whom?" [in theses] discursive forms of boundary-drawing between "law" and "non-law"'.

The fourth cornerstone concerns the normative dimension informing the jurisprudence of process. Despite some different emphases among its authors, this normative component is generally driven by a purposive drive towards immanent or policy values, which gives the jurisprudence of process an evaluative grip on legal developments.[41] The final corollary is the most salient, influential, and yet controversial pillar of the jurisprudence of process: the prevalence that it gives to procedural arrangements over substantive ones in the configuration of legal-political orders. The legal process school at Harvard is usually regarded as the poster child in these respects due to their open affirmation of this idea.[42]

This proceduralist model of legitimacy informing the jurisprudence of process has been the object of stringent jurisprudential criticism. At the national level, these criticisms have been mainly focused on the de-politicising effects that this model has on legal outcomes.[43] At the international level, its ingrained apologetic tendencies to regard whatever represents good foreign policy for the USA (or any state that is circumstantially exerting hegemonic power at the global level) by itself lawful.[44] These stringent criticisms certainly make the jurisprudence of process – as a potential ground for the study of European transnational private law – controversial. They are also particularly relevant to keep in sight for reflective study of the foreign reach of EU law that has been openly regarded as having become a (more-or-less benevolent) 'global regulatory hegemon'.[45]

Nonetheless, from a recollective standpoint, it is relevant to underscore that in its original formulation this prevalence given to process was not based on some ready-made account of '(input or throughput) legitimacy', 'social welfare',

[41] See, eg, at the international level, HD Lasswell and MS McDougal, 'Legal Education and Public Policy: Professional Training in the Public Interest' (1943) 52 *The Yale Law Journal* 203; and HD Lasswell and MS McDougal, 'Jurisprudence in Policy-Oriented Perspective' (1966) 19 *University of Florida Law Review* 486. At the transnational level, see Jessup (n 26) 33–34, 71. For some specialised studies on these normative dimensions informing the scholarship of Hart and Sacks, WN Eskridge Jr , 'Nino's Nightmare: Legal Process Theory as a Jurisprudence of Toggling between Facts and Norms' (2012) 57 *Saint Louis University Law Journal* 865; and CL Barzun, 'The Forgotten Foundations of Hart and Sacks' (2013) 99 *Virginia Law Review* 1.

[42] 'These institutionalized procedures and the constitutive arrangements establishing and governing them are obviously more fundamental than the substantive arrangements in the structure of a society, if not in the realization of its ultimate aims, since they are at once the source of the substantive arrangements and the indispensable means of making them work effectively' Hart and Sacks (n 2) 3–4. In the same vein at the international and transnational levels, see respectively Jessup (n 26) 35–36, 70–71.

[43] G Peller, 'Neutral Principles in the 1950's' (1987) 21 *University of Michigan Journal of Law Reform* 561; MJ Horwitz, *The Transformation of American Law, 1870-1960: The Crisis of Legal Orthodoxy* (Oxford, Oxford University Press, 1992) 271: 'the legal process materials symbolize the moment in post-war history at which the New Deal lawyers' conception of the "common interest" came to be thoroughly transformed from one of substance to one of procedure'.

[44] OR Young, 'International Law and Social Science: The Contributions of Myres S McDougal' (1972) 66 *American Journal of International Law* 60; RA Falk, 'Casting the Spell: The New Haven School of International Law' (1994) 104 *Yale Law Journal* 1991; and BH Weston, O Schachter, WM Reisman, RA Falk, and MS McDougal, 'McDougal's Jurisprudence: Utility, Influence, Controversy' (1985) 79 *Proceedings of the Annual Meeting (American Society of International Law)* 266.

[45] Bradford (n 1) 3–4, 7, 21, 24, 64, 81, 249, 265, 288: arguing that 'the Brussels Effect is therefore not only pervasive today, but there is a convincing argument that it will persist, extending the EU's regulatory hegemony into the foreseeable future'. In this vein, see also, HW Micklitz, 'Epilogue: the Role of the EU in the External Reach of Regulatory Private Law – Gentle Civiliser or Neoliberal Hegemon?' in M Cantero and HW Micklitz (eds), *The Role of the EU in Transnational Legal Ordering: Standards, Contracts and Codes* (Cheltenham, Edward Elgar Publishing, 2020).

'constitutionalism', 'good governance' or any other value that is taken for granted and merely imposed on practice as it has become in many natural law-driven contemporary pleas for proceduralisation.[46] Nor is it driven by a disdain for substance. It is rather driven by the understanding that process is a condition for substance. In other words, the prevalence of process is driven by the understanding that in order to tackle substantive questions of common concern, the first political question that any social group needs to address is how and by whom those substantive decisions are going to be made.

This first political question is usually addressed through the design (or re-design) of institutions with suitable competences to duly tackle these substantive questions or the institutionalisation of relevant procedures for doing so among existing institutions. These dynamics of legal-political representation thereby largely operate through 'institutionalised normative orders' (MacCormick) or modes of 'institutionalised authoritative collective action' (Lindahl). These institutionalised activities are nevertheless susceptible of socio-political contestation on substantive grounds by the participants in or affected by those institutionalised practices and thus stand in a dialectical relationship with their own negation, which may eventually prompt modes of institutional reproduction, obliteration, or transformation.[47] This signals part of the theoretical depth of the jurisprudence of process since its original formulation, as process arrangements are in this sense constitutive.[48]

In sum, the jurisprudence of process emerged during the 1950s as a post-formalist and post-realist approach within modern law and legal thought, which nevertheless productively blended several of the key formalist and realist insights, such as law's social basis, its normative dimension, and its constitutive properties. Its key innovative move is the view of law as an interactive and dynamic process of authoritative decision-making among different institutions rather than a set of merely abstract and self-fulfilling norms. This conception of law is paralleled with at least five core

[46] For a discussion, see P Zumbansen, 'The Incurable Constitutional Itch: Transnational Private Regulatory Governance and the Woes of Legitimacy' in MA Helfand (ed), *Negotiating State and Non-State Law: The Challenge of Global and Local Legal Pluralism* (Cambridge, Cambridge University Press, 2015); and B Kingsbury, M Donaldson and R Vallejo, 'Global Administrative Law and Deliberative Democracy' in A Orford, F Hoffman and M Clarke (eds), *The Oxford Handbook of the Theory of International Law* (Oxford, Oxford University Press, 2015).

[47] I borrow the notion of 'institutionalised normative orders' from Neil McCormick and the notion of 'institutionalised authoritative collective action' from Hans Lindahl, whose work I read as a continuation of this tradition for the contemporary landscapes of national or post-national law: *cf*, N MacCormick, *Institutions of Law: An Essay in Legal Theory* (Oxford, Oxford University Press, 2007); and H Lindahl, *Authority and the Globalisation of Inclusion and Exclusion* (Cambridge, Cambridge University Press, 2018). In this vein, see also J Black, '"Says Who?" Liquid Authority and Interpretive Control in Transnational Regulatory Regimes' (2017) 9 *International Theory* 286.

[48] It is worth retrieving the (in)famous quote from Hart and Sacks highlighted above to stress this point: 'These institutionalized procedures and the *constitutive arrangements establishing and governing them* are obviously more fundamental than the substantive arrangements in the structure of a society, if not in the realization of its ultimate aims, since *they are at once the source of the substantive arrangements and the indispensable means of making them work effectively*' Hart and Sacks (n 2) 3–4 (emphasis added). With respect to the New Haven School, see in this vein H Saberi, 'Love It or Hate It, but for the Right Reasons: Pragmatism and the New Haven School's International Law of Human Dignity' (2012) 35 *Boston College International and Comp Law Review* 59, reviewing the 'antifoundational foundationalism' upon which the New Haven School relies; Bianchi (n 18) 96–97: analysing how the New Haven School account of law 'expresses a dialectical process between authority and power, the two basic concepts that the movement attempted to reconcile through its methodology'.

analytical pillars or cornerstones: (1) a pragmatic focus on concrete 'problems' rather than first principles; (2) a socio-legal purview of the basis and sources of law; (3) a contextual approach to legal developments; (4) its normative dimension driven by a purposive drive towards immanent or policy values; and (5) the prevalence given to process and institutive arrangements due to their constitutive properties. These five pillars thus operate as the theoretical and methodological cornerstones that give shape to the jurisprudential edifice of the process tradition.

Even if the jurisprudence of process had its most salient articulation and influence in US law and legal thought, it is important to stress that this jurisprudential edifice is not exclusively a US patrimony. The development of the jurisprudence of process as a tradition has an entrenched and significant relationship with European law and legal thought as well. To conclude this section, the chapter briefly elaborates on at least two marks of this relationship. This first mark is genealogical. The second mark is structural.

The genealogical mark involves how most of the referred analytical pillars or cornerstones of the jurisprudence of process relate with eminent ancestors and successors in European legal thinking that have distinctively built upon and further develop its original formulation. As to its ancestors, for instance, it has been noted that in their pluralist account of law and legal developments, the lineages of process-based legal theory can be traced to European strands of legal anthropology or sociological jurisprudence and the towering figure of Eugen Ehrlich in particular.[49] Nonetheless, the insights of the jurisprudence of process on the *jurisgenerative* capacity of social practices and the inter-institutional dynamics that drive modern lawmaking possibly find their most direct European predecessors in the institutionalist legal theories advanced during the early twentieth century by prominent European scholars in Italy,[50] France,[51] and Germany.[52] Whether in its legal pluralist or institutionalist variants, as a tradition the jurisprudence of process has in this sense some deep roots in European legal thinking.[53]

[49] Kennedy (n 25) 251. The reference is to E Ehrlich, *Fundamental Principles of the Sociology of Law* [1913] (Transaction Publishers, 1962). For a retrospective on Ehrlich's contemporary relevance, see M Hertogh (ed), *Living Law: Reconsidering Eugen Ehrlich* (London, Bloomsbury Publishing, 2008); and G Teubner, 'Global Bukowina: Legal Pluralism in the World Society' in G Teubner (ed), *Global Law Without a State* (Brookfield: Dartmouth, 1997) 3–28. Legal pluralism is of course a much wider tradition in itself within European law and legal thought. For a reconstruction of this tradition, see VM Muniz-Fraticelli, *The Structure of Pluralism: On the Authority of Associations* (Oxford, Oxford University Press, 2014).

[50] S Romano, *L'ordinamento giuridico* [1917] (Sansoni, 1962); and, for a recent English translation, S Romano, *The Legal Order* (Oxfordshire, Routledge, 2017). On the jurisprudential breakthrough and the significance of Romano's work, see S Tschorne, 'What is in a Word? The Legal Order and the Turn from "Norms" to "Institutions" in Legal Thought' (2020) 11 *Jurisprudence* 114.

[51] M Hariou, 'The Theory of the Institution and the Foundation: A Study in Social Vitalism [1925]' in A Broderick (ed), *The French Institutionalists: Maurice Hauriou. Georges Renard, Joseph T. Delos* (Boston, Harvard University Press, 1970). See, in general, Broderick, ibid.

[52] C Schmitt, *On the Three Types of Juristic Thought* [1934] (Wesport, Praeger Publishers, 2004). For a specialised study of the transition from a 'decisionist' to an 'institutionalist' legal theory in Schmitt's jurisprudence, see M Croce and A Salvatore, *The Legal Theory of Carl Schmitt* (Cheltenham, Routledge, 2013).

[53] For a reconstruction of these pluralist/institutionalist lineages in European legal thinking, and its projections into US law and legal thought through the influential work of Robert Cover at Yale Law School, see M Loughlin, *Political Jurisprudence* (Oxford, Oxford University Press, 2017), chapter 6 on 'Law as Institution'.

The same applies to some of its most salient successors. Within its legacy, the jurisprudence of process tradition comprises some of the most prominent figures in US legal theory during the twentieth century, such as Lon Fuller,[54] Philip Selznick,[55] and Ronald Dworkin.[56] Yet it also comprises prominent European figures as well. As revisionist studies have recently documented, this partly includes HLA Hart.[57] But probably the closest and most prominent successors of the jurisprudence of process within Europe are Neil McCormick, Jurgen Habermas, Niklas Luhmann, and Gunther Teubner due to their elaboration of institutional grounds of lawmaking and their overall commitment to process and proceduralisation as a way to enhance the epistemic qualities of legal decisions, whether in national[58] or post-national contexts.[59] Alongside the seminal scholarship of Joseph HH Weiler, who likewise based his account on a 'theory of equilibrium' among legal and political institutions structuring European integration, it is largely through their influential accounts of legal theory that the 'jurisprudence of process' came to shape pervasive modes of legal thinking regarding the role of law in the 'constitution of Europe' as a peculiar kind of post-national polity and its subsequent transformations.[60]

The second mark of the relationship between the jurisprudence of process and European law is equally or perhaps even more relevant. This mark concerns how the account of law advanced by the jurisprudence of process, as an institutionalised and dynamic process of authoritative decision-making, has had a foundational place and

[54] LL Fuller, 'Positivism and Fidelity to Law: A Reply to Professor Hart' (1958) 71 *Harvard Law Review* 630–72. See also, for an illuminating review of the jurisprudence of Fuller underscoring this aspect, K Rundle, *Forms Liberate: Reclaiming the Jurisprudence of Lon L Fuller* (London, Bloomsbury Publishing, 2012).

[55] P Selznick, 'Sociology and Natural Law' (1961) 6 *Natural Law Forum* 84. See also, for the latest instantiation of this overall agenda in legal sociology, P Selznick, *A Humanist Science: Values and Ideals in Social Inquiry* (Stanford, Stanford University Press, 2008).

[56] VA Wellman, 'Dworkin and the Legal Process Tradition: The Legacy of Hart & Sacks' (1987) 29 *Arizona Law Review* 413–74.

[57] GC Shaw, 'HLA Hart's Lost Essay: Discretion and the Legal Process School' (2013) 127 *Harvard Law Review* 666; and N Lacey, 'The Path Not Taken: H.L.A. Hart's Harvard Essay on Discretion' (2013) 127 *Harvard Law Review* 636. See also, on the overall context informing Hart's journey to the USA and his experience within the 1956–1957 Legal Philosophy Discussion Group at Harvard where he engaged with the emergent legal process school, N Lacey, *A Life of H.L.A. Hart: The Nightmare and the Noble Dream* (Oxford, Oxford University Press, 2004) ch 8; and GC Shaw, 'The Rise and Fall of Liberal Legal Positivism: Legal Positivism, Legal Process, and H.L.A. Hart's America, 1945-1960' PhD thesis (Oxford, University of Oxford, 2013), available at https://ora.ox.ac.uk/objects/uuid:e7ea644b-0d13-4a60-8993-e4119404a5ca.

[58] See N MacCormick and O Weinberger, *An Institutional Theory of Law: New Approaches to Legal Positivism* (London, Springer Science & Business Media, 1986); Habermas (n 9); N Luhmann, *Law as a Social System* [1993] (Oxford, Oxford University Press, 2004); and G Teubner, *Law as an Autopoietic System* (Blackwell, 1993). See also, in general, M La Torre, *Law as Institution* (London, Springer Science & Business Media, 2010).

[59] See N MacCormick, *Questioning Sovereignty: Law, State, and Nation in the European Commonwealth* (Oxford, Oxford University Press, 2002); J Habermas, 'A Political Constitution for the Pluralist World Society?' (2013) 40 *Journal of Chinese Philosophy* 226; and G Teubner, *Constitutional Fragments: Societal Constitutionalism and Globalization* (Oxford, Oxford University Press, 2012).

[60] See, in general, J Weiler, *The Constitution of Europe: 'Do the New Clothes Have an Emperor?' and Other Essays on European Integration* (Cambridge, Cambridge University Press, 1999); and M Dawson, *New Governance and the Transformation of European Law: Coordinating EU Social Law and Policy* (Cambridge, Cambridge University Press, 2011).

role in the practical configuration of EU legal reasoning as a driving force of European polity-building. Drawing upon methods from critical sociology, Antoine Vauchez has recently documented how the social imaginary of the EU as a post-national polity has been largely driven in practice by a diverse set of influential 'Euro-lawyers' based upon a vernacular of institutional autonomy, supranationalism, and a purposive role of law attuned to policy values related to internal-market building. That vernacular is nevertheless not theorised by Vauchez. As I have shown elsewhere, that vernacular relates to an understanding of the place and role of law in the process of European integration that largely corresponds with the conception of law and basic tenets informing the jurisprudence of process.[61] The jurisprudence of process thus represents the structure upon which these Euro-lawyers had been (and largely still are) more or less consciously operating when 'brokering Europe'.[62]

Due to this foundational place and role that the jurisprudence of process and European law have reciprocally had at genealogical and structural levels, as a living tradition the jurisprudence of process can thus nowadays be considered as an integral part of the European legal heritage and thereby culturally suitable to inform studies of European transnational private law. This section has shown how this tradition goes well beyond mere appeals to standards of due process or natural justice in legal/political decision-making as in much of contemporary appeals to proceduralisation. It also showed why this tradition includes a distinctive and innovative account of law that encompasses the national, international, and transnational levels. Yet to what extent and upon what bases may this jurisprudential tradition inform the agenda of a European transnational private law? That is the question that this chapter now tackles.

III. ENGAGING WITH EUROPEAN TRANSNATIONAL LEGAL PROCESSES

The previous section outlined the basic components or contours of the 'jurisprudence of process' as a distinctive strand of modern legal theory and its relationship with EU law and legal thought. Among other points, the previous section signalled that the 'jurisprudence of process' represents the vernacular upon which EU legal thinking and developments have largely proceeded. By moving from the abstract realm of theoretical lineages of contemporary legal thought to the particular realm of case studies, this section takes one further step in the argument. It does so by expounding on the suitability of the legal process as a framework to identify, understand, and assess different instantiations of the foreign reach of EU law through the notion of European transnational private law.

[61] Vallejo (n 23).

[62] A Vauchez, *Brokering Europe: Euro-Lawyers and the Making of a Transnational Polity* (Cambridge, Cambridge University Press, 2015): stressing that: 'the "field effect" is not to be found in the judicial coup of an "invisible college" of Euro-lawyers taking over power and designing this or that public policy, than in the field's specific contribution in the shaping of cross-sectoral and inter-institutional frames of understanding Europe's fragmented polity, thereby providing a privileged locus for the metamorphosis of the inchoate set of treaties, institutions, and groups into one new polity'.

For this purpose, the section draws from the several specialised studies on the foreign reach of EU private law within this edited volume or related literature and interconnects them through the lens of process jurisprudence as outlined in section II. By relating the abstract to the concrete, the section reviews the ways in which different European transnational legal processes concerning issues of private law are currently taking shape and highlights how several patterns, (dis-)continuities, and gaps emerge. In this way, the section seeks to invite and inspire future pathways for development of the research agenda on European transnational private law based on a jurisprudence of process register.

Yet this range of studies does not stand in a theoretical vacuum. Anu Bradford and Joanne Scott have developed pivotal accounts of how and why EU law is achieving a foreign reach beyond EU frontiers. This has been informed by several case studies tracing this phenomenon in varied socio-economic realms. Using the lens of European transnational private law informed by the 'jurisprudence of process' (that is, European transnational legal processes), this section relates the several chapters in the present volume with that range of pivotal studies on the foreign reach of EU law. This in turn illuminates how such a lens can contribute to expanding and nuancing the insights drawn from Bradford and Scott's studies on the phenomenon in at least three distinctive ways.

A. Conceptually – From an International Relations Paradigm to a Transnational Relations Paradigm that Critically Encompasses the Constitutive Role of Private Law

Much of the literature on the external dimension of EU law has been driven by an international relations paradigm. This is a paradigm where the object of analysis is largely centred upon relations between and among the EU, its Member States, foreign governments, and established international institutions, such as international organisations or international courts and tribunals, as relevant actors. In line with the anthropomorphic assumptions of the legal discipline, these actors are usually conceived as separate and unified entities that normally operate through unilateral, bilateral, or multilateral modes. It is also a paradigm largely structured upon a multi-level imaginary of how global governance is conducted. This is a structure where interactions between the EU and foreign countries or regions are generally represented on a horizontal plane, while the EU's interactions with its Member States or international institutions in developing or implementing foreign policy agendas are generally represented on a vertical plane. In their focus on a distinctive set of actors, norms, and modes of foreign agency, the external dimension of EU law as an emergent field of legal studies and practice thereby becomes largely driven by a conceptual framework generally associated with public law.

The pivotal studies of Bradford and Scott are apt illustrations of this characterisation. Bradford conceives the Brussels effect essentially as a unilateral mode through which EU law is travelling abroad, which, as a market-driven phenomenon, largely proceeds on a horizontal plane with respect to foreign countries or regions.[63] This occurs through two distinct ways that usually proceed in tandem. One is the *de facto* Brussels effect, where EU law travels beyond EU frontiers via transnational corporations that under certain conditions are prompted to *de facto* align their production or operations abroad with EU norms. Bradford explains that this means of EU law's foreign reach is unilateral, because 'no regulatory response by foreign governments is needed; [under the referred-to conditions,] corporations have the business incentive to extend the EU regulation to govern their worldwide production or operations'.[64] Global market forces carrying the Brussels effect thus appear as largely naturalised within this framework, while transnational corporations, albeit key actors for its operation, are represented as mere carriers of EU norms concerning market regulation abroad.

The second is the *de jure* Brussels effect. According to this second variant, a EU legal rule or institution that originally travelled *de facto* through leading corporations ends up becoming *de jure* adopted or institutionalised by competent regulators within foreign legal regimes. This usually happens due to lobbying by these transnational corporations that carried the EU norm to ensure a level playing field with their local competitors in foreign countries (which Bradford terms the 'strict' notion of the *de jure* Brussels effect), or can also happen in relation with other concurrent means or factors (that is, the 'broad' notion of the *de jure* Brussels effect).[65] As a 'market-driven mechanism', Bradford analytically distinguishes the Brussels effect as a unilateral means of foreign reach of EU law from other means that are 'treaty-driven', whether they are 'bilateral' (such as treaties or other agreements with foreign governments) or 'multilateral' (through influencing policy choices of international or global governance institutions).[66] The analysis thus focuses on a distinctive set of actors and modes of foreign agency.

[63] 'The term the "Brussels Effect" refers to the EU's unilateral ability to regulate the global marketplace … While acknowledging that other forms of the EU's global influence exist, this book generally reserves the term the Brussels Effect to capture the phenomenon where the markets are transmitting the EU's regulations to both market participants [*de facto*] and regulators [*de jure*] outside the EU.' Bradford (n 1) 1.

[64] Bradford (n 1) 2–3: '*de facto* Brussels Effect is the primary focus of this book and the core of [its] theoretical discussion in chapter 2' where Bradford elaborates on each of its enabling conditions or causes: (i) market size; (ii) regulatory capacity; (iii) stringent regulations; (iv) inelastic targets; and (v) legal, technical, or economic non-divisibility of the referred product or conduct.

[65] This distinction between 'strict' and 'broad' notions of the *de jure* Brussels effect is relevant because, in contrast with the 'strict' approach, the broader notion of the *de jure* Brussels effect '-including the diffusion of EU norms through international treaties and institutions- … has not been extensively examined except in narrow policy areas and with respect to selected jurisdictions.' By adopting this broader notion, Bradford aims 'to show how pervasive the *de jure* emulation of EU regulations is and how the *de jure* Brussels Effect complements and interacts with the de facto Brussels Effect. Together, this will hopefully offer a more comprehensive picture of the EU's influence.' Bradford (n 1) 2–3 (and for illustrative references from the case studies contained in the book), 94–96.

[66] Bradford (n 1) 82–91. It is relevant to clarify that Bradford advances the Brussels effect as a general 'theory of unilateral regulatory power' that is only circumstantially applicable to the EU nowadays. As Bradford explains, 'While developed to explain the Brussels Effect and the EU's role as a global regulatory hegemon, the conditions discussed in this chapter are generic as opposed to EU-specific, and hence designed to explain any jurisdiction's ability to unilaterally supply rules for the global marketplace. In this sense, they should outlive the EU's regulatory hegemony and also help us explain if and when such a hegemony might come to an end or be displaced by another unilateral global regulator, [such as the]

These categories and overall representation are also present in the influential scholarship of Joanne Scott. Albeit already figuring in her seminal essay,[67] these categories are most visible in her latest take on the phenomenon expressed in a co-edited volume with Marise Cremona on 'EU Law beyond EU borders'. In their introductory essay to a set of specialised studies in varied policy fields, Cremona and Scott explain that this 'global reach of EU Law' proceeds through different means. They used the agency-based model to classify these means as unilateral (which comprises 'the extraterritorial application of EU law, the presence of territorial extension, and the so-called "Brussels Effect"'), bilateral ('in the form of agreements with third countries or third country agencies'), or multilateral (through 'the EU's engagement with multilateral fora and the negotiation of international legal instruments'). As in Bradford's transition from a *de facto* to a *de jure* Brussels effect in its 'broader' variant, Cremona and Scott also end up stressing 'the need to appreciate the relationship between these different modes of EU action – unilateral, bilateral and multilateral – and the ways in which they interact' in shaping this global reach of EU law.[68]

This public law framework has been also largely informing other specialised studies on the external dimension of EU law. Some studies have mainly focused on the horizontal extension of EU law to foreign countries or regions in certain policy fields through unilateral or bilateral modalities.[69] Others have focused on the vertical plane regarding how the interactions between the EU and multilateral institutions at the international level are either shaping the global governance agendas of these institutions or are reciprocally shaping the EU's own domestic agendas.[70] Like Bradford and Scott, other studies have generally encompassed the horizontal and vertical spatial planes by either focusing on specific policy fields[71] or on a particular type of actor.[72] In any of their variants, the use of such a public law framework aligns this range of studies with the type of issues driving the established fields of EU External Relations Law and EU Foreign Relations, whether in their focus on

"Washington Effect" or the "Beijing Effect" – as long as the United States or China had the combination of the market power, the regulatory capacity, and the political will to generate stringent regulations, together with the desire to pursue inelastic targets that are non-divisible across jurisdictions.' Bradford (n 1) 4, 64.

[67] Scott, 'Extraterritoriality and Territorial Extension in EU Law' (n 3) 89, 108: explaining that 'while many EU measures giving rise to territorial extension are unilateral, they are characterized by an international orientation nonetheless' because 'the EU uses also uses territorial extension both to prompt the emergence of international (bilateral or multilateral) agreements'.

[68] Cremona and Scott, 'Introduction – EU Law Beyond EU Borders' (n 15) 1–3.

[69] See, eg, Rodrigues (n 4); Giegerich (n 4) pt 4; Hadjiyianni (n 4); L Pantaleo, *The Participation of the EU in International Dispute Settlement: Lessons from EU Investment Agreements* (Berlin, Springer, 2018); and Ankersmit (n 4).

[70] See, eg, Eritja (n 4); M Cremona, A Thies, and RA Wessel (eds), *The European Union and International Dispute Settlement* (London, Bloomsbury Publishing, 2017); KE Jørgensen and KV Laatikainen (eds), *Routledge Handbook on the European Union and International Institutions: Performance, Policy, Power* (Berlin, Routledge, 2013); and Kochenov and Amtenbrink (n 17). In the case of the latter, see mainly C Eckes, *EU Powers Under External Pressure: How the EU's External Actions Alter its Internal Structures* (Oxford, Oxford University Press, 2019).

[71] A Bakardjieva, M Mårtensson, L Oxelheim, and T Persson (eds), *The EU's Role in Fighting Global Imbalances* (Cheltenham, Edward Elgar Publishing, 2015); and Fahey (n 4) focusing on the Area of Freedom, Security, and Justice (AFSJ).

[72] Hofmann, Vos, and Chamon (n 4).

questions of legal validity or competence of the EU or its Member States to act in a certain foreign policy domain[73] or their capacity to influence foreign policies and global governance agendas.[74]

By instead concentrating on the place and role of EU private law and civil society institutions within this phenomenon, the present volume, and the overall research project in which it is embedded, can be understood as transcending the 'international relations' paradigm towards a renewed 'transnational relations' paradigm. Notwithstanding pioneering work on transnational law by Jessup and his successors, the move from international to transnational relations as a renewed paradigm has only gained exponential traction and development within foreign affairs studies since the *fin de siècle*. This renewed paradigm departed from the observation that a diverse fauna of non-state entities held a significant place and role in the exercise of legal-regulatory authority within several domains of external affairs – whether it is, for instance, international trade, security, migration, or development. These non-state entities include formal organisations, such as transnational corporations, chambers of commerce, NGOs, and labour unions, as well as more informal professional networks or advocacy groups that were, through different means, significantly shaping foreign policies and dynamics of co-operation and resistance in these global governance realms. This insight prompted the analytical need to move beyond the focus on states or international institutions as objects of enquiry – whether in its intergovernmental or supranational variants – as a condition to understand the dynamics of foreign policy, world politics, and its concomitant legal developments.[75]

This broader focus has triggered a growing interest in the place and role of private law within this post-national context.[76] Beyond the public law frame of reference that has been informing the seminal work of Scott and broader literature on the external dimension of EU law, in this vein, one of the marks of the FiDiPro project informing

[73] See, eg, M Cremona and A Thies (eds), *The European Court of Justice and External Relations Law: Constitutional Challenges* (London, Bloomsbury Publishing, 2014); P Koutrakos, *EU International Relations Law* (Bloomsbury Publishing, 2015); E Neframi and M Gatti, *Constitutional Issues of EU External Relations Law* (Nomos Verlag, 2018); M Andenas, L Pantaleo, M Happold, and C Contartese (eds), *EU External Action in International Economic Law: Recent Trends and Developments* (Springer Nature, 2020); and WT Douma, C Eckes, PV Elsuwege, E Kassoti, A Ott, and RA Wessel, *The Evolving Nature of EU External Relations Law* (The Hague, TMC Asser Press, 2021).

[74] S Keukeleire and T Delreux, *The Foreign Policy of the European Union* (London, Bloomsbury Publishing, 2022); and KE Jorgensen, AK Aarstad, E Drieskens, K Laatikainen, and B Tonra, *The SAGE Handbook of European Foreign Policy* (Los Angeles, SAGE, 2015).

[75] For some influential studies in this renewed transnational relations framework, see JN Rosenau and E-O Czempiel (eds), *Governance Without Government: Order and Change in World Politics* (Cambridge, Cambridge University Press, 1992); S Strange, *The Retreat of the State: The Diffusion of Power in the World Economy* (Cambridge, Cambridge University Press, 1996); and S Sassen, *Territory, Authority, Rights: from Medieval to Global Assemblages* (Princeton, Princeton University Press, 2006). See also, more recently, W Mattli and N Woods (eds), *The Politics of Global Regulation* (Princeton, Princeton University Press, 2009); and DD Avant, M Finnemore, and SK Sell (eds), *Who Governs the Globe?* (Cambridge, Cambridge University Press, 2010).

[76] For some prominent accounts, see R Michaels and N Jansen, 'Private Law beyond the State? Europeanization, Globalization, Privatization' (2006) 54 *The American Journal of Competition Law* 843–90; P Zumbansen, 'Private Ordering in a Globalizing World: Still Searching for the Basis of Contract' (2007) 14 *Indiana Journal of Global Legal Studies* 181; R Wai, 'The Interlegality of Transnational Private Law' (2008) 71 *Law and Contemporary Problems* 107; and H Muir Watt, 'Private International Law beyond the Schism' (2011) 2 *Transnational Legal Theory* 347.

the present book has been to illuminate the relevance of EU private law within this phenomenon and contemporary developments in EU external relations law.[77] This focus is taken up by the several chapters in this volume that trace and evaluate the foreign reach of EU private law within several socio-economic realms, such as finance (Chadwick, chapter nine and Macacci, chapter 10), trade (Mataija, chapter 11), tax (Pantazatou, chapter 12), labour (Liukkunen, chapter six), non-discrimination (Möschel, chapter seven), and sustainability (Ulfbeck, chapter 13 in addition to Salminen, Rajavuori, and Eller in chapter 14). This distinctive focus has been paralleled by an emerging interest in other EU private law doctrines and institutions within this phenomenon, whether related to traditional private law fields,[78] modes of transnational private regulation,[79] and dispute resolution.[80] As discussed in section II and as the epigraph of Hart and Sacks highlights, this emphasis on the integral place and role of private law and ubiquitous modes of private ordering by civil society institutions has also been one of the marks of the jurisprudence of process tradition since its original formulation.

Yet the socio-legal purview of the jurisprudence of process on legal sources and its insights regarding the constitutive place of law also signal its critical pedigree for the study of EU private law and its constitutive role within foreign or global market relations and orders. Beyond the seeming naturalisation of global market forces underpinning the configuration of the 'Brussels effect', which depicts transnational corporations and regulatory dynamics as merely driven by these forces, from this insight and purview the jurisprudence of process rather underscores how the purportedly spontaneous orderings of markets are legally constituted as well as the pivotal role that private law doctrines and institutions play in this respect. Market orderings are thus premised upon private law institutions and the socio-political practices underpinning them.[81] In highlighting the institutional nature and thus constitutive

[77] See, eg, M Cremona and HW Micklitz (eds), *Private Law in the External Relations of the EU* (Oxford, Oxford University Press, 2016); L de Almeida, M Cantero, and HW Micklitz, 'Institutional and Normative Co-operation in Private Law: Beyond the Hague Conference towards Standard Setting Organizations' in RA Wessel, J Odermatt (eds), *Research Handbook on the European Union and International Organizations* (Cheltenham, Edward Elgar Publishing, 2019); and Cantero and Micklitz (n 45). For a broader account of the relationship of the present volume to the overall FiDiPro agenda and publications, see the introductory chapter by A Beckers, HW Micklitz, R Vallejo, and P Letto-Vanamo in this book.

[78] P Franzina, *The External Dimension of EU Private International Law After Opinion 1/13* (Cambridge, Intersentia, 2017).

[79] M Avbelj, *The European Union under Transnational Law: A Pluralist Appraisal* (London, Bloomsbury Publishing, 2018).

[80] JRM Dona and N Lavranos (eds), *International Arbitration and EU Law* (Cheltenham, Edward Elgar Publishing, 2021); and K von Papp, *EU Law and International Arbitration: Managing Distrust Through Dialogue* (London, Bloomsbury Publishing, 2021). See also, within the specific domain of investment disputes or energy law, C Baltag and A Stanič (eds), *The Future of Investment Treaty Arbitration in the EU: Substance, Process and Policy* (Alphen aan den Rijn, Kluwer Law International BV, 2020); J Berger, *International Investment Protection within Europe: The EU's Assertion of Control* (Oxfordshire, Routledge, 2020); and MD Boeck, *EU Law and International Investment Arbitration: The Compatibility of ISDS in Bilateral Investment Treaties (BITs) and the Energy Charter Treaty (ECT) with the Autonomy of EU Law* (Leiden, Brill, 2022).

[81] K Pistor, *The Code of Capital: How the Law Creates Wealth and Inequality* (Princeton, Princeton University Press, 2019); S Deakin, D Gindis, GM Hodgson, K Huang and K Pistor, 'Legal Institutionalism: Capitalism and the Constitutive Role of Law' (2017) 45 *Journal of Comparative Economics* 188; ATF Lang, 'The Legal Construction of Economic Rationalities?' (2013) 40 *Journal of Law and Society* 155.

role of law is where the jurisprudence of process tradition meets old and contemporary insights on law and political economy.[82]

The way these private law institutions are conceived and designed thereby have the capacity to shape and eventually transform the power dynamics among participants in markets orders as well as the overall socio-political practices underpinning these orders within and beyond the EU.[83] Several chapters within the present volume highlight this constitutive potential of EU private law (including the chapters by Ulfbeck, chapter 13 and that by Salminen, Rajavuori, and Eller in chapter 14), yet others problematise it for different reasons (such as the chapters by Chadwick, chapter nine and Möschel, chapter seven). Alongside the transition from an 'international relations' paradigm to a 'transnational relations' paradigm, this signals the need to trace and critically reflect upon the constitutive roles of EU private law in making these market forces and shaping market relations beyond the EU. This entails configuring a research agenda on European transnational private law informed by insights from constructivism and international political economy that can thereby be seen as a continuation of the jurisprudence of process tradition within the contemporary landscapes of post-national law and policy.[84]

B. Analytically – A Renewed Taxonomy of the Foreign Reach of EU Private Law

The second way in which the notion of European transnational legal processes contributes to ongoing studies on the foreign reach of European private law is by widening and deepening our understanding of the different modalities through which EU law is travelling abroad. The specialised literature has used different angles to map and

[82] P Zumbansen, 'Economic Law: Anatomy and Crisis' (2021) 1 *Journal of Law and Political Economy* 462; PF Kjaer, 'The Law of Political Economy: An Introduction' in PF Kjaer (ed), *The Law of Political Economy: Transformation in the Function of Law* (Cambridge, Cambridge University Press, 2020); and J Britton-Purdy, DS Grewal, A Kapczynski, and KS Rahman, 'Building a Law-and-Political-Economy Framework: Beyond the Twentieth-Century Synthesis' (2019) 129 *Yale Law Journal* 1784. See also, for their relationship with earlier institutional accounts of law, B Fried, *The Progressive Assault on Laissez Faire: Robert Hale and the First Law and Economics Movement* (Harvard, Harvard University Press, 1998).

[83] Among other private law institutions, see, eg, R Walsh, *Property Rights and Social Justice: Progressive Property in Action* (Cambridge, Cambridge University Press, 2021); AC Cutler and T Dietz (eds), *The Politics of Private Transnational Governance by Contract* (London, Routledge, 2017); and D Danielsen, 'Beyond Corporate Governance: Why a New Approach to the Study of Corporate Law is Needed to Address Global Inequality and Economic Development' in U Mattei and JD Haskell (eds), *Research Handbook on Political Economy and Law* (Cheltenham, Edward Elgar Publishing, 2015) 195–204. See also, in general, RM Unger, *What Should Legal Analysis Become?* (Paris, Verso, 1996); and A Beckers, KH Eller and PF Kjaer, 'The Transformative Law of Political Economy in Europe' (2022) 1 *European Law Open* 749: explaining that 'micro actions need to be systematically linked to a concept of society, its overall level of coherency, and institutional dynamics' and how 'this link is provided by legal institutions understood as meso-level formations linking micro and macro. […] A transformative law of political economy ought to look at the most central institutions that constitute, with legal and political means, a particular economic system and its distributive patterns'.

[84] In this vein, see Calliess and Zumbansen (n 20) chapter 2, 111: expounding why and how 'transnational law regimes … are characterised by a combination and, in fact, inseparability of coordinative ("private") and regulatory ("public") dimensions in the *substantive* dimension of law'.

characterise these diverse modes of EU law's foreign diffusion. These angles largely correspond with the traditional focus of their respective disciplinary camp. Political scientists, for instance, have generally focused on the mode of power involved. This had led to an ongoing debate within political science literature on the phenomenon driven by concurrent representations of the modes of power informing the foreign reach of EU law and policies, whether this power is represented in ethical, economic, or epistemic terms.[85] In line with one of the cornerstones of process jurisprudence, however, the importance has been stressed of paying due attention within this debate to context instead of relying on a single perspective to explain the source of power that is driving the application of EU law and policy abroad.[86]

Building upon the anthropomorphic assumptions of the legal discipline, legal scholars have rather tended to focus on the modes of agency involved. As reviewed above, a key taxonomy in these respects has been whether EU law is achieving a foreign reach through unilateral, bilateral, or multilateral means, depending on whether the EU requires the consent of one or more representatives to extend its laws abroad. This agency-based characterisation by legal scholars of the foreign reach of EU law is implicitly supplemented with a spatial representation of the different planes in which these modes of foreign reach proceed. The key parameters here are whether this foreign reach proceeds in a horizontal plane towards foreign states and regional institutions or in a vertical plane towards international or global governance institutions broadly conceived.

As this section elaborates, the process approach and transnational paradigm underpinning the notion of European transnational private law enables us to widen our perspectives on and understanding of the foreign reach of EU law in at least four specific ways. The first way is that it enables us to distil some intricacies between the *de facto* Brussels effect advanced by Bradford and the categories of 'extraterritoriality' and 'territorial extension' advanced by Scott as different unilateral means for the foreign reach of EU law. Distilling these intricacies enables us to thematise a key legal question for the external reach of EU law: could and should the EU be held accountable and eventually responsible for the impacts of its laws abroad through the *de facto* Brussels effect?

The second way is that the socio-legal purview of sources informing the jurisprudence of process enables us to expand the range of bilateral means through which the EU is travelling abroad. According to this broader conception of sources, these bilateral means would also encompass ubiquitous modes of technocratic outreach by EU governmental or administrative authorities that are significantly shaping market orderings and private relations abroad through soft law or even less formalised modes of policy cooperation in several socio-economic sectors, as chapter three by Hans-W Micklitz on regulated industries powerfully illustrates.

[85] See I Manners, 'Normative Power Europe: A Contradiction in Terms?' (2002) 40 *Journal of Common Market Studies* 235; C Damro, 'Market Power Europe: Exploring a Dynamic Conceptual Framework' (2015) 22 *Journal of European Public Policy* 1336; and M Young and P Ravinet, 'Knowledge Power Europe' (2022) 44 *Journal of European Integration* 979.

[86] AR Young, 'The European Union as a Global Regulator? Context and Comparison' (2015) 22 *Journal of European Public Policy* 1233.

The third analytical contribution that the notion of European transnational legal processes makes is to refine the understanding of the multilateral channels through which it is travelling abroad. As this section elaborates, this requires supplementing the 'vertical' account taken by most specialised studies on the foreign reach of EU law with a 'diagonal' account of the EU's foreign legal dissemination through international or global governance institutions.

Fourthly and finally, the triad account of the agency-based model is also relevant for what it conceals. Drawing upon the conceptual transition from an international to a transnational paradigm of foreign relations informing our proposed framework to study European transnational legal processes, two renewed modes of foreign reach are advanced: societal modes of foreign reach through private ordering or private regulation, and collateral modes of foreign reach through comparative legal transplants and processes of legal convergence.

On those bases, this section proposes a renewed taxonomy for the systematic study of the foreign reach of EU law. This taxonomy includes five distinctive means. Building upon the agency-based categorisation advanced by Bradford and Scott, those means are:

1) unilateral means of foreign reach through 'extraterritoriality', 'territorial extension', or the *de facto* Brussels effect;
2) bilateral means of foreign reach through treaties or other agreements between the EU and foreign countries or groups of countries;
3) multilateral means of foreign reach through international or global governance institutions;
4) societal means of foreign reach through non-state actors and private ordering; and
5) collateral means of foreign reach through legal transplants and processes of legal convergence.

Alongside this taxonomy, this section elaborates on each of the insights related to European transnational legal processes outlined above. It also highlights their special relevance from the perspective of private law with reference to some of the chapters in this volume and broader studies on the foreign reach of EU law as a basis for future development of the research agenda on European transnational private law.

i. Foreign Reach of EU Private Law Through Unilateral Modes

The unilateral means for the foreign reach of EU private law generally includes mechanisms of 'extraterritoriality', 'territorial extension', as well as the '*de facto* Brussels effect' respectively advanced by Scott and Bradford. In contrast to the factual basis of the Brussels effect, the hypotheses of 'extraterritoriality' and 'territorial extension' advanced by Scott are indeed two diverse legislative techniques that the EU uses to extend its laws abroad. The former entails applying EU law to persons or circumstances with no connection to EU territory, such as its nationality-based jurisdiction over human trafficking offenders established by the Human Trafficking Directive (2011) or its effects-based jurisdiction over certain derivatives transactions as established by the European Market Infrastructure Regulation (2012).[87] The hypothesis of 'territorial extension' in turn conveys situations where there is some initial connection to EU territory, which at the same time triggers application of EU law to foreign conduct, persons, or legal systems. As Scott explains, while hypotheses of extraterritoriality in EU law are the exception, those of 'territorial extension' are ubiquitous across several fields of EU law and usually operate on a 'transaction-level', 'firm-level', or 'country-level' basis, or through some combination of these.[88] As explained above, they are all unilateral because none of these mechanisms requires the acquiescence or consent of the foreign country or region for application of EU law within their territories.

From the perspective of private law, it is important nevertheless to stress that this triad of unilateral means is one of the key sources for the study of European transnational private law because it analytically represents different instances through which EU law is shaping private relations or market orders abroad via intervening in the configuration of core private law institutions.[89] In the case of what Scott categorises as 'extraterritoriality', a good illustration is the 'bonus cap' introduced by the Prudential Supervision Directive (2013) for managers of credit institutions and financial investment firms, including their foreign subsidiaries, thereby impacting on issues of foreign corporate governance, labour law, and financial regulation.[90] In the case of 'territorial extension', a vivid illustration is the extensive corporate governance and operational requirements that the Ship Inspection Regulation (2009) imposes on 'recognised [private] organisations' in order to perform these inspections on behalf of the EU, which 'encompass all legal entities that contribute to ensuring that the organisation in question provides cover for their services worldwide'. It also encompasses widespread techniques in several domains of EU private law where access to the EU market for foreign services or products is made conditional on recognition of the equivalence of foreign laws in terms of their capacity to ensure compliance with certain production or commercialisation processes.[91] Finally, in

[87] See Art 10(1) of Directive 2011/36/EU of the European Parliament and of the Council of 5 April 2011 on preventing and combating trafficking in human beings and protecting its victims, and replacing Council Framework Decision 2002/629/JHA (Human Trafficking Directive) [2011] OJ 101/1; and Arts 4(l)(a)(iv) and 11(4) of Regulation (EU) No 648/2012 of the European Parliament and of the Council of 4 July 2012 on OTC derivatives, central counterparties and trade repositories (European Market Infrastructure Regulation) [2012] OJ L201/1. For a discussion of these and other examples, see Scott, 'Extraterritoriality and Territorial Extension in EU Law' (n 3) 94–96; and J Scott, 'The Global Reach of EU Law' in Cremona and Scott (eds) (n 15) 23–24.

[88] For a survey and analysis of these cases, see Scott, 'Extraterritoriality and Territorial Extension in EU Law' (n 3), 96–123; and Scott (n 87) 24–29.

[89] On the notion of private law and its different conceptions that are driving our study of European Transnational Private Law, see chapter 2 by A Beckers in this volume.

[90] See Arts 92 and 94 of Directive 2013/36/EU of the European Parliament and of the Council of 26 June 2013 on access to the activity of credit institutions and the prudential supervision of credit institutions and investment firms, amending Directive 2002/87/EC and repealing Directives 2006/48/EC and 2006/49/EC (Prudential Supervision Directive) [2013] OJ L176/338 discussed by Scott (n 87) 23.

[91] See Arts 2(c) and 4(3) of Regulation (EC) No 391/2009 of the European Parliament and of the Council of 23 April 2009 on common rules and standards for ship inspection and survey organisations (Ship Inspection Regulation) [2009] OJ L131/11 and some of the examples of this recognition of equivalence technique discussed by Scott (87) 25–28. On the use of mutual recognition as a modified mode of 'extraterritoriality' or 'territorial extension' within the field of EU financial law, with ample discussion of the EU and US positions and interactions in these respects, see P Davies, 'Financial Stability and the Global

the case of the '*de facto* Brussels effect', a good illustration is how EU approaches to consumer health and safety in the fields of food and chemicals are disciplining related production or commercialisation processes in several foreign countries or regions.[92] Thus, as analytically different modes of foreign EU legal unilateralism, 'extraterritoriality', 'territorial extension', and the '*de facto* Brussels effect' all represent an integral part of the phenomenon that the notion of European transnational private law signifies.

Yet one key question is whether and, if so, how these different unilateral means for the foreign reach of EU law are related, as well as why this is relevant. Anu Bradford has stressed the importance of categorically distinguishing the *de facto* Brussels effect from the hypothesis of 'extraterritoriality' and 'territorial extension' advanced by Joanne Scott. This is because only under 'extraterritoriality' and 'territorial extension' would the EU be directly or intentionally applying its laws to foreign countries or regions.[93] These hypotheses of 'extraterritoriality' and 'territorial extension' thus convey an active and deliberate imposition of its norms by the EU over subjects abroad through these legislative techniques as if they were within its own borders or territory. In contrast, according to Bradford the *de facto* Brussels effect would signify a merely involuntary or unintended application of EU law abroad driven by impersonal market forces.[94] This lack of agency would therefore undermine if not exclude any mode of legal responsibility or political accountability of the EU for the consequences of the Brussels effect.

Drawing upon insights from the jurisprudence of process, I would like to raise some qualifications to Bradford's distinction between purportedly intentional (that is, 'extraterritoriality' and 'territorial extension') and unintentional ('the *de facto* Brussels effect') manifestations of EU legal unilateralism, as a way of showing what the notion of European transnational private law inspired by this tradition adds to the discussion. One can qualify this distinction between intentional and unintentional modes of the unilateral outreach of EU law in at least two ways. The first way is by showing how 'territorial extension' and the *de facto* Brussels effect can be conjoined rather than necessarily standing apart. As recently advanced by Scott, the category of 'legal non-divisibility' as a condition for the operation of the Brussels effect is an ambivalent category that overlooks the extent to which this is deliberately generated by the EU legislator through 'territorial extension' techniques, whether in its

Influence of EU Law' in Cremona and Scott (eds) (n 15). See also, for a specialised study of these techniques in the field of environmental law, Hadjiyianni (n 4).

[92] For a review of these cases, see Bradford (n 1) chapter 6.

[93] Bradford (n 1) 67–68: '… the Brussels Effect is not the only manifestation of the EU's unilateral influence. The EU also exerts unilateral influence over foreign actors through legislative techniques such as extraterritoriality or territorial extension. Through these instruments, the EU seeks to directly apply its own regulations to foreign actors. These techniques are distinct from the market-driven harmonization associated with the Brussels Effect … As a threshold matter, the Brussels Effect should be distinguished from these other unilateral mechanisms of influence.'

[94] See, eg, Bradford (n 1) 6: noting that the *de facto* Brussels effect explains how 'unilateral regulatory globalization occurs when the law of one jurisdiction migrates into another in the absence of the former actively imposing it or the latter willingly adopting it'; and xiv explaining that different from many other forms of global influence, through the Brussels effect 'the EU does not need to impose its standards coercively on anyone – market forces alone are often sufficient to convert the EU standard into the global standard as companies voluntarily extend the EU rule to govern their worldwide operations'.

'firm-level' or country-level' varieties. To the extent that the category of legal non-divisibility 'fails to capture the "legislated" as opposed to the contingent nature of this phenomenon', its presence will 'often reflect a choice that the EU legislature has made … embodied in the substance of EU law'. For these reasons, Scott concludes, through these pervasive modes of 'territorial extension' that 'the EU may be viewed as taking an active step to ensure that the conditions for the emergence of the Brussels Effect are met'.[95] This is a sharp point, which nevertheless implicitly insulates the EU against any contestation for the operation of the Brussels effect in any other hypothesis.

Yet my second qualification comes from Bradford's own findings. Even if one may regard the *de facto* Brussels effect as an unintentional mode of the unilateral legal outreach of EU law beyond those cases of deliberate legal non-divisibility highlighted by Scott, nevertheless – as highlighted by Bradford – the EU has become increasingly aware of this foreign reach of EU law through the Brussels effect.[96] There is thus a growing degree of consciousness within and beyond EU institutions of the significant political power that the EU unilaterally exerts over several socio-economic realms beyond its frontiers through the *de facto* Brussels effect.[97] Given that one of the insights of the legal process tradition is how socio-political power and authority usually stand in a dialectical relationship that is utterly carried and institutionalised through law, one could thus expect that the growing awareness of this 'unique, and highly penetrating power to unilaterally transform global markets' currently wielded by the EU is or will become legally shaped through an evolving European transnational private law that may come to assert renewed conditions for its valid and legitimate exercise. The doctrinal category of 'complicity' recently advanced by Joanne Scott to assess the EU's responsibility for the impacts of its foreign policies or the category of 'network responsibility' recently advanced by Rónán Condon could be understood in this line.[98]

ii. Foreign Reach of EU Private Law Through Bilateral Modes

This conveys situations where EU law travels as a result of different types of international agreements between the EU and foreign states or regions. These agreements

[95] Scott (n 87) 31–35.

[96] This growing awareness has been illustratively documented by Bradford through the review of several statements from EU institutions related to diverse legislative instruments and regulatory programmes, which indicates 2007 as a turning point with the publication of the Commission's working paper on 'The External Dimension of the Single Market Review'. See Bradford (n 1) 18–24: noting how 'In its early decades – beginning in the 1960s but continuing well into the 2000s – the EU's external influence can thus best be viewed as an incidental by-product of its internal motivations. However, more recently, a conscious external agenda has emerged to complement the EU's internal regulatory agenda.'

[97] As Anu Bradford stresses, through the Brussels effect 'the EU wields significant, unique, and highly penetrating power to unilaterally transform global markets'. This is relevant because in a world where 'it is increasingly difficult to exert raw military power or even rely on economic sanctions or conditional incentives embedded in trade or loan agreements … regulatory power is one of the few areas where unilateralism still works.' Bradford (n 1) xiv, xvi.

[98] See Scott (n 87) 41–63; and R Condon, *Network Responsibility: European Tort Law and the Society of Networks* (Cambridge, Cambridge University Press, 2022).

can be general international treaties, such as the salient Accession, Partnership, or Preferential Trade Agreements that the EU has established with several foreign countries or regions, which usually include provisions that shape private relations in several socio-economic domains. It can also be specific agreements of a sectoral nature, such as the Energy Community Treaty, the Treaty Establishing the Transport Community, the EU External Aviation Policy, or Sustainable Fishing Partnership Agreements, which require foreign countries or regions to apply parts of the EU acquis in a given regulatory domain.[99] Yet it can also be less formalised modes of technocratic outreach or other modes of policy co-operation that EU administrative authorities regularly exercise within several domains through trans-governmental networks beyond traditional diplomatic channels, whether for reciprocal collaboration in policy matters, capacity-building, or provision of technical assistance concerning legal developments or enforcement. For the purposes of our study, all these avenues are regarded as bilateral means for the foreign reach of EU law because in all these cases the potential application of EU law abroad requires at least some degree of formal (not necessarily to imply less asymmetrical) consent or at least willingness on the part of the foreign country or region to implement EU law as part of a broader collaboration scheme with the EU.

To the extent that through this range of bilateral means the EU is shaping foreign private relations and market orders with a focus on core private law institutions, they also represent a key source for the study of European transnational private law. The most vivid illustration comes from Accession Treaties, which usually entail complete application of the *acquis communautaire* to countries that are joining the EU, thereby impacting most of their private relations and market orderings that fall within EU spheres of competence.[100] From its six original Member States, the series of accession treaties has enabled the EU to currently extend the 'visible hand' of EU private law to 27 European countries.[101] Moreover, as part of the ongoing 'enlargement strategy', which requires a transition period where prospective Member States need to show their capacity to integrate EU law within their own territories, several domains of EU private law are gradually permeating the orders of several non-EU candidates, such as Albania, Montenegro, Serbia, Turkey, and Ukraine, or prospective candidates, such as Georgia or Kosovo.[102] Accession Treaties have thus been one of the most prominent avenues for the bilateral extension of EU law within the European continent and with potential inroads into Asia (for example, Turkey and Georgia).

[99] See 'The Energy Community Treaty', available at https://eur-lex.europa.eu/EN/legal-content/summary/the-energy-community-treaty.html; 'The Treaty Establishing the Transport Community', available at https://eur-lex.europa.eu/legal-content/EN/TXT/PDF/?uri=CELEX:22017A1027(01)&rid=1; several legal materials comprising the EU 'External Aviation Policy', available at https://transport.ec.europa.eu/transport-modes/air/international-aviation/external-aviation-policy_en; and on the 'Sustainable Fishing Partnership Agreements', available at https://oceans-and-fisheries.ec.europa.eu/fisheries/international-agreements/sustainable-fisheries-partnership-agreements-sfpas_en.

[100] On the significance of these EU private law impacts with respect to the private law orders of its Member States, see HW Micklitz, *The Politics of Justice in European Private Law: Social Justice, Access Justice, Societal Justice* (Cambridge, Cambridge University Press, 2018).

[101] For a chronological list of Accession Treaties, see 'Accession Treaties', available at https://eur-lex.europa.eu/collection/eu-law/treaties/treaties-accession.html.

[102] See EU 'Enlargement Strategy', available at https://commission.europa.eu/strategy-and-policy/policies/eu-enlargement_en.

Yet other types of international treaties have also had a notable place for the extension of parts of EU private law within and beyond the European continent. One manifestation has been prominent modes of economic partnership, association agreements, and bilateral trade agreements that the EU has subscribed to with several foreign countries or regions (including countries as diverse as Israel, Mozambique, Japan, Morocco, and the Palestinian Authority) as well as key strategic countries or regions, such as Canada (Comprehensive Economic and Trade Agreement), Singapore, Australia, India, Mercosur, and the UK. In addition, the EU has subscribed to similar agreements of a diverse nature, such as 'customs unions' (Andorra, Turkey), or 'global agreements' (Mexico). Particularly relevant among these are agreements that the EU has subscribed to with non-EU border countries with the aim of enhancing European stability and prosperity, whether under the Agreement on the European Economic Area (Iceland, Liechtenstein, and Norway) or the European Neighbourhood Policy.[103] In diverse ways and with different emphases, through all of these agreements the EU has been either exporting parts of its rules or principles concerning internal market disciplines and relations abroad or gradually pursuing some degree of convergence towards EU law.[104] As chapter 11 by Mataija further elaborates, this makes these agreements one of the main avenues for the external reach of EU law and places the EU in a relative position of authority regarding modes of regulatory remote control of processes of production and commercialisation beyond its frontiers.[105]

A second manifestation appears in less salient agreements yet equally relevant mechanisms for the bilateral export of EU rules and market disciplines. These are different types of sectoral agreements that the EU has subscribed to with several foreign countries or regions concerning specific socio-economic domains. They are relevant from the perspective of private law because they involve a significant degree of transposition of or convergence towards EU norms and principles regarding certain specific markets. Prominent examples are the Energy Community Treaty,[106] the Treaty establishing the Transport Community,[107] and Sustainable Fishing Partnership Agreements.[108]

A related yet different bilateral way through which EU law is travelling abroad is through varied transgovernmental networks of policymakers and other regulatory officials or stakeholders. This is related because this range of epistemic communities usually also operates in specific legal fields or regulated markets. But it is different

[103] European Commission, 'European Neighbourhood Policy', available at https://commission.europa.eu/strategy-and-policy/policies/european-neighbourhood-policy_en.

[104] For different perspectives into this theme, see D Bouris and T Schumacher (eds), *The Revised European Neighbourhood Policy: Continuity and Change in EU Foreign Policy* (Berlin, Springer, 2016); S Poli, *The European Neighbourhood Policy – Values and Principles* (Oxfordshire, Routledge, 2016); and D Schade, *The EU in Association Agreement Negotiations: Challenges to Complex Policy Coordination* (Oxfordshire, Routledge, 2019). See also, S Gstöhl and S Schunz, *Theorizing the European Neighbourhood Policy* (Oxfordshire, Taylor & Francis, 2016).

[105] On this regulatory technique, see also P Mertenskotter and RB Stewart, 'Remote Control: Treaty Requirements for Regulatory Procedures' (2018) 104 *Cornell Law Review* 165.

[106] 'Energy Community,' available at www.energy-community.org/aboutus/whoweare.html.

[107] 'Transport Community,' available at www.transport-community.org/about-us/.

[108] European Commission, 'Sustainable Fishing Partnership Agreements,' available at https://oceans-and-fisheries.ec.europa.eu/fisheries/international-agreements/sustainable-fisheries-partnership-agreements-sfpas_en.

because these modes of transfer do not happen through formal, bilateral agreements, but usually through less formalised instruments such as codes of conduct, guidelines, or memorandums of understanding, as well as unofficial conventions or practices among officials. Within the jurisprudence of process framework, these types of instruments and practices do have an established place as pertinent sources of analysis due to their contextual and socio-legal relevance. Typically this foreign reach of EU law proceeds as part of reciprocal collaboration between EU governmental or administrative officials on certain policy matters, including provision of technical assistance concerning regulatory rulemaking or enforcement, as well as capacity-building.[109] The specialised study by Micklitz highlights part of this phenomenon concerning regulated industries, yet other studies on the external dimension of EU law have stressed their prominent role in the external dimension of EU competition law[110] and controversial migration agreements between the EU and some border countries or regions.[111]

iii. Foreign Reach of EU Private Law Through Multilateral Modes

This conveys situations where EU law travels to foreign countries or regions of the world through international or global governance institutions. These institutions comprise classic international actors, such as international organisations or international courts and tribunals. They also include a range of other entities that do not necessarily fit within the doctrine of sources of international law but play a prominent role in the development of international law and policy on issues of private law beyond the state. These are usually signified by the broader category of global governance institutions. These global governance institutions include institutionalised networks of policymakers that are non-treaty based, such as the Basel Committee on Banking Supervision or the International Organization of Securities Commission (IOSCO), as well as hybrid (public-private) organisations, such as the Codex Alimentarius Commission or the Internet Corporation for Assigned Names and Numbers (ICANN). These are all multilateral because they involve resolving issues or advancing positions among three or more constituents in a governance dynamic that also encompasses the interests and pedigree of the multilateral institution itself beyond those of their respective constituents or stakeholders.

As noted previously, the relationship between EU law and global governance institutions as well as the place and role of the EU as an international legal actor are themes that have been widely analysed in EU legal scholarship. These themes have been taken up by the specialised literature on the foreign reach of EU law to characterise this foreign reach through multilateral means as one largely defined by instances where the EU participates in international forums or collaborates with global governance institutions for the implementation and dissemination of international

[109] For a specialised study on these technocratic modes of foreign reach of EU law, see S Lavenex, 'The Power of Functionalist Extension: How EU Rules Travel' (2014) 21 *Journal of European Public Policy* 885.

[110] G Monti, 'The Global Reach of EU Competition Law' in Cremona and Scott (eds) (n 15).

[111] B Ryan, 'The Migration Crisis and the European Union Border Regime' in Cremona and Scott (eds) (n 15).

norms within or beyond the EU. An illustrative example is the account provided by Cremona and Scott where discussion of this multilateral means is largely circumscribed by the participation of the EU in international fora and how in its external dimension the EU acts in 'support of the adoption and application of international law'.[112] The relationship is thus generally limited to the EU and international institutions in a vertical plane, where the EU would either perform as an originator for the development or as an agent for the global dissemination of international law. A similar approach to this multilateral means is followed by Bradford.[113] This is a means where the influence of the international relations paradigm *vis-à-vis* the transnational relations paradigm is thus most visible.[114]

Yet this characterisation can be misleading for two main reasons. One is that it may include instances where the EU is the agent rather than the principal concerning certain international or foreign (rather than strictly European) legal developments, as some of the previous references indicate. This would entail analytically muddling the external dimension of EU law as a distinctive phenomenon with instances where the EU is merely performing as an agent of international or global governance institutions in implementing or disseminating their norms. One example comes from the field of accounting standards, where the early embrace of International Financial Reporting Standards (IFRS) by the EU and its ultimate dissemination throughout the world can relate to a distinctive US influence in the institutional and procedural design of the International Financial Reporting Standards Foundation.[115] Another example comes from chapter seven by Möschel in this volume that illustrates this when warning that any perceived global reach of EU non-discrimination law may in fact be the globalisation of a US construct by the EU. In other words, to the extent that EU non-discrimination law is exported to foreign countries or regions, the EU would not be the principal but a mere agent in these transnational legal processes.[116]

The second reason why this characterisation can be misleading is that tracing the vertical relationships between the EU and global governance institutions is only half the story. If one wants to study the foreign reach of EU law through multilateral means, one would need to trace not only the extent to which EU law or regulatory positions were uploaded to global governance institutions. One also needs to trace the extent to which these EU positions were then downloaded or disseminated to foreign countries or regions by these global governance institutions or other actors within those transnational legal processes. Rather than spatially 'vertical,' this sequential upload/download movement reveals that this means of foreign reach is better conceived as 'diagonal' given that EU law is attaining a foreign reach *through*

[112] Cremona and Scott, 'Introduction – EU Law Beyond EU Borders' (n 15) 1–3.

[113] See, eg, Bradford (n 1) 12, 72–74.

[114] For an overview of these multilateral channels, see the thorough study by M Cremona, 'Extending the Reach of EU Law: The EU as an International Legal Actor' in Cremona and Scott (eds) (n 15).

[115] S Botzem, *The Politics of Accounting Regulation: Organizing Transnational Standard Setting in Financial Reporting* (Cheltenham, Edward Elgar Publishing, 2012); and K Camfferman and SA Zeff, *Financial Reporting and Global Capital Markets: A History of the International Accounting Standards Committee, 1973–2000* (Oxford, Oxford University Press, 2007).

[116] For a more differentiated account of the external dimension of EU non-discrimination law, see Giegerich (n 4) pt IV.

multilateral institutions located at the international or global governance level. It is under these sequential upload/download movements that one can thus fully grasp whether and to what extent EU private law is indeed shaping markets or other socio-economic realms within foreign countries or regions *through* multilateral institutions, which chapter 10 by Macacci in this volume highlights concerning the foreign reach of EU financial law through IOSCO.[117]

iv. Foreign Reach of EU Private Law Through Societal Modes

The three previous categories build upon the agency-based model that is well established in the literature on the foreign reach of EU law and the international relations paradigm that largely underpins it. Yet the transition from an international towards a transnational relations paradigm informing the project of a European transnational private law suggests the relevance of thematising at least two additional means for this foreign reach. One of them is the foreign reach of EU law through societal means, which conveys situations where EU law travels to foreign countries or regions of the world through private actors or civil society institutions.

The role of private actors as agents of EU foreign legal dissemination is not new within the specialised literature. For instance, Bradford ascribes a central place and role to transnational corporations operating in the EU as transporters of EU law to foreign countries or regions and thereby accomplishing a *de facto* and potentially also the *de jure* Brussels effect.[118] Scott also underscores the important place that corporate groups with some territorial link to Europe occupy as a mechanism for triggering the 'firm-level territorial extension' of EU law to their worldwide operations.[119] Furthermore, Cremona and Scott also mention some instances where the EU draws upon other legal capacities of non-state actors to export its rules, such as maritime classification societies.[120] Therefore, private actors and civil society institutions already form an integral part of the landscape of the foreign reach of EU law.

What does the transnational relations paradigm informing European transnational private law add to this landscape? In the case of Cremona and Scott these references to the role of private actors and civil society institutions as mechanisms for extending 'EU law beyond EU borders' are largely marginal or anecdotal. This contrasts with the prominent role that private actors and civil society institutions play in different realms of contemporary socio-economic governance that the transnational relation paradigm highlights.[121] For these reasons, from a transnational private

[117] In a similar vein concerning the external dimension of EU financial law *through* global governance institutions, see M De Bellis, 'Reinforcing EU Financial Bodies' Participation in Global Networks: Addressing Legitimacy Gaps?' in Hofmann, Vos and Chamon (n 4).

[118] Bradford (n 1) xv: underscoring from the outset how the Brussels effect 'demonstrates that the EU's greatest global influence may not be through multilateral mechanisms and political institutions, but instead through unilateral actions, facilitated by markets and private corporations'.

[119] Scott (n 87) 25–26; and Scott, 'Extraterritoriality and Territorial Extension in EU Law' (n 3) 107.

[120] Cremona and Scott, 'Introduction – EU Law Beyond EU Borders' (n 15) 13–14.

[121] P Zumbansen, 'The Ins and Outs of Transnational Private Regulatory Governance: Legitimacy, Accountability, Effectiveness and a New Concept of "Context"' (2012) 13 *German Law Journal* 1269; F Cafaggi, 'Transnational Private Regulation: Regulating Global Private Regulators' in S Cassese (ed), *Research Handbook on Global Administrative Law* (Cheltenham, Edward Elgar Publishing, 2016); P Paiement, *Transnational Sustainability Laws* (Cambridge, Cambridge University Press, 2017).

law perspective one can posit that this role of private actors and civil society institutions is worth being thematised as a distinctive means or mechanism of EU foreign legal dissemination.

But how should the role of private actors and civil society institutions be thematised? Scott largely circumscribes the analysis to one structure of private action: more/fewer hierarchical structures represented by single organisations or corporate groups. But this is not the only possible structure of private action. In addition to hierarchies, the societal means category also includes modes of private action structured as markets, as in widespread instances of regulatory competition for the regulation of transnational markets (think of the current regulatory race among several organisations to standardise the notion of 'green investments'),[122] as well as networks, as in the ubiquitous modes of contractual networks that form widespread global supply chains in several industries.[123]

Furthermore, while Bradford largely circumscribes the role of private actors as mere carriers or ruletakers of EU law, whether in their *de facto* application to their foreign production or commercialisation processes or their *de jure* dissemination within foreign regions, this overlooks how this may also involve a significant rule-making dimension. In other words, the engagement of EU law with private actors and civil society institutions as agents for their foreign legal dissemination can have a relevant *jurigenerative* aspect that is worthy of distinctive attention. It is this 'dark private legal space' that this chapter wishes to bring into the spotlight for analysis and scrutiny in the study of European transnational private law through the notion of its foreign reach through societal means.[124]

Within the present volume, one prominent example comes from chapter 14 by Salminen, Rajavuori, and Eller. In analysing how the EU draws upon value chains to extend its laws abroad, the chapter eloquently identifies three waves of EU legislation and regulation in these respects. These waves largely correspond with unilateral and bilateral modalities of the external reach of EU law, yet, as the chapter also highlights, a crucial societal dimension is also operating in parallel that needs to be understood and assessed. How are these policy mandates being implemented by lead firms and other civil society actors within these supply chains? What types of instruments and mechanisms are they using and why are they using them? And with what implications and potential for reform or contestation? These are some of the questions that the 'dark space' of societal private law suggests.

[122] See, eg, H Eidenmüller (ed), *Regulatory Competition in Contract Law and Dispute Resolution* (London, Bloomsbury Publishing, 2013); and JM Smits, 'A Radical View of Legal Pluralism' in L Niglia (ed), *Pluralism and European Private Law* (London, Bloomsbury Publishing, 2013).

[123] A Beckers, 'The Invisible Networks of Global Production: Re-Imagining the Global Value Chain in Legal Research' (2020) 16 *European Review of Contract Law* 95; KH Eller, 'Private Governance of Global Value Chains From Within: Lessons From and For Transnational Law' (2017) *Transnational Legal Theory* 1; M Amstutz, 'Contract Collisions: An Evolutionary Perspective on Contractual Networks' (2013) 76 *Law and Contemporary Problems* 169; and G Teubner, *Networks as Connected Contracts* (London, Bloomsbury Publishing, 2011). See also, in general, K Ladeur, 'Towards a Legal Theory of Supranationality – The Viability of the Network Concept' (1997) 3 *European Law Journal* 33.

[124] A Beckers, 'EU Law's Dark Private Legal Space: Researching Private Regulators and the Importance of Legal Doctrine' (2022) 18 *European Constitutional Law Review* 657.

A similar phenomenon is captured in chapter 13 by Ulfbeck from a different angle. As Ulfbeck discusses, we seem to be at a hinge moment within European tort law that is increasingly evolving to instil due diligence duties for several types of commercial actors who are expected to disseminate them throughout their supply chains. While this is already prominent in the realm of lead transnational corporations in global supply chains, a similar transformation is taking shape for banks as part of the EU sustainable finance strategy[125] and digital platforms in the light of the Digital Services Act.[126] To the extent that these private actors are expected to implement policy mandates through rulemaking, monitoring, and enforcement activities throughout their supply chains or spheres of competence, these represent prominent societal means through which EU law is attaining an external dimension through an emerging 'private administrative law'.[127]

These modes of foreign reach are also neither 'vertical' nor 'horizontal,' but operate 'diagonally'. Yet this 'diagonal' means does not proceed 'upwards' *through* multilateral institutions as recently discussed. It is a diagonal that rather proceeds 'downwards' through private actors or civil society institutions that are fulfilling a key role in the foreign dissemination of EU law through co-regulatory practices in ways that neither Bradford nor Scott properly capture. Apart from the several examples drawn from the different chapters of this volume referenced above, another example is the case of the Society for Worldwide Interstate Financial Telecommunications (SWIFT), which occupies a key place and role for the fulfilment of contractual obligations and the overall operation of the transnational financial system.[128]

v. Foreign Reach of EU Private Law Through Collateral Modes

The second renewed means for the extension of EU law beyond its frontiers consists of cases where a foreign country or region decides to formally integrate EU law within their own legal system. This can be because this foreign country or region directly adopts or applies an EU norm or institution – an instance to be thematised as a case of 'legal transplant'. It can also be because a foreign country or region decides to emulate or approximate its laws to those of the EU without directly transposing them – an instance to be thematised as a case of 'legal convergence'. Whether operating through legal transplants or convergence, these means for the foreign reach of EU law are conceived as 'collateral' because they require an active role by the competent

[125] European Commission, 'Strategy for Financing the Transition to a Sustainable Economy', available at https://finance.ec.europa.eu/publications/strategy-financing-transition-sustainable-economy_en.

[126] European Commission, 'Digital Services Act', available at https://digital-strategy.ec.europa.eu/en/policies/safer-online.

[127] R Vallejo, 'After Governance? The Idea of a Private Administrative Law' in Kjaer (n 82).

[128] SWIFT has been in the spotlight lately due to its key role in implementing international sanctions against Russia in the context of the war on Ukraine: see, 'Ukraine: EU Agrees to Exclude Key Russian Banks from SWIFT', available at https://ec.europa.eu/commission/presscorner/detail/en/ip_22_1484. See also, more broadly, H Farrell and AL Newman, 'Weaponized Interdependence: How Global Economic Networks Shape State Coercion' (2019) 44 *International Security* 42; and A Nölke, *Capital Claims: Power and Global Finance* (Oxfordshire, Routledge, 2022), chapter 10 on 'Geoeconomic Infrastructures: Building Chinese-Russian Alternatives to SWIFT'.

authorities within the foreign country or region rather than necessarily of the EU itself.

This is not a means of global reach thematised by Scott either in her original essay or in its latest iteration within the edited volume with Cremona. Nevertheless, Scott and Cremona mention several instantiations of it, such as widespread emulation or EU leverage for foreign adoption of the EU model of data protection law.[129] Within the framework of the Brussels effect, this 'collateral' means is explicitly considered by Bradford as part of the so-called 'strict version' of the *de jure* Brussels effect, albeit not studied or thematised.[130] Nevertheless, Bradford reviews several instantiations of this 'collateral' means of foreign legal dissemination, highlighting problematic issues, including how 'the actual effectiveness of the *de jure* Brussels Effect is difficult to measure in precise terms'.[131] Drawing upon the re-flourishing field of comparative law as the twin sister of transnational legal studies, it is my contention that many of these issues can be productively addressed by conceptualising them as foreign reach of EU law by collateral means of 'legal transplants' and processes of 'legal convergence' – broadly conceived.[132]

The literature suggests several ways through which EU law is shaping foreign private relations and market orderings, whether through legal transplants or legal convergence. The chapters in this volume by Beckers (chapter two) and Letto-Vanamo (chapter five), for instance, discuss how 'legal transplants' and more or less official processes of 'legal convergence' were a prominent way through which European private law travelled abroad during the nineteenth century alongside codification movements. Key in these respects are the global dissemination of the 'civil law tradition' and the 'common law tradition' from Europe towards specific countries or regions around the globe.[133]

There are other contributions that nevertheless highlight other collateral modes through which EU private law has been travelling abroad. One is the prominent traction that EU data protection and internet law has been gaining abroad through modes of direct legal transplant or gradual processes of legal convergence.[134] Other studies highlight the transplant of specific rules, such as 'the right to be forgotten' established by the European Court of Justice (ECJ) in *Google Spain*,[135] while other studies rather focus on the transplantation or convergence of key EU legal

[129] Cremona and Scott, 'Introduction – EU Law Beyond EU Borders' (n 15) 5, 9: noting how 'in third countries as the EU acquis is used as a model to incentivise the adoption by third countries of "adequate" data protection laws'.

[130] As Bradford explains, this 'strict version' parallels what David Vogel influentially coined as the 'California Effect' and 'will therefore not be revisited in detail in this book'. Bradford (n 1) 3.

[131] Bradford (n 1) 75–80.

[132] For this broad conception of legal transplants and processes of legal convergence, see M Siems, *Comparative Law*, 3rd edn (Cambridge, Cambridge University Press, 2022) ch 10. On comparative law as the twin-sister of transnational law, see RA Miller and P Zumbansen (eds), *Comparative Law as Transnational Law: A Decade of the German Law Journal* (Oxford, Oxford University Press, 2012).

[133] In this vein, see, in general, P Glenn, *Legal Traditions of the World: Sustainable Diversity in Law*, 5th edn (Oxford, Oxford University Press, 2014).

[134] C Kuner, 'The Internet and the Global Reach of EU Law' in Cremona and Scott (eds) (n 15).

[135] A Reich, 'The Impact of the Court of Justice of the European Union on the Israeli Legal System' in A Reich and HW Micklitz (eds), *The Impact of the European Court of Justice on Neighbouring Countries* (Oxford, Oxford University Press, 2020).

institutions abroad.[136] As established concepts in comparative legal studies, the categories of legal transplants and processes of legal convergence transcend the mere institutionalisation of the rule/institution to analyse their functionality and therefore their effectiveness or capacity to adapt or transform after the transplant. In this sense, the notion of legal transplants and processes of legal convergence represents a productive framework to overcome some of the limitations of these collateral modes of EU diffusion outlined above and the strict notion of the Brussels effect in particular.[137]

In sum, as this overview signals, these five means convey distinctive ways through which EU law is travelling abroad. Although they are analytically distinctive, none of these operate in isolation from each other. As Bradford and Scott have thoroughly emphasised, it is key to charting and understanding the way they interact within different socio-economic realms. Several chapters in this volume are also illustrative in these respects. For instance, while the focus of chapter 11 by Mataija is on how the EU is using bilateral means of free trade agreements to exert modes of regulatory remote control over related processes of production and policymaking in foreign regions of the world under the auspices of World Trade Organisation law, it also highlights how – through certain instruments of domestic trade – the EU is also instilling modes of 'co-regulation' and 'territorial extension' to spread its own market disciplines in different sectors, such as fisheries and money-laundering. Likewise, chapter seven by Möschel points to an interplay of 'extraterritoriality', 'legal transplants', and modes of 'co-regulation' as means of enhancing but also hindering adoption of EU non-discrimination law abroad.

This is also one of the key insights of the legal process as a jurisprudential tradition. Given that law is not a set of norms but a process of authoritative decision-making, it is crucial to study the different channels through which legal developments take place. This is because this range of channels provides distinctive insights into when, how, and why these rules matter, as well as the way that perceived interests may be adapted or even transformed alongside this diverse set of transnational interactions. By highlighting five distinctive channels and illustrating them by reference to some of the specialised studies on the foreign reach of EU law both within and beyond this volume, the present chapter thus seeks to offer an analytical point of departure for future studies on European transnational private law.

C. Theoretically – From Abstract Validity and Policy Influence to a Pragmatic Engagement with Institutional Functions, Practices, and their Implications.

The final way in which the notion of a European transnational private law grounded in the jurisprudence of process contributes to ongoing studies on the foreign reach

[136] KJ Alter, 'The Global Spread of European Style International Courts' (2012) 35 *West European Politics* 135–54; KJ Alter, LR Helfer, and O Saldías, 'Transplanting the European Court of Justice: The Experience of the Andean Tribunal of Justice' (2012) 60 *The American Journal of Comparative Law* 629.

[137] See, in general, TS Goldbach, 'Why Legal Transplants?' (2019) 15 *Annual Review of Law and Social Science* 583; and MM Siems, *Convergence in Shareholder Law* (Cambridge, Cambridge University Press, 2007).

of EU law is by extending the theoretical scope of those studies to other relevant aspects of the phenomenon. This is done by supplementing the prevalent focus on competences of the EU or its Member States concerning external relations matters and charting institutional interactions between the EU and foreign government or global governance institutions in at least three distinct ways. These are as follows:

i. a renewed focus on the purposive functions that these European transnational legal processes perform or are meant to achieve;
ii. how these functions or values are shaped 'in context' by studying concrete institutional practices surrounding them; as well as
iii. their material or cultural implications.

As this sub-section elaborates, each of these additional aspects of analysis are in line with the range of pillars or cornerstones informing the jurisprudence of process outlined in section II and thus would represent an integral part of a research project on European transnational private law sustained upon those basic tenets.

Bradford and Scott address the question of functions in different yet related ways. Beyond a particular discussion in some of the specific case studies, Bradford thematises this question of functions in one of the final chapters that generally discusses the normative desirability or justification of the Brussels effect. The function that EU law purposively seeks to perform beyond its frontiers in this account is correlated with a broad parameter of 'welfare', understood as a combination of social welfare and respect for foreign political autonomy based on rational choice grounds.[138] Scott and Cremona mainly focus on the function of law within European transnational legal processes rather than the function of the processes themselves. Nevertheless, they also highlight some immanent tensions between EU interests and the normative values that are purposively driving these EU legal endeavours beyond its frontiers. I now relate the notion of European transnational private law with each of these themes advanced by Scott and Cremona in tandem.

Regarding the first theme, one of the novel contributions that Scott and Cremona make to the study of the foreign reach of EU law is their systematic account of the enabling and constraining functions that law performs in this respect. There are several manifestations to this. The enabling function is mainly represented by the permissive approach that the Court of Justice of the European Union (CJEU) has taken in several cases regarding the foreign reach of EU law, prompting novel forms of socio-economic or political integration with foreign countries or regions as well as innovative techniques for the enforcement of EU law beyond its frontiers. These include integration through Trade and Association Agreements as well as conditionality or mutual recognition techniques that have channelled complementary agreements with regulatory authorities to ensure compliance with EU law abroad.[139]

[138] Bradford (n 1) ch 8: concluding that 'whether the Brussels Effect is positive or negative depends on individual preferences that vary across policy areas, individuals' socioeconomic and cultural backgrounds, values, and ideologies' yet 'on balance, the Brussels Effect is more likely to generate net benefits that are valuable – even if not uniformly in all instances and for all the people'.

[139] Cremona and Scott, 'Introduction – EU Law Beyond EU Borders' (n 15) 11–14.

The constraining function operates at different levels. While international law as applied by the CJEU has only marginally constrained the EU's foreign reach, EU Law's so-called 'principle of autonomy' has represented a significant hindrance. As Cremona and Scott explain, this principle has constrained the foreign reach of EU law whether through bilateral or multilateral means whenever these international agreements or resolutions jeopardise the decision-making capacities of EU institutions or the primacy of the CJEU in the interpretation of EU law, unless some 'disconnection clause is established'. At the same time, while EU and international human rights constrain the foreign reach of EU law at the procedural and substantive levels, these have rather operated as enabler and driver of this foreign reach as signalled by the active agenda that the EU has pursued to secure European conceptions of the right to privacy in foreign data protection laws or abolition of the death penalty throughout the globe (to which one could add the 'trade and …' turn in international trade law, as stressed in chapter 11 by Mataija).[140] In highlighting how law empowers and at the same time restrains the authority of the EU to regulate relations or practices beyond its frontiers, in line with the jurisprudence of process Cremona and Scott thus show how law shapes and is in many ways constitutive of its 'global regulatory hegemony' (Bradford).

While this constitutive role of EU law can generate much political appeal for those seeking reformist or transformative avenues for change, it is relevant to keep in sight that this constitutive role is usually devised from the perspective of EU law itself and thereby prone to express some ingrained institutional or epistemic biases. The proceduralisation of the external dimension of EU law through institutionalising standards of good governance within these legal processes beyond EU frontiers can certainly help ease some of the biases in making EU authorities more 'responsive', and EU law more 'reflexive' towards the interests of foreign countries or regions. But there are inherent limits or blind spots to that responsiveness or reflexiveness. This is because the decision-making powers still rely on EU authorities that are making those decisions from an EU perspective and are circumstantially subject to the socio-political constraints of a European context. Some relevant biases are therefore likely to remain, as previous debates regarding the capacity to restrain creeping EU competences through instituting a principle of subsidiarity or to genuinely constitute modes of private governance beyond the state have continuously reaffirmed.[141]

While institutions can eventually transform, the jurisprudence of process shows that these 'structural biases' underpinning legal-political institutions are often hard, if not impossible, to overcome.[142] This suggests a need to keep under critical scrutiny any substantive value underpinning (or that according to many authors should still underpin) the pervasive 'global regulatory hegemony' that the EU is exerting

[140] ibid 14–17.

[141] See AE de Noriega, *The EU Principle of Subsidiarity and Its Critique* (Oxford, Oxford University Press, 2002); and E Meidinger, 'Law and Constitutionalism in the Mirror of Non-Governmental Standards: Comments on Harm Schepel' in C Joerges, IJ Sand and G Teubner (eds), *Transnational Governance and Constitutionalism* (London, Hart Publishing, 2004).

[142] M Koskenniemi, 'The Politics of International Law – 20 Years Later' (2009) 20 *European Journal of International Law* 7.

in several socio-economic domains, whether this is guided by some ready-made parameters of 'welfare,' 'legitimacy', 'justice', 'constitutionalism', 'good governance' or other substantive value that purposively seeks to 'include the other'.[143] To avoid falling prey to cynical anti-formalism, part of the scholarly and practical effort is to promote a 'culture of formalism' within these diverse legal processes beyond EU frontiers to give the necessary space and horizon for active socio-political engagement towards institutional change or transformation.[144] As Salminen, Rajavuori and Eller's chapter argues with respect to the foreign reach of EU law through supply chains, private international law plays a key role in this respect given the EU's long experience in using it to manage pluralism by enhancing socio-political autonomy and at the same time promoting integration.[145] Yet especially with those subaltern groups and grassroots movements that resist becoming co-opted by the predominant technocratic or policy parlance, such as indigenous peoples and other modes of non-extractive or local production, awareness of this inherent perspectiveness suggests that in some situations the best way of including is paradoxically by excluding the 'other' through modes of 'a-legality' to preserve them in their otherness.[146]

This ambivalent role of human rights or other purposive values directly connects with the second contribution that Cremona and Scott make with respect to these functional elements: the tension between EU interests and values that underpins this foreign reach of EU law. Building upon some of the contributions to their volume, Cremona and Scott highlight how promotion of democratic and rule-of-law values, as well as human rights, has been one of the main functions guiding the external agenda of the EU in seeking their global dissemination. This function finds its legal basis in Articles 3(5) and 21 Treaty on European Union and has led to widespread characterisation of the EU as a 'union of values', which relates to an enduring perception regarding the foreign role of the EU whether in earlier characterisations ('Normative Power Europe') or some of its most recent instantiations ('Good Global Actor').[147]

While it may be in the EU interest to promote its values abroad, Cremona and Scott also highlight some problematic interests underlying that purportedly noble quest. These interests include subjecting foreign countries or regions to international legal frameworks that constrain their range of developmental strategies. It also includes requiring from foreign countries or regions a level of compliance with international legal standards that the EU follows less rigorously (that is, double standards). Even more problematically, it also includes diverting or shielding its own responsibility

[143] J Habermas, *The Inclusion of the Other: Studies in Political Theory* (Cambridge, MIT Press, 1998). In this vein, see I Koivisto, 'Varieties of Good Governance: A Suggestion of Discursive Plurality' (2014) 27 *International Journal for the Semiotics of Law – Rev int'le de Sémiotique juridique* 587.

[144] M Koskenniemi, *The Gentle Civilizer of Nations: The Rise and Fall of International Law 1870–1960* (Cambridge, Cambridge University Press, 2004) 494 ff.

[145] In this vein, see R Michaels, 'Post-Critical Private International Law' in H Muir Watt and DP Fernández Arroyo (eds), *Private International Law and Global Governance* (Oxford, Oxford University Press, 2014).

[146] H Lindahl, *Fault Lines of Globalization: Legal Order and the Politics of A-Legality* (Oxford, Oxford University Press, 2013).

[147] See, respectively, Manners (n 85); and Fahey and Mancini (n 4).

for violation of international law, as in the agreements that the EU has made with key countries to prevent migratory inflows into the EU as part of its controversial 'Global Approach to Migration and Mobility'.[148] Beyond these specific contradictions between EU foreign policies and its declared stance as a purported 'union of values', Scott and Cremona conclude by highlighting how in its external dimension the EU experiences a pervasive tension concerning whether 'it would be unreasonable to expect third countries to accept the EU's political interests as universal values' as well as how to 'ensure that it operates in compliance with its own self-proclaimed values'.[149]

The jurisprudence of process tradition offers certain guidelines to address these questions on how to generate such a transnational legal normativity. As a matter of institutional design, alongside enabling socio-political 'interaction' within the specific regime by empowering more actors to engage with the content and impacts of certain decisions through proceduralisation, the theory identifies two supplementary ways to enhance this normativity. One is to multiply interpretative fora for the elaboration of underspecified norms or generation of new norms within or beyond the specific regime, as a way to trigger institutional awareness and contestation towards the content or implications of those legal commitments. Among other issues, this places the lawyerly focus on opening up doctrines of 'standing' throughout European transnational legal processes. The third way is to subsequently promote the internalisation of the mentioned interpretations whether through social, political, or legal avenues, such as information campaigns, lobbying, strategic litigation, or other modes of legal/political mobilisation. These mechanisms (that is, interaction, interpretation, and internalisation), which encompass several actors, norms, institutions, and means of communication between them, thus represent three recursive steps for enhancing legal integrity and an overall 'fidelity to law' throughout transnational legal processes.[150]

As a matter of theoretical and methodological standpoint, this tradition also points to the relevance of avoiding use of some fixed or ready-made parameter of legitimacy to assess institutional practices. The framework rather requires appraising how legitimacy is actually 'constructed and contested' by those participants in these institutional practices through socio-legal methods.[151] In other words, with respect to the tensions between interests and value highlighted by Cremona and Scott, a European transnational private law informed by such a neopragmatic jurisprudence of process would draw attention to how neither interests nor values are immaculate or pre-defined within these institutional dynamics, but they are usually made and re-defined through *praxis*. This entails a post-idealistic and a post-materialistic account of institutional practices that renews the theoretical perspectives and

[148] For a specialised study on the latter, see Ryan (n 111).

[149] Cremona and Scott, 'Introduction – EU Law Beyond EU Borders' (n 15) 2–4; with reference to Ryan (n 111) 3.

[150] HH Koh, 'Transnational Legal Process' (1996) 75 *Nebraska Law Review*, 181–208; and HH Koh, 'Why Do Nations Obey International Law' (1996) 106 *Yale Law Journal* 2599.

[151] J Black, 'Constructing and Contesting Legitimacy and Accountability in Polycentric Regulatory Regimes' (2008) 2 *Regulation & Governance* 137.

parameters of analysis regarding the question of promotion or compliance with EU values on the external dimension of EU law, as:

> … it should be obvious that a 'non-ideal' refection on problems of praxis does not deny the importance of "ideals" or values but proposes a different way of realising them. To put it simply, this approach is neither some form of political (or scientific) 'realism' at basement prices, nor is it an endeavour, such as analytical ethics, which elaborates on the principles of morality. A non-ideal approach to acting does take values seriously but proceeds by not providing ideal targets against which the actual order can be assessed, but by identifying specific failures. It diagnoses them, and prescribes a remedy that need not be universally applicable but that might 'work' because of 'local' or historical conditions. [In this sense,] … praxis directs our attention to the *Aufgaben*, that is tasks that are given and entrusted to us, which must be 'taken care of' – by correcting again and again the problems that come up because our understandings and capacities are limited – while we strive to go on with our individual and collective projects.[152]

There may be something distinctively (and tragically) European about these non-ideal trade-offs,[153] and chapter five by Letto-Vanamo in this volume reminds us from a historical perspective of the relevance of this pragmatic, contextual engagement with European transnational legal processes in its emphasis on 'glocalised' studies of European transnational private law.[154] Yet, as Harold Koh has lately stressed, as a theoretical framework the jurisprudence of process is driven by aspirations that 'are not just analytic, but transformative'. This conveys the constitutive aspect of the account in generating transnational legal normativity. While from an observational standpoint transnational law appears as a seamless web of complex interactions among different players, as a framework of analysis the goal of transnational legal processes is 'not simply to ratify existing practice but to elevate it'. In this sense, transnational legal processes transcend a mere naturalistic focus on explaining how states or other transnational institutions behave within foreign policy domains. It seeks to uncover why these institutions behave in a certain way and particularly the distinctive role of law in shaping their behaviour. To comprehend the interaction between law and policy within the complex landscapes of contemporary transnational law, Koh powerfully asserts, we need to move beyond the mere assertion that [EU] law matters. We rather need to trace 'how and why [EU] law matters in this brave new world'.[155]

[152] Kratochwil (n 37) 285, 288, 291.

[153] Middelaar (n 8): 'Classic American history is at heart a morality play of right versus might. Russia's is a cynical chronicle of might versus might. China's is a well-arranged harmony. European history has given us a tragic awareness that politics very often is right versus right – peace versus justice, equality versus safety, liberty versus democracy. We Europeans do not play to win but to minimize losses.'

[154] Letto-Vanamo, in this book, stressing that 'what also needs to be studied, in spite of practical and methodological difficulties, are local conditions (social, cultural, geographic) under which the process of cultural translation and thus localisation of potentially global normative knowledge has been or could be reproduced'. For concrete illustrations on why this approach is relevant and how to pursue it, see also M Goodale and SE Merry (eds), *The Practice of Human Rights: Tracking Law between the Global and the Local* (Cambridge, Cambridge University Press, 2007).

[155] HH Koh, 'Transnational Legal Process and the "New" New Haven School of International Law' in JL Dunoff and MA Pollack (eds), *International Legal Theory* (Cambridge, Cambridge University Press, 2022) 115–18: explaining how this 'idea of normativity connects the Transnational Legal Process School to the "Constructivist" School of international relations. Unlike interest theorists, who tend to treat state

This points to the importance of supplementing ubiquitous calls for proceduralisation or establishing a transparent regulatory quality framework for considering the interests of foreign communities, countries, or regions in the external dimension of EU law. The basic proposition of process jurisprudence that regards law as a process of authoritative decision-making rather than a mere set of abstract rules suggests and has eloquently shown that not everything is decided when a certain EU legal act or decision is issued. Much more remains at stake and can be gained through careful socio-legal research on the social, economic and political context of the legal act, as well as concurrent regulatory initiatives, or their respective implementation and enforcement avenues, as it is in any of these instances through which significant policy choices, reformist drives, or modes of resistance towards a given decision can also be channelled.[156] A research agenda on European transnational private law informed by the jurisprudence of process tradition can thus open new avenues of qualitative socio-legal research beyond merely generalist appeals to enhancing the reflexivity, responsiveness, or discursiveness of EU legal acts through their proceduralisation. It is key for these purposes to conceive the foreign reach of EU law as a dynamic and open-ended process that unfolds in a transnational context.[157]

These insights directly correlate with the pragmatic visions of legality that have been informing the jurisprudence of process since its origins. As explained in section II, these visions sought to overcome a purely formalistic and purely realistic view of law as a set of primary rules backed by sanctions, by highlighting how modern legal systems usually involve processes of authoritative decision-making driven by policy mandates that are continuously implemented, reshaped, and resisted throughout recursive and multipolar cycles that involve different types of actors and institutions. The vision of law implicit in these processes is the legal pragmatism underpinning the post-war synthesis of legal formalism and legal realism, which sees law and legal developments as inherently connected to the practical resolution of social problems. As elaborated in section II, this is the vision that provided the intellectual background in which Jessup articulated the very notion of transnational law in his landmark Stork Lectures of 1956.

Drawing inspiration from Jessup and his current legacies in contemporary developments on transnational law and transnational legal studies, throughout studies on European transnational legal processes one can finally seek to retrieve this seminal motivation by asking: what are the social needs that EU law is seeking to safeguard

interests as exogenously given, constructivists have long argued that states and their interests are socially constructed […].'

[156] J Black, 'Critical Reflections on Regulation' (2002) 27 *Australian Journal of Legal Philosophy* 1; Eskridge (n 28); SF Moore, *Law as Process: An Anthropological Approach* [1978] (LIT Verlag Münster, 2000).

[157] P Zumbansen, 'Can Transnational Law be Critical? Reflections on a Contested Idea, Field and Method' in E Christodoulidis, R Dukes and M Goldoni (eds), *Research Handbook on Critical Legal Theory* (Cheltenham, Edward Elgar Publishing, 2019): 'Transnational law challenges the possibility of [legal] coherence by scrutinising the dynamics at the heart of a legal field. The law with which we engage in this space of self-critique is never complete or "finished". Rather, as legal "field", it is an unstable ground on which competing claims are negotiated with regard to values, societal expectations, doctrinal coherence and "system" as well as the field's openness to future challenges. Seen that way, a legal field prompts an inquiry also into the process through which we reengage with what law is, should be, can be.'

throughout this range of voyages beyond its internal market? Chapter 14 by Salminen, Rajavuori, and Eller, for example, highlights the interplay between free commerce and geo-security as cutting across the three types of regulatory approaches to value chains informing the varied EU initiatives. Chapter 13 by Ulfbeck places the focus on evolving conventions on social and environmental sustainability beyond EU frontiers as driving recent developments in European (regulatory) tort law.

Why is this relevant? On the one hand, this renewed functional dimension enables us to consider legal/regulatory effectiveness an additional parameter for assessment, which in turn opens a series of relevant questions. Is the EU effectively fulfilling the purported social needs that it claims to safeguard in its external dimension? To what extent may other regulatory approaches or strategies be better suited for doing so? Are these social needs something that the EU ought to fulfil? Who is winning and who is losing as a result of these foreign regulatory engagements? Some of these questions have been raised by several contributors to this volume. Beckers, for instance, closes chapter two by stressing how a research agenda on European transnational private law requires a 'complementary analysis from the perspective of those affected together with a related discussion on what European transnational private law means from the outside'. Chadwick likewise in chapter nine provocatively highlights how EU law has become the agent of financial markets driven by the interests of capital.[158] All these questions relate to the social basis/impact of law that is one of the hallmarks of the jurisprudence of process.

Nevertheless, through studies of European transnational private law one can seek to cast normative questions wider by extending them from material to cultural implications. As to this cultural dimension, a key question is whether and to what extent the external dimension of EU private law is affecting core notions of private law and overall private law cultures of foreign countries or regions. Hans Micklitz has addressed this question in the internal dimension concerning the relationship between EU private law and the private law institutions and cultures of its Member States.[159] In connection with the FiDiPro project, this analysis of the extension of EU private law's 'visible hand' beyond EU frontiers has been gradually taken to certain foreign countries or regions, such as EU neighbouring countries,[160] parts of Asia,[161] Africa,[162] and Latin America.[163] Nevertheless, these are still relatively specific accounts, focused on certain market relations (B2C) or legal institutions (the ECJ). The present volume has significantly expanded this research scope by focusing on other types of institutions, such as EU administrative agencies (Micklitz), EU legislation (Salminen, Rajavuori,

[158] Chadwick, in this book: 'EU law is not governing financial markets; EU law (and policy) is *on the market*.'.

[159] See, in general, Micklitz (n 100); and HW Micklitz, 'The Visible Hand of European Regulatory Private Law – The Transformation of European Private Law from Autonomy to Functionalism in Competition and Regulation' (2009) 28 *Yearbook of European Law* 3.

[160] Reich and Micklitz (n 135).

[161] M Durovic, G Howells A Janssen, HW Micklitz (eds), *Consumer Protection in Asia: Past Present Future*, (Oxford, Hart Publishing, 2022).

[162] HW Micklitz, T Naude and C Twigg-Flesner (eds), 'Special Issue on Consumer Law and Policy in Africa' (2018) 41 *Journal of Consumer Policy* 303.

[163] M Barata, L Bernstein, C Lima Marques and HW Micklitz (eds),'Special Issue Consumer Law in South America' (2022) 45 *Journal of Consumer Policy* 1–147. See also, in general, chapter 8 by Micklitz in this book on the external dimension of EU consumer law.

and Eller), or private regulators (Chadwick), as well as other types of market relations, such as labour (Liukkunen), creditors (Macacci), and suppliers or affected communities (Ulfbeck). Nevertheless, much more terrain remains to be covered and appraised to fully reckon with the cultural effects of European transnational private law.[164]

IV. THE PROSPECTS OF A EUROPEAN TRANSNATIONAL PRIVATE LAW: GEOPOLITICS AND POST-COLONIAL ENCOUNTERS BETWEEN GOVERNANCE AND GOVERNMENTALITIES

To what extent, if at all, can the jurisprudence of process distinctively sustain (that is, justify and orient) current and future enquiries on the external dimension of EU law through the notion of European transnational private law? In its foundational aspiration, this has been the research question driving the present chapter. To answer this question, the chapter started by reviewing the basic tenets of the jurisprudence of process tradition through recollective engagement with some of its pioneering formulations in the national, international, and transnational levels and discussed its foundational place and role in the constructivist configuration and evolution of the EU as a political project. On these bases, the chapter underscored at least three distinctive contributions that the jurisprudence of process makes as a foundation for the study of the foreign reach of EU law as a phenomenon.

Building upon the seminal scholarship of Bradford and Scott, as well as other legal and non-legal studies on the phenomenon, the chapter first underscored the importance of transiting from an international relations paradigm driven by a public law rationale that is predominant in the literature to a transnational relations paradigm that also encompasses and critically reflects upon the constitutive place of private law in terms of global or foreign market orders and the socio-political relations underpinning them. This retrieves some of the jurisprudence of process insights on the constitutive place of law and connects the jurisprudence of process framework with earlier insights from institutional accounts of law and contemporary studies on law and political economy in national and transnational governance.

The second contribution was an expanded taxonomy of the different modes through which EU private law is travelling beyond EU frontiers by drawing upon the socio-legal purview of legal sources informing the jurisprudence of process tradition and contemporary developments of comparative law as a twin sister of transnational law. These include salient 'societal' and 'collateral' modalities, as well as refined accounts of the nowadays established 'unilateral,' 'bilateral', and 'multilateral' modes of foreign reach of EU law. As shown in section III.B, this renewed taxonomy

[164] In this vein, see the illuminating work that Julian Arato has been engaged in with a similar kind of examination from the perspective of international investment law, by analysing and appraising how international investment law has been transforming key private law institutions throughout the globe. See mainly J Arato, 'The Private Law Critique of International Investment Law' (2019) 113 *American Journal of International Law* 1; J Arato, 'The Elastic Corporate Form in International Law' (2021) 62 *Virginia Journal of International Law* 383; and J Arato, K Claussen, JmLee, and G Zarra, 'Reforming Shareholder Claims in Investor-State Dispute Settlement' (2023) 14 *Journal of International Dispute Settlement* 242.

contributes to expanding and nuancing the study of each of these modalities through which EU law is travelling beyond EU frontiers as well as their relationships.

Drawing upon the pragmatic, contextual, and purposive tenets of process jurisprudence, the chapter finally suggested the importance of innovating on the way European transnational legal processes are studied in at least three specific ways. Against the tendency of the literature to devise an abstract and ready-made normative parameter from which to assess the practice – whether it is 'welfare', 'legitimacy', 'justice', 'constitutionalism', or 'good governance' – the chapter first underscored the importance of pragmatically analysing how these normative commitments or other values are constructed, contested, and ultimately rearticulated or 'cared-for' (*Aufgaben*) by the relevant participants in practices within the respective contexts and non-ideal conditions in which they are operating. Second, the chapter suggested the importance of extending the focus beyond ubiquitous appeals to the proceduralisation of EU rulemaking and an expanded EU regulatory quality assessment to integrate foreign interests and perspectives in the foreign reach of EU law to the overall legal or regulatory processes involved. In this vein, the chapter underscored how tracing and fostering different venues of legal interpretation and mechanisms for the internalisation of these interpretations at all stages of the regulatory process can contribute to generating the sort of transnational legal normativity by the foreign reach of EU law with the principles or normative aspirations that purportedly guide them. This entails moving from the relatively trivial assertion that EU law matters abroad to a more refined and tangible understanding of how and why EU law matters throughout the world.

Lastly, and as a complement to the tendency in the literature to focus on questions of reciprocal policy influence between the EU and other international players, the chapter stressed the relevance of tackling contentious questions regarding regulatory effectiveness as well as the material and cultural implications of the foreign reach of EU law in different socio-economic realms. The chapter drew upon several of the chapters in this volume and other literature on the phenomenon, including the seminal works by Bradford and Scott, to illustrate the relevance of each of these points. If the EU's recent geopolitical awakening, as van Middelaar has argued, is indeed marked by a 'post-pax Americana' that conveys a new 'age of encounters with other great powers, and civilisations that demands pluralistic thinking', the present chapter shows that the process tradition is particularly suited for that style of pluralistic thinking through its recollective engagement with the origins of the jurisprudence of process in national and post-national contexts as well as its interventions in contemporary studies on the foreign reach of EU law. In synthesis, the present chapter has shown that, as a post-formalist and post-realist account of law and legal thinking, which emerged as part of the inter-institutional dynamics of lawmaking and implementation within highly pluralistic contexts within and beyond the state, the jurisprudence of process has the capacity to productively guide current and future studies on European transnational private law through its pragmatic, socio-legal, contextual, purposive, and constitutive purview or analytical apparatus.

Yet the chapter has also underscored some of the blind spots or limitations of the jurisprudence of process. One is ingrained in the very notion of transnational law as a manifestation of the jurisprudence of process in the post-national context.

Although the volume has used the notion of transnational law to frame our enquiries and deliberately taken an EU perspective to understand and assess the role of EU private law outside the internal market, these relationships cannot be represented in a mere dualistic way as based on a sharp inside/outside binary. What the exponential development of transnational law and transnational legal studies has shown is that the contemporary legal landscape is more plausibly conceived through the image of a complex network with different 'nodes' or lawmaking institutions. This image signals that the notion of transnational law is productive for studying the foreign reach of EU law because it critically reminds us that these European transnational legal processes cannot be studied as a one-way street (that is, from the EU towards the outside), but requires multi-polar, pluralistic thinking rather than mere dualistic thinking.[165] Section III.B.iii offered several examples of perceived modes of the foreign reach of EU law that were the result of previous modes of foreign legal-political influence over Europe. The overall point is that in principle there is nothing wrong in appropriating a legal transplant, to the extent that this is a conscious and justified choice rather than a casual incorporation by perceived description.

A second blind spot is the inherent perspective of these judgements concerning the different modalities and desirability of the ways that EU law is travelling abroad. This entails that the purposive drive to pragmatically find novel, fairer ways to 'include the other' (Habermas) in European transnational legal processes also requires cultivating a reflective awareness that at times the proper way to include is by excluding others from these processes in order to preserve them in their otherness through modes of 'a-legality' (Lindahl). This hints at a certain irony underpinning the jurisprudential foundations of European transnational private law, as they would thereby inevitably rely to some extent upon post-foundational grounds.[166]

This reflective awareness is particularly relevant for the study of the encounters between EU law on those of foreign countries or regions, as these are prone to be politically charged encounters. This is not only due to the developmental strategies or distributive issues that may contingently be at stake. Even if grounded upon a pragmatic quest to construct geopolitical authority and enhance modes of socio-political enfranchisement or integration of foreign countries or regions with EU external policies, it is also because these encounters take place against the backdrop of long, deep, and pervasive histories of European colonialism that only recently are being duly unveiled, appraised, and recognised.[167] This new 'age of encounters with other

[165] G Shaffer, 'Transnational Legal Process and State Change' (2012) 37 *Law & Social Inquiry* 229. For an illustrative application, see J Lander, *Transnational Law and State Transformation: The Case of Extractive Development in Mongolia* (Berlin, Routledge, 2019).

[166] On contemporary developments of post-foundational political theory, see O Marchart, *Post-Foundational Political Thought: Political Difference in Nancy, Lefort, Badiou and Laclau* (Edinburgh, Edinburgh University Press, 2007); E Wingenbach, *Institutionalizing Agonistic Democracy: Post-Foundationalism and Political Liberalism* (Oxfordshire, Routledge, 2016); and F Wilhelm, *Political Difference and Global Normative Orders* (Berlin, Springer International Publishing, 2022).

[167] SR Larsen, 'European Public Law after Empires' (2022) 1 *European Law Open* 6; L Salaymeh and R Michaels, 'Decolonial Comparative Law: A Conceptual Beginning' (2022) 86 *Rabels Zeitschrift für ausländisches und internationales Privatrecht (RabelsZ)* 166. See also, for a broader retrospective, M Koskenniemi, *To the Uttermost Parts of the Earth: Legal Imagination and International Power 1300–1870* (Cambridge, Cambridge University Press, 2021).

great powers, and civilisations' (van Middelaar) is, in other words, almost inevitably an age of post-colonial encounters, which brings a distinctive level of gravitation and responsibility for whoever claims to be authoritatively speaking in the name of 'Europe' on a comparative or global stage.[168]

Critique does not need to decay into political cynicism but may render a refreshing and creative awakening in the search for a renewed *raison d'être* for the EU beyond its frontiers (De Burca). As this chapter has shown, studying the external dimension of EU law through the pragmatic, socio-legal, contextual, purposive, and constitutive analytical cornerstones informing the jurisprudence of process can significantly contribute to this renewed awakening. Yet this quest for *telos*-building also requires complementing the prevalent focus on EU transnational *governance* and its reflexive, experimental features through process and proceduralisation with an eagerness to explore how, at the same time, this 'new governance mode of foreign policy'[169] translates into different EU transnational *governmentalities* within diverse socio-economic sectors. This can be done through granular attention to the *dispositif* of instruments, technologies, mechanisms, discourses, and rationales informing these policy processes and the institutions underpinning them.[170]

Rather than a theory or method, governmentality is better conceived as an analytical toolbox driven by a distinctive set of questions regarding these *dispositifs* of governing that are 'amenable to precise answers through empirical inquiry'.[171] As an analytical approach that equips us to understand law and governance beyond inter-institutional dynamics of power and authority, governmentality in this sense is a suitable and valuable complement to the jurisprudence of process framework to scrutinise the pathways and implications of EU law beyond its frontiers. In contrast to the jurisprudence of process, what governmentality adds to the picture is a distinctive focus on [EU] transnational governance 'as an eminently practical activity that can be studied, historicised and specified at the level of the rationalities, programmes, techniques and subjectivities which underpin it and give it form and effect'.[172] This elicits a productive way to critically discover refreshing insights in the quest for a renewed *raison d'être* in at least three distinctive ways.

The first way is through the potential configuration of new cartographies of power. One of the distinctive features of governmentality is its capacity to trace and engage with modes of political power beyond institutionalised politics or institutionalised

[168] P Singh, 'The Private Life of Transnational Law: Reading Jessup from the Post-Colony' in P Zumbansen (ed), *The Many Lives of Transnational Law: Critical Engagements with Jessup's Bold Proposal* (Cambridge, Cambridge University Press, 2020).

[169] De Burca, 'EU External Relations (n 17); J Zeitlin (ed), *Extending Experimentalist Governance?: The European Union and Transnational Regulation* (Oxford, Oxford University Press, 2015); M Dawson, 'New Governance in the EU after the Euro Crisis – Retired or Reborn?' in M Cremona and C Kilpatrick (eds), *EU Legal Acts: Challenges and Transformations* (Oxford, Oxford University Press, 2018).

[170] For an overview, see M Foucault, *The Birth of Biopolitics: Lectures at the Collège de France, 1978-1979* (Palgrave Macmillan, 2008); and T Lemke, *Foucault's Analysis of Modern Governmentality: A Critique of Political Reason* [1997] (Brooklyn, Verso Books, 2019).

[171] N Rose, PO'Malley, and M Valverde, 'Governmentality' (2006) 2 *Annual Review of Law and Social Science* 83, 85.

[172] W Walters, *Governmentality: Critical Encounters* (Oxfordshire, Routledge, 2012) 2.

governance. This is particularly relevant for a research agenda on European transnational private law where much of EU policymaking is being shaped and mediated through prominent private actors and civil society institutions, as well as non-binding instruments or unofficial practices – as the present volume documents. This readily places the foreign reach of European private law within studies of international governmentality that have proven proficient in generating novel purviews of the types of power games and overarching strategies informing these undercurrents of contemporary geopolitics on several socio-economic realms.[173]

The second way is through its creative, refreshing potential. Rather than fulfilling an explanatory or predictive aim, as an analytical toolbox the function of governmentality is mainly diagnostic. With its microscopic attention to governmental practices within and beyond government, governmentality is:

> highly capable of registering all manner of subtle (and not so subtle) shifts in the rationalities, technologies, strategies and identities of governance – shifts that are often overlooked or dismissed by perspectives that focus all their theoretical attention on the so-called bigger picture.[174]

Due to this attention to granular discursive/material practices rather than on particular agents or totalising structures, and its sensibility towards subjugated alternatives driven by its genealogical engagement with the historiographies of these practices, the analytical tools of governmentality are prone to confront us with unexpected insights that may 'prompt us to revise and amend existing concepts, fashion new analytical tools' and, in general, 'open up new ways of understanding social and political problems'.[175]

The third and final way is through its reconstructive, identity-building prospects. Foucault's governmentality shares with the jurisprudence of process tradition its drive for seeking to reconcile some key dualities as a matter of lived experience, such as: structure/transformation, background/transcendence, and object/objective. Similar to the emphasis of the jurisprudence of process on historiographical dynamics based on socio-political struggles, Foucault devises in this way an experiential mode of socio-political critique.[176] This suggests how governmentality complements the jurisprudence of process in proposing a 'critical ontology of ourselves' that can be key for renewed modes of identity-building and socio-political emancipation in the EU's relentless search for itself beyond its frontiers.[177]

[173] S Guzzini and IB Neumann (eds), *The Diffusion of Power in Global Governance: International Political Economy Meets Foucault* (New York, Palgrave Macmillan, 2012).

[174] Walters (n 172) 3.

[175] ibid 5 and chapter 4; and M Dean, *Governmentality: Power and Rule in Modern Society* (SAGE, 2010) ch 2. In this vein, see also, A Orford, 'In Praise of Description' (2012) 25 *Leiden Journal of International Law* 609.

[176] T Lemke, 'Critique and Experience in Foucault' (2011) 28 *Theory, Culture & Society* 26; T Lemke, *Foucault, Governmentality, and Critique* (Paradigm Publishing, 2012).

[177] '... the concept of governmentality is animated by this critical ethos: it is concerned to make intelligible the limits and potentials of who we are and have become, and the ways our understanding of ourselves is linked to the ways in which we are governed, the ways in which we try to govern ourselves and others, and the ways in which this occurs under forms of knowledge postulated as truth by various authorities. By becoming clear about the limits, we open up the possibility of an action to accept or reject them,

Against the temptation of reductively characterising the foreign reach of EU law as *this* or *that*, this book and the notion of European transnational private law informing it shows how complex yet pervasive is the engagement of EU private law alongside transnational policy processes that coalesce from and towards the EU. It also shows how heterogeneous are the place, role, and impacts of EU private law within this range of policy fields. The use of the jurisprudence of process as a framework and governmentality as a toolbox to trace and analyse these and other places or roles of EU private law 'in action' represent in this sense at least two complementary avenues for the progressive development of European transnational private law as a field of study and as a roadmap for searching and instilling tactical interventions within these modes of transnational legal ordering as a matter of practical lawyering.

to show their contingent nature, or to add up the costs of transgressing them. Above all, the point of a critical ontology of ourselves and our present is to make us clear on these risks and dangers, these benefits and opportunities, so that we might take or decline to take action'. Dean (n 175) 14. On this reflective and reconstructivist aspect concerning the foreign reach of EU private law, see R Vallejo, 'Voyaging Through Standards, Contracts, and Codes: the Transnational Quest of European Regulatory Private Law' in Cantero and Micklitz (n 45).

Legal History

5

The European and the Transnational in Historical Perspective

PIA LETTO-VANAMO*

I. INTRODUCTION: TRANSBORDER LEGAL HISTORIES

LAW WITHOUT THE state belongs to the main objects of scholarship in legal history. Not only medieval and so-called pre-modern local law (often labelled as Indigenous law) but also universal or transborder normative systems, such as Roman law and Canon law, have been studied intensively. Characteristic of these studies have been a European positionality and a quite homogenous concept of law. Since the early 2010s, however, global approaches and new perspectives have been advocated towards transnational legal histories. At the same time, the old narratives (histories), focusing on the birth of the idea – or ideal type – of law as rational, secular, and formal/positive, or seeing legal history as the history of the scientification (*Verwissenschaftlichung*) of law have been questioned. At least, rethinking has been proposed. This also concerns methodologies to reconstruct transnational legal formations.

Still, two main (interconnective) histories remain dominant. The first – inspired by the ideas of Max Weber and also playing an important role in legal theory – is that of the emergence or triumph of so-called modern law. This is referred to especially in discussions of the rationale as well as of the validity and legitimacy of European legal order(s), as well as in discussions on the autonomy of legal norms. Thus, the highpoint of modernisation is the law of the nation state, with parliamentary legislation standing at the top of the hierarchy of legal sources. The other main narrative is better than the former, embedded in debates of transnational law, but also facing problems, for instance geographical restrictions. It has also been popular among private law scholars arguing for academic bottom-up proposals for harmonisation of current

* Professor emirata, Faculty of Law, University of Helsinki.

European (Union) law, or for the concept of transnational European law.[1] This is the history about the emergence of the medieval universities and of so-called 'learned law' in Europe. At the centre is the reception of Roman law as a unifying element of European private law systems, especially in the era of the so-called Roman-Canon *ius commune* (mainly twelfth to fifteenth centuries). Some scholars, however, also refer to the importance of the 'second reception' – that of Roman-German legal scholarship (especially the so-called Pandectists) of the nineteenth century.

The first history understates the role of legal scholarship, the substantial continuities in modern private law systems based on the impact of former legal doctrine. Indeed, the landmarks of national legislation, especially the civil law codifications of the nineteenth and twentieth centuries, were drafted by a trained elite, and to a great extent based on legal concepts, classifications, and ideas of previous centuries.[2] The second narrative, too, faces problems. Europe is identified foremost as the reception area of Roman private law and described as a historical combination of Romanic and Germanic elements.[3] At the same time, the concept of Europe is restricted to its Western parts alone, thus never really acknowledging Northern and Eastern Europe. Moreover, one has to remember that several variations existed of the *ius commune*, and several ways and grades of Roman-law influence on legal orders or on judicial argumentation or on legal scholarship. Yet, in European harmonisation projects, references to the Roman *ius commune* narrative easily lead to disregard of the fact that EU private law as transnational legal normativity is more often about regulation of specific economic sectors – for instance, banking or energy – than about classic private-law areas.[4]

American comparative law scholar Harold Berman, however, recalls the Europe of Roman law, and substitutes Roman law with another transborder legal system: Canon law. His focus is mainly on late medieval history, and on the history of European public law, which was influenced by medieval Canonists.[5] Berman gains the support of scholars who accept Canon law as the first 'common law' of Europe. However, this has been questioned by Reinhard Zimmermann, a Roman and comparative law scholar, and the former director of the Max Planck Institute of Comparative and

[1] See an interesting contribution to the discussion: N Jansen, *The Making of Legal Authority. Non-Legislative Codifications in Historical and Comparative Perspective* (Oxford, Oxford University Press, 2010).

[2] M Jansen and R Michaels, 'Private Law and the State: Comparative Perceptions and Historic Observations' (2007) 71 *Rabels Zeitschrift für ausländisches und internationales Privatrecht* 345–97; see also K Luig, 'Die Kontinuität allgemeiner Rechtsgrundsätze. Das Beispiel der clausula rebus sic stantibus' in R Zimmermannn (ed), *Rechtsgeshichte und Privatrechtsdogmatik* (Erlangen, Müller Verlag, 1999).

[3] It relies on the old Romanist approach of Paul Koschaker and his followers. See esp P Koschaker, *Europa und das römische Recht* (Tübingen, Mohr Siebeck, 1947); F Wieacker, *A History of Private Law in Europe* (Oxford, Clarendon Press, 1966) and P Grossi, *A History of European Law* (Hoboken/NJ, Wiley-Blackwell, 2010); see also, and esp the chapter on 'Europe of Helmut Coing'; T Duve, 'Von der Europäischen Rechtsgeschichte zu einer Rechtsgeschichte Europas in globalhistorischer Perspektive' (2012) *Rechtsgeschichte Legal History* 18–59 and K Tuori and H Björklund, 'Introduction', in Kaius Tuori and H Björklund (eds), *Roman Law and the Idea of Europe* (London, Bloomsbury Academic, 2019).

[4] See HW Micklitz in chapter 8 of this book.

[5] H Berman, *Law and Revolution* (Cambridge/Mass, Harvard University Press, 1983); see also T Giaro, 'The East of the West, H J Berman and Eastern Europe' (2013) *Rechtsgeschichte Legal History* 193–97.

Private Law in Hamburg, who objects that the medieval popes could not have been successful in their creation of Canon law, and in the reorganisation of the world, had they not been able to resort to Roman law.[6] According to Berman, 'Western legal tradition' emerged during the late Middle Ages as a transnational legal culture, which was pluralistic, but essentially based upon Canon law. In any case, Canon law was the law of all the faithful regardless of their citizenship, nationality, or subjection to any other centre of power (domination). In modern terms, Canon law was the first transnational law in history. It was a supra-territorial system and also had an impact on contract law – arguing for freedom of contract and launching the principle of *pacta sunt servanda* applicable to all agreements. At the same time, it was a system to make use of many instruments of legal communication (recommendations, advice of counsel, *concilia*, and the like), which today would be considered typical elements of transnational soft law.[7] Berman's concept of Western legal tradition also includes the Common Law of England: Both systems were influenced by values of Christian morality as well as by such legal institutions as self-government or personal rights. How much substantive legal unity vanished because of the Reformation and Counter-Reformation is still debated among legal historians today.

In the following, both the Weberian and Romanist histories are 'respected'. However, for analysis of the history of (European) transnational law, their (at least geographically) updated versions are needed. Furthermore, Weber's idea of domination (*Herrschaft*) is of importance in studies of history of non-state law. For instance, in analysis of medieval legal pluralism the idea of many centres of domination (city councils, the Catholic Church, and so on) is very useful. Hence, one may argue that the medieval legal system was a combination – or a multi-layered network – of several normative orders, based on different sources of domination. Law was status-based, with different legal rules applied simultaneously in one geographical area. People were subject to the local statutes of their city or to the customs and laws of the place where they lived. In addition, noblemen were subject to feudal law and privileges, while peasants could be subject to manorial law. Many artisans had to obey the local customs and statutes of their guilds. Merchants did international business according to a supposedly universal *lex mercatoria*.[8] At the same time, everybody was subject to the universal Canon law.

My methodological inspirations, however, are mainly taken from the global approach advocated by Thomas Duve, who (at the time of writing, spring 2023) is director of the Max Planck Institute of Legal History and Legal Theory in Frankfurt am Main. In particular, his ideas of multi-normativity and cultural translation of

[6] R Zimmermann, 'Das römisch-kanonische ius commune als Grundlage europäischer Rechtseinheit' (1992) *Juristenzeitung* 8–20.

[7] See further T Giaro, 'Medieval Canon Lawyers and European Legal Tradition. A Brief Overview' (2021) *Review of European and Comparative Law* 157–87.

[8] On debates of the medieval *lex mercatoria*, see, eg, A Cordes, 'Auf der Suche nach der Rechtswirklichkeit der mittelalterlichen Lex mercatoria' (2001) *Zeitschrift der Savigny-Stiftung für Rechtsgeschichte: Germanistische Abteilung* 168–84; see also A Cordes, 'Lex maritima? Local, Regional and Universal Maritime Law in the Middle Ages' in W Blockmans, M Krom and J Wubs-Mrozewicz (eds), *The Routledge Handbook of Maritime Trade around Europe 1300–1600: Commercial Networks and Urban Autonomy* (London, Routledge, 2017) 69–85.

normative knowledge (of different epistemic communities) are opening new horizons to studies of transnational law, in terms of both its history and its future developments.[9] As argued by Duve, the global approach also might help to explain the present world order, with its globalisations and fragmentations of legal regimes, and with the presence of a polysemic and seemingly universal language of law, deeply shaped by power asymmetries. It might also raise awareness of law as a tool and part of the historical process of globalisation in all its ambivalences.[10]

II. FROM THE EUROCENTRISM TO A GLOBAL PERSPECTIVE

A. Deconstructing the Old Histories

Duve would like to deconstruct the grand narratives with an effort to be free from the traditional European position and situate European legal history in a global perspective. Thus, the aim is to de-centre and de-Europeanise legal historiography, at the same time emancipating legal history from the conceptual heritage of nineteenth- and twentieth-century European scholarship. As a result, national legal histories may also be seen in a broader framework, with Europe as a global region, interconnected with other areas.[11] For instance, the period of nation-building in Europe was a period of globalisation of law and legal thought: The main monuments of nation-building – codifications and constitutions – were parts of legal communication with a global dimension. With increasing international trade and communication, not least with European colonialism and legal imperialism and the considerable growth of academia, (ideas of) codes and constitutions from different parts of the world circulated and were translated, literally and culturally, into each national reality.

A wider perspective, however, has demonstrated that the internationalisation of law and legal scholarship led to what has been called the 'Europeanisation of the world'. Consequently, studies of the reception of European law and references to expert cultures and elite networks have dominated – for instance – scholarship of Latin American and Asian legal history. Formerly colonised countries have written their legal histories mainly in terms of a pre-history to their inclusion in a colonial empire. Only few studies of legal history of Latin America exist that include a substantial portion of the legal past before European colonisation. Furthermore, 'how cultural translation of the knowledge'[12] acquired from Europe took place in judicial or everyday practices, and what adaptations and transformations occurred in

[9] See esp T Duve, 'Rechtsgeschichte als Geschichte von Normativitätswissen' (2021) *Rechtsgeschichte Legal History*, 41–68, and T Duve, 'What is Global Legal History' (2020) *Comparative Legal History* 73–115.

[10] Duve, *Comparative Legal History* (n 9) 96.

[11] However, a 'global perspective' could require even more. According to Duve, for instance, a global perspective on the history of early modern colonial Hispanic American law would not only have to integrate the Americas into larger spatial contexts, including Europe, Asia and Africa, but it would also have to integrate the colonial period into a larger narrative of local and imperial legal histories of Indigenous peoples or of other social groups; Duve, *Comparative Legal History* (n 9) 103.

[12] Terminology by Duve.

the process of 'translating knowledge' and, above all, what role transplanted law had, has remained mostly in the dark.

Today, a new field of legal history with transnational scope is emerging, especially in southern Europe (Spain, Portugal) and in Anglo-American academia, often starting from an interest in their own colonial past.[13] In addition, the Max Planck Institute is hosting several research projects with global / transnational focus.[14] As a result, histories are being written of the process of trans-nationalisation and globalisation of law – overcoming national perspectives.[15] Their aim is to argue, similarly to Duve, for decentring and decolonising legal historiography and for overcoming the Eurocentrism embedded in academic concepts, practices, and institutional frameworks of legal history. Especially interesting – but highly challenging – are projects where local histories, such as the legal history of Angola or Cape Verde, former Portuguese colonies, are studied from a global perspective.[16]

Two major dimensions of global legal history can be distinguished: a legal history in a global historical perspective, and a global legal history as a history of the globalisation of law. The first of these is based on a deconstructive approach, while the second is based on a reconstructive approach. For studies of foundations of transnational law, the reconstructive approach is worthy of note. Hence, in historical analysis of the formation of legal regimes on a larger spatial scale, the role of communication – that is, reconstruction of various spaces of communication – shaped by transnational epistemic communities or resulting from formal or informal 'empires', are central.

Looking at the research tradition, one can observe that the processes of globalisation or trans-nationalisation of law are often described through ideas of circulation of thoughts, legal transplants, or transfers. Furthermore, comparative studies have highlighted the consequences of the processes of communication under Western 'legal imperialism'. In any case, European legal institutions, ideas, and methods have been important elements of political and economic expansion, integration, and globalisation. As noted, in the nineteenth and twentieth centuries codifications and constitutions were translated and integrated into different legal and political systems, thus contributing to mixing between different legal traditions. Religious expansion and missions, as well as economic integration and increasing (maritime, overseas, global) commerce and trade were the main drivers of entanglements and

[13] See, eg, AM Hespanha, 'Is There Place for a Separated Legal History? A Broad Review of Recent Developments on Legal Historiography' (2019) *Quaderni Fiorentini per la storia del pensiero giuridico moderno* 7–28. On the history of colonial law, see, eg, MS Bilder, *The Transatlantic Constitution: Colonial Legal Culture and the Empire* (Harvard, Harvard University Press, 2004).

[14] See, eg, the (joint) research project hosted by the Max Planck Institute, 'Glocalising Normativities. A Global Legal History (15th – 21st Century)', available at www.lhlt.mpg.de/joint-project/glocalising-normativities.

[15] eg, Japanese legal historians drew on German concepts to write Japanese legal history but are now developing their own analytical and comparative frameworks. After many decades of Eurocentric colonial historiography, South African legal history has been given a different interpretation by leaving the colonial perspective and putting it into a wider framework, see further Duve, *Comparative Legal History* (n 9) 95.

[16] See, eg, M Dias Paes, R Razente Sirotti, J de Matos Ngãla, M Espíndola Souza *Os processos judiciais e a escrita da história em África. Uma bibliografia* (2022) *Max Planck Institute for Legal History and Legal Theory Research Papers* 13.

unification on a global scale. According to Duve, at least since the eighteenth century there have been many indicators of the emergence of multiple and overlapping global legal regimes that gave rise to and shaped legal institutions. These legal regimes were based on economic, political, and religious expansion and/or they came with the new international organisations,[17] and thus were foundations for the emergence of 'a polysemic, highly heterogeneous not all-encompassing and not at all innocent' international language of law on a global scale.[18]

B. Towards New Methodologies

Even so, a global legal history with its own methodologies is missing. For the methodology, at least three key words may be fundamental: communication, multi-normativity, and 'glocalisation' – being useful in studies of foundations of transnational law more generally, too. The role of communication has been mentioned above. Multi-normativity refers mainly to multi-normative knowledge, not only to law, while global legal history (especially as the history of globalisation of law) is studied mainly as processes of knowledge production, understood as 'translation' of normative, theoretical, and practical knowledge on a global scale. At the same time, the challenge is to understand the interplay between the global and the local: the mechanisms of cultural reproduction between the global and the local, or as spelled out by Duve, the 'glocalisation' of normative knowledge. The term 'multi-normativity' or 'multi-normative knowledge' argues for widening the horizon[19] towards very different kinds of normative knowledge, seeing legal knowledge as a way of doing something with rules and cases and other legal materials. An earlier proposal for 'new horizons' of colonial legal history was put forward by Argentinian legal historian Victor Tau in 1997. He argued for a new methodology and the future orientation of Spanish colonial law, namely *derecho indiano*. This would mean going beyond legal norms and law as state hegemony and using a broader array of sources. The 'legalist' culture should be substituted by a 'juridical' culture, while the history of learned jurists and the circulation of (printed) books would be needed. As demonstrated later in this chapter, current comparative research has raised awareness of circulation of ideas and juridical practices and also helped place *derecho indiano* into a broader perspective.

Consequently, the object of a global legal history as a history of knowledge is all knowledge that influences the production of normativity as well as the results of this process itself – regardless of whether normative knowledge would be labelled as social norms, religious norms, legal norms, implicit or explicit knowledge of a

[17] On the history of international organisations see, eg, M Herren, 'Introduction: Towards a Global History of International Organizations' in M Herren (ed), *Networking the International System: Global Histories of International Organizations* (Basel, Springer, 2014) 1–12.

[18] Duve, *Comparative Legal History* (n 9) 99.

[19] V Tau Anzoátegui, *Nuevos horizontes en el estudio del derecho indiano* (Buenos Aires, Instituto de Investigaciones de Historia de estudios historico-jurídico, 1997).

theoretical or practical nature, or even of objects and artefacts or events to which normativity is ascribed. Yet, as a conceptual framework, multi-normativity refers to different modes of normativity. Not only theories need to be analysed but also different modes of practice performed by different epistemic communities (which are also communities of practice). For this, various sources – state and private – are useful. Finally, the relation between local and global sources needs to be studied. Thus, the term 'glocalisation' refers to the fact that production of normative knowledge happens with acts on a local level.[20] Even globally circulating knowledge must be localised. Hence, what is also to be studied are the local conditions under which cultural translation and thus localisation of potentially global normative knowledge is being reproduced, which challenges the legal historians to interdisciplinary and cross-disciplinary studies.

As examples of global legal histories, the history of Canon law and the history of international law[21] could easily be mentioned. As noted, Canon law studies have been labelled as studies of the formation of a transnational legal regime. According to Duve's theoretical approach, this regime was formed both by globalisation and by localisation of normative knowledge, and its translation into larger spaces and different legal cultures with contributions from various actors. At the same time, studies of the history of Canon law – as well as the history of international law – inform us about the formation of a common legal language, legal vocabulary, that enables communication between different legal cultures[22] and even makes up a universal code of legality.[23]

C. Understanding the Legal

What Duve proposes for global legal history is quite well suited to studies in European – even national or local – legal histories, too. Not only in (new) colonial law research but also in studies of medieval or so-called premodern law in Europe, the need is, crucially, to overcome a state-bound, legalistic notion of law, as well as for awareness of the complexity of the concept of law. This also concerns the foundations and current developments of trans-border or transnational law.

Indeed, a never-ending challenge to legal history is to understand the legal. A major part of daily life, even conflict resolution, in many spaces and times has not been regulated by legal norms stemming from state or secular authorities. It has rather been regulated by norms, institutions, and practices that European or Euro-American historiography considers to be 'social', or refers to as religion, as customs, or as traditions. Thus, to declare 'modern' European state-bound law as the main

[20] On 'glocalisation' of European consumer law, see HW Micklitz in chapter 8 of this book.

[21] See esp the role of the School of Salamanca that is integrated into a larger picture in T Duve, JL Egio Carcia and C Birr (eds), *The School of Salamanca. A Case of Global Knowledge Production* (Boston, Brill Nijhoff Leiden, 2021) 1–32.

[22] More generally on the historical and cultural dependence of the law's ratio, see Kaarlo Tuori, *Ratio and Voluntas. The Tension Between Reason and Will in Law* (London, Routledge, 2011).

[23] As an interesting contribution to the topic, see M Koskenniemi, *To the Uttermost Parts of The Earth. Legal Imagination and International Power 1300–1870* (Cambridge, Cambridge University Press, 2021).

reference point of legal history, and to operate with the dichotomy between law and non-law or not-yet-law, are quite the opposite of what is needed for a global legal history – and for topical and critical legal history in general. Furthermore, the idea of multi-normative knowledge (production) connected to ideas of communication within different epistemic communities and cultural translation are useful in analysis of transnational law and its role in the development of national / local legal systems.

As an example, discussions about the characteristics of so-called (European) customary law or legal customs – that is, norms not obtaining their validity from the state or any source of higher authority – are worthy of mention.[24] This may highlight the methodological and practical challenges also faced in global legal history with the idea of multi-normativity. It is not easy to find the 'legal' and the 'global' in local sources of practices, for example in former European colonies in Africa, stemming from times prior to colonisation.

As is known, researching history is closely connected with interpretation. When historians try to understand, try 'to do right by' the object of their research – the ideas and institutions of the past – and interpret it, at the same time they argue for that interpretation. The same easily concerns comparative law scholars interested in foreign legal systems. Interesting ideas on this can be found in *Rechtsgeschichte als Kunstprodukt. Zur Entbehrlichkeit von 'Begriff' und 'Tatsache'* by German legal historian and the former Director of the Frankfurt Max Planck Institute, Michael Stolleis.[25] According to Stolleis, by engaging in linguistic analysis legal historians are doing 'translations' as they try to understand how certain legal terms have been used in a foreign context. At the same time, when we explain the meaning of an expression, we translate it. However, operating with legal concepts (eg ownership) can easily lead to misunderstandings if one assumes that above legal sources stands a supra-historical level to which linguistic findings belong. This is especially a danger when studying legal phenomena. Legal language is bound by tradition; it changes slowly and is even resistant to changes. Too easily legal historians, who are usually educated in law, are led to believe that they can identify in old (foreign) texts phenomena that are familiar to them from the current (own) legal system. Too quickly meanings of past circumstances are changed into current ones, and seemingly similar legal problems are defined ineptly with identical concepts. At the same time, it is quite impossible to discuss, for instance, dispute settlement without using legal concepts and terminology (vocabulary), current and former ones, since they are links to professional discussions about law.

[24] See especially M Pilch, *Der Rahmen der Rechtsgewohnheiten. Kritik des Normensystemdenkens entwickelt am Rechtsbegriff der mittelalterlichen Rechtsgeschichte* (Wien, Böhlau, 2009); J Weitzel, 'Ein zweiter Paradigmenwechsel?' (2010) *Rechtsgeschichte Legal History* 62–66; K Kroeschell, 'Rechtsgewohnheiten' – und wie es dazu kam' (2010) *Rechtgeschichte Legal History* 58–61; see also P Letto-Vanamo, 'Dispute, Procedure and Sanction: Some Remarks on Dispute Settlement in Swedish Medieval Laws' (2013) *Law and Disputing in the Middle Ages: Proceedings of the 9th Carlsberg Academy Conference on Medieval Legal History* 155–64.

[25] M Stolleis, Würzburger Vorträge zur Rechtsphilosophie, Rechtstheorie und Rechtssoziologie 22 (Baden-Baden, Nomos Verlag, 1997).

To speak about interpretation is almost impossible without touching upon problems concerning language, also being at the centre of 'the new legal history'. In any case, it is well known that language has both a present-day and a long-term function. It is a tool of daily communication and a tool of cultural accumulation. Today, legal language is a special, professional, and very often a specialist-to-specialist language. However, legal language emerged before the legal profession was born. It is possible to speak of the 'language of legal life', which can be understood as a functional language connected not only to the typical content but also to the typical functions and practices of the legal domain. More generally, legal language is bound to special ways of acting and to formal positions.[26]

Often, terms relating to the field of procedural law are older than those of substantive law. Procedures, rituals and forms have played an important role in the understanding of law; different communities perform different modes of practice reflecting their norms, or in terms of Duve, normative knowledge. Indeed, it can be argued that law – opinion or consensus about the 'right law' in the case concerned – emerged through 'court' procedures. Moreover, early law emerged mainly through practices of local communities rather than through binding precedents or legislation in the modern sense. Thus, the law did not always mean stated/given law. We can talk of law that was factually applied; law also could be *mos*, *ritus*, or *usus*. Hence, customary or Indigenous law is impossible to characterise by reference to a modern system of abstract norms. Again, the early judgment can be labelled mainly as procedural.[27] It did not find or create any substantive legal condition, but it confirmed how to proceed further, for example, that the accused should swear an oath. At the same time, the difference between norm and fact was small. No authoritative norms as such forced parties to behave in a certain way.

Still, the question remains: how could early law be broken if substantive norms did not exist? My answer would be that although early judgments did not mention anything about substantive norms, this does not imply an absence of ideas about law – they might be also called normativity or normativities. Even pure proof-decision relied on ideas about what one could do and in what circumstances. Thus, it is possible to understand many procedures in customary/Indigenous law as a special type of substantive law (norms) with procedural functions. Hence, we can assume that substantive issues were also discussed during early 'court' sessions. Still, it was uncertain which opinion on the substance of law then *in concreto* became the norm in an individual case.

Anyhow, the most crucial question is how law or opinions on law could be ascertained – and even more, how they can be found in Indigenous sources. People's thinking was concrete and depended on oral communication. This also concerns dispute settlement, discussions on law. Legal communication happened in places where law was dispensed, and the aim was that lost consensus should be recovered

[26] This can be seen, eg, in the terms (in German) *Rechtssprechung* or (in Swedish) *rättegång*. Similarly, in the German and Swedish languages, law (*Recht, rätt*), means right (*richtig, riktig*), but *rätt* was and is also synonymous with the word 'court' (in German, *Gericht*).

[27] Letto-Vanamo (n 24) 155–64.

through concrete discussions.[28] It is also possible to assume that no legal order or legal authority existed outside this communication. One opinion on law was against another opinion, and outside court sessions legal opinions were equal. To have an opinion enforced it should be shared; and to be imposed as a sentence (which was then the law in the particular case) it should pass a formal process. The intimate relationship between law and procedural practices is at least partly a corollary of oral communication, but it also grows from the non-authoritative nature of the law. Because 'broken (consensus on) law' had to be rebuilt through court procedure, the shared opinion of the community was important. Consensus, however, did not mean idyllic harmony. It emerged through negotiations, through participation in court sessions, or sometimes in so-called inspections. As long as dispute settlement involving (state) authorities is absent, the decision needs to obtain authority from forms, and from participation. Although law(s) could be cast in written form, as was the case in many places in the Middle Ages, the legitimacy of the court sentence did not rely on the written word – even if the sentence had been similar to the words found in the medieval texts.

III. TRANSNATIONAL EUROPEAN LAW

A. Roman Law as Transnational Legal Knowledge

In spite of the methodological problems discussed above, the history of Roman law as transnational private law could quite easily be analysed with Duve's toolkit. The challenges, however, start if the traditional geographical scope is opened towards East and North. Then, the role of Roman law knowledge should be analysed in the context not (only) of the *ius commune* but (also) of Roman-German legal scholarship, not forgetting modern civil-law codifications. These reshaped the authority of Roman law but did not derogate from its substantial influence.

Looking at Classical Roman law (roughly from the first century BCE until the end of the third century CE), one can recognise that it was dominated by juristic opinions as the main legal source. Furthermore, the ancient principle of legal personality was based on the transborder applicability of law. The oldest Roman *ius civile* meant originally a legal system reserved to the citizens (*cives*) or members of the Roman community (*civitas*). Thus, the Romans always 'carried' their law with them.[29] At the same time, the original Roman meaning of *ius privatum* is literally 'privately made law', that is, a legal order produced autonomously by private parties without intervention by state agencies. Hence, the opinions or the law of the Roman jurists can be categorised as a private legal order based mainly on the activity of advising private clients. All these juristic pieces of advice, as well as additional interpretations given by (other) jurists, were purely private opinions.

[28] See further J Weitzel: 'Der Grund des Rechts in Gewohnheit und Herkommen' in D Willoweit (ed), *Die Begründung des Rechts als historisches Problem* (Munich, Oldenbourg Wissenschaftsverlag, 2000) 137–52.

[29] See, eg, T Giaro, 'Transnational Law and its Historical Position', *Studia Iuridica 2016* (University of Warsaw) 73–86, esp 74.

The second century lawyer Gaius told of Roman-law sources speaking of the laws of the Roman peoples in the plural (*iura populi Romani*) – conceptually the Roman state was identified with the Roman people. The laws could be the product of different actors (for example, the Roman assemblies, the senate, the emperor), and they also consisted of opinions from legal scholars (*responsa prudentium*). Later came political interventions and formal governmental control, but still Roman law has become famous for a high degree of autonomy from political government.[30] Roman law, however, also provides a history of the increasing public domination of private law. The *Corpus Juris Civilis* (CJC) was established 529–534 under imperial domination by Justinian I. and later formed the point of reference for the *ius commune*. Its most influential parts are the Digest (*Digesta*, in Greek *Pandectae*), a collection of juristic writings, mostly dating back to the second and third centuries, and the *Institutiones*, a textbook, largely based on *Institutiones* of Gaius. The other two parts, the *Codex* and *Novellae*, consist of (imperial) legislation.

The revival of Roman law in Northern Italy from the twelfth century happened due to interpretive studies of the CJC. Consequently, the so-called reception of Roman law took place in the continental area of Western Europe. It was no mechanical transfer of an ancient legal body. Reception consisted rather of intellectualisation (*Verwissenschaftlichung*) of legal knowledge, during which the law – first Roman law and later also local law/s – became the object of scholarly systematisation and university studies. As noted above, supranational or transnational Canon law was applied by the Church throughout the whole (Western) world. Additionally, Canon law was taught at the medieval universities alongside the newborn and 'cosmopolitan' Roman law that reigned above or alongside status-based and local law(s). In contrast, Roman law based on studies (knowledge) of the *Corpus Juris Civilis* and its glosses was not the law of any institution. In its beginning, it lived somewhere in abstract space, at higher levels where only professors and their best pupils could live and work. Nor did it find its application in courts, but for some rare exceptions. Thus, imaginary speculations on imaginary cases could lead to heated disputations in the universities, but it all remained somewhat unreal and theoretical. Nor was anybody amazed or shocked when Roman maxims were quoted or applied entirely out of context. In the ecclesiastical courts, however, Canon law, influenced by Roman law terms and rules, was applied to everyday (clerical and even secular) life.

Gradually, legal science – a body of jurisprudence – was developed. Medieval scholars studied and explained the compilation of Justinian, in which the legal wisdom of Antiquity lay buried. They constructed a scholastic science of the law on the foundations of the CJC, and already in the twelfth century teaching in Roman law, closely connected with that in Canon law, spread beyond the Italian frontiers. A new European legal science was born. Better to say, it was scholarly legal practice, common to learned 'legists' of Roman law and canonists all over Latin Christendom – usually entitled the *ius commune*.

[30] See further Jansen and Michaels (n 2) 358–65.

Still, the authority of Roman law was different. No particularly Roman-law courts existed, in contrast to the ecclesiastical Canon-law courts, and it might not be appropriate to speak either of ancient or medieval Roman law (*ius commune*) as an independent normative order. Generally speaking, medieval scholars but also many university-trained lawyers in practice treated the CJC as an authoritative text, as a holy book. For them, Roman law was a common academic legal 'language'. The *Corpus Juris Civilis* was, first and foremost, the authoritative textual point of reference of common legal knowledge with its terminology, concepts and classifications.

Looking closer at 'local translations' of Roman law knowledge, differences between European regions are great. However, it is possible to see that private law of the medieval European cities especially was influenced by Roman law terminology and in some cases also by its rules, applied by university-trained judges and advocates. At the same time, guild statutes were integrated into the legal systems of cities. Feudal law was quite early on integrated by legal scholars into the *ius commune* – at least partly.[31] The *lex mercatoria* again had its roots in different local and international customs, but also in Roman law.

B. Codifications and German Scholarship as Transnational Legal Knowledge

The history of Roman law as transnational European law is typically seen to end with the civil law codifications of the eighteenth and nineteenth centuries. A civil law codification amounted to emphasis on a new nation-state identity and membership of the continental European legal tradition, as it still does today. This again makes it difficult to analyse and understand non-civil code systems, such as those of the Nordic countries. Furthermore, in European narratives, codifications are presented according to an ascending order of rationality, freedom, and economic liberty. As a historical phenomenon, private law codifications have their origin in legal scholarship but are motivated by a need to reform and unify the whole regional or national legal system.[32] In fact, codifications drafted by legal experts have seldom brought about dramatic substantive changes in private law. The legal system retains large parts of its autonomy – although the development of private law has shifted from scholars and local judges to the state.[33]

From a European – even a global – perspective, the most important outcome of codifications has been relative structural, systematic and substantive uniformity of private law reaching far beyond national borders.[34] A similar unifying role was

[31] eg, it is well known that feudal rights were explained in terms of quasi-Roman property law (*dominium directum – dominium utile*), which had consequences even in the Swedish legal practice of the 17th and 18th centuries.

[32] This happened in a time when the normative status of Roman law had become unclear.

[33] Jansen and Michaels (n 2) 377–81.

[34] On the History of (European) Codifications, see P Caroni, *Gesetz und Gesetzbuch, Beiträge zu einer Kodifikationsgeschichte* (Basel, Helbing & Leichtehahn, 2003). On Latin-American codification history see, eg, FJ Andrés Santos, 'Napoleon in America? Reflections on the Concept of Legal Reception in the Light of the Civil Law Codification in Latin America' in T Duve (ed), *Entanglements, Legal History: Conceptual Approaches, Global Perspective on Legal History1* (Frankfurt, Max Planck Institute for Legal History, 2014).

played by German, Roman law-based, legal scholarship, so-called Pandect science, which in the second half of the nineteenth century inspired legal scholars in Europe, including Eastern and Northern Europe. The new paradigm was invented by Gustav Hugo (1764–1844) and taken up by Friedrich Carl von Savigny (1774–1861) and the Historical School. The unifying element in both is (substantial, terminological, and systematic) knowledge of Roman law, which was more or less translated into local circumstances via codification drafting and/or systematising national/regional private law.

Today, for instance, former socialist countries in Europe have a new civil code, drafted according to the German, Swiss and/or French models. Furthermore, civil-law codifications exist in countries outside Europe, and not only because of their colonial history. Even China has been drafting a new civil code. At the same time, an opposite trend to the codification movement is observable. One could speak about de-codification when private law, dedicated to sector-specific regulation (for example, regulation of banking and energy), refuses to recognise the superiority of the civil code, which then loses its traditional central place within a legal system. Special norms are forming several – and often transnational – microsystems (or normativities), which are only loosely connected to any code. In fact, codification and de-codification are not merely contradictory concepts (unity vs fragmentation); they are two entirely different modes of functioning of any current legal system. De-codification is adapted to a dynamic service society and expresses the contemporary trend towards a pluralistic and polycentric system. According to Polish legal historian Tomasz Giaro, current de-codification, together with Europeanisation and globalisation, have rehabilitated the extra-governmental mechanism of lawmaking. This again appears very similar to the method of Roman jurisprudence, its autonomous law production, taking place outside of the realms of statutory law, consisting mainly in juristic reinterpretations of previous interpretations.[35]

The nineteenth-century codifications (such as the Austrian *Allgemeines Bürgerliches Gesetzbuch*, ABGB, 1812, and the French *Code Civil*, 1804) provoked Roman law to a second reception, attributed to Savigny[36] and the Historical School. Now, (Roman) civil law received scientific treatment based on the all-embracing Pandect system, dividing civil law into five parts ('books').[37] To realise the creative role of modern legal doctrine the Pandectists had to abandon the medieval idea of ancient Roman law as *ratio scripta*. According to ideas of legal positivism, legal scholars grounded their work on legal texts in force. For French writers, the texts were those of the Civil Code. For Germans, they were Roman law texts, especially in the Digest (*pandectae*) based on the idea of its modern use (*usus modernus pandectarum*). According to Savigny and his followers, although the texts were Roman, they expressed the *Volksgeist*, the mind or spirit of the German people, the

[35] T Giaro, 'Roman Law Always Dies with a Codification' in A Dębiński and M Jońca (eds), *Roman Law and European Legal Culture* (Lublin, 2008) 15–26.

[36] See esp FC Savigny, *Vom Beruf unserer Zeit zur Gesetzgebung und Rechtswissenschaft* (Olms Verlag, 1814).

[37] Giaro (n 35) 20–21; see also P Haferkamp, 'Pandektistik und Gerichtspraxis' (2011) *Quaderni Fiorentini* 179–211.

ultimate source of German law. German jurists, such as Savigny, Georg Friedrich Puchta (1798–1846) and Bernhard Windscheid (1817–1892), built on the Roman (-German) texts an intellectual private law system that became clear and consistent.[38] At the same time, legal scholarship continued to be the most important legal actor in Germany. Until the new civil code, the *Bürgerliches Gezetzbuch* (BGB, 1900), came into force, the writings of legal scholars were understood as a source of law (in the meaning of *Juristenrecht*).[39]

Hence, the law by its very nature was a 'living organic entity that moved and changed with the spirit of the people', the *Volksgeist*. Since the scope of the *Volksgeist* was national, it was possible to establish national private law without a legislator and without offending the regimes of the various territorial states. Actually, the Historical School, with its concentration on reception (the modern use) of Roman law in Europe but also focusing on disseminating and localising law in space and time, was a national but at the same time transnational effort.[40] Savigny was known world-wide.[41] Rudolf von Jhering, again, conceptualised Roman law as world law, while his writings were translated[42] and read far beyond the borders of traditional Roman-law Europe. Furthermore, national legal histories were seen as a particular historical formation, shaped by a distinct national spirit (*Volksgeist*), but expressing universal principles. They were written with a clear consciousness about the transnational past and the present vocation of national law.[43]

C. Geography of Transnational Legal Knowledge

i. Eastern Europe

As we have seen, European legal histories have their own geographies. Often Eastern European countries are left out of Romanist histories, while the Nordic countries are

[38] See further P Haferkamp, 'Die sogenannte Begriffsjurisprudenz im 19. Jahrhundert – "reines" Recht?' in O Depenheuer (ed), *Reinheit des Rechts* (Göttingen, VS Verlag, 2010) 79–99.

[39] According to 19th century German legal scholars, legal science was perceived as not only a receptive activity but also a productive one; legal scholars were creators of the law. And even though the drafters of the new legislation, the BGB (1900), were not academics themselves, they were heavily influenced by writings of the dominant contemporary school of legal thought, the Pandectists.

[40] Duve, *Comparative Legal History* (n 9) 78.

[41] See, eg, J Rückert and T Duve (eds), *Savigny International*? Savignyana 13 (Frankfurt am Main, Vittorio Klostermann, 2015).

[42] See esp R Jhering, *Geist des römischen Rechts I–III* (Leipzig, Breitkopf and Hartel, 1865); Jhering's *Kampf um's das Recht* (Wien, Hanse, 1872) has been translated into more than 20 languages. See also K Zweigert, K Siehr, 'Jhering's Influence on the 'Development of Comparative Legal Method' (1971) *The American Journal of Comparative Law* 215–31 and on the development of his theoretical thinking, J Rückert, 'Das Methodenorakel Rudolf von Jhering (1818–1892)' (2019) 219 *Archiv für die zivilistische Praxis* 457–87.

[43] Duve, *Comparative Legal History* (n 9) 78–79. According to Duve, due to the still strong historical method of legal scholarship, this also meant learning about the legal histories of other countries and even world areas and relating one's own national legal history to these other legal cultures. The search for the particular 'national spirit' was only possible by creating images of and differences from the others; see also M Reiman, *Historische Schule und Common Law, Die deutsche Rechtswissenschaft des 19. Jahrhunderts im amerikanischen Rechtsdenken* (Berlin, Duncker & Humblot, 1993) 56–73 and MH Hoeflich, 'Savigny and his Anglo-American Disciples' (1989) *American Journal of Comparative Law* 17–37.

left out of both Romanist and 'modernisation' histories. During the pre-codification period, Roman law in Europe had three zones of influence: The Western part of the continent, Eastern and Northern Europe, and England.[44] A lack of early general reception of Roman law (*ius commune*) with university-trained judges and other legal actors distinguishes the other areas from the Western one. However, this defect was partly compensated during the nineteenth century with a transfer of Western codes and legal scholarship.

In the East, the learned judge remained unknown until the nineteenth century. Justice was administered by noble lay judges in Eastern Central Europe, whereas in Russia and in South-Eastern Europe by Orthodox clerics.[45] Due to Canon law and town law, however, East-Central Europe was more integrated into Western legal culture than South-Eastern Europe and Russia.[46] With the Christianisation of Poland and Hungary in the eleventh and twelfth centuries, Canon law began to apply, becoming the link to Roman law, too.[47] Another bearer of Roman law was German town law when numerous towns and villages were established. Magdeburger rights were granted in more than 100 cities, first in Poland and Lithuania but later also in Ukraine and Moldavia. Still, knowledge of Roman law was scarce.

As noted, the most important outcome of modern civil codes has been the relative uniformity of private law reaching far beyond national borders. A similar harmonising role was played by German Pandect science, which embraced Eastern Europe in the second half of the nineteenth century. In the Polish territories the Prussian *Allgemeines Landrecht* (ALR), the Austrian Civil Code (ABGB) and the French Civil Code (*Code civil*) were *ratione imperii*.[48] In the Balkan peninsula the reception of Western civil codifications swept away the old feudal customary laws a few decades later than in East-Central Europe. In Russia, legal 'Westernisation' was in private and constitutional law but limited mainly to the doctrinal level as well as to the cassation judicature of the Ruling Senate in St Petersburg, which stood under the influence of German Pandect science. The Pandect influence culminated in Russian drafts of a civil code,[49] published in 1905 and 1913, which took into consideration the French

[44] See also R Zimmermann, 'Der europäische Charakter des englischen Rechts' (1993) *Zeitschrift für Europäisches Privatrecht* 4–50.

[45] In more detail see T Giaro, 'Some Prejudices about the Legal Tradition of Eastern Europe' in B Sitek, JJ Szczerbowski and AW Bauknecht (eds), *Comparative Law in Eastern and Central Europe* (Cambridge Scholar Publishing, 2003) 26–50 and T Giaro, 'Legal Tradition of Eastern Europe. Its Rise and Demise' (2011) *Comparative Law Review* 2–23; see also T Giaro, 'Europa und Pandektenrecht' (1993) *Rechtshistorisches Journal* 326–45.

[46] About Roman Law in Russia, see M Avenariuss, *Fremde Traditionen des römischen Rechts. Einfluß, Wahrnehmung und Argument des ›rimskoe pravo‹ im russischen Zarenreich des 19.* Jahrhunderts (Göttingen, Wallstein, 2014) and criticism of it by T Giaro: 'Russia and Roman Law' (2015) *Rechtsgeschichte Legal History* 309–19.

[47] Giaro, 'Some Prejudices about the Legal Tradition of Eastern Europe' (n 45) 29.

[48] On the history of private law codification in Hungary, see J Balogh, 'Debates in Articles (Positions in the Legal Literature on the Possibilities of Private Law Codification, 1866–1900)' (2020) *Journal of European History of Law* 126–37.

[49] As a brief history of Russian and Soviet civil codification, see D Poldnikov, 'The Formalistic Pattern of Soviet Civil Codification as A Chapter in European Legal History' (2020) *Journal of European History of Law* 53–60.

Civil Code and the Baltic Code of Private law, compiled in 1864 by Friedrich Georg von Bunge.[50]

In the East, however, codifications could not be considered as a compromise between the old and the new law or between local customs and Roman law, as was the case in the West.[51] The change was more radical. Indigenous law was replaced by a foreign law, customary law replaced by statutes, while norms proper to given social orders were replaced by a unitary code, and the lay judge by a professional one. At the same time, modernisation and professionalisation of legal education in Eastern Europe occurred.[52]

For an understanding of legal development in the Eastern part of Europe, the peculiarities of so-called modernisation should also be noted. While modernisation in the West took a long time, Eastern Europe saw a clash between Western legal transfers and pre-industrial societies. Thus, the nineteenth century brought with it a breach of local traditions. For instance, most Balkan states[53] changed their outdated Byzantine model overnight in favour of modernised Western ones – to codifications – in order to ensure legal unity of their territory. The new model of legislation and the state monopoly on legal training and adjudication disempowered the Orthodox Church. Legal modernisation through imported codifications, however, could not induce effective social change. The traditional Balkan societies remained incomplete: unlike Prussia and Bohemia, they had no middle class – nor, like Russia, Hungary, or Poland, an aristocracy. In the absence of a middle class, legal reforms undertaken from above did not lead to an efficient social transformation. In fact, the Balkan modernisation of the nineteenth century remained nearly symbolic. At the same time, the modernisation of East Central Europe was more successful.[54]

During the inter-war period between 1918 and 1939, the intense circulation of Western European legal models continued (except in Soviet Russia), and Eastern Europe dismissed its old law. The new Western codes – the German BGB, the Swiss ZGB and Swiss code of obligations – determined the preparatory works. The achievements were not particularly great, and the simple receptions, typical of the nineteenth century, were now sometimes substituted by a synthesis of Western models. The Polish Code of 1933 was the greatest achievement of the European doctrine of private law

[50] See further on the Code drafted by Friedrich Georg von Bunge, M Luts-Sootak, 'Zur Verortung des Baltischen Privatrechts (1864/65) unter den europäischen Privatrechtskodifikationen' in G Hamza, M Hlavačka, K Takii (eds), Rechtstransfer in der Geschichte, *Internationale Festschrift für Wilhelm Brauneder zum 75. Geburtstag* (Berlin, Peter Lang, 2019).

[51] Giaro is referring to the codification idea of the father of the Code Napoleon, Giaro, 'Some 'Prejudices about the Legal Tradition of Eastern Europe' (n 45) 26–50. See also T Giaro, 'Modernisierung durch Transfer – Schwund osteuropäischer Rechtstraditionen' in T Giaro (ed), *Modernisierung durch Transfer im 19. und frühen 20. Jahrhundert, Rechtskulturen des modernen Osteuropa, Traditionen und Transfers* I (Frankfurt am Main, Vittorio Klostermann, 2006) 275–342.

[52] Moscow 1755, Kiev 1834 and St Petersburg 1819, but in South-Eastern Europe later: Athens, 1832, Bucharest 1864, Sofia 1892, Belgrade 1904; in East Central Europe the old universities were revitalised.

[53] See, eg, M Kargjoziva-Finkova and C Takoff, 'The Bulgarian Legal System from 1878 until World War I' in Giaro (ed), *Modernisierung durch Transfer* (n 51) 129–44, and S Sarkic, Constitutional and Legal History of Serbia 1804–1914 in Giaro (ed) *Modernisierung durch Transfer* (n 51) 201–23.

[54] Giaro, 'Some Prejudices about the Legal Tradition of Eastern Europe' (n 45) 40–41.

between the wars: The drafters came from all parts of formerly partitioned Poland with a knowledge of Austrian, French, Roman, and German and Swiss law – and indeed the Polish Code was well received in other European countries.

In so-called real socialism, the old law was first adjusted by general clauses and vague concepts. The general clauses (especially the socio-economic scope of a right) preserved their role even after new codifications of civil law (Czechoslovakia 1950 and 1964, Hungary 1959, Soviet Russia and Poland 1964 and East Germany 1975). The new 'socialist legal family', however, covered a non-homogeneous territory belonging partly to the border area of the reception of Roman law, partly to the Byzantine world and partly to the area occupied during the nineteenth century by codifications and Pandect Science.[55] Poland and Hungary proved most faithful to the so-called civil-law tradition. They justified the cultivation of Pandect science 'with the hermeneutic distinction between the traditional forms of the socialist content'.[56] In addition, Soviet civil law, in particular the Russian code of the NEP period (New Economic Policy of the 1920s), was drafted by pre-revolutionary jurists in a traditional manner. After World War II, truly socialist codes were promulgated only in 1964 by Czechoslovakia and 1975 by East Germany.

ii. Northern Europe

Especially problematic are European narratives of transnational knowledge with Roman law and codifications when studying the history of law of the Nordic Countries.[57] Canon law and the very few scholars with studies at universities in Southern Europe and Germany were certainly important in forming legal thinking in the North in the Middle Ages. Both also played a significant role in the process of recording local law, which mostly occurred in the twelfth and thirteenth centuries, similarly to many other European countries.[58] Traces of Canon law can be seen especially in sections on family and inheritance of Nordic medieval laws.

Perhaps the best Nordic example of 'glocalisation' of transnational normative knowledge, though, is the Rules of Judges drafted by Olaus Petri in the first decades of the sixteenth century, and still today printed in the first pages of law books in Sweden and Finland. Olaus, who later became an important reformer, had studied at the University of Wittenberg and was familiar with both Canon law and Roman law. He also well knew local circumstances in Sweden, in line with which he formulated the Rules. Thus, many ideas of Canon law and even of Roman law are seen in the

[55] Giaro, 'Some Prejudices about the Legal Tradition of Eastern Europe' (n 45) 45–46.

[56] ibid 47.

[57] Today Denmark, Finland, Iceland, Norway, and Sweden. Scholars comparing European legal systems tend to put the Nordic countries together as one legal group, and often also as a subfamily of the continental European civil law family. The peculiarities of development of the Nordic legal system(s) are explained by referring to a certain historical delay of the European mainstream. See also P Letto-Vanamo and D Tamm, 'Nordic Legal Mind' in P Letto-Vanamo, D Tamm, BO Gram Mortensen, *Nordic Law in European Context* (Basel, Springer, 2019) 1–19.

[58] See, eg, Introduction to the English translation of the *Liber legis Scaniae*, D Tamm (ed), *The Liber legis Scaniae. The Latin Text with Introduction, Translation and Commentaries* (London, Routledge, 2018) 1–10.

Rules, whereas for instance procedural rules – especially rules of evidence (in Roman-Canon procedural law with detailed rules on torture) – are translated in circumstances where university-trained judges familiar with nuanced procedural rules were totally missing.[59]

For a long time, Nordic societies were small and homogenous, without big cities and their bourgeoisie. Thus, the main forums for legal communication until the seventeenth century were the local assemblies (*ting*). They worked without trained lawyers for resolution of local, minor conflicts – usually based on local practices (especially many ways for the parties and the local community to participate) and local norms (customs). At the same time, the early reception of Roman law (*ius commune*) was missing. Since the fifteenth/sixteenth century it has been possible to study law at Nordic universities, but students were very few and a university-trained legal profession and legal science[60] are phenomena of the nineteenth century.[61] Civil law codifications are missing, too: The Nordic countries have been resistant to large-scale law projects in terms of systematic collections of law covering general principles and more detailed rules in several areas, with the aim of being the main source of private law. Within the civil law, issues such as contracts, marriage, or succession have been regulated by more or less independent acts, of which many are the results of common Nordic drafting and exchange of ideas.[62] At the same time, general doctrines (*allgemeine Lehren*) of law have been developed mainly by legal scholarship, but in cooperation with other legal actors.

German legal scholarship and the drafting of the BGB, however, were well known in the Nordic countries and revived the old discussion about codifying civil law. In 1899, the Danish professor Julius Lassen took the opportunity to launch the idea of creating a modern Danish civil code.[63] He was much driven by his interest in German systematic legal thinking but was also critical of the way the new German Code was drafted. In this connection, he also mentioned that a common Nordic civil code should be the final goal. Creating a code, and even more a Nordic code, would have been a big issue, and much scholarly and practical work would have been needed before such a project could seriously have been considered. Thus, the very few Nordic lawyers did not see such a project as possible or useful, and prioritised flexibility in law.

Similarly, later proposals for a common European civil code also met attitudes among Nordic legal professionals – often characterised as pragmatic – that were more

[59] See further H Pihlajamäki, Olavus Petri (1493–1552), 'Transplanting Foreign Law in Reformation Sweden' in KÅ Modéer and H Vogt, *Law and the Christian Tradition in Scandinavia. The Writings of Great Nordic Jurists* (London, Routledge 2020) 90–104.

[60] In Denmark at the end of the 18th century but elsewhere somewhat later.

[61] Furthermore, Nordic legal culture was later professionalised. And more generally, for a long time one could speak of non-expert or lay-dominated cultures. This again has defined court systems and legal procedures but could also explain at least partly why Nordic legal culture is even today characterised by the term 'pragmatism'.

[62] Nordic Meetings of Lawyers have been held since 1872; see in more detail P Letto-Vanamo and D Tamm, 'Cooperation in the Field of Law' in J Strang (ed), *Nordic Cooperation. A European Region in Transition* (London, Routledge, 2016) 92–107; there are also Nordic associations and/or yearly meetings for scholars and other lawyers, eg in administrative law, criminal law, and contract law.

[63] Letto-Vanamo and Tamm (n 57) 101–102.

sceptical than enthusiastic. Even today, Nordic lawyers prefer discrete acts, which are easier to formulate and more flexible to change and amend, and which do not govern the law and legal thinking too much but allow pragmatism and judicial and scholarly interpretations to meet practical ends. Indeed, the non-existence of wide and complicated civil codes has also made Nordic legislative cooperation possible – and guaranteed its success.

Anyhow, Nordic law – and especially Nordic legal scholarship – are heavily indebted to the efforts of German scholarship of the nineteenth century to create a method of developing the law based on profound thinking, on systematic coherence, and on legal concepts. This ideal, however, was gradually superseded by the idea of the law as serving practical, social purposes. Nevertheless, it is quite impossible to think of the history of Nordic legal scholarship without Roman–German influences. When modern Danish, Swedish, or Finnish legal science emerged during the nineteenth century, German-Roman law-based classifications and concepts were diligently adapted. Thus, German legal literature, rather than the idea of codification, formed a link to the idea of a private law system furthering coherence within national law.

Savigny, Jhering and Windscheid were well known by Nordic scholars. Additionally, those lawyers who were instrumental within Nordic legal cooperation would have had a common background based on German legal literature, even if they represented different Nordic legal systems. Still, when national private law scholarship emerged in the Nordic countries during the nineteenth century, this happened mostly by adapting ideas of the Historical School and the Pandect system, quite often also by relying heavily on texts by German legal authors. For instance, the above-mentioned Lassen was strongly inspired by Windscheid, and the first handbook on Finnish civil law written by Robert Montgomery (1889)[64] was in many parts a direct translation of Windscheid's *Lehrbuch des Pandektenrechts*.[65] These writings were channels for knowledge of Roman law and its vocabulary, still visible in Nordic legal systems.

IV. EUROPEAN LAW BEYOND EUROPE

The geography of legal history referring to influences and adaption of transnational legal knowledge is topical not only in the context of the 'peripheries' of the European continent discussed above. Increasing interest in the colonial past among legal scholars has resulted in studies on transfer of European legal institutions to Latin America and Africa as well as on Indigenous law – before and after the colonial period. The history of transnational law both as transborder European law and as non-state, Indigenous law has been dealt with. In the following, I will briefly highlight some current scholarly debates on Latin American legal history. The focus is mainly on Spanish America.

[64] R Montgomery, *Handbok i Finlands allmänna privaträtt I* (Helsinki, Edlund, 1889).
[65] B Windscheid, *Lehrbuch des Pandektenrechts I–III* (Düsseldorf, Julius Buddeus, 1870).

Latin America is quite often conceptualised only as a geographical region. Sometimes, shared historical experiences, a common culture, religion and language/s or combinations of these have been pointed out. Many – even historians – have identified Latin America only in terms of peoples and things originating from Europe.[66] Today, this is radically changing, and most scholars tend to include in it a rich variety of peoples and cultures as well as their interactions.

As a term, 'Latin America' has a long history – and it has seldom been neutral. Most probably, it was invented by local actors but soon after taken up first by the French and then by other foreign actors, who tended to lend the term interpretations that classified its community as backward and traditional. Thereafter, opposition between Anglos and Latins was also translated as one contrasting Protestants with Catholics and whites with persons of mixed race. Some of these characterisations have also influenced the way Latin America has been treated by international agencies, in transnational litigation and international arbitration: it has often been conceived as a space where a huge gap existed between law and its implementation, inefficiencies, corruption, excessive legal formalism, and where European norms were said to have been adopted but failed to materialise.[67] Thus, Latin America has often been seen as a case of failed modernisation.

Scholars, however, are today using the term quite neutrally, which seems to allow more than national narratives, and point out various connections between cultures and regions. In one of the latest publications on Latin American legal history, edited by Thomas Duve and Tamar Herzog, the perspective is global and opposing Eurocentrism.[68] At the same time, the focus is on production of normative knowledge by different actors and institutions. Thus, not only the legal experience of multiple regions and peoples are highlighted but also religious (mainly Catholic) normativity, normativities created and implemented in the social space of the household[69] or by communities living in parallel to the colonial or modern state. Often, the emphasis is on studying attempts to implement norms that were created elsewhere and under radically diverse circumstances but that needed to be translated and concretised ('glocalised') so as to fit local circumstances that included a large Indigenous population and the enslaved, who practiced their own laws.

This is a novel horizon in studies of the legal history of Latin America, and follows the theoretical paths of Duve's proposal for a global approach discussed above. At the same time, it might be influenced – not only by methodological changes in legal history scholarship but also by current developments in Latin American countries towards a legal/normative pluralism validating Indigenous rights and cultural

[66] See, eg, WD Mignolo, *The Idea of Latin America* Malden (Hoboken, Blackwell, 2005) and M Tenorio-Trillo, *Latin America: The Allure and Power of an Idea* (Chicago, University of Chicago Press, 2017).

[67] See, eg, D López Medina, 'The Latin American and Caribbean Legal Traditions. Repositioning Latin America and the Caribbean on the Contemporary Maps of Comparative Law' in M Bussani and U Mattei (eds), *The Cambridge Companion to Comparative Law* (Cambridge, Cambridge University Press, 2012) 344–67.

[68] T Duve and T Herzog (eds), *The Cambridge History of Latin American Law in a Global Perspective* (Cambridge, Cambridge University Press, 2024).

[69] T Duve and T Herzog, 'Introduction' in Duve and Herzog (eds) (n 68) 1–17.

differences by their new constitutions (for example, in Bolivia and Mexico) and other legislation.

Before discussing Latin American legal pluralism (including Indigenous law as transnational law) and its history, another subject will be addressed, namely *derecho indiano* and its transnational/ local nature, currently under quite intensive debate among legal historians. This might also open an interesting perspective on the competition between different regulative techniques, and on the problematic issue of legal transfers; even better than a short history of Latin American private law with emergence of modern codifications. *Derecho indiano* is a term used among scholars in Spanish to refer to the legal system in force in the Spanish colonies during the early modern period (especially the sixteenth to eighteenth centuries).[70] It distinguishes a particular area of study tending to conceal connections that the law in Spanish America had with Spanish and other European law. Hence, the research tradition of *derecho indiano* has – like any national or regional legal history – highlighted its particularity instead of denoting its similarities with (or differences from) other colonial systems or European law more generally; Comparative studies on Spanish colonial law have been lacking until recent years.

In recent years, the particularity of *derecho indiano* has been questioned.[71] For instance, the most improved reference point in the studies on content and development of *derecho indiano* of Heikki Pihlajamäki, a comparative legal historian from Finland, has been the massive amount of European regulation produced by the chanceries of early modern kingdoms, towns, and other legislating entities:[72] Like today, different areas of societal and economic life needed detailed regulation – for example, religion, security and public order, agriculture, industry and commerce, traffic, construction, culture and sciences, as well as control of the poor and the marginalised. In many European countries and regions, so-called police ordinances attempted to create and maintain public order, discipline, and stability, but at the same time to promote the well-being of society. Thus, the emergence of police regulation was linked to the rise of the modern state and modern absolutism.

Spain was no exception to this general European tendency and, according to Pihlajamäki, the development of Spanish colonial law also followed the development of police law in general. Indeed, the need for constant and rapid regulatory changes was even greater in the American lands, which were distant and internally heterogenous. The regulation technique of police law was extremely well suited for such circumstances. As he points out, the whole legislative ideology changed; corresponding to the general trend in European statutory law, Spanish colonial law was mainly police regulation. Traditional normative techniques – legal scholarship, court decisions, and codes – had to be supplemented with special regulation. They were not

[70] See in more detail H Pihlajamäki, 'The Westernization of Police Regulation: Spanish and British Colonial Laws Compared' in T Duve and H Pihlajamäki, *New Horizons in Spanish Colonial Law. Contribution to Transnational Early Modern Legal History* (Frankfurt am Main, Max Planck Institute for Legal History, 2015) 97–124.

[71] eg, see Tau (n 19).

[72] Pihlajamäki 2015; see also information (June 2023) of the research project Comparing Early Modern Colonial Laws: England, the Netherlands, Portugal, and Spain, available at www.helsinki.fi/en/researchgroups/comparing-early-modern-colonial-laws.

quick and detailed or flexible enough to master the multitude of new circumstances and peoples to which the law needed to apply. Instead, the core of Spanish colonial law, *derecho indiano*, came to be based on police regulation, of which Spaniards already had plenty of experience on the Iberian Peninsula. In theoretical terms, police regulation (not always categorised as law but rather as administration) was a European normative institution, a legal transfer translated into new social and political circumstances.

Police law can also be found in other colonies. Interestingly, however, police regulation in Spanish America was, according to Pihlajamäki, different from police law in British America, where the bulk of regulation was drafted and issued in the colonies themselves, reflecting the relative independence of the British colonies from London. In the Spanish colonies, however, the majority of regulation continued to flow from the Council of the Indies (*Consejo de las Indias*) right up to the end of the colonial period, thus reflecting the centralised nature of the Spanish Empire.

For her part, Tamar Herzog, a legal scholar and historian specialised in Latin-American history, has analysed Spanish American legal historiography from the perspective of discussions on legal pluralism. In the article 'Latin American Legal Pluralism: The Old and New',[73] the main question is whether current Latin American constitutional legal pluralism should be understood as a new phenomenon or whether it only demonstrates continuity from the colonial past. According to Herzog, the most common scholarly narrative (that of the 1960s and 1970s), has divided Spanish American society into two separate legal and political spheres. The Spanish republic included Spaniards who obeyed Spanish law and Spanish judges. The second was an Indigenous republic that included Indigenous natives who obeyed their own authorities and customary law. They were separate but not equal. Indigenous communities received judicial autonomy only as long as their law and customs were not contrary to Spanish law and morality. Nonetheless, the idea was not easy to implement in practice – for instance, it was not easy to define who was who and to which group the individual belonged.[74]

This, again, was not only a Spanish American phenomenon but common to many other 'empires', too.[75] According to Latin American scholars of the 1990s – especially those familiar with European legal history scholarship – the co-existence of several legal systems and distinct jurisdictions was a common feature. It was embedded in the very nature of the early modern state, which was a conglomerate made up of a plurality of communities with multiple powers and with a plurality of authorities with power (domination) over people. As noted above in this chapter, all individuals were under the jurisdiction of more than one single, unified authority. They belonged to a family, religious community, professional guild or association, were residents or citizens of a village, town or city, belonged to a particular estate, were (Indigenous) natives of certain regions, and so on. In each one of these capacities, they were under

[73] T Herzog, 'Latin American Legal Pluralism: The Old and New' (2021) *Quaderni Fiorentini* 705–36.
[74] ibid 706–708.
[75] On studies of legal pluralism in empires see, eg, LA Benton and RJ Ross (eds), *Legal Pluralism and Empires, 1500–1850* (New York, New York University Press, 2013).

distinct normativities and authorities. Thus, awareness of the distinct nature of (all) early modern societies led Latin American legal historians to insist that in colonial Spanish America multiple Spanish and multiple Indigenous 'republics' coincided. The right to exercise jurisdiction, however, did not necessarily dictate the law to apply – Indigenous authorities could implement Indigenous customary law but also Spanish law, and vice-versa.

The existence of various legal regimes typical of the *ancien régime* in Europe and its colonies came to be questioned in the eighteenth century. This happened mainly by monarchs wishing to create a new type of polity where citizens would be directly tied to the emperor (sovereign) rather than to intermediate bodies. This, however, did not succeed before the French Revolution with the ideas of a new legal subject who was legally equal to all others and of new (parliamentary) legislation by the representatives of the people.[76] The (French) revolutionary proposals were disseminated across the globe, including the new – since the beginning of the nineteenth century – independent Latin American states. In practice, however, most states failed to ensure the primacy of state law, to abolish the rights of different (Indigenous and other) communities, or to guarantee legal equality.[77] Regardless of the equality of citizens and state monopoly as the main principles, Indigenous communal structures and legal orders persisted either because the state so willed or so did the members of these groups – or both combined. Former (Indigenous) native structures continued to shape daily lives in many communities, where state normativity and state authorities were either completely absent or were accompanied or even replaced by communal authorities and norms.

Quite provocatively, Herzog traces identification of the persistence of Indigenous, native law as 'legal pluralism' to Anglophone legal anthropologists, who wished to demonstrate the endurance of Indigenous legal structures despite colonialism and despite the theoretical exclusion of state law and proposed that European domination never managed to annihilate Indigenous normativities, which survived colonialism and often re-emerged in post-colonial times.[78] In sum, the first generation of scholars of legal pluralism were mostly interested in the survival of Indigenous (native) law. To the second generation belonged those who argued that all societies have been plural with the coexistence of various legal systems; still, there was a difference between the 'natural' state of affairs and the colonial and post-colonial situation, in which European normativity existed side by side with Indigenous legal spheres. By the late twentieth century, the third generation of legal pluralists added new scenarios to the discussion, referring for instance to today's Europe with a so-called multicultural turn, as well as to the increasing role of non-state law through regulations issued by international bodies and other transnational entities. Common to all these approaches, however, is the wish to decentre state law.

[76] The promise of legal equality was never fulfilled; distinctions based on gender, civic, state and religions survived.

[77] See in more detail Herzog (n 73) 715–17: Actually, at the end of the 19th century (and later) many Latin American countries adopted measures which instituted distinctions between different types of citizens and which assigned a particular status to Indigenous inhabitants.

[78] Herzog (n 73) 720–21.

Anyhow, ideas of legal pluralism with a focus on cultural differences argued by legal anthropologists have been largely espoused by contemporary Latin American political actors and their observers: Since the late twentieth century, legal pluralism includes – also in constitutional texts – the 'right to be different' (for instance in Bolivia in 1994 and Ecuador in 1996 and 1998). Legal norms and conflict resolution systems thus demonstrate the multi-ethnic, multi-cultural, and multinational character of the state. Still, recognition of legal diversity has not been absolute: state normativity has remained superior. Nonetheless only limited studies are available as to how new ideas and processes have affected Indigenous law. Additionally, the assumption that Indigenous law would be easy to identify and uphold has been questioned. For instance, empirical studies have demonstrated that during the colonial period both the Spanish and Indigenous authorities could use Indigenous law; Spanish and Indigenous judges borrowed and blended Spanish and Indigenous law, and their own visions about what was just and possible.[79] It is also known that in some places, following the abolition of oral law and the legitimation of Indigenous normativity, village communities openly deliberated as to what their customs should be. Negotiations between different social and ethnic groups resulted in norms that harmonised Indigenous law with local, state and international law.

At any rate, complex processes of transformation and adaption were released, and they absorbed external influences and inputs. Empirical studies have shown that the Indigenous law that resulted represented, not so much a move to legitimise the Indigenous legal sphere but, rather, a social process that allowed the national system to develop new instruments to promote the inclusion of social actors that surrounded it.[80] Thus, the new Indigenous law was not substantially different from or opposing state law.

Today, a modern Latin American group identity can be seen as a result of complex interactions between local, state, and international norms, governmental agencies, intergovernmental agencies, missionaries, anthropologists, the church and international organisations. Yet, according to Herzog, current legal pluralism is new – not a continuation of or return from the old regime – expressing a novel political desire to acknowledge and validate a wish for auto-determination of mainly ethnic groups and the understanding that no auto-determination is possible without the capacity to declare and apply the law. Yet, at the same time, it differs from colonial (and premodern European) practices, which recognised the particularities of ethnic groups but also cities, professional associations, estates, families and so on, thus having a modern understanding of what can and should be recognised as right-bearing groups.[81]

[79] ibid 727.

[80] ibid 728–29; see also C Tornhill, C Calabria, R Cespades, D Dagbanja and EO'Loughlin, 'Legal Pluralism? Indigenous Rights as Legal Constructs' (2018) *University of Toronto Law Journal* 440–93.

[81] At the same time, it is battling between the idea of legal equality with the emergence of distinct legal personalities, with a distinct set of rules.

V. CONCLUSIONS

It is problematic to use history as a model or argument for current or future phenomena and their development. Only seldom can the meanings of past circumstances be changed into current meanings or define seemingly similar problems or practices with identical concepts. That said, the thoughts of transnational and global legal history discussed in this chapter might help us to understand the current world order, with globalisation and fragmentation of legal regimes, and with the presence of a seemingly universal vocabulary of law, shaped by power asymmetries. This might also make us better aware of 'law' as a tool of historical processes of globalisation.

In particular, the roles of transnational institutions (such as the Catholic Church), as well as formal and informal epistemic communities (for example, medieval or nineteenth-century academia) as actors and bearers of global normative knowledge are worthy of analysis. Today, international organisations, global networks (for instance, among consumer-law or business-law scholars, or constitutional-law judges or electronic libraries and databanks) cannot be forgotten when discussing multinormative knowledge (theoretical or practical) production and legal regimes.

The 'producers' might be global, or national but acting across borders, and the normativities multi-faceted (such as conventions, model codes, recommendations, standards, and theories). At any rate, global normative knowledge must be implemented and culturally glocalised in local acts. All legal regimes have their histories which need to be studied, but what also needs to be studied, in spite of practical and methodological difficulties, are local conditions (social, cultural, geographic) under which the process of cultural translation and thus localisation of potentially global normative knowledge has been or could be reproduced. Especially challenging are discussions about the (meaning of) law and its historical and local variations. For professional discussion, legal vocabulary is necessary. But not always do past practices and thoughts reflect the Weberian ideal type of so-called modern (state) law and its rationalities, as is the case with present 'soft law', discussed in several chapters of this book.

Part II

Legal Fields

6

Transnational Labour Law and Private Labour Governance – Regulatory Formula for European Works Councils Revisited

ULLA LIUKKUNEN*

I. INTRODUCTION

THE DEVELOPMENT WHERE collective labour relations are becoming increasingly decentralised is a global phenomenon. Decreasing trade union density and weakening organisational power of traditional regulatory actors in the arena of labour regulation reflect the changing environment of rule-setting for labour relations.[1] As individualisation and privatisation are gaining wider space in labour standards creation, they call for rethinking mechanisms of labour governance. They also challenge the traditional premises of labour protection, both nationally and across borders.

Increasing diversity of norm-setting is characteristic of a legal environment where transnational labour standards are being created between private actors. However, in transnational settings, points of departure of this diversity are different from those of domestic settings. To understand these points of departure, private labour governance needs to be viewed not only through its outcomes but also through the regulatory mechanisms and normative layouts that enable private

* Professor of Labour Law and Private International Law, Faculty of Law, University of Helsinki.

[1] Although collective agreements function differently in different bargaining regimes, general trends point to transformation of bargaining regimes. See, eg, U Liukkunen (ed), *Collective Bargaining in Labour Law Regimes: A Global Perspective* (Cham, Springer, 2019); T Araki and S Laulom, 'Organization, Productivity and Well-being at Work' in G Casale and T Treu (eds), *Transformations of Work: Challenges for the Institutions and Social Actors* (Wolters Kluwer, 2019).

labour governance itself.[2] In this effort, the cross-border dimension of employee participation based on Europeanised norm-making offers so far unexplored perspectives to transnational labour governance.

Cross-border employee participation rights are integrated in their transnational normative environment by privatised rule-making. This involves contractual arrangements whose role in labour governance has been expanding. Transnational normative settings where employee participation rights operate manifest a contractualisation of labour standards as a profound characteristic. The extension of voluntarism has been visible in the development of transnational company agreements signed by multinational enterprises, on the one side and, on the other side, international trade unions as well as collective bodies of employee representation, global or European Works Councils (EWCs), adding another layer of transnational social dialogue for private labour governance.

Developments in private labour governance require a more precise look into what voluntarism in transnational settings is all about. Domestically, in search of stronger labour institutions, the rationale of voluntarism intertwined with expanding contractual arrangements has prompted major concern among labour law scholarship. Accordingly, in line with traditional thinking, contractualisation has been first and foremost discussed in terms of limiting the scope of contracting parties' discretion in order to ensure weaker party protection. Moreover, it has been largely doubted whether employee representatives are able to articulate labour rights claims in the transnational juridification spheres of multinational enterprises.

From the normative perspective on transnational labour law, another approach is needed. European legal integration can be viewed as a normative process that supplies norms which become deployed in various ways in transnational regulatory settings. In these particular settings, labour standards are approached predominantly from a contractual standpoint when mechanisms of labour governance are being built. Understanding regulatory patterns in transnational labour law requires enlarging the view on formation of cross-border labour relations and their extraterritorial reach.

Noting Jessup's point of departure, namely that transnational law governs 'all law which regulates actions or events that transcend national frontiers', so that both public and private international law are included, as well as other rules which do not wholly fit into such standard categories, this chapter focuses on cross-border legal relations between private parties as well as regulation targeting transnational settings, with an emphasis on private labour governance.[3] In the following, transnational labour governance is examined through a normative development which is typically viewed as belonging to the sphere of the internal market, but whose influence

[2] In the EU context, this involves paying heed to modes of governance discussed in the context of the creation of European private law in ways that set them against the multi-level governance structures of the EU and call for new methods of construction of a Union of shared fundamental values. See F Cafaggi and H Muir-Watt, 'Introduction' in F Cafaggi and H Muir-Watt (eds), *Making European Private Law: Governance Design* (Cheltenham, Edward Elgar Publishing, 2008) 9.

[3] See PC Jessup, *Transnational Law* (New Haven, Yale University Press, 1956) 2. See also P Zumbansen, 'Transnational Law' in J Smits (ed), *Encyclopedia of Comparative Law* (Cheltenham, Edward Elgar Publishing, 2006).

reaches transnational settings where private governance dominates. The normative development under scrutiny is viewed as a more or less self-standing process of private actors in the transnational settings where they operate.[4]

The normative frames through which private labour governance is built in global value chains involve complex contractualisation of labour relations.[5] European legal integration is a development which should be contextualised against transnational regulatory settings. In a transnational scene, employee participation as a governance mechanism needs to be approached through the positioning of workplace democracy regulation in the industrial relations context. But employee participation also needs to be approached as a factor that features transnational ways of regulating labour issues in building mechanisms for a cross-border collective voice.

A. Private Labour Governance and Extension of Voluntarism

When EU legislation on EWCs was created in the late 1990s, it started an era of regulating cross-border employee participation on a transnational level.[6] The regulatory formula adopted was based on a multi-layered 'contractual voluntarism',[7] which has become a contested characteristic of transnational labour standards creation. Voluntarism in market-based governance lays preference to contracting clauses over binding normativities, whereas in industrial democracy voluntarism has not earlier formed a profound regulatory pattern. In evaluations of the regulatory formula concerning EWCs one of the characteristics is that voluntarism as a regulatory approach is often equated with or hidden under 'flexibility' or 'shared responsibility' of the parties.[8]

Mechanisms of private labour governance that the use of voluntarism fleshes out raise critical perspectives as to the development of EU labour law, where EWCs have traditionally been positioned in the category of employee participation dependent on state law frames and the traditional portrait of industrial democracy. What is often lacking from the picture is viewing these institutions of employee participation against how labour relations are shaped in transnational settings. Understanding of this development has remained fragmented and its consequences have not been addressed by the EU legislature in attempts to further construction of the normative dimension of Union social policy. Moreover, these attempts have failed to pay sufficient heed to cross-border conditions of labour protection.

[4] See also B Burkett, 'The International Labour Dimension: An Introduction' in JDR Craig and SM Lynk (eds), *Globalization and the Future of Labour Law* (Cambridge, Cambridge University Press, 2006) 40–42.

[5] See also D Taglioni and D Winkler, *Making Global Value Chains Work for Development* (Washington DC, World Bank, 2016) 12.

[6] See Council Directive 94/45/EC of 22 September 1994 on the Establishment of a European Works Council or a Procedure in Community-Scale Undertakings and Community-Scale Groups of Undertakings for the Purposes of Informing and Consulting Employees [1994] OJ L254/64.

[7] See W Streeck, 'Industrial Citizenship under Regime Competition: The Case of the European Works Councils' (1997) 4 *Journal of European Public Policy* 643–64.

[8] See W Lecher, B Nagel and HW Platzer (eds), *The Establishment of European Works Councils: From Information Committee to Social Actor* (London, Routledge, 1999).

For labour law, be it domestic or transnational, the question of institutions that are capable of developing and upholding social protection is a pressing issue. As cross-border bodies of employee representation, EWCs belong to the sphere of transnational labour law. They have adopted roles through which transnational contractual developments move beyond the normative framework originally set by the EU legislature.[9] These are developments where EWCs participate in negotiating transnational company agreements with multinationals that concern issues beyond information and consultation and where, under certain circumstances, EWCs can transform into global works councils.

Institutional characteristics of EWCs need to be viewed through cross-border regulatory frameworks and the interplay between them. Roles that EWCs have assumed demonstrate that means of transnational labour governance have become increasingly complicated, often placing contractual arrangements to the forefront instead of mandatory rules of law. Accordingly, exploring cross-border employee participation and its effects requires a contextualisation that crosses state law frames because both creation and usage of labour standards take place in transnational settings. As Zumbansen emphasises, in an analysis of transnational legal developments, the context of law moves to the centre.[10]

With the growing power of transnational regulatory actors, the possibility of defining regulatory space in territorial terms is decreasing. In transnational settings, private regulators largely focus on rule-making in ways that distance them from public regulatory frameworks. Normatively, the essential question appears not to be how to isolate cross-border labour protection from economic pressure but how to better integrate labour protection in economic governance. Challenges posed by market-based governance and changes in regulatory modes are intertwined in a blurred search for counterbalance or a struggle for social justice.[11]

In transnational settings, private regulation of social protection is filtered through regulatory frames that illustrate expansion of party autonomy.[12] This calls for closer attention to contractualisation of labour standards to unveil preferences that are given priority in related contracting processes. In cross-border employee participation, EWCs as bodies created for information and consultation purposes have become harnessed for private labour governance through contractual arrangements governing a broadening array of substance. Transnational settings offer a new perspective on employee participation when observed against the contractualisation of which it has become part in the EU.

[9] As Cafaggi emphasises, the transfer of rule-making power is not the only form affecting its redistribution. See F Cafaggi, 'New Foundations of Transnational Private Regulation' (2011) 38 *Journal of Law and Society* 20–40.

[10] According to Zumbansen, context has become a factor that forms a crucial part of assessing the legal nature of norms and the processes of creating and implementing them. P Zumbansen, 'The Ins and Outs of Transnational Private Regulatory Governance: Legitimacy, Accountability, Effectiveness and a New Concept of "Context"' (2012) 13 *German Law Journal* 1269–70.

[11] See A Blackett and A Trebilcock, 'Conceptualizing Transnational Labour Law' in A Blackett and A Trebilcock (eds), *Research Handbook of Transnational Labour Law* (Cheltenham, Edward Elgar, 2015) 4.

[12] It can be thought, leaning on Cafaggi's characterisation of the link between governance and regulatory activity being built around the regulatory relationship, that the beneficiaries are outside the legal boundaries but within the regime in question. See Cafaggi, (n 9) 20–46.

B. Developing the Transnational Agenda

The opening of societies and economies has led to a situation where national regulators do not have enough awareness about typical transnational situations and thus cannot create rules that would correspond to them.[13] Similar problems are noticeable in regional regulatory efforts. The need for a better understanding of the transnational legal environment and its impact on social protection connects to the need for a better understanding of contractualised labour governance in building protective normative frames based on uniform labour standards. While privatisation and contractualisation are essential characteristics of transnational settings where labour standards find their application in cross-border work constellations, so far there is little understanding of how this should influence the ways private labour governance is approached in regulatory arenas where public actors seek to enhance labour protection.

Nor have transnational strategies towards labour protection been elaborated to pinpoint loopholes of protection in cross-border settings.[14] While contractualisation essentially shapes the position of workers in different parts of global value chains, the heightened role of contractualisation draws attention to institutions that affect the efficiency and functioning of contracts in different countries.[15] Privatisation of labour standards also has a bearing on the weakening role of international labour standards created by the International Labour Organization (ILO).[16] While public regulators highlight the particular role of fundamental labour rights as defined by the ILO,[17] this emphasis is characterised by lack of attention to the consequences of expanding voluntarism in terms of labour protection in transnational settings.

There is a broad consensus that fundamental labour rights should be central in defining the content of the objective of decent work.[18] However, efforts to advocate

[13] See J Basedow, *The Law of Open Societies: Private Ordering and Public Regulation in the Conflict of Laws* (Brill, Leiden, 2015) 61.

[14] See U Liukkunen, 'Decent Work and Private International Law' (2022) 86 *Rabels Zeitschrift für ausländisches und internationales Privatrecht* 899–902. For examples of elaboration that build on the ways EWCs have brought about transnational law 'in action' and related procedures, see S Sciarra, 'Collective Exit Strategies: New Ideas in Transnational Labour Law' in G Davidov and B Langille (eds), *The Idea of Labour Law* (New York, Oxford University Press, 2011) 416–19.

[15] See A Paula Cusolito, R Safadi, and D Taglioni, *Inclusive Global Value Chains: Policy Options for Small and Medium Enterprises and Low-Income Countries* (World Bank and OECD, 2016) 79–81.

[16] U Liukkunen, 'SDG 8: Decent Work and Economic Growth' in R Michaels, V Ruiz Abou-Nigm and H van Loon (eds), *The Private Side of Transforming our World: UN Sustainable Development Goals 2030 and the Role of Private International Law* (Cambridge, Intersentia, 2021) 269–77.

[17] See ILO Declaration on Fundamental Principles and Rights at Work and its Follow-up, adopted 18 June 1998, amended 10 June 2022. Fundamental labour rights include freedom of association and effective recognition of the right to collective bargaining, elimination of all forms of forced or compulsory labour, effective abolition of child labour, and elimination of discrimination in respect of employment and occupation, and a safe and healthy working environment.

[18] This is also illustrated in the way SDG 8 of UN Agenda 2030 and its sub-targets are composed and concretised. See Resolution adopted by the UN General Assembly on 25 September 2015: Transforming our World: The 2030 Agenda for Sustainable Development (A/RES/70/1). See also U Liukkunen, 'The ILO and Transformation of Labour Law' in T Halonen and U Liukkunen (eds), *International Labour Organization and Global Social Governance* (Cham, Springer, 2021) 27.

sustainability through the decent work objective have remained piecemeal and lacked a strong normative focus. In the EU, related thematising of fundamental labour rights has typically occurred in contexts that relate to requirements set for third, non-EU countries, so that the external perspective has dominated and the tendency has been to link promotion of these rights to the external policy objectives of the Union.[19] The view that the idea of rights protection and decent work can be presented as distinctively different in intra-EU situations as compared with extra-EU situations is present in setting goals for EU transnational social policy.[20]

On a global level, the impact of transnational norm-setting draws attention to the limited role of fundamental labour rights in private labour governance. The ILO's Decent Work Agenda lacks a transnational dimension which would encompass cross-border contracts.[21] Shying away from cross-border normative developments also has to do with not addressing the consequences of enlarging voluntarism as a point of departure for committing to core labour standards in transnational settings. Ways to enhance fundamental labour rights protection in transnational settings need to be sought and the ILO should take a leading role in this search.[22]

The new voluntarism in labour relations reflects market-based governing regimes whose value-settings penetrate global value chains and would require more precise normative responses. UN-initiated work for regulating the social dimension of global supply chains reflects worries about lack of coverage of sufficient social protection.[23] However, regulatory efforts appear to be largely based on a worn-out understanding of the world of work. Mere references to the ILO 1998 Declaration and the MNE Declaration[24] remain insufficient because binding normativities encompassing labour protection should be directly connected to the framework of transnational regulatory developments detached from the traditional models of regulation that ILO labour standards typically rely on.[25]

[19] See Liukkunen (n 14) 885–86.

[20] See also European Commission, Communication from the Commission to the European Parliament, the Council and the European Economic and Social Committee on Decent Work Worldwide for a Global Just Transition and a Sustainable Recovery, COM(2022) 66 final; *cf* European Commission, Communication from the Commission to the European Parliament, the Council, the European Economic and Social Committee and the Committee of the Regions: The European Pillar of Social Rights Action Plan, COM(2021) 102 final.

[21] The Decent Work Agenda was adopted by the ILO in 2008, see ILO Declaration on Social Justice for a Fair Globalization, adopted by the International Labour Conference, 97th Session, Geneva, 10 June 2008, amended 2022.

[22] See Liukkunen (n 14) 876–904.

[23] See Resolution 26/9, adopted by the UN Human Rights Council 14 July 2014, Elaboration of an International Legally Binding Instrument on Transnational Corporations and Other Business Enterprises with Respect to Human Rights, A/HRC/RES/26/9; Chairmanship of the Open-Ended Intergovernmental Working Group Established by the Human Rights Council Resolution A/HRC/RES/26/9, *Elements for the Draft Legally Binding Instrument on Transnational Corporations and other Business Enterprises with Respect to Human Rights* (2017); UN Human Rights Council, *Report on the Eight Session of the Open-Ended Intergovernmental Working Group on Transnational Corporations and other Business Enterprises with Respect to Human* Rights, A/HRC/52/41 (2022).

[24] See ILO Tripartite Declaration of Principles concerning Multinational Enterprises and Social Policy, adopted 16 November 1977, and amended November 2000, March 2006, March 2017 and November 2022.

[25] See ILO, *Gap Analysis of ILO Normative and Non-Normative Measures to Ensure Decent Work in Supply Chains* (2021) 25.

In regulatory efforts of a regional nature, there is a similar tendency to simplify the transnational dimension of private labour governance to be noticed, but the points of departure differ. Development of cross-border employee participation as a governance mechanism in the EU is premised on a functioning internal market. The regulatory approach to EWCs has prompted considerable research which focuses on EU law and related state law frames that are relevant to the realisation of employee participation rights.[26] Studies frequently adopt a European or sector-specific perspective towards EWCs, whereas what is lacking is a normative perspective which would reach transnational settings and their extraterritorial dimension. So far in the current search for stronger labour governance institutions, no attempt has been made to conceptualise EWCs so as to address the regulatory formula adopted as a cross-border legal construction so that the role of transnational settings becomes central in the analysis.[27]

Unveiling the regulatory formula of the EU requires exploring normativities that EWCs manifest in the context of the transnational agenda to be developed for labour law. In this effort, transnational normativities become essential to understanding the nature of the cross-border context where transnational settings form regulatory spaces.[28] As forming transnational labour standards often bears a connection to contractualisation, the transnational labour law agenda needs to build a perspective on private ordering that acknowledges contractualisation of the elements of labour governance which have traditionally been viewed as belonging to the public law area. The same agenda also needs to encompass a labour law-oriented approach to the market and economy so that the particular underpinnings that labour law offers are not blown away.[29]

One of the basic problems in understanding the evolution of transnational normativities is the absence of private international law considerations.[30] Labour law lacks a perspective on cross-border regulatory frameworks where these considerations play a role in ways that shape the space for legal harmonisation. Partial harmonisation of substantive law combined with the use of private international law techniques has been used in the EU to ensure acknowledgment of the public interest in circumstances where market-based governance dominates.[31] Subject-specific choice-of-law rules have been used in certain parts of internal market law in ways that enlarge the roles of private international law in legal

[26] See V Pulignano and J Waddington, 'Management, European Works Councils and Institutional Malleability' (2020) 26 *European Journal of Industrial Relations* 5, 5–21.

[27] See U Liukkunen, 'Introduction' in U Liukkunen (ed), *Employment and Private International Law* (Cheltenham, Edward Elgar, 2020) xxviii.

[28] ibid xxvii–xxviii.

[29] See also R Dukes, *The Labour Constitution: The Enduring Idea of Labour Law* (Oxford, Oxford University Press, 2014) 209.

[30] On challenges in the field of international labour law posed to private international law by transnational normative developments, see Liukkunen, 'Introduction' (n 27).

[31] See, eg, U Liukkunen, 'Collision Between the Economic and the Social – What Has Private International Law Got to Do with It?' in P Letto-Vanamo and J Smits (eds), *Coherence and Fragmentation in European Private Law* (München, Sellier European Law Publishers, 2012).

integration.[32] Transnational regulation embraces and produces normativities that are independent of the state-centred context where private international law of labour relations traditionally operates and is needed to identify and resolve collisions that occur. Private international law also plays a role in regulatory approaches that influence how contractualisation of labour standards takes place in transnational settings.

The field of labour law places a strong emphasis on national legal practices and their institutional contexts and the debate on transnational labour law has been evolving from that particular frame.[33] As to regional assessments of transnational developments, these tend to highlight regulatory approaches within relatively uniform state entities when setting general points of departure for labour protection.[34] In such contexts, the question of regulatory frameworks and their interplay is often addressed from the underlying perspectives deriving from state law frames, in turn leading to difficulty in pinpointing the consequences of regulatory developments in transnational settings.

With transnational normativities, institutions of labour governance also need a rethink.[35] There is a need to build a perspective on privatised labour governance in order to understand how the regulatory formula of EWCs is influenced by transnational settings where these bodies of employee participation operate. In essence, the particular mode of regulation developed by the EU has enabled the birth of a transnational institution which shapes the use of labour standards in a legal environment characterised by cross-border regulatory multi-connectivity.

The legal environment where EWCs operate highlights the mutual connectivity of regulatory frameworks in shaping transnational labour governance and its influence on the protective sphere of the cross-border dimension of law. Viewing EWCs in terms of transnational labour governance requires developing a theoretical framework for their conceptualisation which moves beyond analyses that highlight the level of the integrated market. In the following, EWCs are first analysed in the internal market context in order to understand the purposes of regulation and after that they are analysed against transnational settings. This approach involves a broader theoretical view on their function and the regulatory formula enabling that function.

[32] U Liukkunen, 'Managing Legal Diversity in the EU: The Case of Subject-Specific Conflicts Rules' (2012) 20 *European Review of Private Law* 1045–74.

[33] See Blackett and Trebilcock (n 11), where a wide-ranging conception of transnational labour law is adopted as a point of departure.

[34] See also KVW Stone, 'Labor and the Global Economy: Four Approaches to Transnational Labor Regulation' (1995) 16 *Michigan Journal of International Law* 987–1006. *cf* MF Finkin, 'International Governance and Domestic Convergence in Labor Law as Seen from the American Midwest' (2001) 76 *Indiana Law Journal* 1043–72.

[35] eg, Estlund describes the variety and cumulative weight of barriers towards changes characteristic of US labour law in CL Estlund, 'The Ossification of American Labor Law' (2002) 102 *Columbia Law Review* 1527–1612. This isolation is recognisable even in broader developments beyond individual states and influences approaches to institutional labour governance.

II. EMPLOYEE PARTICIPATION IN THE EU – A REGIONAL ENTERPRISE

In general, employee participation may refer to a wide range of mechanisms and modes of regulation through which employee involvement can be arranged.[36] Employee participation has gradually established itself as one of the core areas of EU labour law. EU law has not only brought about a cross-border dimension to the employee participation systems of the EU Member States but also set a minimum level of domestic rights to information and consultation. The EU legislature's current approach to developing employee participation rights is based on the view that participation rights are fundamental social rights, and they are also reflected in the EU social pillar.[37] However, the influence of constitutionalisation has remained a question which is not addressed from the standpoint of the role of EU law in transnational settings.

On the whole, the importance of cross-border employee participation is not matched by corresponding rights in transnational settings, as is demonstrated by the wide use of voluntarism in adopted regulatory approaches. Despite an active regulatory strategy, EU law on employee participation has been maintained as an enterprise of and within the internal market.[38] Consequently, legal integration as a regional enterprise is typically viewed in the Union from the perspective of producing harmonisation of rules that protect and create minimum rights for EU workers – while the extraterritorial impact of regulatory efforts is overlooked. In the same vein, non-EU workers remain beyond the horizon.

Even where cross-border participation rights are viewed as a part of the region-centred regulatory approach developed by the EU, they would simultaneously require that heed be paid to the specific characteristics of the transnational settings where they operate. The regional nature of cross-border participation rights is accentuated as these rights concern personnel of undertakings as well as groups of undertakings of a certain size in the European Economic Area (EEA) states. EWC legislation only applies when these undertakings and groups are located in the EEA, including those that operate partly inside and partly outside that area.

In the EU, the use of regulatory policies that affect transnational labour governance forms part of internal market governance. The internal market is based on a regional regime which seeks to guarantee the four EU fundamental economic freedoms. The system, as such, involves a tension between economic and social interests.

[36] On the variation of terminology and its conceptual basis in changing socio-economic contexts, see, eg, R Markey and K Townsend, 'Contemporary Trends in Employee Involvement and Participation' (2013) 55 *Journal of Industrial Relations* 4, 475–78.

[37] The right to information and consultation is acknowledged as a fundamental labour right in the EU Charter of Fundamental Rights, which was made binding by the Treaty of Lisbon. According to Art 27 of the Charter, 'workers or their representatives must, at the appropriate levels, be guaranteed information and consultation in good time in the cases and under the conditions provided for by Community law and national laws and practices'. The Charter does not, however, include the right to employee representation in company administration.

[38] See also MA Moreau, 'The Originality of Transnational Social Norms as a Response to Globalisation' in B Bercusson and C Estlund (eds), *Regulating Labour in the Wake of Globalisation: New Challenges, New Institutions* (Oxford and Portland, Hart Publishing, 2008) 266.

EU labour law has notably served the political economy of the market.[39] The aim to strengthen European competitiveness and the European economy permeates the idea of integration and the aims of EU social policy are often filtered through it.

The EU's choice for its ultimate policy goals has affected how employee participation rights have developed. The criticism of moving away 'from legal prescription to bargaining in the shadow of the market' refers to deficiencies recognised in the European system of employee participation.[40] A central problem in developing employee participation rights has been that conflicting goals are pulling legislative development in different directions, with the market-oriented approach at the one end and, at the other, the aim of securing labour rights. The EU legislature has often opted for the market, which is particularly evident in legislative projects involving employee representation in company administration and pan-European company forms.[41] This tendency has also affected EU regulatory policies that influence labour rights protection in transnational settings.

The European aim of promoting development of employee participation rights as a tool for anticipating and managing changes can be viewed as a part of the wider context where responses are sought to counter the harsh social outcomes of economic developments in the internal market. In certain respects, however, EU law's perception of collective labour rights has proven to be contradictory. The striving for supremacy of the fundamental economic freedoms is something that has come to possess particular normative characteristics. These were made most explicit in the *Viking*[42] and *Laval*[43] judgments. In the area of employee participation, the sought-for certain balance between fundamental economic freedoms and fundamental social rights has largely been built on continuance of existing participation rights as sought by the EU legislature. This has involved efforts at relieving tensions between the economic and the social in a controlled manner by less-discussed means of private international law techniques.[44]

III. TRANSFORMATION OF COLLECTIVE VOICE: A CROSS-BORDER SCENE

To a notable extent, EU legislation on employee participation rights builds on maintaining existing Member State legislative traditions and related diversity.

[39] See S Giubboni, *Social Rights and Market Freedoms in the European Constitution: A Labour Law Perspective* (Cambridge, Cambridge University Press, 2006) 163.

[40] Streeck (n 7) 643–54.

[41] Securing continuity of employee representation in company administration has proved to be complicated and has prolonged legislative processes and related decision-making in the EU. This was visible, eg, in the work of the so-called Davignon group, which attempted to find a solution to the deadlock in the preparation of SE legislation as regards employee representation in SEs. See Group of Experts, European Systems of Worker Involvement (with regard to the European Company Statute and the Other Pending Proposals), Final Report, May 1997.

[42] Case C-438/05 *International Transport Workers' Federation and Finnish Seamen's Union v Viking Line ABP and OÜ Viking Line Eesti* [2008] OJ C51/11.

[43] Case C-341/05 *Laval un Partneri Ltd v Svenska Byggnadsarbetareförbundet, Svenska Byggnadsarbetareförbundets avdelning 1, Byggettan and Svenska Elektrikerförbundet* [2007] ECR I-11767.

[44] See Liukkunen (n 31).

The regulatory approach acknowledges that each national labour law model is deeply embedded in the related industrial relations and labour market model developed through different evolutionary stages.[45] But when EU legislation on employee participation has brought about a cross-border participation dimension at the level of multinational undertakings, it has departed from this and made industrial relations models confront each other in transnational settings. What should be noted is that maintenance of traditions has been coupled with voluntarism in the adopted regulatory approach.

The development of EWCs has often been evaluated from the highlighted context of the trade union movement and the Europeanisation of industrial relations.[46] One of the aims of the original EWC Directive was to establish transnational information and consultation procedures within multinational undertakings and groups of undertakings operating in the EEA but there were also aims that connect the legislative outcome to the social partnership.[47] One of these aims was to foster negotiations between the social partners within multinational undertakings. Another was set to encourage trade unions to invest both more material and more political resources at the European level.[48]

In EU labour law, employee participation rights have typically been developing across borders in two ways. Firstly, participation rights have been extended to cover the cross-border area. The central managements of multinational undertakings and groups of undertakings of a certain size have been placed under an obligation to inform and consult employees in a timely manner.[49] Secondly, EU labour law has built an approach highlighting that cross-border restructuring should be carried out without diminishing existing employee participation rights.

Not only employee representation at board level but also employee information and consultation have become elements of advancing sustainable corporate governance. At the same time, the EU legislative framework has remained fragile so that cross-border corporate restructuring may endanger employee representation at board level. The diversity of national regulatory models enables companies from different Member States participating in restructuring to seek corporate arrangements that enable them to avoid or terminate employee representation at board level.[50] Moreover, although EWC legislation on cross-border information and consultation applies in transnational settings, this involves noteworthy limitations.[51]

[45] See U Liukkunen, *Globalisaatio, EU ja henkilöstön osallistuminen. Tutkimus globalisaatiojuridiikasta ja eurooppaoikeudesta erityisesti rajat ylittävissä yritysjärjestelyissä* (Helsinki, Edita, 2005) 337.

[46] See, eg, J Waddington, *European Works Councils and Industrial Relations: A Transnational Industrial Relations Institution in the Making* (New York, Routledge, 2010).

[47] The original EWC Directive was adopted in 1994.

[48] See Waddington (n 46) 219–22. See also Preamble to Directive 94/45/EC (n 6).

[49] Also the fact that the right to information and consultation is considered a fundamental right highlights the timeless nature of information and consultation.

[50] Additionally, the case law of the European Court of Justice (CJEU) on freedom of establishment has come to offer some possibilities for circumventing board-level employee representation through establishing a company under the law of a Member State which does not have a system of board-level employee representation. Illustrative of this development is the CJEU judgment in Case C-208/00 *Überseering BV v Nordic Construction Company Baumanagement GmbH (NCC)* [2002] ECR I-09919.

[51] eg, multinational enterprises that operate simultaneously on several continents may observe the European model and provide related participation rights only in their units located in the EEA area.

The role of EWCs in EU social policy has been built on regulatory choices that essentially detach from the traditional state-bound way of viewing participation rights. The Recast Directive of 2009 (Recast EWC Directive)[52] followed the original EWC Directive of 1994, which entrenched the right to information and consultation for personnel of multinational groups of undertakings and undertakings operating in the EEA. Like its predecessor, the Recast EWC Directive applies to them when they have at least 1,000 employees – including at least 150 in at least two EEA states. The employee participation model set forth is based on contractual arrangements: the purpose is to reach agreement for an EWC consisting of employee representatives from each EEA country where the group of undertakings or undertaking in question has a certain number of employees. Alternatively, the parties may agree on some other form of employee information and consultation.

While EWCs are often characterised as an institutional innovation modelled on the national participation systems of the Member States, Germany and France in particular, the Directive emphasises freedom of contract in forming the applicable employee participation model. This approach has been criticised as anticipating the decline of industrial democracy and related employee rights.[53] The emphasis on party autonomy has been seen as a sign of EU labour law becoming more neoliberal and dictated by the market.[54] Evaluations of the legislative outcome have also been critical because the number of EWCs has remained modest and their role as the workers' voice has not been strong.[55] A central question of controversy, which the Recast EWC Directive did not alter, is the three-year negotiation period given to the parties for the purpose of agreeing on an EWC.[56]

According to the Recast EWC Directive, EWCs are to be informed and consulted on transnational issues.[57] The Directive also includes a definition of information and consultation. The manner in which information and consultation are to be performed cannot be determined by the contracting parties themselves but the manner in which information is given and consultation is carried out have to fulfil the criteria in the Directive. However, the Directive does not clearly state the time when informing and consulting should take place, although the demand for them to be timely is crucial for the materialisation of participation rights.[58] Moreover, a further criticism is that,

[52] Directive 2009/38/EC of the European Parliament and of the Council of 6 May 2009 on the Establishment of a European Works Council or a Procedure in Community-scale Undertakings and Community-Scale groups of Undertakings for the Purposes of Informing and Consulting Employees (Recast) ('Recast EWC Directive') [2004] OJ L122/28.

[53] See Streeck (n 7) 643–64.

[54] See Lecher et al (n 8) 7–8.

[55] See Pulignano and Waddington (n 26) 5–21.

[56] Only after such a long time can the secondary provisions of the Directive be applied, ie, fallback provisions can be used to arrange for information and consultation.

[57] See Art 1(4) of Recast EWC Directive (n 52), which is supplemented by Rec 16, included in the Directive on the initiative of the European Parliament. The Recital has been considered to have exceptional weight in relation to the content of the EWC Directive. This can also be seen in that certain Member States, such as Finland and Sweden, have included the content of the Recital in their legislation transposing the Directive.

[58] Despite certain improvements, the reform of the Directive has prompted criticism for not meeting the aims set for it. See, eg, S Laulom, 'The Flawed Revision of the European Works Council Directive' (2010) 39 *Industrial Law Journal* 2, 202–208. In 2023, the European Commission launched a first-stage consultation of European social partners on a possible revision of the Directive.

in terms of timing, legal obligations deriving from company law may de facto take precedence over obligations deriving from employee participation regulation.[59]

IV. RECONCEPTUALISING COLLECTIVE VOICE

While recent economic and labour market developments have put added pressure on domestic labour law systems, this has not translated into growing attention to cross-border regulatory needs. Yet, uncertainties created by global competition and, above all, the fact that undertakings are making quick changes in business locations, have maintained anticipating and managing changes as a key challenge for the social dimension of European integration. Although typically viewed as local issues, anticipating and managing changes connects to multi-level regulatory structures that shape transnational settings in multiple ways, most notably when undertakings having cross-border operations make decisions affecting employees in a country other than where those employees are working.[60]

EU-level efforts to mitigate the social effects of corporate restructuring have been increasingly linked to adjusting to changes in corporate decision-making structures so that employee participation is largely regulated from the standpoint of social adaptation. Moreover, with the diversity of situations, cross-border corporate restructuring and its complex nature have created a demand for better anticipation and management of changes in situations where employees in the EEA area are affected.[61] The response by the EU has been based on a transnational reconstruction of collective voice through the EWC regulatory formula. Its unintentional outcome, namely that EWCs have acquired transnational roles in private labour governance, reaches the social impact of restructuring processes. Transnational company agreements that EWCs participate in typically address the social consequences of restructuring when these agreements are made to govern European personnel of the undertaking or group in question.[62]

Self-organised activities of EWCs have become highlighted in that EWCs have assumed tasks that derive from their transnational operational framework, in which they communicate with the central management beyond their role as a cross-border institution of information and consultation.[63] Although EWCs can sometimes

[59] See Pulignano and Waddington (n 26) 12.

[60] Moreau has highlighted that anticipating changes involves several phases and complex interrelations between different actors as well as a need to build effective forms of regulation. See MA Moreau, 'European Solidarity and Labour Law. Some Thoughts Stemming from the Question of Restructuring Europe' in L Magnusson and B Stråth (eds), *European Solidarities: Tensions and Contentions of a Concept* (Brussels, Peter Lang, 2007) 116–19.

[61] See also MA Moreau and JJ Paris, 'The Role of the European Works Councils during Restructurings. The Lessons of the AgirE Project' in MA Moreau, S Negrelli and P Pochet (eds), *Building Anticipation of Restructuring in Europe* (Brussels, Peter Lang, 2009) 173.

[62] U Liukkunen (n 1).

[63] See also the characterisation by Dukes and Streeck of labour law being 'in a pronounced way' participatory law which is developed not only by the state but also by its subjects, which either may or may not seek to balance the asymmetries between them in terms of their market and organisational power. R Dukes and W Streeck, *Democracy at Work: Contract, Status and Post-Industrial Justice* (Newark, Polity Press, 2022) 40.

function in ways that decrease their original role, they can also acquire roles that manifest transnational institutional power enabled in developments which start from their establishment through the particular regulatory framework created by the EU legislature.[64] As bodies of employee participation, they demonstrate the development of transnational labour governance which has to do with the regulatory framework they stem from, which in turn is, to a certain extent, built on private international law technique.[65] When assuming roles in transnational labour governance EWCs bring out capacities built on their institutionalisation enabled by the particular regulatory framework for cross-border employee information and consultation.

V. NORMATIVE LAYOUT BEHIND EWCS – THREE LEVELS OF REGULATION

EWCs offer a perspective on private labour governance that builds on a normative construction of the transnational institutions of labour relations.[66] They offer a particular perspective on the influence of the extension of party autonomy to contract-based labour standard-setting deriving from a particular institutional and legal architecture which in turn is enabled by the way private international law rules have been used by the EU legislature for integrationist purposes. Against this, the Recast EWC Directive can be viewed as setting a particular regulatory frame, which in transnational settings produces transnational normativities. The regulatory formula is based on a complex construction of voluntarism, which suggests a fundamental rethink of how employee participation is regulated when the EU builds industrial democracy and labour governance for cross-border purposes.[67]

The normative framework for the establishment and operations of EWCs is also a telling example of the characteristics of neo-voluntarism in transnational labour law.[68] The regulatory formula is a multi-level construction involving several opportunities of choices for the parties to negotiations and eventual agreement for an EWC. The Directive comprises three levels of regulation that can be viewed as constituting a kind of nested circle.[69] Inside the circle stands the mandatory core, that is, mandatory

[64] On ways of using EWCs so that their industrial democracy function is lessened, see Pulignano and addington (n 26) 10–11.

[65] The Recast EWC Directive, like its predecessor, is built on the idea that the conflicts rules include determining the Member State whose national transposition legislation becomes applicable to the group of undertakings or undertaking in question.

[66] See DM Trubek, J Mosher and JS Rothstein, 'Transnationalism in the Regulation of Labor Relations: International Regimes and Transnational Advocacy Networks' (2000) 25 *Law & Social Inquiry* 1187–1211.

[67] According to the Report published by the European Commission, '[t]he priority given to the negotiated formula within the companies for their establishment and operation is at core of the success of EWCs from their early days'. See Report of the Group of Experts: Implementation of Recast Directive 2009/38/EC on European Works Councils (European Commission, 2010) 6.

[68] See W Streeck, 'Neo-Voluntarism: A New European Social Policy Regime?' (1995) 1 *European Law Journal* 31–49.

[69] U Liukkunen, *Yritystoiminnan muutokset ja yhteistoiminta. Tutkimus kansallisesta ja transnationaalista työoikeudesta* (Helsinki, Forum Iuris, 2013) 251–52.

provisions on the procedures for agreeing on and implementing information and consultation procedures as well as the operation and rights of an EWC.

In the middle are the semi-mandatory provisions of the Directive. These include provisions on adjusting EWC operations to structural changes and integrating the information and consultation procedure into national-level procedures. If there are no provisions on adjustment in the EWC agreement, or if several agreements apply but with conflicting adjustment provisions, negotiations on a new agreement are launched. Similarly, when the information and consultation procedure for an EWC is integrated into national procedures, it is to be based on the EWC agreement. If the agreement does not state how integration takes place, the information and consultation obligations are carried out at both the EWC level and the national level.

The fall-back solution offered by the Directive is also connected to voluntarism.[70] The Appendix to the Directive consists of provisions on subsidiary requirements that concern the establishment, composition and competence of an EWC.[71] These secondary provisions can be generally considered as semi-mandatory, and they apply if the central administration and the special negotiation body (SNB) representing the personnel so agree, or if the central administration refuses to launch negotiations for an EWC agreement or, thirdly, if agreement cannot be reached in negotiations.[72] The secondary provisions can only be applied if certain procedures laid down in the Directive are adopted first.[73]

The outermost part of the nested circle of the three levels of regulation in the Directive comprises dispositive provisions that contain issues which are negotiable in the EWC agreement. These provisions include, for example, the Directive's optional list of items that should be taken in the agreement. Because the operative framework for EWCs is transnational, rules adopted by the Member States to transpose the Directive are meant to only offer a general framework on which EWCs may tailor transnational operating procedures that suit their operating environments. The Directive does not suggest what EWCs should do if they are offered an opportunity to participate in negotiating transnational company agreements or other kinds of company-specific documents.[74]

The multi-layered regulatory approach sketched out above is based on extensive freedom of contract. This enables observation of the individual characteristics of each undertaking and group of undertakings in their EWC agreements. The regulatory frame enables EWCs to create their own substance and rules in an agreement between the SNB and central management. At the same time, negotiations for specific contractual arrangements are not built in a void but are surrounded by and interact with various normative frameworks. These frameworks can be viewed as providing a broader normative context for the operations of EWCs, shaping them as bodies of transnational labour governance that act beyond the jurisdiction of the EU.

[70] See also Streeck (n 7) 643–52.
[71] See Annex I to Recast EWC Directive (n 52).
[72] ibid Art 7.
[73] The personnel must at least establish an SNB and propose negotiations to the central administration.
[74] There is also no EU legislation on the legal effects of the operations of EWCs in such a context.

A. Contractual Freedom and Transnational Institutionalisation

It has often been stressed that EWC legislation builds on a procedural regulatory approach instead of a substantive one.[75] Party autonomy connects to this in ways that intertwine procedural and institutional processes.[76] The EU regulatory approach highlights party autonomy to an extent that enables a wide array of institutional outcomes and, as a result, EWCs form a heterogeneous entity.[77] As we have seen, the regulatory approach enables variations that differ from each other, for example in the structure and composition of EWCs. Behind the variations, the different characteristics of undertakings can be recognised but also an interaction between and among the different kinds of industrial relations systems and related regulatory frames.[78]

EWCs offer a transnational context for the meeting of different legal traditions present in Member States' employee participation models. To a certain extent, these can be viewed as manifesting a kind of transnational fusion of national industrial relations models as well as related ideas and ideologies. As they build on normative regimes strongly affected by their transnational environment, EWCs become detached from a certain spatial location as decisive to the functions they perform. Contractual freedom shapes the way EWCs are built but it also affects their transnational institutionalisation.

Freedom of contract can be utilised in different ways in an EWC agreement.[79] The wide extent of party autonomy entrusted to the negotiating parties is demonstrated by the fact that the content of the EWC agreement agreed upon may be weaker than the rights provided by the secondary provisions of the Recast EWC Directive in questions relating to the EWC or to informing and consulting employees.[80] There are also opportunities to utilise freedom of contract for more protective and inclusive purposes. For example, the number of personnel representatives in an EWC can be agreed to include workers' representatives in a more balanced manner than the requirements of the Directive would stipulate. Emphasis on freedom of contract is also significant with respect to the effects on the tasks that EWCs may assume outside

[75] See, eg, M Weiss, 'The Development of Employee Involvement in the EU: Lessons to Be Learned' in V Pulignano and F Hendrickx (eds), *Employment Relations in the 21st Century: Challenges for Theory and Research in a Changing World of Work* (Alphen aan den Rijn, Wolters Kluwer, 2020) 183. Deakin considers the EWC Directive as an example of a regulatory approach highlighting procedural orientation to law and seeking to advance autonomy at the level of self-regulatory systems of law, and hence diverse local level approaches to regulatory problems. See S Deakin, 'Regulatory Competition versus Harmonization in European Company Law' in DC Esty and D Géradin (eds), *Regulatory Competition and Economic Integration: Comparative Perspectives* (Oxford, Oxford University Press, 2001).

[76] See also Lecher et al (n 8) 178–81.

[77] See Weiss (n 75) 184.

[78] On conceptualising EWCs in terms of a 'multi-level structure' of workplace industrial relations in multinational enterprises, see HW Platzer, 'Approaching and Theorising European Works Councils: Comments on the Emergence of a European Multi-Level-Structure of Employee Involvement and Participation' in M Hertwig, L Pries and L Rampeltshammer (eds), *European Works Councils in Complementary Perspectives: New Approaches to the Study of European Interest Regulation* (Brussels, European Trade Union Institute, 2009) 49.

[79] The Directive only includes a non-binding list of things that must be included in the agreement.

[80] See Art 6(4) of Recast EWC Directive (n 52).

the geographical scope of the Directive. In an EWC agreement, the right to information and consultation can be expanded to cover personnel outside the EEA to cover the personnel of an entire undertaking or group of undertakings so that a globally operating works council can be formed.

Contractual freedom has come to play a transformative function in transnational settings where transnational company agreements on labour and social issues are negotiated and concluded between multinationals and EWCs. EWCs take part in drafting and implementing not only transnational agreements but also company-specific corporate social responsibility documentation. When drafting and executing such company-specific documents, EWCs act outside their tasks set out by the legal framework as laid down by EU law and further shape the transnational social partnership.

B. Party Autonomy in Arranging Employee Participation Through Negotiations for an EWC

Essentially, the legal framework for negotiations concerning an EWC agreement derives from national norms that have transposed the Recast EWC Directive in the EEA state where the central management is located. As noted, the Directive sets boundaries for voluntarism in that, when parties fail to reach agreement, secondary provisions on informing and consulting employees become applicable. Ultimately, employee participation must be arranged in accordance with these provisions if the employees demand participation rights and an agreement cannot be reached on these. If two-thirds of the personnel decline an information and consultation procedure, they can choose not to have it. Yet the primary option is to reach agreement through negotiations between the central management and the SNB.

As noted, in negotiations for the establishment of an EWC, the freedom of contract provided by the Recast EWC Directive can be utilised in different ways. At the one extreme, freedom of contract can be argued as allowing for a lightweight EWC. It is even possible to agree that no information and consultation procedure will be adopted at all. In such cases it is not mandatory to apply the secondary provisions of the Directive either. At the other extreme, freedom of contract can be used to create a more comprehensive system of information and consultation which takes into account the special features of the individual undertaking or group of undertakings and may, for example, extend the information and consultation procedure to parts of the undertaking or of the group that are located beyond the EEA, or even to the whole of the undertaking or group globally.

Freedom of contract also has other noteworthy dimensions. It can be used in seeking a balance between an EWC's representativeness and its transnationality of operations. The EU regulatory formula of EWCs enables arrangements where the number of representatives of employees from each country is changed to the effect that the number of employees from the country where the undertaking or the group has most of its staff is reduced or levelled out for the benefit of the smaller countries. Such a move may be made in order to better balance employee representation and transnationality. The regulatory formula also enables extending participation rights to workers from non-EEA states who are in the sphere of EWC legislation and also taking into account gender and non-discrimination issues in the composition of the EWC.[81]

VI. CROSS-BORDER REGULATORY FRAMEWORKS AND THEIR INTERPLAY

Once concluded, an EWC agreement does not function in a normative void but can be viewed as a part of group- or company-specific normative regimes.[82] These regimes are influenced by cross-border regulatory frameworks, creating a normative context which also shapes the operation of EWCs, including situations that do not fall within the sphere of issues agreed upon in the EWC agreement. Moreover, international framework agreements and other transnational company agreements are shaped by the regulatory framework.[83] With conclusion of such agreements, EWCs as private regulatory actors move beyond the regulatory framework set by EU legislation and establish transnational labour standards on their own terms, independently from their regulatory basis as set by EU law.[84]

Creation of EWCs based on broad contractual autonomy is enabled by the regulatory formula which builds on a particular private international law approach.[85] The influence of private international law rules penetrates the regulatory approach, but choice-of-law rules also affect private rule-making which EWCs take part in. These rules determine which EEA state's law applies to the establishment of an EWC.[86] The private international law approach adopted has enabled creation of the particular regulatory formula based on applying each EU Member States' national legislation along with harmonised rules based on the Recast EWC Directive.[87]

The European regulatory architecture of cross-border employee participation rights relies on the mechanism built on choice-of-law rules. The role given to private international law in the regulatory formula behind EWCs can be linked to the materialisation of private international law.[88] When private international law is to a certain extent used by the EU legislature in a manner which differs from its

[81] See also S Mangold, 'Hybrid Transnational Self-Regulation' (2019) 40 *Comparative Labor Law & Policy Journal* 454–55. According to Art 6(2)(d) of the Recast EWC Directive the composition of EWCs takes into account the need for balanced representation of employees, including with regard to gender.

[82] See MA Moreau, 'The Reconceptualization of the Employment Relationship and Labour Rights through Transnationality' (2013) 34 *Comparative Labor Law & Policy Journal* 697–714.

[83] International framework agreements form a specific group of transnational company agreements and typically seek to ensure respect for fundamental labour rights.

[84] See also I Schömann, 'The Impact of Transnational Company Agreements on Social Dialogue and Industrial Relations' in K Papadakis (ed), *Shaping Global Industrial Relations: The Impact of International Framework Agreements* (Hampshire, Palgrave Macmillan, 2011) 30–31; Sciarra (n 14) 416–17.

[85] See also E Pataut, 'Collective Agreements in Europe: European Social Dialogue and Contractual Autonomy' in J Basedow, C Su, M Fornasier and U Liukkunen (eds), *Employee Participation and Collective Bargaining in Europe and China* (Tübingen, Mohr Siebeck, 2016).

[86] See Liukkunen (n 45) 293–97.

[87] The former is used to define, eg, how employee representatives are to be determined on the basis of national laws.

[88] See Liukkunen, (n 45) 293–97.

traditional use, this is often explained as relating to maintaining diversity of national laws. However, this involves also using choice-of-law rules so that the outcome of applying them is considered in terms of substantive law interests and the rules drafted can also produce protective underpinnings.[89] Arguably, the particular use of choice-of-law rules contributes to adjusting the operation of EWCs to private governance mechanisms dominant in transnational settings. But at the same time, the EU regulatory model also affects labour rights in ways that make realising those rights dependent on contractualised labour governance.

VII. EWCS AS A MANIFESTATION OF TRANSNATIONAL LABOUR LAW

Labour law has been somewhat hesitant to involve the discourse of circulation and reception of legal models.[90] It was Kahn-Freund who put forward the claim that transplants cannot really succeed in the field of collective labour law because they are so strongly connected to power relations in society.[91] Although later comparative labour law scholarship has become more at ease with legal transplants, it often highlights the close relationship between employee participation institutions and domestic power relationships.[92] Nevertheless, the development of cross-border employee participation rights related to the transnational legal environment has created an interaction between industrial relations traditions on a transnational level.

The traditions of different employee participation systems and industrial relations models meet in the operations of EWCs. In order for different conceptions of participation to penetrate the conditions for transferability set by the transnational normative frame of EWCs, national traditions have to adjust to each other. The resulting constellations can be approached from the perspective of transnational legal transplants. They highlight the need for a nuanced understanding of the criteria for transferability and different stages of transferability in multi-layered governance structures where the legal environment is of a transnational nature.

In the operation of EWCs, an interaction occurs between different labour market traditions that reconciles these traditions. In a way, traditional discourse has to give way to transnational discourse, which brings new meanings and links between national models related to cross-border participation rights. From the transnational

[89] See also U Liukkunen, 'The Method of Understanding and an Internal Viewpoint – On the Interface between Comparative Law and Private International Law' (2007) 2 *Zeitschrift für Vergleichende Rechtswissenschaft* 141, 144–46.

[90] On legal transplants and transplantation, see A Watson, *Legal Transplants: An Approach to Comparative Law* (Edinburgh, Scottish Academic Press, 1974). Watson emphasised the value of comparative law in terms of understanding legal changes, writing '… for me the main value of comparative law as an academic discipline is the insights it gives into legal change and into the relationship of law and society' in A Watson, *Legal History and a Common Law for Europe: Mystery, Reality, Imagination* (Stockholm, Institutet för rättshistoriska forskning, 2001) 117.

[91] See O Kahn-Freund, 'On Uses and Misuses of Comparative Law' (1974) 37 *MLR* 1, 1–27. See also Stone (n 34) 1005–06.

[92] See also B Hepple, 'Can Collective Labour Law Transplants Work? – The South African Example' (1999) 20 *Industrial Law Journal* 2–3.

perspective, EWCs should not be seen as conclusively dependent on the national legislation of the state where the central management is located in terms of how they are shaped and how they function. EWCs function in a transnational operational environment and the legal rules applicable to them should be seen against this context.

An EWC is profoundly different from the works council institutions known in certain European employee participation systems. It can be considered a flexible transplant created by the EU legislature that adjusts, on the one hand, to the legal system of the Member State that is the state of origin or the host state, and, on the other hand, to the normative regime of the undertaking or group of undertakings.[93] This means that, generally, EWCs could be understood as representing a transition, firstly, from transplants at the level of national systems to transplantation within transnational law, and, secondly, from EU law to transplantation that takes place on the level of the laws of the Member States. Such transplantation can be viewed as taking place in two phases in the sense that, after the Member States implemented the Recast EWC Directive, through transnational negotiations and eventually also their operation, EWCs adjust not only to a company-specific normative regime but also to the corporate culture and social as well as the business environment.[94]

When legal mobility materialises in transnational settings, legal transplants originating in EU law cannot be looked at solely from the viewpoint of national or EU law. EWCs can be considered as an example of transplantation in transnational law. They manifest transplants that are integrated into transnational law, that is, into EU law and the normative regimes of multinational undertakings and groups of undertakings. Notably, an EWC starts to truly take form institutionally only after the EWC agreement on it has been concluded.[95]

When analysing legal transplants, Graziadei has taken up the influence of global actors that actively produce strategies of legal change and are involved in the making of a transplant.[96] EWCs demonstrate how transplantation to transnational law can take place so that institutional structures are created in transnational settings. The normative regimes of multinational undertakings do not solely base themselves on national, regional or international norms, while multinationals themselves shape their regimes through autonomous choices.[97] In terms of transnational labour law, EWCs can be regarded as an EU-level regulatory construction that has

[93] See Liukkunen (n 69) 260.

[94] ibid 260–61.

[95] The agreement may provide only a loose framework for the development and operation of the EWC. See ibid 263.

[96] M Graziadei, 'Comparative Law, Transplants and Receptions' in M Reimann and R Zimmermann (eds), *The Oxford Handbook of Comparative Law*, 2nd edn (Oxford, Oxford University Press, 2019) 473. *cf* Zumbansen (n 10) 1281, taking up actors, norms and processes 'in which law appears to be caught up'.

[97] '… extraterritoriality does little to prevent the rules governing employment relations in one country from taking root elsewhere, from shaping foreign labor market norms, institutions, and practices, and from being reproduced, in their original or mutant forms, in foreign systems of labor law. The result is the extraterritorial projection "by other means" of labor law and policy – a form of extraterritoriality that has the potential to enhance as well as undermine labor standards in global enterprises'. HW Arthurs, 'Extraterritoriality by Other Means: How Labor Law Sneaks Across Borders, Conquers Minds, and. Controls Workplaces Abroad', *Comparative Research in Law & Political Economy. Research Paper No. 25/2010* (2010) 102.

the potential to influence a multinational undertaking's operations beyond their role as the bodies of information and consultation, and represent the interests of the entire personnel.[98]

Altogether, EWCs suggest that the transnational dimension of law brings new perspectives to the transplantation discourse. An EWC can be regarded as a flexible transnational transplant created by the EU legislature and adjustable, on the one hand, to the legal system of the 'host country' and, on the other hand, to the normative regime of the undertaking or group of undertakings. In essence, EWCs can be viewed as representing a shift away from transplants between national systems to transplants within transnational law. In a way, there are two phases, as after transposition of the Directive by the Member States, undertakings modify the EWCs based on the particular regulatory framework to make them fit their own normative regimes.[99]

VIII. NORMATIVE REGIONALISM AND PRIVATE LABOUR GOVERNANCE

The regulatory formula of EWCs, which emphasises voluntarism in organising employee participation in a cross-border context, is based on a different ideology from that based on equal collective rights for all employees. The regulatory framework manifests that developing a transnational social model predominantly on the basis of voluntarism encompasses mutually reinforcing norm-making processes that highlight the contractual nature of standard-making. Operation in transnational settings links EWCs to privatised norm production where a market-based governance regime dominates.

Reconciling cross-border employee participation and transnational labour governance requires rejection of intra-regional and extra-regional perspectives on EU labour law as the sole point of departure in exploring the extraterritorial influence of EU law. Emphasis on regionalism in the discourse of transnational labour law hinders viewing the consequences of neo-voluntarism in transnational settings.[100] Consequently, inability to see beyond regional transformations has a bearing on the social protection the EU aims at. The EU legislature focuses in particular on employee participation rights within the internal market, which in internal market law development means also regulating cross-border legal relations from the highlighted perspective of European integration as a regional enterprise.[101] Even though it is clear that regionalism is already accentuated because the EU is based on regional integration, the impact of transnational legal developments, reflected by EWCs, on labour standards should be examined against transnational settings in order to understand profound changes in the ways protective frameworks are involved.

[98] See also Lecher et al (n 8).
[99] See Liukkunen (n 69) 260–61.
[100] See generally Stone (n 34) 987–1028.
[101] A telling example is the regulatory approach adopted in the EU pieces of legislation that govern European companies, European Co-operative Societies, and cross-border mergers.

From the viewpoint of globally operating enterprises, the regulatory formula of EWCs presents a regional governance model with a remarkably strong emphasis on flexibility. However, transnational normative structures that have an effect on the outcome of cross-border contractual arrangements derive from outside EU law as well. Regulatory space for contractual arrangements on employee participation is a precondition for transnational labour governance based on a certain reinterpretation of the normativity of labour standards. Voluntarism, which is strongly associated with market-oriented rationalism, has become a point of departure for creating mechanisms to manage labour relations. For states, moves towards better labour protection require an acknowledgement of transnational regulatory developments that leave less room for mandatory law but highlight contractual freedom instead.

The Recast EWC Directive shies away from situations where EWCs get the opportunity to negotiate a transnational company agreement. Similarly, the Directive does not regulate the legal effects of such agreements. Although EWCs are set up for the purpose of information and consultation and involve the aim of engaging employee interest on a European level, their role in private labour governance as bodies representing employees expands beyond those aims towards global labour governance with the negotiated agreements they become parties to.[102] Depending on the formation of regulatory space in the transnational operational environment, EWCs may even gain a role in negotiating an international framework agreement which opens a horizon on advocating social protection on a global scale.

IX. CONCLUSION

Cross-border contractual arrangements in transnational labour governance highlight voluntarism but also interactions between the regulatory frameworks involved.[103] Protective imbalances that underlie contractualisation of labour relations often make the ideal of balanced governance distant as privatisation of norm production shifts the focus from demands of continuity of labour protection to contractualised choices of protection or non-protection. This is also visible in the regulatory formula of EWCs developed for cross-border employee participation in the EU. Extending employee participation rights to transnational settings has strongly reflected change anticipation and management in the internal market but the emphasis on voluntarism in how information and consultation can be established has come to have an even broader bearing on transnational labour governance. The EWC legislation of the Union can be viewed as a channel enabling broad use of voluntarism connected to the different roles that EWCs may acquire in transnational settings where a particular normative context is formed through interaction among cross-border regulatory frameworks.[104]

[102] See also M Weiss, 'Re-Inventing Labour Law?' in Davidov and Langille (n 14) 54.

[103] See also C Scott, F Cafaggi and L Senden, 'The Conceptual and Constitutional Challenge of Transnational Private Regulation' in C Scott, F Cafaggi and L Senden (eds), *The Challenge of Transnational Private Regulation: Conceptual and Constitutional Debates* (Malden, Wiley-Blackwell, 2011) 6.

[104] The way different norms interact is often viewed in simplistic and statistical ways. See Moreau who highlights the 'process of articulation' between norms: Moreau (n 82) 697–705.

To see transnational settings simply as an extension of domestic or regional spheres of regulation in terms of enhancing labour protection is misleading.[105] When contracts, often formed in a networked manner, carry a cross-border nature, this shifts them from the regulatory sphere of the one and only state. Analysing private labour governance against transnational settings demonstrates a certain change in the ways employment contracts are placed in global supply chains under the influence of networked contractualisation.[106] Private labour governance builds on the idea of interconnected regulatory frameworks through which work is regulated by contracts and contracts are organised. As norm-setting is increasingly being transferred to private actors, the transnational structures of regulation produce privatisation of labour standards where voluntarism as set forth by EU law on industrial democracy alters the traditional parameters of making choices that affect workers' rights.

Labour governance in transnational settings alters the space for the normativity of labour law.[107] Transnational settings emphasise contractual freedom and change the regulatory context of the formation of labour rights. With the particular context of transnational labour governance, the idea of labour law that labour protection does not function on a purely voluntary basis has to be placed in a cross-border perspective where transnational regulatory developments highlight preferences based on choices between private parties. Therefore, public regulatory interventions need to be constructed so that the particular nature of transnational settings is taken into account.[108] With the regulatory formula connected to multi-level voluntarism, EWCs demonstrate that the transnational labour law agenda remains open-ended by nature in ways that alter the traditional space for contracting in making use of labour standards. Its loopholes cannot be caught without taking into account cross-border regulatory modes and their highlighted contractual frames.

As cross-border participation rights have added a transnational dimension to employee information and consultation, EWCs offer a view on the characteristics of transnational settings that escape traditional categorisations and conceptualisations of domestically oriented labour law. The regulatory formula adopted by the EU has enabled the birth of the institution of a collective labour voice that can develop into a social actor negotiating transnational company agreements on social protection of workers either regionally or even with a global reach.[109] Although their mode of operation gives them an identity and integrates them in the operational model

[105] See H Arthurs, 'Making Bricks Without Straw: The Creation of a Transnational Labour Regime' in G de Búrca, C Kilpatrick and J Scott (eds), *Critical Legal Perspectives on Global Governance: Liber Amicorum David M Trubek* (Oxford, Hart Publishing, 2014) 142.

[106] It has been viewed as the influence of extra-territorial normative developments. See Moreau (n 82) 697–706.

[107] See also Arthurs (n 105) 138–39.

[108] See also A Blackett, 'Architects, Landscapers, and Gardeners in the Transnational Futures of International Labor Law' in P Zumbansen (ed), *The Oxford Handbook of Transnational Law* (Oxford, Oxford University Press, 2021) 601–602.

[109] See also T Treu, *Labour Law and Social Policies: An Agenda for Transnational Research* (21st World Congress of the International Society for Labour and Social Security Law, 15–18 September 2015, Cape Town) 14–17.

of the undertaking or group of undertakings in question, EWCs should be seen as actors of privatised labour governance that shape the extraterritorial reach of labour standards. Transnational settings where EWCs are formed and act are where both the weaknesses and the potential of EWCs and their regulatory formula meet each other.

The idea of transnational labour protection through private governance is different from transnational labour protection in private governance. In European legal integration, modes of labour governance need to be developed with that in mind.[110] While normative regimes of multinational undertakings shape transnational norm-setting in private governance, unmasking the influence of regulatory frameworks deriving from specific labour law frames, such as those constructing the regulatory formula of EWCs, shows how the transnational context rearranges traditional pillars of labour protection.

The impact of the transnational legal environment on labour rights has to be viewed against transnational settings in order to understand profound changes in the ways protective frameworks are shaped by transnational labour governance. Contractual commitments that shape private labour governance are often misleadingly viewed without placing them into the transnational legal environment where they function within multiple regulatory frames that reaffirm party autonomy. Privatisation and contractualisation highlight regulatory frames that interact in transnational settings and contribute to private labour governance. Weaker party protection through private labour governance requires that the characteristics of contractualisation be viewed in their particular normative context in order to understand how labour standards and the protection they afford are shaped under the influence of transnational settings.

[110] See also Sciarra (n 14) 418–19.

7

The Absence of Anti-Discrimination Law in the Global Reach of EU (Private) Law

MATHIAS MÖSCHEL*

I. INTRODUCTION: THE 'BRUSSELS EFFECT' AND ANTI-DISCRIMINATION LAW

THIS CONTRIBUTION INTENDS to explore the private law dimension of EU anti-discrimination law[1] and its role in (re-)shaping global markets and legal orders. Framed in terms of questions, what is the global (private) law reach of EU anti-discrimination law and how far does EU anti-discrimination law contribute to the 'Brussels effect'[2] (that is, the Europeanisation of global commerce)? Answering such questions is not straightforward – for various reasons.

First, while anti-discrimination law certainly has a private law dimension, especially as to its labour and social law aspects, it also has administrative law, criminal law, constitutional law, and human rights law dimensions. It is not always easy to separate these diverse dimensions neatly, especially considering the cross-border context that EU law operates in.

* Associate Professor, Central European University (CEU, Vienna). The author would like to thank Hans-Wolfgang Micklitz and Anna Beckers for helpful discussions and references provided for this chapter, as well as the interview partners from various European companies who took the time to discuss the global practice and relevance or absence of EU anti-discrimination law in their daily work. All errors or omissions are mine.

[1] I use this expression to refer to the body of anti-discrimination provisions contained inter alia in the EU Charter of Fundamental Rights as well as the EU's various Anti-Discrimination Directives, such as Council Directive 97/80/EC of 15 December 1997 on the burden of proof in cases of discrimination based on sex [1998] OJ L 014/6; Directive 2000/43/EC of 29 June 2000 implementing the principle of equal treatment between persons irrespective of racial or ethnic origin [2000] OJ L180/22; Directive 2000/78/EC of 27 November establishing a general framework for equal treatment in employment and occupation [2000] OJ L303/16; and Directive 2006/54/EC of 5 July 2006 on the implementation of the principle of equal opportunities and equal treatment of men and women in matters of employment and occupation (recast) [2006] OJ L204/23.

[2] A Bradford, *The Brussels Effect – How the European Union Rules the World* (Oxford, Oxford University Press, 2020).

Second, while the logic and regulatory aspects of anti-discrimination law and its effects throughout the internal market and on the private law of EU Member States have been problematised and commented upon – especially in German scholarship[3] – the *external* effects of EU anti-discrimination law in (re-)shaping global markets have not attracted much attention.

Third, in the external dimension, it is at times difficult to differentiate between EU anti-discrimination law's private and more regulatory – including public law – aspects. That private regulatory law in this external dimension is opaque has already been stated elsewhere.[4] EU anti-discrimination law forms part of that grey zone inasmuch as it is partly social policy or employment law and partly a regulatory framework. In addition, the EU's self-styled role as a human rights promoter adds a public law dimension to this picture, given that anti-discrimination is also a fundamental rights principle, thus making it especially hard to isolate, identify and distinguish anti-discrimination law's influence in the private law domain beyond EU borders.

Fourth, and linked to the previous point, EU anti-discrimination law stems from hybrid roots, especially in areas concerned with nationality- and sex-based discrimination. While initial anti-discrimination measures, especially based on nationality and sex, were adopted to further economic ends relating to the creation and sustainability of the EU single market, later on the fundamental rights logic became more prevalent, as evidenced by the case law of the Court of Justice of the European Union (CJEU)[5] and the enshrinement of the principle of non-discrimination in the EU Charter of Fundamental Rights (for example, in Article 21). However, anti-discrimination law's comparatively recent fundamental rights and public law goals continue to overlap with older market-motivated and private law aspects, both internally and externally.[6]

This contribution will attempt to navigate these muddied waters so as to better understand the place of EU anti-discrimination law in global markets and orders. Section II will look at this in relation to more traditional understandings of the external dimension of EU law and EU institutions, focusing primarily on institutional EU law mechanisms such as accession, international agreements, and the case law of the CJEU. Section III will then move to a less explored external dimension, posing the question: is the private law regulatory dimension of EU anti-discrimination law 'exported' beyond EU borders by private actors such as EU-based companies?[7]

[3] See, most recently: M Stürner, *Europäisches Vertragsrecht. Institutionelle und methodische Grundlagen, materielles Recht, Kollisionsrecht* (De Gruyter, 2021) 436–53.

[4] HW Micklitz, 'The Internal versus the External Dimension of European Private Law: A Conceptual Design and a Research Agenda' in HW Micklitz and M Cremona (eds), *Private Law in the External Relations of the EU* (Oxford, Oxford University Press, 2016) 14.

[5] Case C-50/96 *Schröder* ECLI:EU:C:2000:72 (10 February 2000), para 57.

[6] See on this hybrid regime: R Xenidis, 'Transforming EU Equality Law? On Disruptive Narratives and False Dichotomies' (2019) 38 *Yearbook of European Law* 2–57.

[7] What will not be explored here is how via the mechanisms of private international law EU anti-discrimination law as implemented nationally might be applicable beyond the EU's borders. On this dimension, see more generally, M Cremona, 'A Triple Braid. Interactions between International Law, EU Law and Private Law' in Micklitz and Cremona (n 4) 33–55 and JD Lüttringhaus, *Grenzüberschreitender Diskriminierungsschutz – Das internationale Privatrecht der Antidiskriminierung* (Tübingen, Mohr Siebeck, 2010).

Overall, the conclusion is that – for various reasons that I outline in the explanatory conclusions – EU anti-discrimination law does not play a major role in the global market. In stark contrast to other areas of EU law, the 'Brussels effect' is not really felt in this domain.

II. SEARCHING FOR EU ANTI-DISCRIMINATION LAW IN THE EU'S EXTERNAL DIMENSION

The external dimension of EU anti-discrimination law can be found in several places. This section will start by considering the accession process (point a), then move on to consider various kinds of EU external action (point b), while the third and final point will consider the possible influence of CJEU judgments beyond EU borders (point c).

A. Accession

The most obvious and visible external manifestations of EU anti-discrimination law in private law and in global markets result from accession proceedings involving (potential) future EU Member States. First and foremost, accession is supposed to guarantee access to the market on the same terms as other Member States (that is, without discrimination on the basis of nationality). More recently, however, various anti-discrimination law directives follow fundamental rights-based rather than solely market integration-based paradigms, which alongside the EU Charter of Fundamental Rights now constitute an integral part of the *acquis communautaire* and thus part of the 'rules of the club' which any acceding Member State must abide by. It is thus neither theoretically nor practically novel to analyse this aspect much further. Hence, I will only provide some pertinent examples of this phenomenon below.

While the textual standards for accession first developed in the 1993 Copenhagen criteria and later codified in Article 49 of the Treaty of Maastricht do not explicitly mention anti-discrimination, the condition remains that the 'principles of liberty, democracy, respect for human rights and fundamental freedoms, and the rule of law' must be respected as a prerequisite to EU membership. Here, fundamental rights could be construed as encompassing areas of anti-discrimination legislation which conform to fundamental rights-based paradigms. Thus, one may presume that both the market-driven rules on nationality discrimination and the prohibition on favouring a country's own goods, services or employees, as well as fundamental rights-driven issues relating to gender, race, disability, religion or age discrimination are all included in the accession criteria.

Indeed, current accession procedures involve (formal) checklists. These require adoption of EU anti-discrimination law provisions, and via progress reports the European Commission monitors prospective Member States' advances in this domain. For example, progress in reports on Turkey, which has been attempting to join the EU for longer than any other prospective Member State,[8] one can find references to anti-discrimination law from 1998 onwards. These references have increased both numerically and qualitatively over the years.[9]

Recent accession reports for other countries reflect the fact that, to some extent, the enlargement procedure has been streamlined through Stabilisation and Association Agreements, which aim to prepare prospective Member States for accession.[10] The issues of anti-discrimination and equality appear both in these agreements and in European Commission progress reports for these candidate countries.

As far as monitoring of implementation goes, Albania's 2020 Progress Report notes that 'the legal and policy framework is generally aligned with EU standards' but that 'the Law on protection against discrimination needs to be improved in a number of aspects' and also that 'effective implementation of the national strategy and action plan 2016–2020 on gender equality is hampered by a persistent funding gap'.[11]

Montenegro's 2020 Progress Report only mentions the market-based aspects of anti-discrimination twice, while all other references to anti-discrimination law are concerned with labour rights and fundamental rights. Crucially, this report refers to the importance of anti-discrimination legislation for the *acquis*, stating that: '[t]he labour law and the linked anti-discrimination law are planned to be further aligned with the EU acquis in this area during 2020' and notes 'its relevance both as a structural reform measure, and as one of the key pieces of legislation to align with the EU acquis, implementation and monitoring of the labour law should be a priority'.[12]

All the above demonstrates that anti-discrimination law undoubtedly has a direct effect on future Member States' private law and its regulation within the context of EU accession. How each state adapts to (and resists) such integration varies from state to state (as do the precise measures implemented), but the idea is that the Member State will be *acquis*-compliant by the moment of accession. It also means that, for as long as non-Member States are interested in EU accession, EU law and its anti-discrimination provisions exerts at least some influence on private law and markets

[8] These can be found at the following: 'Türkiye Reports Prepared by the European Commission' (*AB Başkanlığı | T.C. Dışişleri Bakanlığı Avrupa Birliği Başkanlığı*), available at www.ab.gov.tr/regular-progress-reports_46224_en.html.

[9] While the 1998 Regular Progress Report for Turkey (www.ab.gov.tr/files/AB_Iliskileri/Tur_En_Realitons/Progress/Turkey_Progress_Report_1998.pdf) contains only seven references to 'discrimination', and these deal equally with equality between men and women and internal market rules, in the Turkey 2020 Report (www.ab.gov.tr/siteimages/trkiye_raporustrateji_belgesi_2020/turkey_report_2020.pdf) there are 21 references to 'discrimination', of which only two deal with market related issues with the majority concerning group based discrimination (eg, discrimination against women, LGBTQI, Roma, religious minorities, and disabled people).

[10] 'Stabilisation and Association Agreement' (*European Neighbourhood Policy and Enlargement Negotiations*), available at https://neighbourhood-enlargement.ec.europa.eu/enlargement-policy/glossary/stabilisation-and-association-agreement_en.

[11] Albania 2020 Report, 33, available at https://ec.europa.eu/neighbourhood-enlargement/sites/default/files/albania_report_2020.pdf.

[12] Montenegro 2020 Report, 98, available at https://ec.europa.eu/neighbourhood-enlargement/sites/default/files/montenegro_report_2020.pdf.

beyond the EU's borders. The Turkish example demonstrates that influence-without-accession may occasionally continue almost indefinitely.

B. External Action

It is interesting to consider whether EU anti-discrimination law plays a role in global private law outside the context of the accession process. This section will consider the question: How far does anti-discrimination feature in documents, policies, agreements and/or actions relating to EU external action?

An important indication comes from the 2019 EU Human Rights Guidelines on Non-Discrimination in External Action,[13] which first provide relatively detailed definitions of discrimination that include de jure and de facto discrimination, direct and indirect discrimination, structural discrimination, discrimination by association and assumption, discriminatory profiling, as well as multiple discrimination.[14] In a second step they detail the tools to fight discrimination, ranging from policies, prohibitions, remedies, reasonable accommodation, and affirmative action to monitoring and assessment and national equality bodies.[15] Finally, they also give operational guidance on the principle of non-discrimination and how to deal with it at various levels. In the context of bilateral co-operation, this means addressing issues related to discrimination by assessing, analysing and reporting on the state of discrimination in its partner countries on all prohibited grounds, by including such issues in Head of Mission reports, by making public statements on special international days, by intervening in individual cases or by raising the issue in political dialogue and by informing EU high-level representatives in missions to third countries.[16] In somewhat less detailed ways, these 2019 Guidelines also provide for the EU's engagement in favour of non-discrimination in the context of EU development co-operation and humanitarian assistance,[17] multilateral co-operation,[18] as well as providing guidance for working with civil society.[19] One can say with certainty that this is a valiant attempt at mainstreaming non-discrimination into external action.

For the purposes of analysis here, I will take a limited look at: (i) partnership and association agreements or policies; (ii) (trade) agreements concluded by the EU over recent years; and (iii) specific actions in which non-discrimination has started featuring more prominently.

[13] Council of the European Union, 6337/19, 18 March 2019, available at https://data.consilium.europa.eu/doc/document/ST-6337-2019-INIT/en/pdf.

[14] ibid 8–11.

[15] ibid 12–18.

[16] ibid 20–25.

[17] ibid 25–28.

[18] ibid 29–30.

[19] ibid 31–33.

i. European Neighbourhood Policies

Following on from the analysis of accession proceedings, the next level of external action relates to the EU Neighbourhood Policy (ENP).[20] Launched in 2003, the ENP has undergone various changes over the years so that today the non-EU countries involved can be separated into two main groups: the East[21] and the South.[22]

Regarding the Eastern Partnership in particular, gender equality and non-discrimination are listed as challenges ahead.[23] Moreover, these criteria also figure in a recent series of association agreements containing an annex which references a number of EU law instruments that these states must implement within a given number of years from the date that their agreement with the EU enters into force. Amongst these instruments are EU anti-discrimination law directives.[24] As an example, Georgia adopted anti-discrimination legislation in 2014 to comply with the agreement,[25] demonstrating that the EU has been successfully pushing to expand this body of law beyond its borders and beyond the context of accession procedures. Nevertheless, it seems that the effect is mostly that of introducing legislation with little happening in terms of case law and enforcement, partly also due to the limited or different understanding of anti-discrimination law.[26]

Further, a recent Joint Communication by the European Commission and the High Representative of the Union for Foreign Affairs and Security Policy on the Eastern partnership indicates that the EU will continue to follow up on discrimination-related issues in these partnerships.[27] This Joint Communication highlights the EU's continued focus on 'outstanding issues from the current objectives, notably the rule of law, protection of human rights, the fight against corruption and *discrimination*, the role of an independent media and civil society and *promotion of*

[20] For more information, see www.euneighbours.eu/en.

[21] This group includes Armenia, Azerbaijan, Belarus (suspended in 2021), Georgia, the Republic of Moldova and Ukraine.

[22] This group includes Algeria, Egypt, Israel, Jordan, Lebanon, Libya, Morocco, Palestine, Syria and Tunisia.

[23] '20 Deliverables for 2020: Bringing Tangible Results for Citizens' (*Language selection | European Neighbourhood Policy and Enlargement Negotiations* (*Eastern Partnership*, November 2021), available at https://neighbourhood-enlargement.ec.europa.eu/system/files/2021-11/112021_eap_deliverables_factsheet_2021_eng.pdf.

[24] See, eg, Association Agreement between the European Union and the European Atomic Energy Community and its Member States, of the one part, and Ukraine, of the other part [2014] OJ L161/3; Association Agreement between the European Union and the European Atomic Energy Community and their Member States, of the one part, and Georgia, of the other part [2014] OJ L261/4; Association Agreement between the European Union and the European Atomic Energy Community and their Member States, of the one part, and the Republic of Moldova, of the other part [2014] OJ L260/4; Comprehensive and enhanced Partnership Agreement between the European Union and the European Atomic Energy Community and their Member States, of the one part, and the Republic of Armenia, of the other part [2018] OJ L23/4.

[25] Law of Georgia on the Elimination of All Forms of Discrimination, 2391-IIb, 2 May 2014, available at https://matsne.gov.ge/en/document/view/2339687?publication=0.

[26] See in this sense: N Reich et al (eds), *Autonomy and Antidiscrimination in Private Law – The Experience of the Western Balkans* (SEELS Network, Civil Law Forum for South East Europe, 2014) 33–34.

[27] Joint Communication to the European Parliament, the European Council, the Council, the European Economic and Social Committee and the Committee of Regions, 'Eastern Partnership Policy beyond 2020 – *Reinforcing Resilience – an Eastern Partnership that Delivers For All*', 18 March 2020, JOIN(2020) 7 final.

gender equality' (emphasis added),[28] and declares that '[t]he EU will step up action to combat all forms of discrimination including on grounds of sex, racial or ethnic origin, religion or belief, disability, age or sexual orientation'.[29] This communication was endorsed by the Council in May 2020.[30] The suspension of Belarus from the Eastern Partnership in 2021 and the war in Ukraine in 2022 have profoundly changed the overall reality in that partnership and have propelled Ukraine and Moldova from 'mere' partners to official accession candidates.[31] EU anti-discrimination law thus becomes more directly relevant for those two legal systems.

ii. Agreements

Beyond these partnership agreements, references to anti-discrimination have started to appear in various bilateral or multilateral (trade) agreements between the EU and individual third countries. Here again, one needs to distinguish between the market-driven aspects of anti-discrimination (which are mostly concerned with nationality-based discrimination) and fundamental rights-driven aspects. In agreements, market-driven aspects are present in order to guarantee reciprocal access to each party's respective market, whereas fundamental rights-driven aspects form part of a larger trend towards increased use of human rights clauses in trade agreements.[32]

It is safe to conclude that anti-discrimination provisions in these economic partnership agreements are, unsurprisingly, predominantly (and sometimes exclusively) nationality-related and driven by a market-based logic.[33]

Without pretending to undertake a full analysis of all the EU's external agreements, presumably the first time a human rights clause appeared in an EU external agreement is in the Argentina trade agreement in 1990.[34] In terms of importance, however, one should mention the Cotonou Agreement of 2000, a multilateral agreement between the EU, EU Member States and 79 African, Caribbean, and Pacific countries.[35]

[28] ibid 1.

[29] ibid 15.

[30] Council of the European Union, 'Council Conclusions on Eastern Partnership Policy beyond 2020', 11 May 2020, 7510/1/20 REV 1 COEST 70 CFSP/PESC 357 COPS 135 PROCED 6.

[31] See 'Eastern Partnership' (*European Council of European Union*, 23 June 2022), available at www.consilium.europa.eu/en/policies/eastern-partnership/.

[32] On such human rights clauses and more generally on the EU's human rights conditionality in the literature, see eg: L Bartels, *Human Rights Conditionality in in the EU's International Agreements* (Oxford, Oxford University Press, 2005); and S Velluti, 'The Promotion and Integration Human Rights in EU External Trade Relations' (2016) *Utrecht Journal of International and European Law* 32(83), 41–68. See also the more institutional overview provided by: European Parliament Research Service (EPRS), 'Human Rights in EU Trade Agreements. The Human Rights Clause and its Application' (*EPRS*, July 2019), available at www.europarl.europa.eu/RegData/etudes/BRIE/2019/637975/EPRS_BRI(2019)637975_EN.pdf.

[33] See, eg: the Association Agreement with Chile of 30 December 2002, available at https://eur-lex.europa.eu/resource.html?uri=cellar:f83a503c-fa20-4b3a-9535-f1074175eaf0.0004.02/DOC_2&format=PDF; the Interim Agreement between the EU and Southern and Eastern African Member States of 13 July 2009, available at http://publications.europa.eu/resource/cellar/e0a39709-5456-464c-899d-fd09967436c0.0006.02/DOC_1.

[34] F Martines, 'Human Rights Clauses in EU Agreements' in S Poli (ed), *Protecting Human Rights in the European Union's External Relations* (TMC Asser Institute, CLEER Papers, 2016/5) 37, fn 1.

[35] See 'Cotonou Agreement' (*EUR-Lex – Access to European Union Law*, 3 April 2020), available at https://eur-lex.europa.eu/legal-content/en/TXT/?uri=LEGISSUM:r12101.

This is currently being re-negotiated.[36] The agreement contains the usual market-oriented, anti-discrimination provisions; for example, with regard to migration, it provides that 'each [state] shall accord comparable non-discriminatory treatment to workers who are nationals of a Member State'.[37] It also cautions signatory states against using or enforcing sanitary and phytosanitary measures necessary to protect human, animal or plant life or health as a pretext for arbitrary discrimination or as a disguised restriction on trade,[38] and also warns against discrimination between state parties to the Cotonou Agreement through making investment promotion and protection agreements with third countries.[39] Clearly, these provisions concern trade-related aspects of anti-discrimination on the basis of nationality, so that their potential impact on private law beyond the employment realm is greater.

The issue of anti-discrimination as a question of respect for human rights nonetheless arises quite frequently. Indeed, the Preamble to the Cotonou Agreement mentions the UN's Convention on the Elimination of all Forms of Discrimination Against Women (CEDAW) and the Convention on the Elimination of all Forms of Racial Discrimination (CERD) and, when referring to political dialogue between the parties, the agreement lays down that the focus shall be, inter alia, on combating ethnic, religious and racial discrimination.[40] Further elements of the human rights dimension can be found in its provisions on migration, especially where '[t]he Parties reaffirm their existing obligations and commitments in international law to ensure respect for human rights and to eliminate all forms of discrimination based particularly on origin, sex, race, language and religion'.[41] Other provisions concern child labour and anti-discrimination in respect to employment,[42] as well as humanitarian and emergency assistance which shall be granted 'between victims on grounds of race, ethnic origin, religion, gender, age, nationality or political affiliation'.[43] Some of these provisions may have a (limited) impact on the private law of some of these legal systems.[44]

A more recent and widely debated example of the importance of human rights clauses – and the 'human rights conditionality' inserted by the EU into trade agreements – comes from the CETA Agreement with Canada.[45] As in other trade agreements, one again finds the market-driven, anti-discrimination (nationality-based) provisions. But, in addition to that, some articles provide for more explicitly

[36] See: E Pichon, 'Signature and Conclusion of the New Agreement between the EU and the Countries of Sub-Saharan Africa, the Caribbean and the Pacific (ACP-EU post-Cotonou)' (*Legislative Train Schedule, European Parliament*, 2 August 2022), available at www.europarl.europa.eu/legislative-train/theme-a-stronger-europe-in-the-world/file-signature-of-the-new-eu-acp-agreement-('-post-Cotonou').

[37] Cotonou Agreement, Art 13, para 3.

[38] ibid Art 48, para 1.

[39] ibid Art 15, para 1(b).

[40] ibid Art 8, para 4.

[41] ibid Art 13, para 1.

[42] ibid Art 50, para 1.

[43] ibid Art 76, para 2.

[44] For a critical overview of the EU's involvement as a human rights actor in Africa, see: OU Rutazibwa, 'The Problematics of the EU's Ethical (Self)Image in Africa: The EU as an "Ethical Intervener" and the 2007 Joint Africa–EU Strategy' (2010) 18 *Journal of Contemporary European Studies* 209–28.

[45] See: 'Comprehensive Economic and Trade Agreement (CETA) between Canada, of the one part, and the European Union and its Member States, of the other part' [2017] OJ L11/23–1079. For more details

human rights-related aspects of anti-discrimination. For instance, the CETA provides that '[a] Party breaches the obligation of fair and equitable treatment [...] if a measure or series of measures constitutes [...] targeted discrimination on manifestly wrongful grounds such as gender, race or religious belief'.[46] A specialised committee overviews the content of this obligation to provide fair and equitable treatment and may develop recommendations to a larger committee established under the CETA,[47] with litigation being able to be brought to a specific tribunal created under the CETA.[48]

Some of these provisions will impact upon at least parts of the private law of some of these legal systems, with the proviso that any impact is probably fairly limited and that – so far – the EU has not suspended an international agreement on the basis of violation of a human rights clause.[49]

iii. Actions

In some specific areas of anti-discrimination law, the EU has taken action with some degree of persistence. This is particularly true of gender equality when, in 2010, the European Commission adopted the 'EU Plan of Action on Gender Equality and Women's Empowerment in Development 2010–2015' (also known as the Gender Action Plan I or GAP I).[50] GAP I was followed by GAP II from 2015–2020 and then by the EU's new Action Plan on Gender Equality and Women's Empowerment in External Action 2021–2025 (GAP III).[51] All of these GAPs deal explicitly with the external dimension.

More recently, the EU also adopted action plans with regard to race[52] and an equality strategy with regard to individuals who identify as LGBTQI.[53] However, in these documents the external dimension forms only a small part of the EU's sphere of intervention.

in the literature, see: KL Meissner and L McKenzie, 'The Paradox of Human Rights Conditionality in EU Trade Policy: When Strategic Interests Drive Policy Outcomes' (2019) 26 *Journal of European Public Policy* 1273–91.

[46] CETA, Art 8.10, point 2(d).

[47] ibid Art 8.10, point 3.

[48] ibid Art 8.27.

[49] Recently the European Parliament came close to doing something like this by voting for suspension of the ratification of the EU-China Comprehensive Agreement on Investment, arguably due to sanctions imposed on some MEPs and MPs, but also because of human rights violations by China in its treatment of the Uighur minority: European Parliament Resolution of 20 May 2021 on Chinese countersanctions on EU entities and MEPs and MPs (2021/2644(RSP)).

[50] European Commission, SEC(2010) [2010] 265 final.

[51] See: European Parliament, 'EU Action Plan on Gender Equality' (*Legislative Train Schedule*, *European Parliament*, (n d)), available at www.europarl.europa.eu/legislative-train/theme-women-s-rights-and-gender-equality-femm/file-eu-action-plan-on-gender-equality. However, due to Bulgaria, Hungary and Poland's refusal to endorse the broad mandate, the 'political' conclusions to this Council were not adopted as usual as Council conclusions but 'only' as Presidency conclusions: Council of the European Union, 'Presidency Conclusions on the Gender Action Plan (GAP) III 2021–2025 – An Ambitious Agenda for Gender Equality and Women's Empowerment in EU External Action', 16 December 2020, 13947/20, available at https://data.consilium.europa.eu/doc/document/ST-13947-2020-INIT/en/pdf.

[52] European Commission, 'A Union of Equality: EU Anti-Racism Action Plan 2020–2025', 18 September 2020, COM(2020) 565 final.

[53] European Commission, 'Union of Equality: LGBTIQ Equality Strategy 2020–2025', 12 November 2020, COM(2020) 698 final.

How far these actions will directly impact private law outside of the EU's borders is a different question, but one can see how anti-discrimination law and policy have penetrated the external action of the EU in several ways and thus may influence the global market, whether directly or indirectly.

C. Judicial Dialogue

Another avenue of analysis for exploration of the external influence of EU anti-discrimination law is via the observable influence of CJEU jurisprudence and case law beyond EU borders. The various freedoms and directives enshrining the principle of anti-discrimination, once adopted, are interpreted by the CJEU, so it is no surprise that the EU's highest court has been an influential actor in this area of law. The CJEU has handed down several path-breaking judgments on aspects of anti-discrimination law. These judgments form the basis of much of the law in this area today.[54]

The EU has adopted certain principles of anti-discrimination law from other jurisdictions, including the notion of indirect discrimination (disparate impact) introduced by the famous US Supreme Court *Griggs* judgment,[55] which entered EU law and its various anti-discrimination directives via the United Kingdom (UK).[56] However, this contribution is considering the opposite question, namely: how far have EU anti-discrimination law judgments travelled to non-EU jurisdictions via the informal mechanism of judicial dialogue and the CJEU's soft power, thus influencing the development of anti-discrimination law in the private law domain beyond EU borders?

There are general studies demonstrating that CJEU case law has been influential outside the EU. One recent publication indicates that EU anti-discrimination case law may have a (limited) impact in third countries.[57] The most relevant example mentioned therein comes from Israel, and it concerns the issue of different mandatory retirement ages for men and women. After litigation went all the way up to the Israeli Supreme Court – where EU case law was discussed and relied upon – the Knesset passed legislation which allowed women to retire at the same age as men.[58]

[54] Eg: Case C-43/75 *Defrenne II* ECLI:EU:C:1976:56 (8 April 1976), establishing the direct effect of the equal pay for equal work principle; Case C-144/04 *Mangold* ECLI:EU:C:2005:709 (22 November 2005), holding that the principle of non-discrimination is a general principle of EU law; Case C-267/06 *Maruko* ECLI:EU:C:2008:179 (1 April 2008), holding that excluding same-sex couples from survivor's pensions is direct discrimination; Case C-54/07 *Feryn* ECLI:EU:C:2008:397 (10 July 2008), holding that an employer's public statements that he would not employ immigrants constituted a racially discriminatory hiring practice even when no immigrant actually applied; and Case C-303/06 *Coleman* ECLI:EU:C:2008:415 (17 July 2008), holding that dismissal of an employee who is not disabled but whose child is disabled constitutes discrimination by association.

[55] *Griggs* v *Duke Power Co*, 401 U.S. 424 (1971).

[56] J Suk, 'Disparate Impact Abroad' in E Katz and S Bagenstos (eds), *A Nation of Widening Opportunities: The Civil Rights Act at 50* (Michigan Publishing, 2015) 283–306.

[57] See, eg, most recently: HW Micklitz and A Reich (eds), *The Impact of the European Court of Justice on Neighbouring Countries* (Oxford, Oxford University Press, 2020).

[58] A Reich, 'The Impact of the Court of Justice of the European Union on the Israeli Legal System' in ibid 291–94.

The same publication also cites examples from the Swiss Federal Supreme Court which refer to EU internal market law while adjudicating the right of anti-discrimination of Swiss citizens from one canton before the authorities of other cantons as well as its reliance on the *Kalanke* judgment[59] in a decision on gender quotas.[60] Further afield, a recent chapter on the impact of EU anti-discrimination law in Asia with a specific focus on Hong Kong and India concludes that any impact is fairly limited, and that in any case, there is certainly no *dialogue*, which would (by definition) necessarily involve the CJEU citing case law from Hong Kong and India.[61]

Apart from what we can glean from extant studies, insight could also be gained by inquiring whether CJEU judgments relating to anti-discrimination law are cited in court cases in Eastern Partnership countries that have adopted anti-discrimination legislation in line with partnership agreements. Without being able to conduct a full-blown study on all those countries, few such citations came to light during a cursory perusal of Georgian case law, despite Georgia's implementation of such legislation in 2014.[62] Two judgments by the Georgian Supreme Court concerned with pregnancy discrimination barely mention CJEU case law despite the applicants referring to EU anti-discrimination directives and CJEU jurisprudence in their submissions.[63]

Overall, there is little evidence that CJEU case law on anti-discrimination is exerting a strong influence abroad and thus little support for the conclusion that it significantly impacts the private law regulation of global markets.[64]

To summarise the conclusions drawn throughout section II: outside the context of accession, EU anti-discrimination law as promoted (directly or indirectly) by official and public actors plays a limited and anecdotal role beyond EU borders.

III. SEARCHING FOR EU ANTI-DISCRIMINATION LAW AS EXPORTED BY PRIVATE ACTORS

This section considers an alternative hypothesis regarding the mechanisms by which EU anti-discrimination law in the private law domain 'spreads' beyond EU borders.

[59] Case C-450/93 *Kalanke* ECLI:EU:C:1995:322 (17 October 1995).

[60] F Maiani, 'CJEU Citations in the Case Law of the Swiss Federal Supreme Court' in Micklitz and Reich (n 57) 97.

[61] H Lau and K Loper, 'The European Union as Promoter of Equality in Asia: Beyond Economic Tools of Influence' in T Giegerich (ed), *The European Union as Protector and Promoter of Equality* (Heidelberg, Springer, 2020) 487–502.

[62] See n 25.

[63] Georgia Supreme Court, *N.Sh.* v *Georgian Chamber of Commerce and Industry*, №: ას-1481-1401-2017, 29 August 2018 and *N.Sh., Sh.L.* v *"S.B" Joint Stock Company*, №: ას-1009-2020, 24 December 2020, both available in Georgian at http://prg.supremecourt.ge/CaseCivilResult.aspx. The author would like to thank A Gudadze (LLM in Human Rights Law at CEU – AY 2021/2022) for signaling these judgments to him.

[64] There are even examples of failures to invoke CJEU case law, despite it being raised by the parties in a set of Russian cases dealing with the EU–Russia Partnership and Cooperation Agreement (PCA) provisions in relation to the direct effect of the prohibition against discriminatory treatment of EU citizens' access to justice in Russia, and despite the fact that the EU had already recognised such direct effect on Russian individuals within EU territory. P Kalinichenko, 'The Impact of the Court of Justice of the European Union on the Israeli Legal System' in Micklitz and Reich (n 57) 164–65.

In particular, it considers the possibility that private actors spread rules globally via private lawmaking and evaluates the claim that regulatory intermediaries[65] operating multinationally such as law firms, (big) companies, auditors or similar actors may contribute to the spread of EU anti-discrimination law, albeit in a less visible way. The mechanisms considered here are internal codes of conduct, ethical codes, diversity policies, (sexual) harassment guidelines, supply chain contracts, or similar documents with potential global reach. The question becomes: to what extent do actors that draft and interpret private standards play a fundamental role in translating and exporting (as well as creating and vernacularising) EU anti-discrimination law beyond EU borders?

Previous publications have focused on aspects of the phenomenon of regulatory intermediation in case studies. These publications have, for example, analysed the role of Walmart as a global legislator via its internal labour standards and ethics rules,[66] the application of the Fair Labor Association's Freedom of Assembly rules by Chinese and Vietnamese companies,[67] the transplant of Codes of Vendor Conduct to China via global supply chains,[68] and promotion of human and labour rights in transnational supply chain contracts.[69]

However, few (if any) of these studies focus on EU law and its circulation via these avenues, and even fewer on EU anti-discrimination law in particular. Do such private regulatory intermediaries 'export' EU anti-discrimination law rules across the globe and thus influence, contribute to, or create private law regulations and/or constraints in global markets? And do lawyers educated in EU law export their expertise and understanding of anti-discrimination law abroad, *imposing* it, so to speak, beyond EU borders?

An armchair analysis combined with a few interviews may shed some light on these questions. Indeed, a cursory glance through certain company documents reveals that it is mostly the fundamental rights concerns of anti-discrimination law that come to the fore in this context rather than the market-related aspects that concern the economic integration process. Of course, this does not exclude that market-related, company reputation-enhancing motivations could be behind production of such documents.

It should be noted that references to human rights and anti-discrimination concerns depend on the company and/or the internal document in question. Sometimes these references appear only in a single sentence or section, unaccompanied by additional information or explanation.

[65] See, eg, the special issue of the (2017) 670 *Annals of the American Academy of Political and Social Science* 1–288, which is dedicated to such regulatory intermediaries.

[66] L Catá Backer, 'Economic Globalization and the Rise of Efficient Systems of Global Private Law Making: Wal-Mart as Global Legislator' (2007) 39 *Connecticut Law Review* 1739–84.

[67] P Paiement, 'Jurisgenerative role of auditors in transnational labor governance' (2019) 13 *Regulation & Governance* 280–98.

[68] L-W Lin, 'Legal Transplants through Private Contracting: Codes of Vendor Conduct in Global Supply Chains as Example' (2009) 57 *American Journal of Comparative Law* 711–44.

[69] K Mitkidis, S Perkovic and P Mitkidis, 'Tendencies in Contractual Governance to Promote Human and Labour Rights in Transnational Supply Chains' (2019) 23 *Competition & Change* 397–419.

For example, Article 3.3 on *diversity and Non-Discrimination* of the Code of the Supplier Conduct of the global German telecommunications company, Deutsche Telekom AG, specifies that

> [t]he Supplier shall prohibit and fight negative discrimination based on race, colour, sex, sexual orientation, language, religion, political or other opinion, national or social origin, property, birth or other status and shall promote diversity, equality of opportunity or treatment in employment and occupation.[70]

Interestingly, the internal Code of Conduct of the same company nowhere mentions diversity or anti-discrimination, and only refers to the Code of Human Rights & Social Principles. Under this Code, Deutsche Telekom commits, among other things, to respect and promote human rights including International Labour Organisation (ILO) core labour standards.[71]

Another example of a passing reference to rights and anti-discrimination is Article 3.3 of the section on the *Centrality of the Person – Diversity and Inclusion* in the 2019 Ethics Code of Barilla, a worldwide pasta producer from Italy. This article affirms that 'Barilla supports and respects human rights in its activities and sphere of influence' and that

> Barilla does not tolerate any form of discrimination or exclusion based on *inter alia* age, culture, ethnicity, nationality, religious belief, race, political opinion, civil status, pregnancy, veteran status, gender and sexual orientation, gender identity or its expression, genetic information, health or disability.[72]

Some documents from other companies contain comparatively detailed provisions. For example, the Ethics Code of Essilor Luxottica, a French/Italian global eyewear company, states that '[t]he Group upholds the highest standards in how it runs its activities, notably by respecting Human Rights, labour laws and the environment', and also that Essilor Luxottica 'abides by the International Labour Organisation Convention and the UN Global Compact Principles on Human Rights'.[73] Regarding discrimination specifically, it affirms that 'Essilor Luxottica respects and encourages diversity', that '[e]qual opportunities are guaranteed for employees at all levels irrespective of gender, age, nationality or origin, religion, sexual orientation, marital status, union affiliation or disability' and that '[t]he organization does not tolerate any form of discrimination, intimidation or harassment'.[74]

[70] Deutsche Telekom AG, 'Supplier Code of Conduct' (*api.telekom.me*, 2019) 1, available at https://api.telekom.me/api/FileManager/Download?root=/Tenderi/2022/04012022/Prilog%208%20SCoC.pdf.

[71] ibid 12.

[72] Barilla, *Ethics Code*, 27 February 2019 (author's translation). See 'Codice Etico' (*Barilla Group*, 27 February 2019), available at www.barillagroup.com/media/filer_public/f9/7f/f97fecd5-71e3-4a73-909e-fdcc117802f5/codice_etico_27_febbraio_2019.pdf.

[73] Essilor Luxottica, *Code of Ethics* (30 July 2019) 17, available at www.essilorluxottica.com/governance/code-ethics.

[74] ibid 14.

ENGIE, a French global energy company, has a separate policy on human rights, the *Human Rights Referential*. What is interesting here is that this document refers to the Group's commitment to operate in accordance with international human rights standards wherever it conducts business and, in particular, to abide by the provisions of the 1948 Universal Declaration of Human Rights, the 1966 International Covenant on Civil and Political Rights, and the 1966 International Covenant on Economic, Social and Cultural Rights, as well as the ILO Conventions.[75] Probably as a consequence of its separate internal human rights policy, ENGIE's Code of Ethics is less detailed on questions of human rights and anti-discrimination and 'only' states that the principle of respect for others 'guides the Group's policy for gender equality, respect for private life, promoting diversity and fighting all forms of discrimination, protecting health and safety at work, and in particular preventing and sanctioning all situations of harassment'.[76]

In some rare cases, the information contained in such documents is quite detailed. The Code of Ethics of L'ORÉAL, a French global luxury company, is an example of this, both in terms of content and procedure. Thus, the Code highlights L'ORÉAL's commitment to human rights by referring to the Universal Declaration of Human Rights dated 10 December 1948 and the United Nations Guiding Principles on Business and Human Rights dated 16 June 2011. It also refers to the fact that it has been a signatory to the United Nations Global Compact since 2003, and further professes L'ORÉAL's support for the UN Women's Empowerment Principles.[77] Moreover, the document explains how to apply different rules on 'quality, health and safety standards, labour law, the environment, corruption and money-laundering, data privacy, taxation, accurate communication of financial and non-financial information and fair competition in varying local contexts'. Indeed, the Code states that

> **where local law or customs impose higher standards than those set out in the Code, local law and customs should always apply. If, by contrast, the Code provides for a higher standard, it should prevail, unless this results in illegal activity.**[78]

It is under the heading of *Diversity* that the Code references the issue of discrimination. The Code of Ethics avers that 'L'ORÉAL is an inclusive, equal opportunity employer. We facilitate the professional integration of people who are under-represented in the workforce, in particular people with disabilities and under-represented social and/or ethnic groups'. It continues with the provision that

> We must not – Discriminate or harass/bully on the basis of: – gender – disability – marital status or family situation – sexual orientation – age – political and philosophical opinions – religious beliefs – union activity – ethnic, social, cultural or national origin.

[75] ENGIE, *Human Rights Referential: Commitments and Implementation*, 2014, Commitments No.1 and No. 2, 2–3, available at www.engie.com/sites/default/files/assets/documents/2021-03/Human%20Rights%20Referential%20EV.pdf.

[76] ENGIE, *Ethics Charter*, 5, available at www.engie.com/en/group/ethics-and-compliance/principles-and-commitments/charte-guide-pratique-ethique.

[77] L'ORÉAL, *Code of Ethics. The Way We Work*, 3rd edn, 8, available at www.loreal.com/-/media/project/loreal/brand-sites/corp/master/lcorp/2-group/news-and-documentation/publications/code-of-ethics/codeofethicsenglishus.pdf.

[78] ibid (bold also in the original document).

Concerning the hypothetical question of what is meant by 'discrimination' and whether the Code's definition corresponds with the law of any given country, the explanation states the following:

> The first rule is that L'ORÉAL respects national laws and therefore any employee violating the discrimination laws in their country may be sanctioned. But there may be countries where the law on discrimination does not prohibit certain behaviours which the Company finds unacceptable. For example, L'ORÉAL is opposed not only to direct discrimination, but also to indirect discrimination. Direct discrimination means any action taken with regard to jobs, training, promotions, continued employment or any other aspect of working life which means those affected do not enjoy equal treatment or opportunities. Indirect discrimination is any action which, while apparently neutral, puts anyone with a particular gender, age, disability or other characteristic at a disadvantage compared to others.[79]

Interestingly, this explanation refers to both direct and indirect discrimination, one of the key conceptual distinctions in EU anti-discrimination law.

Now, of course, the bigger (empirical) question is whether (and to what extent) these anti-discrimination rules and standards are actually applied and enforced beyond EU borders by these companies. Many of these internal standards are soft law rules rather than mandatory (reporting) rules of the kind enshrined in the US Foreign Corrupt Practices Act or even optional (reporting) rules contained in the UK's 2015 Modern Slavery Act. This may change with the 'European Due Diligence Act'[80] and its mandatory rules, though anti-discrimination law does not seem to be playing an important role in current versions of this draft directive.

IV. (TENTATIVE) EXPLANATORY CONCLUSIONS

To summarise, there is little evidence that EU anti-discrimination law has a global reach in markets and private law. This conclusion holds regardless of whether official/public channels or private mechanisms are being considered. Several plausible explanations can be offered for this.

First, it has been convincingly – and critically – demonstrated that anti-discrimination is a fundamental element of the legal construction of European society and the European Union.[81] However, anti-discrimination, coupled with EU fundamental freedoms, was introduced primarily as an adjunct to the establishment of the European internal market. Goods, services and persons are supposed to circulate within these boundaries without discrimination on the grounds of nationality. Over the years, additional grounds were added, prompting Münch to state that '[w]ith the freedoms and anti-discrimination as guiding principles, the CJEU has contributed to the paradigm change which shifted the focus away from the national collective welfare and status groups toward the inclusion of empowered individuals'.[82]

[79] ibid 30.

[80] European Parliament Resolution of 10 March 2021 with recommendations to the Commission on corporate due diligence and corporate accountability (2020/2129(INL)), available at www.europarl.europa.eu/doceo/document/TA-9-2021-0073_EN.html.

[81] R Münch, *Die Konstruktion der Europäischen Gesellschaft* (campus, 2008) esp 92–106.

[82] ibid 105.

This may explain why the external effects of anti-discrimination law have mostly concerned – and have been mostly limited to – accession procedures and partnership agreements.

Second, anti-discrimination law is a contested concept. It would be fair to say that it has often been viewed or portrayed as a legal irritant of American import rather than as something quintessentially European,[83] particularly in Germany[84] and certain Central and Eastern European (CEE) countries.[85] This perception of anti-discrimination law as a foreign irritant may have made exporting EU anti-discrimination law as a European creation more difficult, thus limiting its influence on private law globally.

Third, different EU Member States interpret and apply anti-discrimination law differently, thus making it tricky to export a unitary vision of it upon the global market. This is not to deny that there are minimum standards and 'common denominators' of anti-discrimination law that apply throughout the EU, as demonstrated by EU directives concerning discrimination and the CJEU's affirmation that the principle of non-discrimination is a general principle of EU law.[86]

However, it is also true that some doctrinal and political discussions have arisen out of anti-discrimination law that have drawn attention beyond the expert field of anti-discrimination lawyers. One example to be mentioned is the various approaches to race discrimination: in Ireland and the (formerly EU) UK, collecting racial statistics to fight discrimination is allowed, whereas in most mainland European countries this practice is prohibited. This leads to different approaches and understandings of anti-discrimination law and varying levels of difficulty in proving racial discrimination.

Another example of these differences concerns religious discrimination. For instance, national constitutional interpretations of the freedom of religious employers in Germany have led to conflicts with EU anti-discrimination law.[87]

[83] On this see B Havelková B and M Möschel, 'Introduction. Anti-Discrimination Law's Fit into Civil Law Jurisdictions and the Factors Influencing it' in B Havelková and M Möschel (eds), *Anti-Discrimination Law in Civil Law Jurisdictions* (Oxford, Oxford University Press, 2020) 1–27.

[84] On German resistance to anti-discrimination law, see, eg: JF-J Säcker, '"Vernunft statt Freiheit": die Tugendrepublik der neuen Jakobiner' (2002) *Zeitschrift für Rechtspolitik* 286; J Braun, 'Übrigens – Deutschland wird wieder totalitär' (2002) *Juristische Schulung* 424–25; D Straub, 'Drohen amerikanische Verhältnisse?' (2005) 2 *Arbeit und Arbeitsrecht* 65; K Adomeit, 'Political Correctness – jetzt Rechtspflicht!' (2006) *Neue Juristische Wochenschrift* 2169; W Phillip, 'Ein verfassungswidriges Monstrum – Die Antidiskriminierungsstelle des Bundes' (2006) *Neue Zeitschrift für Verwaltungsrecht* 1235.

[85] On the limitations of the transfer of anti-discrimination law via the *acquis communautaire* to various CEE countries, especially with regard to gender equality, see, eg: C Chiva, 'The Limits of Europeanisation: EU Accession and Gender Equality in Bulgaria and Romania' (2009) 10 *Perspectives on European Politics and Society* 2, 195–209 and B Havelková, *Gender Equality in Law: Uncovering the Legacies of Czech State Socialism* (Oxford, Hart Publishing, 2017). See also the refusal by Bulgaria, Hungary and Poland to endorse the broad mandate from the "political' conclusions to the European Council on adopting the GAP III, which were not adopted as usual as Council conclusions but 'only' as Presidency conclusions: Council of the European Union, 'Presidency conclusions on the Gender Action Plan (GAP) III 2021–2025 – An ambitious agenda for gender equality and women's empowerment in EU external action', 16 December 2020, 13947/20, available at https://data.consilium.europa.eu/doc/document/ST-13947-2020-INIT/en/pdf.

[86] See most famously: *Mangold* (n 54).

[87] See the cases where this (potential) conflict arose: Case C-414/16 *Egenberger* ECLI:EU:C:2018:257 (17 April 2018) and Case C-68/17 *IR v JQ* ECLI:EU:C:2018:696 (11 September 2018). For a recent discussion

In a similar vein, the question whether headscarf bans at the workplace are religious discrimination or an admissible means of enforcing *laïcité*, customer wishes, or company neutrality policies have been raised before the CJEU. The CJEU has declined to prohibit these bans in principle on various occasions.[88] Most recently, it held that

> Directive 2000/78 allows account to be taken of the specific context of each Member State and allows each Member State a *margin of discretion* in achieving the necessary reconciliation of the different rights and interests at issue, in order to ensure a fair balance between them (emphasis added).[89]

There may thus be differences in how anti-discrimination law plays out in companies or with private employers, depending on the EU borders but in the different Member States in which they operate in.

Continuing with the example of headscarf bans, the *Achbita* case illustrates some of the problems inherent in enforcing uniform application of anti-discrimination law even within the EU, let alone beyond it. This judgment involved a receptionist in a global company (G4 Solutions) who was fired under internal workplace regulations which prohibited employees from wearing any visible signs of their political, philosophical or religious beliefs and/or from engaging in any visible observance of such beliefs.[90] The CJEU indicated that such an internal rule might constitute indirect discrimination on the grounds of religion,

> unless it is objectively justified by a legitimate aim, such as the pursuit by the employer, in its relations with its customers, of a policy of political, philosophical and religious neutrality, and the means of achieving that aim are appropriate and necessary, which it is for the referring court to ascertain.[91]

Now, if G4 Solutions introduced such a neutrality policy, would it and/or could it be globally applicable, thus allowing neutrality policies compatible with EU anti-discrimination law to circulate?. While this may be an extreme example, it illustrates some of the issues that might arise for those hoping for any degree of uniformity in the application of EU anti-discrimination law by regulatory intermediaries.

Fourth, as some of the above-mentioned examples of internal company documents demonstrate, when operating beyond EU borders in a global market, multinational companies are more inclined to invoke global human rights instruments than EU anti-discrimination law directives.[92] Lack of EU anti-discrimination law in the internal

on this see: A Tischbirek, 'A Double Conflict of Laws: The Emergence of an EU "Staatskirchenrecht"?' (2019) 20 *German Law Journal* 1066–78.

[88] Case C-157/15 *Achbita* ECLI:EU:C:2017:203 (14 March 2017); Case C-188/15 *Bougnaoui* ECLI:EU:C:2017:204 (14 March 2017); and Joined Cases C-804/18 and C-341/19 *WABE and MH Müller Handel* ECLI:EU:C:2021:594 (15 July 2021).

[89] *WABE and MH Müller Handel*, ibid, para 88.

[90] *Achbita* (n 88).

[91] ibid paras 44 and 45.

[92] The Organisation for Economic Co-operation and Development (OECD) Guidelines for Multinational Enterprises also refer to such documents and not to EU anti-discrimination law when dealing with discrimination. See OECD Guidelines for Multinational Enterprises, 2011 Edition, esp paras 51–54, available at www.oecd.org/corporate/mne/48004323.pdf.

regulations governing EU companies' global operations may not come as a complete surprise. Indeed, for them it might be more appropriate to utilise global anti-discrimination and human rights initiatives formulated at the UN level[93] rather than within the geographically limited EU framework and setting.[94]

Legal(istic) reasons can also be offered for referring to global instruments rather than EU law. The role of lawyers acting as in-house counsel, corporate lawyers, or auditors may be of relevance in explaining the circulation or non-circulation of EU anti-discrimination law via private companies. In particular, in-house counsel play a certain role in the process of drafting internal policies and codes.[95] They work in close co-operation with internal, non-legal units that might be affected by these documents both at the central level and locally, and then make determinations as to how far a specific code or policy ought to apply in a given national and legal context.[96] These legal experts are aware that rules have a bounded geographical scope, which explains why references to anti-discrimination law concern global instruments rather than EU ones: the presumption is that most states have ratified these conventions and thus their relevance and applicability beyond EU borders is broader.

This does not mean that in-house counsel, corporate lawyers, or auditors who have been educated in EU anti-discrimination law never consider EU legislation when drafting, interpreting, and enforcing internal soft law rules in non-EU countries. There certainly are situations in which EU law applies indirectly via these company codes and policy documents, especially in situations when the national law of a given non-EU country is silent on a given issue. Thus, when elaborating internal guidelines on (sexual) harassment in a French global energy company, internal units drew upon definitions in the ILO Convention on Violence and Harassment,[97] but they also considered the fact that such harassment is prohibited under various EU anti-discrimination directives. These guidelines or policies may not be relevant where their provisions conflict with national laws, or where national laws provide better protection than internal policy. But the weight given to EU law beyond EU borders may be

[93] See, eg, the 'UN Stereotype Alliance' (www.unstereotypealliance.org/en/membership/overview); the United Nations Global Compact (www.unglobalcompact.org/); or the French language 'entreprises pour les droits de l'Homme' (www.e-dh.org/fr/membres.php).

[94] This justification was more or less explicated in an interview on 31 January 2022 with the VP of Human Rights at a French global luxury brands company.

[95] A different question is: why do global companies adopt such policies, and is this due to compliance with mandatory rules or is it a voluntary move? The answer lies somewhere in between, and at times what starts as a list of norms which are adopted voluntarily as internal soft law rules for the prevention of ethical risks is later transformed into mandatory requirements. Anticipating regulatory trends has ethical, marketing, and compliance advantages in the long run for companies, especially when these 'soft' company policies (eg on sexual harassment or on supply chains) later become hard law which competitors with less foresight may have to rush to comply with at considerable expense. In this sense, an interview on 11 February 2022 with the Deputy to the Ethics, Compliance and Privacy Directory at a French global energy company.

[96] As explained in an interview on 21 January 2022 with the Ethics Project Director of a French global luxury brand company and also in another interview on 11 February 2022 with the Deputy to the Ethics, Compliance and Privacy Directory at a French global energy company.

[97] ILO, C190, Violence and Harassment Convention, 2019 (No. 190).

greater where the relevant jurisdiction's law is silent, thus indicating that EU law rules could become indirectly relevant if an employee works in such a company in such a non-EU country.[98]

These preceding explanatory paragraphs may also help in understanding why EU anti-discrimination law is not part of the Brussels effect, referred to in the Introduction to this contribution, in global markets and private law. As Bradford explained, that effect is most visible with a combination of market size, regulatory capacity to develop stringent rules, inelastic targets as well as 'when a company's benefits of adhering to a single standard exceed the benefits of taking advantage of laxer standards in other markets'.[99] When looking at EU anti-discrimination law, one cannot say that these rules are stringent or inelastic even within the EU. As just mentioned, the EU anti-discrimination law directives set certain minimum standards and provide EU Member States some flexibility and elasticity in how to implement them that accommodate the differing interpretations existing in that context. Moreover, the cost/benefit calculation of companies to take advantage of laxer (or non-existent) anti-discrimination law standards in other markets is certainly also an element to consider. Whether it is an explicit calculation or simply an unwanted consequence is a different story and study. However, despite all the official language of human rights in EU external action and also of private companies adopting internal documents on human rights standards, they either remain soft law, or monitoring and enforcement are insufficient to exert pressure to make the benefits of a single standard exceed the downsides of adhering to them.

As an overall conclusion, the impression is that EU anti-discrimination law is rather absent in the global reach of EU (private) law. Such an unambiguous role is observable only in non-EU countries interested in accession and thus subject to the prerequisite of conforming to the *acquis communautaire*. In the other situations analysed here, EU anti-discrimination law's reach in EU (private) law beyond EU borders is at best indirect and negligible.

[98] This example was mentioned during an interview on 11 February 2022 with the Deputy to the Ethics, Compliance and Privacy Directory at a French global energy company.

[99] Bradford (n 2) xvii.

8

The External Dimension of European Consumer Law

HANS-W MICKLITZ*

I. EU CONSUMER LAW IN CONTEXT

CONSUMER POLICY IS the product of the consumer society that developed and arose first in the United States, then in Europe and from there spread around the world.[1] Promoted by the Organisation for Economic Co-operation and Development (OECD) and then by the European Union (EU), consumer law and policy bears a strong Western outlook. It is stamped through with the understanding and the needs of Western democratic societies. The rise of the consumer society produced new types of problems to which the democratic legislatures reacted so as to increase protection of weaker parties. When the United Nations (UN) and later the World Bank stepped in, the outlook and design of consumer law and policy changed in that the needs of non-Western countries were better taken into account.

However, we can observe a current tension between two models of consumer law and policy. At the one end stand Westernised models of consumer law and policy, promoted most strongly by the EU through its neighbourhood and trade policy, as well as through activist development aid agencies of Western states at the one end. Contrary to its origin the EU uses consumer law for market-building purposes, within the EU and beyond the EU. At the other end stand programmes and activities of international organisations, such as the UN and the World Bank, which promote a somewhat different kind of consumer policy and law, putting more emphasis on health and safety, sustainability and consumer finance.

*Professor of Economic Law, Robert Schuman Centre, European University Institute. The chapter combines and elaborates joint research, see G Howells, C Lima Marques, T Naude and M Barata, the two introductions to the special issues on Africa and Asia in 'Dissemination of Consumer Law in Africa, Asia, Americas and Australia' (2018) 41 *Journal of Consumer Policy* 4, 303–307; South America in 'An Introduction to the Issue of Consumer Law in South America' (2022) 45 *Journal of Consumer Policy* 3, 1–6.

[1] M Durovic and HW Micklitz, *Internationalisation of Consumer Law – A Game Changer* (Berlin, Springer, 2017).

This chapter puts the focus on the role of the European Union and its potential impact on the development of consumer law in three major regions: Africa, Asia and Latin America. It is based on the premise that the EU, which started as a latecomer, has now turned into a forerunner that bundles Western legal thought on consumer law and policy, thereby infiltrating international organisations and countries around the world.

A. Body of EU Consumer Law

From the mid-1980s on, the EU developed a dense net of directives and regulations. These serve market-building purposes and can be understood as the nucleus of a European Consumer Code.[2] The general part, applicable to all types of consumer contracts, consists of Directive 93/13/EEC on unfair terms[3] and Directive 2005/29/EC on unfair commercial practices.[4] The specific part is built around an enlarged understanding of the consumer contract, enlarged because the EU has harmonised the modalities of contract conclusion, through Directive 2011/83 on doorstep selling and distance selling,[5] Directive 2002/2065/EC[6] (under revision) on distance selling in financial services, through price labelling (98/7/EC) and the E-commerce Directive (2000/31/EC),[7] revised through the Digital Services Act (Regulation 2065/2022).[8] In addition, the EU has step by step been harmonising particular types of contracts: consumer credit (2008/48/EU,[9] under revision), package tours (2015/2302/EU)[10] and

[2] L Krämer, 'The Origins of Consumer Law and Policy at EU Level' in HW Micklitz (ed), *The Making of European Consumer Law and Policy* (Oxford, Hart Publishing, 2021).

[3] Council Directive 93/13/EEC of 5 April 1993 on unfair terms in consumer contract (Control of Unfair Terms Directive) [1993] OJ L95/29.

[4] Directive 2005/29/EC of the European Parliament and of the Council of 11 May 2005 concerning unfair business-to-consumer commercial practices in the internal market and amending Council Directive 84/450/EEC, Directives 97/7/EC, 98/27/EC and 2002/65/EC of the European Parliament and of the Council and Regulation (EC) No 2006/2004 of the European Parliament and of the Council (Unfair Commercial Practices Directive) [2005] OJ L149/ 22.

[5] Directive 2011/83/EU of the European Parliament and of the Council of 25 October 2011 on consumer rights, amending Council Directive 93/13/EEC and Directive 1999/44/EC of the European Parliament and of the Council and repealing Council Directive 85/577/EEC and Directive 97/7/EC of the European Parliament and of the Council [2011] OJ L304/64.

[6] Directive 2002/65/EC of the European Parliament and of the Council of 23 September 2002 concerning the distance marketing of consumer financial services and amending Council Directive 90/619/EEC and Directives 97/7/EC and 98/27/EC [2002] OJ L271/16.

[7] Directive 2000/31/EC of the European Parliament and of the Council of 8 June 2000 on certain legal aspects of information society services, in particular electronic commerce, in the Internal Market (Directive on Electronic Commerce) [2000] OJ L178/1.

[8] Regulation (EU) 2022/2065 of the European Parliament and of the Council of 19 October 2022 on a Single Market For Digital Services and amending Directive 2000/31/EC (Digital Services Act) (Text with EEA relevance) [2022] OJ L277/1.

[9] Directive 2008/48/EC of the European Parliament and of the Council of 23 April 2008 on credit agreements for consumers and repealing Council Directive 87/102/EEC [2008] OJ L133/66.

[10] Directive (EU) 2015/2302 of the European Parliament and of the Council of 25 November 2015 on package travel and linked travel arrangements, amending Regulation (EC) No 2006/2004 and Directive 2011/83/EU of the European Parliament and of the Council and repealing Council Directive 90/314/EEC [2015] OJ L326/1.

time shares (2008/122/EU),[11] digital content and consumer sales (2019/770[12] and 2019/771[13]). Similar to its fragmented approach in contract law, the EU adopted Directive 85/374/EC on product liability[14] as a segment of the overall field of tort law. The Omnibus Directive (2019/2161/EU)[15] modernised diverse bits and pieces of EU consumer law.

In the decade from 2011–2020, the European Commission concentrated its energy on harmonising individual and collective enforcement. The EU adopted Regulation 861/2007[16] on small claims and Directive 2008/52/EC[17] on mediation, the ADR Directive (2013/11/EC)[18] and the Regulation on Online Dispute Resolution (524/2013/EC)[19] – the last two under revision. Recommendation 2013/396/EC on collective redress was transformed into Directive 2020/1828[20] on representative action. Litigation-based harmonisation is complemented by Regulation 2017/2394[21] on co-operation in transborder enforcement of consumer law.

B. Extension of EU Consumer Law Beyond EU Territory

Right from the beginning, EU consumer law has struggled with its external reach, most prominently in private law relations, when early EU consumer law directives dealt with the applicable law in private law relations that tied the EU consumer to

[11] Directive 2008/122/EC of the European Parliament and of the Council of 14 January 2009 on the protection of consumers in respect of certain aspects of timeshare, long-term holiday product, resale and exchange contracts (Text with EEA relevance) [2008] OJ L33/10.

[12] Directive (EU) 2019/770 of the European Parliament and of the Council of 20 May 2019 on certain aspects concerning contracts for the supply of digital content and digital services (Text with EEA relevance) [2019] OJ L136/ 1.

[13] Directive (EU) 2019/771 of the European Parliament and of the Council of 20 May 2019 on certain aspects concerning contracts for the sale of goods, amending Regulation (EU) 2017/2394 and Directive 2009/22/EC, and repealing Directive 1999/44/EC (Text with EEA relevance) [2019] OJ L136/28.

[14] Council Directive 85/374/EEC of 25 July 1985 on the approximation of the laws, regulations and administrative provisions of the Member States concerning liability for defective products (Product Liability Directive) [1985] OJ L210/29.

[15] Directive (EU) 2019/2161 of the European Parliament and of the Council of 27 November 2019 amending Council Directive 93/13/EEC and Directives 98/6/EC, 2005/29/EC and 2011/83/EU of the European Parliament and of the Council as regards the better enforcement and modernisation of Union consumer protection rules (Text with EEA relevance) [2019] OJ L328/7.

[16] Regulation (EC) No 861/2007 of the European Parliament and of the Council of 11 July 2007 establishing a European Small Claims Procedure [2007] OJ L199/1.

[17] Directive 2008/52/EC of the European Parliament and of the Council of 21 May 2008 on certain aspects of mediation in civil and commercial matters [2008] OJ L136/3.

[18] Directive 2013/11/EU of the European Parliament and of the Council of 21 May 2013 on alternative dispute resolution for consumer disputes and amending Regulation (EC) No 2006/2004 and Directive 2009/22/EC (Directive on Consumer ADR) [2013] OJ L165/63.

[19] Regulation (EU) No 524/2013 of the European Parliament and of the Council of 21 May 2013 on online dispute resolution for consumer disputes and amending Regulation (EC) No 2006/2004 and Directive 2009/22/EC (Regulation on Consumer ODR) [2013] OJ L16/1.

[20] Directive (EU) 2020/1828 of the European Parliament and of the Council of 25 November 2020 on representative actions for the protection of the collective interests of consumers and repealing Directive 2009/22/EC (Text with EEA relevance) [2020] OJ L409/1.

[21] Regulation (EU) 2017/2394 of the European Parliament and of the Council of 12 December 2017 on cooperation between national authorities responsible for the enforcement of consumer protection laws and repealing Regulation (EC) No 2006/2004 (Text with EEA relevance) [2017] OJ L345/1.

a non-EU business. Enlargement in all celestial directions and a strong focus on market-building forced the EU – much more than national legislatures – to take into account the potential external reach of EU consumer law rules and to establish mechanisms that deal with the interaction between EU law and the laws of non-EU countries. It is hard to identify clear patterns, as the external reach of consumer law depends on the degree to which the EU has managed to complete the Internal Market through an appropriate set of private and public law rules.

EU consumer law can be divided into private and public law and, depending on its character, the nature of its extension changes. The core of EU law is consumer contract law together with product liability. Private law thinking dominates. The focus is put on the individual consumer and protection of their economic interests. Public law comes in through health and safety, where consumer law goes hand in hand with market-building and where business and the Member States operate as law enforcers. The public law dimension prevails in enforcement of the collective interests of consumers beyond EU territory.

Even the first generation of EU consumer law directives touched upon the EU's external reach through insertion of European (sic) international private law rules aiming at protecting the rights of consumers within the Internal Market. The Rome I Regulation 593/2008[22] and the Rome II Regulation[23] have led to a harmonised body on the applicable law in cross-border litigation. These have to be read together with Brussels I (Regulation 44/2001, recast 1215/2012)[24] on jurisdiction and execution, which, read together, establish the far-reaching impact of EU consumer law once the EU consumer engages in private law relations with non-EU business. Brussels I allows the EU consumer – even in transnational litigation – to invoke the court where they reside and to insist on transposed EU consumer law as the applicable law due to the universal applicability of Rome I and Rome II.[25]

Looking into the external reach of EU consumer law beyond international private law rules, a striking difference exists between EU law on regulated markets (banking and finance, energy, electronic communication and transport) and EU consumer contract law. EU law on regulated markets is characterised by strong political efforts to extend the scope and reach of the four sectoral rules beyond EU territory.[26] Thereby the EU unfolds and exerts pressure on non-EU countries to adapt their rules to EU requirements on consumer protection within the four sectors. Outside and beyond regulated markets, one needs to distinguish between countries to which the EU is bound through trade agreements and those which have applied for membership. In the case of those which have applied for membership, the EU ties the prospect of membership

[22] Regulation (EC) No 593/2008 of the European Parliament and of the Council of 17 June 2008 on the law applicable to contractual obligations (Rome I) [2008] OJ L177/6.

[23] Regulation (EC) No 864/2007 of the European Parliament and of the Council of 11 July 2007 on the law applicable to non-contractual obligations (Rome II) [2007] OJ L199/40.

[24] Regulation (EU) No 1215/2012 of the European Parliament and of the Council of 12 December 2012 on jurisdiction and the recognition and enforcement of judgments in civil and commercial matters (recast) (Brussels I) [2012] OJ L351/1.

[25] HW Micklitz and P Rott, 'Verbraucherschutz' in *Dauses/Ludwigs, Handbuch des EU-Wirtschaftsrechts: 54. Ergänzungslieferung*, Stand 10 (Munich, C.H BECK, October 2021).

[26] See HW Micklitz in chapter 3 of this book.

to alignment of candidate states with the body of EU consumer law.[27] In the case of countries to which the EU is tied through trade agreements, consumer law is missing, although there is a tendency in more recent trade agreements to give consumer law more weight.[28]

Analysis of the law of regulated markets highlights the importance of European agency which – often in co-operation with the European Commission – is developing international soft law agreements. Consumer law is different, though. The European Commission has no enforcement powers. EU law leaves it to the Member States whether they put enforcement of collective interests into the hands of public agencies or consumer organisations, or both. Member States are not obliged to establish agencies, not even in the context of transborder co-operation. Austria and Germany rely on private law enforcement through their consumer organisations, internally and within the EU. The Consumer Protection Co-operation network (CPC) is an attempt to merge the two different enforcement cultures in terms of transborder litigation within the EU. Under the current regime, the European Commission can alert national authorities and co-ordinate their action in order to tackle practices that harm a large majority of EU consumers. This is followed by negotiation with the business(es) concerned, directly at EU level. However, the EU cannot take regulatory action against market participants. Article 32 Regulation 2017/2394 empowers the EU to conclude agreements with third countries setting out mutual assistance arrangements, establishing exchange of confidential information (relevant for consumer law enforcement) and exchanging staff programmes. The EU has established bilateral co-operation with China, Japan and the United States on product safety, typically in the form of Memoranda of Understanding.[29] Of particular relevance is co-operation with China which aims at monitoring imports of unsafe toys in particular and which brings the EU into a prominent position. The Economic Partnership Agreement between the EU and SADC (the Southern African Development Community) aims to promote harmonisation towards international safety standards.[30] The biannual CPC report does not deal with co-operation by the CPC network with non-EU authorities.[31] ICPEN, the International Consumer Protection and Enforcement Network established by OECD,[32] brings together consumer agencies from around the world, not only members of OECD but also many authorities from the three regions under investigation. ICPEN and not the CPC-network is the key actor in

[27] M Karanikic, HW Micklitz and N Reich (eds), *Modernising Consumer Law. The Experience of the Western Balkan* (Baden-Baden, Nomos, 2012).

[28] See below.

[29] See, Bilateral Cooperation on the EU Commission's website, available at https://commission.europa.eu/business-economy-euro/product-safety-and-requirements/product-safety/international-cooperation-product-safety/bilateral-cooperation_en#china.

[30] Art 56(f). For the updated text of this document see https://trade.ec.europa.eu/access-to-markets/en/content/epa-sadc-southern-african-development-community#:~:text=The%20EU%2DSADC%20Economic%20Partnership,states%20can%20benefit%20your%20trade.

[31] Commission Staff Working Document (final), *Biennial overview of actions carried out by national authorities under Regulation (EU) 2017/2394 on consumer protection cooperation and key market trends that might affect consumers' interests in the future*, Brussels, 8.4.2022 SWD (2022) 108.

[32] See International Consumer Protection and Enforcement Network (ICPEN) website, available at https://icpen.org/protecting-consumers-worldwide.

co-ordination of consumer law enforcement. Here the European Commission does not have the same status as the members: it acts as an observer only, due to lack of genuine enforcement powers.

II. METHODOLOGY

Investigating the potential reach of EU consumer law beyond EU territory requires a methodology which allows for investigating whether EU consumer law has made its way into the consumer laws of non-EU countries. The EU is not actively promoting export of the body of consumer law through policy programmes or EU financed projects. One obvious possibility to study external reach was to look into foreign national laws and their historical roots. However, not much research is available on consumer law and policy outside Australia, the EU and the USA, with the exception of Latin America in Spanish or Portuguese and India,[33] and what little there is has hitherto been limited. The aim of the FiDiPro Project was to close that gap through research on consumer law in Africa, Asia, and Latin America on the interaction with European consumer law and policy.[34] In 2017 we organised three conferences: in Hong Kong with Geraint Howells; in Cape Town (South Africa) with Tjakie Naude; and in Porto Alegre (Brazil) with Claudia Lima Marques.[35] Without their network and input it would never have been possible to bring so many researchers together and make the project work.

A. Common Template

We, the organisers of the conferences, jointly developed a common template. This template was meant to allow for guaranteeing comparability. All national reporters were asked to start with socio-economic background information on the history of their country and the overall development of consumer legislation. The aim was not to receive doctrinally sophisticated analyses, but to understand the baseline of national consumer laws and their practical relevance. The template distinguished between first and second generations of consumer law. *First generation consumer law* is associated with the four basic consumer rights set out in the declaration of President Kennedy in 1962 (the rights to safety, to be informed, to choose, and to be heard), broken

[33] HW Micklitz and C Twigg-Flesner, 'Editorial: Think Global – Towards International Consumer Law' (2010) *Journal of Consumer Policy* 33, 201–207.

[34] Distinguished as research of scientific excellence, the project receives funding under the Finland Distinguished Professor (FiDiPro) funding programme at www.helsinki.fi/katti/english/FiDiPro_project.htm.

[35] HW Micklitz, T Naude and C Twigg-Flesner (eds), 'Special Issue on Consumer Law and Policy in Africa' (2018) *Journal of Consumer Policy* 41(4), 303–471; M Mathios, HW Micklitz, LA Reisch, J Thøgersen and C Twigg-Flesner (eds), 'Celebrating 40 Years of the Journal of Consumer Policy: The Future of Consumer Law and Policy – Internationalisation, Digitalisation and Sustainability' (2020) *Journal of Consumer Policy* 43(1), 1–248; M Barata, L Bernstein, C Lima Marques and HW Micklitz, 'An Introduction to the Issue on South America' (2022) *Journal of Consumer Policy* 45(1), 1–6; M Durovic, G Howells, A Janssen and HW Micklitz (eds), *Consumer Protection in Asia* (London, Bloomsbury Publishing, 2022).

down into legislation on unfair terms (boilerplate contracts), unfair and misleading commercial practices, sale of goods, product liability and individual, collective and private, and public enforcement. *Second generation consumer law* added the law on contracts for telecommunication, energy, transport and financial services. In order to gain insights into the law in action, the template set up *three case studies on product liability, consumer products, and telecommunication services*. Whilst the distinction between first and second generation consumer law turned out to be useful, the three case studies were overly conceived of against a Western understanding of consumer problems. In that sense, the common template might well have influenced the type of results presented. Looking back, it would have been useful to put more emphasis on collecting information from within the regions.

B. Project Limits

One of the major limits turned out to be language barriers. Within the EU, English serves as a lingua franca, even after Brexit. This is similar in the Asian countries. However, Africa is divided, with English and French being the two major foreign languages spoken in Africa, and little to zero interaction between the two Africas. The choice fell on English speaking South Africa. In Latin America, the lingua franca is Spanish and Portuguese. The conference languages were English and Spanish and most of the contributions had to be translated into English.

The three regions under investigation cover 118 countries, Latin America 13, Africa 54, Asia 51. English speaking Africa is represented by eight countries, namely Ethiopia, Ghana, Kenya, Nigeria, the Seychelles, South Africa, Tanzania, and Uganda; Latin America by six jurisdictions, namely Argentina, Brazil, Chile, Cuba, Peru, and Uruguay, complemented through MERCOSUR (Mercado Común del Sur); and Asia by 12 countries: in *South Asia* (India); *East Asia* (China, including the special administrative regions of Hong Kong and Macau, Japan, South Korea); *South East Asia* (Myanmar, Malaysia, Thailand, Vietnam, Indonesia, and Singapore) plus Australia. The choice is in no way systematic or guided by any rationale criteria other than preparedness and availability to join the project.

III. FRAMEWORK OF ANALYSIS

A. Socio-Economic and Political Background

In Europe, consumer law developed together with the rise of the consumer society, mainly from the late 1960s on. Consumer law formed an integral part of Western social welfarism, introduced to protect the weaker party. The EU stepped in when the welfare state and therewith consumer law were on the decline. Consumer law in the EU was first and foremost a tool to complete the Internal Market from 1986 on. Thereby the EU deprived national consumer law of its protective outlook. Consumer protection law became consumer law. This is not to say that European consumer law does not bear a social element. But whether or not this is correct is subject to disagreement in European legal scholarship.[36] It is near to impossible to provide a serious account of socio-economic and political development in the three regions under investigation. The condensed insights should nevertheless serve as a reminder of broader differences.[37]

After independence from the Spanish and Portuguese crowns throughout the nineteenth century, the six Latin American jurisdictions dealt with a period of profound political, social and economic change. Until the 1980s, the economy was centralised, unstable democracies were in place, or authoritarian regimes were in power. This meant that in most cases many public utilities and services were provided or distributed by the state, which *per se* delayed the need to regulate the relationship between private supplies and distributers. The strengthened role of the state in the Latin American region was justified by public policy goals, including increasing production and availability of essential goods. From the 1980s on, the industrial privatisation years marked the beginning of a new social, cultural and economic era for the region, where governments began to take consumers' interests into consideration in their legislative and political programmes. Not surprisingly, this period of socio–economic transformation had a strong impact on the legislative setting of these countries, including contract dynamics and consumer relations. This transformative period influenced the degree of codification and the role and function of consumer law.

The array of countries that belong to South Asia and East Asia are extremely heterogeneous in size, in their economic power, their per capita income and not least their history. Despite all these differences they all share development of a consumer society which has been compressed into a shorter time span than in the West.[38] The consumer society is now pervasive throughout many parts of Asia. In China, the country with the largest population, Hong Kong, Japan, South Korea and Singapore are seen as shopping tourist destinations as they have reputations for high consumer standards. Admittedly, the markets are developed to a different degree, but everywhere is a sense that development of consumption will form an important part of the economy going forward. Middle class affluence brings increased demand for quality products and services, while safety scandals have brought about an understanding that consumer protection is needed to protect all, but especially the most vulnerable. This is recognised particularly in the Association of Southeast Asian Nations (ASEAN) taking action in the field of consumer protection and the raft of measures introduced in many states.

In Africa too, consumer law is on the rise, though with a time delay of 10 to 20 years. The eight countries are markedly heterogenous in size, economic power and legal tradition. The Ethiopian legal order is influenced by Italian law, Ghana, Kenya, Nigeria and Uganda by English common law and Tanzania by German law.

[36] For a critical point of view, see M Hesselink, 'EU Private Law Injustices' (2022) *Yearbook of European Law*, available at https://doi.org/10.1093/yel/yeac005; For a more positive view, see, HW Micklitz, *The Politics of Justice in European Private Law* (Cambridge, Cambridge University Press, 2018).

[37] With particular emphasis on the importance of the Financial Crisis in 2008 and the role of consumer law in the economic development, see the contributions in CL Lima Marques and D Wai (eds), *Consumer Law and Socioeconomic Development, National and International Dimensions* (Berlin, Springer, 2017).

[38] F Trentmann, *Empire of Things* (London, Penguin, 2016) 355 et seq.

South Africa and the Seychelles are mixed jurisdictions combining English common law with Roman-Dutch law in the case of South Africa, and with French law (the Napoleonic Code) in the case of the Seychelles. Consumer protection legislation is a recent development in English-speaking Africa, with many countries only promulgating reasonably extensive or comprehensive consumer legislation for the first time this century and others not having done so yet (as discussed further below).

B. Two Economies, One Law

Consumer law around the world is based on a one-size-fits-all approach. The overall addressee is 'the consumer', independent of their economic resources and their intellectual capacities. No conceptual distinction is drawn between different groups of consumers and their particular needs in terms of protection through the law. In the EU the distinction between the responsible and the vulnerable has gradually gained ground. However, there is no European policy insight that seems ready to take the distinction seriously and rethink consumer law and policy along the line of that distinction.

Many less developed economies display a deep divide between those consumers who can afford Westernised – often imported – products and those with scarce resources who have to buy local products that are often counterfeited and substandard. The potential impact of a divided economy and a society divided on elaboration of an appropriate consumer law features among key topics that are under-discussed, under-researched and under-theorised. The all-dominating one-size-fits-all consumer law approach neglects economically and socially vulnerable consumers who least benefit from high consumer protection standards. The only effort to investigate the impact on consumers of the two economies has been undertaken in Georgia,[39] which concluded an association agreement with the EU and is supposed to integrate EU consumer law into its own legal system. The Regulatory Impact Assessment demonstrated how a one-size-fits-all-consumer law, based on EU standards, risks deepening the divide in the Georgian economy and in Georgian society. The counterargument, put forward by economics, is that high standards are needed to compete for production and sales of high value-added goods.[40] This would mean that the only way for Georgia out of the misery of a divided economy would be to take over the higher consumer standards provided so as to be competitive. Whilst this might be true in theory, the vulnerable consumer appears as a kind of collateral damage. However, similar trends in terms of divided economies can be observed in the Western world to a steadily increasing degree.

[39] Regulatory Impact Assessment of the Draft Law of Georgia on Consumer Rights Protection 2019. The Regulatory Impact Assessment was conducted and the report was prepared at the initiative of the Committee on European Integration of the Parliament of Georgia, with the financial and technical assistance of the Deutsche Gesellschaft für Internationale Zusammenarbeit (GIZ).

[40] M Porter, 'The Competitive Advantage of Nations' (*Harvard Business Review*, March–April 1990), available at https://hbr.org/1990/03/the-competitive-advantage-of-nations.

C. Making of Consumer Law

In the Western world, consumer law-building is usually associated with the post-Kennedy declaration period, the 1960s in the United States and a decade later in Europe and Australia. In the old democracies, no link exists between the constitution and consumer law-building. Notable exceptions in Europe are Portugal and Spain, where consumer law and policy formed an integral part of the democratisation of these societies after the end of dictatorship.

The critical mass of eight African states is too small to make meaningful comments. Many African states gained their independence only after the World War II, from the 1950s on. Consumer law-building did not feature among the priorities and only gradually gained momentum after the new millennium. Most of the consumer laws in Africa were adopted in the 2000s and 2010s, with South Africa being the first mover in 2009. There and in Kenya, adoption of a consumer code went hand in hand with or followed upon the elaboration of a new constitution. In South Africa the democratic order was adopted in 1996. The position is different in Asia, where the number of countries investigated is higher than in Africa but still not sufficient. From the 13 countries investigated, India and China take a prominent position. India's consumer law, which dates back to 1986 and was fully revised in 2019,[41] was heavily promoted through Indian academia[42] and attracted much attention in the Western world. China followed suit in 1993. Both laws were linked to economic and political reforms and both enjoy great influence in Asia. The only region of the world which shows relative homogeneity is Latin America, where the analysis covers six out of 13 countries and where adoption of consumer laws is often the result of democratisation processes.

Brazil is the front–runner in the development of consumer law in Latin America, with its particular focus on the vulnerable consumer[43] and its basis is present in the Federal Constitution, which determined the establishment of a Consumer Protection Code (articles 5°, XXII,170, V, and 148 of the Constitution of the Federative Republic of Brazil). Following a period of economic growth in the 1970s, which failed to overcome social inequalities, interest groups and social movements pushed for better treatment – and recognition – of consumer rights and in 1978 for the creation of the first public agency for consumer protection: the Consumer Protection Executive Group, known as the PROCONS. More than a decade later, the Brazilian Consumer Protection Code was adopted, influenced by the legislative experience of Quebec, Mexico, France, Spain, Portugal and Germany, as well as by early EU legislation.

In Perú, the consumer defence movement began with the 1979 Constitution, which was approved after a long authoritarian regime characterised by democratic instability, increased state intervention in the economy and nationalisation. The reforms under Alberto Fujimori led to the privatisation of state-owned companies, reduction

[41] AR Patil, *Commentary on Consumer Protection Act 2019* (London, Thomson Reuters, 2022).

[42] See various articles in the *Journal of Consumer Policy*, which is widely read around the world. There is also the *International Journal on Consumer Law and Practice*, which is published in India and which is increasingly choosing to integrate non-Indian contributions, available at https://repository.nls.ac.in/ijclp/.

[43] M Cantero Gambito, 'Latin America' in G Howells et al (n 35) 489 at 493.

of public subsidies and promotion of free competition. Against this reform background, Perú enacted a Consumer Protection Act in 1991.

In Argentina, the years of dictatorship between 1976 and 1983 were followed by periods of hyperinflation, currency devaluation and economic crisis. During the 1990s a set of neoliberal policies (in various shades) was implemented, mostly known for privatisation waves and for downgrading workers' rights. In 1993/94 consumer law was integrated in the Argentinian Constitution, resulting in consumer protection rules bearing a constitutional nature.

In Chile, democratic reconstruction paved the way for adoption of a Consumer Protection Act in 1997, after six years of parliamentary discussions.

Uruguay was the last country in MERCOSUR to pass consumer protection legislation only at the beginning of the new millennium.

The construction of an incipient International Private Consumer Law, within the scope of MERCOSUR, has been influenced by regulations issued by the EU on definition, international jurisdiction and the law applicable to transnational consumer contracts. Cuba, a socialist country, is a unique case as it was one of the last remaining Spanish colonies in America, and hence remained under Spanish rule and rules for a longer period. The weaker and later development of consumer protection reflects the socio-economic and political background of the country. A major step was adoption of the Cuban Civil Code of 1987. This later Code reflects a strong influence from EU consumer law, as well as deferred impact of international movements.

D. Legislators, Courts, Administrations and Consumer Organisations

Setting aside Japan, a remarkably conspicuous aspect is that two actors who play a key role in the development of consumer law in the Western world are by and large missing: the courts and consumer organisations. Courts were at the forefront in the development of consumer law in the USA, in Western European and – more recently – Central and Eastern European countries, and – last but not least – also in the EU itself through the European Court of Justice. One of the major battlefields of consumer law in which the courts played a key role was product liability. Many key cases decided in the courts concerned the liability of car manufacturers,[44] pharmaceuticals in the aftermath of the thalidomide catastrophe,[45] and tobacco.[46] Even at the EU level, it needed the European Court of Justice to tackle the social problem of consumers evicted from their home during the financial crisis in 2008/2009 because they could no longer pay their mortgages or were unable to repay loans concluded in foreign currency (Swiss francs in particular).[47] Litigation in the courts quite often

[44] R Nader, *Unsafe at Any Speed* (New York, Grossman, 1965).

[45] Thalidomide Scandal, https://en.wikipedia.org/wiki/Thalidomide_scandal.

[46] G Howells, *The Tobacco Challenge: Legal Policy and Consumer Protection* (Farnham, Ashgate, 2011).

[47] F Gómez and M Artigot, 'Ex-Post Fairness Controls and Contract Design: The Spanish Experience' in K Mathis and A Tor (eds), *Consumer Law and Economics. Economic Analysis of Law in European Legal Scholarship* (Cham, Springer, 2021) 133; M Jazon, 'Judicial Governance by Unfair Contract Terms Law in the EU: Proposal for a New Research Agenda for Policy and Doctrine' (2020) *European Review of Private Law* 28(4), 909–30.

served as a last resort for the victims of consumer harm to seek compensation and justice. The country reports demonstrate that national courts did not play a similar role. Consumer law very much remains in the hands of governments not only with regard to lawmaking but also in terms of law enforcement. One branch of government – the judiciary – is by and large excluded.

A similar observation can be made on the role and function of the consumer organisations, though only with regard to Africa and Asia. In a perfect world, consumer organisations would grow out of the heart of society, would be sponsored and monitored by members of civil society. In the Western world, the role and function of consumer organisations vary considerably, in particular with regard to their political and economic power.[48] Many Western democratic states subsidise consumer organisations to such a degree that they look much more like outsourced branches of government than civil society organisations. Some states, such as Hong Kong, Macau and Singapore, have state-backed Consumer Councils that might provide a similar function. These are different from grassroots consumer organisations, though. In Asian countries – setting aside Japan and perhaps to some extent India, Malaysia and Taiwan – consumer organisations are by and large out of the picture in terms of three aspects, namely consumer politics, the making of consumer law, and enforcement of consumer law through collective action. Even if they exist and even if the respective law provides for rights granted to consumer organisations, their practical importance is limited. The consequences are far-reaching: consumer law is not really anchored in civil society, perhaps in the form of individual expectations, but not institutionally anchored through organisations that claim to speak for the consumer society in the countries concerned.[49] A similar conclusion can be drawn as to the role and function of consumer organisations in the African countries.

E. Substance of Consumer Law

The substance of consumer laws around the world looks very similar. They cover the first and second generation of consumer laws to a varying degree. They share in common that the similarity is greater in newer fields of consumer law, those which arose together with consumer rights rhetoric and consumer policy. In comparison, EU consumer law is far ahead of the curve so far. In terms of the core of common law and civil law, though – such as sales contracts, handling of unfair terms or non-contractual liability (tort) – differences between consumer laws around the world are deepening.[50]

All legal orders have a system of liability for contractual non-conformity derived from civil law code traditions or from the English Sales of Goods Act. The respective

[48] S Nessel, 'Consumer Policy in 28 EU Member States: An Empirical Assessment in Four Dimensions' (2019) 42 *Journal of Consumer Policy* 455–80.

[49] HW Micklitz and G Saumier, 'Enforcement and Effectiveness of Consumer Law – General Report' in HW Micklitz and G Saumier (eds), *Enforcement and Effectiveness of Consumer Law* (Cham, Springer, 2018) 3–45.

[50] M Cantero Gambito, 'Latin America' and T Naude, 'African Perspective', both in G Howells et al (n 35) 489–500 and 501–14.

rules are typically non-mandatory and can be contracted out of through standard terms. If there are particular rules on sales contracts in consumer laws, they tend to transform default rules into mandatory law. However, there is surprisingly little development of a sales regime modelled on EU reforms. The first consumer sales directive, dating back to 1999, was transposed into the legal orders of EU Member States. One might have assumed that the consumer laws under investigation are inspired directly by the EU or indirectly via the legal orders of the former colonial powers who had to adapt their rules.

However, only in Macau and Singapore could such a link be found.[51] In South Africa, the rules on non-conformity in the Consumer Protection Act are not derived from the English Sale of Goods Act or from its counterpart in Civil Codes, but created afresh by drafters with long term influence over other African laws. These rules are more radical than the EU Directive: the consumer may not only choose between refund, replacement or repair for six months from the date of delivery, but may also claim their rights against the manufacturer, importer and distributor who do not deal with the consumer directly.

The elaboration of appropriate rules on product liability belongs to the core of the first generation of consumer law. The EU Directive, agreed upon in the mid-1980s, has been described as one of the most successful European legal exports, at least on paper.[52] This is certainly true not only true for Asia, but for many consumer laws under investigation.[53] To varying degrees of depth, national reforms have been inspired and developed in line with the EU Product Liability Directive. The Directive operated as an impetus for reform alongside knowledge of US developments. Concrete solutions combine foreign and internal elements. Home-grown solutions, for instance, as developed in South Africa, to some extent influenced by the EU Directive, unfolded influence in Kenya and Zimbabwe. However, as in so many jurisdictions outside North America, having strong substantive laws does not ensure that victims have access to justice. The number of cases reported from the various consumer laws is amazingly low.

Unfair terms regulation lies somewhere between product liability and sales law as regards the extent to which national laws have been adapted to the needs of consumers. Promoting substantive fairness can also be underpinned by prohibiting specific unfair terms. Often such prohibitions relate to controls on exclusion clauses, to unilateral amendments or to forced arbitration. Some of the controls in Asian common-law states, such as Hong Kong and Singapore, reflect the UK's Unfair Contract Terms Act 1977. The EU Directive on Control of Unfair Terms was not a force for approximation of African, Asian and Latin American laws to the same extent as the Product Liability Directive, except for Chile, Cuba, South Korea, the Seychelles and, to a limited extent, South Africa. The gap is even deeper in terms of so-called abstract control, the possibility for regulatory agencies or consumer organisations (or both)

[51] A Loke, 'The Lemon Law and the Integrated Enhancement of Consumer Rights in Singapore' (2014) *Singapore Journal of Legal Studies* 285–306.

[52] M Reimann, 'Product Liability in a Global Context: The Hollow Victory of the European Model' (2003) 2 *European Review of Private Law* 128–54.

[53] M Cannarsa, 'Product Liability' in G Howells et al (n 35) 365–74.

to pre-emptively monitor standard terms through a stop-order mechanism so as to prohibit their further use. Where the possibility exists, as in South Africa, the legislation is clumsily worded and the possibility of regulatory authorities taking proactive steps is not foregrounded. The overall finding resembles that from product liability: that is, there is little evidence that unfair terms legislation as far as it exists at all has led to extensive regulatory action and litigation.

Information is central to most consumer protection regimes. In comparison to Europe, the position in the three regions under investigation looks underdeveloped or at least in patchwork form. EU law has set a high benchmark in the duo consisting of the Unfair Commercial Practices Directive[54] – with its obligation not to omit material information – and the Consumer Rights Directive,[55] with its positive information obligations in sales and service contracts. Information duties in the consumer laws under investigation are, if at all, derived from a duty not to mislead. In some jurisdictions this also extends to obligations in relation to omissions. Pre-contractual duties, especially in financial services contracts, complement the existing body of rules. A consumer right to information, as expressed in the Kennedy declaration and later translated into the EU Consumer Rights Directive, is the exception to the rule and, if it exists, it is unclear how it operates in practice. China, Macau, South Korea (in e-commerce), Taiwan and Vietnam provide examples of states that have extensive mandated pre-contractual information duties.

Rights of withdrawal are another area where the rest of the world seems to lag behind Europe. EU consumer law grants consumers a right to withdrawal from doorstep and distance selling contracts, from consumer credit and time share contracts. Such rights exist in Asia China, Japan, Macau, Vietnam, Thailand, Malaysia as well as in Africa in Kenya and South Africa. Overall, however, they are less well-developed not only in the countries under investigation, but even in areas of the world that have a track record for adopting consumer laws, such as North America and Australasia. Where rights of withdrawal exist in Asia, Africa and Latin America, they tend to be limited to doorstep and occasionally to distance selling,[56] although one might find counter examples as in South Africa. In Brazil, the right to withdrawal applies only for purchases made outside a commercial establishment, such as by telephone, internet and at home.

Misleading and unfair commercial practices lie on the cusp of private and public law. In the Western world, contract and tort law were originally used to handle these commercial practices. The EU set a high benchmark with the Unfair Commercial Practices Directive, which covers unfair, misleading and aggressive advertising and sales promotion. Specialised laws in the three regions started by focusing on specific practices but increasingly broadened the scope to cover misleading, unfair and aggressive practices. Commercial practices legislation in Australia, Hong Kong, India, Japan, and Singapore was influenced by US, Canadian and Australian laws and

[54] Directive 2005/29/EC of the European Parliament and of the Council of 11 May 2005 concerning unfair business-to-consumer commercial practices in the internal market [2005] OJ L149/22.

[55] Directive 2011/83/EU of the European Parliament and of the Council of 25 October 2011 on consumer rights [2011] OJ L304/64.

[56] M Atkins and E Webb, 'Information Duties and the Right to Withdrawal' in Howells et al (n 35) 319–40.

more recently by the EU Directive. The overall trend is towards more sophisticated enforcement structures away from criminal sanctions to allow for civil law remedies such as injunctions.[57] A still unresolved issue is whether individual consumers should have individual rights to combat unfair and misleading practices and even claim compensation. Again, EU law takes the lead. However, EU Member States are struggling as to how to implement the newly introduced right to individual redress.

The right to safety is another legacy of the Kennedy declaration. In 1972 the USA set a long standard benchmark with regard to regulation of product safety. Twenty years later the EU adopted the Product Liability Directive. Malaysia was an early adopter of a general safety obligation. Product safety information from the countries under investigation is scarce, although there are similarities between developments in the Western world and the three regions investigated. Controlling unsafe products developed through measuring and labelling techniques, sometimes connected to regulation of technical standards.[58] Consumer safety laws exist in Hong Kong and Macau, copying EU inspired reforms by the UK and Portugal. Japan and Singapore have established sophisticated regimes linked to pre-market controls. In many Asian countries national standardisation bodies exercise a strong influence on product safety culture. India allows unsafe goods to be withdrawn from the market or recalled if in the hands of consumers. However, the most common regulatory powers are post-market control measures. ASEAN is promoting co-ordination of its members' product safety regulation.[59] In Africa, attempts are underway to introduce product safety regulation. However, these are still limited, even in a fairly developed country like South Africa, which has no safety standards for certain consumer goods.[60] Even where sufficient standards exist, problems often arise with enforcement.[61]

F. Enforcement of Consumer Law

By far the most important problem is consumer law enforcement. The law enforcers are Member States' authorities or consumer associations, or both. The remedies are an action for injunction and, more recently, representative actions, including collective redress. Outside agencies and the courts, the EU has managed to establish a third layer through alternative forms of dispute resolution. However, even EU law is a long way from an all-embracing sophisticated enforcement regime, as expounded in works such as that of Ayres and Braithwaite that advocate a pyramid of levels of regulatory enforcement.[62]

[57] HW Micklitz, 'Commercial Practices: A Comparative Perspective' in Howells et al (n 35) 389–406.

[58] M Rizzi, 'The Evolution of Consumer Product Safety Policy and Regulation in India' (2017) *Journal of Consumer Policy* 40(3), 389–412.

[59] L Nottage and S Thanitcul, 'Consumer Product Safety Law' in Howells et al (n 35) 437–52.

[60] T Naude, 'Dissemination of Consumer Law and Policy in South Africa' in Howells et al (n 35) 416.

[61] See, eg, ibid; C Duwuona-Hammond, 'Consumer Law and Policy in Ghana' (2018) *Journal of Consumer Policy* 41, 333–54, esp 341–42.

[62] I Ayres and J Braithwaite, *Responsive Regulation* (Oxford, Oxford University Press, 1992); F Cafaggi and HW Micklitz (eds), *New Frontiers of Consumer Protection – the Interplay between Private and Public Enforcement* (Mortsel, Intersentia, 2009).

The gap between the law in the books and its impact in practice is well-documented and particularly significant in relation to consumer protection law, though not limited to the three regions under investigation.[63] Consumers all over the world have to be ready to fight for their rights, individually or collectively, and public agencies or consumer organisations, or both, should defend the collective interests of consumers. One difference might result from the degree to which countries rely on adversarial litigation or on more harmonious forms of conflict resolution.[64] Politeness and respect for authority and hierarchies are certainly features that one recognises from even a casual acquaintance with Asia. However, some caution is required before embracing the notion that Asian consumers shun litigation. This may be true for certain sectors of society and with regard to less confrontational means of dispute resolution, such as mediation.

Legal regimes all over the world are experimenting with new procedures and institutions to assist consumers seeking access to justice outside the courts or through the courts than through specifically designed small claims procedures. Mediation has been adopted as a mechanism to enhance dispute resolution in many countries, such as the Hong Kong Consumer Council, the Korean Consumer Dispute Settlement Commission, Macau's Consumer Council Centre for Arbitration of Consumer Conflicts, the Consumer Disputes Mediation Service run by local authorities in Taiwan, and the mediation role of the Vietnam Consumer Protection Association. In Indonesia, the Consumer Dispute Settlement Agency allows consumers to choose between mediation and arbitration. Arbitration is widespread in relation to financial services (Hong Kong's Financial Dispute Resolution Scheme, Singapore's Financial Industry Dispute Resolution Centre, and Taiwan's Financial Ombudsman Institute). Thailand and Hong Kong have introduced small claims procedures. Singapore builds mediation into its small claims procedure. Hong Kong has also adopted a novel procedure for accelerated hearing of claims involving tourists. By contrast, there are also examples of special consumer tribunals, such as in India and in Malaysia. In some African countries, mediation is also widely used by specialised agencies such as ombuds, and only if that is unsuccessful will these make a ruling.[65]

The dominant actors in the enforcement of consumer laws in the three regions are public agencies. Sometimes these are independent consumer agencies, at other times they are linked to other fields of the law such as competition. There is also regulatory overlap with competing competences. Many agencies have limited resources. The scale of the resource problem is often related to the wealth of the economy. There seem to be limited moves to more modern forms of enforcement, for example suing undertakings rather than simply relying on the criminal law or administrative fines. Collective redress remains by and large underdeveloped. In South Africa, courts fashioned rules for class actions (initially outside of the consumer protection field), before

[63] Micklitz and Saumier (n 49).

[64] AHY Chen, 'Mediation, Litigation, and Justice: Confucius Reflections in a Modern Liberal Society' in DA Bell and H Chaibong (eds), *Confucianism for the Modern World* (Cambridge, Cambridge University Press, 2003) 259.

[65] See, eg, T Naude and J Barnard, 'Enforcement and Effectiveness of Consumer Law in South Africa' in Micklitz and Saumier (n 49).

the Consumer Protection Act introduced widely worded class actions. These have not been extensively used in the consumer context, however.

IV. OVERALL ASSESSMENT

A. Colonial Past

Europe's colonial past is omnipresent in a chapter which aims at analysing the external reach of European consumer law. The EU inherited the colonial legacy. The famous banana conflict demonstrated in a nutshell how the ties between the former colonial powers and the now independent states influenced the building of a European development policy. In 1986 all former colonial powers had joined the EU. This made it easier for the EU to co-ordinate the foreign relations of its members. This is not the place to discuss trade policies. However, in the narrow field of consumer law and the potential export of European consumer law on former colonies, the EU took a backstage role.

The countries under investigation could be divided into those having been colonised and those having remained free. Some of them were colonised by more than one power. In English-speaking Africa, the British Empire was the dominating power, in Latin America it was Spain and Portugal. With the exception of (most of) China, Japan and Thailand, the countries under review in Asia were colonised chiefly by the British Empire, France, the Netherlands or Spain. Colonial times have left deep legacies in the three regions. The House of Lords, today the UK Supreme Court or the French Cour de Cassation, are reference points for interpretation of the UK Sale of Goods Act or the respective provisions in countries with a civil code. Beyond the former colonial powers, the reports pointed to Australia, Canada, the USA and often to the United Nations Consumer Guidelines. Western influence, however, can also be traced in countries with no colonial legacy.

The developing consumer law has to be merged with existing common law or civil law systems, or both. Throughout the various fields of consumer law, but in particular in consumer sales law and unfair commercial practices law, common law and civil law traditions are omnipresent, not least in terms of judicial redress.[66] EU consumer law – this is one of the major findings – made its way into legal orders around the world indirectly. Countries with a colonial past imported EU consumer law via the legal orders of their former colonial power: the UK, France, Netherlands and Spain. The perception prevails that they are borrowing from the old legal systems to which they remain connected, without necessarily knowing that the adaptation processes in these countries were triggered by the EU and without excluding the option that they may have developed autonomous meanings. There are only rare examples where EU law has had a direct impact on the development of consumer law in the countries under investigation.

The analysis demonstrates a correlation between economic and political independence and preparedness to overcome the historical legacy, to disconnect from the

[66] M Cantero Gambito, 'Access to Justice with Regard to Asia' in Howells et al (n 35) 407–36.

former colonial power and to engage in a much more open exchange of the possible pros and cons of common-law and civil-law systems in terms of elaboration of consumer laws, as is the case in Singapore and (parts of) China. Here, path dependency is much looser anyway as the consumer society leads to a relatively homogeneous set of consumer issues which require similar answers. Depending on the perspective and on the degree of scrutiny, one might be surprised by the relatively homogeneous legal answers to consumer problems throughout the three regions. Path dependency, however, is stronger and stubborner when consumer law interferes in the core of the common-law or the civil-law system, such as consumer sales law or control of standard terms. Here the old legacies remain visible, whether they result from the colonial past or not. China, Japan and Singapore may serve as outstanding examples, where the historical legacies are weakening. These countries can no longer be classified as common-law or civil-law countries, as their legal orders combine all sorts of elements depending on the relevant subject matter.

B. EU and UN Consumer Guidelines

The unanimous adoption of the UN Consumer Guidelines in 1985 is one of the greatest success stories of consumer advocacy, and the then International Organisation of Consumer Unions (IOCU), nowadays Consumers International (CI). Lars Broch, who later became IOCU's director, was given the mandate to present a first draft, which might help to understand the considerable attention that consumer lawyers devoted to a decisive move in geopolitics. However, attention was very unevenly spread around the world. Crudely speaking, the UN Guidelines resonated much more strongly in what is today called the Global South than in the Global North. Many African, Asian and Latin American countries felt inspired and encouraged by the adoption of the UN Guidelines to initiate legislative measures. By that time, consumer law and policy were on the retreat in the USA with the move from President Carter to President Reagan and in Europe through the growing influence of Thatcherism. For 20 years the USA had used the OECD as a catalyst to promote adoption of consumer laws in Western Europe.

This was the perfect moment in time for the European Commission to fill the void and to take over consumer law and policy not only from the Member States but also from the OECD. Quite apart from the UN Guidelines, the European Commission developed its own agenda and via the Single European Act received a powerful instrument by way of Article 114, paragraph 3 of the Treaty on the Functioning of the European Union – to complete the Internal Market at a high level of consumer protection. The following two decades turned into the heyday of consumer law in Europe. Euro-centrism was the result. The UN Guidelines fell by the wayside, at least in the Global North. The Global South, together with open minded Western states, advocated for the greening of the UN Guidelines in 1998 and for an overhaul in 2015 so as to integrate universal services.[67] In particular, the latter move towards a stronger

[67] M Durovic, 'International Consumer Law: What Is It All About?' (2020) 43 *Journal of Consumer Policy* 125–43.

focus on vulnerable consumers, on those who suffered from the liberalisation and privatisation of former incumbents and who had difficulty in gaining access to water, electricity, electronic communication and banking at affordable prices might have contributed to public recognition of the UN Guidelines as a model which takes the concerns of the Global South seriously.

In terms of consumer politics, it looks as if the EU missed the boat in two respects – the need to merge consumer policy with environmental concerns and the need to reintegrate a strong social dimension into consumer policy through the call for universal services. The greening of European consumer law entered politics with the von der Leyen Commission, 20 years after the revised UN Guidelines. Universal services do not form an integral part of European consumer policy. This is not to say that EU law does not deal with universal services at all – just not in consumer law. The rules are scattered and vary according to context.[68] Six years ago, United Nations Conference on Trade and Development (UNCTAD) set up an intergovernmental group of experts 'to monitor the application and implementation of the guidelines, provide a forum for consultations, produce research and studies, provide technical assistance, undertake voluntary peer reviews, and periodically update the guidelines'.[69] The EU is not a member of the United Nations. However, an ad hoc agreement between the EU and the UN grants the EU a position which comes close to membership. The Directorate General just represents the EU in the intergovernmental group which mainly works on consumer policy. Despite its shaky formal status, the European Commission manages to co-ordinate positions between the Member States, in particular in product safety, and operates as one of the key drivers within UNCTAD. This is very different from the European Commission's role in ICPEN.

The intellectual community of consumer lawyers still looks highly compartmentalised, broken down into national, European and international communities. An editorial 10 years ago in the *Journal of Consumer Policy* tried to shift the focus away from European consumer law to international law, in order to broaden the perspective beyond Europe.[70] However, the call to redirect the intellectual discourse – in the Western world towards the rest of the world and in particular to UNCTAD, the World Bank and OECD – largely failed. Again, it might very well be that Brexit will be the game changer. The UK is no longer a member of the CPC network but has strengthened its position in the international arena for instance in ICPEN, OECD and UNCTAD.

C. EU and Regional Organisations – OHADA, MERCOSUR and ASEAN

Regional organisations could theoretically be the target of closer co-operation, in particular when these regional organisations include consumer law and policy among

[68] HW Micklitz, *Politics of Justice in European Private Law*, Part IV (Cambridge, Cambridge University Press, 2018).

[69] UNCTAD, Intergovernmental Group of Experts on Consumer Protection Law and Policy, available at https://unctad.org/topic/competition-and-consumer-protection/intergovernmental-group-of-experts-on-consumer-protection.

[70] Twigg-Flesner and Micklitz (n 33) 201–207.

their political objectives. Potential candidates are OHADA (Organisation for the Harmonisation of Business Law in Africa) in French speaking Africa,[71] and the African Continental Free Trade Area which only recently started,[72] as well as MERCOSUR in Latin America and ASEAN. The first reaches beyond the scope of the chapter. Comparable to the European Economic Community, MERCOSUR, created in 1991, aims at establishing a common market for over 300 million consumers in Argentina, Brazil, Paraguay and Uruguay, later joined by Venezuela and Bolivia.[73] MERCOSUR is a trade agreement but does not aim to harmonise consumer law; it is a process of economic integration aiming at building a common market. However, it needs to consolidate the so-called four freedoms of circulation, namely: merchandise, services, workers, and foreign investment. Composed initially of Argentina, Brazil, Paraguay, and Uruguay, it was created by the Treaty of Asunción, in 1991. Subsequently, in 2012, Venezuela was incorporated into the bloc as a full member and since 2015 Bolivia has been in the process of joining. Given the much later debut of MERCOSUR as an economic bloc, it is not surprising that EU consumer law has played an inspirational role for MERCOSUR rules on conflicts of law. The pending EU–MERCOSUR Trade Agreement does not deal with consumer policy matters.

However, the South East ASEAN countries – Brunei, Cambodia, Indonesia, Laos, Malaysia, Myanmar, Philippines, Singapore, and Taiwan – are not only tied together to some form of regional market-building, they are also gradually moving towards a cautious form of harmonisation of consumer law.[74] The deeper reason might be that these countries are exporting their products to Europe as well as elsewhere, and have to abide by the production standards of importing countries. Consumers within ASEAN are then indirectly benefiting from the economic interaction between ASEAN and the Western world.[75] The EU is not envisaging co-operation with ASEAN, but the EU has concluded or is about to conclude major trade agreements with Singapore, as well as Japan and Singapore. Consumer law and policy forms an integral part. Based on mutual respect for the right to regulate consumer law within the respective territories, the agreements provide for exchange of information and co-operation.

D. EU Evidence-Based Policy

In the Western world, evidence-based policymaking,[76] sets out the conditions which determine reform of consumer law. A perfect starter would be a kind of stock-taking

[71] See Organization For The Harmonisation Of Business Law In Africa, available at https://www.ohada.org/en/#.

[72] The AfCFTA has not yet intimated a concern with harmonisation of consumer law, see https://au-afcfta.org/.

[73] CL Marques, LK Vieira and SS Barocelli (eds), *Los 30 años del MERCOSUR: avances, retrocesos y desafíos en materia de protección al consumidor* (Madrid, IJ Editores, 2021).

[74] L Nottage et al, *ASEAN Consumer Law, Harmonisation and Co-operation* (Cambridge, Cambridge University Press, 2019) 11.

[75] A Bradford, *The Brussels Effect: How the European Union Rules the World* (Oxford, Oxford University Press, 2020).

[76] P Cairney, *The Politics of Evidence-Based Policy Making* (Basingstoke, Palgrave MacMillan, 2017).

of the socio-economic situation in the countries concerned. What kind of problems do consumers suffer from? What are the most urgent problems? Who is in need of protection? Is the existing law fit for use? To anticipate the result – none of the countries of the Global South disposes of solid data in order to be able to answer these questions. The situation is not so different in the Global North. The EU is trying to remedy the situation through the Eurobarometer and through evidence-seeking in preparation for consumer law reforms. The decade-long promotion within the EU might gain pace internationally through the recently adopted OECD Guidelines.[77]

Evidence-based consumer policy does not necessarily presuppose a genuine political democratic dimension, whether it serves to stabilise the market and the government as in China[78] or whether consumer law is part of a programme to democratise a country – such as in Greece, Portugal, Spain or in Argentina and Brazil. It might very well be that the open texture of consumer law – its multifunctional usability – from correcting deficits in the market to questioning inequality in society, contributes to its success and helps to explain its relative homogeneity. This can be seen as a strength as it increases political acceptability for consumer protection measures. The chameleon character, however, can also be seen as a weakness as it makes promoters believe that consumer law is 'a-political', only bound to the existence of markets, independent of the political regime which constituted the market.

With regard to the countries investigated, it seems fair to assume that none of them undertook this kind of stock-taking. Otherwise, the data would have become known in one way or the other. It equally means that governments and parliaments are operating from the idea that the consumer society produces similar problems whatever the country might be. This is both correct and wrong. It is correct, as mass production leads to nearly identical problems provided products are available throughout the countries. Dieselgate is a wonderful example. The social and economic problem – consumers being cheated through misleading information, to put it politely – concerns all consumers who bought these cars, independent from where they live. However, the assumption is wrong in that there are differences depending on whether countries are exporters or importers of consumer mass production and whether national countries are leaders in the chain or are rather at the lower level.[79] These differences are not visible in the existing body of consumer laws. Trade law and consumer law are not interlinked. Neither production nor transportation or distribution form part of consumer law. Globalisation of the economy, however, is making it possible for the first time ever to understand consumption as being an integral part of the global value chain, upwards to production and downwards to recycling.[80]

[77] See www.oecd.org/gov/building-capacity-for-evidence-informed-policy-making-86331250-en.htm.

[78] Trentmann (n 38) 355 et seq.

[79] For an overview, however, with a view on companies not on countries, see J Salminen and M Rajavuori, 'Transnational Sustainability Laws and the Regulation of Global Value Chains: Comparison and a Framework for Analysis' (2019) 26 *Maastricht Journal of European and Comparative Law* 602–27; A Beckers and HW Micklitz, 'Une perspective holistique sur la réglementation des chaînes d'approvisionnement mondiales' (2020) 3 *Revue Internationale De Droit Economique* 343–59.

[80] R Ravalli, *Externalities of Production in GVCs: An EU Consumer Perspective*, PhD thesis (European University Institute, Florence 2022).

E. EU Effects and Concluding Remarks

A constant theme in analysis of the interaction between EU consumer law and the consumer law of Africa, Asia and Latin America is recognition of the trade-off between the benefits that come with a more universal cross-country approach to consumer protection law as against the costs associated with legal constructs that do not recognise and bend to local cultural, technical, and economic circumstances. The development of consumer law in the EU is one example of a one-size-fits-all approach, which yields tensions between the centre (the old) and the periphery (the new Member States)[81] and which neglects economic, social and cultural differences.[82]

European consumer law appears to be a rather homogeneous block of well-developed consumer rights that could easily serve as a model, or at least as a source of inspiration, for other regions in the world. EU consumer law presupposes the existence of an open regional market – in EU language, the Internal Market – which requires a high level of consumer protection. The consumer contributes to market-building, be it the confident consumer or even the weak consumer.[83] There are substantial differences between market-building and consumer protection in the other regional markets around the world. MERCOSUR comes closest to a model where market-building and consumer protection interact. In this part of the world, consumer protection and consumer law carry a strong political message. In Brazil the consumer code intermingles with democratisation.[84] Consumer law is not about risk-free consumption, but serves as a tool to promote civil rights. It is much harder to identify such a clear label for the role and function of consumer law in Africa.[85] The law is divided between the English and the French speaking part, with little to no interaction. The colonial past is present in the way consumer law is perceived. Quite often, it is the common law that sets the basic standards combined with national consumer codes that cherry-pick from other consumer laws around the world adapted to the particular need of that country. The result is great diversity even within the English-speaking part. What holds true for Africa seems to be true for India. This huge country is tied together by one consumer law and strong national courts which often use consumer law for promoting political objectives. However, the common law continues to be the basis of the Indian legal system, on top of which consumer law sits uneasily.[86]

[81] K Kukovec, 'Law and the Periphery' (2015) 21 *European Law Journal* 406–28; R Manko, 'Delimiting Central Europe as a Juridical Space, a preliminary Exercise in Critical Legal Geography' (2019) 89 *Acta Universitatis Lodziensis Folia Iuridica* 63–80.

[82] T Meyer, 'Apples and Peaches – Consumer Protection Goes East' (2020) 43 *Journal of Consumer Policy* 77–83.

[83] G Howells, C Twigg-Flesner and T Wilhelmsson, *Rethinking European Consumer Law* (Abingdon, Routledge 2017).

[84] C Lima Marques, 'International protection of Consumers as a Global or a Regional Policy' (2020) 43 *Journal of Consumer Policy* 57–75.

[85] J Naude, 'Fragmentation Versus Convergence of Consumer Law Within One Legal System and Across Legal Systems: An African Perspective' (2020) *Journal of Consumer Policy* 43(4), 11–33; J Naude, 'Dissemination of Consumer Law and Policy in South Africa' (2018) *Journal of Consumer Policy* 41(4), 411–34.

[86] N Reich, 'Reflections on Hans Micklitz' Plea for a "Movable System" (of Consumer Law) – Anything to Learn from the Experiences of Indian Consumer Law?' in K Purnhagen and P Rott (eds), *Varieties of European Economic Law and Regulation, liber amicorum for Hans Micklitz* (651–74) (New York, Springer, 2010).

Asia and the USA show similarities despite huge cultural differences. ASEAN countries are intensifying efforts to build a stronger integrated market.[87] It goes without saying that the importance of consumer protection increases as the volume of cross-border exchanges grows. Once more, the focus is on the market, albeit in a way that differs from the European understanding of market integration and social regulation. Consumer law in Asia is much closer to US consumer law. Both Asian countries and the United States tend to focus on economic efficiency, downplaying the need to protect the weaker party. Consumption turns into a means to promote economic growth. The similarities should not be overstated. China stands out in that consumption serves as a substitute for political action. Seen this way, consumer law in China is also a political tool, but not for democratisation.[88]

EU consumer law has had an impact on the development of national consumer laws in Asia. The impact is direct, provided EU legislative activities are hitting the spirit of the age, such as the Product Liability Directive. Mostly, however, the impact mitigates indirectly through former colonial ties. If the colonial power is a member of the EU, the country might adjust its law to the consumer law of the colonial power, which in fact is EU law. Overall, it seems that the link between EU consumer law and national consumer laws is closer in new legal fields of the law, whereas core rules on contract and tort in national private law orders remain rather resistant against external influences. Such an insight offers opportunities for the EU – but also responsibilities – in regulation of the digital economy. So far, however, the EU has not yet developed a clear-cut approach on the kind of protection consumers require in the digital economy. The General Data Protection Regulation[89] has yielded 'consumer data protection'.[90] With some optimism, one might suggest that in Africa, too, the growing tendency to adopt data protection laws[91] will lead to an approximation of data protection and consumer law.

The Digital Market Act, the Digital Services Act and the Artificial Intelligence Act affect the consumer, but they do not yet establish a sufficient level of consumer protection. This will be achieved through the 'Digital Fairness initiative',[92] which consumer advocates might want to see realised in a Digital Fairness Act. In contrast to digitisation, EU consumer law lags behind in terms of development of sustainable consumption and a sustainable consumer law. However, initiatives are underway that might be studied attentively far beyond the EU.

[87] Nottage et al (n 74).

[88] D Wei, 'From fragmentation to Harmonization of Consumer Law: The Perspective of China' (2020) 43 *Journal of Consumer Policy* 35–56.

[89] Regulation (EU) 2016/679 of the European Parliament and of the Council of 27 April 2016 on the protection of natural persons with regard to the processing of personal data and on the free movement of such data, and repealing Directive 95/46/EC (General Data Protection Regulation) (Text with EEA relevance) [2016] OJ L119/1.

[90] H Helberger, F Zuiderveen Borgesius and A Reyna, 'The Perfect Match? A Closer Look at the Relationship between EU Consumer Law and Data Protection Law' (2017) 54 *CML Review* 1427–65.

[91] A Roos, 'Data Privacy Law' in DP van der Merwe (ed), *Information and Communications Technology Law*, 3rd edn (LexisNexis, 2021) 387–530, at 476–77; P Boshe and M Hennemann, *Data Protection in Northern African Countries* (Konrad Adenauer Stiftung, 2022), available at www.kas.de/documents/265308/265357/Study+-+Data+Protection+Laws+in+Northern+Africa+%282022%29.pdf/9593d6ad-84c2-40ac-fee0-bd1c5464cf42?version=1.1&t=1668249386554; M Hennemann, R Atuguba, P Boshe and S Afua Dei-Tutu, *African Data Protection Laws – Regulation, Practice, and Policy* (Berlin, De Gruyter, 2023).

[92] Digital Fairness – Fitness Check on Consumer Law, available at https://ec.europa.eu/info/law/better-regulation/have-your-say/initiatives/13413-Digital-fairness-fitness-check-on-EU-consumer-law_en.

Finance

9

Transnational European Private Law and the Governance of Global Finance: Confronting Financialisation

ANNA CHADWICK*

IT IS ARGUED that the European Union (EU) has become 'the world's largest regulatory power' across a range of industries and sectors, including agriculture and food, industrial chemicals, and telecommunications.[1] In addition to its powerful and internationally unique regulatory capacities, the EU is the world's largest consumer market, hence, it has been argued that 'market forces alone are sufficient to convert EU standards into global standards'.[2] When it comes to global financial markets, however, the picture is more complex. It is widely acknowledged that the project of creating a single *internal* EU market for financial services, along with the EU's response to the financial and sovereign debt crises, has 'produced nearly two decades of constant legislating in the financial domain'.[3] Nevertheless, the EU has historically acted as a 'rule-taker' in the context of *global* financial regulation. As Quaglia uncovers in her in-depth appraisal of the EU's contributions to rulemaking for finance, in

> some (very few) cases, the EU 'uploads' its financial services rules internationally; in other (very many) cases, the EU 'downloads' international financial rules domestically; in other cases, the EU actively 'cross-loads' its rules to other jurisdictions, or passively 'cross-loads' rules from other jurisdictions (mainly the US); finally, in some instances, private sector governance prevails.[4]

* Senior Lecturer, School of Law, University of Glasgow.

[1] W Jacoby and S Meunier, 'Europe and the Management of Globalization' (2010) 17 *Journal of European Public Policy* 3, 299–317, 306 citing D Drezner, *All Politics is Global: Explaining International Regulatory Regimes* (Princeton/New Jersey, Princeton University Press, 2007).

[2] A. Bradford, 'Exporting Standards: The Externalization of the EU's Regulatory Power Via Markets' (2015) 42 *International Review of Law and Economics* 158, 165.

[3] A Newman and D Bach, 'The European Union as Hardening Agent: Soft Law and the Diffusion of Global Financial Regulation' (2014) 21 *Journal of European Public Policy* 430–52, 435.

[4] L Quaglia, *The European Union and Global Financial Regulation* (Oxford, Oxford University Press, 2014).

Multiple factors can explain the EU's comparative lack of influence as a political and regulatory actor in the field of global finance. The EU's internal financial market only came to fruition in the 2000s, and it remains under-developed and fragmented. Individual (current and former) Member States, as opposed to the EU as a whole, hold leading positions as independent global financial centres in the global political economy.[5] The EU is also a relative late-comer in terms of formal representation in many supranational governance fora, and it is not yet an official member of the Organisation for Economic Cooperation and Development (OECD) or the International Monetary Fund (IMF), as membership of both organisations is currently reserved for states. In other influential bodies for international financial governance, such as the G20, the Financial Stability Board, and the International Organisation of Securities Commissions (IOSCO), the EU is represented *alongside* its Member States. Longstanding internal divergences between EU Members concerning how finance should be governed have inhibited the EU from speaking with a single voice in matters of global financial regulation, and EU politicians and regulators have often been acting in the shadow of the United Kingdom (UK), which has developed important regulatory clout in international circles owing to the centrality of the City of London to the global financial services industry.[6]

As both Quaglia and Karremans underscore, the global financial crisis generated a shift of regulatory authority from the national to the supranational level, expanding and significantly strengthening the competences of EU institutions.[7] Alongside the United States (US), the EU has become one of two dominant players driving forward the G20 regulatory agenda of restoring stability to the global financial system through enhanced powers of supervision and through harmonised regulations.[8] A 2016 Resolution of the EU Parliament calls on European actors to focus on the global competitiveness of the EU's financial sector when making policy at European and international level, and mandates that the EU 'should seek full membership of international economic and financial institutions where this has not yet been granted and is appropriate (e.g. in the cases of the OECD and the IMF)'.[9] In addition to enhancing its regulatory influence on the global stage, the advent of Brexit has been a key factor prompting the EU to enhance the competitiveness of its capital markets. In response to Brexit and the

[5] According to one influential index, London is the second most important global financial centre after New York, and Luxembourg is seventeenth. 'GFCI 29 Rank' (*Longfinance.net*), available at www.longfinance.net/programmes/financial-centre-futures/global-financial-centres-index/gfci-29-explore-data/gfci-29-rank/.

[6] See N Moloney, '"Bending to Uniformity": EU Financial Regulation with and without the UK' (2017) 40 *Fordham International Law Journal* 5.

[7] J Karremans, 'The ISDA and the Containment of Financial Regulation in Europe' (European Studies Association paper) 1 citing Quaglia (n 4), available at www.eustudies.org/conference/papers/download/605.

[8] 'G20 Leaders' Statement' (Pittsburgh, 2009), available at www.g20.utoronto.ca/2009/2009communique0925.html.

[9] 'Report on the EU Role in the Framework of International Financial, Monetary and Regulatory Institutions and Bodies' (2015/2060(INI)) Committee on Economic and Monetary Affairs Rapporteur, paras 6–9.

new constitutional separation between the EU and its 'investment banker', the City of London,[10] the EU has been advancing the development of the European Capital Markets Union (ECMU). Albeit that the question of the EU overtaking London as a global financial centre is continually answered in the negative, wholesale market-based finance is growing in the EU, and the EU is reported to be determined to develop substitutes for UK-based wholesale market business going forward.[11]

In this evolving global context, many are now looking to the EU to act as a moderating force in the governance of global finance. As Jacob and Meunier observe, rather than making Europe 'fit for globalization', there is hope that the EU might pursue an agenda of making 'globalization fit for Europe' by supplanting 'ad hoc globalization', based primarily on the removal of regulations, 'with rule-based globalization that seeks to channel, regularize, and sometimes limit certain aspects of competition'.[12] There is evidence that the EU is already acting as a force to shelter its citizens from some of the impacts of a liberalised financial model. Alongside the US, EU policymakers committed to addressing 'excessive levels of financial speculation' in instruments linked to commodity prices at the G20 summit in Pittsburgh in 2009.[13] Although progress has been very slow and has encountered strong resistance from some Member States, since 2013, the EU Commission has been driving forward an agenda to implement an EU-wide financial transactions tax in order to 'limit undesirable market behaviour and consequently stabilise markets'.[14] In more recent years, the EU has positioned itself as a leader in the move towards green finance.[15] The EU's new Sustainable Finance Disclosure Regulation (SFDR), implemented in March 2019, imposes significant environmental, social, and governance disclosure requirements on EU institutional investors that are responsible for substantial capital flows.[16]

Much of the analysis of the impact of the EU on the governance of global finance to date has centred on the somewhat restrictive question of whether the EU is a 'rule-maker' or a 'rule-taker' in the context of global financial regulation, and, more recently, on how effective the EU will be in cross-loading its regulatory rules to other jurisdictions via equivalence regimes.[17] The narrow focus on financial regulation underplays the more complex legal processes by which

[10] N Moloney, 'EU Financial Market Regulation after the Global Financial Crisis: "More Europe" or more Risks?' (2010) 47 *CML Review* 1317–83.

[11] ibid.

[12] Jacoby and Meunier (n 1) 304.

[13] G20 Leaders (n 8).

[14] Proposal for a Council Directive implementing enhanced cooperation in the area of financial transaction tax (COM/2013/71).

[15] See the contributions to this collection on the EU's Sustainable Finance Directive.

[16] Regulation (EU) 2019/2088 of the European Parliament and of the Council of 27 November 2019 on sustainability-related disclosures in the financial services sector ('Sustainable Finance Directive') [2019] OJ L317/1.

[17] P Davies, 'Financial Stability and the Global Influence of EU Law' in M Cremona and J Scott, *EU Law Beyond EU Borders* (Oxford, Oxford University Press, 2019); N Moloney, 'Capital Markets Union, Third Countries, And Equivalence: Law, Markets, and Brexit' in D Busch, E Avgouleas and G Ferrarini (eds), *Capital Markets Union in Europe* (Oxford, Oxford University Press, 2018).

financial activity in and beyond the EU is co-ordinated and enabled. The operations of financial markets and the capacities of agents within them depend on a much wider array of legal regimes than are typically made visible in the literature on financial regulation, notably contract law; laws governing the taking of collateral; and corporate and bankruptcy laws.[18] What is more, the character and operations of global financial markets are shaped to a significant extent by the norm-generating practices of networks of private actors who produce contractual devices, develop regulatory norms, and elaborate the infrastructure through which financial transactions are realised. So what, if any, influence does the EU exert over the processes of *transnational private lawmaking* that are acknowledged to play a highly influential role in the governance of global finance? Does the post-crisis regulatory framework in the EU really strengthen EU authority both vis-à-vis transnational private interests and vis-à-vis its Member States, as has been suggested?[19] Or might the post-crisis financial regulations operate to entrench the influence that a narrow subset of transnational private actors is able to exert over lawmaking processes within the EU?

In section I of the chapter, I address some of the conceptual ambiguities that arise from investigating the role of the EU – a public body – in making, or influencing the making of, transnational law, which is typically understood to be elaborated by *private* actors. I then survey some of the existing literature that has studied the interrelationship between the EU and transnational private law in the field of financial services. In section II, after drawing together the insights from this literature, I re-affirm that the EU's mode of developing regulations for financial markets effectively institutionalises and proceduralises processes of transnational norm-making that are dominated by sector-specific interests. In seeking to locate an explanation for this development, I then argue that one important reason why the governance of global finance in the EU is structurally vulnerable to capture by the interests of transnational financial actors is that no inquiry is made by EU political actors into what global finance actually *is*. From the perspective of scholars writing on the phenomenon of financialisation, banks and financial institutions in the EU are not just creating and trading financial 'products' and selling financial 'services' in wholesale and retail markets: they are (re)producing a social model of financialised capitalism that extends an extraordinary range of capabilities upon a narrow constituency of beneficiaries to generate credit, to redirect financial flows, and to exert influence over the policy-making of elected governments and regional governance bodies, such as the EU. In section III, I offer some reflections as to why the EU as a legal and political actor appears to be locked into a de-politicised model for understanding and regulating global finance, and I ask whether there is anything special about the EU that makes it particularly well adapted to, or vulnerable to, a 'symbiotic'[20] relationship

[18] K Pistor, *The Code of Capital: How the Law Creates Wealth and Inequality* (Princeton New Jersey, Princeton University Press, 2019).

[19] Karremans (n 7) at 1.

[20] T Juutilainen, 'EU Securitisation Regulation: Legal Ordering in Symbiosis with Transnational Bodies' in M Cantero Gamito and HW Micklitz, *The Role of the EU in Transnational Legal Ordering: Standards, Contracts and Codes*, Anonymous Translator (Northampton, Edward Elgar Publishing, 2020).

with the development of transnational private law. In the concluding section of the chapter, I offer some final reflections on the broader marketising effects of EU lawmaking in the field of finance.

I. EUROPEAN TRANSNATIONAL PRIVATE LAW AND GLOBAL FINANCIAL GOVERNANCE: EXPLORING THE TERRAIN

A significant proportion of the literature on the governance of global finance tends to employ a binary distinction between *financial regulation* – which is issued by public authorities, such as state and EU regulatory agencies, and which determines the rules pursuant to which financial institutions can operate and trade financial products – and the *transnational private law* generated by corporate and financial actors to determine the nature and scope of the obligations owed by private actors to one another, or to create guidelines for conduct in private markets. Transnational private law is commonly understood to be produced through the activities of private associations which, through repeated interactions in networks, generate norms that increasingly condition behaviour in particular contexts, leading to forms of regulation that have a binding effect, even though they are not generated, at least in the first instance, through the lawmaking apparatus of the state. Another feature of transnational legal ordering is that it is identified with activities performed by what Cutler and Dietz described as '"governance communities" or "global law communities", based on a sector-specific logic … The resulting private legal regimes are responsive to the rationality of the sector-specific community.'[21] Transnational private law takes a variety of forms, and can range from standard form contracts to soft law codes of corporate responsibility. Two key topics debated in the literature on transnational private law are the extent to which 'transnational' law can meaningfully be said to be 'beyond the state', and if and how norm generation and the creation of standard form contracts by private actors comes take on broader qualities of regulation or governance.[22]

The reason that transnational private lawmaking in the field of global finance has attracted such attention from scholars is that this form of lawmaking is understood to result in the creation of normative and regulatory orders that *replace, transcend, or capture* the law-making apparatus of states, or other public lawmaking bodies, creating a constitutional conundrum, as important economic and social functions of governments come to be directed by the interests of a narrow sector of the citizenry. To take the example of the International Swaps and Derivatives Association (ISDA), considerable attention has been paid to how this private association of derivatives traders 'creates the rules' for the global derivatives market through

[21] AC Cutler and T Dietz (eds), *The Politics of Private Transnational Governance by Contract* (London, Routledge, 2017); G-P Callies and P Zumbansen, *Rough Consensus and Running Code: A Theory of Transnational Private Law* (London, Hart Publishing, 2010).

[22] G Teubner, 'Global Bukowina: Legal Pluralism in the World Society' in G Teubner, *Global Law Without a State* (Dartmouth, 1997); R Michaels and N Jansen. 'Private Law Beyond the State? Europeanization, Globalization, Privatization' (2006) 54 *American Journal of Comparative Law* 843.

innovations in contract law that stipulate what is to be done in cases of default, pre-loading its interpretations as to how its contracts should be enforced into judicial forums, and restricting opportunities for interpretation of terms by judges that could generate uncertainty in the market. It is also widely noted that ISDA has gone so far as to produce model legislation for states to ensure that its interpretations of how the outstanding transactions between contracting parties ought to be dealt with when a bankruptcy occurs are followed by governments. Nevertheless, as other scholarship on transnational lawmaking by actors such as ISDA has underscored, a defining feature of the purportedly 'transnational' contract law that underpins the enormous global derivatives market, and more broadly, laws regulating the use of collateral for a wider range of financial transactions, is that they are grounded in the domestic laws of two concrete jurisdictions. Parties elect 'New York Law' or the law of England and Wales in their standard form contracts, ensuring that if there is a dispute, the contracts 'touch down' in derivatives-friendly jurisdictions.[23]

Upon an initial appraisal, attempting to uncover the operations of a European, or EU, transnational private law for global finance generates some conceptual ambiguities. Processes of lawmaking in the EU are characterised by idiosyncratic forms of inter-governmental and supranational co-ordination that take as their point of departure the founding treaties of the Union. If transnational law is law generated by private actors which are understood to operate in some sense 'beyond the state', as has been widely suggested, then it is not clear, at least at the outset, how transnational law relates to lawmaking processes at the EU, which is a governance body that operates under a relatively rigid constitutional framework that is the result of agreement between Member States. What is more, the EU is most obviously influential in terms of generating *financial regulation* to integrate financial markets and to govern finance within the territory of the EU. This means that the law that the EU generates is not obviously 'transnational' in terms of its geographical scope, and, more significantly, that it takes a form that is not commonly understood to be characteristic of transnational law – ie it is not contracts, codes, and standards – it is legislation (Regulations and Directives) and detailed regulatory rules (Regulatory Technical Standards). In addition, with respect to the development of standard form contracts that *are* widely acknowledged to have a transnational character, the EU appears to be very much on the side lines with regard to the private law that forms the basis of financial transactions. The standard form contracts that have attracted such interest for their regulatory qualities by scholars of transnational law have been developed primarily by actors using contract law from Common Law jurisdictions, although this is changing post-Brexit.[24]

[23] R Wai, 'Transnational Liftoff and Juridical Touchdown: The Regulatory Function of Private International Law in an Era of Globalization' (2002) 40 *The Columbia Journal of Transnational Law*; JP Braithwaite, 'Standard Form Contracts as Transnational Law: Evidence from the Derivatives Markets' (2012) 75 *MLR* 779.

[24] ISDA is now developing standard form Masters' Agreements grounded in the law of France and Ireland. See ISDA, 'ISDA Publishes French and Irish Law Masters Agreements' (Press release, 3 July 2018), available at www.isda.org/2018/07/03/isda-publishes-french-and-irish-law-master-agreements/.

As an emerging body of scholarship has demonstrated, however, the binary understanding of lawmaking that might emerge from an initial appraisal of the concepts of 'Financial Regulation' and 'Transnational Private Law' misses the critical interplay between EU financial regulations and the transnational ordering practice of financial actors. I will now offer a brief overview of the findings of five authors, each of whom has studied a different dimension of the EU's relationship to processes of transnational private lawmaking in the field of global finance.

A. Energy Exchanges

Lucila de Almeida mobilises a conceptual framework that distinguishes a twofold process – codification and intrusion – to characterise the role of the EU in the context of the new post-crisis regulations for the trading of energy contracts on the European Power Exchange. De Almeida's study of the EU Regulation on Wholesale Energy Market Integrity and Transparency (REMIT)[25] demonstrates that, when enacting its regulatory forms, the EU frequently 'codifies' transnational law by creating regulations 'that mirror prior established practices of the organized market, for example the definition of certain standard contract terms such as 'spot', 'day-ahead' and 'two-day-ahead'.'[26] In the post-crisis context, however, the EU exhibits a strong tendency towards more overt regulation of trades, thus it also introduces measures of 'intrusion' – measures that impose changes on the behaviour of market participants, creating wider changes in market practice.[27] One example of intrusive regulation in the case of REMIT is the redistribution of monitoring duties among actors involved in the market.[28] Perhaps the most significant finding of de Almeida's study relates to how through this process of regulation, the EU produces what she describes as 'the standardization of standard contracts': it produces a situation in which energy exchanges start reviewing their standard agreements to transcribe new provisions of EU law into the wording of these contracts, meaning that the chambers of commerce which review the contracts have 'no choice other than to take into account the rules of EU law as they are the terms of the contract'.[29] To make use of Quaglia's terminology in the field of financial regulation,[30] in addition to a process of EU lawmakers 'uploading' interpretations from formerly privatised interactions into formal rulemaking, the EU's interaction also results in transnational private actors 'downloading' content into their private contracts, resulting in far-reaching changes in market practice.

[25] Regulation (EU) No 1227/2011 of the European Parliament and of the Council of 25 October 2011 on wholesale energy market integrity and transparency [2011] OJ L326/1.

[26] L de Almeida, 'Standardization of Standard Contracts: Fairness in EU Energy Exchanges' in Cantero Gamito and Micklitz (n 20) 156.

[27] ibid.

[28] ibid 175.

[29] ibid 160.

[30] Quaglia (n 4).

B. Securities Regulation

Juutilainen works with a different conceptual toolbox in his research into the Securitisation Regulation[31] and its implications for transnational private law. As opposed to focusing on the impact of the EU's regulations on a specific market, or on the behaviour of private actors, when exploring 'primary transnationalisation', Juutilainen explores the interaction between the EU and organisations at the global level, namely, the Basel Committee on Banking Supervision (BCBS) and the IOSCO, 'both of which exemplify transnational bodies in financial regulation'.[32] Juutilainen finds that while the Securitisation Regulation represents internally oriented and formal EU lawmaking, it builds on 'much broader expert work, including at the global level', resulting in a symbiosis that 'appears mutualistic in that all parties are able to advance their aims, while the exact source of regulatory ideas or influence is often difficult to pinpoint'.[33] Juutilainen relates these developments to what Mügge describes as 'the emergence over the years of a transatlantic circle of financial regulators, experts, and professionals who share a common understanding of the regulatory world they inhabit'.[34] In contrast to de Almeida's study, which describes a process of the EU uploading transnational norms into its regulations from the established practices of market actors (the energy exchanges), Juutilainen uncovers a mechanism whereby EU regulators are co-producing regulatory norms together with private associations in supranational governance fora, and then downloading them into its legislative frameworks. To reference Quaglia once more, there are no purely 'inter-governmental' policies or regulations that the EU downloads into its jurisdiction: rather, EU lawmakers jostle for influence alongside transnational actors to set the regulatory agenda in the first place. As with de Almeida, Juutilainen also draws attention to a reflexive interaction between EU lawmaking by demonstrating that the Securities Regulation can produce 'secondary transnationalisation' through the export of its provisions, policy choices and underlying values to other regulatory regimes.[35]

Three other notable studies on the role of EU in the context of transnational financial law are advanced by Marcacci, who investigates the product governance regimes iterated under the new Markets in Financial Instruments Directive II (MiFID II),[36] Tot, who examines the Financial Collateral Directive',[37] and Karremans,

[31] Regulation (EU) 2017/2402 of the European Parliament and of the Council of 12 December 2017 laying down a general framework for securitisation and creating a specific framework for simple, transparent and standardised securitisation, and amending Directives 2009/65/EC, 2009/138/EC and 2011/61/EU and Regulations (EC) No 1060/2009 and (EU) No 648/2012 [2017] OJ L347/35.

[32] Juutilainen (n 20) 180.

[33] ibid 181.

[34] ibid 189, citing D Mügge, 'Introduction' in D Mügge (ed), *Europe and the Governance of Global Finance* (Oxford, Oxford University Press, 2014) 3–4.

[35] ibid 196.

[36] Directive 2014/65/EU of the European Parliament and of the Council of 15 May 2014 on markets in financial instruments and amending Directive 2002/92/EC and Directive 2011/61/EU [2014] OJ L173/349.

[37] Directive 2002/47/EC of the European Parliament and of the Council of 6 June 2002 on financial collateral arrangements [2002] OJ L168/43.

who studies the influence of ISDA on the development of the post-crisis regulations for over-the-counter (OTC) derivative markets.[38]

C. Product Governance under MiFID II

In a similar finding to those of de Almeida and Juutilainen, Marcacci argues that the EU 'plays a doublehatted role' with regard to the development of financial product governance. In his reading, the EU first contributes to the transnational regulatory debate by defining the content of new rules in advance; and it later 'hardens' transnational soft rules, in this instance, the standards of IOSCO, 'by incorporating and deepening them into its legislative body'.[39] Marcacci is particularly interested in what he calls 'the regulatory context of product governance', namely, how MiFID II, 'with a view to protecting investors, directly affects intrafirm processes and procedures'.[40] He finds that product governance was first conceptualised by the British in 2012, and was then shared and agreed upon at transnational level in 2013, and then turned into hard law through EU legislation – namely MiFID II – in 2014. 'The EU law has thus worked as a regional stabilizer of locally conceived and then transnationally shared policy strategies', he concludes.[41] In addition to harmonising locally conceived rules for the EU market, like Juutilainen, Marcacci also describes a process of symbiosis at the supranational level whereby 'the Union and domestic authorities first define policy strategies, and discuss and diffuse them at transnational level through IOSCO' – a process in which 'the regional (EU) and transnational (IOSCO) levels influence and inspire each other. As a final stage, detailed EU rules become regulatory standards for investment firms'.[42]

D. Financial Collateral

In contrast to the authors surveyed thus far, Tot sees less influence for the EU as a political actor in the development of the regulations for collateral arrangements. The taking of financial collateral is foundational to the execution of the trillions of contracts that form the basis of global financial markets. Prior to the introduction of the EU's Financial Collateral Directive, the arrangements for taking collateral had been overwhelmingly governed by the standard Master Agreement that is used in the European cross-border repo market: the Global Master Repurchase Agreement (GMRA), which is prepared and published by the International Capital Market Association (ICMA) and the Securities Industry and Financial Markets Association

[38] Karremans (n 7) 2.
[39] A Marcacci, 'Standardizing Intrafirm Processes Worldwide: Product Governance between IOSCO and the EU' in Cantero Gamito and Micklitz (n 20) 200.
[40] ibid 201.
[41] ibid 218.
[42] ibid 219.

(SIFMA). As with the standardised contracts produced by ISDA for the OTC derivatives market, the GMRA exhibits those functions that are seen to be particularly distinctive and interesting by scholars of transnational law: the regime for collateral developed by ICMA and SIFMA is grounded in privately developed, *sui generis* contracts that seek to formalise a privately developed market practice through the production of, and widespread adherence to, a standardised contractual agreement in order to provide certainty for market actors. The objective of the Financial Collateral Directive was to create a minimum EU legal regime for the provision of financial collateral in bilateral financial collateral arrangements.[43] Although Tot describes a processes of consultation between the EU and ISDA in the lead-up to the Regulation, he finds that many provisions of the Financial Collateral Directive represent 'a level of reception of the financial market practice embodied in the various standard master agreements' drawn up by the international financial market associations that indicates that 'the true legislator of the European financial market in the field of financial collateral is the financial market itself'.[44]

Tot's analysis underlines that in this context, the EU Regulation does not displace the reversal of the widely-shared notion of how lawmaking should operate in constitutional terms that is seen to be effected through transnational private lawmaking. In the case of collateral, private actors had not only created a new market through innovative private transnational contracts, developing norms that governed their own interactions, but they successfully institutionalised their practices at EU level, formalising a legal status quo in which national laws had come to be conceived as 'burdens and unnecessary formalities',[45] as barriers to lawmaking that was initiated through the prerogatives of private actors.

E. OTC Derivatives

As opposed to studying how the EU has engaged with existing transnational private law when developing post-crisis regulatory rules, Karremans concentrates instead on how a transnational private actor, ISDA, has deliberately sought to influence EU lawmaking in the field of finance. Karremans immediately highlights that the development of detailed regulatory rules for finance by the EU both constitutes 'a challenge to the private self-regulatory that the ISDA has established between the 1980s and 2000s', and also presents 'a solution to one of the traditional challenges faced by international traders of financial products, namely the uncertainty associated with the fragmentation of different legal jurisdictions'.[46] In his survey of the interactions between ISDA and the EU, Karremans identifies similar dynamics to those discussed in the work of de Almeida, Juutilainen, Marcacci, and Tot.

[43] I Tot, 'Financial Market Lex Mercatoria And Its Influence On The Financial Collateral Directive' (2018) *Intereulaweast*, V:1, 39.
[44] ibid 37.
[45] ibid.
[46] Karremans (n 7) 2.

Karremans shows that ISDA was influential in the supranational governance fora in which the post-crisis regulatory agenda was crystalised, welcoming the regulatory initiatives of the G20, and promoting itself 'as an interlocutor of the reform of the regulatory framework of the international financial system'.[47] Indeed, Karremans survey of the more than 30 policy documents produced by ISDA in which the association expresses its position on the European legislative initiatives in the OTC-derivative markets uncovers that ISDA was actively promoting two of the core regulatory objectives of the post-crisis financial regulations of the G20 – the use of central counterparty clearing for bilateral trades and transparency – as far back as 2008, in advance of the Pittsburgh Summit in 2009 at which the G20 agenda was made public.

> As early as October 2008, ISDA made the following statement in a letter to the Federal Reserve Bank of New York:
>
> > (…) the end state across derivatives needs to include some form of these components to make OTC derivative processing more scalable, transparent and resilient. The seven goals are as follows: – Global use of central counterparty processing and clearing to significantly reduce counterparty credit risk and outstanding net notional positions (…). (ISDA, 31 October 2008).[48]

As with Tot, beyond the diagnosis of 'symbiosis' that Juutilainen and Marcacci identify, Karremans' study suggests that ISDA, the transnational private actor, has substantially shaped the post-crisis policy agenda in the EU from the outset. On the other hand, though ISDA actively promoted some of the regulatory solutions that were then taken up by EU and US policymakers, the EU regulations for OTC derivative markets also have the intrusive characteristic described by de Almeida: the key measure, 'centralized counter-party clearing', produces a rupture in the formerly private law arrangements that had previously governed the enormous OTC Market by interposing a regulated body, a clearing house (in practice, another large financial institution) between the formerly bilateral trades. Again, however, in parallel with dynamics identified by de Almeida, the clearing house function replicates the role of commodity futures exchanges, which are frequently characterised as a private ordering solution developed by commercial hedgers using futures contracts (the precursor to OTC derivatives) in the nineteenth century in the US on regulated exchanges, such as the Chicago Board of Trade. To make use of Quaglia's terminology once more, the EU regulations, like those in the US, thus upload and transpose a governance measure that was previously developed as a private ordering solution on the domestic level into a new edifice of regional financial regulations for the now global derivatives market. To rehearse the findings of Juutilainen, the question of where regulatory ideas come from – the 'exact source of the regulatory ideas'[49] – becomes even more difficult to pinpoint when the longer-standing practices of private actors in formerly domestic futures exchanges are brought into the picture.

[47] Tot (n 43) 8.
[48] ibid.
[49] Juutilainen (n 20) 181.

Although ISDA has continually expressed support for the development of a harmonised EU regime, this does not mean that it shares all of the goals of the EU regulatory agencies. As Karremans underlines, 'The controversies with public regulators, as we shall see, emerged gradually in the scope and the modalities within which central clearing was going to be implemented.'[50] Here, it is possible to see the emergence of the dynamic described by Tot, whereby the critical dependency of regulators on knowledge about market practices that can only be furnished by transnational private actors leads to a form of regulatory capture. As Karremans underlines, quoting Biggins and Scott, 'Considering that the CCP obligations require an assessment of the eligibility of specific derivatives for central clearing, public regulators needed the advice of market insiders for establishing such eligibility criteria.'[51] Consequently, Karremans concludes that while it is true that ISDA's regulatory authority has 'partially been curbed, in the sense that today it is no longer the sole or principal rule-maker in derivative-markets', the expertise of ISDA in the functioning of these markets 'allows it to remain a powerful interlocutor for governments and public authorities'.[52] Indeed, while new European regulatory agencies such as the European Securities and Markets Authority (ESMA) are playing important new roles as 'central public authorities' in one of the world's largest financial market jurisdictions, ESMA is 'forced to rely on the sectorial expertise provided by market actors'.[53]

II. CRITICALLY EVALUATING THE ROLE OF THE EU IN THE CONTEXT OF THE DEVELOPMENT OF TRANSNATIONAL PRIVATE LAW

The picture that emerges from the discourse of G20 leaders concerning developments in financial governance in the post-crisis era is one of a large-scale intervention by governments to regulate global finance in accordance with political – and indeed social – objectives. Developments in the EU context would appear to corroborate this narrative. The creation of a European System of Financial Supervision (ESFS) in 2010 in response to the findings of the Larosière Report is widely regarded as instituting a paradigm shift towards the further Europeanisation and centralisation of public supervision in the area of financial services in which the European Supervisory Authorities (ESAs)[54] 'avail themselves of far-reaching powers to govern the financial services industry' in line with a particular regulatory mission: to enhance investor protection and to reinforce stable and well-functioning financial markets.[55] It is acknowledged in the financial regulation literature that what results from

[50] Karremans (n 7) 8.

[51] ibid 7–8 citing J Biggins and C Scott, 'Public-Private Relations in a Transnational Private Regulatory Regime: ISDA, the State and OTC Derivatives Market Reform' (2012) 13 *European Business Organization Law Review* 340.

[52] ibid.

[53] ibid.

[54] The ESFS is composed of the three sectoral ESAs – ESMA, the European Banking Authority (EBA) and the European Insurance and Occupational Pensions Authority (EIOPA) – plus the European Systemic Risk Board (ESRB) and national supervisory authorities.

[55] O Cherednychenko, 'Cooperative or Competitive? Private Regulators and Public Supervisors in the Post-Crisis European Financial Services Landscape' (2016) 35 *Policy and Society* 103–14, 105.

these interventions is not a neat shift away from self-regulation by transnational private actors in 'deregulated' markets towards a world in which regulators control each aspect of a financial market. As Cherednychenko underlines, '[C]ontrary to the traditional dichotomy between self-regulation by private actors and command and control regulation by public actors', there is, in fact, a great deal of 'interplay between the two in governing financial services in a multi-level EU legal order': public regulators and private actors both co-operate and compete with each other in this context.[56] Nevertheless, the strong presumption in the regulatory literature is that the EU is setting the agenda and creating rules for its internal market, and, by extension, that it is reshaping the rules for the governance of finance on a global scale. Looking through the lens of transnational private law, by contrast, what immediately becomes visible is that through its regulatory interventions the EU is not introducing new laws, rather, it is *changing the character of the law* that has hitherto governed the market.

In their evaluation of the significance and effects of the EU's regulatory interventions for global financial governance, Newman and Bach find that the EU is effectuating a large-scale transformation in the nature of the law governing global finance through the hardening of formerly soft law rules. As they write, 'Across multiple issues in global finance, the European Union (EU) acts as a legalization mechanism that transforms soft law from informal transnational best practice into embedded rules backed by domestic law'.[57] As each of the authors surveyed above has suggested, by moving to enact more detailed regulations for energy exchanges, for securities regulation, for financial collateral arrangements, for financial product governance, and for OTC derivatives market, EU regulators are hardening and proceduralising forms of transnational private lawmaking, thereby formalising and concretising the operations of these distinct financial markets, and also legitimating them on the basis that regulators are now supervising financial agents in the market. Turning now to the central question that animates this chapter, the crux of the matter is whether these developments – the hardening, proceduralising, harmonising, and institutionalising – functions that the authors ascribe to the interactions between the EU and transnational private lawmaking combine to empower the EU to act as a moderating force over global financial markets or not.

The new EU regulations have clearly instituted significant changes in market practice with regard to the contracts and legal architectures developed by transnational private actors that form the basis of markets for financial derivatives, repurchase agreements (REPOs), and other types of financial transaction. Financial actors must now consider and develop responses to these detailed centralised regulations when developing new financial products and services. Thus, in addition to a formalising and harmonising role with regard to transnational private lawmaking, the EU is also playing a more productive role: it is inducing changes in how transnational private actors go about developing new financial products and offering them to the market. For example, ISDA has produced a number of protocols to explicitly help

[56] ibid 104.
[57] Newman and Bach (n 3) 431.

its members ensure that their portfolios of contracts comply with the regulatory technical standards of ESMA relating to heightened margin requirements, and portfolio reconciliation and dispute resolution obligations.[58] In a similar dynamic to earlier processes in which the EU sought to make its Member States 'fit' for the EU, such as through the adoption of new constitutional articles, or the creation of specialised parliamentary and governmental bodies dealing with European politics,[59] the EU is forcing the same kind of internal reordering onto transnational private actors. These actors, like the Member States before them, are 'incorporating the European legal system into their self-description', by referring to this regulatory system in the way that they produce contractual instruments and in the way that they are required to order themselves internally in order to comply with the regulations.[60]

On the other hand, switching from a regulatory lens to a focus on transnational private lawmaking reinforces that financial regulators in the EU are acting in a context in which the nature of these financial markets, their terms of operation, and their role in the global political economy have largely already been established through the prior actions of networked agents. All of the authors describe how the EU, in instituting a regulatory process for a specific domain of finance – energy futures, securities, financial products, collateral, derivatives – largely lifts a pre-constituted understanding of the market into its regulatory process, importing the terms and instruments and processes used by the private actors. The consequences of the EU's interventions vary between the different markets, but there are common trends of codification and proceduralisation, whereby terminology that was previously used by private actors to define their engagement becomes a regulatory language that it used to make the operations of the market in question legible to regulators, who then introduce new requirements – such as the use of monitoring measures, centralised clearing, or reporting requirements – to try to control what is happening in specific areas of the market activity. Thus, when the EU uploads market practices and formalises them as more regulated exchanges, it legitimises and lends power to a processes of rulemaking that have been largely shaped by the interpretations of sector-specific communities as to how these markets operate, which can have a constraining impact on how they can be regulated. Furthermore, the work of each of the authors discussed earlier suggests that the EU seems to be creating new pathways to institutionalising its engagement with transnational private associations by enrolling them in successive consultation exercises, and by deferring to their expertise on the technical questions concerning how markets work.

While the epistemological hurdle that EU regulators face when trying to 'know' complex financial markets in order to regulate them seems to enhance the authority of transnational private actors, enabling them to load their preferences into the EU's regulatory architectures, the approach taken by the EU to financial governance is also linked to its wider policy agenda. The EU can only introduce limited changes to the process of buying and selling energy contracts, creating securities, developing

[58] For a full list of ISDA protocols, see www.isda.org/protocols/.

[59] M Jachtenfuchs, 'Democracy and Governance in the European Union' (*European Integration Online Papers*, 1997) 5, available at http://eiop.or.at/eiop/texte/1997–002a.htm.

[60] M Albert, 'Governance and Democracy in European Systems: On Systems Theory and European Integration' (2002) 28 *Review of International Studies* 293, 302.

financial 'products', producing financial collateral, and trading derivatives because it is concerned to promote the public good of global financial stability while maintaining the competitiveness and profitability of the EU's markets with respect to those of competitor jurisdictions. From the perspective of the literature on financialisation, the problem with a regulatory strategy based on enhancing financial stability and maintaining market competitiveness is that the financial 'products' and 'services' that the EU has been seeking to provide by generating a single market for financial services over multiple decades are not nearly as bland and uninteresting as their description might suggest. The EU's newly empowered financial regulatory agencies create stipulations for how the trades are made by the parties and require them to take into account specific regulations relating to systemic risk and transparency, but they make no investigation into *what is being traded* in these contracts. For critical scholars working on the phenomenon of financialisation, at a minimum, the financial products and services developed by large financial institutions are furthering the increased liberalisation of financial capital and its movement in and out of different markets and jurisdictions, which has far reaching implications for the collection of tax, for the stability of currencies, and for levels of sovereign indebtedness. A substantial interdisciplinary literature demonstrates that financialised capitalism represents a highly unstable and politically controversial model for growing the economy, and is persuasively linked to rising levels of income inequality,[61] the intensification of wage stagnation, and a lack of public spending on services, the entrenchment of a debt-driven model of spending,[62] and the transfer of income from the 'real' sector to the financial sector through products such as consumer investment schemes and pension funds.[63] As scholarship on the broader impacts of the monumental global market in derivatives has underlined, derivatives are not just financial instruments that protect financial and commercial institutions from a range of market 'risks' (exchange rate risk, interest rate risk, energy price movements) and enable some degree of speculative investment. Rather, derivatives are a financial technology through which processes of sentiment-driven market volatility increasingly interact with a wide range of systemically significant' prices[64] – exchange rates, interest rates, energy prices, prices for food staples, property markets, and stock prices – enabling financial communities to effectively govern markets and, simultaneously, to constrain the capabilities of governments to challenge logics of financialisation.[65]

[61] N Fligstein and T Shin, 'The Shareholder Value Society: Changes in Working Conditions and Inequality in the U.S., 1975–2000' in K Neckerman (ed), *Social Inequality* (New York, Russell Sage Foundation, 2004); T Picketty, *Capital in the 21st Century* (Cambridge Massachusetts, Harvard University Press, 2013); Pistor (n 18).

[62] C Lapavitsas, *Profiting without Producing: How Finance Exploits Us All* (London, Verso, 2013); W Streeck, *Buying Time: The Delayed Crisis of Democratic Capitalism*, Anonymous Translator (London, Verso, 2014).

[63] A Dixon, 'The Rise of Pension Fund Capitalism in Europe: An Unseen Revolution?' (2008) 13 *New Political Economy* 249–70.

[64] R Hockett and S Omarova, 'Systemically Significant Prices' (2016) 2 *Journal of Financial Regulation* 1, 1–20.

[65] D Bryan and M Rafferty, *Capitalism with Derivatives: A Political Economy of Financial Derivatives, Capital and Class* (Basingstoke, Palgrave Macmillan, 2006); D Wigan, 'Financialisation and Derivatives: Constructing an Artifice of Indifference' (2009) 13 *Competition & Change* 157.

From the perspective of the financialisation literature, by accepting this world of inter-locking financial contracts, and by merely seeking to 'channel, regularize, and sometimes limit certain aspects of competition' within those markets, in its efforts to regulate finance, the EU is largely entrenching a political economic model that privileges the interests of an influential group of financial institutions. Integrated financial markets are commonly praised for 'enlarging the opportunity sets of lenders and borrowers' and for 'diversifying idiosyncratic risks away from the national economies, thereby contributing to financial stability'.[66] Yet, integration of EU financial markets has occurred primarily in the form of market-based banking, as opposed to consisting in an expansion of retail services.[67] Even if retail services are further integrated, the claim that the welfare of citizen consumers will be enhanced by greater access to credit has a flipside: the increased indebtedness of citizens, companies, and governments means that forms of financial discipline come to exert greater influence over everyday life. As Riles underscores in her critique of the limits of current approaches to conceptualising and governing finance, financial regulation is 'not some isolated set of technical problems in need of a quick fix' but a piece of a wider financial apparatus: 'a template for social, economic and political life that stretches from welfare policy to the governance of universities, from development policy to the management of prisons'.[68] Fraser, a leading scholar of financial capitalism, rejects the core argument underlying the need for expanded and integrated financial markets – that finance produces economic growth – as false. In her argument, finance 'penetrates and sucks value from every sector' exacerbating the exploitation of the majority of citizens around the world, in and beyond the EU.[69]

Overwhelmingly, the EU's perspective – whether it is iterated by the EU Commission, by the G20, or by individual governments – is addressed to the inter-related goals of enhancing the growth and development of 'deep', liquid financial markets; ensuring global financial stability; preventing the build-up for systemic risk; and enhancing consumer protection. The result is that a very narrow set of seemingly self-evident goals – ensuring consumer safety and protection – is met through legal techniques that operate to sideline other potentially more penetrating approaches to product approval. For example, Omarova argues in the US context that certain financial products, like OTC derivatives, should be pre-tested and approved for their contribution to beneficial commercial hedging or destabilising speculation prior to their introduction into the market.[70] Indeed, as Karreman's study underlines, transnational private actors are determined to prevent the EU from conducting investigations

[66] 'The Quest for Financial Integration in Europe and Globally', Speech by Mr Agustín Carstens, General Manager of the Bank for International Settlements at the Eurofi Financial Forum, Helsinki, 12 September 2019, available at www.bis.org/speeches/sp190912.htm.

[67] P Lysandrou and T Ranjbaran, 'Financialisation Reinforced: The Enduring Legacy of the Covid Pandemic' in E Stockhammer et al, 'Financialisation: Continuity and Change' (2021) 2 *Review of Evolutionary Political Economy* 2, 389–401, 400.

[68] A Riles, 'New Approaches to International Financial Regulation' (2014) *Cornell Law School Research Paper* No. 15-03, 33.

[69] N Fraser, 'A New Form of Capitalism? A Reply to Boltanski and Esquerre' (2017) *New Left Review*.

[70] ST Omarova, 'License to Deal: Mandatory Approval of Complex Financial Products' (2012) 90 *Washington University Law Review*.

into the nature of what is being traded in financial markets. In its communications to the EU, ISDA insists that 'We believe that the regulatory focus should therefore be on process uniformity, legal uniformity and standardization of documentation; not product uniformity. Non standardized products are not inherently more risky than plain vanilla products'.[71] As scholarship that has highlighted the extensive liberties that are being taken with private law in the development of financial products would underline,[72] and as Pistor's penetrating study into the role of private lawyers and financial institutions in innovating around key modules of law – property, contract, collateral, and bankruptcy laws – underscores, the ability of actors to develop new, non-standardised financial products is central to the ongoing process in which capital is coded, and novel ways of protecting wealth are elaborated.[73]

On a strong reading of the findings from the scholarship on the relationship between the EU and the development of transnational private law in the context of financial governance, the EU has become a kind of institutional host for a socially parasitic form of financial capitalism. Arguing in this vein, critical scholars have suggested that the ECMU is a technical project that further entrenches a problematic over-reliance on private capital as a driver of growth and constructs EU capital markets on the premises of the same socially irresponsible financial model that led to the global financial crisis.[74] However, the question remains whether there is anything specific about the EU as a regional governance body and lawmaking that makes it a particularly attractive institutional host for this kind of financial model. In light of the urgency of developing rules to stabilise the global financial system and to prevent it from collapsing in the years after the crisis, some of the trends observed in which the EU simply 'uploads' and 'cuts and pastes' norms that were developed through market practices into its regulations are perhaps unsurprising. Thus far, the literature on the relationship between the EU and transnational private law has sidestepped an important question, which is whether there is anything special about the EU as an entity, or as a lawmaking actor, that makes it structurally aligned with a sector-specific understanding of the nature of global finance. I will now offer some reflections on this important dimension of the debate.

III. TRANSNATIONAL EUROPEAN PRIVATE LAW AND FINANCIALISATION – FOUNDATIONAL FLAWS?

Many political and lawmaking authorities at local, national and supranational levels now rely on intense consultation with private stakeholders when developing

[71] ISDA's Response to European Commission consultation on OTC derivatives, 31 August 2009, cited by Karremans (n 7) 13.

[72] H Collins, 'The Revolutionary Trajectory of EU Contract Law Towards Post-National Law' in S Worthington et al (eds), *Revolution and Evolution in Private Law* (Oxford, Hart Publishing, 2018) 315, 321.

[73] Pistor (n 18).

[74] B Braun and M Hübner, 'Fiscal Fault, Financial Fix? Capital Markets Union and the Quest for Macroeconomic Stabilization in the Euro Area' (2018) 22 *Competition & Change* 2, 117–38; N Haerter, 'Ceci n'est pas un Capital Markets Union: Re-Establishing EU-Led Financialization' (2020) 24 *Competition & Change* 248–67.

laws and policies for an interconnected global economy. Given that many of those stakeholders are large transnational corporations and financial institutions, it would seem reasonable to assume that lawmaking at all levels, and not just at the level of the EU, is likely to be co-developed with transnational private actors to some degree. As scholars writing on the phenomenon of New Public Management have argued, the economic and political crisis in the 1970s 'paved the way for neoliberal governments and policies that aimed to solve the problem of "government overload" by means of privatising public enterprises, contracting-out public services, and commercialising the remaining public sector'.[75] In response to the postulated 'ungovernability of society', New Public Management reforms aimed to enhance the reliance on the self-regulating capacity of private markets, which resulted in a move in many polities to forms of public-private partnership for the delivery of public services.[76] According to Torfing and Sørensen, one of the results of this political shift is that 'the national space for making and amending public policy is transgressed as policies are increasingly being uploaded to and downloaded from international policy arenas through complex processes of policy learning and policy diffusion'.[77] Multilateral action through which 'a plethora of public and/or private actors collaborate in order to pool and exchange their resources and competences' is argued to be becoming inevitable in response to the growing 'fragmentation, complexity and dynamism of our present societies'.[78]

One of the problems with the suggestion that the EU can become a moderating force in the governance of global finance is that the EU is acting in a global political economy that is structurally oriented towards dynamics of sector-specific regulation, or, to use another lens, 'club governance'.[79] For some scholars, notably those influenced by Systems Theory, the developments in the EU are part of a broader structural characteristic that is inherent in the evolution of complex societies. Legal scholars who have built on the insights of Systems Theory have developed persuasive theoretical explanations for processes of 'constitutional fragmentation' and 'societal constitutionalism', that are premised on an understanding that although all social systems form part of a complex social whole, they all operate according to communicative codes, or 'systems languages', which result in the progressive institutionalisation of sector-specific logics.[80] A key finding of this literature is that the political system can 'no longer claim supremacy over, or be representative of, other social systems'.[81] Scholars of transnational law suggest that

[75] J Torfing and E Sørensen, 'The European Debate on Governance Networks: Towards a New and Viable Paradigm?' (2014) 33 *Policy and Society* 329–44, 331.
[76] ibid.
[77] ibid 330.
[78] ibid 331.
[79] P Knaack, 'Innovation and Deadlock in Global Financial Governance: Transatlantic Coordination Failure in OTC Derivatives Regulation' (2015) 22 *Review of International Political Economy* 1217–48, 1239.
[80] G Teubner, *Constitutional Fragments: Societal Constitutionalism and Globalization* (Oxford, Oxford University Press, 2012).
[81] Albert (n 60) 298.

critiques of transnational private lawmaking that seek to unmask the public origins of the (purportedly) private legal regimes from which complex systems of economic regulation depart are insufficiently attuned to the complexity of social relations under conditions of global capitalism.[82] From this perspective, critiques of the EU's democratic deficit that highlight its structural reliance on technocratic decision-making elide the fact that many ostensibly more democratic decision-making bodies may be equally deficient. Other analysts nonetheless continue to stress that it is political choices of governments – however fragmented and denationalised they might be – that give institutional and legal life to the lawmaking preferences of sector-specific communities and financial elites. This alternative reading is found in the work of Knack, who argues that, in determining the architectures for the current supranational governance of global finance, governments deliberately 'eschewed any attempts at using or creating a broadly representative organization firmly rooted in international public law, and put a minilateral club-like government network in charge of coordinating global regulatory reform instead'.[83] The minilateral approach involves a small set of stakeholders, allowing for the development of financial standards that 'sideline potential veto players among developing countries', and secure the ascendence of 'transnational operations of government networks based on soft law' that also 'allow the executive branch to circumvent domestic veto players to a large extent'.[84]

While it would seem clear that the dynamics between policymakers, regulators, transnational private actors in the EU are far from unique, it has nonetheless been suggested by a number of scholars that key institutional features of the EU may indeed be responsible for giving further institutional life to a sector-specific way of understanding finance. In their recent examination of the ECMU,[85] Braun and Hübner argue that the EU suffers from a 'structural capacity gap' that 'severely limits the capacity of both national and supranational actors to provide a core public good: macroeconomic stabilization'.[86] In their analysis, not only is a foundational feature of the EU – its lack of a common fiscal policy – identified as a driver of a financialised economic model, but the EU is also seen to be structurally vulnerable to 'technocrats, think tanks, and financial-sector lobbyists', who 'through the strategic use of knowledge and expertise, established securitization and market-based finance as solutions to the European Monetary Union's governance problems'.[87]

[82] As Zumbansen writes in response to critiques that seek to uncover the public underpinnings of 'transnational' contract law, how useful a critique that points to the political underpinnings of a formalist approach to understanding contract only to try to reintegrate contractual governance into a larger framework of legal and political theory under circumstances 'in which the sites of democratic politics have become de-centered, fragmented, and denationalized?'. Zumbansen, 'The Law of Society: Governance Through Contract' (2007) 14 *Indiana Journal of Global Legal Studies* 191.

[83] Knaack (n 79) 1239.

[84] ibid.

[85] The ECMU has been described as a multi-faceted project, which, 'though more than thirty proposed measures, is designed to strengthen financial intermediation via capital markets, or, in other words, to deploy bond, equity, venture capital, and securitization markets towards a goal of financing 'real' economic activity'.

[86] Braun and Hübner (n 74) 118.

[87] ibid 118.

Braun and Hübner further contend that the single market project, which is 'enshrined in the Treaty of Rome and thus in the EU's institutional DNA', not only drives forward a politically contentious mode of political economy, but that it has to be done through the specific legal form of regulation.[88] The complaint is that a foundational flaw with the EU with regard to its legitimacy as a lawmaking actor lies in its institutional structure, which authorises the EU to issue regulations but only in regard to a limited field of action stemming from the competences that have been conferred on it by its Member States. For Braun and Hübner, the EU's return to reliance on a discredited model of securitised finance through the ECMU initiative is a consequence of its limited field of competence, which requires it to deploy regulatory powers to try to make private financial markets function to service the public goal of providing macroeconomic stability in light of its inability to institute a common fiscal policy.

Braun and Hübner's argument is in dialogue with a long-standing debate about the significance of the perceived imbalance between the constitutional commitment in the Treaty of Rome to the creation of a single market, which requires the removal of restrictions on the free movement of goods, people, services, and capital,[89] and the EU's limited mandate to regulate in prescribed areas. For a number of influential scholars, the EU's constitutional commitment to economic integration and its character as a regulatory state is predicated on a neoliberal worldview which regards economic integration as 'not only a necessary reaction to the requirements of a natural process of economic globalization but also an explicit normative goal'.[90] The consequence of this is that the EU has institutionalised a particular kind of economic constitution that 'legitimates the activity of the EU in a number of functional areas and at the same time limits the extension of EU competencies to what is necessary for coping with economic interdependencies'.[91] Other authors, notably Majone, rebut the understanding of the democratic deficit that is seen to extend from the foundational structures of the EU, which empower it primarily to develop economic laws and regulations based on 'negative integration', in which barriers to economic transactions are dismantled and new markets are created.[92] Majone asserts that, as a regulatory state, the EU is only authorised to produce regulation to address market failures, resulting in policy outcomes that are 'Pareto-efficient (where some benefit and no one is made worse off)', rather than redistributive or value-allocative measures (where there are both winners and losers).[93] In his assessment, the EU should embrace its nature, which he suggests is that of a technocratic regulatory agency – a 'fourth branch of government' that functions much like regulatory agencies at the domestic level in Europe, such as telecoms agencies, competition authorities,

[88] ibid 105.

[89] European Union, Treaty Establishing the European Community (Consolidated Version), Rome Treaty, 25 March 1957, Art 3(a).

[90] Jachtenfuchs (n 59) 8.

[91] ibid 8–9.

[92] G Majone, *Regulating Europe* (London, Routledge, 1996). G Majone, 'Europe's "Democratic Deficit": The Question of Standards' (1998) 4 *European Law Journal* 5–28.

[93] Follesdal and Hix citing Majone, 'Europe's "Democratic Deficit"', ibid. A Follesdal and S Hix, 'Why there is a Democratic Deficit in the EU: A Response to Majone and MoravcsiK' (2006) 44 *Journal of Common Market Studies* 533–62, 536.

central banks' – and should focus not on enhancing its democratic credentials, but on improving this particular style of technocratic rulemaking.[94] As Follesdal and Hix underline, however, Majone's position is predicated on a false notion that economic efficiency is a universal good and that it does not have the kind of distributive consequences that Majone himself acknowledges should be weighed and considered by democratic decision-making bodies.[95] In fact, the EU has consistently tried to make its decision-making less technocratic and more democratic in response to critiques of its democratic deficit. According to Torfing and Sørensen, the European Commission and influential academic commentators 'recommended the creation of governance networks, partnerships and other forms of participatory governance. The argument was that the involvement of private stakeholders would help to enhance input- and output-legitimacy'.[96] Thus, in its attempt to move away from a regulatory state that is 'integrated through law', the EU has become 'integrated through governance', incrementally enrolling private actors in its decision-making in an array of regulatory fields.[97] Herein lies one explanation for the oft-diagnosed 'technocratic' character of the EU and the perception that, as a political and lawmaking actor, the EU is characterised by a 'strong degree of both internationalization and functional differentiation':[98] in an attempt to enhance its democratic credentials, the EU has shifted towards an institutionalised model of stakeholder consultation, but its constitutional foundations result in these processes being carried out through a segmented approach that reflects an ongoing attempt to integrate specific markets for goods, services, and capital.

So what does this mean for the specific case of the relationship between the EU, transnational private law, and global finance? The first point to note is that the constitutional basis from which the EU departs in trying to govern financial markets is one that is committed to a liberalised model of integration through the removal of barriers. As Moloney underscores, the EU's capacity to engage in penetrating financial regulation is precarious, as it risks overstretching the EU's competence in the area of financial regulation, which is

> almost always based on Article 114 of the Treaty on the Functioning of the EU, which contains the EU competence to adopt harmonizing measures for the purposes of the establishment and functioning of the internal market, or on similar competences related to free movement.[99]

As a number of legal challenges spearheaded by the UK on over-reach by the EU have underlined,[100] the Article 114 competence has been used to 'support an array of

[94] G Majone, 'The European Community: An "Independent Fourth Branch of Government"?' *EUI Working Paper SPS No 94/17* (Florence, European University Institute, 1993).

[95] Follesdal and Hix (n 93).

[96] Torfing and Sørensen (n 75).

[97] R Vallejo, 'Voyaging through Standards, Contracts, and Codes: The Transnational Quest of European Regulatory Private Law' in Cantero Gamito and Micklitz (n 20) 293.

[98] Jachtenfuchs (n 59) 3.

[99] Moloney (n 6) 1357.

[100] As Molony discusses, 'In four high-profile cases, relating to the bankers' bonus rules, the proposed financial transaction tax, the powers of the new European Securities and Markets Authority (ESMA), and the "location policy" adopted by the ECB in relation to central clearing counterparties (CCPs),

measures that have pushed at the boundaries of what has traditionally been characterized as a "harmonizing" measure for the support of the single market'.[101] Hence, EU regulators, albeit that they are more empowered in the post-crisis context, are nonetheless treading a careful line when developing rules, and are thus incentivised to adopt detailed regulatory standards that conform to industry expectations about the needs of specific financial markets in order to avoid lawsuits. What is more, albeit that the EU is now perceived to be taking on a much more active role in trying to govern the 'unruly' financial markets that operated prior to the crash in 2008, as a consequence of its long-standing agenda for liberalising finance and removing barriers to cross-border activity, the financial markets and activities that the EU now seeks to regulate are so complex and so deeply enmeshed with the global economy that the EU is structurally dependent upon transnational private associations that act on behalf of market actors to understand the impacts of its more coercive regulatory interventions. The result is that the EU often lifts a preconstituted understanding of how the market works into its regulatory structures, and, owing to concerns about its democratic deficit and its lopsided evolution as a regulatory state, it has further institutionalised an engagement with private actors in order to legitimate the adoption of increased powers by centralised ESAs. While a broad array of stakeholders is invited to consult with ESAs in the development of new regulatory rules, powerful transnational private associations have a significant advantage in terms of both expertise and resources over other constituencies, such as non-governmental organisations (NGOs), in trying to push their preferences on how the rules should be interpreted.

This is part of the explanation for the EU's symbiotic relationship with transnational private lawmaking for global finance. However, while a lot of the literature surveyed on the role of the EU in the development of transnational private law focuses on the post-crisis context, in which the power of transnational actors is established, the EU can also be seen to have constituted that power owing to its *sui generis* attempts to create a single market for financial services. The EU has progressed through multiple phases of engagement with financial markets based on its underlying commitment to enhancing economic integration. The first agenda was the EU's 'market making' liberalisation phase that was iterated initially through attempts in the 1960s through to the 1980s to achieve 'extensive harmonisation', and, when this did not result in integrated financial markets, by an accelerating move that involved changes to institutional voting procedures[102] and the shift to the use of minimal harmonisation and mutual recognition[103] in the 1980s following the jurisprudence of the European Court

it challenged the competence of the European Union to act … While it was unsuccessful in all apart from the ECB case, the actions underline the UK's monitoring role in relation to EU competence and the risk of over-reach.' ibid 1357.

[101] ibid 1357.

[102] The 1986 Single European Act changed the decision-making process (from unanimity to qualified majority) in European institutions (31 December 1992).

[103] The principle of mutual recognition enabled products or services that had been lawfully produced and marketed in one Member State to be granted free access throughout the internal market, without the imposition of further conditions by the regulatory authorities of other members.

of Justice (ECJ) in the *Cassis de Dijon* (1979) case.[104] Here, then, EU institutions started pioneering mechanisms that enabled a trade in financial products without any investigation or consideration of the wider purposes and effects of these financial 'services' by national governments or regulatory agencies.

The drive to create an integrated single financial market in the EU was then advanced significantly through the Financial Services Action Plan (FSAP) in 2005,[105] which entailed a comprehensive upgrading programme of 43 Directives and Regulations, mainly on wholesale markets. This regulatory push resulted in the creation of a market for financial services that enabled providers of banking, insurance and investment services to offer their services throughout all of the EU under a single licence. Again, with the purpose of integrating markets and overcoming regulatory barriers, the EU developed innovative strategies to facilitate market access during this period. Two such legal innovations are particularly worthy of note: the passporting system; and the Lamfalussy process. The EU system of regulatory passports allows regulated financial actors to operate cross-border on the basis of authorisation and supervision in their 'home' Member States.[106] Nine different regulatory passports developed through a series of EU Directives in the 1990s – late 2000s allow institutions operating within the EU to provide different kinds of financial services within the EU market on the same terms as financial institutions originating in a particular Member State.[107] At the legislative level, since 2001, the macro design of EU financial regulation follows the 'Lamfalussy model', which segments financial regulation into a hierarchy of different norms and institutional levels.[108] The Lamfalussy approach was adopted by the EU in 2001 'as a means for expediting the law-making process in the financial regulation area (which was then receiving serious policy and political attention for the first time)'.[109] As Moloney underlines, the Lamfalussy process means that one of the major channels for influence over EU lawmaking for finance is 'technocratic rather than overtly political and relates to the massive and fast-growing corpus of level 2 administrative law'.[110] While expert-dominated groups do not have the power to adopt level 2 administrative rules, as this power rests with the Commission, 'they propose administrative rules to the Commission (based on mandates contained in legislation) and advise the Commission on their content'.[111] The result of these activities by the EU was the creation of a financial market that was sufficiently 'deep and liquid' so as to

[104] Case 120/78 *Rewe-Zentral AG v Bundesmonopolverwaltung für Branntwein* ('Cassis de Dijon') EU:C:1979:42, [1979] ECR 649.

[105] Commission Communication of 11 May 1999 entitled 'Implementing the framework for financial markets: action plan' COM(1999) 232.

[106] Moloney (n 6) 1335.

[107] 'What is Passporting and Why does it Matter?' (*UK Finance*), available at www.ukfinance.org.uk/sites/default/files/uploads/pdf/BQB3-What-is-passporting-and-why-does-it-matter-UKF.pdf.

[108] The different levels are as follows: Level 1 are legislative rules; Level 2 administrative rules; Level 3 soft law and supervisory convergence measures; and Level 4 enforcement of Member State compliance by the Commission.

[109] Moloney (n 6) 1341.

[110] ibid.

[111] ibid.

justify further liberalization and financial deregulation in the years leading up to the financial crisis.[112]

Following the events of the financial crisis and European sovereign debt crisis, it was recognised that the permissive approach to the integration of financial services that had been pushed through by means of regulatory strategies and innovative legal techniques stemming from the EU's original competences has produced a situation in which 'regulatory liberalization is not matched by supervisory co-ordination'.[113] This resulted in the deregulatory model being superseded by a catalogue of new regulatory schemes to harmonise financial supervision and to further empower European regulatory agencies: the ESA system. However, while it is undoubtedly the case that EU financial regulation has become significantly more granular and administrative in nature due to these reforms, owing to the former approach of the EU that categorises the activities of financial institutions in terms of product development and the provision of services, when EU regulatory agencies were established and tasked with exercising more enhanced supervisory powers to govern the integrated financial market, the characteristics of those markets – interdependency, high levels of product complexity, grounded in financial collateral, predicated on widespread securitisation, and connected via futures and derivatives contracts to a wide array of 'systemically significant prices' – had already been established by the financial institutions empowered by previous iterations of the EU's rules. Hence, taking a longer view, it becomes clear that the terrain in which transnational private actors have been developing practices on the use of financial collateral, the trading of derivatives and other financial products have been facilitated by an EU agenda intent on integrating financial markets in spite of political differences on the kind of capitalism that the EU should incentivise – a terrain in which a politically contentious economic model is described in neutral terms of delivering financial 'products' and 'services'.

I will now conclude the chapter by offering some final reflections on a striking possibility that emerges when the relationship between the EU, transnational private lawmaking, and global finance is studied in tandem with the literature on financialisation. I would like to suggest that if the question becomes not what is the impact of EU law on rulemaking, on or within other legal regimes (supranational governance fora, regimes of mutual recognition, or by co-regulating markets with private financial actors), but what are the effects of EU rulemaking on global financial markets, or on the political economy of finance, a strikingly different picture to the portrait of an increasingly influential EU taking a lead in the development of sustainable finance emerges: EU law is not only governing financial markets; EU law (and policy) is also *on the market*. Through the creation of a single currency, the permissive, compartmentalised, and specialised approach that the EU has taken to the development and trading of wholesale financial services (investment; securities; derivatives; private pensions), and the legitimacy that the EU confers on what is a deeply contentious

[112] Moloney (n 10) 1324–25.
[113] ibid.

model for pursuing economic growth, the EU (its policies, and its regulatory choices) has become a node in a global network of free moving capital. An under-explored external effect of EU law in the context of global finance is to turn the EU into a brand: a label that will attract some investors and deter others, depending on how the EU performs politically and economically with respect to the overriding objective of delivering on financial yield.

IV. CONCLUDING REFLECTIONS: THE EU ON THE FINANCIAL MARKET?

The impression garnered from policy statements and academic literature on the EU's role in governing finance is that the EU is an increasingly influential political actor that is introducing large scale policy initiatives, such as the ECMU and the Sustainable Finance Directive,[114] to steer the operations of its internal financial markets and exert greater influence in the field of global financial regulation. Yet, as discussed earlier in the chapter, the operations of diverse-but-integrated EU and global financial markets for instruments such as government bonds, currencies, commodity derivatives, energy contracts, and interest rate swaps have largely been elaborated at the initiative of transnational private actors enabled by permissive legal regimes, and their character has been assumed in, and further legitimised by, EU regulations that now seek to supervise certain aspects of their operations. When further consideration is given to the question of what is being traded in these markets, and when their operations are taken together with the creation of a single currency – described by analysts at the New Bureau for Economic Research as 'the single most important event for *international financial markets* since the collapse of the Bretton-Woods system of fixed exchange rates' (emphasis added)[115] – the impression that the primary effect of EU lawmaking in this area is to build greater capacity to regulate and supervise and interconnected financial markets become open to challenge.

So what *are* financial actors doing when they are providing financial services and trading in wholesale financial markets? Economic literatures tend to focus on how financial activity 'mitigates risks' and 'frees up liquidity' and, owing to the ability of dispersed communities of investors to uncover information about 'fundamentals' in underlying economy, leads to 'price discovery' for underlying assets. As referenced above, sociologists who have studied finance contest the presentation of the activity of financial market actors as being about discovering prices based on information about 'fundamentals'. Rather, according to the Social Studies of Finance (SSF) literature, geographically dispersed but legally and electronically networked financial actors interact as interpretative communities who, though wider process of enculturation into specific (and contestable) ways of understanding value – such as through training and use of particular formulae for pricing – produce and

[114] Sustainable Finance Directive (n 16).

[115] JP Danthine et al, 'Capital Markets after the EMU: A First Assessment' (National Bureau of Economic Research Working Paper 8044, 2000) 3.

disseminate information about the assets whose value they presume to 'measure', intervening and thereby creating price 'signals' that feed into the development of technologies that further justify their assumptions, and that create feedback loops and patterns for particular assets – technologies which are nonetheless influenced by location-specific trading cultures and are embedded in financial institutions that have their own *sui generis* cultures.[116] It is also important to stress that different kinds of traders approach this work differently: fundamentals traders purport to be processing and aggregating information about intrinsic value; momentum traders consciously look for patterns based on historical time series data of market performance; and arbitrage traders 'test ideas about the correspondence between two securities (or bonds or indexes or derivatives)',[117] and can help to bring about new correlations between previously uncorrelated prices in the underlying economy.[118] In order to do this, the traders engaged in fundamentals and arbitrage trading seek out information about changes in policy and economic environments that can influence the relative value of different assets. They use a variety of sources in this effort, as websites advising trading novices relate: statements from central banks on interest rates and directions in monetary policy; announcements from governments regarding policy changes relating to tax or to labour markets; commodity and currency prices; predictions from other financial traders, and more besides.[119] As Riles summarises, SSF scholars have shown that the result of these practices is that 'market truths or givens – from the rationality of economic actors to public trust in national currencies – are performatively produced through particular institutional arrangements, through the widespread usage of certain economic theories, and through carefully crafted public statements of government officials'.[120]

What, then, might be the effect of the EU bringing together the multiple different economic and monetary profiles of EU Member States through the creation of a single currency that is now also traded as a financial asset on global forex markets? Relatedly, what is the effect of then expanding the capacities of financial markets to evaluate and trade a wide range of other assets based on different indicators of aspects of EU economic performance – stocks, food commodity prices, energy prices – by smoothing away regulatory barriers for the efficient trade in financial products and services? It is only possible to gesture to these other consequences of EU lawmaking in the field of financial markets in this chapter; more research will be needed, nevertheless, a number of key dynamics are in evidence.

First, even in the years of preparation for the EMU, liberalised financial markets have played a role in helping to police Member States in line with the requirements

[116] M Callon (ed), *The Laws of the Markets* (John Wiley & Sons, 1998); D MacKenzie, *An Engine, Not a Camera: How Financial Models Shape Markets* (MIT Press, 2006); K Knorr-Cetina and A Preda, *The Sociology of Financial Markets* (Oxford, Oxford University Press, 2005).

[117] D Beunza, and D Stark. 'Tools of the Trade: The Socio-Technology of Arbitrage in a Wall Street Trading Room' (2004) 13 *Industrial and Corporate Change* 2, 375.

[118] ibid 372.

[119] For a list of indicators that effect the euro, see J Nguyen et al, '5 Economic Reports that affect the Euro' (*Investopedia*, 31 January 2022), available at www.investopedia.com/articles/fx/11/5-reports-fx-traders-use.asp.

[120] Riles (n 68) 34.

for fiscal rectitude set out as conditions for membership, notably adopting the Maastricht guidelines on government deficits '(not to exceed 3% of GDP)' as a 'common language' for making decisions as to where to invest.[121] In early 1997, for instance, investors analysed Italy's fiscal actions very closely, asking 'will this get them below 3% or not?'[122] In some ways, this is an example of the EU using financial markets to enact its policies, nevertheless, it is also a powerful example of how by making it easier to move capital into and out of different EU economies, and by removing barriers and making regulations more transparent, the EU's action have resulted in the policies of EU Member States – and the EU itself – becoming variables that inform financial trading strategies. Second, nations with greater levels of resident investment are typically more insulated from financial market pressures,[123] thus, a well-noted effect of integrating EU financial markets and empowering financial actors to trade in diverse markets using a single currency is that some governments lost part of their 'captive audience' in this transition, as institutional investors rebalanced portfolios away from domestic assets.[124] As a result, it was anticipated that governments would have to 'make greater efforts to make their bonds attractive to European investors'.[125] Yet financial markets did not only start a process of more intensively appraising the policy positions and economic environments of different Member State governments as a result of this shift: they also took into consideration the wider economic and monetary governance frameworks of the EU and started pricing assets based on this new information. The result was that in spite of the enduring differences across EU governments in their fiscal policy positions, 'borrowing costs converged dramatically because market participants assumed that the single currency's survival rendered sovereign risk somewhat irrelevant', and traders began to price Greek and Italian debt similarly to Dutch and German debt.[126] As opposed to financial markets enforcing discipline against fiscally irresponsible governments, as had been anticipated, it was more advantageous, at least at this time, for these interpretative communities to fuel a debt-based economic model by masking national differences and by enabling higher levels of sovereign borrowing.

In addition to elected governments needing to be mindful as to how financial markets will 'vote' on their policies and EU legislation becoming a variable that is priced into financial assets, it is also evident that investors watch EU policymakers for announcements and act to induce changes in the relative values of different stocks of EU companies. The greater convergence and harmonisation of action by the EU makes the task of traders easier, as pricing stocks based on reports issued by centralised economic and financial agencies, as opposed to reports issued in multiple

[121] L Mosley, 'Government Financial Market Relations After EMU: New Currency, New Constraints? (2004) 5 *European Union Politics* 181–209, 185.
[122] ibid.
[123] Mosley (n 121) 188.
[124] ibid 188–89.
[125] ibid 189.
[126] L Mosley, 'Still Afraid of Footloose Finance? Exit and Voice in Contemporary Globalization (2017) 8, available at https://ssrn.com/abstract=3058317.

different formats by policy actors working in a multitude of different languages, is less burdensome. A study by Bechtel and Schneider on the relationship between EU policy statements and asset pricing in the defence sector lends empirical support to the view that

> financial markets indeed evaluate the substance of Euro- pean Council meetings and react to those summit decisions that consolidate EU military capabilities and the ESDP (European Security and Defense Policy) when they update their beliefs about the expected profitability of an asset.[127]

In their view, this process can help to uncover the economic effects – 'that is, the economic winners and losers of political decisions'.[128] However, the SSF literature would suggest that financial market actors interpret these developments in line with their own interests, meaning that markets *produce* particular economic effects in response to these announcements and *create* winners and losers based on their own interpretative frameworks, which, as just demonstrated in the case of sovereign debt, do not always amount to an accurate pricing of some objective measure of 'risk', but result in calculated decision informed by their own assumptions, ideological frameworks, and prerogatives.[129]

If traders buy and sell assets and enter into new markets based on the issuance of statements from the ECB or the European Commission, or in response to regulations developed by ESMA, and if their activities in turn shape and influence EU decision-making, and translate the effects of EU decision-making in the wider economy through the interpretive communities of investors, does this not suggest that EU law and policy is up for sale on global financial markets? Does it not mean that, in addition to being the source of rulemaking, the EU also the object of dense networks of trillions of financial contracts – a variable to be taken into account in the drafting of the contracts that its regimes operationalise, legitimate, and enable? The effects may be variegated, and it is clear that this dynamic is not unique to the EU, but, as this chapter has demonstrated, the EU is pushing to harmonise regulations, to develop its capital markets, and to pursue financial and monetary integration in spite of its constitutional constraints. The EU is compensating for its reputation as an overly technocratic body by enrolling private actors into the development of its new regulatory technical standards. Yet the political economies for which the EU is developing harmonised financial regulations remain diverse, and their legal systems, tax systems, and exposure to imports and exports and commodity price movements are distinct. Traders and banks in the EU and beyond now increasingly price financial assets in a single currency that has been shown to have particular distributive impacts on the diverse Member States. In its early years, the euro's role on foreign exchange markets closely resembled that of the German deutschemark in terms of its share in global foreign exchange trading, the tightness of spreads, its volatility vis-a` -vis the dollar and the yen, and its role

[127] M Bechtel and G Schneider, 'Eliciting Substance from "Hot Air": Financial Market Responses to EU Summit Decisions on European Defense' (2010) 64 *International Organization* 199–223, 199.
[128] ibid 207.
[129] ibid 217.

as an anchoring currency.[130] This was the desired trajectory for the euro, as the EU wanted to create a strong and stable currency like the mark, but as de Grauwe and Streeck both argue, the loss of control over monetary policy on the part of Member States, and the unified (and high) interest and exchange rates of the new currency, had very different impacts on countries in Southern Europe as contrasted with those in Northern Europe.[131] The fact that the fortunes of many diverse constituencies and Members States within the EU are now bound together not only through a single currency, but through a currency that is being priced on financial markets, suggests that developments in the EU relating to legislation and policy reform will be translated by particular interpretative communities into price signals that have far reaching and complex effects on diverse Member States.

The mission of the EU is to smooth out regulatory frictions and to improve the capacities of financial market actors to allocate capital and to price risk, but financial markets, exemplified by the role of arbitrage traders, thrive on *exploiting differences*. As the SSF literature has shown, if all of these actors are using the same formulae to price risk, how can a profit be made? 'The more the formulae diffuse to perform the market', Beunza and Stark conclude, 'the more one's profits depend on an original performance. That is, the premium shifts to innovation'.[132] The financial contracts through which these innovations are created are not grounded in a pan-EU private law; they are elaborated based on modules of property law, contract law, collateral law, and bankruptcy law that have been moulded out of the laws of specific states – sovereigns which area outside of the EU (the UK and the US), or Member States whose private laws have accommodated industry preferences for these standard form contracts[133] – by the lawyers who 'paper the trades' and produce the necessary legal infrastructure to create financial assets and operationalise distinct financial markets.[134] In making intra-EU financial investment and capital mobility easier, the interaction between EU financial regulation and transnational private law creates the perfect legal terrain for finance to 'penetrate and suck value from every sector',[135] as suggested by Fraser, and to continue to make a profit out of exploiting the remaining legal, economic, and financial differences of distinct EU Member States. When dynamics of financialisation in the global political economy

[130] G Galati and K Tsatsaronis. 'The Impact of the Euro on Europe's Financial Markets' (2003) 12 *Financial Markets, Institutions & Instruments* 165–222, 167.

[131] As De Grauwe emphasises in his discussion of the design flaws of the euro, the employment of a common nominal interest rate was too high for countries experiencing inflows of capital: 'the booming Southern European countries (including Ireland) experienced systematically higher inflation rates and increases in unit labour costs than in the rest of the Eurozone. These booms led to large current account deficits in the South and surpluses in the North. It is important to stress here that the booms in the South allowed the Northern European countries to accumulate large current account surpluses. These were financed by credit that the Northern European countries granted to the South'. P De Grauwe, 'Design Failures in the Eurozone: Can they be Fixed?' (20133) EQS Paper No. 57, available at http://eprints.lse.ac.uk/53191/1/LEQSPaper57.pdf. See also W Streeck, *How Will Capitalism End? Essays on a Failing System* (Verso, 2016) chapter 7.

[132] Beunza and Stark (n 117) 372.

[133] As discussed earlier, in the aftermath of Brexit, new ISDA Master Agreements are being fashioned out of the laws of France and Ireland (n 24).

[134] See Pistor (n 18).

[135] Fraser (n 69).

are confronted, it becomes clear that, by pursuing an agenda of liberalising and deepening its financial markets, stabilising them and making them more transparent and governable through financial regulation, the EU is also sending signals to global financial market actors who evaluate the performance of the EU brand and assess implications for their portfolios according to their own sector-specific rationality. In addition to transnational private actors needing to re-order themselves in response to the EU's lawmaking, this would imply that the EU is also empowering transnational private actors to produce economic data and variables that will then force forms of reordering onto the EU as it responds to changes in its economic environment.

10

The Growing Influence of the EU on Global Securities Regulation and Foreign Private Relations

ANTONIO MARCACCI*

I. SETTING THE SCENE: THE INVISIBLE LINK BETWEEN GLOBAL STANDARDS AND PRIVATE LAW

THIS CHAPTER ANALYSES the growing influence of the law of the European Union (EU) on the production of global rules and its indirect consequences into private law, taking global securities regulation as the field of study. By 'transnational securities regulation' this chapter means the standards covering transnational, cross-border securities markets,[1] including derivatives.[2] These standards

*Senior Compliance Expert at an EU Global Systemically Important Bank and Lecturer (*Lehrbeauftragter*) at Leipzig University and at Passau University, Germany. Dr Marcacci holds a PhD in Laws from the European University Institute, Florence, and is currently based in Munich, Germany. The views expressed in the chapter are those of the author and do not necessarily represent the views of his current and/or past employers. The chapter has greatly benefited from the interview held in 2021 with Dr Carlo Comporti, CONSOB Commissioner, to whom the author's heartfelt thanks go. Importantly, no opinion or idea expressed in the chapter can be linked to Dr Comporti, to whom only that information as explicitly mentioned in specific footnotes can be attributed. This chapter builds on and revises research previously published in: A Marcacci, *Transnational Securities Regulation – How it Works, Who Shapes it* (Springer, 2023), the editor(s) (if applicable) and the author(s) 2022, reproduced with permission of the licensor (Springer).

[1] 'International securities market standards are created to establish co-operative agreements with regulators from foreign jurisdictions, to export national regulatory frameworks to under-regulated or ineffective regulated foreign financial centers, or to promote common regulatory frameworks between national jurisdictions.': D Kempthorne, *Governing International Securities Markets: IOSCO and the Politics of International Securities Market Standards* (University of Waterloo, 2013) 16.

[2] On the scope of securities regulation as delimited by the International Organization of Securities Commissions (IOSCO), 1996 Reform of By-Laws – Explanatory Memorandum (1996). Also 'The words "securities markets" are used in the Methodology, as the context permits, to refer compendiously to the various market sectors, including markets for derivatives that are securities. The same interpretative convention applies to the use of the words "securities regulation"': IOSCO, IOSCO Online Self-Assessment Questionnaire (2021), available at www.iosco.org/online-methodology-2017/.

have a hybrid nature: they are substantially public but formally private.[3] This hybrid nature reflects that of the only global standard-setter producing this kind of transnational rules, the International Organization of Securities Commissions, IOSCO.

IOSCO can be defined as a flexible *transnational* – given its global, cross-border and multilateral membership – and *transgovernmental* – since its full members are public regulatory agencies[4] – club[5] or network.[6] Flexibility mainly stems from IOSCO's lack of binding regulatory powers, its consensus-based, standard-making procedures, and its ability to co-operate with other institutions. But flexibility also stems from IOSCO's particularly unorthodox legal nature. This emerges through the combination of an autonomous general secretariat established without an international treaty but governed by internal by-laws;[7] an incorporation statute of the host jurisdiction that defines IOSCO as a private-law, non-profit association; and derived standards that, despite being non-binding and of a private-law nature, have a substantial public-law effect, being addressed to public regulatory authorities. Puzzlingly enough, such standards with a substantial public-law effect may affect traditional private law, as indeed this chapter shows.

The key issues that this chapter investigates indeed concern the growing influence of EU law on production of global securities standards and its indirect impact on private law. The chapter examines three case studies: investor protection, credit rating agencies (CRA), and financial benchmarks (FBMs).

[3] It is worth noting that a different perspective exists, purely grounded in private law and focusing on holding securities via intermediaries and the affected holders' rights. That perspective falls outside the scope of this chapter. Comprehensive analyses of intermediated securities are offered in P-H Conac et al, *Intermediated Securities. The Impact of the Geneva Securities Convention and the Future European Legislation* (Cambridge, Cambridge University Press, 2013); T Keijser, *Transnational Securities Law* (Oxford, Oxford University Press, 2014). For German readers, see also U Bertschinger, 'The Hague Convention on the Law Applicable to Certain Rights in Respect of Securities Held with an Intermediary – ein Schritt zur Vereinheitlichung des Rechts der Wertschriftenmärkte' in *Privatrecht und Methode : Festschrift für Ernst A Kramer* (Heinrich Honsell, et al eds, 2004).

[4] IOSCO's full members 'are the national securities commissions or similar governmental bodies with significant authority over securities or derivatives markets in their respective jurisdictions'. IOSCO, 'About IOSCO' (2021), available at www.iosco.org/about/?subsection=about_iosco.

[5] Zaring already defined IOSCO as a club in 2005: D Zaring, 'Informal Procedure, Hard and Soft, in International Administration' (2005) 5 *Chicago Journal of International Law* 562, with further references in fn 64. Also: GRD Underhill, 'Keeping Governments Out of Politics: Transnational Securities Markets, Regulatory Cooperation, and Political Legitimacy' (1995) 21 *Review of International Studies*; RS Karmel and C Kelly, 'The Hardening of Soft Law in Securities Regulation' (2009) 34 *Brooklyn Journal of International Law* 883, 1–71, esp 944; and C Brummer, 'Post-American Securities Regulation' (2010) 98 *California Law Review*.

[6] On transnationalism and transgovernmentalism, and networks: RO Keohane and JS Nye, 'Transgovernmental Relations and International Organizations' (1974) 27 *World Politics* 39; A-M Slaughter, 'The Real New World Order' (1997) 76 *Foreign Affairs* 183; A-M Slaughter, 'Government Networks: The Heart of the Liberal Democratic Order' in GH Fox and BR Roth (eds), *Democratic Governance and International Law* (Cambridge, Cambridge University Press, 2000); A-M Slaughter, *A New World Order* (Princeton, Princeton University Press, 2009); K Raustiala, 'The Architecture of International Cooperation: Transgovernmental Networks and the Future of International Law' (2002) 43 *Virginia Journal of International Law*; B Kingsbury et al, 'The Emergence of Global Administrative Law' (2005) 68 *Law and Contemporary Problems* 15; P Craig, *UK, EU and Global Administrative Law: Foundations and Challenges* (Cambridge, Cambridge University Press, 2015).

[7] IOSCO, 'By-Laws of IOSCO' (2011), available at www.iosco.org/about/?subsection=by-laws.

The methodological perspective underpinning the choice of the three case studies is the indirect connection between global standards and private law / private parties. Each case study shows a private-law nature although being subject to global standards with a substantial public-law effect. The more traditional private-law topic of investor protection, which shapes relations between service providers and consumers/investors, is accompanied by standards covering provision of information services on the part of market players, CRAs, and FBMs. These standards even acquire a transnational 'supervisory spirit', thus merging public and private, local and transnational. For each case, the chapter highlights the increasing influence of the EU on IOSCO normative production, with particular regard to the (partially waning) influence of the United States of America (USA). The chapter closes by raising an intriguing question worth further investigation in the near future: is EU law able somehow to penetrate third-country private law regimes by influencing IOSCO normative production?

II. THE INTERNATIONAL ORGANIZATION OF SECURITIES COMMISSION – IOSCO

As mentioned above, IOSCO is the only[8] global organisation in the world that gathers public securities regulators and is officially committed to setting securities standards for global securities markets, infrastructures, investors, and intermediaries.[9] Alongside standard-setting, IOSCO co-ordinates its members' efforts in cross-border enforcement through a sophisticated mechanism of co-operation and information-sharing. Importantly, IOSCO is not established through a traditional international treaty but, instead, is incorporated in Spain as a private-law, non-profit association, and is governed by internal by-laws.[10] Despite this, IOSCO has an autonomous general secretariat headquartered in Madrid.

The organisation's key members are public regulatory authorities tasked with securities regulation and supervision, and come from almost all jurisdictions around the world – it currently covers 95 per cent of financial markets.[11] For this reason, it

[8] Other organisations set standards for stock markets and exchanges. A leading example of these is the World Federation of Exchanges (WFE) [on the WFE, see M Blair et al, *Financial Markets and Exchanges Law*, 3rd edn (Oxford, Oxford University Press, 2021)].

[9] The transnational financial area is split along the traditional lines of securities, banking, and insurance sectors, with the Basel Committee on Banking Supervision covering the banking sector and the International Association of Insurance Supervisors covering the insurance sector. This structure reflects the domestic separation of oversight responsibilities in many jurisdictions, as Newman and Posner point out: 'the legacies of domestic regulatory institutions created pressures that worked against centralization in international regulation': A Newman and E Posner, *Voluntary Disruptions: International Soft Law, Finance, and Power* (Oxford, Oxford University Press, 2018) 47. In 2012, Mc Lucas defined IOSCO as 'basically a forum for the establishment of a framework for the globalization of markets': J Stocker, Interview with William McLucas – Securities and Exchange Commission Historical Society – Oral History Project (2012) 18, available at http://3197d6d14b5f19f2f440-5e13d29c4c016cf96cbbfd197c579b45.r81.cf1.rackcdn.com/collection/oral-histories/20120305_McLucas_William_T.pdf.

[10] IOSCO, 'By-Laws of IOSCO' (n 7).

[11] IOSCO, 'About IOSCO' (n 4).

has also been defined as an 'umbrella organization',[12] where the authorities joined in the organisation meet to discuss and co-operate on common issues, up to the point that 'communication and cooperation may lead to convergence in approaches'.[13] Due to its discussion-driven structure, Dalhuisen highlights that IOSCO is 'also a think-tank […] for securities regulation'.[14]

Public regulatory agencies are key members of IOSCO. They collectively agree on IOSCO standards through consensus. While IOSCO works for global regulatory convergence, it does not have the power to adopt prescriptive instruments and adopts its standards through a consensus-based approach. Following the 2021 Organisation for Economic Co-operation and Development (OECD) classification,[15] IOSCO adopts policy instruments (such as statements, declarations, and communiqués); incentive instruments (such as best practices, guidelines, and codes of practice); technical standards, which '[d]raw upon specialised knowledge',[16] and supporting instruments, which '[b]ridge policy instruments with modes of practical implementation'[17] and are meant to help members in their implementation efforts. As a result, in terms of substance IOSCO's standards have a public-law nature and are 'deliberately broad'.[18] They represent a clear example of soft law,[19] in that they are 'are not binding and do not give rise to any legal rights or obligations',[20] are not directly enforceable as such,[21] and compliance with them is formally voluntary.[22]

[12] LS Terry, 'Preserving the Rule of Law in the 21st Century: The Importance of Infrastructure and the Need to Create Global Lawyer Regulatory Umbrella Organization' (2012) *Michigan State Law Review* 35–68, esp 741. In a 2012 interview for the Securities and Exchange Commission Historical Society, William McLucas, former Director of Enforcement for the Securities and Exchange Commission, defined IOSCO as 'basically a forum for the establishment of a framework for the globalization of markets', McLucas/Stocker Interview (n 9).

[13] Terry (n 12) 744.

[14] JH Dalhuisen, *Dalhuisen on Transnational Comparative, Commercial, Financial and Trade Law Volume 3: Financial Products, Financial Services and Financial Regulation* (Oxford, Hart Publishing. 2019) 593.

[15] OECD, *Compendium of International Organisations' Practices: Working Towards More Effective International Instruments* (OECD Publishing, 2021).

[16] ibid 24.

[17] ibid.

[18] 'The organization explicitly acknowledges that there is no single prescription or roadmap to good regulation in the field of securities. […] Instead, these principles articulate an aspirational statement of the core elements of an essential securities regulatory framework', Brummer (n 5) 340.

[19] For soft-law definition, see C Chinkin, 'Normative Development in the International Legal System' in D Shelton (ed), *Commitment and Compliance: The Role of Non-Binding Norms in the International Legal System* (Oxford, Oxford University Press, 2000). 31. On soft law and international financial law: C Brummer, 'How International Financial Law Works (And How It Doesn't)' (2011) 99 *Georgetown Law Journal*; Karmel and Kelly (n 5).

[20] IOSCO, 'By-Laws of IOSCO' (n 7).

[21] On non-enforceability of soft law: F Dialti, 'Main Differences and Similarities Between Standards and Legal Rules in the Area of Financial Regulation' (2005) 4 *Euredia : revue européenne de droit bancaire et financier* 357.

[22] Generally, on voluntary compliance with standards, Padoa-Schioppa rightly summarised that: 'Standards constitute an informal mode of governance; they are formulated under a consensus principle by those to whom they are addressed; and compliance with them is voluntary': T Padoa-Schioppa, 'Self vs. public discipline in the financial field' (*European Central Bank*, 2002), available at www.ecb.europa.eu/press/key/date/2002/html/sp020520.en.html.

As a result of the characteristics outlined above, IOSCO can be labelled a flexible *transnational* and *transgovernmental* club[23] or network.[24] The former feature is due to the organisation's global, cross-border, and multilateral membership. The latter is linked to the fact that IOSCO's full members are public regulatory agencies.[25] Even more importantly, IOSCO has a particularly unorthodox legal nature. Although the incorporation statute of the host jurisdiction – Spain – defines IOSCO as a private-law, non-profit association; the organisation's non-binding standards (of a private-law nature) have a substantial public law effect due to the fact that they are addressed to public authorities.

Historically speaking, IOSCO is of American origin. With the US Securities and Exchange Commission (SEC) 'believ[ing that] transgovernmental cooperation serves important US interests',[26] IOSCO's origins are rooted in the pan American forum called the Inter-American Conference of Securities Commissions – IACSC –[27] whose first meeting was held in Caracas[28] in September 1974, and is funded by the International Finance Corporation (IFC).[29] The IACSC became IOSCO in 1983 with regulators from France, Indonesia, South Korea, and the United Kingdom (UK) becoming official members a year later.[30] From an historical point of view, the USA was the driving force behind the establishment of IOSCO[31] and its first regulatory commitments. The following case studies will show that, on the one hand, the EU has been able to emerge as an alternative regulatory power while, on the other hand, the USA still plays an important role, albeit less hegemonic than before.

III. RETAIL INVESTOR PROTECTION

Retail investor protection is one of those fields of securities regulation where private law plays an important role. In the USA, private enforcement procedures and

[23] Zaring (n 5) 562, with further references in fn 64. Also: Underhill (n 5); Karmel and Kelly (n 5) 944; Brummer (n 5).

[24] On transnationalism, transgovernmentalism, and networks: Keohane and Nye (n 6); Slaughter, 'The Real New World Order' (n 6); Slaughter, *Government Networks* (n 6) ; Slaughter, *A New World Order* (n 6; Raustiala (n 6) ; Kingsbury et al (n 6); Craig (n 6).

[25] IOSCO's full members (n 4).

[26] Raustiala (n 6) 2–51, esp 34.

[27] Also called the Inter-American Association of Securities Commissions in: AA Jr Sommer, 'IOSCO: Its Mission and Achievement Symposium: Internationalization of Securities' (1996) 17 *Northwestern Journal of International Law & Business*.

[28] IOSCO Annual Report (2010).

[29] This information was reported by Mr IM Pollack, SEC Commissioner from 1974 to 1980, to R Bismuth: R Bismuth, *La coopération internationale des autorités de régulation du secteur financier et le droit international public* (Bruylant. 2011) 293.

[30] IOSCO, 'About IOSCO' (n 4).

[31] In this sense, also Jordan: 'The initial phase of IOSCO's standard-setting activities was a time of US hegemony in capital markets regulation; for one thing, few jurisdictions had a dedicated regulatory framework for the operation of domestic capital markets. […] At the time, the US regulatory framework represented the gold standard, a notion that US regulators (and some financial economists) were happy to promote. International standards subsuming US regulation would represent best practice and could

remedies – above all securities class actions[32] – are complementary to the public enforcement tools handled by the SEC.[33] On the other side of the Atlantic, EU law has been producing an increasing volume of public law rules that have been influencing and penetrating domestic private law regimes.[34] Given the soft and public-law nature of its standards, IOSCO has been relatively cautious when producing rules on the matter. On the one hand, it has adopted several sets of standards with a growing level of detail since the early 1990s. On the other hand, the organisation has always recognised the crucial importance of domestic solutions tailored to the specific characteristics of home markets.

At least before the 2008 crisis, the US regulatory framework strongly – although not exclusively – relied on a 'philosophy of full disclosure',[35] which embraced the so-called 'rational expectations investor'[36] model. The latter was developed under the influence of the law and economics school[37] and views investors as behaving 'like members of the species homo economicus: they are cool, calculating, and purely self-interested actors'.[38] Importantly, the US system of retail investor protection is basically a 'bifurcated regulatory regime'[39] and this is to a certain extent reflected in early IOSCO standards. This comprises, on the one hand, broker-dealers that have not been generally subject to a private-law fiduciary duty towards their customers but, instead, to an obligation of fair dealing[40] developed by self-regulatory organisations – the suitability rule – where service providers are required to know whether

be emulated in emerging and other economies around the world, producing convergence to the ideal' in C Jordan, *The New Internationalism? IOSCO, International Standards and Capital Markets Regulation* (Centre for International Governance Innovation ed, 2018) 13. Also P-H Verdier, 'The Political Economy of International Financial Regulation' (2013) 88 *Indiana Law Journal* 1405–73, esp 1434.

[32] On this topic see the leading analysis by SJ Choi, et al, *The Screening Effect of the Private Securities Litigation Reform Act* (*Law & Economics Working Papers Archive: 2003-2009*. 69. 2007).

[33] Arthur Levitt, a former chair of the SEC, clearly describes the complementary interplay between public and private enforcement mechanisms in the US Securities Regulation regime: '[P]rivate actions also provide a "necessary supplement" to the Commission's own enforcement activities by serving to deter securities law violations. Private actions are crucial to the integrity of our disclosure system because they provide a direct incentive for issuers and other market participants to meet their obligations under the securities laws.' Testimony of Arthur Levitt Concerning Litigation Reform Proposals before Subcommittee on Telecommunications and Finance Committee on Commerce (1995).

[34] DellaNegra provides a leading analysis of this phenomenon: F DellaNegra, *MiFID II and Private Law: Enforcing EU Conduct of Business Rules* (Oxford, Hart Publishing, 2018).

[35] *SEC v Capital Gains Research Bureau*, Supreme Court of the United States (1963).

[36] On the model: LA Stout, 'The Investor Confidence Game' (2002) 68 *Brooklyn Law Review*. On IOSCO and the efficient market hypothesis, also C Jordan, *Transnational Law: Practice Inspiring Theory* (Melbourne, Melbourne Law School, 2011).

[37] Stout explains that the rational expectations investor model is strongly interconnected with the law and economics school: 'legal scholars who specialize in securities regulation have been strongly influenced over the past two decades by the "law and economics" school of analysis. The law and economics school, in turn, relies on a model of investor behavior that I will call the "rational expectations" investor model' Stout (n 36) 6–7.

[38] ibid 7.

[39] A Tuch, 'Conduct of Business Regulation' in N Moloney et al (eds), *The Oxford Handbook of Financial Regulation* (Oxford, Oxford University Press, 2015) 547; also, ML Fein, *Securities Activities of Banks*, 4th edn (Wolters Kluwer, 2011) 5–42, esp 17.

[40] Securities and Exchange Commission – SEC, Study on Investment Advisers and Broker-Dealers (2011) 59.

a recommended security suits their customer's investment profile.[41] On the other hand, investment advisors are instead subject to a common-law fiduciary duty and its traditional private law remedies.[42] This bifurcation has only recently been attenuated with adoption of the SEC Regulation Best Interest.[43]

The European landscape is substantially different. Taking stock of the fact that there is no 'federal' contract law at the European level, Directive (EC) 2004/39 on markets in financial instruments ('MiFID I')[44] introduced public-law disclosure and conduct-of-business duties. Information disclosure follows the US paradigm but, with the enactment of MiFID II,[45] has become extensively detailed due to several hard- and soft-law pieces adopted by the European Commission and the European Securities and Market Authority, ESMA.[46] More importantly, conduct-of-business rules[47] have been conceived as supervisory tools which amount to 'administrative enforcement of private law'[48] or a 'European supervision private law'.[49] Against this backdrop, MIFID II Product Governance took a leap forward with a heteronomous framework that reaches firms' internal processes and arrangements aimed at protecting investors *before* the conclusion of a contract (*ex-ante* product testing) and *during* performance of the contract (ongoing product testing). The objective is to minimise to the greatest possible extent the sale of unfit products to (a predetermined category of) clients.[50] Investment firms must proceduralise into their formal intra-firm practices all PG obligations and track all the way through.

The influence of the US regulatory regime was clear in the first IOSCO standards touching on retail investor protection. The first ever document on the matter was the 1990 International Conduct of Business Principles,[51] which recognised that the source of conduct-of-business rules can be either professional – that is,

[41] Financial Industry Regulatory Authority – FINRA, FINRA Rule 2111 (Suitability) FAQ (2008).

[42] See A Marcacci, *Regulating Investor Protection under EU Law – The Unbridgeable Gaps with the U.S. and the Way Forward* (Palgrave Springer, 2018).

[43] 17 CFR § 240.15l-1 – Regulation Best Interest (2019).

[44] Directive (EC) 2004/39 of the European Parliament and of the Council of 21 April 2004 on markets in financial instruments amending Council Directives 85/611/EEC and 93/6/EEC and Directive 2000/12/EC of the European Parliament and of the Council and repealing Council Directive 93/22/EEC ('MiFID I') [2004] OJ L145/1.

[45] Directive 2014/65/EU of the European Parliament and of the Council of 15 May 2014 on markets in financial instruments and amending Directive 2002/92/EC and Directive 2011/61/EU (recast) ('MiFID II') [2014] OJ L173/349.

[46] For a previous analysis of mine concerning this topic, see Marcacci (n 42).

[47] For a previous analysis of mine concerning this topic, see ibid.

[48] HW Micklitz, 'Administrative Enforcement of European Private Law' in R Brownsword et al (eds), *The Foundations of European Private Law* (Oxford, Hart Publishing 2011).

[49] OO Cherednychenko, 'Public Supervision over Private Relationships: Towards European Supervision Private Law?' (2014) 22 *European Review of Private Law*.

[50] Cherednychenko rightly points out that the EU lawmaker has come to the conclusion that 'intervention through consumer empowerment at the point-of-sale alone is insufficient to stop products which may cause significant detriment to individual consumers and the financial market as a whole from reaching consumers. The idea behind the new product-oriented approach, therefore, is to deter the creation of investment products which are likely to cause such problems through product development oversight': OO Cherednychenko, 'Freedom of Contract in the Post-Crisis Era: Quo Vadis?' (2014) 10 *European Review of Contract Law* 390–421, esp 401.

[51] IOSCO, 'International Conduct of Business Principles' (1990), available at www.iosco.org/library/pubdocs/pdf/IOSCOPD8.pdf.

self-regulation – or governmental, thus raising the US model to an international standard. Tellingly, IOSCO cautiously recognised that domestic transpositions of its principles can take different forms: 'laws; regulations; internal rules within a company or institution; unwritten principles and customs; case law'.[52]

This caution is particularly important because it takes into account the role that domestic private laws play on retail investor protection.

Nevertheless, in the early 2000s, IOSCO began considering new tendencies coming from the EU, later enshrined in MiFID I. In particular, the 2003 Regulatory and Investor Protection Issues Arising from the Participation by Retail Investors in (Funds-of) Hedge Funds[53] Report handled issues deriving from selling complex instruments in retail markets. First, it defined retail investors as a residual category, comprising 'investors other than those normally referred to as "professional", "qualified" or "sophisticated" investors'.[54] Second, it hinted at the option of banning complex instruments for retail investors, an approach that was officialised in the 2004 MiFID I.[55] Another 2003 Report even raised the issue of 'misconduct/mismanagement in the marketing and selling processes by firms'[56] and heralded the EU law approach on mis-selling.

A more robust change in tone took place after the 2008 crisis, when two reports adopted in 2013 substantially modified IOSCO's approach towards retail investor protection. The first report[57] introduced nine principles regarding suitability requirements that IOSCO Members should develop in their home jurisdictions. The entire framework of the report, despite revolving around complex financial products, clearly reflected the general 2004 MiFID approach. The second report, although written for a specific market section, revolves around the need to enhance investor protection all 'along the value chain'[58] of a product, from creation to issuance to distribution to investment, following an approach close to the MiFID II Product Governance. With these two reports, IOSCO shifted from basically focusing on full disclosure and transnational co-operation in *ex-post* public enforcement to including regulatory law duties on intra-firm policies and procedures aimed at protecting investors *before* the point of sale, that is, before a contract is concluded. These intra-firm policies and procedures are domestically supervised by public authorities and designed (but not limited to) *ex-ante* public enforcement, that is, before a provider-customer dispute arises.

As a result, the new approach adopted by IOSCO seems to be influenced by EU law, though without severing ties with the USA. Nevertheless, a sense of unease started

[52] ibid 7.

[53] IOSCO, 'Regulatory and Investor Protection Issues Arising from the Participation by Retail Investors in (Funds-of) Hedge Funds' (2003), available at www.iosco.org/library/pubdocs/pdf/IOSCOPD142.pdf.

[54] IOSCO, 'Investment Management Risk Assessment: Marketing and Selling Practices' (2003) 3, available at https://www.iosco.org/library/pubdocs/pdf/IOSCOPD156.pdf.

[55] MiFID I (n 44).

[56] IOSCO (n 54) 3.

[57] IOSCO, 'Suitability Requirements With Respect to the Distribution of Complex Financial Products' (2013), available at www.iosco.org/library/pubdocs/pdf/IOSCOPD400.pdf.

[58] IOSCO, 'Regulation of Retail Structured Products – Final Report' (2013) 1, available at www.iosco.org/library/pubdocs/pdf/IOSCOPD434.pdf.

brewing in the USA. Two SEC Commissioners took a strong stance against the first report[59] stating that they 'objected to [its] publication [...] and, therefore, that the Final Report was not approved by the Commission'.[60] The Commissioners pointed out that the report did 'not accurately reflect the relevant law in the U.S. Nor should the U.S. regulatory regime conform to the Final Report'.[61] A year later, one of the two Commissioners openly criticised IOSCO (and the Financial Stability Board – FSB):

> These international organizations were born out of legitimate efforts to engage in constructive multilateral dialogues on matters of mutual interest, including financial regulation. However, following the financial crisis, they have taken on a new and more opaque character, and in some cases, they have attempted to arrogate to themselves regulatory powers that properly reside with sovereign governments.[62]

Taking into account the particular interplay between private and public law in the USA and the EU-leaning approach adopted by IOSCO, this reaction does not come as a complete surprise, at least content-wise.

IV. CREDIT RATING AGENCIES

Credit Rating Agencies – CRAs – are private firms that assess the financial soundness of issuers and borrowers, including financial products such as securities and loans. Their ratings are:

> opinion(s) on the creditworthiness of a debt issue or issuer. The rating does not provide guidance on other aspects essential for investment decisions, such as market liquidity or price volatility. As a result, bonds with the same rating may have very different market prices.[63]

Notwithstanding that CRAs have claimed for years that their ratings do not constitute investment recommendations but are, rather, opinions,[64] their impact on financial markets and investors has become progressively clearer[65] to the point that lawmakers and regulators in the USA and the EU eventually stepped in.[66] While some key CRAs run a global business, they are always incorporated in a particular jurisdiction. Against this backdrop, IOSCO adopted transnational standards, even before the USA and the EU had been able to enact their own domestic legislation.

[59] IOSCO (n 57).

[60] Securities and Exchange Commission, 'Statement Concerning Publication by IOSCO on January 21, 2012 of the Final Report on "Suitability Requirements with respect to the Distribution of Complex Financial Products"' (2013), available at www.sec.gov/news/statement/2013-spch012213dmgtaphtm.

[61] ibid.

[62] Securities and Exchange Commission, 'Closing Remarks at the SEC's 24th Annual International Institute for Market Development' (2014), available at www.sec.gov/news/speech/2014-spch041614dmg.

[63] JG Katz et al, *Credit Rating Agencies: No Easy Regulatory Solutions* (World Bank, 2009).

[64] ibid 1.

[65] Also in terms of behavioural science: F Amtenbrink and K Heine, 'Regulating Credit Rating Agencies in the European Union – Lessons from Behavioural Science' (2003) 2 *The Dovenschmidt Quarterly*.

[66] 'Lacking domestic regulatory templates on these activities, neither the US nor the EU were able to upload their domestic rules as international standards': L Quaglia, *The European Union and Global Financial Regulation* (Oxford, Oxford University Press, 2014) 106.

Interestingly, that on CRAs has been the first set of IOSCO standards directly addressed to private parties, thus to a certain extent directly penetrating domestic private law. Vitally, this case study sheds further light on the increasing impact of EU Law on IOSCO's regulatory outcome and, to some extent, on the decreasing influence of the USA.

Although the most important CRAs in the world have traditionally been incorporated in the USA, the US lawmaker was particularly reluctant to adopt a thorough regulatory framework that would grant the SEC far-reaching powers. In 1997, an important proposal for a new regulation was put forth,[67] which would have given the SEC significant powers to determine the status of domestic CRAs. However, this proposal was never adopted and only in 2006 did Congress adopt the Credit Rating Agency Reform Act.[68] The Act had two main points of focus: first, clear procedural steps and requirements to apply for and register as a nation-wide agency; second, a fight against rating abuses via empowering the counterparts of nationwide agencies.[69] In 2009, in the early aftermath of the 2008 crisis, the SEC changed its own rules and required higher standards of disclosure, record-keeping, and reporting, and introduced new restrictions and controls on situations likely to lead to conflicts of interest.[70] Importantly, notwithstanding the slowness of the US lawmaker, the SEC was already in the driving seat of the CRA Task Force (CRA TF) that IOSCO established in 2003[71] and the USA played a leading role at least until the 2008 crisis.[72]

As for the EU, the bloc did not have common legislation on this topic before adoption of the CRA Regulation[73] in 2009. In March 2005, the Committee of European Securities Regulators (CESR) advised the European Commission (EC) not to move forward with a legislative proposal, to co-operate with the SEC,[74]

[67] Securities and Exchange Commission – SEC, Release No. 34-39457 (1997).

[68] Credit Rating Agency Reform Act, Pub.L. 109–291.

[69] E Conte and F Parmeggiani, *The Regulation of Credit Rating Agency Across USA and EU: Different Systems, Same Concerns* (2008) 5.

[70] Katz et al (n 63) 5.

[71] IOSCO, 'Report on the Activities of Credit Rating Agencies' (2003) 1, available at www.iosco.org/library/pubdocs/pdf/IOSCOPD153.pdf.

[72] Brummer offers a detailed background of the political discussions about CRAs at global level especially in the aftermath of the 2008 crisis: C Brummer, *Soft Law and the Global Financial System: Rule Making in the 21st Century*, 2nd edn (Cambridge, Cambridge University Press, 2015) 290–97. Although from the perspective of the Basel II Accord and how it leverages credit ratings, De Bellis also highlights the leading role of the US regulatory framework: '[T]he reference to credit-rating agencies in Basel II comes from the U.S. domestic tradition; hence, this global linkage does not innovate vis-a-vis the national tradition but simply transplants a tool well-known domestically': M De Bellis, 'Public Law and Private Regulators in the Global Legal Space' (2011) 9 *International Journal of Constitutional Law*, esp 447. Also Jordan: 'The 2004 IOSCO CRA Code was, in fact, hardly international at all; it was narrowly determined by the issues surrounding the three large CRAs in the United States and represented a deft play on their part to deflect domestic regulation in the face of perceived failures associated with the collapse of Enron and WorldCom': Jordan (n 31) 7.

[73] Regulation (EC) No 1060/2009 of the European Parliament and of the Council of 16 September 2009 on credit rating agencies Regulation (EC) No 1060/2009 of the European Parliament and of the Council of 16 September 2009 on credit rating agencies [2009] OJ L302/1.

[74] 'CESR stresses the need for a common worldwide approach on the treatment of CRAs. CESR acknowledges that the US SEC is currently assessing a possible review of the NRSRO system. Before any decision is taken on any side of the Atlantic, either by the European Commission or by the SEC, CESR encourages

and to rely on the CRAs' voluntary compliance with the IOSCO CRA Code.[75] In December 2005, the CESR issued a press release which confirmed its 'pragmatic approach'[76] based on voluntary participation by CRAs and on monitoring of regulatory developments (such as the Capital Requirements Directive), while paying special attention to key topics such as issuers and investor protection.[77] Importantly, the CESR outlined a hands-off approach to overseeing compliance by CRAs with the IOSCO CRA Code, a procedure based on co-operation between CRAs and the CESR.[78] Significantly, the crisis that started unfolding in 2007 after the Commission Communication would have reversed this approach. In 2008, the European Commission decided to propose a regulation on CRAs, highlighting that 'legislation [*in particular, a regulation*] is the best option to ensure a common framework throughout the EU and an efficient counterbalance to other important jurisdictions, notably the US'.[79] The first CRA Regulation (CRAR 1),[80] approved in April 2009, introduced common rules on registration and supervision of CRAs that went beyond the IOSCO Code at the time. Alongside the more traditional co-ordination and guidance tasks, the first CRA Regulation assigned to the CESR direct responsibility for registration of CRAs[81] and shared responsibility for their supervision,[82] marking a drastic turnaround from the CESR's early position on this issue. With the establishment of ESMA in 2010, the 2011 CRA Regulation (CRAR 2)[83] clarified the CESR's responsibilities and shifted these onto ESMA.[84] As a result, ESMA now has extensive powers on three elements: registration, perimeter, and supervision,[85] acting as the sole EU supervisor of CRAs. Importantly, the power to grant a CRA a licence now rests with the ESMA board and the current Regulation envisages certification of third-country CRAs under the precondition of a Commission equivalence decision on a third-country regulatory regime. Certification of CRAs in third countries has expanded the supervisory powers of the EU centralised supervisor beyond EU borders, reaching US shores.

a close co-ordination between the different regulators and hopes to continue to be an active party in this process.' Committee of European Securities Regulators (CESR), CESR's technical advice to the European Commission on possible measures concerning credit rating agencies – Ref: CESR/05-139b (2005).

[75] See ibid.

[76] CESR, CESR's dialogue with Credit Rating Agencies to review how the IOSCO code of conduct is being implemented – Ref: 05-751 (2005).

[77] See ibid.

[78] ibid at 1.

[79] European Commission, 'Proposal for a Regulation of the European Parliament and of the Council on Credit Rating Agencies' Brussels, 12.11.2008 COM(2008) 704 final 2008/0217 (COD) (2008).

[80] CRA Regulation (n 73).

[81] ibid Art 15.

[82] ibid Chapters II and III.

[83] Regulation (EU) No 513/2011 of the European Parliament and of the Council of 11 May 2011 amending Regulation (EC) No 1060/2009 on credit rating agencies [2011] OJ L145/.

[84] For a critical appraisal of the 2011 Regulation: IH-Y Chiu, 'Regulatory Governance of Credit Rating Agencies in the EU: The Perils of Pursuing the Holy Grail of Rating Accuracy' (2013) 4 *European Journal of Risk Regulation*.

[85] European Securities and Markets Authority – ESMA, 'Credit Rating Agencies' (2021), available at www.esma.europa.eu/supervision/credit-rating-agencies/supervision.

As for IOSCO standards, in September 2003 its CRA TF first issued the IOSCO Statement of Principles Regarding the Activities of Credit Rating Agencies,[86] followed by the first version of the Code of Conduct Fundamentals for Credit Rating Agencies[87] in 2004 (revised in 2008). In 2006 the CRA TF was asked to examine 'the codes of conduct of 32 CRAs of varying size, focus, and methodologies from seven jurisdictions'.[88] The results of that examination were issued in the 2007 consultation report.[89] This was the first time that IOSCO openly carried out an implementation assessment *directly* on private parties, that is, service providers incorporated as companies in their home jurisdictions. The 2007 report had found that a number of CRAs had 'substantially implemented the IOSCO CRA Code',[90] including the three largest CRAs in the world.[91] While a larger group had only partially implemented the IOSCO Code, a 'relatively large group (which mostly included smaller CRAs) had only minimal or non-existent implementation of the IOSCO CRA Code'.[92]

A reading of the 2003 Principles and the first version of the Code suggests similarities with the then-traditional approach of the SEC and, above all, with the content of the 1997 proposed regulation.[93] Both the 2004 Principles/Code and the 1997 proposed regulation focused on the same facets, namely the reliability and credibility of ratings, adequate internal processes and procedures, the handling of confidential and non-public information, and qualified staff. Moreover, the broad discretion that the SEC enjoyed for many years is in a way transposed into IOSCO's document when it clearly states that the formal legal instrument through which licensing activity is carried out is not important, but the requirements a company must meet to be registered as a CRA. Such flexibility, already a characteristic of the US system, was adopted by IOSCO in 2004, with the US-led disclosure paradigm being the driving force behind the 2008 revision.[94]

Nevertheless, subsequent important reforms of the IOSCO CRA Code, in particular establishment of colleges of supervisors and inclusion of registration and oversight programmes, have contributed to making the Code much more EU-leaning.[95] In 2013,

[86] IOSCO, 'IOSCO Statement of Principles Regarding the Activities of Credit Rating Agencies' (2003), available at www.iosco.org/library/pubdocs/pdf/IOSCOPD151.pdf.

[87] IOSCO, '2004 Code of Conduct Fundamentals for Credit Rating Agencies' (2004), available at www.iosco.org/library/pubdocs/pdf/IOSCOPD180.pdf.

[88] IOSCO, '2009 A Review of Implementation of the IOSCO Code of Conduct Fundamentals for Credit Rating Agencies' (2009) 5, available at www.iosco.org/library/pubdocs/pdf/IOSCOPD286.pdf.

[89] IOSCO, '2007 Review of Implementation of the IOSCO Fundamentals of a Code of Conduct for Credit Rating Agencies' (2007), available at www.iosco.org/library/pubdocs/pdf/IOSCOPD233.pdf.

[90] IOSCO, '2009 Review' (n 88).

[91] Moody's Investor Services, Standard and Poor (S&P), and Fitch Ratings: IOSCO, '2007 Review of Implementation' (n 89) 8.

[92] IOSCO, '2009 Review' (n 88).

[93] SEC, Release No. 34-39457 (1997) (n 67).

[94] 'Consistent with the US regulatory approach, the revisions producing the 2008 IOSCO CRA Code were disclosure-based. [...] These revisions reflected concerns very specific to the US derivatives markets, which had risen to prominence in the Bear Stearns fiasco': Jordan (n 31) 7.

[95] As Jordan correctly points out: 'the CRA Regulation looped back into the revised 2015 IOSCO CRA Code of Conduct. These European influences, with their different balancing of private and public interests and relative indifference to disclosure-based regulatory approaches, immediately put the 2015 revisions of

the IOSCO board took a bold step – that Pagliari had somehow forecast in 2012[96] – and issued the Final Report on Supervisory Colleges for Credit Rating Agencies,[97] which consolidated the work already started by the standing committee on CRAs and poured into a previous 2012 consultation report.[98] In the final report, the board put forth a recommendation to establish supervisory colleges for globally active CRAs, following the guidelines contained in the IOSCO Principles Regarding Cross-Border Supervisory Cooperation.[99] The opening meetings of the supervisory colleges for the three largest CRAs were held in late 2013: while the US SEC chaired the colleges for S&P and Moody's, ESMA chaired the college for Fitch.[100] As Jordan[101] also highlights, the establishment of supervisory colleges was an ESMA win in its new position as EU-wide supervisor for CRAs.

Finally, in early 2014, a proposal for a revised CRA Code was published. Comments and feedback contributed to the new 2015 CRA Code,[102] which is still in force. Major contributions came from the supervisory experiences of IOSCO Members and from 26 CRAs based in Argentina, Brazil, Canada, Chile, the EU, Japan, Mexico, and the USA,[103] although key CRAs were (and still are) incorporated in the USA. Unlike previous revisions, consensus was not easy to achieve, with an opening disclaimer reaffirming that participating authorities retained the power to adopt diverging domestic standards.[104] Importantly, the new Code has taken into account 'the emergence of CRA registration and oversight programs' at the domestic level – two elements of particular importance in the EU CRA Regulation – and 'is intended to work in harmony with CRA registration and oversight programs and to continue operating as the international standard for CRA self-governance'.[105]

the IOSCO CRA Code of Conduct at odds with US approaches': Jordan (n 31) 10. Jordan also offers a comparative table between IOSCO 2008 and 2015 Codes and the EU CRA Regulation giving grounds to a growing EU influence.

[96] 'The crisis has thus gradually shifted the responsibility to monitor and enforce compliance with the IOSCO code of conduct from market pressures to the hands of public regulatory authorities': S Pagliari, 'Who Governs Finance? The Shifting Public–Private Divide in the Regulation of Derivatives, Rating Agencies and Hedge Funds' (2012) 18 *European Law Journal* 20.

[97] IOSCO, 'Supervisory Colleges for Credit Rating Agencies – Final Report' (2013), available at www.iosco.org/library/pubdocs/pdf/IOSCOPD416.pdf.

[98] IOSCO, 'Supervisory Colleges for Credit Rating Agencies – Consultation Report' (2012), available at www.iosco.org/library/pubdocs/pdf/IOSCOPD397.pdf.

[99] IOSCO, 'Principles Regarding Cross-Border Supervisory Cooperation' (2010) 7, available at www.iosco.org/library/pubdocs/pdf/IOSCOPD322.pdf.

[100] IOSCO, '2015 Code of Conduct Fundamentals for Credit Rating Agencies' (2015), available at www.iosco.org/library/pubdocs/pdf/IOSCOPD482.pdf.

[101] Jordan (n 31).

[102] IOSCO, '2015 Code of Conduct' (n 100).

[103] ibid 4–5.

[104] ibid as opening stage: 'Certain authorities may consider rule proposals or standards that relate to the substance of this report. These authorities provided information to IOSCO or otherwise participated in the preparation of this report, but their participation should not be viewed as an expression of a judgment by these authorities regarding their current or future regulatory proposals or of their rulemaking or standards implementation work. This report thus does not reflect a judgment by, or limit the choices of, these authorities with regard to their proposed or final versions of their rules or standards.'

[105] ibid 4.

Loss of prestige after the 2008 crisis[106] and, above all, the 2010 establishment of a single EU agency acting as a pan-EU supervisor for CRAs, have contributed to shifting IOSCO's internal balance of power in this specific area. The result is that a document initially conceived as 'US-styled' has turned into a global normative background that justifies domestic authorities in supervising foreign private companies,[107] as is the case for ESMA and the US CRAs.[108] In particular, EU (public) law has been able to influence IOSCO standards and, through them and extraterritorial clauses, even to penetrate the US legal system and indirectly apply to private parties incorporated in the USA.

V. FINANCIAL BENCHMARKS

Financial Benchmarks (FBMs) are a crucial source of information concerning underlying assets and, for this reason, strongly contribute to increasing transparency and liquidity in securities markets.[109] IOSCO defines FBMs as:

> prices, rates, indices or figures that are: a) Made available to users […]; b) Calculated periodically […] by the application of a formula or another method of calculation to, or an assessment of the value of, one or more underlying assets, prices or certain other data, including estimated prices, rates or other values, or surveys; and c) Used for reference for [several] purposes […].[110]

Importantly, FBMs are provided by private parties called FBM Administrators. This is a 'natural or legal person that has control over the provision of a benchmark and in particular administers the arrangements for determining the benchmark, collects and analyses the input data, determines the benchmark and publishes it'.[111]

Notwithstanding the 'ubiquitous feature'[112] that FBMs have gained in modern financial markets, this topic was largely unregulated until the 2012 Libor scandal.

[106] JE Fisch, 'Top Cop or Regulatory Flop? The SEC at 75' (2009) 95 *Virginia Law Review*; Brummer (n 5). With reference to the 1990s, Jordan writes that 'At the time, the US regulatory framework represented the gold standard, a notion that US regulators (and some financial economists) were happy to promote': Jordan (n 31) 4. With reference to loss of prestige, Jordan writes that: 'The decade that followed sorely tested this conviction [that of the US securities regulation being a model for the world], beginning with the corporate governance failures of Enron and Worldcom and culminating only a few years later with the near collapse of the US, and world, financial system': C Jordan, *International Capital Markets: Law and Institutions* (Oxford, Oxford University Press, 2014) 6.

[107] On the same wavelength, 'It is hard to escape the conclusion that these particular standards are not "international" at all. With the benefit of hindsight, it may be that pressures for these particular standards are a response to failure, for a number of reasons, to adopt regulation at the national level in the United States': Jordan (n 31) 9.

[108] ESMA, 'Non-EU Credit Rating Agencies' (2021), available at www.esma.europa.eu/supervision/non-eu-credit-rating-agencies.

[109] G S Fletcher, 'Benchmark Regulation' (2017) 102 *Iowa Law Review* 1929, 1930–81, esp 1943.

[110] IOSCO, 'Financial Benchmarks – Consultation Report' (2013) 48, available at www.iosco.org/library/pubdocs/pdf/IOSCOPD399.pdf.

[111] Regulation (EU) 2016/1011 of the European Parliament and of the Council of 8 June 2016 on indices used as benchmarks in financial instruments and financial contracts or to measure the performance of investment funds and amending Directives 2008/48/EC and 2014/17/EU and Regulation (EU) No 596/2014 ('Financial Benchmarks Regulation') [2016] OJ L171/.

[112] Fletcher (n 109) 1930.

IOSCO stepped in, in order to find common solutions to the challenges created by the scandal. At least at the beginning, the USA and the UK – de facto acting as the leading EU jurisdiction – were proposing two different approaches: while the UK preferred a transaction-based approach, the USA was leaning more towards an approach based on market bids or offers.[113] The IOSCO released its Principles for Financial Benchmarks[114] in July 2013. Here, Principle 7, although favouring the transaction-based method, took quite a diplomatic approach that did 'not preclude Benchmark Administrators from using executable bids or offers as a means to construct Benchmarks where anchored in an observable market consisting of Bona Fide, Arms-length transactions'.[115] Subsequently, the FBM TF released the important assessment methodology – IOSCO Principles for Financial Benchmarks[116] in January 2014 to test the degree of implementation of IOSCO standards on the part of FBM Administrators. This conferred on the standards a 'supervisory spirit',[117] that was tested directly on private parties through specific implementation reviews.[118] In February 2015, IOSCO released its Review of the Implementation of IOSCO's Principles for Financial Benchmarks,[119] which covered 36 benchmarks and related administrators, and the Report on Guidance on the IOSCO Principles for Financial Benchmarks,[120] which introduced a basis for harmonising compliance disclosure by benchmark administrators.

IOSCO standards are sufficiently high-level to be implemented in different fashions. Indeed, the EU and the USA have followed diverging – somehow conflicting – paths. To begin with, the European approach is prescriptive rather than reactive.[121] This means that the EU has transposed IOSCO standards through imposition of detailed duties on predetermined categories, with *ex-ante* supervision and enforcement taking the driving seat vis-à-vis *ex-post* enforcement. This is a substantial departure from the US 'traditional' or 'reactive'[122] approach, which sees that US regulators mainly intervene *after* a wrongdoing has occurred, thus treating FBM manipulation like any

[113] Interview with Dr Carlo Comporti, CONSOB Commissioner, March 2021.

[114] IOSCO, 'Principles for Financial Benchmarks' (2013), available at www.iosco.org/library/pubdocs/pdf/IOSCOPD415.pdf.

[115] ibid 11.

[116] IOSCO, 'Assessment Methodology – IOSCO Principles for Financial Benchmarks' (2014), available at https://www.iosco.org/library/pubdocs/pdf/IOSCOPD444.pdf.

[117] Dr Comporti (n 113) directly defines these standards as 'de facto supervisory standards'.

[118] See: IOSCO, 'Review of the Implementation of IOSCO's Principles for Financial Benchmarks by Administrators of Euribor, Libor and Tibor' (2014), available at www.fsb.org/wp-content/uploads/r_140722a.pdf; IOSCO, 'Second Review of the Implementation of IOSCO's Principles for Financial Benchmarks by Administrators of EURIBOR, LIBOR and TIBOR' (2016), available at www.iosco.org/library/pubdocs/pdf/IOSCOPD526.pdf; IOSCO, 'Review of the Implementation of IOSCO's Principles for Financial Benchmarks by WM in respect of the WM/Reuters 4.p.m Closing Spot Rate' (2014), available at www.iosco.org/library/pubdocs/pdf/IOSCOPD451.pdf; IOSCO, 'Second Review of the Implementation of IOSCO's Principles for Financial Benchmarks in respect of the WM/Reuters 4 p.m. Closing Spot Rate' (2017), available at www.iosco.org/library/pubdocs/pdf/IOSCOPD553.pdf.

[119] IOSCO, 'Review of the Implementation of IOSCO's Principles for Financial Benchmarks' (2015), available at www.iosco.org/library/pubdocs/pdf/IOSCOPD474.pdf.

[120] IOSCO, 'Report on Guidance on the IOSCO Principles for Financial Benchmarks' (2016), available at www.iosco.org/library/pubdocs/pdf/IOSCOPD549.pdf.

[121] Fletcher (n 109).

[122] See ibid.

other traditional form of market manipulation. As a result, the USA has transposed IOSCO standards on FBMs via conventional regulation on market manipulation,[123] instead of an *ad hoc* piece of legislation. Nevertheless, the point of contention mainly revolves around the extraterritorial rules enshrined in the EU Financial Benchmarks Regulation. EU law mandates that US benchmark administrators that want to have their index used in the EU seek either recognition or endorsement.[124] US regulators were not happy – to say the least – with the EU extraterritorial mechanism,[125] but this was still implemented in Europe. Similar to the CRA case, although IOSCO standards have not pushed the USA towards the European direction, they have to some extent absorbed the EU approach. This approach has been reinforced by extraterritorial rules that provide the EU authorities with an indirect footprint in the USA, even affecting private parties incorporated in that jurisdiction.

VI. CONCLUSIONS: THE EMERGENCE OF THE EU AS A GLOBAL REGULATORY POWER AND ITS INDIRECT INFLUENCE ON PRIVATE LAWS OUTSIDE THE EU

This chapter revolves around three case studies that show the growing influence of the EU and its normative production on transnational standards for global securities markets. The standards under scrutiny are those adopted by IOSCO, the only global standard-setter bringing together public regulators from around the world. Here domestic authorities agree via consensus on standards aimed at promoting best practices at the local level and on enforcement co-operation at the cross-border level.

While IOSCO standards have an intrinsic public law nature, the three case studies analysed in this chapter – investor protection, credit rating agencies, and financial benchmarks – have clear ramifications in private law regimes. The standards examined in the three case studies provide a basis for regional/national public law rules aimed at shaping market relations, subsequently followed by functional use of national private law, viewed as a means of constituting an efficient and competitive market.[126] Viewed from this perspective, standards on retail investor protection contribute to indirectly shaping relations between investment service providers and investors; standards on FBMs and CRAs promote market efficiency through tougher rules on disclosure and access to information. Both functions were traditionally covered by private law rules and remedies, while public law rules now play a significant (if not even predominant) role.

[123] From a general standpoint: Commodity Futures Trading Commission – CFTC, Remarks of Chairman Timothy Massad before the Natural Gas Roundtable (Washington, DC) (2015), available at www.cftc.gov/PressRoom/SpeechesTestimony/opamassad-23.

[124] Financial Benchmarks Regulation (n 110).

[125] H Jones, 'U.S. Under Pressure to Match EU Rules on Market Benchmarks' (Reuters, 2014). Also CFTC (2015) (n 123).

[126] On regulatory private law: HW Micklitz, 'The Visible Hand of European Regulatory Private Law – The Transformation of European Private Law from Autonomy to Functionalism in Competition and Regulation' (2009) 28 *Yearbook of European Law*.

Importantly, in each of the three case studies the EU has been able to influence IOSCO standards, even overcoming the traditional hegemonic role of the USA. At least in one case, the impact on IOSCO standards of EU regulatory solutions has been coupled with extraterritorial rules which can significantly extend the reach of EU regulatory law to private parties incorporated abroad, in particular in the USA. This growing influence of the EU on IOSCO standards and its fortification via extraterritorial rules has indeed encountered some critical reactions – sometimes explicit – on the part of US rule-makers. This does not come as a surprise since the result appears to be the indirect influence of EU regulatory law on private parties incorporated in the USA and governed under the US private law regime.

At the end of this chapter an intriguing question emerges: is EU law able to somehow penetrate third-country private law regimes by influencing IOSCO normative production? Although the depth of this phenomenon remains to be explored and carefully analysed, it can already be assumed that EU financial law, although intrinsically public, shows the potential to penetrate third-country private law regimes and indirectly affect private parties incorporated in third countries.

International Trade and Taxation

11

Leveraging EU Trade Agreements and Legislation to Influence Regulation Abroad

MISLAV MATAIJA*

I. EXTRATERRITORIALITY AND EXTERNAL EFFECTS

THE ABILITY OF EU law to, incidentally or even intentionally, produce effects in other jurisdictions, has been well explored in the literature. Most famously, Anu Bradford has described the so-called 'Brussels effect', by which the need to comply with EU law requirements leads to a global alignment of the behaviour of producers and service suppliers to (high) EU standards.[1]

Bradford's analysis does not focus on overt attempts by the EU legislator to extend its rules to conduct abroad, although such rules would of course lead to similar (or even more extensive) effects in practice. Bradford's framework is, to a large extent, agnostic of the legislator's intention.[2]

Others have, however, focused on such practices. Thus, Joanne Scott provides a detailed overview of the many examples of EU legislation with external effects, distinguishing between 'territorial extension' and 'pure' extraterritoriality (in a nutshell: the existence of a 'trigger' linking the subject-matter of the measure to the EU jurisdiction).

As Scott herself recognises, however, there is some tension between the two concepts, and criticisms of one can extend to the other. Notably, as Scott explains,

* Member of the Legal Service, European Commission. All views are personal and do not necessarily represent those of the European Commission.

[1] A Bradford, *The Brussels Effect: How the European Union Rules the World* (USA, Oxford University Press, 2020). There are also numerous sector-specific studies of this phenomenon. See, eg, B Annegret and M Römer, 'Externalizing Europe: The Global Effects of European Data Protection' (2018) 21 *Digital Policy, Regulation and Governance* 1, 32–43; M Lehmann, 'Legal Fragmentation, Extraterritoriality and Uncertainty in Global Financial Regulation' (2017) 37 *OJLS* 2, 406–34.

[2] I Hadjiyianni, 'The European Union as a Global Regulatory Power' (2021) 41 *OJLS* 1, 243–64, at 246.

'although it is the existence of an initial point of territorial connection that sparks EU law into life, some of the transactions governed by EU law will, when taken individually, have no territorial connection with the EU in the end'.[3] Moreover, while EU rules tend to be grounded on a territorial trigger, Scott recognises that these links are recently becoming more tenuous, reaching the conduct of non-EU actors that takes place entirely abroad.[4] With this in mind, examples of 'territorial extension' can prove to be just as controversial as those of straight-out extraterritoriality. Nevertheless, Scott argues that a grounding on international standards, or at least openness towards them, provides more justification for the EU's approach.

II. EXTERNAL EFFECTS OF EU LEGISLATION

In practice, examples of rules intended to produce external effects proliferate in the regulatory practice of the EU, for example in environmental, financial and IT regulation.

Many of these examples have been discussed in the literature. Scott herself discusses numerous examples in the areas of banking and finance, transport, and environmental law.[5] Ankersmit lists three examples of EU measures regulating production processes abroad, on leghold traps, illegal fishing and conflict diamonds.[6] Others have analysed, for example, the revision of the Renewable Energy Directive to address de-forestation,[7] or the proposal for a Carbon Border Adjustment Mechanism (CBAM).[8]

Among the more recent examples is the 'Fit for 55' package, a flagship Commission project aimed at reducing carbon emissions, which contains a number of rules not only with clear external effects but also with a clear external orientation. This includes a more ambitious Emissions Trading System, amendments to the Renewable Energy Directive which allow for the tracking of emissions-saving criteria for imported fuels, and a ReFuelEU Aviation Initiative which would impose fuel sustainability standards on fuel suppliers. The Impact Assessment of the latter expressly justifies EU-level action by stating that 'spill-over effects are also likely to occur more easily, whereby third countries may

[3] J Scott, 'Extraterritoriality and Territorial Extension in EU Law' (2014) 62 *The American Journal of Comparative Law* 1, 87–126, at 124.See also J Scott, 'The New EU "Extraterritoriality"' (2014) 51 *CMLR* 5.

[4] Scott, 'The New EU "Extraterritoriality"', ibid 1344.

[5] Scott, 'Extraterritoriality and Territorial Extension' (n 3) 114, Table 4; Scott, 'The New EU "Extraterritoriality"' (n 3) 1363–64, Table II.

[6] L Ankersmit, *Free Trade, Fair Trade, and Green Trade in and with the EU: Process-Based Measures within the EU Legal Order* (Cambridge, Cambridge University Press, 2017) 43 et seq.

[7] M Limenta, 'Palm Oil for Fuels: WTO Rules and Environmental Protection' (2020) 15 *Global Trade and Customs Journal* 7.

[8] Directive (EU) 2018/2001 of the European Parliament and of the Council of 11 December 2018 on the promotion of the use of energy from renewable sources (recast) [2018] OJ L328; CG Leonelli, 'Export Rebates and the EU Carbon Border Adjustment Mechanism: WTO Law and Environmental Objections' (2022) 56 *Journal of World Trade* 6.

consider adopting similar measures'.[9] Perhaps most prominently, the proposed CBAM aims at ensuring that 'the price of imports reflects more accurately their carbon content' and preventing carbon leakage, which is premised on 'embedded emissions', released in the production of the good and looks at the carbon price paid in the country of origin.[10]

Another example is the Taxonomy Regulation, which creates a classification system for economic activities based on their environmental sustainability, extending certain reporting obligations to third country undertakings. Similarly, the Corporate Sustainability Reporting Directive requires non-EU companies with branches or subsidiaries in the EU that achieve a certain level of revenue in the EU to report on their environmental, social and governance impacts, including at group level.[11] The proposed Corporate Sustainability Due Diligence Directive would go a step further, requiring certain third country companies active in the EU market to conduct due diligence of certain adverse human rights and environmental impacts, not just of their own activities but across their supply chains, and to take appropriate measures to address such impacts. In addition, due diligence obligations of EU companies over their supply chains can indirectly impact the activities of their suppliers. This would amount to *facto* regulation, on a global scale, of sustainability-related practices of some suppliers of goods and services to EU companies.[12]

The legislative proposal on European green bonds[13] contains rules concerning the designation of certain bonds as linked to environmentally sustainable projects (including where those projects are located abroad). It also provides for a set of rules regulating third country reviewers of the actual sustainability of such bonds.

Important recent 'gatekeeper' regulations on digital platforms (the Digital Services Act and the Digital Markets Act)[14] are among many examples of acts that impose obligations on certain actors active in the EU market, regardless of their place of establishment. These acts are certain to have spill-over effects on those platforms' way of doing business globally.

As these examples make clear, there is an increasing tendency to use EU legislation to address, in particular, production processes abroad. None of these would

[9] Commission Staff Working Document, Impact Assessment Accompanying the Proposal for a Regulation of the European Parliament and of the Council on ensuring a level playing field for sustainable air transport, SWD(2021) 633 final, 14 July 2021, section 3.3, p 23.

[10] Proposal for a Regulation of the European Parliament and of the Council establishing a carbon border adjustment mechanism, COM(2021) 564 final, 14 July 2021, Explanatory Memorandum, section 1.

[11] Directive (EU) 2022/2464 of the European Parliament and of the Council of 14 December 2022 amending Directive 2013/34/EU, Directive 2004/109/EC, Directive 2006/43/EC and Regulation (EU) No 537/2014, as regards corporate sustainability reporting [2022] OJ L322/15.

[12] Proposal for a Directive of the European Parliament and of the Council on Corporate Sustainability Due Diligence and amending Directive (EU) 2019/1937 (COM/2022/71 final).

[13] Proposal for a Regulation of the European Parliament and of the Council on European green bonds (COM/2021/391 final).

[14] Regulation (EU) 2022/2065 of the European Parliament and of the Council of 19 October 2022 on a Single Market For Digital Services and amending Directive 2000/31/EC (Digital Services Act) [2022] OJ L277/1; Regulation (EU) 2022/1925 of the European Parliament and of the Council of 14 September 2022 on contestable and fair markets in the digital sector and amending Directives (EU) 2019/1937 and (EU) 2020/1828 (Digital Markets Act) [2022] OJ L265/1.

obviously constitute 'extraterritoriality', as there is in each case at least some sort of 'trigger' (to use Scott's terminology) that provides a link to the EU jurisdiction: imports of goods, movement into the EU, provision of services to the EU or revenue generation in the EU – if not by the addressee himself, then by someone in the same supply chain. The strength of the 'trigger' varies, and issues of compatibility with international trade law may therefore be more frequent than before. This brings us to the topic of the next section.

III. CONFLICTS? 'EXTRATERRITORIAL' REACH OF EU REGULATION AND INTERNATIONAL TRADE LAW

National measures regulating methods of production or processes abroad – known in WTO jargon as 'processes and production methods' (PPMs) – have been a long-standing source of controversy. This problem goes beyond domestic measures that conflict with trade law disciplines (eg a ban on importing products containing harmful substances). It refers to domestic measures that treat imports less favourably, in law or in fact, by targeting the way in which the good or service was produced in a third country. A sub-group of such measures expressly recognises certain methods of third country domestic *regulation* at the expense of others, creating not just a conflict (however likely) but also recognition premised on modes of regulation comparable to those of the EU itself. Yet another group may focus on the manufacturer or provider, rather than its country of origin, and impose on them certain requirements. For example, imported products can be treated more favourably in case their manufacturer complies with a particular standard.

In these cases, the key distinction is between so-called 'incorporated' (or product-related) PPMs – which can be seen or otherwise have an impact on the product or service itself – and 'unincorporated' ones – which do not leave such a trace. An 'unincorporated' PPM comes close, in some ways, to an extraterritorial measure. To use again Scott's terminology, unincorporated PPMs might seem to create no 'trigger' with the regulating jurisdiction.

The classic two WTO cases illustrating this problem are *US – Tuna (Mexico) (Tuna – Dolphin)* and *US – Shrimp*. In each case, the facts were relatively similar: for sustainability reasons, the United States banned the imports of the relevant product if it was fished, in the country of origin, in a way considered to be unsustainable by the United States, and illegal in the United States.

The General Agreement on Tariffs and Trade (GATT) Panel in *Tuna – Dolphin* found:

> If Article XX were interpreted to permit contracting parties to deviate from the obligations of the General Agreement by taking trade measures to implement policies, including conservation policies, within their own jurisdiction, the basic objectives of the General Agreement would be maintained. If however Article XX were interpreted to permit contracting parties to take trade measures so as to force other contracting parties to change their policies within their jurisdiction, including their conservation policies, the balance of rights and obligations among contracting parties, in particular the right of access to markets, would be seriously impaired. Under such an interpretation the

> General Agreement could no longer serve as a multilateral framework for trade among contracting parties.[15]

By contrast, in *US – Shrimp*, the Appellate Body overturned similar reasoning, adopted by the panel in the same case, as follows:

> In the present case, the Panel found that the United States measure at stake fell within that class of excluded measures because Section 609 conditions access to the domestic shrimp market of the United States on the adoption by exporting countries of certain conservation policies prescribed by the United States. It appears to us, however, that conditioning access to a Member's domestic market on whether exporting Members comply with, or adopt, a policy or policies unilaterally prescribed by the importing Member may, to some degree, be a common aspect of measures falling within the scope of one or another of the exceptions (a) to (j) of Article XX. Paragraphs (a) to (j) comprise measures that are recognized as exceptions to substantive obligations established in the GATT 1994, because the domestic policies embodied in such measures have been recognized as important and legitimate in character … It is not necessary to assume that requiring from exporting countries compliance with, or adoption of, certain policies (although covered in principle by one or another of the exceptions) prescribed by the importing country, renders a measure a priori incapable of justification under Article XX.[16]

Thus, there is no reason to think that a measure is excluded from justification just because it seeks to create external effect, or pursues 'territorial extension'. Ever since this Report, the notion that regulating production methods in third countries is *a priori* WTO-inconsistent has been, for all intents and purposes, rejected.[17] This does not mean, however, that such measures will always be justified either. Indeed, WTO jurisprudence still expresses quite some scepticism towards territorial extension, which can also be partly explained through rules of customary international law on extraterritorial jurisdiction. In that same Report, the Appellate Body left open the question of whether the provisions of Article XX(g) of the GATT contain an 'implied jurisdictional limitation', such that domestic measures in which the nexus with the regulating jurisdiction – or 'trigger' – is weaker or non-existent, might be condemned.[18]

On the basis of this jurisprudence, Bartels has argued that 'Article XX is to be read consistently with the rules governing a WTO Member's right to exercise legislative jurisdiction over activities and things located outside of its territory', meaning that it should 'apply to save various trade measures designed to promote and protect

[15] GATT Panel Report, *United States – Restrictions on Imports of Tuna* (DS29/R), para 5.26. See also Panel Report, *Indonesia – Certain Measures Affecting the Automobile Industry* (DS54), para 14.143; Panel Report, *United States – Standards for Reformulated and Conventional Gasoline* (DS2), para 6.11.

[16] Appellate Body Report, *United States – Import Prohibition of Certain Shrimp and Shrimp Products* (DS58) (hereinafter '*US – Shrimp*') para 121.

[17] R Howse and D Regan, 'The Product/Process Distinction – an Illusory Basis for Disciplining "Unilateralism" in Trade Policy' (2000) 11 *European Journal of International Law* 2, 249–89.

[18] *US – Shrimp* (n 16) para 133. See also L Ankersmit, JC Lawrence, and GT Davies, 'Diverging EU and WTO Perspectives on Extraterritorial Process Regulation' (Spring 2012) *Minnesota Journal of International Law Online* 40–42.

human rights outside of the territory of the regulating Member'.[19] In other words, it is fair to say that that the extraterritorial effects of a measure are not necessarily a red flag, but merely one of several factors that will be assessed when applying one of the justifications in Article XX, as well as its *chapeau* which calls for a non-discriminatory application of restrictive measures.

Despite all this, there still seems to be an implicit expectation in the trade law community that such measures will have to be pure as the whitest snow in order to benefit from justification.

A fragment of this type of thinking may be seen in *Argentina – Financial Services*, a case which is also as interesting as the first example of this discussion in the area of services (arguably, a more interesting one for the future as many measures with external effects are taken precisely in this area). In that case, the panel took a positive view of domestic rules that distinguish between service providers from different countries based on 'regulatory aspects', ie whether they were co-operative in terms of tax enforcement. It considered that these regulatory aspects could be taken into account at the stage of likeness, meaning that two providers were not comparable due to the different regulation to which they were subject in the country of origin – making discrimination permissible. The Appellate Body disagreed, noting that the GATS (General Agreement on Trade in Services) national treatment provision does not exempt measures intended to '"neutralize" a "regulatory" competitive advantage, namely, one that results from the regulatory framework in the country of origin of certain foreign service suppliers'.[20] In itself, this does not mean that regulating processes abroad in the area of services is presumptively illegal (as it may have been considered to be, for goods, in the GATT and early-WTO era). It does, however, show lingering doubts towards the projection of domestic regulatory concerns on third countries. In fact, the finding is reminiscent of the old *US – Gasoline* panel, which rejected the view that imports are not discriminated against because they were treated the same as the products of certain 'similarly situated' domestic producers. That panel held that such an interpretation

> would mean that the treatment of imported and domestic goods concerned could no longer be assured on the objective basis of their likeness as products. Rather, imported goods would be exposed to a highly subjective and variable treatment according to extraneous factors.[21]

As demonstrated by the examples above, the EU is more likely than many other WTO Members to be on the receiving end of challenges to regulations of 'unincorporated PPMs' or 'extraterritorial' measures. And indeed, some EU measures in that category have already been challenged. One example is *EC – Seal Products*, concerning the EU's prohibition of seal products coupled with exceptions for certain categories of seal products. While the prohibition itself is of course not the type of

[19] L Bartels, 'Article XX of GATT and the Problem of Extraterritorial Jurisdiction The Case of Trade Measures for the Protection of Human Rights' (2002) 36 *Journal of World Trade* 2 at 402.

[20] Appellate Body Report, *Argentina – Financial Services* (DS453), paras 6.145 and 6.151.

[21] Panel Report, *United States – Standards for Reformulated and Conventional Gasoline* (DS2), para 6.12.

measure we are concerned with here, some of the exceptions were: the EU accepted seal products produced from seals hunted in particular ways (for purposes of marine resource management) and by certain groups (certain indigenous communities). While the Appellate Body accepted that the resulting different treatment between imports based *de facto* on their country of origin could be justified on the basis of public morals under Article XX(a) of the GATT, the justification failed under the chapeau of Article XX as the details of the design of the EU's exceptions potentially led to 'arbitrary or unjustifiable discrimination' between imports from different sources.[22]

Another example is the ongoing dispute with Indonesia in which it is claimed that the EU's restrictions on use of palm oil in biofuels, meant to address global deforestation, is indirectly discriminatory, favouring other products such as soybeans despite their comparable risk profile.[23]

And one could speculate, based on the examples above, that future cases of this sort are more likely to concern services rather than goods. In addition, the focus of many recent measures on environmental sustainability, in particular climate change, make it more likely than ever that EU measures will be addressing regulatory concerns that are not reflected in the product itself.

When that happens, however, the EU will not be facing an insurmountable legal barrier. The risk that externally-focused measures face is not so much a prohibition of 'unilateralism' or 'extraterritorial' regulation (although this remains somewhat untested in the GATS), but rather a tricky, case-by-case challenge of designing such measures in an even-handed way.

IV. INTERNATIONAL TRADE LAW AS LEVERAGE FOR EXTERNAL EFFECTS

Thus we come to the main argument advanced in this chapter: these days, rules of international and domestic trade law are tools for, and not just obstacles to, the externalisation of domestic regulatory concerns through measures such as the ones listed above.

I will trace this trend through several examples, taken (a) from international trade agreements and (b) from EU domestic trade instruments.

A. Free Trade Agreements

The aspect of EU trade policy that has so far attracted the most interest from the point of view of our topic is the expansion of the EU's recent 'deep and comprehensive' trade agreements to issues such as sustainability (labour and environment), coupled with dedicated dispute settlement provisions for their enforcement. These provisions

[22] Appellate Body Report, *EC – Seal Products* (DS401), section 5.3.3.3.
[23] *European Union – Certain measures concerning palm oil and oil palm crop-based biofuels* (DS593).

require the contracting parties to comply with certain sustainability requirements, notably by ratifying and complying with certain core international treaties. For example, in a recent dispute based on the EU-Korea Free Trade Agreement (FTA), the panel of experts concluded that Korea infringed its sustainability commitments by failing to ratify four fundamental International Labour Organisation (ILO) conventions and by failing to ensure freedom of association in its labour legislation.[24] I do not propose to treat that topic here *as such*, as it mostly concerns the 'extension', through EU trade agreements, of certain international treaties, and not of EU domestic laws as such.[25]

There are, however, examples where EU trade agreements actually 'extend' EU legislation, or reinforce its external effects.

i. Direct Extension Through Trade Agreements

The EU's association agreements are, in large part, trade agreements, in that they grant asymmetric market access to the association country as part of a broader package that involves not just market access commitments on the other side but also wide-ranging legal and governance reforms and alignment with EU rules.

A particularly salient example are the rules on 'internal market treatment' in the EU–Ukraine agreement.[26] Under these rules, when EU institutions find that Ukraine has fully aligned its laws with the EU acquis in four listed sectors (Financial Services, Telecommunication Services, Postal and Courier Services and International Maritime Transport Services), the Trade Committee set up by the agreement may decide that the Parties grant each other internal market treatment in that sector, requiring the removal of certain restrictions on freedom of establishment and free provision of services. Importantly, the approximation obligation extends to new rules adopted by the EU (Annex XVII, Article 5).

Such mechanisms also exist in other trade agreements. Most famously, the European Economic Area Agreement requires alignment with EU legislation, as does the Northern Ireland Protocol to the EU–UK Withdrawal Agreement.

Through this technique, the EU uses trade agreements to expressly require other contracting parties to modify their legislation in line with EU rules.

ii. Indirect Extension Through Mutual Recognition and Regulatory Co-operation

Some of the FTAs recently concluded or negotiated by the EU, like the EU–Canada Comprehensive Economic and Trade Agreement (CETA) or the EU-Japan Economic

[24] Report of the Panel of Experts, Proceeding constituted under Article 13.15 of the Eu-Korea Free Trade Agreement, available at https://circabc.europa.eu/ui/group/09242a36-a438-40fd-a7af-fe32e36cbd0e/library/d4276b0f-4ba5-4aac-b86a-d8f65157c38e/details.

[25] For more details, see, eg, L Bartels, 'Human Rights and Sustainable Development Obligations in EU Free Trade Agreements' and R Leal-Arcas and CM Wilmarth, 'Strengthening Sustainable Development through Regional Trade Agreements' both in J Wouters et al (eds), *Global Governance through Trade: EU Policies and Approaches* (Cheltenham, Edward Elgar Publishing, 2015).

[26] Association Agreement between the European Union and the European Atomic Energy Community and their Member States, of the one part, and Ukraine, of the other part [2014] OJ L161/3.

Partnership Agreement, show promise in the techniques of regulatory co-operation and mutual recognition, which are also permitted and encouraged within the WTO framework but have so far failed to gain significant traction in a multilateral setting. FTAs enable more developed instruments, since they tend to be concluded among like-minded partners. In EU–Japan, for example, there is the possibility for the parties to engage in regulatory co-operation on a voluntary basis, which means that they would need to 'consider, to the extent feasible, any regulatory approach by the other Party on the same or a related matter',[27] and consider applying 'common principles, guidelines, codes of conduct, mutual recognition of equivalence and implementing tools, to avoid unnecessary duplication of regulatory requirements such as testing, qualifications, audits or inspections' as well as co-operation in international fora 'with a view to developing and promoting the adoption and implementation of international regulatory standards, guidelines or other approaches'.[28]

A related example is the co-operation between accreditation and conformity assessment bodies. For example, a bilateral agreement concluded in the framework of CETA[29] allows EU and Canadian products to be certified by the accreditation and conformity assessment bodies of the EU for compliance with Canadian standards, and vice versa.

Yet another example are mutual recognition agreements (MRAs) for regulated professions. Compared to the WTO (GATS) framework, recent FTAs offer more detailed and better structured frameworks allowing professional bodies to put in place mutual recognition schemes, for easier access to each other's markets. The 'authorities' that are recognised in this framework could very well be private or semi-private professional associations, the only requirement being that they are domestically empowered to admit practitioners to a profession. These bodies are encouraged to recommend MRAs, which can be adopted by a committee set up for this purpose (ie no need to ratify additional agreements). Thus, MRAs set up a sort of co-regulatory system with an important role for professional associations, and can lead to regulatory alignment.[30]

iii. Reinforcing EU Domestic Territorial Extension Measures

Interestingly, the EU has used trade agreements not just to require alignment with other rules of international law (eg ILO conventions) or with its own legislation (such as in the case of association agreements), but also to reinforce separate EU legislation which itself involves 'territorial extension'.

[27] Agreement between the European Union and Japan for an Economic Partnership, Article 18.12.5.

[28] ibid Article 18.13.

[29] Comprehensive Economic and Trade Agreement between the EU and Canada (CETA) – Protocol on Conformity Assessment.

[30] Council Decision (EU) 2023/2467 of 23 October 2023 on the position to be taken on behalf of the Union within the Joint Committee on Mutual Recognition of Professional Qualifications established under the Comprehensive Economic and Trade Agreement (CETA) between Canada, of the one part, and the European Union and its Member States, of the other part, as regards the adoption of a decision on an agreement on the mutual recognition of professional qualifications for architects [2023] OJ L2023/2467, available at ELI: http://data.europa.eu/eli/dec/2023/2467/oj.

One example of this technique are the rules on IUU fishing.

Article 16.8 of the EU–Japan Economic Partnership Agreement requires the parties to, among other things, 'adopt and implement their respective effective tools for combating [IUU] fishing, including through legal instruments, and, where appropriate, control, monitoring and enforcement, and capacity management measures'. There are other instruments of international law that deal with IUU fishing, which are however for the most part soft law, with the notable exception of the FAO (Food and Agriculture Organisation) Agreement on Port State Measures to Prevent, Deter and Eliminate Illegal, Unreported and Unregulated Fishing.[31] Another globally important instrument, however, is the EU's own IUU Fishing Regulation, which sets up a system of 'yellow and red cards' for countries that, in the EU's view, do not sufficiently co-operate in the fight against IUU fishing, potentially leading to a ban from the EU market. At the same time, the EU is pushing for the conclusion of a WTO fisheries subsidies instrument, which would include disciplines on IUU fishing. Hence, the rules on IUU fishing in the Economic Partnership Agreement go hand in hand with the EU's own legislation which seeks to extend certain standards to third countries.

A similar example can be found in the anti-corruption chapter of the EU–Mexico draft 'agreement in principle'.[32] That chapter requires both parties to have effective anti-money laundering rules, in line with international instruments like the Financial Action Task Force (FATF) Recommendations on Transparency and Beneficial Ownership of Legal Persons and Arrangements. The parties must also implement in national law the concept of 'beneficial ownership' to ensure that information on beneficial ownership is available to relevant actors.

Obligations on customer due diligence are imposed on financial institutions and national authorities. All this fits rather neatly with the EU's own Anti-Money Laundering Directive,[33] which also imposes a number of requirements on tracking beneficial ownership and customer due diligence. Importantly, it also fits with certain 'territorial extension' elements of that Directive. Its Annex II lists factors of 'potentially lower risk' which can justify less intensive customer due diligence obligations. Some of those are linked to the country of registration, establishment or residence of the customer. For third countries, this means having an effective anti-money laundering system, or requirements to combat money laundering 'consistent with the revised FATF Recommendations'. Hence, while the two instruments are not expressly linked, it is clear that the trade agreement reinforces the 'territorial extension' set out in the Directive, and vice versa.

[31] TH Tai, K Shih-Ming, and H Wan-Chun, 'International Soft Laws against IUU Fishing for Sustainable Marine Resources: Adoption of the Voluntary Guidelines for Flag State Performance and Challenges for Taiwan' (2020) 12 *Sustainability* 15, 6013.

[32] Provisions on Anti-corruption in the context of the Modernisation of the EU-Mexico Association Agreement, available at www.gob.mx/cms/uploads/attachment/file/416576/33._Anticorrupci_n.pdf.

[33] Directive (EU) 2015/849 of the European Parliament and of the Council of 20 May 2015 on the prevention of the use of the financial system for the purposes of money laundering or terrorist financing, amending Regulation (EU) No 648/2012 of the European Parliament and of the Council, and repealing Directive 2005/60/EC of the European Parliament and of the Council and Commission Directive 2006/70/EC, as amended [2015] OJ L141/73.

B. EU Domestic Trade Instruments

A less explored question is to what extent EU's own trade law instruments are used for the purpose of territorial extension. This does not refer simply to trade as leverage for regulatory ends. As already discussed, there are many examples of EU legislation using market access as leverage to achieve regulatory ends abroad. In that sense, EU 'territorial extension' instruments are very often 'trade' instruments. Some examples are the Seals Regulation, the use of the Emissions Trading System in aviation, or EU regulations on timber.[34] What I would like to look at is narrower: EU legislation that is more generally centred on trade issues, often adopted directly on the basis of Article 207 Treaty on the Functioning of the European Union (common commercial policy). This goes beyond regulating the marketing (and thus importation) of specific products and services, which is part and parcel of regulating the EU's internal market. And indeed, just as the EU's trade agreements have increasingly expanded to 'trade and' issues like sustainability, so has the EU's trade acquis. I give two examples here.

i. The EU's Generalised System of Preferences (GSP)

The EU's 'GSP' and 'GSP+' rules are a well-known example of conditionality in EU trade policy. Thus, they are to some extent a parallel with the already discussed rules in the EU–Ukraine Association Agreement: closer ties and improved market access are the reward for alignment of domestic rules with EU requirements.

The GSP is based on provisions of the WTO Agreement (Enabling Clause), which elaborate on an exemption from most-favoured-nation disciplines which allows WTO Members to provide preferential access to their markets for the trade of developing and least-developed countries. The Enabling Clause itself[35] does not provide for any sort of conditionality. It does not require beneficiaries to jump through any hoops. It does, however, allow for that possibility and includes disciplines against abuse: its paragraph 6 provides that

> developed countries shall exercise the utmost restraint in seeking any concessions or contributions for commitments made by them to reduce or remove tariffs and other barriers to the trade of such countries, and the least-developed countries shall not be expected to make concessions or contributions that are inconsistent with the recognition of their particular situation and problems.

The EU's own rules do provide for certain requirements, depending on the degree of market access afforded. Most interesting for our purposes is the so-called GSP+ (or the 'special incentive arrangement'), under which beneficiaries obtain additional market access in exchange for ratifying and, to put it simply, generally upholding and

[34] C Ryngaert and M Koekkoek, 'Extraterritorial Regulation of Natural Resources: A Functional Approach' and D Geraets and B Natens, 'Governing through Trade in Compliance with WTO Law: A Case Study of the European Union Timber Regulation' both in Wouters et al (n 25).

[35] Decision of 28 November 1979 (L/4903), available at www.wto.org/english/docs_e/legal_e/enabling1979_e.htm.

complying with, a number of international conventions on human rights, labour rights, environmental sustainability, trade in narcotics and corruption. In addition, all of the preferential arrangements (including GSP+) may be withdrawn temporarily on a number of grounds, such as failure to comply with anti-money laundering conventions, or 'unfair' trading practices (such as subsidies declared to be WTO-inconsistent).

Previous work has assessed the EU's use of its common commercial policy, through the GSP, to unilaterally pursue good governance and sustainability in third countries. Spotty enforcement, not just as an effectiveness concern but also possibly rising to the level of a difference in treatment between beneficiaries, has been a target of criticism.[36] Even authors that find examples of positive effects in target countries conclude that this success is far from universal.[37] The GSP has been amended several times, notably in order to remove a WTO consistency found in the WTO dispute *EC – Tariff Preferences*, due to the discriminatory treatment of certain beneficiaries. There is an ongoing discussion on further reforms, potentially by strengthening conditionality.[38]

It is beyond the scope of this chapter to enter into the discussion of how well the GSP and GSP+ schemes are functioning. What is clear, however, is that this is an example of an EU trade instrument that is expressly used for purposes of 'territorial extension'.

ii. Regulation on Foreign Subsidies

The recently adopted Regulation on Foreign Subsidies[39] tackles distortive subsidies granted by third countries to undertakings active in the EU internal market. In practice, it may cover a subsidy originally granted in a third country, the benefit from which can be said to flow to an undertaking established in the EU (eg EU subsidiaries) or even established elsewhere but merely 'active' in the EU, ie engaging in an economic activity in the internal market.

This instrument can create a trade-law mediated external impact of EU regulatory law. The premise is a relatively broad definition of a subsidy, similar to that in WTO law, which may cover different types of regulatory interventions in third countries that provide a benefit to a third country assuming (industry or sector-level) specificity: for example, the foregoing of revenue otherwise due or the provision of goods or services by public actors other than central government, or by private actors whose conduct can be attributed to the third country. Thus, what is at stake are not only

[36] L Beke and N Hachez, 'The EU GSP: A Preference for Human Rights and Good Governance? The Case of Myanmar' in Wouters et al (n 25) s 2.2.

[37] J Yap, 'One Step Forward: The European Union Generalised System of Preferences and Labour Rights in the Garment Industry in Bangladesh' in Wouters et al (n 25).

[38] European Commission, Inception Impact Assessment, 'Towards the Future Generalised Scheme of Preferences Regulation Granting Trade Advantages to Developing Countries', available at https://ec.europa.eu/info/law/better-regulation/have-your-say/initiatives/2136-Trade-preferential-tariff-scheme-between-the-EU-and-developing-countries-update-_en.

[39] Regulation (EU) 2022/2560 of the European Parliament and of the Council of 14 December 2022 on foreign subsidies distorting the internal market [2022] OJ L330/1.

'classic' subsidies such as grants or below-market financing, but also the provision of state resources in various forms. In markets with a high degree of state intervention, the conduct of state-owned enterprises or undertakings to which public functions have been delegated (including, possibly, forms of co-regulation) may be caught.

This doesn't directly impose or even push for any specific mode of regulation, much less EU-like regulation. But it may push towards a different method of organisation of production, or a lesser level of state involvement, that resembles more closely the EU model. Moreover, the EU may find itself in the position of scrutinising or disciplining the conduct of actors straddling the public-private divide, such as co-regulators. It could even be said that the EU engages in 'territorial extension' of sorts of its internal state aid regime.[40]

In that sense, it is interesting to note that the proposal sets out a number of rather intrusive remedies that is, in some respects, more reminiscent of antitrust than state aid. For example, it would authorise the Commission to seek commitments, or to impose 'redressive measures', consisting in rather specific conduct such as engaging in FRAND (fair, reasonable and non-discriminatory) licensing, publishing research and development results, divesting, or offering access to certain infrastructure. While not directly imposing its rules, those remedies would clearly seek to align the conduct of the undertaking to what would be expected of an EU market actor, subject to EU rules in areas like competition law.

V. PRIVATE LAW AND THE EXTERNAL LEVERAGE OF TRADE LAW

To what extent can the mechanism just described be relevant to private law? Arguably, there are two possible mechanisms. First, the EU rules being extended may very well be rules of private law. The likelihood of this being the case depends, of course, on how broad our understanding of 'private law' is – which is, of course, one of the core themes of the entire European Regulatory Private Law project. For obvious reasons, it is not very likely that classic rules of private law such as contract, tort, or property rules would be relevant here. Looking somewhat more broadly, however, already the examples listed above suggest that certain areas of 'regulatory private law' are implicated. For example, certain international trade agreements, like EU–Ukraine, require the implementation by third countries of EU financial regulations. A similar example are the rules on customer due diligence in the fight against money laundering, contained in agreements such as EU–Mexico as well as in internal EU legislation engaging in territorial extension.

A different mechanism is private not in the sense of the substance of the rules being extended, but in the sense of the actors involved. Indeed, the use of a territorial extension technique is, essentially, premised on the regulator's inability to enforce its rules directly. It thus imposes its requirements indirectly on actors that are not within easy reach; typically, these would be either third countries or private actors located

[40] See recitals 1–5 of the Proposal; for example: 'In particular, the new tool complements Union State aid rules which deal with distortions in the internal market caused by Member State subsidies.'

in third countries, or private actors within the regulating jurisdiction that engage, for example, in business relationships abroad. Thus, private action may be leveraged, and private actors may become gatekeepers, or proxy regulators. Customer due diligence by financial institutions also serves to illustrate this tendency. A different example is the reliance on (private) professional bodies in the negotiation of mutual recognition agreements. From a more speculative point of view, one could also see the Regulation on Foreign Subsidies as a way of indirectly re-organising business activities of firms abroad, including market actors sufficiently linked to the state which are described as 'public bodies' and hence potential *providers*, not just recipients of subsidies, to align with EU practices.

VI. CONCLUSION

There is no empirical measure of how often the EU enacts rules in pursuit of 'territorial extension' to either regulate processes in third countries or influence third countries' regulation, in the area of trade or otherwise. Nevertheless, anecdotally it seems quite clear that this is happening more often than ever before, and with more far-reaching effects. It also seems to be more prevalent in services regulation, not just in the area of goods.

It is too early to tell what to make of this move in normative terms. Nevertheless, several conclusions can be drawn.

First, conflicts with international trade law may be more likely in the future, including in the areas of services. While the debate on such 'extraterritorial' regulation is rather long-standing, there is little recent jurisprudence, especially with respect to services. It is therefore still relatively unclear how such measures should be designed to avoid violating international trade law disciplines. It is clear that there is no *a priori* prohibition, but the weaker the links with the regulating jurisdiction, the more likely it is that these measures will fall foul of the requirements of Article XX of the GATT (or equivalent GATS provisions, for services measures). It may be especially difficult to ensure even-handed treatment of products or processes in various third countries.

Second, it is unlikely that the trend will be reversed. There is, on the one hand, a strong push to include rules going beyond pure trade-liberalising obligations in trade agreements. Rules on sustainability, mutual recognition and regulatory cooperation, unlike pure 'negative integration' provisions, must by definition be underpinned by detailed normative content. Those benchmarks can refer to other instruments of international law (like ILO conventions, in the area of sustainability). But they are also increasingly to be found in the EU's own legislation, some of which is itself engaging in 'territorial extension' by conditioning the treatment of products, services and undertakings of third countries on compliance with certain regulatory requirements. On the other hand, more extensive legislation in areas where international spill-overs and externalities are more likely, such as environmental issues or finance, makes it more likely that the EU legislator will seek to address third country undertakings and processes.

Third, a careful balance will need to be struck between effectively pursuing regulatory objectives and avoiding protectionism. Especially, the EU legislator will need to avoid the trap of assuming that EU undertakings, services and products are sufficiently regulated so as not to give rise to concerns; international trade law requires an even-handed approach between different third countries as well as between domestic and foreign actors. In this regard, international standards – be they public or private ones – may be particularly important as a way of grounding such measures on objective considerations.

12

What Role for the EU in (Re-)Shaping Global Tax Ordering?

KATERINA PANTAZATOU*

I. INTRODUCTION: THE 'PRIVATE LAW' VS 'PUBLIC LAW' DEBATE IN TAX LAW

ONE MAY WONDER how a chapter on taxation fits within the scope of a volume on 'European Transnational Private Law'. Indeed, as a rule, taxation for most legal cultures falls within the public law realm.[1] However, even in these cultures, the vicinity of tax law to private law cannot be contested. This vicinity can take a number of expressions, such as the private law consequences of transactions that are critical for tax law[2] and, vice-versa, the impact of taxation on corporate and business decisions (locational, investment, profit shifting).[3] The existence of fiscal barriers may dissuade a corporation from (re-)locating to or investing in another state, while, on the contrary, the existence of tax incentives may prompt a corporation to pursue investing in a state through specific vehicles.

Tax law was not always considered (and it is still not universally accepted) as belonging in the public law realm. In England, in the sixteenth century, taxes were not considered as a representation of state power over individuals, but instead were perceived as a private gift from the taxpayer to Parliament, and as such were considered to be a private transaction.[4]

Today, however, most legal cultures place tax law in the scope of public law, as it either represents the relationship between the state and taxpayers,[5] and/or because it

* Associate Professor in Tax Law, University of Luxembourg. Many thanks to Arthur Bianco for his valuable research assistance. All errors remain my own.

[1] RE Barnett, 'Foreword: Four Senses of the Public Law-Private Law Distinction' (1986) 9 *Harvard Journal of Law & Public Policy* 271.

[2] V Thuronyi, K Brooks and B Kolosz, *Comparative Tax Law* (Wolters Kluwer, 2016) 300.

[3] MP Devereux and R Griffith, 'Evaluating Tax Policy for Location Decisions' (2003) *International Tax and Public Finance* 10, 107–26; J Lintner, 'Effect of Corporate Taxation on Real Investment' (1954) 44 *The American Economic Review* 2 520–34.

[4] MJ Horwitz, 'History of the Public/Private Distinction' (1981–82) 130 *University of Pennsylvania Law Review* 6, 1423–24.

[5] A Harel, 'Public and Private Law' in M Dubber and T Hörnle (eds), *Oxford Handbook of Criminal Law* (Oxford, Oxford University Press, 2016) 1–3 and S Dorigo, 'The Rule of Law and Tax Law: The Case of the Abuse of Law' (2020) 12 *Italian Journal of Public Law* 2, 184.

(primarily) aims at ensuring the funding of government activities and as such is paramount to the functioning of the state, and/or because it represents the state's power over persons (natural and legal).[6]

Other legal cultures, however, together with elements of legal scholarship, have underlined the autonomous (or quasi-autonomous) character of tax law, because of its own sets of rules in comparison to a more unified public law.[7] At the same time, in stressing the proximity of tax law to private law, they note that tax law regulates relationships among economic actors, private or public,[8] and that private law protects not only the interests of private actors but often the public good itself.[9]

Despite the absence of universal categorisation, the relationship between tax law and private law cannot be overstated. Tax law most often relies, as a basis for taxation, on a taxpayer's private law transactions. In most jurisdictions, the tax law classification of a transaction follows its private law classification.[10] In some jurisdictions, such as Canada, priority is given to private parties' preference to follow what they consider to be the most tax-advantageous solution in their transactions.[11] This, in turn, has impacted on how anti-tax avoidance rules have been implemented in those states, and have resulted in Canadian judges being more hesitant to requalify a private law classification for tax purposes.[12]

The rule, however, remains that, in certain situations, tax law would intentionally deviate from the private law classification of certain transactions, by purposely putting it aside in favour of its own interpretation of the taxable event. This happens very often in the context of the application of anti-abuse rules linked to the principle of 'substance-over-form' or of 'economic reality' where tax enforcement requires the private law classification to be disregarded and to be replaced by what tax law considers to be the 'real' transaction. Other tax laws may simply disregard private-law choices made by the taxpayer. This often happens in anti-tax avoidance rules, of which thin capitalisation rules are a representative example: for the purpose of combating tax avoidance, states have set up such a rule that allows the administration to disregard a taxpayer's choice of financing itself through debt by not granting them the usual interest deduction available.[13]

[6] See, eg, LH Levison, 'Public/Private Law Distinction in the Courts' (1989) 57 *George Washington Law Review* 6, 1593, where the author claims that public law distinguishes itself via state access to prerogatives unavailable to private individuals, eg taxation.

[7] A Maniatis, 'Tax Evasion' (2018) *e-Journal of Science & Technology* 2–4, see also F Reimer, 'Public Law and Economy, Annual Report 2012 – Germany' (2012) *IUS Publicum Network Review* 3; M Lemonnier, 'Interpretation of the Tax Law in France. Selected Problems' (2017) 3 *Financial Law Review* 5.

[8] JS Wilkie and PW Hogg, 'Tax Law Within the Larger Legal System' (2015) 52 *Osgoode Hall Law Journal* 2, 465.

[9] M Rosenfeld, 'Rethinking the Boundaries between Public Law and Private Law for the Twenty First Century: An Introduction' (2013) 11 *International Journal of Constitutional Law* 1, 126.

[10] W Barker, 'The Disconnect between Tax Concepts and the World of Fact: State Law as the Gatekeeper' (*Penn State Dickinson Law*, 2018) 133: '(…) the private law characterization is the tax law characterization of the facts.'

[11] P Cornut St-Pierre, 'L'évitement fiscal vu sous l'angle du droit civil: le privé est politique!' in Y Emerich and L Saint-Pierre Harvey (eds), *Le Public en droit privé* (Yvon Blais, 2019) 167–74.

[12] ibid.

[13] FH Fuller, 'Business Purpose, Sham Transactions and the Relation of Private Law to the Law of Taxation' (1962–63) 37 *Tulane Law Review* 3.

Besides the detachment of tax law from private law in certain cases, such as the abuse example referred to already, tax law directly or indirectly influences the choices that taxpayers (private parties) make.[14] In this sense, tax effects may supersede private law considerations in informing the choices individuals make, a situation referred to as a 'knock-on effect' of tax law on private law.[15] The relationship between tax law and private law may also be illustrated in the context of corporate governance, whereby directors are obliged, under the duty of care, to maximise shareholders' profits, possibly by adopting tax strategies with that in mind. This 'obligation' is, however, subsequently curtailed by the need for directors (and the corporation as a whole) to comply with all laws on anti-tax avoidance, reporting and 'corporate social responsibility'. Below it will be explained how EU tax law and international tax law (if it exists) have shaped this relationship between private law and tax law which in its broadest form can entail absolute freedom for private parties to use tax law in their best interest, or in its strictest form an insurmountable obstacle for private parties to structure their legal relationships at will.

II. 'GLOBAL TAX GOVERNANCE', THE EU AND OTHER ACTORS

It is arguable whether, in the realm of taxation, one can speak of 'world' or 'global markets'. The same applies to terms like 'global tax governance' or the 'international tax regime'.[16] Being at the core of state sovereignty, taxation is usually one of the last policy areas to succumb to supranational co-ordination efforts. Accordingly, states, even EU Member States, are eager to maintain their taxing rights and tax policy preferences, which are delineated around their stance towards tax competition. Accordingly, tax competition-friendly states are concentrated on facilitating and attracting taxpayers (corporations, small and medium-sized enterprises (SMEs), multinational enterprises (MNEs) and/or individuals) and capital whereas the rest are usually designated as 'high tax jurisdictions'. Next to the 'low tax jurisdictions', another category may be identified, that of states which employ harmful tax practices that are traditionally seen as tax havens.[17]

While states' stance towards tax competition is very much used in their classification in different categories, there is no agreement on how to define tax competition. Some scholars put the emphasis on the mobility of taxpayers that leads governments to reduce taxation to attract them,[18] whereas others, such as Steichen, focus on the

[14] Several works, especially in the field of economics, can be cited here. See, eg, JK Mackie-Mason, 'Do Taxes Affect Corporate Financing Decisions?' (1990) 45 *The Journal of Finance* 5, 1471–93.

[15] J Bungaard, 'On Tax Law and Private Law Relations' (*Stockholm Institute for Scandinavian Law*, 2009), available at https://scandinavianlaw.se/pdf/44-4.pdf.

[16] Note that whether an 'international tax regime' exists at all is debatable in tax scholarship. See R Avi-Yonah, 'Tax Competition, Tax Arbitrage and the International Tax Regime' (2007) *Bulletin for International Taxation* 130–38 and D Rosenbloom, 'International Tax Arbitrage and the "International Tax System"' (2000) *Tax Law Review* 137–66.

[17] The 1998 OECD Report on Harmful Tax Competition uses the following phrasing '[…]tax havens and harmful preferential tax regimes, collectively referred to as *harmful tax practices*', at 8.

[18] I Roxan, 'United Kingdom' in W Schön (ed), *Tax Competition in Europe* (IBFD, 2003) 485.

interdependence of the fiscal decisions of one country on another.[19] By implication, defining 'good' and 'harmful' tax competition – a potential benchmark in the typology of states – becomes even more problematic. Faulhaber suggests that tax competition could be classified by reference to the tools used by countries to compete with each other (for example, statutory tax rate, effective tax rate, secrecy) or by reference to the things they compete over (such as competition for investment, for tax revenue, for establishment of corporations).[20] Thus, a third classification of states in the international arena could be premised on their stance vis-à-vis harmful tax competition (however this is defined).

At the core of this classification, the role of the *taxpayer* vis-à-vis the *state* is essential. This relationship between states and taxpayers is often antithetical in that usually both parties pursue maximisation of their revenues, either by raising and collecting taxes due (states) or by structuring their businesses in such a way as to minimise their tax burden (taxpayers). The one goal usually only works at the expense of the other. In some instances, however, states are willing to disregard the fiscal function of taxation, that is, the revenue the taxes will bring in, in exchange for all indirect revenue that will be produced through an MNE's establishment or investment in a given state, as several examples of MNEs paying very little tax in their state of residence show.[21]

One could, further, attempt a categorisation on the basis of the most influential states in setting out 'international tax policy', assuming one exists.[22] There is no doubt that in this classification the USA emerges as the most influential player from the emergence of 'international tax governance'[23] over the years via several initiatives, revisions and policy choices.[24] The discussion below aims to show how the EU has evolved from a simple observer and follower of different initiatives at global level to a regulatory influencer in its own right.

A. International Level: The OECD and Double Tax Conventions

Increasing globalisation, trade liberalisation, digitalisation and ample techniques offered for tax avoidance have made 'domestic only' situations rather rare for the taxpayer. Given that states are able to levy taxes on their residents (residence taxation)

[19] A Steichen, 'Tax Competition in Europe or the Taming of the Leviathan' in Schön (n 18) 45.

[20] L Faulhaber, 'The Trouble with Tax Competition: From Practice to Theory' (2018) 71 *Tax Law Review* 311.

[21] For a discussion on this, see C Hadjipanayi, 'Is Aggressive Tax Planning Socially Irresponsible?' (2015) 10 *Intertax* 544.

[22] See (n 16).

[23] See, eg, R Eccleston, *The Dynamics of Global Economic Governance. The Financial Crisis, the OECD and the Politics of International Tax Cooperation* (Cheltenham, Edward Elgar Publishing, 2012) 134, according to whom 'since the 1960s the broad contours of international tax cooperation have been defined by changing US policy references'.

[24] See indicatively, C Radaelli, 'Game Theory and Institutional Entrepreneurship: Transfer Pricing and the Search for Coordination International Tax Policy' (1998) 26 *Policy Studies Journal* 4, 603–19; J Sharman, *Havens in a Storm. The Struggle for Global Tax Regulation* (Ithaca, Cornell University Press, 2006).

or on income that arises in their territory (source taxation), it becomes clear that a taxpayer that engages in cross-border activity may be subject to double taxation (juridical double taxation) or their income may be taxed twice (economic double taxation). To eliminate this fiscal barrier and to facilitate cross-border activity and investment, Double Tax Conventions (DTCs) are concluded between different states and are implemented into domestic laws in accordance with the states' constitutional traditions. DTCs constitute the core of international taxation and together with domestic tax laws have shaped what has traditionally been referred to as 'the international tax regime' that forms a significant part of international law (both treaty-based and customary).[25]

DTCs are usually based on different Model (Tax) Conventions (MC), the most notable being the OECD MC for developed countries and the UN MC for developing countries. Some countries, like the United States of America (USA), draft their DTCs on the basis of their own MC.

Currently, more than 3,000 DTCs exist worldwide and their main purpose is to provide relief from double taxation between two states and to prevent tax evasion.

The importance of those treaties is tremendous at a global level, because the main function of these DTCs is to allocate taxing rights between the competing states. For instance, if a dividend arises in state A and is paid to a shareholder in state B, it is the DTC between the two states that will decide which of the two states maintains its taxing right and if/which one has to give it up. Most of these treaties are negotiated on the basis of the OECD MC, making the OECD the protagonist of the international tax regime. Both the OECD MC and its Commentary are revised and amended on a more or less regular basis. These updates often include answers to definitional or interpretative matters or even consideration of tax issues that arose in the meantime due, for instance, to technological advances. Because of the long and burdensome process of negotiating and adopting the treaties, some states apply a dynamic interpretation to their treaties following these amendments, thus escaping the need to go through this process frequently.

Consequently, the significance of the OECD in developing international tax norms cannot be overstated, in the same way that the USA's political influence cannot be overlooked in this development.[26] As the OECD Secretary General remarked, 'the success of the OECD MC was based on the capacity to adapt international tax rules to the changing business environment, the enhanced participation of the business community and the progressive involvement of nonmember countries'.[27]

The Committee on Fiscal Affairs (CFA), which is the OECD's arm responsible for tax matters, is composed of country representatives, usually high-level officials

[25] See (n 16).

[26] See Radaelli (n 24), who describes how changing US preferences led to revisions of transfer pricing guidelines in the OECD and Sharman (n 24), who shows how withdrawal of US support contributed to the 1998 OECD Harmful tax competition project. Similar, see L Hakelberg, *The Hypocritical Hegemon – How the United States Shapes Global Rules against Tax Evasion and Avoidance* (Cornell University Press, 2020) who argues that the USA, through imposition of the FATCA, has inadvertently been the motor behind BEPS.

[27] A Gurria, OECD Secretary-General, Remarks at Conference on the 50th Anniversary of the OECD Model Tax Convention (8 September 2008).

in national treasuries and tax administrations. Decisions are made by consensus and, therefore, they may often be very general. The complexity of the relationship between the EU and the OECD can be showcased in the works of OECD committees, including the CFA, where the performance of individual states and the EU is assessed by their/its peers. While the relationship between the EU and the OECD started off on a competitive basis, the slow but steady integration of the European Commission in the OECD and the better understanding of each other's role led to a more co-operative spirit.[28] Despite this progress, the Commission's quasi-membership in the OECD[29] cuts both ways, in that it can urge the development of policies that would be difficult to promote successfully within the differing political circumstances of the EU but it can also be reviewed by the EU members of the OECD for possible failures.[30]

Besides work done on the tax treaty level, the OECD issues recommendations that express the political will of the member countries to follow the recommendations in their domestic policy and publishes reports that provide legal analysis on certain issues. One such example was the publication of the report on 'Harmful Tax Competition: An Emerging Global Issue', which created an international sensation by seeking to address two fundamental problems in international taxation: tax havens and harmful preferential tax regimes.[31] The impact of the Report has been controversial in tax scholarship, partly because it was left to the participant states to decide whether they wished to apply any defensive measures (whether in a co-ordinated manner or not) against these harmful tax practices.[32] This freedom in applying sanctions may have deprived the Report of its effectiveness, although the Report was positively perceived, from a counterfactual perspective, for preventing taxpayers from shifting their profits offshore.[33]

While over 40 jurisdictions were identified as meeting the OECD tax haven criteria in June 2000, in 2002 the list comprised only seven states and in May 2009, the OECD Committee on Fiscal Affairs removed all three remaining jurisdictions (Andorra, the Principality of Liechtenstein and the Principality of Monaco) in light of their commitments to implement OECD standards of transparency and effective exchange of information and the timetable they set for implementation.[34]

[28] P Carroll and A Kellow, 'The OECD' in KE Jørgensen and KV Laatikainen (eds), *Routledge Handbook on the European Union and its Institutions* (Routledge, 2013) 248.

[29] Under the Supplementary Protocol to the Convention on the Organisation for Economic Co-operation and Development (14 December 1960), the European Commission 'shall take part in the work of that Organisation'. Despite the Commission's pleas to become a full member of the OECD, the Commission was eventually allowed full access to the OECD's deliberations, enabling it to participate and speak at any OECD meetings without being invited, with the sole exception of meetings dealing with the internal organisation of the OECD, including the key Budget Committee.

[30] Carroll and Kellow (n 28) 249.

[31] OECD, 'Harmful Tax Competition, An Emerging Global Issue' (1998), available at www.oecd.org/ctp/harmful/1904176.pdf.

[32] OECD, 'Harmful Tax Practices: The 2004 Progress Report' (OECD, 2004).

[33] R Avi-Yonah, 'The OECD Harmful Tax Competition Report: A Retrospective after a Decade' (2009) 34 *Brooklyn Journal of International Law* 783, 789–91.

[34] For the process of removing all states from the list of uncooperative jurisdictions, see www.oecd.org/countries/andorra/list-of-unco-operative-tax-havens.htm.

Several other actions and reports followed but the breakthrough came in 2013 with discussion of the Base Erosion and Profit Shifting (BEPS) project.[35] Throughout its actions it is worth noting that the OECD has been open and inclusive in its work by bringing together different voices to discussions on international tax issues, including business representatives.[36] This inclusion, however, has come at the cost of establishment of over-general principles and the concession of opt-outs and reservations in order for agreement to be reached.[37] Thus, OECD works usually provide the basic structure for technical rules on which all agree, leaving other issues for further, usually bilateral, negotiation.[38]

B. The EU Level: Actors and Instruments

The need to improve market integration via taxation was contemplated as long ago as the 1960s, when the Commission called for harmonisation of corporate tax systems, bases and rates as an antidote to tax competition.[39] The 'Neumark report' already highlighted the – still present – challenge of reconciling

> fiscal or financial disparities hindering the free play of competition between the Member States on the one hand, and the expediency of not interfering in the policy of the Member States anxious to maintain national peculiarities arising from natural conditions and/or historical evolution on the other hand.[40]

For most of its existence, the EU had been rather inward-looking with regard to tax governance. This was partly because of the focus it had placed on its internal affairs, notably (economic) integration and with that purpose in view, increasingly ambitious plans for harmonisation in the corporate tax sector.[41] The Union had a limited toolbox to limit or eliminate intra-EU tax obstacles, notably EU primary law – primarily consisting of general principles of EU law, the fundamental freedoms and state aid provisions as well as the possibility of adopting EU secondary law – but this toolbox was restrained by the unanimity requirement of Article 115 Treaty of the Functioning of the European Union (TFEU). Indeed, lack of further integration has been attributed to the impossibility of reaching consensus at the Council due to the competing interests and traditions of the different Member States.[42]

[35] See below, section III.B.i.

[36] HJ Ault, 'Reflections on the Role of the OECD in Developing International Tax Norms' (2009) 34 *Brooklyn Journal of International Law* 757, 779.

[37] Note that countries may indicate reservations or observations to the provisions of the OECD MC.

[38] Ault (n 36) 780.

[39] Commission of the European Communities (1967) 'Program for the harmonization of direct taxes: communication by the Commission'. Bulletin of the EC, Supplement 8, 6–22.

[40] Report of the Fiscal and Financial Committee (Neumark Report) 1962.

[41] By the mid-1990s, only two directives in corporate taxation had been adopted, namely Council Directive 90/435/EEC of 23 July 1990 on the common system of taxation applicable in the case of parent companies and subsidiaries of different Member States [1990] OJ L225/6–9 and Council Directive 90/434/EEC 1990 on the common system of taxation applicable to mergers, divisions, transfers of assets and exchanges of shares concerning companies of different Member States [1990] L225/1–5.

[42] Several Member States including France and Germany traditionally favoured higher income tax rates and more tax transparency, whereas Member States such as Ireland, Luxembourg and the Netherlands

The Member States' bilateral relationships or their relationships with third states were regulated – in addition to the free movement of capital – by bilateral DTCs. Thus, the limited secondary legislation adopted by the mid-2000s had very little to do with the EU's (and its constituent Member States') relationships with third states, for which DTCs and, by implication, OECD tax norms and trends played a much more important role.

In light of the deeply disappointing results in this policy area, a new strategy was launched in the early 1990s based on efficiency and tax neutrality.[43] European tax policy would no longer target over-ambitious projects for corporate tax harmonisation but would from that time onwards be curbed to eliminate distortionary domestic taxes, to be assessed on a case-by-case basis, in order to provide a level playing field. Such an *ad hoc* 'tax neutrality' approach, aiming at selective elimination of domestic tax obstacles, would have resulted in gains for companies and costs to be borne by states. Consequently, this 'top-down' imposition of tax neutrality would favour the taxpayer at the expense of the participating states.[44]

As the existing secondary law removed very few and specific obstacles in the internal market – notably double taxation arising in highly specific contexts – the 'duty' of removing those barriers was shifted to the Court of Justice of the European Union (CJEU). Thus, the CJEU became the motor of integration using mainly non-discrimination and market access principles and the fundamental freedoms. For a long while, the CJEU was the principal integration catalyst in that it consistently found most national measures that could hinder fundamental freedoms incompatible with EU law.[45] This trend lasted until the mid-2000s. The consequence was that Member States felt that they were losing their tax sovereignty to a non-EU competence but also that they felt much more limited by comparison to third states, to which they often had to give up their taxing rights due to free movement of capital.

Alongside the CJEU, the Code of Conduct for business taxation[46] – an expression of the 'open method of coordination' approach[47] – was adopted as part of

are often depicted as 'de facto' tax havens within the European Union due to the many tax advantages they offer to taxpayers, including very low or 'zero' tax rates, exemptions from taxation and other benefits, see, eg, European Parliament, 'Tax Crimes: Special Committee Calls for a European Financial Police Force' (Press Release, 27 February 2019), noting that '[s]even EU countries (Belgium, Cyprus, Hungary, Ireland, Luxembourg, Malta and The Netherlands) display traits of a tax haven and facilitate aggressive tax planning'.

[43] European Commission, 'Guidelines on Company Taxation' (20 April 1990).

[44] Despite 'moderation' of the approximation goals by the Commission, achieving tax neutrality in a heterogeneous bundle of tax systems would require a certain degree of approximation of different tax laws, as distortions and obstacles, eg, double taxation and withholding taxes, could be caused by the mere interaction of two different tax systems.

[45] For a breakdown of the case law in direct taxation and the Court's political and economic considerations, see K Pantazatou, 'Economic and Political Considerations of the Court's Case Law Post Crisis: Another Example from Tax Law and the Internal Market' (2013) 9 *Croatian Yearbook of European Law and Policy* 77–118.

[46] European Union (1998) 'Council Conclusions of the ECOFIN Council Meeting on 1 December 1997 Concerning Taxation' [1998] OJ C2/1–6.

[47] CM Radaelli, 'The Code of Conduct Against Harmful Tax Competition: Open Method of Coordination in Disguise?' (2003) 81/3 *Public Administration* 513–31.

the Commission's 'Package to tackle harmful tax competition in the EU'.[48] The Code emerged as a political necessity to reconcile conflicting interests among the participant states and at the same time – similar to the OECD Report – to tackle harmful tax competition *at EU level* in a co-ordinated fashion. The Code targets 'potentially harmful' tax measures on business – regulations and administrative practices as well as provisions – which are 'unfairly' competitive by virtue of 'a significant effect on the location of business activity'.[49] Since the Code is not legally binding, the Member States adopting it undertook a political pledge to abolish tax incentives which were not in line with good fiscal behaviour (rollback clause) and to refrain from introducing new ones (standstill clause).

III. THE 'GLOBAL CHANGE'

A. The Financial Crisis as a Catalyst Towards a Big Shift

In the first decade of the twenty-first century, the EU was still occupied with the removal of tax obstacles in the internal market. Despite the subtle change in CJEU case law around 2005,[50] corporations were still the main beneficiaries of the way the CJEU interpreted the fundamental freedoms and the lack of restrictive secondary EU law.[51] Furthermore, at the time, bank and tax secrecy were still a matter for Member States to decide and the traditional 'culprits' of aggressive tax practices in the EU could maintain these practices by reason of a lack of any binding legal measures on exchange of information and anti-tax avoidance practices. Thus, it was *the constituent Member States of the EU*, rather than the EU itself, that played a role in the global markets either because they appeared as attractive destinations for establishment and investment (for example, Ireland and Luxembourg) and/or because they fiercely opposed these policies and pushed for a change within the institutional setup of the EU (for instance, Germany and France). Bilateral relationships with the outer world were regulated on the basis of DTCs that, at least for EU Member States, followed the OECD MC. In contrast, relationships with third countries qualifying as tax havens were not yet positively viewed, nor entirely eliminated either.

The *financial crisis* that broke out in 2008 functioned as a catalyst in the rise of the G20 as a central international actor in tax policymaking and in the subsequent and related development of an EU direct tax law framework. The emergence of the G20 as a new and fertile model for tax policymaking was celebrated for its wider inclusion of states, yet the USA and Europe continued to dominate a

[48] European Commission, Communication: 'A Package to Tackle Harmful Tax Competition' (5 November 1997) COM (1997)564 final.

[49] ibid, Annex 1, C. The Code's coverage of 'business taxes' appears to be quite broad, although manifestly excluding indirect taxes and direct taxes on individuals.

[50] S Kingston, 'A light in the Darkness: Recent Developments in the ECJ's Tax Jurisprudence' (2007) 44 *CMLR*; Pantazatou (n 45).

[51] Existing directives at the time were rather facilitative for corporations, aiming at removing tax obstacles.

virtually impervious institutional architecture of tax policymaking in the form of the OECD.[52]

The need for more revenue for states hard-hit by the financial crisis, together with a series of tax and financial scandals,[53] shifted the focus at a *global level* to curbing tax avoidance practices in order to ensure enough revenue, but also to appease public opinion. Awareness of the huge inequalities that were exposed through leaked information that arose due to tax avoidance and tax evasion practices by wealthy individuals and MNEs, created a feeling of injustice among citizens, SMEs and governments that did not pursue these practices. Indicatively, the European Commission reported in 2012 that every year around one trillion euros were lost to tax evasion and tax avoidance in the EU.[54] Counteracting this feeling of injustice created by tax avoidance practices thus became a fundamental priority not only at EU level but at *a global level* as well. Thus, the focus shifted to combating tax avoidance, in order to ensure that profits were taxed where they should be, that is, either where economic activity took place or where value was created but not in low-tax or no-tax jurisdictions. To achieve this, abolishing bank secrecy and solidifying and enhancing exchange of taxpayers' information became a priority.

With this purpose in mind, the OECD developed the Common Reporting Standard (CRS) in 2014, in response to the G20. In line with the CRS, financial institutions have to regularly report all capital income held by non-resident individuals and entities, as well as their account balances and automatically exchange that information with other jurisdictions on an annual basis, effectively abolishing bank secrecy. The general consensus is that it was the USA, as a major economic player, which deserves credit for this major regulatory breakthrough.[55] It did so in 2009 by adopting the Foreign Account Tax Compliance Act (FATCA) that obliged foreign financial institutions to automatically report to the Internal Revenue Service (IRS) on the income of non-resident US customers. The penalty for failing to do so would be a 30 per cent withholding tax on the payments the institution receives from US sources. By 2014, the USA had concluded bilateral FATCA agreements with more than 100 jurisdictions, including traditionally 'non-cooperative' jurisdictions.[56] Despite this framework, which could be seen as the precursor to the CRS, it has

[52] A Christians, 'Taxation in a Time of Crisis: Policy Leadership from the OECD to the G20' (2010) 5 *Northwestern Journal of Law & Social Policy* 19, 19.

[53] See, eg, LuxLeaks files (2014), database available at www.icij.org/investigations/luxembourg-leaks/explore-documents-luxembourg-leaks-database/; Panama Papers (2016), ICIJ investigation, available at www.icij.org/investigations/panama-papers/; Paradise Papers (2017), ICIJ investigation, available at www.icij.org/investigations/paradise-papers/.

[54] European Commission, 'Clamping Down on Tax Evasion and Avoidance: Commission Presents the Way Forward' (6 December 2012), available at https://ec.europa.eu/commission/presscorner/detail/en/IP_12_1325.

[55] See indicatively, Hakelberg (n 26); W Lips, 'Great Powers in Global Tax Governance: A Comparison of the US Role in the CRS and BEPS' (Globalizations SocArXiv ewd3j, Center for Open Science, 2018); P Emmenegger, 'The Long Arm of Justice: U.S. Structural Power and International Banking' (2015) 17 *Business and Politics* 3, 473–93; L Hakelberg, 'Coercion in International Tax Cooperation: Identifying the Prerequisites for Sanction Threats by a Great Power' (2016) 23 *Review of International Political Economy* 3, 511–41.

[56] Hakelberg, ibid.

been shown in fact there was no reciprocity in the exchange of information under FATCA agreements.[57] This resulted in a situation where the USA would receive the requested data, without disclosing equivalent information on non-residents to its treaty partners.[58]

Despite the first step towards greater tax transparency, the tax avoidance problem worsened with the continuous rise of digitalisation and the possibility for MNEs to operate in different states without having a physical presence there – and thus also without being taxable there. This latter problem was no longer only a problem vis-à-vis non-OECD countries, some of which traditionally employed harmful tax practices, but also an inherent tax problem for all countries not hosting headquarters of the big tech companies.

In light of the increasing possibilities for tax avoidance and the need for more revenue, on 19 July 2013 the OECD published its action plan on BEPS. What was, until very recently, a national matter – namely, to counteract abusive tax practices through General Anti-Avoidance Rules (GAARs) or Specific Anti-Avoidance Rules (SAARs), such as Controlled Foreign Corporation (CFC) rules – had now become the subject of a co-ordinated approach through the BEPS initiative. The BEPS project started off as a highly ambitious joint project of the OECD and G20 countries, aiming to set up an international framework to combat tax avoidance by MNEs using base erosion and profit-shifting tools, that is, tax avoidance strategies to exploit gaps and mismatches in tax rules to artificially shift profits to low-tax or no-tax locations.[59] The project was initiated in 2013 and in 2015 the OECD presented 15 Actions ranging from taxation of the digital economy (Action 1) to dispute resolution between countries (Action 14), all of which aim to 'equip governments with domestic and international instruments to address tax avoidance, ensuring that profits are taxed where economic activities generating the profits are performed and where value is created'.[60]

Currently, the Inclusive Framework on BEPS brings together over 140 countries and jurisdictions, including many developing countries, to collaborate on *implementation* of the BEPS Package. While it has been acknowledged that the main source of these tax avoidance schemes is the interaction among existing different rules, rather than one rule per se (or the absence thereof), the goal of the BEPS package is to tackle – in a co-ordinated manner – the *causes* and *circumstances* creating BEPS practices, rather than just suppressing the actual use of BEPS practices.[61] Out of the 15 Actions of the BEPS Action Plan, four of them contain a minimum standard, which means that there is an implementation obligation. These four Actions concern the fight against harmful tax practices and the spontaneous exchange of information on advance tax rulings (Action 5), the inclusion of abuse clauses in

[57] Hakelberg, ibid; A Christians, 'What You Give and What You Get: Reciprocity under a Model 1 Intergovernmental Agreement on FATCA' (2013) *Cayman Financial Review*.

[58] ibid.

[59] OECD, 'Action Plan on Base Erosion and Profit Shifting' (*OECD Publishing*, 2013), available at www.oecd.org/tax/beps/.

[60] See OECD BEPS, available at www.oecd.org/tax/beps/beps-actions.htm.

[61] European Parliament, 'Understanding the OECD Tax Plan to Address "Base Erosion and Profit Shifting" – BEPS', Briefing, June 2017, 3.

double taxation agreements (Action 6), country-by-country reporting (Action 13) and dispute resolution mechanisms (Action 14). Implementation of minimum standards across countries is regularly reviewed and monitored by the Inclusive Framework on BEPS in order to ensure timely and accurate implementation, thus safeguarding a level playing field.

Despite good intentions at international level and the undeniable success of the OECD in its inclusiveness and consensus, the BEPS outcome has been met with criticism by some for failing to efficiently address tax avoidance.[62] For some, dissatisfaction with the non-reciprocal Automatic Exchange Of Information (AEOI) by the USA and the BEPS project's failure to limit tax avoidance in the Common Market has motivated the European Commission and several Member States to push for a common reaction and consequently for the EU to take the lead.[63]

B. The (New) Role of the EU

The EU could not be left outside this global movement in terms of curbing tax avoidance practices that affected the EU as a whole or had an impact on its individual Member States. Even before publication of the final BEPS reports, several EU Member States were urging the EU to take action and agree on co-ordinated implementation of the BEPS project. These urgings were preceded by the European Council's conclusions in December 2014 that had also emphasised the need to fight tax avoidance at both global and EU levels.[64] One year later, in December 2015, the Economic and Financial Affairs Council (ECOFIN) welcomed the recommendations of the BEPS reports and committed to an EU BEPS roadmap for the future.[65] In line with the Council's conclusions, preference should be given to implementing those actions through EU legislation over possible parallel soft-law discussions.[66] This could be achieved, according to the Council, on the basis of existing directives, especially the Interest and Royalty Directive recast and/or proposal that had long been under development by the Commission, in the shape of the Common (Consolidated) Corporate Tax Base (CCCTB).[67] Yet the role of the Code of Conduct Group should not be undermined in framing and following a '*complementary* soft law approach'.

While most EU Member States are members of the OECD and/or of the Inclusive Framework, the EU wished to establish a regional playing field with regard to anti-tax avoidance *that would bind not only its Member States but, this time, would*

[62] See, eg, T Büttner and M Thiemann, 'Breaking Regime Stability? The Politicization of Expertise in the OECD/ G20 Process on BEPS and the Potential Transformation of International Taxation' (2017) 7 *Accounting, Economics, and Law: A Convivium* 1, 449; Hakelberg (n 55).

[63] Hakelberg (n 26) 132.

[64] See 'Outcome of the Council Meeting Economic and Council Affairs' (*Council of the EU*, 9 December 2014), available at www.consilium.europa.eu/media/24527/146136.pdf.

[65] See 'Council Conclusions on Corporate Taxation – Base Erosion and Profit Shifting' (*Council of the EU*, 8 December 2015, available at www.consilium.europa.eu/en/press/press-releases/2015/12/08/ecofin-conclusions-corporate-taxation/.

[66] ibid.

[67] ibid.

also have an impact vis-à-vis third states. That would, supposedly, bring back to the EU the revenue that was lost to tax havens or other low-tax jurisdictions but, at the same time, it would also curb certain Member States' tax preferences and would oblige them to introduce anti-tax avoidance measures that were not in place before.[68] As neither existing secondary legislation,[69] nor the extensive anti-abuse doctrine for direct (and indirect) taxation developed by the CJEU[70] provided a sufficient anti-avoidance framework, the Council encouraged a hard-law approach, in particular in relation to certain BEPS Actions.[71] Thus, the options for implementing the BEPS Actions were limited to an 'EU-wide' reaction that would be expressed through adoption (by unanimity) of binding secondary legislation or a 'Member State' reaction that would resemble the reaction of all states members of the Inclusive Framework and would be translated into international co-operation and subjection to peer review monitoring.

i. Secondary EU Law: Going Beyond the Minimum Standard

To the surprise of many, the EU proceeded not only by adopting ground-breaking directives but also by going beyond the minimum standard(s) mandated by BEPS. This was translated via two main (strands of) legislative initiatives that can be discerned, namely adoption of the Anti-Tax Avoidance Directive(s) (ATAD)[72] and expansion of the Directives on Administrative Cooperation (DACs).[73] While an analysis of these directives does not constitute the focus of this chapter, it is worthwhile to briefly explain how these EU cornerstones against tax avoidance came into being and how they affected the global tax order in taxation.

The ATAD has been characterised by many as the turning point in the history of EU tax legislation.[74] The ATAD establishes a *minimum framework* that Member

[68] There are plenty of examples of Member States, traditionally pictured as favourable to tax competition, that did not have certain types of SAARs in place. One such example is Luxembourg which, until the introduction of the Anti-Tax Avoidance Directive(s), did not have any CFC rules in place.

[69] Some directives provided for anti-abuse rules, applicable in their specific context: see, eg, the beneficial ownership clause in the Council Directive 2003/49/EC of 3 June 2003 on a common system of taxation applicable to interest and royalty payments made between associated companies of different Member States [2003] OJ L157/49–54 (Interest and Royalty Directive).

[70] See Joined Cases C-115/16, C-118/16, C-119/16 and C-299/16 *N Luxembourg 1* ECLI: EU:C:2019:134 and Joined Cases C-116/16 and C-117/16 *T Danmark* ECLI: EU:C:2019:135 (the '*Danish Beneficial Ownership Cases*'). See also Case C-6/16 *Eqiom and Enka* ECLI:ECLI: EU:C:2017:641 and Joined Cases C-504/16 & C-613/16 *Deister Holding* ECLI:EU:C:2017:1009; Case C-196/04 *Cadbury Schweppes and Cadbury Schweppes Overseas* ECLI: EU:C:2006:544.

[71] Notably, Actions 2 (hybrid mismatches), 3 (Controlled Foreign Company rules), 4 (interest limitation rules), 6 (general anti-abuse rule), 7 (permanent establishment status) and 13 (country by country reporting).

[72] Directive 2016/1164 Laying down Rules against Tax Avoidance Practices that Directly Affect the Functioning of the Internal Market [2016] OJL193/1.

[73] DAC 1 (Directive 2011/16/EU); DAC 2 (Directive 2014/107/EU); DAC 3 (Directive (EU) 2015/2376); DAC 4 (Directive (EU) 2016/881); DAC 5 (Directive (EU) 2016/2258); DAC 6 (Directive (EU) 2018/822); DAC 7 (Directive (EU) 2021/514) and DAC 8, the 'compromise text' of which was adopted by the Council on 18 May 2023. DAC 8 deals with implementation of the OECD rules on the Crypto-Asset Reporting Framework and introduces amendments to the Common Reporting Standard.

[74] P Pistone, 'The Meaning of Tax Avoidance and Aggressive Tax Planning in European Union Tax Law: Some Thoughts in Connection with the Reaction to Such Practices by the European Union' in AP Dourado (ed),

States have to implement in order to cope with tax avoidance practices that, according to its title, 'directly affect the functioning of the internal market'. This constitutes the first co-ordinated effort to interpret specifically the G20/OECD BEPS goals, as it constitutes a 'regional' implementation of the BEPS holistic approach, which is much more consistent with the BEPS' spirit than the unilateral measures that have been taken by some EU Member States.[75] It thus results in curtailing – if not eliminating – the tax practices and incentives adopted by countries traditionally engaging in tax competition within the Union.[76]

It is the first time in the history of EU direct taxation that a directive has such a broad scope; the ATAD applies to all taxpayers that are subject to corporate tax in a Member State, including permanent establishments of third country entities. As it aims to lay down rules against erosion of tax bases in the internal market and shifting profits out of the internal market, it lays down rules of substantive law that go far beyond the reach of existing directives in the field of direct taxation both quantitatively and qualitatively.[77] It hence focuses on different practices that could facilitate tax avoidance and thus establishes general rules on limitations to the deductibility of interest, exit taxation, a general anti-abuse rule, controlled foreign company rules and rules to tackle hybrid mismatches. The general aim is not only to counter tax avoidance practices but also to avoid creating other obstacles to the market such as double taxation.[78]

The uniqueness of this unprecedented undertaking is, further, backed by the 'fast-track' timeframe within which the ATAD was adopted, despite the unanimity obstacle enshrined in Article 115 TFEU. This was not only due to the need to fulfil the timeframe for BEPS implementation, but is in itself symptomatic of the level of urgency felt across EU Member States to respond to the challenges raised by globalisation and digitalisation of the economy.[79]

As a consequence, the ATAD limits the Member States' sovereignty in the techniques they can employ to attract capital. Despite its scope, the repercussions of the ATAD go far beyond the internal market, as they also regulate the behaviour of Member States, as well as those that have traditionally been perceived as hubs for particular types of investment or establishment, vis-à-vis third states. To illustrate this, one can draw an example from Articles 7 and 8 of the ATAD that introduce mandatory CFC rules for all Member States. CFC rules aim, through different methods, at reducing the benefits of establishing in low-tax jurisdictions and not repatriating profits in order to trigger taxation at the 'home' jurisdiction.

Prior to the ATAD, several Member States did not have CFC rules, and it is believed that – especially for non-high-tax jurisdictions – introduction of the ATAD

Tax Avoidance Revisited in the EU BEPS context (Amsterdam, IBFD, 2017), and D Gutman (et al), 'The Impact of the ATAD on Domestic Systems: A Comparative Survey' (2017) *European Taxation* 2.

[75] AP Dourado, 'The EU Anti Tax Avoidance Package: Moving Ahead of BEPS?' (2016) *Intertax* 44, 440.

[76] E Kemmeren, 'Where is EU Law in the OECD BEPS Discussion?' (2014) 4 *EC Tax Review* 190.

[77] Gutman et al (n 74).

[78] Rec 5, Council Directive (EU) 2016/1164.

[79] R de la Feria, 'Harmonizing Anti-Tax Avoidance Rules' (2017) 3 *EC Tax Review* 110.

may harm their competitiveness.[80] Accordingly, corporate freedom to benefit from establishing in lower-tax jurisdictions will be curtailed, even more so if they used CFC in third states. This is because where an EU company has established a CFC in a third country, the ATAD gives Member States the option to disregard the 'economic substance' of the company (if it exists), and still apply the CFC rule to it, thus treating it less favourably than intra-EU situations. The first amendment to the ATAD, 'ATAD 2',[81] specifically targets third countries and – notably – hybrid mismatches arising between Member States and third countries, in an effort to ensure that income will not escape taxation in both countries due to the mismatch.[82] Because of the ATAD, income arriving from third countries will thus be subject to stricter rules across Member States, in order to ensure that it does not escape taxation.

The same applies with the mandatory harmonised exit tax under Article 5 of the ATAD. The introduction of exit taxes was not foreseen in the OECD BEPS Action Plan but, once again, found its way into binding EU law. While the CJEU has a long history of providing guidelines to Member States as to how to structure their exit taxes so as to be 'EU law compliant',[83] it may come as a surprise that this barrier to freedom of establishment and capital is imposed on corporations through the ATAD, even in cases where cross-border relocations are not tax-driven.[84]

However, *in reality*, the practical positive impact with respect to the new rules that had to be adopted by Member States[85] is potentially quite limited due to lack of closer harmonisation of the anti-avoidance rules as a consequence of the number of options granted in the Directive.[86] Several academic commentators have thus noted that they rather expect greater fragmentation of the internal market compared to the situation prior to the Directive.[87] Additionally, the Commission's 2020 Implementation Report[88] showed a significant divergence in implementation with respect to the various options provided for in the Directive, although that report did not yet include exit taxation or anti-hybrid rules. However, when assessing the success of ATAD implementation, this criticism must be balanced against the alternative of even greater fragmentation that would have resulted from completely uncoordinated development anti-avoidance rules to implement the BEPS consensus.

[80] See A Rust, 'Controlled Foreign Company Rule (Articles 7 and 8 ATAD)' in W Haslehner and K Pantazatou et al (eds), *A Guide to the Anti-Tax Avoidance Directive* (Cheltenham, Edward Elgar, 2020) 174–99, 198.

[81] Council Directive (EU) 2017/952 of 29 May 2017 amending Directive (EU) 2016/1164 as regards hybrid mismatches with third countries [2017] OJ L144/1–11.

[82] Those hybrid mismatches refer, in general terms, to avoiding paying taxes through 'loopholes' that, in general, lead to double deductions (in both states) or a deduction in one state without inclusion in the tax base of the other state.

[83] For exit taxes levied on corporations see notably, Case C-371/10 *National Grid Indus* EU:C:2011:785; Case C-164/12 *DMC* EU:C:2014:20; Case C-657/13 *Verder LabTec* EU:C:2015:331.

[84] S Peeters, 'Exit Taxation: From an Internal Market Barrier to a Tax Avoidance Prevention Tool' (2017) *26 EC Tax Review* 122.

[85] Note that several Member States already had many of these SAARs in place.

[86] See W Haslehner and K Pantazatou, 'Assessment of Recent Anti-Tax Avoidance and Evasion Measures (ATAD & DAC6)', Study for the FISC Committee of the European Parliament, 21.

[87] Rust (n 80) 199.

[88] Report from the Commission to the European Parliament and the Council on the Implementation of Council Directive (EU) 2016/1164 of 12 July 2016, COM(2020) 383 final.

Similarly, the DACs encapsulate the EU's response to the need for greater tax transparency, a key goal at international and EU level and one of the pillars of the 15 BEPS Actions. According to the OECD, 'tax transparency is about putting an end to bank secrecy and tax evasion through global tax co-operation'.[89] All DACs constitute implementations of commitments accepted by OECD members in connection with the BEPS project and they are premised on extensive reporting and AEOI among Member States to combat tax avoidance and evasion. It has been argued that, because in the EU these BEPS commitments have been translated into binding legislation that goes beyond the BEPS minimum standard, they may harm the EU Member States' competitiveness in that much more information will be required from MNEs and exchanged within the EU, arguably making the EU a less attractive destination for MNEs and their capital.[90] This degree of transparency, however, may also function in favour of these multinational corporations in that they will have access to a much bigger bulk of information regarding the European operations of foreign MNE groups.[91]

Pending an elaborate analysis of these two major pillars of EU anti-tax avoidance, one can already note two main findings; first, that the EU has gone well beyond the BEPS recommendations in that a) it established a binding legal framework rather than a 'recommendation' or 'guidelines' and b) in terms of scope, this binding legal framework goes well beyond the minimum standard established by BEPS. In the opposite situation, a highly rigid legal framework would risk undermining the tax competitiveness of the EU as a whole and its individual Member States as it would effectively deprive them of any tax incentives for investment and (re)location. It would also have very little chance of being adopted. The result is *a hybrid* outcome that, compared to the previous situation, certainly makes the EU more tax avoidance-proof. At the same time, it allows EU Member States to continue some of their previous practices.[92] It remains to be seen, however, whether these harmonisation efforts will harm the EU's competitiveness as a whole and whether they will contribute to corporations moving away from the continent in search of less rigid and less strict anti-avoidance requirements.

ii. Twist in Existing Primary Law: State Aid Law

A second item in the EU's toolbox was to be found in primary law. State aid law had always been used in the field of taxation. However, in order to be used in a BEPS context, it had to be reinvented. In this context, it was the European Commission that employed state aid law provisions to scrutinise tax rulings and

[89] See 'Tax Transparency – OECD BEPS', available at www.oecd.org/tax/beps/tax-transparency/>.

[90] See, eg, 'DAC 6' and the obligations it imposes on intermediaries. See also K Pantazatou, 'Effective Implementation of the ATAD: Information Collection, Exchange and Monitoring through DAC 6' in Haslehner and Pantazatou et al (n 80) 277–303.

[91] R Lyal, 'Transparency and Exchange of Information: BEPS in EU Legislation – More advanced Standards or Distortion?' in AM Jimenez (ed), *The External Tax Strategy of the EU in a Post-BEPS Environment* (IBFD, 2019) 125–48, 147.

[92] eg, 'financial undertakings' may be exempted from a series of ATAD provisions such as the interest-limitation rule.

Advance Pricing Agreements (APAs). A series of high-profile cases was brought before the General Court (GC),[93] many of which subsequently came before the CJEU.[94]

While the Commission had previously dealt with transfer pricing cases,[95] this was the first time that it delved into such specific transfer pricing analyses, combining accounting, economics, EU law and international law. Inevitably, the reviewing EU Court(s) were also called upon to apply this analysis when deciding whether tax rulings and APAs were compatible with Article 107 TFEU.

It has been repeatedly argued that by employing these tools, the Commission is trying to create anti-tax avoidance tax policy, especially in areas where all other tools (fundamental freedoms, secondary law and the Code of Conduct) do not seem to work.[96] In doing so, the Commission has often had to push the boundaries of EU law and consider that the Arm's Length Principle[97] is a general principle enshrined in Article 107 TFEU. In this way, it would enable intervention in the way Member States tax their undertakings, in particular MNEs. The effect of these investigations and cases has not been limited only to within the EU but has also impacted on third states where multinational giants have their residence, notably the USA,[98] and has resulted in outcomes not seen favourably by those third states that do not have similar rules in place.[99]

While the GC has decided in favour of the Member State at issue – with the exception of the *Fiat* case – this has only been a pyrrhic victory, as the GC has already confirmed not only its right to review any Member State's tax rulings regarding their consistency with national law but has also affirmed the legitimacy of taking into account OECD transfer pricing guidelines when analysing correct implementation of the arm's-length standard.[100]

[93] See, eg, Judgments of the General Court: T-816/17 '*Amazon*' ECLI:EU:T:2021:252; T-755/15 '*FIAT*' ECLI:EU:T:2019:670; T-760/15 and T-636/16 '*Starbucks*' ECLI:EU:T:2019:669; T-778/16 and T-892/16 '*Apple*' ECLI:EU:T:2020:338.

[94] Note that all of these cases, with the exception of *Starbucks*, are currently pending before the CJEU, on appeal from the General Court.

[95] Joined cases C-182/03 and C-217/03 *Belgium and Forum 187 ASBL v Commission* [2006] ECLI:EU:C:2006:416, para 96. In its decision challenged before the EU Courts, the Commission had, however, explicitly noted that 'when determining transfer prices, the Belgian administration must base itself on the OECD reports'.

[96] PJ Wattel, 'Regulation and Effects of Fiscal State Aid in Third-State Relations' in Jimenez (n 91) 149–69, 150; M Tenore, 'APAs and State Aid: A New Era of European Tax Law?' in D Weber (ed), *EU Law and the Building of Global Supranational Tax Law: EU BEPS and State Aid* (IBFD, 2017) 201–23, 201; C Peters, 'Tax Policy Convergence and EU Fiscal State Aid Control: In Search of Rationality' (2019) 28 *EC Tax Review* 1, 6–17; E Traversa and A Flamini, 'Fighting Harmful Tax Competition through EU State Aid Law: Will the Hardening of Soft Law Suffice?' (2015) *European State Aid Law Quarterly* 323–30.

[97] The Arm's Length Principle is an international standard which states that, where conditions between related enterprises are different from those between independent enterprises, profits which have accrued by reason of those conditions may be included in the profits of that enterprise and taxed accordingly.

[98] See, eg, *Apple* (n 93).

[99] Note that according to WTO law, specific export subsidies are prohibited, thus escaping the broad framework of state aid rules.

[100] W Haslehner and K Pantazatou, 'Luxembourg Cases' in M Lang et al (eds), *CJEU Recent Developments in Direct Taxation 2021* (Vienna, Linde, 2022) 98.

iii. Tax Havens

In the fight against abusive tax practices, the EU has been maintaining its own blacklist of tax havens since 2017.[101] The list – updated by the Council twice a year – includes only non-EU Member States. The background to its adoption can be traced back to the European Commission's External Strategy for Effective Taxation, which aimed to prevent profit shifting away from the EU and safeguard a predictable business environment.[102]

The non-EU Member States included on the list are those that do not meet EU standards of 'tax good governance', which in broad terms means the criteria of tax transparency, fair taxation and implementation of anti-BEPS measures.[103] The most recent list of 4 October 2022 includes 12 countries,[104] many fewer than the first list published in 2017. In selecting those identifying criteria, the 'tax good governance' agenda has relied on the Code of Conduct criteria.[105] It is noteworthy that the criteria advanced by the Code of Conduct and subsequently adopted in the context of the 'EU blacklist' to define harmful tax practices are not identical to those included in the 1998 OECD Report on Harmful Tax Competition.[106] In this sense, the EU seems to be going beyond the minimum consensus agreed by the OECD countries on what constitutes harmful tax competition by adopting stricter criteria and by expanding its list of un-cooperative countries when the OECD removes all countries from its (equivalent) list.[107] Despite the soft-law character of the EU Code of Conduct, the defensive measures against blacklisted countries constitute real sanctions that may be suffered by several states that cannot meet the EU Code of Conduct criteria.[108] Thus, the EU emerges as a 'global regulator' in terms of harmful tax practices, towards both the (other) OECD members that have not agreed on these standards but also towards other states that cannot meet them either because they may have a legitimate interest to utilise their tax systems to attract investment from other jurisdictions, or

[101] The EU list of non-cooperative jurisdictions can be found here: www.consilium.europa.eu/en/policies/eu-list-of-non-cooperative-jurisdictions/.

[102] European Commission, Communication from the Commission to the European Parliament and the Council, 'An External Strategy for Effective Taxation', COM (2016) 24 (28 January 2016).

[103] Council Document 15429/17, Council Conclusions on the EU list of non-cooperative jurisdictions for tax purposes (5 December 2017).

[104] See www.consilium.europa.eu/media/24527/146136.pdf. The countries currently figuring on the list are: American Samoa, Anguilla, Bahamas, Fiji, Guam, Palau, Panama, Samoa, Trinidad and Tobago, Turks and Caicos Islands, US Virgin Islands, Vanuatu.

[105] The Code of Conduct for business taxation was set out in the conclusions of the Council of Economics and Finance Ministers (ECOFIN) of 1 December 1997, OJ C2, 6 January 1998, see above under section III.B.

[106] See W Haslehner and P Schwarz, 'Harmful Tax Competition from the European Union towards Third Countries?' in Jimenez (n 91) 265, who point out that the EU Code of Conduct includes a criterion of 'substance' and a reference to the 'accepted principles of profit determination' that are not included in the 1998 OECD Report.

[107] ibid 266.

[108] One category of these defensive measures includes non-tax 'penalties', notably the cut-off of these countries from access to EU funds. The second category includes tax measures directed to the residents of one such state or to a taxpayer that has dealings with such a state. These measures include, but are not limited to, non-deductibility of costs, CFC rules, application of withholding taxes and a reversed burden of proof.

because they do not have the (administrative) capacity to deal with such sophisticated rules.[109]

IV. FUTURE/OUTLOOK

A. Digitalisation

Out of all the tax challenges which the BEPS Actions address, those that caused considerable unrest and discussion in the international and EU worlds are those that relate to digitalisation. Discussion on how best to address these challenges has spurred a series of proposals for directives by the Commission and intense international debate.

As early as 2018, the EU seemed to be 'in competition' with the OECD in releasing the first comprehensive proposals relating to taxation of the digital economy. In 2018, the Commission published proposals for two Council Directives on taxation of the *digital economy*[110] and one (non-binding) Commission Recommendation relating to corporate taxation of a *significant digital presence*.[111] These proposals came immediately after the release of the 2018 OECD Interim Report on the tax challenges arising from digitalisation.[112] In light of lukewarm reactions by Member States, the Commission withdrew the proposals and in 2020 announced a legislative proposal for a digital levy as an EU own resource that was supposed to be published in summer 2021. The announcement of an EU digital levy proposal was met with particular scepticism by the USA for unfairly discriminating against US companies.[113] Allegedly, in April 2021, after the USA stepped into the debate, the Commission signalled that it planned to take a 'soft' approach that did not interfere with the OECD process.[114] Eventually, delivery of the proposal was postponed until global consensus could be reached at OECD level on Pillar 2, which constitutes the current bone of contention.

Currently, at both EU and international level, the discussion focuses on what is commonly called 'Pillar 1' and even more so on 'Pillar 2' solutions. These pillars are part of the OECD Inclusive Framework proposals; i) to address the tax challenges that arise from digitalisation of the economy and constitute an extension of BEPS

[109] ibid.

[110] European Commission, Proposal for a Council Directive laying down rules relating to the corporate taxation of a significant digital presence, 21 March 2018, COM (2018) 147 final; and European Commission, Proposal for a Council Directive on the common system of a digital services tax on revenues resulting from the provision of certain digital services, 21 March 2018, COM (2018) 148 final.

[111] European Commission Recommendation of 21 March 2018 relating to the corporate taxation of a significant digital presence, COM(2018) 1650 final.

[112] OECD, 'Tax Challenges Arising from Digitalisation – Interim Report 2018' (OECD Publishing, 2018).

[113] Politico, 'EU to Postpone Digital Tax Proposal' (12 July 2021), available at www.politico.eu/article/eu-to-postpone-digital-tax-proposal/.

[114] R Christie, 'International Tax Debate Moves from Digital Focus to Global Minimum' (*Bruegel Blog Post*, 27 May 2021), available at www.bruegel.org/2021/05/international-tax-debate-moves-from-digital-focus-to-global-minimum/.

Action 1; and ii) to tax the world's biggest and most profitable companies where they operate. The interrelated policy goals of the two pillars are, therefore, to address the remaining BEPS challenges and to halt tax avoidance and excessive tax competition between jurisdictions.[115]

In this context, Pillar 1 focuses 'on new nexus and profit allocation rules to ensure that, in an increasingly digital age, the allocation of taxing rights with respect to business profits is no longer exclusively circumscribed by reference to physical presence'.[116] Thus, under Pillar 1 the aim is to shift taxation on large digital service providers to the countries were the sale takes place. In contrast, Pillar 2 arguably pursues an even more ground-breaking goal, namely establishment of a minimum global tax rate.[117] Pillar 2, or the Global Anti-Base Erosion (GloBE) Rules aim to ensure that large multinational enterprises pay a minimum level of tax on the income arising in each of the jurisdictions where they operate.

In October 2021, 136 out of 140 members of the OECD/G20 Inclusive Framework officially agreed on certain key parameters to reallocate some taxing rights to market jurisdictions (under Pillar 1) and introduce global minimum effective taxation (under Pillar 2).

While the technical details of implementation, at least for Pillar 1, remain to be agreed, the BEPS Inclusive Framework released the Pillar 2 Model Rules on 20 December 2021. One day later, the EU Commission published its proposal for a Directive on Pillar 2 (the 'GloBE Directive'). Almost one year after the European Commission published its proposal for a Directive setting out rules on ensuring a global minimum level of taxation for multinational groups active in the EU, the GloBE Directive was unanimously adopted on 15 December 2022,[118] having as its main purpose to put 'a floor to competition over corporate income tax rates through the establishment of a global minimum level of taxation'.[119] The adoption of EU binding legislation to implement the OECD Pillar 2 Model Rules is even more remarkable if one considers that the USA has – so far – failed to adopt similar implementing rules.[120]

[115] European Commission, Proposal for a Council Directive on ensuring a global minimum level of taxation for multinational groups in the Union, COM (2021) (22 December 2021), available at <https://ec.europa.eu/taxation_customs/system/files/2021-12/COM_2021_823_1_EN_ACT_part1_v11.pdf.

[116] OECD, 'Tax Challenges Arising from Digitalisation – Report on Pillar One Blueprint' (14 October 2020), available at www.oecd-ilibrary.org/taxation/tax-challenges-arising-from-digitalisation-report-on-pillar-one-blueprint_beba0634-en.

[117] OECD, 'Tax Challenges Arising from the Digitalisation of the Economy – Global Anti-Base Erosion Model Rules (Pillar Two) (21 December 2021), available at www.oecd.org/tax/beps/tax-challenges-arising-from-the-digitalisation-of-the-economy-global-anti-base-erosion-model-rules-pillar-two.pdf.

[118] Council Directive (EU) 2022/2523 of 14 December 2022 on ensuring a global minimum level of taxation for multinational enterprise groups and large-scale domestic groups in the Union [2002] OJ L328/1–58 (hereinafter the 'GloBE Directive'). The big news on the historical agreement was announced before the official written procedure at the Council on 15 December, resulting in different dates appearing in various (official and news) outlets. See, eg, the press release by the European Commission on 13 December 2022, available at https://ec.europa.eu/commission/presscorner/detail/en/ip_22_7674.

[119] GloBE Directive, ibid, Preamble, Rec 2.

[120] The recent proposed changes to the current US global minimum tax – the tax on global intangible low-taxed income – and the recently enacted tax reconciliation bill, the 'Inflation Reduction Act', have not included any rules on Pillar 2.

Despite the seemingly fast process, especially by EU standards,[121] the adoption process was not uncontentious. The (unanticipated) adoption of the Directive was preceded by the expressed willingness by five large Member States to move ahead with swift implementation of Pillar 2 'by any possible means'.[122] This indirect call for co-operation found several proponents, who entertained the idea of moving ahead under the enhanced co-operation regime (Article 20 TEU),[123] if Hungary – one of the two main hold-out Member States together with Poland – continued to veto the proposal.[124] In addition, the UK's commitment to proceed with the adoption of Pillar 2, and publication of its draft legislation towards this purpose in June 2022, put more pressure on the EU.

Given the complexity of the rules and their expressed alignment with the OECD Pillar 2 Model Rules, one of the main problems that arose was the role of the OECD Model Rules and subsequent explanatory documents, in the interpretation and application of secondary EU law. Recital 19a in the Preamble to the Directive explicitly provides that:

> [I]n implementing this Directive, Member States should use the 'Tax Challenges Arising from the Digitalisation of the Economy Global Anti-Base Erosion Model Rules (Pillar Two)' agreed by the OECD/G20 Inclusive Framework on BEPS and the explanations and examples in the OECD Commentary on the GloBE Rules under Pillar Two, as well as the GloBE Implementation Framework [...] as a source *of illustration or interpretation* in order to ensure consistency in application across Member States to the extent that they are consistent with the provisions of this Directive and with Union law.

As a result, several Member States have drafted their implementing laws making express reference to the OECD Model Rules and the accompanying Commentary[125] and Administrative Guidance.[126] This is largely problematic not only from a political perspective – as it showcases the deference of these states to the OECD '*Model Rules*' and accompanying documents, but also from a legal perspective in that after adoption of the Directive guidance has found its way into domestic law(s) concealed under the disguise of uniform interpretation across the Union.

In these ground-breaking advances for the future of digital taxation as well as the (minimum) taxation of MNEs, the EU has maintained a dubious role. On the one

[121] Under Art 115 TFEU, adoption of directives in direct tax matters in the EU requires unanimous approval by all 27 Member States. Several initiatives by the European Commission have either been abandoned or have been put on hold for many years because of the impossibility of reaching unanimous approval (see, eg, the CC(C)TB).

[122] On 9 September 2022, France, Germany, Italy, the Netherlands, and Spain, issued a joint statement, in the context of ECOFIN's informal meeting in Prague at that time, signalling their willingness to move ahead swiftly with implementation of Pillar 2, see EY Tax Alert, 'Five Major EU Member States Commit to Swift Implementation of Pillar Two by any Possible Legal Means' (*EY*, 13 September 2022), available at www.ey.com/en_gl/tax-alerts/five-major-eu-member-states-commit-to-swift-implementation-of-pi.

[123] Enhanced co-operation under Art 20 TEU requires a minimum of nine Member States to co-operate.

[124] J Barros, 'EU Watch: Pillar Two Directive Gaining New Momentum' (2002) *Tax Journal*.

[125] OECD Commentary to the Global Anti-Base Erosion Model Rules (Pillar Two) (March 2022), available at www.oecd.org/tax/beps/tax-challenges-arising-from-the-digitalisation-of-the-economy-global-anti-base-erosion-model-rules-pillar-two-commentary.pdf.

[126] OECD Administrative Guidance on the Global Anti-Base Erosion Model Rules (Pillar Two) (February 2023), available at www.oecd.org/tax/beps/agreed-administrative-guidance-for-the-pillar-two-globe-rules.pdf. Note that the OECD Administrative Guidance was published *after* adoption of the Directive.

hand, it rushes to advance binding legislation in the form of directives, while on the other hand it appears to simply copy the OECD proposals without having thoroughly thought through the repercussions of these proposals on the EU as a whole and the individual Member States. Indicative of this is the absence of an impact assessment of the effects of Pillar 1 and 2 on the EU and the Commission's reliance on the OECD impact assessment.[127] One can only speculate but this could be either because of the strong position of the European Commission in the OECD, where it has already contributed to policy outcomes, or to the concurrence of the Commission's and the OECD's priorities that are now further supported by the OECD aegis.

B. Corporations and Corporate Law

At the same time the Commission revealed its ATAD 3 (or 'Unshell') proposal that aims to counter the abusive use of shell companies.[128] As explained in the draft proposal, 'legal entities with no minimal substance and economic activity continue to pose a risk of being used for improper tax purposes, such as tax evasion and avoidance, as confirmed by recent massive media revelations'.[129]

It is clear from the scope of the Directive, that – if it is adopted – it will intersect substantially with EU corporate law and specifically with the anti-abuse doctrine developed from the *Centros* judgment onwards.[130] As the Court ruled in *Centros*, a letterbox company, devoid of any economic activity, does not necessarily have to be abusive. Since then, the anti-abuse doctrine has been developed by the CJEU in both indirect[131] and direct tax cases,[132] culminating in the so-called 'Danish beneficial ownership' cases.[133] Under the anti-abuse 'tax doctrine', the need for 'economic reality' or, put differently, 'genuine economic activity' or 'substance' appears to be a necessary requirement for a corporation or a transaction to come within the scope of freedom of establishment.[134] As the CJEU ruled in the Danish cases,

> [t]he *absence of actual economic activity* must […] be inferred from an analysis of all the relevant factors relating, in particular, to the management of the company, to its balance

[127] See, eg, European Parliament resolution of 29 April 2021 on digital taxation: OECD negotiations, tax residency of digital companies and a possible European Digital Tax (2021/2010(INI)) that calls on the European Commission to 'complete its own impact assessment on the effects of Pillars One and Two on revenue collection for the Member States and to inform the Council and Parliament about its findings […]'.

[128] European Commission, Proposal for a Council Directive laying down rules to prevent the misuse of shell entities for tax purposes and amending Directive 2011/16/EU, COM(2021) 565 final (22.12.2021).

[129] ibid 1.

[130] Case C-212/97 *Centros* EU:C:1999:126.

[131] See Case C-110/99 *Emsland Stärke* and C-255/02 *Halifax and Others*.

[132] Note that several scholars suggest that the Court does not apply the same anti-abuse doctrine in direct and indirect tax cases. See indicatively, F Vanistendael, 'Halifax and Cadbury Schweppes: One Single European Theory of Abuse in Tax Law?' (2006) *15 EC Tax Review* 195 and B Kiekebeld, 'Anti-Abuse in the Field of Taxation: Is There One Overall Concept?' (2009) *18 EC Tax Review* 144.

[133] See *Luxembourg* (n 70) and *Danmark* (n 70).

[134] See Case C-196/04 *Cadbury Schweppes and Cadbury Schweppes Overseas* ECLI:EU:C:2006:544 and in agreement, K Lenaerts, 'The Concept of "Abuse of Law" in the Case Law of the European Court of Justice on Direct Taxation (2015) *3 Maastricht Journal of European and Competition Law* 322.

> sheet, to the structure of its costs and to expenditure actually incurred, *to the staff that it employs and to the premises and equipment that it has.*[135]

While the requirement of physical presence appears to be at odds with the *Centros* line of case law, the proposed 'Unshell' directive aims to put an end to the dichotomy created by the two lines of case law (company law[136] and tax law[137]) by suggesting, in essence, that if an entity fails to provide evidence that it meets the *minimum substance requirements*, then it will be considered as an artificial arrangement, along the lines of the *Cadbury Schweppes* judgment. The taxpayer, however, may rebut the presumption of abuse, under the proposal and in line with CJEU case law, if they show valid commercial justifications for the arrangement.

The 'Unshell directive', if adopted, will not disallow the use of 'letterbox companies' but it will instead require the Member States that have in place arrangements with a shell entity to disregard any tax benefits stemming from secondary EU law or the DTCs of the Member State where the shell entity is resident. The tax consequences vary depending on whether the Member State at issue is the state of the shell entity, the state of the shareholder or the ultimate source state.[138] Despite focusing on withdrawing any tax benefits for shell companies, the Unshell directive is expected to have a broader impact on letterbox companies for removing one of their fundamental *raisons d'être* in the EU.

V. CONCLUSION: THE EU AS A 'GLOBAL TAX ACTOR'?

This chapter aimed to show the role and the evolution of the EU as a 'global tax actor'. It placed the EU as a whole and its constituent Member States in an evolutionary and contextual framework in order to show if – and, if so, how – the EU has affected international tax policy or the 'international tax regime'.

The interests and policy goals of the EU and the OECD have not always coincided. While the EU could be considered as a strong 'observer' party in the OECD works, the USA has traditionally been the main trend-setter. To this has contributed the inward-looking outlook of the EU for most of its years of existence, as expressed via the antithetical goals of both removing tax obstacles via hard law and abolishing Potentially Harmful Tax Regimes via soft law. The choice of instruments was a result of the Member States' diverging priorities and stances vis-à-vis tax competition and the subsequent inability to reach consensus on whether – and, if so, how – to tame their tax competition practices. Thus, priority was given to the Member States through lack of legislative action by reason of their will to 'maintain their

[135] *Luxembourg* (n 70) para 131.

[136] Suggesting that there is no requirement of physical presence in order to fall within the scope of freedom of establishment as confirmed in *Centros and Polbud* (Judgment of 25 October 2017, C-106/16 *Polbud – Wykonawstwo* EU:C:2017:804).

[137] Suggesting that lack of physical presence may lead to the arrangement qualifying as abusive for lacking 'actual economic activity'.

[138] For a discussion see P Pistone (et al), 'Abuse, Shell Entities and Right of Establishment: A Plea for Refocusing Current Proposals and Achieving Deeper Coordination within the Internal Market' (2022) *World Tax Journal* 187.

tax sovereignty' and to taxpayers' freedom(s) via removal of tax obstacles, notably through CJEU case law.

However, a series of events – the financial crisis, tax scandals, the USA's non-reciprocity in the exchange of information, and global developments triggered by all these events – contributed to making the EU more 'outward-looking'. This coincided with the turn that was observed on both sides of the Atlantic in prioritising combating tax avoidance through a new co-operative and inclusive framework, namely that of BEPS.

In BEPS 'atypical competition', it appears that it is the OECD and the Inclusive Framework that have been the trend-setters and standard-setters. However, very often, despite the solutions and policy recommendations contemplated at a global (and inclusive) level, the states involved – including the dominant USA, are hesitant in implementing these ground-breaking rules (such as Pillar 1 and, until recently, Pillar 2). This 'varied' reaction to OECD proposals may create uncertainty across states and taxpayers and increase the danger for unilateral measures that will threaten to affect not only application of the DTCs between Member States and allocation of taxing rights (and revenues across states), but also the coherence of the international tax framework as we know it. The signature of the Multilateral Instrument (MLI) that allows all signatory governments to simultaneously modify existing bilateral tax treaties in a synchronised and efficient manner to implement the tax treaty measures developed during the BEPS Project, can be considered as a great success for the OECD. The MLI has been signed by all Member States and by 99 states (so far) in total, but not the USA. Its particular design that allows for reservations (opt-ins and opt-outs) has contributed to its popularity but has taken away from its efficiency and coherence.

In contrast, while the EU seems to anticipate agreement at international level before acting or convincing the Member States about its necessity, it appears to be at the forefront in terms of implementation, by adopting binding legislation that transposes not only BEPS minimum standards but very often going beyond those. In addition, it has also incorporated BEPS 'recommendations' in its binding legislation. This could possibly be justified on grounds of 'global decision' dressing and/or actual agreement and the need at EU level to make the EU as 'tax avoidance-proof' as possible. Possibly, the pinnacle of this compliance has been witnessed with the adoption of the GloBE Directive and explicit reference to the OECD works for its interpretation.

The EU taking the 'implementation lead' has repercussions for its constituent Member States, third states and corporations. Not only does it signal – for the first time – that the EU is speaking with one voice in tax matters in the context of its external tax policy, but it also creates some legal certainty for taxpayers as to the intentions of the Union and its constituent Member States.

With regard to the Member States, the shift in focus has come at the expense of the competence of Member States to define their tax practices so as to become as competitive as possible. In this sense, traditionally 'tax-competitive' Member States, such as Ireland, the Netherlands and Luxembourg, have lost some of their attractiveness due to recently adopted secondary EU law. While the European Commission, through its drafting strategy, has allowed for several carve-outs and leeway in implementation, the compulsory introduction of CFC rules and exit taxes, for instance, has limited the pool of available tax tools for the Member States. This, together with the very broad exchange of information framework, may indeed harm the competitiveness not only of individual Member States but also of the EU as a whole in that corporations – whether they operate in the digital sector or not – may stop using the EU for their establishment(s) or investments. In this sense, the EU appears to be choosing promotion of fair tax competition values versus its financial interests.[139]

Corporations, and MNEs in particular, have also witnessed their – traditionally widely interpreted – freedom of establishment being seriously curtailed due to anti-tax avoidance practices and the continuously growing exchange-of-information framework. Establishing in low-tax jurisdictions, relocating, or contemplating aggressive tax planning either comes at a cost or is (now) forbidden. This turn towards curtailment of tax avoidance and tax abuse has clearly taken its toll on the private aspect of tax law and has tipped the scales towards further detachment of tax law from private law, where private parties' freedom of choice as to their place of residence, investment and structure of transactions is severely limited in comparison to the past.[140]

As a solution to the divide between tax law and private law, some authors have advocated integrating tax law into certain branches of private law; the underlying idea being that instead of introducing more tax regulation, changes should take place at the level of private law so that tax avoidance is attacked at its core.[141] Interestingly, at EU level, the same idea of integration was considered for an amendment to Directive (EU) 2017/1132 on certain aspects of company law, notably on cross-border conversions, mergers and divisions. The proposal for the amendment contained a provision which would have inserted Article 86c that would require Member States to deny the right to a cross-border conversion should it constitute 'an artificial arrangement aimed at obtaining undue tax advantages'.[142] The provision was removed in the final version of the amending Directive, following criticisms of the potential integration of a tax-specific rule in a company law instrument.[143] Recent initiatives in the area of tax law appear to confirm this 'autonomy of tax law' and the advocating of an expanding web of tax laws that will inevitably impact on company law, without the latter necessarily following up.[144]

[139] M Cremona and J Scott (eds), *EU Law Beyond EU Borders – the Extraterritorial Reach of EU Law* (Oxford, Oxford University Press, 2019) 2.

[140] For the relationship between tax law and private law, see above, under section II.

[141] See, eg, in the field of IP Law: A Blair-Stanek, 'Intellectual Property Law Solutions to Tax Avoidance' (2015) 62 UCLA Law Review 1.

[142] Proposal for a Directive amending Directive (EU) 2017/1132 as regards cross-border conversions, mergers and divisions, COM/2018/241 final – 2018/0114 (COD), 25 April 2018.

[143] G van Gelder, 'The Polbud-Case and New EU Company Law Proposal: Expanding the Possibilities for Cross Border Conversion in Europe' (2018) 27 *EC Tax Review* 5, 264.

[144] One such example is the ATAD 3 proposal which appears to deprive letterbox companies of a big part of their tax advantages, without, however, company law following up on the debate between the 'real seat' and 'incorporation' theories.

Consistent with promotion of fair tax competition and its 'tax good governance agenda', the EU has further taken a much stricter stance than the OECD against 'blacklisted' tax havens. It has thus emerged as an international tax actor vis-à-vis third countries – and in particular, tax havens – by applying real 'defensive measures'.[145]

While in the past, the EU, as opposed to the USA, could not be considered as an 'influential superpower' in the field of international tax law, the EU now has its own role in the (tax) world, namely that of an 'initiator' and an 'effects-oriented' regulator. This role is designated by an ambitious plan to turn the EU *as a whole* into an anti-tax avoidance hub. It is doubtful whether the EU can go beyond this qualification and become the predominant global tax actor.

Taxation constitutes a highly specialised area that is difficult to compare to other policy areas, such as product regulation. At the same time, the EU only relatively recently adopted a binding legal framework that has turned it into the first region globally to apply – and often go beyond – BEPS standards. This makes it difficult to consider the Union, as early as now, a global influencer – we do not yet know if other states/regions will follow the EU example, or whether the EU and the constituent Member States will strictly enforce this legal framework. After all, both the choice of legal instrument (directives) and their content (several opt-outs and choices) allow leeway to Member States in implementation. Thus, if one had to attribute to the EU a special role, it should be the one of 'global initiator'. It is doubtful if the EU possesses the necessary characteristics in the tax world that would make it a 'global regulatory power' in Bradford's words.[146] Not only because 'regulatory' would be a misnomer for 'taxation' but also because of its inability to meet at least two conditions: inelastic targets and non-divisibility.[147] Taxation is primarily elastic as it enables taxpayers to move their capital wherever it would enjoy the most beneficial treatment. This, of course, applies only to certain types of taxes (such as taxes on certain types of income and capital) but to a much lesser extent to other taxes, such as taxes on income from employment or from immovable property, that would hardly cause migration of the taxpayer or sale of their property.[148] Similarly, the requirement of non-divisibility would hardly be applicable in taxation – a taxpayer cannot 'export' another state's tax system.[149] It can pursue its values by avoiding transactions that would fall under the vague term 'tax avoidance' but it could not contribute to the globalisation of 'good tax governance'. Also seen realistically, corporations would most likely structure their activities and transactions in such a way so as to benefit from the most

[145] AM Jimenez, 'Preface' in Jimenez (n 91) xvii and U Gonzalez de Frutos, 'The EU and OECD Contend to Lead Global Tax Governance' in ibid 122 who rightly notes that the OECD standard represents a 'strikingly' low threshold, especially after the Paradise Papers revelations.

[146] A Bradford, *The Brussels Effect: How the European Union Rules the World* (Oxford, Oxford University Press, 2020) 25 et seq.

[147] I am referring here to the five conditions discussed in Bradford, ibid, that must be met cumulatively for the Brussels effect to flourish.

[148] ibid 48–53. In the aforementioned cases it is doubtful whether a taxpayer would move their residence and employment just by reason of the applicable taxes (unless they were operating in the area of the digital economy where a move for digital nomads is much easier), and the same would apply to immovable property. The same would be applicable with Value Added Tax (VAT).

[149] ibid 53–58.

favourable tax regime. Even if they are established in a state with strict anti-tax avoidance rules, it is likely that, as long as they have the possibility to channel their profits and capital in a low-tax jurisdiction, they would do so.[150]

Thus, if one had to locate the fundamental norm the EU aims to export to the world, this would be anti-tax avoidance. It remains to the MNEs to show whether the EU made the right choice to move forward with a series of stringent binding measures that aim to curb most remaining possibilities for tax avoidance. However, the EU's determination to go beyond the rest of the world in pursuit of its values showcases not only the EU's consistency but also its confidence that it has more to offer besides an attractive tax framework.

[150] This is, of course, an unlikely scenario, as the anti-tax avoidance legal framework of said state would attempt to dissuade this behaviour.

Sustainability

13

Climate Change in Tort Law? The New Regulatory and External Effect of Suits against Private Actors

VIBE ULFBECK*

I. SETTING THE SCENE: EUROPEAN CLIMATE CHANGE LITIGATION

CLIMATE-CHANGE LITIGATION ORIGINATED in the United States (USA/US) but over recent years several suits have been brought in Europe, in particular against European governments.[1] The cases take many shapes and some of them have the direct goal of forcing governments to make more ambitious carbon reduction strategies.[2] In this regard, the big breakthrough in Europe came with the Dutch *Urgenda* ruling of December 2019.[3] In this case, brought by the non-government organisation (NGO) Urgenda against the Dutch state, the Dutch Supreme

*Professor in Private Law, Faculty of Law, Centre for Private Governance (CEPRI), University of Copenhagen.

[1] A fairly updated overview of various types of climate-change litigation in different jurisdictions can be found in F Sindico and M Möise Mbengue (eds), *Comparative Climate Change Litigation: Beyond the Usual Suspects* (Berlin, Springer, 2021). For a good overview of European climate-change suits against states, see also C Gottlieb, 'Climate Claims against Governments in Europe' (2021), available at www.clearygottlieb.com/-/media/files/alert-memos-2021/climate-change-litigation-in-europe-increasing-judicial-scrutiny-over-state-climate-policies.pdf.

[2] Other cases have concerned the public authority duty to take into consideration climate aspects when granting permissions and licences, see, eg, the UK case *R (Friends of the Earth Ltd and Ors) v Heathrow Airport Ltd* [2020] EWCA Civ 2014 and in general M Spitzer and B Burtscher, 'Liability for Climate Change: Cases, Challenges and Concepts' (2017) 8 *Journal of European Tort Law* 137, 141–42, categorising these cases as more 'ordinary', 'bread and butter' cases. In a recent Norwegian case, the Supreme Court found that granting an oil exploitation licence did not violate the Norwegian Constitution, see E Columbo, 'Climate Change and the Individual: A Norwegian Perspective' in Sindico and Möise Mbengue (n 1) 91–117, 97.

[3] Hohe Raad 20 December 2019, ECLI:NLHR:2019:2006, unofficial English translation ECLI:NL:HR 2019:2007 ('*Urgenda*').

Court found the basis for such a claim in human rights law. More precisely, it found that Articles 2 and 8 of the European Convention on Human Rights (ECHR) should be interpreted in such a way that these provisions oblige the contracting states to do 'their part' to counter the danger of climate change[4] and that the Dutch state was obliged to achieve a reduction of at least 25 per cent of its carbon emissions by 2020.[5] The Court furthermore combined the duty found in human rights law with an injunction and ordered the state to adjust its legislation to achieve this goal.[6] The case has been regarded as a breakthrough in terms of establishing the link between climate change and human rights[7] and as an example of a case that – from a constitutional law perspective – demonstrates that courts can play a role in this area without acting as a legislator in disguise that oversteps the boundaries of the judiciary.[8] As such, the case has been a source of inspiration for several parallel suits in Europe over recent years.[9]

Whereas the ultimate goal of a suit against a state is to make it enact legislation that will change the behaviour of its subjects, including companies, one might also ask whether suits could simply be brought – more efficiently – directly against these companies, forcing them to reduce carbon emissions. With 90 major private carbon emitters being responsible for over 30 per cent of global industrial green house emissions[10] one might think they should be an obvious target.

Whereas international treaties and human rights obligations can form the basis of claims against states, these frameworks are not binding on private parties. This brings tort law into play. And in fact, tort law suits against private actors have also emerged in Europe, to some extent inspired by *Urgenda* which at district court level *did* rely on tort law in establishing the basis for imposing reduction requirements.[11]

[4] ibid legal ground 5.8.

[5] ibid legal ground 8.3.5.

[6] ibid legal ground 8.2.1: 'If the government is obliged to do something, it may be ordered to do so by the courts, as anyone may be, at the request of the entitled party' (Art 3:296 Dutch Civil Code (DCC)).

[7] For an early analysis of this relation, see A Gouritin, 'Potential Liability of European States under the ECHR for Failure to take Appropriate Measures with a View to Adaptation to Climate Change' in M Faure an M Peeters (eds), *Climate Change Liability* (Cheltenham, Edward Elgar, 2011).

[8] The Court itself found that it had not overstepped its boundaries because it had not decided on the specific content of the legislation to be enacted, *Urgenda* (n 3) legal ground 8.2.6. See further, eg, J Spier, 'The "Strongest" Climate Ruling Yet': The Dutch Supreme Court's *Urgenda* Judgment (2020) 67 *Netherlands International Law Review* 319–391, 334.

[9] eg, in Belgium, the Brussels Court of First Instance has ruled that based on the general tort law duty of care principle in the Belgium Civil Code Arts 1382 and 1383 as well as human rights obligations, the Belgian Government is obliged to take measures to meet more ambitious reduction targets in 2025, 2030 and 2050, see *VZW Klimaatzaak v Kingdom of Belgium* & others no 2015/4585/A (17 June 2021). Also the German Constitutional Court has found that the German constitution obliges the state to protect the climate and aim at climate neutrality, see BVerfG, Beschluss des Ersten Senats vom 24. März 2021–1 BvR 2656/18 – Rn. 1-270, available at www.bundesverfassungsgericht.de/e/rs20210324_1bvr265618.html.

[10] R Heede, 'Tracing Anthropogenic Carbon Dioxide and Methane Emissions to Fossil Fuel and Cement Producers' 1854–2010 (2014) 12 *Climatic Change* 229–41.

[11] The District Court had originally found that the Dutch state breached its tort law duty of care under Art 6:162 towards the Dutch people by not having a sufficiently ambitious carbon reduction policy when measured against scientific IPCC reports, *Urgenda* (n 3) legal ground 2.3.1.

From the outset, however, fundamental scepticism has been voiced towards the idea of tort law climate-change litigation. For example, Spitzer and Burtscher comment as follows:

> From a tort law perspective, the creation of a duty of care [in the Urgenda ruling] is remarkable. Still, one must not forget that the defendant was the state. Urgenda v. the Netherlands is therefore as far away from private law as duty of care can be ... it is probably no milestone for tort law.[12]

And further, '... if we look at climate change litigation against private entities, we must say that it died where it was born'.[13]

However, as will be shown in the following, the development seems to have gone in a different direction, building widely on the capacity of tort law to exercise regulatory effects and to reach beyond national borders. It is the purpose of this chapter to analyse this development.

II. THE REGULATORY AND EXTRATERRITORIAL CAPACITY OF TORT LAW

Distrust in European private climate-change litigation is understandable if one takes into consideration the classic features of tort law. Firstly, no common European tort law has been developed. At the EU level, legislative approaches have generally been confined to more specific areas such as product liability,[14] environmental liability,[15] liability for competition law infringements,[16] and so on. Private initiatives to try to take a more general approach include the development of the PETL (Principles of European Tort Law)[17] and the DCFR (Draft Common Frame of Reference),[18] but despite these efforts no official unifying codification of EU tort law exists. This largely leaves it to the national legal systems to develop their own autonomous tort law rules. This arguably makes tort law a less powerful tool to apply to a global problem.

Secondly, the classic understanding of tort law is that it deals with the bipolar relationship between the wrongdoer and the victim.[19] Over recent decades, it has also

[12] Spitzer and Burtscher (n 2) 148.

[13] ibid 176.

[14] Council Directive 85/374/EEC of 25 July 1985 on the approximation of the laws, regulations and administrative provisions of the Member States concerning liability for defective products [1985] OJ L210/28.

[15] Directive 2004/35/CE of the European Parliament and of the Council of 21 April 2004 on environmental liability with regard to the prevention and remedying of environmental damage ('Environmental Liability Directive') [2004] OJ L143/47.

[16] Directive 2014/104/EU of the European Parliament and of the Council of 26 November 2014 on certain rules governing actions for damages under national law for infringements of the competition law provisions of the Member States and of the European Union Text with EEA relevance [2014] OJ L349/57.

[17] The principles can be found at www.egtl.org/PETLEnglish.html.

[18] The principles can be found at www.ccbe.eu/fileadmin/speciality_distribution/public/documents/EUROPEAN_PRIVATE_LAW/EN_EPL_20100107_Principles__definitions_and_model_rules_of_European_private_law_-_Draft_Common_Frame_of_Reference__DCFR_.pdf.

[19] ER De Jong, MG Faure, I Giesen and P Mascini, 'Judge-Made Risk Regulation and Tort Law: An Introduction' (2018) *European Journal of Risk Regulation* 9, 6–13; EJ Weinrib, *The Idea of Private Law* (Oxford, Oxford University Press, 2012) 2.

been the general understanding that the main purpose of tort law is to compensate the victim.[20] In this role, tort law is solely backward-looking with a strong focus on how an act by the wrongdoer constitutes a negligent act or omission towards the victim as well as the causal link between that act or omission and the loss suffered by the victim. In this conception, the purpose of tort law is to solve problems between two parties. For this reason, climate-change litigation which concerns public interests – and potentially relations between everyone in society – has also been called 'anti-tort' as compared to tort law in its classic clothing.[21]

However, the ability of tort law also to have effects beyond the relationship between concrete parties in a tort law conflict has also always been recognised. One could speak of the regulatory effect of tort law in its ability to deter unwanted behaviour in the future through the threat of liability in situations similar to examples set in concrete rulings. This deterrent effect of tort law was originally regarded a 'byproduct' of tort law.[22] In contrast, over recent years, it has become clear that limited resources in the public sector do not always allow for efficient enforcement of public law standards.[23] Against this background, interest has increased in the potential of the regulatory role of tort law.[24] A recent very clear example of this is the new proposal for a directive on corporate sustainability due diligence, where tort law plays a central role in enforcing human rights obligations on companies.[25] Tort law, operating on the basis of general 'open standards' that apply to all members of society and that can respond to societal changes and needs, is in many ways well suited for this role.[26] As will be shown in the following, climate-change litigation is an area where

[20] eg, D Kysar, 'The Public Life of Private Law: Tort Law as a Risk Regulation Mechanism' (2018) 9 *European Journal of Risk Regulation* 1, 48–65, 49, pointing out that historically, tort law has been understood to 'provide a private law forum for the airing of grievances, the declaration of norms and the redress of wrongs', P Cane, 'Using Tort Law to Enforce Environmental Regulation?' (2002) 41 *Washburn Law Journal* 427–68, 466: '[the] justification for tort law in the regulatory state must rest on its role as a mechanism for imposing obligations or repair on the basis of ideas of personal responsibility'.

[21] DA Kysar, 'What Climate Change Can Do About Tort Law' (2012) 48 *Environmental Law Reporter News & Analysis* 10739–44, 10739.

[22] Kysar (n 20) 49: '… the threat of liability in tort might provide incentives for actors to alter their behavior but that possibility has not traditionally been identified as a central goal of tort law'.

[23] One speaks of 'the shortcomings of traditional command and control regulation' as generating a need for private enforcement, see, eg, De Jong et al (n 19) 9.

[24] ER De Jong, 'Tort Law and Judicial Risk Regulation: Bipolar and Multipolar Risk Reasoning in Light of Tort Law's Regulatory Effects' (2018) *European Journal of Risk Regulation* 9, 14–33, 24 on 'The (increasing) relevance of multipolar considerations'. Kysar (n 20) 49 draws attention to the law and economics movement as having been successful in changing the view of tort law in the USA so that today its purpose is seen as being *primarily* deterrence. Interest in tort law's regulatory effects is part of broader interest in the regulatory effects of private law, see in general H Micklitz, *The Politics of Justice in European Private Law* (Cambridge, Cambridge University Press, 2018).

[25] Proposal for a directive of the European Parliament and of the Council on Corporate Sustainability Due Diligence and amending Directive (EU) 2019/1937, COM(2022) 71 final 2022/0051 (COD), Art 22. Another clear example of this is provided by the area of competition law where deterrence through private enforcement now also in Europe has become a strong focus point, see, eg, the ruling from the Court of Justice of the European Union (CJEU) on parent company liability for subsidiaries, C-724/17 *Skanska Industrial Solutions and Others* ECLI:EU:C:2019:204.

[26] As noted by Bouwer: 'Private law … does not only deter behavior but also defines what that behavior should be. It also heralds tremendous potential for standards determined as "reasonable" by judges, to inform and supplement law regulation', K Bouwer, 'Lessons from a Distorted Metaphor: the Holy Grail of Climate Litigation' (2020) 9 *Transnational Environmental Law* 2, 347–78, 364. On some of the challenges

the regulatory role of tort law has come to play a decisive role. Moreover, climate-change litigation seems to be adding new dimensions to the regulatory role of tort law: dimensions that go far beyond creating deterrent effects.

In addition, despite the inherent national character of tort law, the effects of these rules may well go beyond national borders. Thus, whereas tort law rules may differ from one national legal system to another, tort law systems across the world also display commonalities in terms of the very basic principles of tort law. This offers an excellent basis for 'cross fertilisation' and invites the idea that a concept developed or refined in one legal system can be 'exported' to another legal system. Moreover, the tort law that is being shaped in the national courts of the EU will inevitably contain traces of sectoral pieces of EU regulation that may not directly contain liability provisions but may nevertheless impact the development of liability standards and shape the contours of a more common EU tort law. This will make concepts more visible to the outside world, thereby also strengthening the potential for transfer of concepts to systems outside of the EU.

Finally, whereas the principle of state immunity procedurally limits opportunities to bring suits against states in foreign courts, these restrictive principles do not necessarily apply to private actors.[27] Rules on jurisdiction, enforcement, and choice of law to some extent open the possibility of suing companies abroad or bringing claims against foreign companies in domestic courts. And whereas states enjoy jurisdiction only in their territory and can implement climate policy regulation only within their national boundaries, multinational companies expand and control their activities across national barriers, so that targeting their activities may have trickle-down effects that could generate real effects not just in the EU but also externally.

To illustrate the increasingly regulatory and extraterritorial role played by tort law in climate-change litigation, the following sections identify three different phases and strategies in tort law climate-change litigation against private actors and offer in-depth analyses of the central cases.

III. FIRST STAGE STRATEGY: BACKWARD-LOOKING CLAIMS FOR DAMAGE COMPENSATION

Some of the first tort law climate-change claims brought against private parties were classic tort law claims for damages for loss allegedly suffered by climate-change phenomena partially caused by private actors.

In *Comer v Murphy Oil*,[28] the claimant contended that emitting activities by energy companies had reinforced the consequences of the Katrina hurricane, eventually leading to the loss of the claimant's home. In *Kavalina v ExxonMobil*

related to norm generation in tort law, see, eg, M Lee, 'The Sources and Challenges of Norm Generation in Tort Law' (2018) *European Journal of Risk Regulation* 9, 24–47, focusing in particular on the challenge of courts applying scientific knowledge in standard-setting. On challenges and limits, see also P Cane, 'Tort Law as Regulation' (2002) 31 *Common Law World Review* 305–31.

[27] Also M Hinteregger, 'Civil Liability and the Challenges of Climate Change: A Functional Analysis' (2017) 8 *Journal of European Tort Law* 238, 246–47.

[28] *Comer v Murphy Oil USA Inc* 607 F.3d 1049 (5th Cir 2010).

Corporation et al,[29] peoples from Alaska claimed that energy companies were responsible for transboundary greenhouse gas (GHG) emissions leading to coastal erosion and melting Arctic ice and eventually displacement and relocation, since their village was threatened. Both cases were basic tort law cases in which the claimants demanded compensation for property loss and economic loss.[30]

From a tort law perspective, these suits face several challenges.

In the concrete cases, the claims were dismissed by the US district courts on the basis of the 'political question doctrine', meaning that the cases raised political questions which it was not for the courts but rather for the legislator to deal with.[31] In a European context, the political question doctrine may also pose barriers, albeit perhaps to a somewhat lesser degree.[32] However, other problems remain.

A basis for liability must be established. Strict liability may to some extent be available, notably under the tort of nuisance in Anglo-American law[33] but the most general and universally recognised principle of liability is fault-based liability.[34] Moreover, with regard to professionals, it is widely accepted that liability is 'objectivised'.[35] This means that with regard to large GHG emitters (the so-called 'Carbon Majors'), the basic question is whether the company's activity has infringed any generally accepted standards of behaviour. Here, it can be noted that, over the years, no laws have prohibited Carbon Major activity. On the contrary, Carbon Majors often provide products of crucial importance to society, such as energy. Moreover, in identifying generally accepted standards of behaviour, the general view is that public law rules and standards may to some extent play a role.[36] With regard to carbon emissions, one of the main points of discussion has been the question of the possible impact of European Emissions Trading Systems (ETS).[37] In the literature, opinions differ on this

[29] *Kavalina v ExxonMobil Corporation et al* 696 F.3d 849, 2012 WL 4215921 (9th Cir 2012).

[30] The claims were brought in the areas of nuisance, civil conspiracy and negligence.

[31] At the appellate level, *Comer* was eventually dismissed and in *Kivalina* it was held that federal legislation pre-empted the claimants federal common law claims, see in general, G Ganguly, J Setzer and V Heyvaert, 'If at First You Don't Succeed: Suing Corporations for Climate Change' (2018) 38 *OJLS* 841, 446–849.

[32] See further below under section VI.

[33] See further below under section IV. Also the Environmental Liability Directive (n 15) on environmental liability with regard to the prevention and remedying of environmental damage, could be considered as a basis of liability. However, it is generally thought not to be a suitable basis for claims concerning carbon emissions for which it was not deigned, see, eg, Hinteregger (n 27) 251.

[34] Reflected in Principles of European Tort Law (PETL) (n 17) Art 4.101. In some jurisdictions, the notion of fault is explicitly split into two parts, an objective one, requiring the unlawfulness or wrongfulness of the act, and a subjective one, requiring blameworthiness on the part of a concrete actor. Even if these two parts of the notion of fault are not explicit, they are generally understood to frame the concept of 'fault', see Hinteregger (n 27) 251, referring to France and Spain as examples of the latter model. As for the comparable Scandinavian model, see, eg, B Eyben and H Isager, *Lærebog i Erstatningsret* (Gothersgade, Djof for Lag, 2019) 96.

[35] See, eg, Hinteregger (n 27) 251.

[36] Reflected in PETL (n 17) Art 4.102 (3): Rules which prescribe or forbid a certain conduct have to be considered when establishing the required standard of conduct.

[37] The system is a carbon trading system that allows companies to emit a certain amount of carbon per year and to trade unused amounts. The system is regulated in Directive 2003/87/EC of the European Parliament and of the Council of 13 October 2003 establishing a system for greenhouse gas emission allowance trading within the Union and amending Council Directive 96/61/EC, with further amendments [2003] OJ L275/46.

argument. Some maintain that a company that does not exceed the allowed amount of emissions under this scheme cannot be held liable.[38] Others contend that observing the level of the ETS system is no guarantee against liability and that likewise the fact that a company stays within the carbon emissions limits in a licence cannot as such rule out tort liability.[39]

Since an objectified approach to establishing a basis of liability for big corporations must be assumed, it must also be assumed that courts will focus on the question of when it could *generally* be expected that those companies would have knowledge about the climate change effects of their activities. Consequently, one might need to distinguish between 'innocent' emissions, predating (general awareness of) the climate crisis and 'guilty' emissions.[40]

Furthermore, in a classic tort law case, the claimant also has to document loss. Here, climate change litigants face the challenge that whereas it is entirely foreseeable that climate change will cause losses in the future, as a starting point, only losses already suffered can be the object of a tort law claim.

Finally, one of the most basic challenges faced by tort law climate-change litigation is the requirement of proof of a causal link between the loss suffered and the negligent act. The general test for causation is the 'conditio sine qua non' test, also called the 'but for' test. According to this test, the wrongdoer's act or omission is only the cause of a certain loss if the loss would not have occurred had it not been for the act or omission by the wrongdoer. This test has posed a basic challenge to climate-change tort claims. Representative of these challenges is the formulation by the Court in *Kivalina* that there was 'no realistic possibility of tracing any particular alleged effect of global warming to any particular emissions by any specific person, entity, [or] group at any particular point in time'. Although some exceptions to the 'but-for' test have been developed, these are not widely used. In climate-change tort cases, the principle that would be most helpful for claimants would be the principle of proportional liability.[41] The principle comes in different versions[42] and has been designed inter alia for situations in which a large number of actors have each delivered a small contribution to causing the damage (minimal causation). In this situation, it would be unjust to apply the principle of joint and several liability and hold each contributor liable for the entire loss. Rather each contributor should be held liable for a part of the loss proportionate to its contribution.[43] Although this legal principle has support in doctrine, only a limited amount of case law has so far supported it.[44]

[38] Spitzer and Burtscher (n 2) 162–64; C van Dijk, 'Civil Liability for Global Warming in the Netherlands' in Faure and Peeters (n 7) 206–26, 215; P van den Biesen, 'Will Civil Society take Climate Changers to Court?' in Faure and Peeters (n 7) 227–36, 234.

[39] Hinteregger (n 27) 254; U Magnus, 'Injunctions against Climate Change?' in OC Ruppel, C Roschmann and K Ruppel-Schlichting (eds), *Climate Change: International Law and Global Governance. Volume 1: Legal Responses and Global Responsibility* (Baden-Baden, Nomos Verlagsgesellsschaft mbH, 2013) 851.

[40] Spitzer and Burtscher (n 2) 167.

[41] See in general, I Gilead, M Green and B Koch (eds), *Proportional Liability: Analytical and Comparative Perspectives* (De Gruyter, 2013).

[42] ibid; PETL (n 17) Arts 3:103, 3:105, 3:106.

[43] Hinteregger (n 27) 256.

[44] B Koch, 'Minimal Causation – Comparative Report' in B Winiger, H Koziol, B Koch and R Zimmermann, *Essential Cases on Natural Causation* (Wien, Springer, 2007) 541–43.

Despite the legal hurdles to overcome, this type of litigation with its focus on damages and its expected deterrent effect was originally praised as a potential 'magic bullet' in climate-change litigation as a more efficient way of achieving climate goals than pursuing legislation and regulation.[45] Being framed as a classic tort law case, based on classic tort law reasoning, the litigation model would probably also hold potential for 'export' to other legal systems. However, an obvious downside of pursuing this classic kind of tort law litigation with regard to climate change is that much climate change damage will only occur in the (distant) future. This means that the deterrent effect of this type of case mainly lies in the risk of being sued in the (distant) future. This risk will only create limited regulatory effect and behavioural change here and now in companies in the EU and across global value chains outside the EU, which is what is needed.[46]

IV. SECOND STAGE STRATEGY: FORWARD-LOOKING CLAIMS FOR FINANCING ADAPTATION MEASURES

In Europe, climate-change litigation against private actors took off following the 2014 Heede study.[47] The study provided a better scientific basis for claiming that emissions to a very large extent originate from the Carbon Majors and when these emissions took place.[48] The study also calculates what percentage of emissions that has been discharged into the atmosphere by concrete private actors.[49]

It is characteristic of the cases in this category that they are not concerned with damage already caused. Rather, the cases are forward looking, giving tort law a stronger regulatory role. The goal is to achieve monetary compensation for costs to cover foreseen necessary preventive measures against the consequences of climate change. As explained above, the forward looking aspect poses a basic challenge for tort law. Thus, normally, tort law only comes into play as a compensatory mechanism when actual loss has been suffered. For example, this is articulated clearly by Pieter Gillaerts: 'Tort law remains compensatory. With no loss, no claim'.[50] Yet, as will be explained below, tort law does manage to play a role in this type of case, in some legal systems more indirectly, and in others more directly.

The most spectacular case in this category is probably the German case of *Lliuya v RWE*, initiated in 2015.[51] In this case, a Peruvian farmer sued RWE, Germany's largest electricity producer, claiming payment of 21,000 US dollars to partly cover

[45] Shi-Ling Hsu, A Realistic Evaluation of Climate Change Litigation through the Lens of a Hypothetical Lawsuit (2008) 79 *University of Colarado Law Review* 3, 701–57, 714. See also Bouwer (n 26) 368 finding that these early cases, had they succeeded, could have been real 'game changers'.

[46] For this view, see also Spier (n 8) 48.

[47] Heede (n 10) 229–41.

[48] More specifically it is said to document that 90 Carbon Majors released more than half of their total contribution after 1988, Ganguly, Setzer and Heyvaert (n 31) 853.

[49] ibid 852, 854.

[50] P Gillaerts, 'Instrumentalisation of Tort Law: Widespread yet Fundamentally Limited' (2019) 15 *Utrecht Law Review* 3, 27–43, 41 with references.

[51] See *Luciano Lliuya v RWE AG* – Climate Change Litigation (climatecasechart.com)http://climatecasechart.com/non-us-case/lliuya-v-rwe-ag/.

expenses in securing his house against the risk of flooding. The risk stems from the glacial lake, Lake Palcacocha, located above the city in which the claimant's house is located, and which is threating to overflow due to rising water levels or glacial ice avalanches. The claimant argues that RWE is partly responsible for this situation through the GHG emissions produced by itself and its subsidiaries over which RWE as the parent company exercises control and that since RWE is responsible for 0.47 per cent of the carbon dioxide (C02) emitted into the atmosphere in the industrial era, RWE is obliged to pay compensation equivalent to 0.47 per cent of the sum necessary to spend on preventive measures.[52]

The case is often described as a tort law case,[53] although technically, it is not. It is not a claim for damages and it is not argued that RWE has acted unlawfully or negligently. Rather, the claim is based on property law principles. More specifically, the claim is based on §1004(1) *Bundesgesetzbuch* (BGB).[54] This provision protects the owner of property from interference with their property which they are not obliged to tolerate. Causing damage to property is clearly 'interference'. However, in this case the claimant asserts that a *risk* of damage may also qualify as 'interference' if it is inevitable that the condition will lead to interference.[55] According to §1004(1) sentence 1, the owner can demand that the disturber eliminates the interference. Interference, which in this case is the risk of the flooding of the house, can only be eliminated by taking costly precautionary measures. Under BGB Article 1004(1) sentence 1, the costs of eliminating interference rests with the disturber.[56] It is on this basis that the claimant argues in favour of a monetary claim against the German power plant station.[57]

[52] V Kumar and W Frank, 'Holding Private Emitters to Account for the Effects of Climate Change: Could a Case Like Lliuya Succeed under English Nuisance Laws?' (2018) 2 *Carbon & Climate Law Review* 110–23, 114–15.

[53] See, eg, W Frank, C Bals and J Grimm, 'The Case of Huaraz: First Climate Lawsuit on Loss and Damage Against an Energy Company Before German Courts' in R Mechler et al (eds), *Loss and Damage from Climate Change, Climate Risk Management, Policy and Governance* (Berlin, Springer, 2019) 475; see also A Hösli,' Milieudefense et al. v Shell: A Tipping Point in Climate Change Litigation against Corporations?' (2021) 11 *Climate Law Review* 195–209, 205.

[54] In German: '(1) Wird das Eigentum in anderer Weise als durch Entziehung oder Vorenthaltung des Besitzes beeinträchtigt, so kann der Eigentümer von dem Störer die Beseitigung der Beeinträchtigung verlangen. Sind weitere Beeinträchtigungen zu besorgen, so kann der Eigentümer auf Unterlassung klagen.

(2) Der Anspruch ist ausgeschlossen, wenn der Eigentümer zur Duldung verpflichtet ist'. English translation: '(1) If ownership is interfered with by means other than removal or retention of possession, the owner may require the disturber to eliminate the interference. If further interference is to be feared, the owner may seek a prohibitory injunction. (2) A claim is excluded if the owner is obliged to tolerate the interference'.

[55] Claimant's writ, page 29 with reference to MuKoBGB. See also A Kling, 'Die Klimaklage gegen RWE – Die Geltendmachung von Klimafolgeschäden auf dem Privatrechtsweg' (2018) *Kritische Justiz* 1–13, 4–5.

[56] MüKoBGB §1004(1) Rn 288: 'Die Kosten der Beseitigung fallen privatrechtlich nach allgM dem Störer zur Last'.

[57] As an exception to §1004(1), it follows from §1004(2) that a claim for cessation of the disturbing activity is excluded if the owner is 'obliged to tolerate the impairment'. This means that if the general interest prevents cessation of an activity that causes disturbance, the disturbance must be tolerated. However, in the German case, it is not cessation of the activity of the power plant that is claimed but only cessation of the risk of flooding of the house.

Although the claim is not technically a tort law claim, it nevertheless resembles a tort law claim in that the claimant seeks monetary compensation. In other ways, too, tort law principles seem to seep into the case. This is particularly relevant with regard to the issue of causation. BGB §1004 does not specify what kind of causal link must be proven between the disturbance (activities by the power plant) and interference (the risk of flooding). Here, it seems that to some extent tort law criteria are relied upon.[58] This was clear in the first instance decision where the Court in Essen dismissed the claim on the basis that the classic tort law 'but for' causation test was not satisfied.[59] The Court did not discuss the appropriateness of this test in a property law-based action.

The appellate Court of Hamm seems to have taken a different perspective altogether. It did not dismiss the case but ordered it to move to the evidentiary phase. In its decision of November 2017,[60] it stated that the case concerned 'the role of the energy companies' operations as active (contributory) causes of flood risk'.[61] More specifically, the Court required an expert opinion to be obtained on five aspects concerning causation:

1) a flood resulting from expansion of lake Palacocha poses a serious threat to the claimant's property;
2) the carbon emissions by the defendant rise into the atmosphere and lead to a higher concentration of GHGs throughout the earth's atmosphere;
3) the result is an increase in global temperature;
4) the increase in average local temperatures accelerates the melting of the Palcaraju Glacier and the volume of water will rise to a level that can no longer be contained by a natural moraine; and
5) the defendant's share in the contributory causation is measurable and calculable and the expert should quantify the correct proportion.[62]

As will be seen, these demands do not correspond to the demands under the classic but-for test. The Court seems to be willing to be satisfied with proof of causation at the more general level.[63]

[58] MüKoBGB §1004 Rn 71: 'Die Rspr.selbst tendiert hier zu schadensersatzrechtlichen Kategorien: adäquate Kausalität …'. See also Magnus (n 39) 850, assuming that tort law criteria on causation apply with regard to §1004 (1) Sentence 2.

[59] Court of Essen decision of 15 December 2016. Firstly, the Court found that RWE emissions were not necessary for the flood risk to exist. It would have existed anyway, due to other emissions and other factors. On a similar line of thinking, see Spitzer and Burtscher (n 2) 167 concerning the situation where a certain threshold (tipping point) has been reached after which every emission no longer contributes. Secondly, the Court found that it would not be possible to trace specific emissions by RWE to the specific flood risk in Peru. More precisely, the Court found that it would be impossible to 'identify anything resembling a linear line of causation from one particular source of emissions to one particular damage', see Court decision, 5. Here, the Court referenced the German Forest Damage case (Waldschadenurteil, Federal Court, III ZR 220/86, 10 December 1987). In sum, the Court's reasoning was clearly based on a traditional 'conditio sine qua non test' resembling the reasoning in the *Kavalina* case described above.

[60] Hamm Court decision of 30 November 2017, available at https://germanwatch.org/sites/germanwatch.org/files/static/20732.pdf.

[61] ibid Section I(3).

[62] ibid Section III.

[63] It has been noted that the most demanding requirement is probably obtaining evidence of 4), ie the existence of a link between global warming and the melting of the particular glacier, since local conditions

In its decision of 1 February 2018,[64] the Court confirmed its 2017 decision and further noted that with regard to §1004(1) Section 1, '… the established interpretation is that, in the case of multiple 'disturbers' each participant must eliminate its own contribution …'.[65]

This claimant thus has a basis for claiming from the defendant a proportionate sum of the total preventive cost. Commentators have found the decision to confirm the principle that 'each person must do his or her share' as expressed in *Urgenda*, whether or not this share constitutes a necessary condition for climate change.[66] However, it is unclear whether the view on causation in the case is also influenced by the fact that the case technically is not a tort law case but a property law case, providing a clearer basis for reaching the conclusion that each disturber must eliminate its own interference with the property ('do its part').

Relying on basic property law principles, combined to some extent with tort law principles, one may ask whether the case could be replicated in other jurisdictions. In Scandinavian law, which historically has often taken inspiration from German private law, basic property law principles are uncodified and their reach thus also uncertain. Basing a claim on neighbouring law would restrict the cases to concerning local nuisances.[67] In contrast, in English law, it has been suggested that the tort of nuisance (private or public) might provide the basis.[68] Whereas private nuisance law may be limited to concerning disputes between private landowners,[69] the tort of public nuisance covers a broader field.[70] Since a claim under English law would be a tort law claim, as a starting point it would be necessary to document harm and loss. However, it has been suggested that a compensatory claim for expenses of preventive

may also play a role, Kumar and Frank (n 52) 119. Here, new attribution science studies may help, see, eg, B Ekwurzel and others, 'The Rise in Global Atmospheric Co2, Surface Temperature, and Sea level from Emmissions Traced to Major Carbon Producers' (2017) *Climatic Change* 579. See also S Marjanac and L Patton, 'Extreme Weather Event Attribution Science and Climate Change Litigation: an Essential Step in the Causal Chain?' (2018) 36 *Journal of Energy and Natural Resources* 265–98.

[64] Hamm Court decision of 1 February 2018, available at https://germanwatch.org/sites/germanwatch.org/files/static/21158.pdf.

[65] Hamm Court decision of 1 February 2018, Section IV.

[66] See, eg, Ganguly, Setzer and Heyvaert (n 31) 855, who with reference to Germanwatch states that the Court declared 'it is enough that its emissions are partially responsible for the actual, present risk'. In line with this, it has also been suggested that the Court either finds that the *conditio sine qua non* test is satisfied since 'without RWE's contribution, the degree and extent of the flood risk would be lowered' or that the *conditio sine qua non* test does not apply in a case of 'cumulative causation', see Kumar and Frank (52) 118. The term 'cumulative causation' is used by the parties in the case although it is not a generally established category in tort law. It seems to cover the situation in which several actors contribute to the same harm without any single actor being responsible for causing the harm. The term seems also to be used in English tort law, see Kumar and Frank (52) 118. In other legal systems, the term 'concurrent causes' would be used to cover this situation, see Hinteregger (n 27) 255–56.

[67] See, eg, for Norwegian law: Columbo (n 2) 103–104.

[68] A very interesting in-depth analysis of this question is found in Kumar and Frank (n 52), on which the following relies.

[69] ibid 112.

[70] In English law, it is defined as 'acts and omissions of the defendant that materially affect the reasonable comfort and convenience of a class of her Majesty's subjects', see Kumar and Frank (n 52) 112 with reference to Lord Denning. Public nuisance claims may be brought either as tort law claims or as criminal law offences, Kumar and Frank (n 52) 112. It is noted that in English law a public nuisance claim may be restricted to subsidiaries as the direct source of emissions, rather than the parent company, Kumar and Frank (n 52) 115.

measures may also be possible under English law as a 'quia timet' mandatory injunction. This is an order to take action to prevent damage that will otherwise occur, such as preventing flooding of private property by investing in protective measures.[71] However, the requirement of causation may also pose problems under English law, which also proceeds from the 'but for' test as a general starting point. The asbestos case of *Bonnington Castings Ltd v Wardlaw*[72] could support the view that, in the case of concurrent (cumulative) causes that all add to the problem without each of them being either a necessary or a sufficient cause, each contributor could still be held liable.[73] However, separate argumentation is needed to reach the conclusion that a claim for a proportionate amount of costs should not be rejected on the basis that awarding such a sum will not prevent the risk from materialising.[74] English law scholars conclude that it may be more difficult but still possible also to bring suits similar to the German one under English law.[75] In line with this, suits of this kind have already been brought under both private and public nuisance law in the USA.[76] In French law, the new Article 1251 in the Code Civil takes preventive costs into account as an item of loss[77] and thus does away with one of the obstacles to bringing adaptation claims on the basis of tort law.

The above might indicate that the 'German model' could to some extent also be 'exportable' to jurisdictions outside the EU that have roots either in German or Common Law traditions. Export could also happen more indirectly through company structures such as those described in the RWE case, where RWE in reality controls several subsidiaries worldwide that would also have to adjust to the effect of a court decision based on (German) property law thinking. The property law model has some advantages. By basing a claim on property law principles – or in Anglo/American law, on nuisance law – the claimant is relieved from proving negligence on the part of the defendant. In addition, by not claiming full compensation for specific loss or injury but only a proportional sum to prevent a risk from materialising, the claimant's burden of proof with regard to causation is reduced to concerning a *contribution* by the defendant, rather than the defendant being the necessary cause of the risk.

[71] For details of this argument, see Kumar and Frank (n 52) 116, 122; G Kaminskaité-Salters, 'Climate Change Litigation in the UK: Its Feasibility and Prospects' in Faure and Peeters (n 7) 165–88, 175.

[72] *Bonnington Castings Ltd v Wardlaw* (1956) AC 613.

[73] Kumar and Frank (n 52) 118.

[74] ibid 122.

[75] ibid 123.

[76] Several of these cases have concerned procedural issues regarding preemption by federal law, see, eg, *County of San Mateo v Chevron Corp*, No. 18-15499 (9th Cir Apr 19, 2022), where three local governments in California had filed separate lawsuits in the California Superior Court making compensatory claims on the basis that the carbon emissions by the defendants cause more severe flooding and sea level rise that jeopardise infrastructure, beaches, schools and communities. The claim is inter alia based on private and public nuisance. The Ninth Circuit ruled that the case should be remanded to state court. See also *City of New York v BP: City of New York v Chevron Corp*, et al., No. 18-2188, 2021 WL 1216541 (2d Cir Apr 1, 2021), preemption by the Clean Air Act; *City of Oakland v BP PLC*, 969 F.3d 895 (9th Cir 2020). Public nuisance claim for compensation for protective measures needed. No complete preemption.

[77] It states that expenses to prevent imminent realisation of damage, in order to avoid aggravation of damage or in order to reduce the effects, constitute an item of loss for which compensation can be claimed. Art 1251 reads (in French): 'Les dépenses exposées pour prévenir la réalisation imminente d'un dommage, pour éviter son aggravation ou pour en réduire les conséquences constituent un préjudice réparable'.

In addition, as compared to classic, backward looking tort case law that can only be initiated once damage has actually been suffered, this type of claim holds somewhat more potential as a regulatory mechanism as suits can be initiated at an earlier phase, namely as soon as a risk of damage can be identified.[78] However, the regulatory effect of this type of claim still consists mainly of a possible deterrent effect.

V. THIRD STAGE STRATEGY: FORWARD-LOOKING CLAIMS FOR CHANGE OF POLICIES

The big potential in tort-based climate-change litigation lies in using tort law as a truly regulatory mechanism that directly claims a change of behaviour with regard to carbon emissions. As explained, normally, tort law is used as a basis for claiming damages for loss already suffered and only by some stretch and partly reshape of claims into proprietary claims may it be possible to cover compensation for preventive measures.[79] However, in a ground-breaking decision from 2021, the Hague District Court used tort law as a basis for ordering Royal Dutch Shell (RDS) to change policy, more specifically to reduce carbon emissions from the entire Shell Group, over which RDS was found to have control, by 45 per cent below 2019 levels by 2030.[80] The Court took a value chain perspective and found that the parent company could be held accountable – in its role as a 'private regulator' – not only for its own emissions (scope 1) but – under certain conditions – also for emissions from subsidiaries and contractual partners (scope 2) and from end users (scope 3). The Court briefly rejected the view that in reaching this conclusion it was acting as a legislator and outside the function of a court.[81] However, the ruling gives tort law a very clear regulatory role that is not only indirectly but 'directly' forward looking. Basically, the Court found that continuing GHG emissions according to company policy would be a negligent act and consequently unlawful. On that basis, the Court imposed an injunction on the company, ordering it to change its policies. Thus, the Court used the part of tort law that concerns the basis of liability and combines it with the law of injunctions to reach the result.

With regard to the basis of liability, the Court took its starting point in the unwritten standard of care, proper social conduct',[82] laid down in Book 6, Section

[78] *cp* Spier (n 8) 49 finding it 'not so very easy to explain why claims for damages should be dismissed, while adaptation costs could be recovered'.

[79] But compare the tort of nuisance which can give rise to both compensatory liability claims and criminal law claims.

[80] ECLI:NL:RBDHA:2021:5339. The decision immediately generated several case comments, see, eg, C Macchi and J van Zeben, 'Business and Human Rights Implications of Climate-Change Litigation: Millieudefensie et al v. Royal Dutch Shell (2021) *Review of European, Comparative & International Environmental Law* 30, 409–15; O Spijkers,'Friends of the Earth Netherlands (Milieudefensie) v Royal Dutch Shell' (2021) *Chinese Journal of Environmental Law* 5, 237–56; CV Ciabardo, 'Climate Change Litigation & Corporate Responsibility. A Comment on "Milieudefensie and Others v. Shell" (2021), available at www.glawcal.org.uk/stories/climate-change-litigation-corporate-responsibility-a-comment-on-milieudefensie-and-others-vs-shell-2021; Hösli (n 53).

[81] Legal grounds 4.1.2 and 4.1.3.

[82] Hösli (n 53) 198.

162 of the Dutch Civil Code. The standard is a broad and open-ended standard similar to those found in many other tort law systems. The standard must be interpreted in order to be applied in a concrete case. In interpreting the standard, the Court resorted to a wide range of criteria.[83] Notably, the Court made use of human rights (ECHR Articles 2 and 8).[84] Whereas in *Urgenda*, the Court found a basis for imposing reduction requirements on the state in human rights law, human rights are not directly binding on companies. Instead, the Court used tort law as 'the missing link'. Thus, by referring to human rights to determine the standard of care, the Court indirectly gave horizontal effect to those rights, although as a general rule human rights only apply vertically as between states and individuals.[85] The Court thus 'assumed' standards that might ordinarily be thought of as belonging to public law.[86] In addition, the Court also relied on UNGPs (United Nations Guiding Principles)[87] for interpreting the tort law standard of care. On this basis, combined with scientific reports, the Court developed the value chain perspective and the notion of scope 1, 2 and 3 emissions.[88] In this way, the Court conveyed legal effect to principles that ordinarily are only thought of as soft law principles or vague quasi legal ideas.[89] Finally, with regard to the argument that observance of the relevant public regulation ought to shield the company from liability, the Court stated: 'The reduction target of the ETS system is not identical to RDS's reduction obligation … RDS cannot rely on the indemnifying effect of the ETS system …'[90]

Having established a basis of liability in tort law, and thereby unlawfulness, the Court moved on to combine this with the law of injunctions and ordered the company to change its company policy to reduce its emissions.[91]

The linking of tort law and the law of injunctions is a technique that is also known in other jurisdictions. Injunctions are sometimes described as an 'in kind' tort law remedy.[92] In Scandinavian law, for example, it is also assumed that injunctions can be used against acts that general tort law would deem 'negligent' (and thereby unlawful).[93] German law uses the general tort law provision in BGB Article 823(1) to identify the 'interests' which an injunction can protect[94] and further requires serious risk of 'wrongful' infringement of these rights. However, what is considered

[83] Summarised in legal grounds 4.4.2.

[84] Legal ground 4.4.9–4.4.10.

[85] For an explanation of this basic starting point, see, eg, V Jentsch, 'Etappensieg bei Klimaklage zur Reduktion von CO2-Emissionen gegen Rohstoffunternehmen' (2021) *Gesellschafts- und Kapitalmarktrecht* (2021) 3, 321–43, 327–29.

[86] For a very clear analysis of the case in this regard, see ibid 327–29.

[87] United Nations Guiding Principles on Business and Human Rights, available at www.ohchr.org/sites/default/files/documents/publications/guidingprinciplesbusinesshr_en.pdf.

[88] Legal grounds 4.4.11-4.4.21 with reference to the UNGP's and 'the Oxford Report'.

[89] Jentsch (n 85) 332–33.

[90] Legal grounds 4.4.46.

[91] The basis for the order is found in Art 3:296 (1) in the Dutch Civil Code which (in translation) reads: 'Where a person is legally obliged towards another person to give, to do or not to do something, the court shall order him, upon a request or claim of the entitled person, to carry out this specific performance, unless something else results from law, the nature of the obligation or a juridical act'.

[92] For a general analysis of injunctions as a tort law remedy, see J Murphy, 'Rethinking Injunctions in Tort Law' (2007) 27 *OJLS* 3, 509–35.

[93] See CS Petersen, P Møgelvang-Hansen and T Riis, *Judicielle forbud/påbud og immaterialretsproces* (Karnov Group, 2015) 42.

[94] Magnus (n 39) 850. Under BGB Art 823(1), protected interests are eg life, bodily integrity and property.

wrongful in a liability context need not necessarily also be wrongful in the context of injunctions.[95] Likewise, one might ask whether the tort law criterion of causation can be transferred to the injunction context. The fact that the case concerns injunctions and not compensation for personal injury or property damage means that the theme of causation slightly transforms. It turns on the relation between the alleged wrongful act and 'the risk of future damage' to property that the claimant wants to address, which is arguably a more general causation theme.[96] In German legal scholarship, it is been observed that 'the defendant's activity must be the cause of actual or threatened infringement'[97] and further that

> [in] a rather general sense, there is a causal link between any activity contributing to climate change and threatened loss of land … On a concrete level it is very problematic to state that, for instance, the emissions of a German energy plant cause the rise of the level of the Pacific Ocean (to what extent)?[98]

Moreover, injunction cases may contain an extra layer of causal questions. Thus, in addition to showing that an infringement caused the risk of loss, it may also be necessary to show that an injunction is both necessary and sufficient to protect the claimant against the risk.[99] In *Millieudefensie*, the Dutch Court addressed this aspect of causation when it noted that the order (to adopt a more ambitious climate policy) could only be rejected if the order could 'not *contribute* [my emphasis] to preventing the alleged imminent infringement of interests'.[100] RDS had argued that a court order would have no effect since the place of the Shell group 'would just be taken by competitors'.[101] The Court took a different view on this, finding that:

> Due to the compelling interests which are served by the reduction obligation, this argument cannot justify assuming beforehand that there is no need for RDS to not meet this obligation. It is also important here that each reduction of greenhouse gas emissions has a positive effect on countering dangerous climate change. After all, each reduction means that there is more room in the carbon budget. The court acknowledges that RDS cannot solve this global problem on its own. However, this does not absolve RDS of its individual partial responsibility to do its part regarding emissions by the Shell Group, which it can control and influence.[102]

Here, the Court seems to do away entirely with the traditional tort law principle on causation embedded in the 'but for' test, not only with regard to the question whether an injunction will protect against risk, but also more generally. Thus, having regard to 'the compelling interests served by the reduction obligation', the fact that

[95] Notably, compliance with licence requirements, although not necessarily a barrier to liability may in German law prevent an injunction, Magnus (n 39) 851. This can be contrasted with the view of the Dutch Court, rejecting that compliance with the ETS system could shield the company against an injunction.

[96] See also van Dijk (n 38) 221–22.

[97] Magnus (n 39) 852.

[98] ibid.

[99] Thus, there could be many ways to protect oneself against risk. In English law, the causal requirement is clearly expressed in relation to the *quia timet* mandatory injunction which as a starting point requires that 'it must be impossible for the claimant to defend himself without the relief granted via a quia timet action', Kumar and Frank (n 52) 122.

[100] Legal ground 4.5.5.

[101] Legal ground 4.4.49.

[102] Legal ground 4.4.49.

Shell's activities are not a necessary condition for the threat is not decisive. For the court, causation 'in a more general sense' seems to suffice, in that it is scientifically established that part of global warming is man-made, that Shell partly contributes to this and that global warming will threaten the Dutch people and specifically the people of Wadden. This simplified reasoning on causation is in line with the *Urgenda* reasoning.[103] The emphasis on the view that RDS must 'do its part' can be seen as a version of 'proportional liability' only in the context of injunctions.[104]

The regulatory role played by tort law here becomes clear in several different respects. By including both human rights and UNGPs in interpreting the standard of care, the decision very clearly uses tort law as a regulatory tool. Human rights are 'imported' into tort law and used not only in support of the result but also to create a standard of care. In this way, tort law becomes an enforcer of human rights and the public policy behind them. The regulatory character of tort law even seeps into the test of causation where the simplified test seems to be legitimised at least in part by the 'compelling interests which are served by the reduction obligation', or strong societal needs. Additionally, use of an injunction as a remedy gives the tort law basis for the claim a clear regulatory effect. RDS is held accountable in its capacity as 'the policy setting entity'[105] and is not just asked to pay compensation to a concrete claimant but to alter its company policy, that is, the private regulatory basis for the company's activities, which will affect not only a specific claimant but a larger number of future potential victims of climate change.

The ruling will also have external effects. Concretely, *Millieudefensie* represents the Dutch residents and the inhabitants of the Wadden region who are particularly vulnerable to flooding, but in addition the ruling will benefit potential climate-change victims in parts of the world other than the Netherlands and – due to the value chain approach in the decision – also subsidiaries and business relations worldwide which will have to adjust to the policies of the lead company.

The concept embedded in *Millieudefensie* of suing the Carbon Majors on the basis of a combination of tort law and the law of injunctions has also already been copied and used in legal systems other than the Dutch legal system.[106] In Germany, Greenpeace has sued Volkswagen, one of the greatest car manufacturers in the world, claiming that the company be ordered to phase out the highly polluting internal combustion engine and to adapt its business strategy to the Paris Agreement.[107] The basis for the claim is a combination of BGB Article 823 (tort law) and

[103] See above in section I on the reasoning in this case.

[104] Perhaps in line with this, J Spier suggests a more lenient standard for proof of causation with regard to injunctions, J Spier, 'Injunctive Relief: Opportunities and Challenges. Thoughts About a Potentially Promising Legal Vehicle to Stem the Tide' in J Spier and U Magnus (eds), *Climate Change Remedies* (The Hague, Eleven International Publishing, 2013) 54.

[105] Legal ground 4.4.4.

[106] An early US case failed for procedural reasons, see *American Electric Power Co v Connecticut* 131 S. Ct. 2527 (2011). The case was dismissed on the basis that the Clean Air Act displaced a federal common law public nuisance claim seeking to reduce CO2 emissions from a fossil-fuel power plant.

[107] See, eg, Greenpeace International, 'Greenpeace Sues Volkswagen for Fuelling the Climate Crisis and Violating Future Freedom and Property Rights' (9 November 2021), available at www.greenpeace.org/international/press-release/50625/greenpeace-sues-volkswagen-for-fuelling-the-climate-crisis-and-violating-future-freedom-and-property-rights/.

Article 1004 (injunctions).[108] A parallel suit has been initiated against Daimler.[109] In France, a coalition of NGOs has initiated a suit against Total before the Nanterre judicial court.[110] They request a judicial injunction against the oil company demanding it make a more ambitious plan for reducing carbon emissions to meet the objectives of the Paris Agreement and in accordance with the French Duty of Vigilance Act.[111] According to Article L.225-102-5 of the Act, the duty of vigilance can be enforced by invoking civil liability. There is no mention in the Act of the use of injunctions. In the case, the basis for claiming an injunction is sought in Article 1252 in the tort law section in the French Code Civil.[112] In other words, here as well the connection is drawn between tort law principles and injunctions. It remains to be seen if this will be accepted by the French Court.[113]

This Court activity clearly reflects export of ideas from one legal system in the EU to another. Arguably, 'export' could also happen to any system outside of the EU that operates a combination of tort law and the law of injunctions.

All of the cases mentioned revolve around the same general idea of obliging companies to create self-regulation for the purpose of meeting the global challenge from climate change. Self-regulation would necessarily target not only the company itself but the entire global value chain over which the company has control. This would include companies outside of the EU and thus lead to a 'transplant' of principles stemming from tort law thinking in EU civil courts to jurisdictions outside of the EU.

The obligation to self-regulate with the goal of keeping the rise in temperatures below the 1.5 degree target of the Paris Agreement may in the future be codified in EU legislation that could reinforce the development described above. Thus, the proposal for a directive on corporate sustainability due diligence obligations with regard to human rights and the environment[114] also imposes a regulatory duty on companies to create self-regulation in the shape of company plans and strategies for this purpose.[115]

[108] For the claim form in German, see www.greenpeace.de/publikationen/vw_klage_final_small_0.pdf. Summary in English, see www.greenpeace.de/publikationen/greenpeace_vs_vw_english.pdf.

[109] See V Waldersee, 'Explainer: Why are BMW and Daimler being Sued over Climate Change?' (*Reuters*, 21 September 2021), available at www.reuters.com/article/climate-change-germany-court-idAFL1N2QM0AI.

[110] See, eg, http://climatecasechart.com/non-us-case/notre-affaire-a-tous-and-others-v-total/.

[111] La loi n° 2017-399 du 27 mars 2017 relative au devoir de vigilance des sociétés mères et des entreprises donneuses d'ordre.

[112] Art 1252 (in French): 'Indépendamment de la réparation du préjudice écologique, le juge, saisi d'une demande en ce sens par une personne mentionnée à l'article 1248, peut prescrire les mesures raisonnables propres à prévenir ou faire cesser le dommage'.

[113] On this issue, see, eg, www.arnaudgossement.com/archive/2020/02/07/devoir-de-vigilance-la-loi-du-27-mars-2017-a-t-elle-pour-obj-6210940.html: '..l'article L.225-102-5 permet l'exercice d'une action en responsabilité contre la société dans les conditions prévues aux articles 1240 et 1241 du code civil. La société responsable devra alors réparer le préjudice *que l'exécution de ses obligations aurait permis d'éviter.* Le texte est néanmoins silencieux concernant le tribunal compétent pour prononcer l'injonction …'.

[114] Proposal for a directive of the European Parliament and of the Council on Corporate Sustainability Due Diligence and amending Directive (EU) 2019/1937, COM(2022) 71 final, 2022/0051 (COD).

[115] See the proposal, Art 15 (1): 'Combating climate change: 1. Member States shall ensure that companies referred to in Article 2(1), point (a), and Article 2(2), point (a), shall adopt a plan to ensure that the business model and strategy of the company are compatible with the transition to a sustainable economy and with the limiting of global warming to 1.5 °C in line with the Paris Agreement. This plan shall, in particular,

VI. HOW TO GIVE EFFECT TO REGULATORY EFFECT?

Given that a duty to create self-regulation in the shape of plans and strategies exists at company level, either on the basis of tort law or on the basis of a forthcoming directive or both, one might ask what will be the legal effect of this type of regulation.

Firstly, the question arises whether a company that lives up to such self-regulation would be protected against further climate claims.[116] If the line of reasoning in *Millieudefense* is followed, it would be possible for an NGO to challenge an internal company policy in a tort law suit to test whether the level of ambition in the policy is sufficient.

Likewise, one might ask to what extent self-regulation would be legally enforceable. Normally, corporate policies do not have self-binding effect.[117] Internal policies created by the company can always be changed by the company.[118] However, it has been argued that these internal policies can influence the standard of care and set the individual standard of care for a particular company.[119] If internal policies are a result of a court decision, and hence not entirely voluntary, this argument must gain in force. On that basis it might be possible to argue that not living up to internal rules created as a response to an injunction should be regarded as constituting a violation of the general duty of care and consequently also as providing the basis for imposing a (new) injunction to live up to company self-regulation.

Moreover, the duty to create such regulation, its existence and the general awareness of companies' climate obligations that the duty to self-regulate creates may have other trickle-down effects. Thus, as has been pointed out in the legal literature, we are already beginning to see a new wave of climate-change litigation cases concerning the 'financial infrastructure' surrounding companies.[120] Cases concern duties of directors and board members to handle climate change risk at the managerial level and duties of investors and financial actors to take climate change risk into consideration when

identify, on the basis of information reasonably available to the company, the extent to which climate change is a risk for, or an impact of, the company's operations.' On the development of a concept of 'Climate Change Due Diligence' see further C Macchi, 'The Climate Change Dimension of Business and Human Rights: The Gradual Consolidation of a Concept of "Climate Due Diligence" (2021) 6 *Business and Human Rights Journal* 93–119.

[116] The proposed directive on corporate accountability contains a 'safe harbour' clause to this effect (Art 22) but it does not apply to climate obligations.

[117] See, eg, A Beckers, *Enforcing Corporate Social Responsibility Codes* (Oxford, Hart Publishing, 2015) 82, noting about self-commitments in general that 'such self-commitments are from the orthodox perspective treated as voluntary in nature that cannot be enforced as a legally binding contract'.

[118] Perhaps for this reason, the view has been expressed that injunctive relief is 'just another form of regulation', Hsu (n 45) 714.

[119] Beckers (117) 178, C Glinski, 'Bridging the Gap: The Legal Potential of Private Regulation' in O Dilling, M Herberg and G Winther (eds), *Responsible Business, Self-Governance and Law in Transnational Economic Transactions* (Oxford, Hart Publishing, 2008) 41–66, 47ff; V Ulfbeck and O Hansen, 'Interplay between Contract and Tort' in V Ulfbeck, A Andhov and K Mitkidis (eds), *Law and Responsible Supply Chain Management* (London, Routledge 2019) 133–45, 137.

[120] Ganguly, Setzer, Heyvaert (n 31) 858–61.

deciding which market players to support.[121] In this way, market developments may force companies to take seriously their climate policies.[122]

VII. SUMMING UP: TOWARDS A TRULY REGULATORY TORT LAW WITH EXTERNAL EFFECTS IN CLIMATE-CHANGE LITIGATION?

The above analysis has drawn a picture of a still stronger regulatory role played by tort law in climate-change litigation. Whereas it has been the general view for decades that tort law may have a deterrent effect but primarily plays a compensatory role in modern society and largely leaves the task of correcting behaviour to areas such as criminal law and public law, climate-change litigation is a very clear example of an area where this is changing. Here, tort law is no longer just a backward looking discipline that provides the basis for payment of compensation for loss suffered. Tort has become forward looking and is used as a basis for claims to prevent future losses. This is seen in claims for monetary sums to establish adaptation measures. However, it is seen even more clearly in claims for sufficiently ambitious self-regulation by companies.

With regard to establishing a basis of liability, it can be observed that this problem 'disappears' if an action is based on property law principles/nuisance law principles, which do not require proof of negligence. In addition, if a claim is based on the duty of care, there is now case law to the effect that the relevant standard is not necessarily dictated by standards that could be deduced from concrete licences or public law regulation aimed at regulating emission trading. In fact, tort law can serve as the 'missing link' and take in more far-reaching international standards and soft law standards that are not normally legally binding upon private parties. However, it can also go beyond international standards and standards found in public law regulation when determining the standard of care. This enables tort law to pay stronger attention to science-based knowledge on climate change and what is necessary to meet the challenge.

The regulatory character of climate-change tort law can be observed not only with regard to the basis of liability but even in relation to the requirement of causation. As pointed out, the content of the requirement of proof of causation in part depends on a more precise framing of the claim. For instance, new types of claims for self-regulation do not demand establishing a link between acts by the wrongdoer and specific loss because no compensation is claimed. It is sufficient to establish a causal

[121] RH Weber and A Hösli, 'Corporate Climate Responsibility – The Rise of a New Governance Issue' (2021) *Sui Generis* 83–92. See also Expert Group on Climate Obligations of Enterprises, *Principles on Climate Obligations of Enterprises* (The Hague, Eleven Publishing, 2018) 198.

[122] It could also be considered whether a court could order a company not only to adopt self regulation but also to secure monitoring the observance of such regulation. Inspiration could perhaps be sought in the model used in competition law concerning commitment decisions, sometimes supervised and controlled by private law firms. For an overview of developments in the EU and national law on commitment decisions in EU competition law and national competition law, see: www.concurrences.com/en/bulletin/special-issues/commitment-decisions/new-article-no90109.

link between the activity of the specific wrongdoer and the general level of carbon emissions. Science provides a still better basis for this. However, in addition, given the pressing societal need to react to climate change, the law may also be showing signs of moving away from strict adherence to the 'but for' test in the direction of acceptance of the concept of proportional liability, as seen in cases concerning claims for adaptation costs and self-regulation. It remains to be seen if this is a more general move that could also benefit the classic tort law case for damage compensation.

Whether the theme in a climate-change tort case concerns the basis of liability or causation, in both regards the claimant may be helped if it is shown that the defendant clearly had knowledge of the impact of the company's activities on climate change. In this respect, a very recent Philippine study[123] is said to document that not only did large carbon emitters have knowledge of the dangerous effects of their activities but they also tried to obfuscate and conceal related scientific evidence.[124] Establishing these facts will not only make it easier to establish a basis of liability, but it may also ease the burden of proof of causation. This can also be seen as an example of the regulatory role played by tort law.

Indeed, the regulatory role of tort law in climate-change litigation is so strong that it has raised the question how far the courts can go. In common law jurisdictions, and in particular in the USA, this theme is addressed under the 'political question' doctrine. Clearly, this principle has a role to play in cases against states, where it can be argued that the question how to legislate is a question for the legislator but not for the courts. However, it may also play a role in suits against private parties. In the USA, the 'political question doctrine' is a formalised principle that requires dismissal of a case that raises political questions.[125] In Europe, the principle is less formalised but courts may find a matter to be injusticiable[126] or be hesitant to impose liability if a liability question involves a question that is for the legislator to decide. Overall, until now, the doctrine seems to have been less of a hindrance to climate-change litigation in Europe than in the USA.[127] This may cause Europe to become a new motor for tort law climate-change litigation.

The effects of this motor will hardly stop at the borders of the EU. Thus, since tort law is a fundamental building block in most legal systems, the idea of basing suits against companies on tort law will often be transferable to other jurisdictions. It has not been the objective of this chapter to provide empirical evidence that export of legal concepts has in fact taken place (yet) but rather to show its potential for development. As described above, suits against private actors on the basis of tort law or in combination with tort law are, for example, currently taking

[123] See National Inquiry on Climate Change Report, May 2022 104, available at https://chr.gov.ph/reports/.

[124] Here, there may be obvious parallels with the asbestos and tobacco litigation some decades ago, see, eg, Ganguly, Setzer, Heyvaert (n 31) 856, making this parallel.

[125] See, eg, ibid 848.

[126] Kumar and Frank (n 52) 114.

[127] See, eg, Bouwer (n 26) 373 noting that by bringing an action in a German court one may avoid the 'political question doctrine'. Compare F Simlinger and B Mayer, 'Legal Responses to Climate Change Induced Loss and Damage' in R Mechler et al (eds), *Loss and Damage from Climate Change* (London, Springer 2019) 179–203, 182, finding the opposite to be the case.

place in the Netherlands, in Germany and in France and the concepts in these cases could be transferable to jurisdictions that are based on the same legal traditions as these systems. Furthermore, however, new concepts developed in civil law systems often have parallels in Common Law, opening up the possibility for export also to common-law jurisdictions. In a wider perspective, the liability standards that are being shaped in the courts of the EU will inevitably contain traces of sectoral EU law developments, such as due diligence standards found in the Conflict Minerals Regulation[128] and the Corporate Sustainability Due Diligence Directive (if adopted) drawing a picture that what is in reality being prepared for export is 'EU tort law'.

Finally, export of ideas also has a more practical side. Whereas new standards imposed on states (as in *Urgenda*) can only be enforced by the state within its own territory, the new regulatory climate-change tort law that is evolving with regard to private actors in Europe in recent years will in practice also have effects outside of the EU through company structures. Thus, many of the big companies that are being sued have subsidiaries and business partners in other parts of the world. In order to comply with the standards set by the new regulatory tort law, parent companies must also take into account carbon emissions from these enterprises and use their leverage to also impose the standards outside the borders of the EU. In this way, too, the new regulatory tort law acquires 'extraterritorial effect'. This 'climate change in tort law' itself means that even if the 'political question' doctrine may stand in the way of suits in the USA and other common-law jurisdictions, the European motor, could in practice – through the back door – spread its effects even to those jurisdictions, including the USA where it all started.

[128] Regulation (EU) 2017/821 of the European Parliament and of the Council of 17 May 2017 laying down supply chain due diligence obligations for Union importers of tin, tantalum and tungsten, their ores, and gold originating from conflict-affected and high-risk areas [2017] OJ L130/1–20.

14

Global Value Chains as Regulatory Proxy: Transnationalising the Internal Market Through EU Law

JAAKKO SALMINEN, MIKKO RAJAVUORI AND KLAAS HENDRIK ELLER*

I. INTRODUCTION: REGULATION ALONG GLOBAL VALUE CHAINS

SINCE THE LATE twentieth century, global value chains (GVCs) have emerged as a predominant form of economic organisation. GVCs can be understood as centrally governed but organisationally and geographically fragmented production networks that channel commodities, knowledge, and capital around the world. Their proliferation has prompted companies and states to develop advanced techniques of governance, seeking to capture the economic, social, and political dynamics of GVCs. In short, GVCs increasingly channel regulation and governance along the chain.

In this chapter, we examine *GVCs as regulatory proxies* in the context of the European Union's (EU) recent sustainability instruments. A flurry of contemporary EU legislation, spanning from conflict minerals to sustainability reporting, has espoused the terminology and operative mechanisms of GVCs to curb companies' social and environmental 'externalities',[1] both within and beyond the Union's territorial borders. Against this backdrop, we identify the primary ways through which the EU utilises GVC-related concepts and embeds them in the legal design of EU regulations and directives in the context of sustainability. We further analyse how the emergent 'GVC turn' in sustainability regulation exposes and forges new modalities

*Jaakko Salminen, Lund University/Copenhagen Business School; Mikko Rajavuori, University of Turku/University of Eastern Finland; Klaas Hendrik Eller, University of Amsterdam. We acknowledge the financial support of the Academy of Finland (grants 324037, 338643, and 338645) and the Dutch Research Council (NWO) (grant VI.Veni.211R.058).

[1] We use this term as descriptively helpful, while acknowledging that thinking of social and environmental effects as 'externality' in the first place pertains to a micro-economic imagination of GVCs that is spurred by private law and private autonomy.

of the EU's transnational regulatory influence. This new regulatory technique – *regulating along the GVC* – provides a fresh perspective on the governance of transnational production and further augments the dominant narratives of the EU's internal and extraterritorial market regulatory strategies and leverage.

This is also what we mean by GVCs as a 'regulatory proxy'. Instead of extending regulation through seeking adoption by foreign regulators or by targeting key foreign actors, the EU now 'only' regulates actors *within* its jurisdiction so that they in turn *privately* extend certain governance measures *outside* the regulating jurisdiction. The GVC, and more specifically, the lead firm and the value-chain governance emanating from it, become a substitute, or proxy, for transnational regulation. Focusing on GVCs allows for a more surgical approach than earlier paradigms of extraterritorial regulation, enabling the targeting of specific strands of global production linked to the regulating jurisdiction by way of chains of contracts. It also allows the regulator to focus on a range of motives, spanning from 'universal' justifications, such as global sustainability, to more 'domestic' issues including security of supply. That said, the political aspirations behind GVC regulation reach far beyond improving the sustainability of selected value chains and amount to a reconfiguration of the EU internal market in a globalised economy and the EU's global regulatory imprint. Similar to the realm of the digital economy where the global interconnections of key platforms elevate EU regulatory efforts to a global level,[2] the 'GVC turn' acknowledges the permeability and global embeddedness of the internal market. An international political economy perspective exposes some of the blind spots and global distributive dynamics behind this new mode of EU regulation under the banner of sustainability.[3] In particular, some of the normative tensions underlying the green transition and the emerging 'geoeconomic order'[4] with intertwined agendas of sustainability and security of supply affect the legitimacy of the EU as a transnational regulatory power.

Drawing on the GVC-governance analytic and related material on value-chain governance, we propose that regulating along value chains can be roughly differentiated into three primary approaches. The first approach focuses on the inside of the regulating jurisdiction but nonetheless can have an extraterritorial so-called 'Brussels effect',[5] either intentionally or unintentionally. Under the second approach, regulators require companies within their jurisdiction to map, track and report on their extraterritorial value chains, thus explicitly extending the regulator's gaze outside its own jurisdiction. Under the third approach, regulators mandate companies not only to map but also to govern their extraterritorial value chains in specific ways, thus explicitly extending the regulator's reach outside the regulating jurisdiction.

[2] On the EU Digital Services Act/Digital Markets Act from a value chain perspective see J Salminen, M Viljanen, K Sobel-Read and KH Eller, 'Digital Platforms as Second-Order Lead Firms: Beyond the Industrial/Digital Divide in Regulating Value Chains' (2022) 30 *European Review of Private Law* 1059–88.

[3] See, eg, A Nissen, *The European Union, Emerging Global Business and Human Rights* (Cambridge, Cambridge University Press, 2022).

[4] A Roberts, H Choer Moraes and V Ferguson, 'Toward a Geoeconomic Order in International Trade and Investment' (2019) 22 *Journal of International Economic Law* 655–76.

[5] See A Bradford, *The Brussels Effect: How the European Union Rules the World* (Oxford, Oxford University Press, 2020).

This rudimentary analytic, we argue, provides an insight into the increasing contestation of transnational space by way of the *transnational extension of EU law and the internal market along GVCs* or, in other words, using lead firms and the governance of their value chains as a proxy for furthering diverse regulatory interests extraterritorially.

The chapter is structured as follows. Section II briefly explains the emergence of GVCs as the dominant contemporary form of transnational economic production, with a focus on contractual private governance mechanisms that underpin their operation. It further notes the reshuffling of states' regulatory toolkits to adapt to the reality of GVC capitalism. Section III reviews earlier theorisations of the extraterritorial reach of EU law. It then builds on these by introducing what we claim is a 'GVC turn' in the transnational extension of EU law and the internal market. The GVC turn is elaborated by way of a comparative evaluation of instruments, techniques and ideologies of regulating along value chains. Section IV draws together the main lessons of the comparative exercise and highlights what the turn to GVCs means for an increasingly contested transnational regulatory space. A short conclusion (section V) ends the chapter.

II. THE 'GVC TURN': A NEW FOCAL POINT FOR GOVERNANCE AND REGULATION

A. GVCs as Infrastructure of a Connected Global Economy

GVCs can be understood as complex and dynamic economic networks in which production crosses at least one border. Since the late twentieth century, GVCs have become basic operative units of economic organisation and transnational production. GVCs are a distinctive stage in the evolution of capitalism and differ considerably from previously dominant forms of production, such as centralised mass production under industrialisation.[6] By spanning across jurisdictions as well as traditional product markets, GVCs create links of interconnectedness between actors, places and economic dynamics, thereby gradually replacing a territorial conception of markets by a functional conception of vertically disintegrated economic co-operation.[7] Currently, around half of global trade takes place in and through GVCs, making them vital institutions of the global economic order.[8]

The proliferation of GVCs is founded on the ideology and practice of specialisation. Firms focus on their most value-producing core competences, such as research

[6] eg W Milberg and D Winkler, *Outsourcing Economics: Global Value Chains in Capitalist Development* (Cambridge, Cambridge University Press, 2013); G Gereffi, *Global Value Chains and Development: Redefining the Contours of 21st Century Capitalism* (Cambridge, Cambridge University Press, 2018).

[7] For one account of the narrative, see R Baldwin, *The Globotics Upheaval: Globalization, Robotics, and the Future of Work* (Oxford, Oxford University Press, 2019).

[8] World Bank, *World Development Report 2020: Trading for Development in the Age of Global Value Chains* (World Bank, 2020); for a compelling critique of the report as 'expansion of neoliberal globalisation couched in the language of global value chains' see J Bair et al, 'Capitalist Crisis in the 'Age of Global Value Chains' (2021) 53 *Environment and Planning A* 1253–72.

and development, product design, marketing and intellectual property.[9] Other, less value-producing aspects of production, such as manufacturing, component design and back-office functions, are outsourced to entities and jurisdictions with the highest added value (or conversely, the lowest costs) related to these tasks. Specialisation thus drives organisational and jurisdictional fragmentation, that is, the fragmentation of primarily local individual entities, as under industrialised models of production, into primarily global collective entities under value-chain capitalism. In this way, firms become the 'lead firms' of their own production networks (or value chains),[10] by choosing which aspects of production are outsourced to global networks of suppliers and which are sourced in-house.[11]

A distinctive factor for understanding the structure and operation of value chains is 'governance'.[12] Specialisation is only feasible if the ensuing collective entities can be effectively governed, or in other words, if the lead firm can ensure the alignment of interests in its value chain with those of its own.[13] These interests typically range from ensuring the basic logistical functioning of the value chain to ensuring value chain-wide adherence to standards of product quality, cost-management and research and development and, increasingly, also sustainability or security of supply.[14] Governance

[9] On specialisation as a path to increased value creation, see, eg, C Krishnarao Prahalad and G Hamel, 'The Core Competence of the Corporation' (1990) 68 *Harvard Business Review* 79–96. On the economics of outsourcing, eg, Milberg and Winkler (n 6). On managerial techniques and ideologies in GVCs see P Gibbon and S Ponte, 'Global Value Chains: From Governance to Governmentality?' (2008) *Economy and Society* 37, 365–92.

[10] For the concept of lead firm, see, eg, G Gereffi, 'Global Value Chains in a Post-Washington Consensus World' (2014) 21 *Review of International Political Economy* 9–37; J Salminen and M Rajavuori, 'Transnational Sustainability Laws and the Regulation of Global Value Chains: Comparison and a Framework for Analysis' (2019) 26 *Maastricht Journal of European and Comparative Law* 602–27. Essentially, lead firms are actors that use various means to align the interests of their supply chains with their own. These are similar to, eg, earlier theories of network forms of organisation, but focus more on certain key actors, ie, 'lead firms', and their effort, skill and power in the alignment process. For networks, WW Powell, 'Neither Market Nor Hierarchy: Network Forms of Organization' (1990) 12 *Research in Organizational Behavior* 295–336. For one early approach to conceptualising how firms govern networks, G Teubner, *Netzwerk als Vertragsverbund: Virtuelle Unternehmen, Franchising, Just-in-Time in sozialwissenschaftlicher und juristischer Sicht* (Baden-Baden, Nomos, 2004). While much focus is now on lead firms as the key avenue of entry into the governance structures of GVCs, this approach has also been criticized, for which, eg, A Beckers, 'The Invisible Networks of Global Production: Re-Imagining the Global Value Chain in Legal Research' (2020) 16 *European Review of Contract Law* 95–117.

[11] This is necessarily a simplification of a complex process depending on, eg, available supplier networks and their competences, trade relations and transport and communication infrastructures. For just some examples, DM Bernhofen, Z El-Sahli and R Kneller, 'Estimating the Effects of the Container Revolution on World Trade' (2016) 98 *Journal of International Economics* 36–50; T Dietz, 'Contract Law, Relational Contracts, and Reputational Networks in International Trade: An Empirical Investigation into Cross-Border Contracts in the Software Industry' (2012) 37 *Law and Social Inquiry* 25–57; T López and others, 'Digital Value Chain Restructuring and Labour Process Transformations in the Fast-Fashion Sector: Evidence from the Value Chains of Zara & H&M' (2021) 22 *Global Networks* 684–700.

[12] eg, J Salminen, 'Contract-Boundary-Spanning Governance Mechanisms: Conceptualizing Fragmented and Globalized Production as Collectively Governed Entities' (2016) 23 *Indiana Journal of Global Legal Studies* 709–42; Salminen and Rajavuori (n 10); KH Eller, 'Private Governance of Global Value Chains From Within. Lessons From and For Transnational Law' (2017) 8 *Transnational Legal Theory* 296–329.

[13] Generally, compare, eg, RM Locke, *The Promise and Limits of Private Power: Promoting Labor Standards in a Global Economy* (Cambridge, Cambridge University Press, 2013); G Gereffi, J Humphrey and T Sturgeon, 'The Governance of Global Value Chains' (2005) 12 *Review of International Political Economy* 78–104; Dietz (n 11); López and others (n 11).

[14] For some examples, see, eg, P Kajüter and H I Kulmala, 'Open-Book Accounting in Networks: Potential Achievements and Reasons for Failures' (2005) 16 *Management Accounting Research* 179–204;

can take the form of corporate or contractual organisation, standard-setting, certification and other co-ordinating devices that ensure a necessary level of control while retaining the benefits of decentralised organisation.[15]

Contractual governance mechanisms are particularly important, and lead firm strategies for controlling contractually organised value chains can be roughly separated into three approaches.[16] The first strategy is contracting based on market price with an individual contract partner. Contract, as it exists in the transnational sphere, allows lead firms to outsource production based on the market-price mechanism as if the world were a unified market (though one with exceptionally little regulation). The second strategy is the extension of standards and monitoring throughout the value chain, thus acknowledging the fragmented production structure hidden behind the initial transaction. The third strategy is an integrated approach where 'relational' or 'capability-building' mechanisms are used to ensure that the entire value chain has the means and capabilities to adhere to required standards of operation. This last kind of governance most clearly transforms a set of seemingly independent entities into a single collective production structure, but even the other strategies entail a lead firm's ultimate control over its value chain in the sense that it is the lead firm that is ultimately responsible for its decision to outsource and on what terms.

In sum, GVCs can be described as a jurisdictionally fragmented network of actors that, paradoxically, is simultaneously centrally co-ordinated by a lead firm, whose governance efforts act as the gravitational force pulling together seemingly independent entities.

B. The Reconfiguration of Regulatory Spaces Along GVCs

The rise of GVCs involves significant economic and political implications. On the one hand, economic development and upgrading – whether on firm or state level – increasingly occurs through access to GVCs.[17] On the other hand, the practices of GVC capitalism have exacerbated asymmetries between lead firms and large buyers with increasing governance power and their supplier firms and workers, thus reducing the autonomy of developing states and firms.[18] In addition to their impact on the

RJ Gilson, CF Sabel and RE Scott, 'Contracting for Innovation: Vertical Disintegration and Interfirm Collaboration' (2009) 109 *Columbia Law Review* 431–61; A Ali, A Mahfouz and A Arisha, 'Analysing Supply Chain Resilience: Integrating the Constructs in a Concept Mapping Framework via a Systematic Literature Review' (2017) 22 *Supply Chain Management* 16–39; Locke (n 13).

[15] Gereffi, Humphrey and Sturgeon (n 13).

[16] See especially J Salminen, 'Towards a Genealogy and Typology of Governance Through Contract Beyond Privity' (2020) 16 *European Review of Contract Law* 25–43, Table 1, 39. The table fleshes out the three approaches based on a collation of earlier material on governance through contract, in particular IR Macneil, 'Contracts: Adjustment of Long-Term Economic Relations under Classical, Neoclassical, and Relational Contract Law' (1978) 72 *Northwestern University Law Review* 854–905; O Williamson, 'Transaction-Cost Economics: The Governance of Contractual Relations' (1979) 22 *Journal of Law & Economics* 233–61; Gereffi, Humphrey and Sturgeon (n 13); Locke (n 13).

[17] Gereffi (n 10); World Bank (n 8).

[18] D Danielsen, 'Trade, Distribution and Development under Supply Chain Capitalism' in A Santos, C Thomas and D Trubek (eds), *World Trade and Investment Reimagined* (London, Anthem Press, 2019) 121–30.

logic of transnational production, GVCs and their individual sites are also a source of great distributive inequality and a target of deep political contestation on national and international levels.[19] GVC-related policies of reshoring have featured prominently on populist and anti-globalist agendas in recent years, while policies such as the Chinese Belt and Road Initiative use GVCs and the connection between firms and infrastructure for geostrategic influence.[20] It is thus no surprise that regulators have started paying close attention to the proliferation and reconfiguration of GVCs in particular since the 2010s.

However, regulators face an elusive regulatory target, as GVCs utilise the 'in-between', or transnational, space between different national jurisdictions and are notoriously difficult to map from a regulatory perspective.[21] An international economic order built around free trade is an essential facilitative factor for the rise of GVCs, and particularly so the transnational recognition and 'detachment' of contracts from their national regulatory embedding.[22] This has on the one hand accelerated the jurisdictional 'lift-off' of GVCs, whereby the applicable regulatory systems for economic operation are decoupled from national regimes.[23] On the other hand, the lead firm-centric transnational production structure relies to a great extent on private governance, such as contracts, that can be even more difficult to understand from the outside for regulators and other actors than the internal workings of a corporate group.[24]

Consider the social or environmental externalities traceable to a GVC. From a regulatory perspective, a marked effect of the organisational and geographic fragmentation of production is the loss of much of the relevance of earlier rules, focused on local corporations (the typical form of organisation for industrial installations) or similarly on local bilateral contracts (the typical form of organising relations between business and labour, consumers and suppliers).[25] Organisational fragmentation, such as strategic outsourcing or gig-work, allows lead firms to override existing rules aimed at mitigating externalities of earlier regulatory paradigms.[26] Jurisdictional

[19] eg, J Bair and F Palpacuer, 'CSR beyond the Corporation: Contested Governance in Global Value Chains' (2015) 15 *Global Networks* S1–S19.

[20] B Kingsbury, 'Infrastructure and InfraReg: On Rousing the International Law "Wizards of Is"' (2019) 8 *Cambridge International Law Journal* 171–86; J Lorenzo, 'A Path Toward Sustainable Development Along the Belt and Road' (2021) 24 *Journal of International Economic Law* 591–608.

[21] P Zumbansen, 'The Disaster Chain: Counter-Mapping Global Value Chains' (2022) 42 *Northwestern Journal of International Law & Business* 303–53.

[22] See, eg, J Paul, 'The Transformation of International Comity' (2008) 71 *Law and Contemporary Problems* 19–38; J Bomhoff, A Brandão de Oliveira and L Biziková, 'Post-War Yearning for Deparochialisation and the Siren of Free Trade: The Bremen v. Zapata Off-Shore Co' in H Muir Watt and others (eds), *Global Private International Law: Adjudication without Frontiers* (Cheltenham, Edward Elgar, 2019).

[23] R Wai, 'Transnational Liftoff and Juridical Touchdown: The Regulatory Function of Private International Law in an Era of Globalization' (2002) 40 *Columbia Journal of Transnational Law* 209–74.

[24] P Zumbansen, 'Lochner Disembedded: The Anxieties of Law in a Global Context' (2013) 20 *Indiana Journal of Global Legal Studies* 29–69.

[25] The many externalities of industrialisation were internalised for example through the 'rise and fall' of freedom of contract in national space. PS Atiyah, *The Rise and Fall of Freedom of Contract* (Oxford, Oxford University Press, 1979). This, however, coincided with the liberalisation of transnational contracts, removing them from the increasing national restraints. Bomhoff, Brandão de Oliveira and Biziková (n 22).

[26] D Weil, *The Fissured Workplace: Why Work Became So Bad for So Many and What Can Be Done to Improve It* (Cambridge/MA, Harvard University Press, 2014).

fragmentation exacerbates the ensuing regulatory arbitrage, allowing lead firms to leverage the even vaster jurisdictional differences in regulation and enforcement.[27] As a result, GVCs, as globally disaggregate, jurisdiction-spanning networks of actors, avoid being pinned under specific jurisdictions.[28] In these conditions, lead firms *outsource not only production* but *also their social, environmental, cultural and economic externalities along the GVC.*

The severing of these externalities from the operation of a GVC is reflected in private governance, such as in the three strategies for controlling contractually-related GVC entities discussed above. This is most obvious with regard to 'fire-and-forget' market-price contracting. Contractual relations and especially sales contracts typically do not need to pay attention to working conditions, labour rights, environmental effects or resource use, or whether parties pay taxes to their local communities.[29] Severance of liability is based on a perceived lack of control over actors connected via contractual market-price mechanisms. The missing connection between GVC actors is compounded by additional tiers of contractual relations: the only constraint that the first market-price contract entails in relation to further tiers of contracts is that of the price and physical quality of goods. What is more, firms are free to use regulatory arbitrage to leverage global regulatory plurality and gaps. This includes not only localisation of contracts in specific jurisdictions, applicable laws and enforcement networks, but also means for contesting national regulation through investor protection that binds states.[30] The end result is a broad freedom to act with impunity with regard to the societal effects of contracts.

Conversely, lead firms may also leverage their governance mechanisms to control and mitigate social or environmental externalities. Consider the two further contractual modes of GVC governance. In today's commerce, it is illusory to imagine the market-price mechanism as following from a 'natural' interplay of market dynamics.[31] Actors need to co-ordinate their relationship at least marginally to ensure that goods and services consistently match diverse expectations. Standards are deployed and compliance with them monitored through auditing and other mechanisms. Typically, a lead firm requires other value chain actors to comply with standards incorporated into their contract along with diverse monitoring mechanisms. The requirements on standards and monitoring are then cascaded throughout the value chain to ensure that the whole fragmented production entity has the same rule book regarding logistical and product-related standards, increasingly including sustainability. The integrated contractual strategy of capability-building takes this approach further. In addition to merely acknowledging the existence of its contractually connected

[27] B Hepple, *Labour Laws and Global Trade* (Oxford, Hart Publishing, 2005).

[28] J Salminen and M Rajavuori, 'Private International Law, Global Value Chains and the Externalities of Transnational Production: Towards Alignment?' (2021) 12 *Transnational Legal Theory* 230.

[29] eg, Luhmann states that contracts 'stabilize a specific difference over time, while being indifferent to anything else' (own translation, original in German). N Luhmann, *Das Recht Der Gesellschaft* (Frankfurt a.M., Suhrkamp, 1993) 459.

[30] For a recent deconstruction of investment law's internal rationales, see D Schneiderman, *Investment Law's Alibis. Colonialism, Imperialism, Debt and Development* (Cambridge, Cambridge University Press, 2022).

[31] R Hockett and R Kreitner, 'Just Prices' (2018) 27 *Cornell Journal of Law & Public Policy* 771–99.

production structure by spreading and monitoring standards throughout, here a lead firm actively governs the value chain by mapping and developing the competences of value-chain actors. This can take place either through *de facto* action that transcends contractual boundaries or through dedicated governance contracts that work above and beyond individual supply chain contracts to connect fragmented actors through explicit contracts, such as the Accord on Fire and Building Safety in Bangladesh.[32]

But just as lead firms are developing techniques of governance along the GVC, so are states. The new modalities of transnational economic production and organisation are increasingly registered and legally re-conceptualised in national regulation particularly with a view to social and environmental sustainability. Since the 2010s, a series of transnational sustainability laws have provided examples of regulatory strategies and mechanisms through which national legislators have sought to conceptualise and rein in GVCs with regard to their sustainability deficits. While diverse in their design, these laws put forward an explicit regulatory intervention that attempts to extend (home) state control more directly over production and GVC practices that take place outside its jurisdiction. In doing so, these national regulations also conceptualise and come to terms with the private governance of GVCs. In the next section, we situate the EU's emerging sustainability regulation in the broader genealogy of the EU's role in shaping markets, internally and globally.

III. A TYPOLOGY OF REGULATING GVCS IN THE EU: DRIVERS, MODES AND IMPLICATIONS

A. EU Regulation of Transnational Production: A Theoretical Outlook

The proliferation of national laws attempting to capture the operation of GVCs is a recent phenomenon, but outward-looking regulation focused on transnational economic operation per se is not new. Antitrust law had early on explored approaches to capturing distortions of the domestic market emanating from abroad, but these focused primarily on maintaining internal cohesion in the regulating jurisdiction.[33] Sanctions aimed at third countries, on the other hand, are clearly focused outside the regulating jurisdiction.[34] And, in many cases, external effects of regulation appear to be incidental. The introduction of local emissions controls or product liability regulation in a key market such as California or the EU,[35] for example, illustrate the

[32] J Salminen, 'The Accord on Fire and Building Safety in Bangladesh – A New Paradigm for Limiting Buyers' Liability in Global Supply Chains?' (2018) 66 *American Journal of Comparative Law* 411–51; J Bair, M Anner and J Blasi, 'The Political Economy of Private and Public Regulation in Post-Rana Plaza Bangladesh' (2020) 73 *Industrial and Labor Relations Review* 969–94.

[33] G Monti, 'The Global Reach of EU Competition Law' in M Cremona and J Scott (eds), *EU Law Beyond EU Borders: The Extraterritorial Reach of EU Law* (Oxford, Oxford University Press, 2019).

[34] M Blessing, *Impact of the Extraterritorial Application of Mandatory Rules of Law on International Contracts* (Helbing & Lichtenhahn, 1999); T Szabados, *Economic Sanctions in EU Private International Law* (Oxford, Hart Publishing, 2021).

[35] D Vogel, *Trading Up: Consumer and Environmental Regulation in a Global Economy* (Harvard, Harvard University Press, 1995) 68–70; Bradford (n 5).

potential impact of domestic regulation and liability frameworks on transnational economic organisation. In the globalised economy, local rules continue to carry major transnational effects.[36]

Since the 2010s the global effects of these local measures have spurred considerable research spanning international trade and investment law,[37] EU and private international law,[38] and law and political economy.[39] Much of this scholarly effort has focused on the regulatory infrastructure of the EU. With the EU being the largest internal market in the world, its regulation, such as product safety standards, directly affects the logic of production processes used by third country operators, given their need to meet EU standards if they wish to be granted market access. Accordingly, EU policy areas as diverse as competition, personal data and environmental protection have long been rife with rationales, mechanisms and regulatory devices that aim at underwriting a functioning internal market but, simultaneously, export the reach of these initiatives beyond its territorial borders.

Naturally, the EU is not the only actor whose regulatory actions extend transnationally and provoke reactions from individuals and companies based in other jurisdictions or from other states. However, it is precisely EU regulatory power that has been identified as a special leverage point of the EU as a global actor, leading the EU to have become a key target for analysing the extraterritorial and transnational dynamics of regulation. There is no shortage of primary EU legislative materials that have been used in these analyses. While some regulatory instruments require exporting *states* to have in place legislation fulfilling EU standards,[40] others target *third-country manufacturers* directly.[41] Similarly, major differences exist between regulatory techniques that aim to cover market-abusive behaviour by third-country operators outside the EU[42] compared to those preventing producers from placing unsafe products on

[36] For a summary, see, eg, D Danielsen, 'Local Rules and a Global Economy: An Economic Policy Perspective' (2010) 1 *Transnational Legal Theory* 49–115.

[37] eg, B Cooreman, *Global Environmental Protection through Trade: A Systematic Approach to Extraterritoriality* (Cheltenham, Edward Elgar, 2017); J Lawrence, *Governmentality in EU External Trade and Environment Policy: Between Rights and Market* (London, Routledge, 2018).

[38] eg, HW Micklitz, 'The Internal versus the External Dimension of European Private Law. A Conceptual Design and a Research Agenda' in M Cremona and HW Micklitz (eds), *Private Law in the External Relations of the EU* (Oxford, Oxford University Press, 2016) 9–31; M Szpunar, 'Territoriality of Union Law in the Era of Globalization' in D Petrlík et al (eds), *Evolution des rapports entre les ordres juridiques de l'Union européenne, international et nationaux. Liber Amicorum Jirí Malenovsky 2020* (Brussels, Éditions Bruylant, 2020) 149–68; J Basedow, *The Law of Open Societies – Private Ordering and Public Regulation of International Relations* (General Course on Private International Law) (Leiden, Brill Nijhoff, 2015) 75 et seqq.

[39] eg, G LeBaron and J Lister, 'The Hidden Costs of Global Supply Chain Solutions' (2021) *Review of International Political Economy* 669–95.

[40] See, eg, Council Regulation 3254/91 of 4 November 1991 prohibiting the use of leghold traps in the Community and the introduction into the Community of pelts and manufactured goods of certain wild animal species originating in countries which catch them by means of leghold traps or trapping methods which do not meet international humane trapping standards (Animal Legtrap Regulation) [1991] OJ L308/1. A comparable mechanism is employed in Regulation 2016/679 of 27 April 2016 on the protection of individuals with regard to the processing of personal data and on the free movement of such data (General Data Protection Regulation (GDPR)) [2016] OJ L119/1.

[41] eg, Regulation 1223/2009 of the European Parliament and of the Council of 30 November 2009 on cosmetic products (Cosmetic Products Regulation) [2009] OJ L342/59.

[42] eg, Regulation (EU) No 596/2014 of the European Parliament and of the Council of 16 April 2014 on market abuse [2014] OJ L173/57.

the internal market. Given the sprawling regulatory infrastructure, it is not surprising that the global effects of EU instruments have been extensively theorised in relation to their explanatory drivers, operative mechanisms and empirical outcomes. While no theoretical account has yet adopted a distinct GVC approach, several recent approaches have examined the transnational operation of the EU's existing regulatory instruments in detail. These typologies enable us to sketch a rough analytical framework against which we can position the EU's recent 'GVC turn' in sustainability regulation.[43]

The most influential recent high-level account explaining the conditions of the global reach of EU regulation is Anu Bradford's *Brussels Effect*. According to Bradford, the EU has become a powerful global regulator precisely 'because it has built an institutional architecture that has converted its market size into a tangible regulatory influence'.[44] In essence, Bradford outlines five conditions – among them being market size, institutional preference for strict standards and focus on inelastic regulatory targets – as key factors unlocking the EU's unique regulatory clout, which materialises either *de facto* or *de jure*. In this scheme, a *de facto* Brussels effect refers to processes whereby third-country operators voluntarily change their behaviour, for instance by revamping entire production lines to meet EU standards even when products are targeted at non-EU markets. By contrast, EU regulation may also invoke a *de jure* Brussels effect, an example being third countries that design national product safety requirements with a view to EU standards through regulatory emulation. At the heart of Bradford's analysis is the empirical analysis of these primary influence mechanisms across policy areas including competition law, data protection and consumer safety.

Another recent account of EU global regulatory power is put forth by Joanne Scott.[45] Unlike Bradford's more empirical focus devoid of legal design analysis, Scott deploys a doctrinally oriented examination of the techniques through which the applicability of EU law is extended beyond the territorial confines of the Union. Her account relies on careful distinctions between truly 'extraterritorial' regulation and regulatory measures that give rise to 'territorial extension'. The latter category is crucial because it covers multiple processes where assessing compliance with EU law 'requires an evaluation of foreign conduct and/or third country law', usually through various 'triggers' that bring foreign conduct within the ambit of EU law.[46]

[43] Due to our focus on transnational production processes, we rely mostly on product-related regulation, thus assigning financial and competition regulation to a lesser role. We acknowledge the importance of, eg, EU competition law in defining the broad contours of the EU's extraterritorial regulatory effects and their doctrinal conceptualisation. For discussion of the potential role of EU competition law on private contracts outside the EU, see, eg, Blessing (n 34); Monti (n 33).

[44] Bradford (n 5); see also I Hadjiyianni, 'The European Union as a Global Regulatory Power' (2021) 41 *OJLS* 243–64. The 'Brussels effect' resembles what Vogel (n 34) 68–70 has termed the 'California effect' in the field of environmental regulation. He argues that regulatory competition ultimately led to a ratcheting up of environmental standards in many US states triggered by progressive Californian regulation. Vogel contrasts this with the inverse 'Delaware effect', which depicts a race towards deregulation in corporate law, see, eg, M Roe, 'Delaware's Politics' (2005) 118 *Harvard Law Review* 2491–2543.

[45] See, eg, J Scott, 'Extraterritoriality and Territorial Extension in EU Law' (2014) 62 *CML Rev* 87; J Scott, 'The Global Reach of EU Law' in M Cremona and J Scott (eds), *EU Law Beyond EU Borders* (Oxford, Oxford University Press, 2019).

[46] Scott, 'The Global Reach of EU Law' (n 45).

These triggers – which may be activated by market access but also, for example, by a transaction concluded with an EU firm in a third country – is most elaborate in the context of financial regulation,[47] but also touches on other fields such as environmental law.[48]

Many other recent typologies complement and illustrate the high-level accounts by Bradford and Scott. For example, Laurens Ankersmit[49] and Ioanna Hadjiyianni[50] have recently provided what are essentially *instrument-level* analyses on the global reach of EU economic and environmental regulation. Ankersmit has identified three basic regulatory strategies that the EU uses to affect production methods beyond its territorial borders. Using the terminology of process-based product rules, these techniques are country-based measures (such as prohibitions on import of goods from a country that lacks adequate environmental legislation in force),[51] producer-based measures (such as preventing goods that fail to comply with certain production rules from accessing the EU market),[52] and consumer-based measures (such as voluntary labelling rules).[53] Similarly, Hadjiyianni's typology relies, on the one hand, on market access-based strategies that materialise as process standards, which in turn may impose mandatory or non-mandatory conditions, cover foreign actors directly or indirectly, and also be based on economic incentives.[54] On the other hand, she draws attention to the variety of compliance techniques and safety valves built into the different regulatory instruments.[55] In combination, these accounts emphasise both the intricacies of legal design that enable the effectiveness of the EU's transnational regulatory efforts and their stated normative zeal of protecting human rights and the environment.[56]

Three broad lessons emerge from these theoretical accounts. First, market access is clearly the lynchpin in the EU's external regulatory strategies. Whether third-country producers internalise EU standards voluntarily because of import restrictions or due to regulatory emulation in their home country, the trajectory of the EU's internal market-building efforts also conditions and shapes its external reach. Second, the concrete instruments used to examine the EU's global regulatory power are exceedingly heterogenous. The operation of competition law and chemical regulation, for example, are based on very different internal and external logics, and thus resist sweeping generalisations. Third, the accounts generally focus on the mechanisms and techniques of governance but skirt normative questions as to the intent and desirability of EU regulation's global effects. In this regard, the sustainability-focused

[47] Scott, 'Extraterritoriality and Territorial Extension in EU Law' (n 45).

[48] Scott, 'The Global Reach of EU Law' (n 45).

[49] L Ankersmit, *Green Trade and Fair Trade in and with the EU Process-Based Measures within the EU Legal Order* (Cambridge, Cambridge University Press, 2017).

[50] I Hadjiyianni, *The EU as a Global Regulator for Environmental Protection* (London, Bloomsbury Publishing, 2019).

[51] eg, Animal Legtrap Regulation (n 40).

[52] eg, Cosmetic Products Regulation (n 41).

[53] Ankersmit (n 49) 26–38.

[54] Hadjiyianni (n 50).

[55] ibid.

[56] For a careful recent examination on this civilising mission, see A Ganesh, *Rightful Relations with Distant Strangers: Kant, the EU, and the Wider World* (London, Bloomsbury, 2021).

accounts analyse 'mission-oriented' regulatory measures with greater affinity and often in relation to accountability mechanisms that ought to be built into regulatory devices designed with global reach in mind.

No theoretical exposition, however, discusses the drivers, techniques and outcomes of EU regulation from a distinct GVC perspective. This does not mean that the paradigm shift prompted by the rise of GVC capitalism has gone unnoticed. Rather, the contemporary realities of transnational production structures animate all accounts of the leverage that the EU enjoys in explicitly steering and harnessing third-country producers to fulfil its regulatory objectives. In our view, however, a dedicated GVC-based approach can augment existing theorisation because of its focus on *lead firms* as entities co-ordinating transnational production through *private governance*. This conceptual move allows us to locate the GVC approach right at the intersection between public and private power, thus highlighting a new, discreet modality of *regulating by way of and along the GVC* as an emerging template for governing transnational production. In the next section, we introduce and discuss recent EU approaches to sustainability regulation from a GVC perspective.

B. The 'GVC Turn' in EU Regulation and its Relation to GVC Governance

Starting around the 2010s, the EU has increasingly adopted GVC terminology in its regulatory efforts. The 'GVC turn' can be identified across many policy areas, but nowhere does the EU's reliance on the concept seem greater recently than under the banner of sustainability. An array of recent EU legislation has mobilised the concepts and operative conditions of GVCs to curb companies' social and environmental externalities both within and beyond the Union's territorial borders. These span from sectoral or thematic approaches, such as conflict minerals,[57] deforestation,[58] forced labour,[59] carbon emissions[60] and investment,[61] to more general 'non-financial'[62]

[57] Regulation (EU) 2017/821 of the European Parliament and of the Council of 17 May 2017 laying down supply chain due diligence obligations for Union importers of tin, tantalum and tungsten, their ores, and gold originating from conflict-affected and high-risk areas (EU Conflict Mineral Regulation (CMR)) [2017] OJ L130/1.

[58] Regulation (EU) 2023/1115 of the European Parliament and of the Council of 31 May 2023 on the making available on the Union market and the export from the Union of certain commodities and products associated with deforestation and forest degradation and repealing Regulation (EU) No 995/2010 (Deforestation Regulation) OJ L150/206.

[59] Proposal for a regulation on prohibiting products made with forced labour on the Union market (COM(2022) 453) (Forced Labour Regulation).

[60] Regulation (EU) 2023/956 of the European Parliament and of the Council of 10 May 2023 establishing a carbon border adjustment mechanism (CBAM) [2020] OJ L130/52.

[61] Regulation (EU) 2020/852 of the European Parliament and of the Council of 18 June 2020 on the establishment of a framework to facilitate sustainable investment, and amending Regulation (EU) 2019/2088 [2020] OJ L198/13.

[62] Directive 2014/95/EU of the European Parliament and of the Council of 22 October 2014 amending Directive 2013/34/EU as regards disclosure of non-financial and diversity information by certain large undertakings and groups (Non-Financial Reporting Directive (NFRD)) [2014] OJ L330/1.

or 'sustainability'[63] reporting and due diligence[64] type instruments, to say nothing of other policy instruments such as the Green Deal.[65] While some of the legislative proposals mentioned here are yet to enter into force, the clear proliferation of GVC language already allows preliminary examination of the drivers, dynamics and potential outcomes of novel regulatory measures, as well as analysis of their potential contribution to theoretical debates on transnational regulation.

Even though 'GVC language' is especially prominent in sustainability instruments, the EU increasingly relies on this and related concepts on other policy verticals. The Covid-19 pandemic and the war in Ukraine, for instance, prompted EU-wide deliberation on instruments aimed at developing security of supply by enhancing the resilience of critical entities,[66] access to critical raw materials,[67] and more broadly, the functioning of the internal market during emergencies.[68] These instruments, as also many related to sustainability,[69] do not always overtly adopt the terminology of '*value* chains' but may refer instead to '*supply* chains' (though see the CRM proposal as a prominent example of GVC language creeping into the field of security of supply). Differences in the disciplinary and theoretical background, usage and legal effects of the terms 'value chain' and 'supply chain' are well-documented.[70]

[63] Directive (EU) 2022/2464 of the European Parliament and of the Council amending Regulation (EU) No 537/2014, Directive 2004/109/EC, Directive 2006/43/EC and Directive 2013/34/EU, as regards corporate sustainability reporting (Corporate Sustainability Reporting Directive (CSRD)) [2022] OJ L322/15).

[64] Proposal for a Directive of the European Parliament and of the Council on Corporate Sustainability Due Diligence and amending Directive (EU) 2019/1937 (COM/2022/71 final; CSDDD). We use this version as the primary basis of our analysis. At the same time the political process is moving on. On 1 December 2022 the Council of the European Union published its own adopted position for negotiations, available at https://data.consilium.europa.eu/doc/document/ST-15024–2022-REV-1/en/pdf. When explicitly so stated, we refer to this instrument. Finally, on 14 December 2023, a provisional political agreement is reported to have been reached by EU co-legislators, for which, eg, see the Council of the EU's press release of the same date, 'Corporate Sustainability Due Diligence: Council and Parliament Strike Deal to Protect Environment and Human Rights', available at www.consilium.europa.eu/en/press/press-releases/2023/12/14/corporate-sustainability-due-diligence-council-and-parliament-strike-deal-to-protect-environment-and-human-rights/. Thus, the CSDDD is poised to take the next step in the legislative process.

[65] Communication from the Commission to the European Parliament, the European Council, the Council, the European Economic and Social Committee and the Committee of the Regions: 'The European Green Deal' (COM/2019/640 final).

[66] Directive (EU) 2022/2557 of the European Parliament and of the Council of 14 December 2022 on the resilience of critical entities and repealing Council Directive 2008/114/EC (CER Directive) [2022] OJ L333/164.

[67] Proposal for a Regulation of the European Parliament and of the Council establishing a framework for ensuring a secure and sustainable supply of critical raw materials and amending Regulations (EU) 168/2013, (EU) 2018/858, 2018/1724 and (EU) 2019/1020 (COM/2023/160 final) (CRM Regulation).

[68] Proposal for a Regulation of the European Parliament and of the Council establishing a Single Market emergency instrument and repealing Council Regulation No (EC) 2679/98, COM(2022)459 (SMEI Regulation). The SMEI took inspiration from the US Defense Production Act of 1950 that both the Trump and the Biden Administration employed to steer national manufacturing of health and medical resources during the Covid-19 pandemic.

[69] Such as the California Transparency in Supply Chains Act and the three UK and Australian Modern Slavery Acts. For these, see, eg, Salminen and Rajavuori (n 10). Notably, while the CSDDD speaks of 'value chains' throughout, the proposed Forced Labour Regulation speaks of 'value chains' in the analysis and the recitals while switching to 'supply chains' in the actual provisions.

[70] J Bair, 'Global Commodity Chains: Genealogy and Review' in J Bair (ed), *Frontiers of Commodity Chain Research* (Stanford, Stanford University Press, 2009). Generally in the sustainability context, see Salminen and Rajavuori (n 10).

Whichever terminology is chosen and however it is legally operationalised, both the EU's sustainability-related instruments and security-driven instruments aim to regulate how firms within the EU *govern production taking place outside the EU*. Our contention is that the EU's different modes of regulating transnational production coincide with the way that transnational production is and can be organised. This raises the question to what extent certain modes of *private governance* can inform – and even be organically coupled to – different modes of GVC regulation.

We have previously analysed a range of mostly national sustainability laws that seek to regulate how lead firms govern their global value chains.[71] Our comparative analysis focused on what kinds of lead firms are regulated, how their value chains are conceptualised from a legal perspective, and what kinds of obligational effects are attached to value-chain governance. After our initial examination it seems that research has focused on three topics in particular. Alongside coverage of new regulatory instruments, research has focused on practical analyses of the effectivities of existing regulation[72] and, building on these, comparative analyses of different types of regulation, for example by differentiating between reporting and so-called mandatory due diligence obligations.[73] However, our understanding is that the important *differences in the modes of transnational traction* of such regulation have not been theorised.[74] In our view, the EU's recent GVC-based regulatory instruments mark a new stage in EU law's role in facilitating an ever more globally embedded internal market and hence also for scholarship on transnational regulation.

The key to our contribution here consists in the three private governance approaches that underpin contractual control over fragmented transnational production: market-price contracting, private governance through standards and monitoring, and capability building.[75] These strategies reflect three 'ideologies' (as in condensed

[71] Salminen and Rajavuori (n 10). The instruments covered included, eg, the California Transparency in Supply Chains Act, the US Federal Dodd Frank Act Section 1502 on conflict minerals, the UK, New South Wales and Australian Federal Modern Slavery Acts, the French *loi de vigilance*, the EU NFRD, and planned Swiss and Dutch regulations.

[72] R McCorquodale and J Nolan, 'The Effectiveness of Human Rights Due Diligence for Preventing Business Human Rights Abuses' (2021) 68 *Netherlands International Law Review* 455–78. Again, this trails extensive debate in relation to the private governance of value chains. J Bair, M Anner and J Blasi, 'The Political Economy of Private and Public Regulation in Post-Rana Plaza Bangladesh' (2020) 73 *ILR Rev*, 969; M Anner and J Bair, 'The Bulk of the Iceberg: A Critique of the Stern Center's Report on Worker Safety in Bangladesh, Penn State Centre for Global Workers' Rights Research Brief 10 February 2016' (2016).

[73] eg, N Bueno and C Bright, 'Implementing Human Rights Due Diligence through Corporate Civil Liability' (2020) 69 *International and Comparative Law Quarterly* 789. Once more, this echoes the earlier differentiation between more voluntary and more binding private governance instruments in the field of sustainability, eg, B ter Haar and M Keune, 'One Step Forward or More Window-Dressing? A Legal Analysis of Recent CSR Initiatives in the Garment Industry in Bangladesh' (2014) 30 *International Journal of Comparative Labour Law & Industrial Relations* 5; M Anner, J Bair and J Blasi, 'Toward Joint Liability in Global Supply Chains: Addressing the Root Causes of Labor Violations in International Subcontracting Networks' (2013) 35 *Competition Labor Law & Policy Journal* 1.

[74] However, for early work on the transnational theorisation of private value-chain governance, eg, Salminen and Rajavuori (n 28); Salminen (n 32).

[75] See section II.A.

world-views and frames of responsibility) of transnational private ordering particularly when applied to externalities of transnational production. The first strategy, 'market-price', entails a refusal to explicitly tackle the transnational effectivities of private governance, even if it is clear that merely setting a price on a commodity can affect, for example, the outsourcing choices of suppliers. The second strategy, 'private governance', entails an acknowledgment of the existence of a transnational production network beyond first-tier contractual partners and a need to understand, map and regulate its extent. The third strategy, 'capability building', is a hands-on acknowledgment that transnational aspects of production are efficiently governable, but only if lead firms invest in governance mechanisms that go beyond the one-sided setting and monitoring of standards.

Consequently, we hypothesise that these three approaches, or ideologies, also coincide with the EU's three approaches to *regulating transnational production along the GVC*. In short, we make an explicit connection with *GVC governance mechanisms*, drawn in part from GVC theory but expanded through legal, economic and empirical work in related fields, and the recent rise of the EU's GVC-driven regulatory efforts in a sustainability context. In our view, the process yields a functional comparative analysis of EU sustainability regulation, with the comparison focusing on how individual instruments utilise the three main approaches to value-chain governance.[76] This, we hypothesise, will provide insights into the inner workings of what seems to be a new wave of transnational regulation focused on regulating along value chains, by using lead firms, their value chains and their value-chain governance as a local proxy for extending the effects of regulation transnationally.

In combination, the three approaches to GVC governance lead to three regulatory approaches. First, regulators can renounce any explicit extension beyond established jurisdictional confines, thus limiting the transnational effects of regulation, at least in name and stated aims if not in practice. Focus is on activities that take place squarely within jurisdictional borders and the traditionally accepted reach of national regulators. In this way, regulators try to maintain their focus within their jurisdiction, even if such regulation may nonetheless acknowledge the existence of extraterritorial parts of GVCs and may have an indirect effect on their operation outside the regulating jurisdiction. This type of regulation is reflected, for example, in national standard-setting that restricts non-compliant imports or other regulations that cut off GVCs at borders, such as EC product safety regulation,[77] the EU chemicals

[76] Thus, following Michaels, we use the functional method to emphasise *difference* in the selected sustainability regulations. R Michaels, 'The Functional Method of Comparative Law' in M Reimann and R Zimmermann (eds), *The Oxford Handbook of Comparative Law* (Oxford, Oxford University Press, 2006) 339–82. The evaluative criterion, as we explained, comes from the realisation that GVC-based regulation should, if true to its source, utilise the private governance mechanisms crucial to GVCs, as reflected, eg, in the GVC governance analytic of Gereffi, Humphrey and Sturgeon and as compared to related governance approaches by, eg, Salminen. Gereffi, Humphrey and Sturgeon (n 13); Salminen (n 16).

[77] Directive 2001/95/EC of the European Parliament and of the Council of 3 December 2001 on general product safety, [2002] OJ L11/45. Other acts may have a similar effect even more indirectly. Related to product safety, eg, the earlier product liability directive (Council Directive 85/374/EEC of 25 July 1985 on the approximation of the laws, regulations and administrative provisions of the Member States concerning liability for defective products), in addition to harmonising the internal market has been argued as raising the barrier for entry into the single market.

regulation REACH[78] and the Carbon Border Adjustment Mechanism (CBAM), and these rules resonate strongly in the debate on the *de facto* and *de jure* Brussels effect.

Second, regulators can initiate information-gathering on transnational production entities and practices. Focus is on asking lead firms to map the extraterritorial extent of their GVCs,[79] disclose their scope and any governance mechanisms in place. In this way, regulators extend their gaze beyond their jurisdictional boundaries, along the lines of GVCs anchored in their jurisdictions. This approach explicitly acknowledges a regulator's interest in seeing beyond its traditionally conceived jurisdictional limits. Aside from many national disclosure regulations, such as the California Transparency in Supply Chains Act and the three Modern Slavery Acts in the UK and Australia, in the EU this approach is reflected by the Non-Financial Reporting Directive (NFRD) and its successor, the Corporate Sustainability Reporting Directive (CSRD).

Third, regulators can require local actors to govern their transnational production networks in specific ways. Focus is on asking lead firms to forge together a particular kind of value chain, with specific, premeditated governance relationships that connect otherwise disparate actors. In this way, regulators explicitly extend not only their gaze but also their hand over production taking place in other jurisdictions. They acknowledge that the transnational dimension of value chains, if conceptualised as a collective entity fragmented over multiple jurisdictions, is efficiently governable through regulation of lead firms domiciled within their jurisdiction. This approach is reflected in due diligence-type regulations, such as the Dodd Frank Act Section 1504 on conflict minerals and the French *loi de vigilance*, and in the EU for example the Conflict Mineral Regulation (CMR), the Deforestation Regulation and the planned Corporate Sustainability Due Diligence Directive (CSDDD).

Against this backdrop, in the next section we suggest an analytical typology focusing on the GVC governance approaches that the EU's recent sustainability instruments deploy when regulating along value chains.

C. EU Transnational Sustainability Regulation: A Framework and Analysis of Regulation Along Value Chains

In this section, we examine select EU regulatory instruments from the perspective of how they exert influence transnationally *along value chains*. Our deeper analysis focuses on three comparatively established and three novel or proposed EU instruments, comprising both regulations and directives. The selected established

[78] Regulation (EC) No 1907/2006 of the European Parliament and of the Council of 18 December 2006 concerning the Registration, Evaluation, Authorisation and Restriction of Chemicals (REACH) [2006] OJ L396/49.

[79] Of course, the legally operationalised 'extent' of the GVC that needs to be mapped is defined by the instrument in question. Salminen and Rajavuori (n 10).

instruments are the REACH Regulation, the Non-Financial Reporting Directive, and the Conflict Mineral Regulation, while the selected novel or proposed instruments are the CBAM Regulation, the CSRD, and the Commission proposal for a CSDDD. Of these, the CBAM entered a transitional phase on 1 October 2023, with expected full implementation by 1 January 2026, while the CSRD entered into force on 5 January 2023 with first reports, concerning the 2024 financial year, expected in 2025. Regarding the CSDDD, a provisional agreement was reached between the EU co-legislators on 14 December 2023, with the process poised to continue.

These instruments reflect three different approaches to how regulatory instruments can exert influence extraterritorially along value chains by way of regulating lead firms and their governance efforts. That three of the instruments are already in force, two are currently being phased in and the last one constitutes a well-debated legislative proposal provides, we hope, a crude future-oriented dimension to our analysis. Our focus on sustainability-related instruments is motivated by sustainability being one of the areas where the EU's regulatory approach is particularly rife with GVC concepts, up to utilisation of 'value chain' (or a partially narrowed version of 'value chain' called 'chain of activities', as under the Council's position) as the key operative mechanism delineating corporate due diligence duties in the CSDDD. Of the selected instruments, only REACH predates GVC terminology. However, REACH is a central figure for Bradford's notion of the 'Brussels effect' and other similar typologies and, we argue, representative of the classic, unintentional – or at least non-explicit – approach to regulating beyond borders where the regulatory focus falls primarily within the regulating jurisdiction.

There is no dearth of additional instruments that could be included in the analysis. The comparison could be extended exponentially by covering more thematic areas or even simply more sustainability-related regulatory instruments both within and without the EU, but we feel that for the purposes of this initial foray a more qualitative approach provides a good starting point. Despite the sustainability focus, the instruments we analyse also intertwine with other drivers and motives for regulating along value chains, such as guaranteeing internal market cohesion and security of supply. By registering these varying motives, we hope our analysis will have sufficient breadth to act as a springboard or roadmap to further, more expansive and detailed evaluations of regulating along value chains across different EU policy verticals.

The instruments are collected in Table 1 (found as an annex to this chapter), which is organised along the lines of our proposed analytical GVC regulation typology. The vertical axis contains key variables we have previously used for comparing GVC regulation, namely a focus on lead firms, value chains and governance obligations.[80] These include the personal and material scope of regulation, the scope of value chains, the duties implied, and the stated objectives of the regulatory instruments. On the horizontal axis, then, we have framed how the instruments fit into the threefold division derived from the private governance of GVCs discussed in sections II

[80] Salminen and Rajavuori (n 10).

and III.B). Following this, regulation building on market-price focused approaches to governance is referred to as 'boundaries' type regulation; regulation building on standards and monitoring based approaches to governance is referred to as 'mapping' type regulation, and regulation building on capability building-based approaches to governance is referred to as 'acting' focused regulation.

We have included the six chosen EU instruments in Table 1, reflecting two examples of all three hypothesised governance/regulation categories. Under each of the three horizontal categories the first example reflects established regulation, while the second example reflects regulation that is being phased in or planned, thus highlighting current and future tendencies. First, in relation to GVC measures focusing primarily within the territorial limits or 'boundaries' of the EU, REACH represents established approaches and CBAM – which is currently being phased in – reflects newer developments. Second, for measures focusing on 'mapping' value chains extraterritorially, we have selected NFRD as an established example and CSRD – which is currently being phased in – as representative of newer developments. Third, in relation to measures focusing on 'acting' upon value chains extraterritorially, that is, eliciting specific forms of control over them, we have selected CMR as a current and CSDDD as a future example.

Our analysis here is meant to be preliminary and primarily highlights the different techniques of transnational extension of regulation along value chains. To this extent, Table 1 seems to confirm our initial hypothesis that we are dealing with a tangible, analytically approachable phenomenon that has central importance to transnational regulation and is markedly different from earlier approaches theorising the external dimension of EU, or indeed other, extraterritorial regulation.

First, the two instruments we see as representing the 'boundaries' model of GVC regulation, REACH and CBAM, acknowledge the fragmented and globalised nature of production while restricting direct regulatory effects within the territory of the regulator. REACH, for example, follows an earlier EU regulatory paradigm that in principle acknowledges the complex nature of production by focusing on a broad category of complementary actors such as manufacturers, importers and downstream users.[81] At the same time, the aim of this technique is primarily to ensure that some relevant value chain actor is within the reach of the regulator by adding the qualification 'within the Community' to each potentially applicable actor type. If, for example, the manufacturer is located outside the EU, then the focus turns to importers. This technique essentially avoids having to focus on value chain actors outside the EU even if these might, from a value chain functional perspective,[82] be a more reasonable regulatory focus. Given that it precedes the GVC turn by some years, REACH quite naturally focuses on the internal market with little if any reflection of any effect it might have outside the EU. However, the instrument is now seen to have a clear 'Brussels effect' on third countries.[83]

[81] eg, similarly to the EC Product Liability Directive.
[82] For the 'functional' perspective on value chain actors, see, eg, Salminen and Rajavuori (n 10).
[83] Bradford (n 5).

This kind of approach, focused on staying within the regulating jurisdiction both through regulatory mechanisms and stated aims may, however, be partially changing. This is to some extent due to the realisation that it is increasingly impossible to rule out the extraterritorial effects of even locally focused EU regulations. Thus the CBAM, while in its regulatory mechanism focusing on EU-internal actors, states in Article 14 of its Preamble that:

> While the objective of the CBAM is to prevent the risk of carbon leakage, this Regulation would also encourage producers from third countries to use technologies that are more efficient in reducing greenhouse gases so that fewer emissions are generated. For that reason, the CBAM is expected to effectively support the reduction of greenhouse gas emissions in third countries.

While the 'boundaries' type of GVC regulation can thus acknowledge globally fragmented production and can even exert an explicitly stated intended effect beyond EU boundaries, it does not require lead firms to directly tackle production taking place outside the EU in any specific manner.

At the same time such regulation may in part help incentivise EU lead firms to map their global value chains and put in place private governance mechanisms that ensure their seamless functioning. This effect, however, should be kept separate from regulatory instruments explicitly requiring lead firms to map extraterritorial parts of their value chains. A marked difference in operative logic exists between instruments that require lead firms to tackle, for example, the sustainability impact of goods once they enter the EU, as under the CBAM, and instruments that more generally require lead firms to map their value chains and know where sustainability impacts arise outside the EU.

Second, the two instruments we see as representing extraterritorial 'mapping' similarly acknowledge the globally fragmented nature of production. However, the mapping function embedded in the NFRD, for example, utilises a very limited understanding of 'value chain'. Focus is on a traditional concept of groups of companies with business relationships covered 'where relevant and proportionate', even if the Commission guidelines on reporting methodology attempt to steer attention away from the wording of the NFRD towards a more expansive conceptualisation of value chains.[84] The CSRD, then, expands the mapping effort further by requiring undertakings to provide descriptions of impacts connected to their 'value chains', even if the concept of value chain used is no doubt still prone to variation in practice. The scope of the mapping exercise is further tied in with growing due diligence obligations, including foregrounding actions to 'identify and track' lead firms' sustainability impacts.[85]

As opposed to 'boundaries' type instruments, 'mapping' type instruments openly acknowledge the need for information on value chains extending outside the EU to

[84] Communication from the Commission, 'Guidelines on non-financial reporting (methodology for reporting non-financial information)' (2017/C 215/01). More generally on the comparative scope of the legal operationalisation of the 'value chain' in the NFRD, see Salminen and Rajavuori (n 10).

[85] CSRD, Art 19a(2).

provide a fair picture of the reality of transnational production in relation to sustainability along the value chain. This is reflected in the way that the instruments require reporting of impacts not only within the EU or cumulative impacts on the border, but rather pinpointing impacts taking place outside the EU. In relation to the NFRD, focus is on the impacts of undertakings on certain sustainability-related indicators. In relation to the CSRD, this idea is developed further with the so-called 'double-materiality principle', which includes not only the sustainability impacts of value chains but also the impacts of sustainability-related events on the resilience of a lead firm's business model.[86] However, the reporting obligations are light and mostly depend on lead firms' willingness to map their value chains.

We cannot stress strongly enough the importance of the value chain 'mapping' project, especially in comparison to the more traditional 'boundaries' type regulations.[87] Knowing the extent of value chains is a crucial starting point for acting. Here, the impact of the two reporting directives might be highlighted by further comparison to security of supply instruments – the CER Directive and the SMEI and CRM proposals – which establish duties on critical lead firms to map their value chains with a view to understanding alternative modes of operation in case access to suppliers is denied in crises. The dearth of facial masks in the early stages of the Covid-19 pandemic provides a tangible example: better awareness of the facial mask value chain might have helped or speeded up possibilities for acting.[88] Thus the transnational extension and invasiveness of 'mapping' type regulations lies in the possibilities for acting upon the value chain information they provide. This makes 'mapping'-style regulation crucial not only for sustainability but also for other interests, including security.

Third, and finally, the two instruments we see as representing 'acting' – the CMR and the planned CSDDD – build on instruments focused on mapping by requiring actors not only to track their value chains but also to deploy mechanisms for their active governance. Again, legal-operative conceptualisations of a value chain may vary, but by our definition these regulations require not only the mapping and monitoring of risks in value chains but their active mitigation as well. Regulatory focus is on explicitly affecting and steering how a lead firm governs its extraterritorial value chain by requiring the lead firm to put in place specific due diligence mechanisms. Similarly to the term 'value chain', 'due diligence' is a broad concept that can entail

[86] CSRD, Preamble 32.

[87] See also KH Eller, 'The Information Architecture of Corporate Accountability' in H Shamir, S Banerjee and T Barkay (eds), *Modern Slavery and the Governance of Global Value Chains* (Cambridge, Cambridge University Press, 2024).

[88] OECD, 'The Face Mask Global Value Chain in the COVID-19 Outbreak: Evidence and Policy Lessons', available at www.oecd.org/coronavirus/policy-responses/the-face-mask-global-value-chain-in-the-COVID-19-outbreak-evidence-and-policy-lessons-a4df866d/; G Gereffi, P Pananond and T Pedersen, 'Resilience Decoded: The Role of Firms, Global Value Chains, and the State in Covid-19 Medical Supplies' (2022) 64 *California Management Review* 46–70.

anything from mapping the value chain, analysing related risks and acting on them to prevent externalities – as under the Deforestation Regulation – to putting in place specific capability building mechanisms to develop value chain integration as under the CMR. Something of the state of the art in this regard is provided by the French *loi de vigilance*[89] or the proposed CSDDD, which both require integration of value chain stakeholders with the lead firm's governance mechanisms.[90]

Due to their orientation, these instruments have little choice but to acknowledge that their regulatory effect extends outside the regulating jurisdiction. In relation to *sustainability* this is generally justified through the notion of global complicity in sustainability deficits.[91] Other motives may, however, also be explicitly integrated into the regulatory mix. For example, the CMR refers in its preamble to security of supply in relation to minerals:

> (8) In its communication of 4 November 2008 entitled 'The raw materials initiative – meeting our critical needs for growth and jobs in Europe', the Commission recognised that securing reliable and undistorted access to raw materials is an important factor for the Union's competitiveness. The raw materials initiative contained in that Commission communication is an integrated strategy aimed at responding to different challenges related to access to non-energy and non-agriculture raw materials. That initiative recognises and promotes financial as well as supply chain transparency, and the application of corporate social responsibility standards.
>
> (15) Union economic operators have, through public consultations, expressed their interest in the responsible sourcing of minerals and reported on current due diligence schemes designed to pursue their corporate social responsibility objectives, customer requests, or the security of their supplies.

[89] Loi du 27 mars 2017 relative au devoir de vigilance des sociétés mères et des entreprises donneuses d'ordre. See, eg, N Cuzacq, 'Le devoir de vigilance des sociétés mères et des entreprises donneuses d'ordre: Acte II, Scène 1' [2015] *Recueil Dalloz* 1049; E Savourey and S Brabant, 'The French Law on the Duty of Vigilance: Theoretical and Practical Challenges Since its Adoption' (2021) 6 *Business and Human Rights Journal* 141–52.

[90] How far *exactly* such instruments require lead firms to go will naturally depend on developing interpretations of the operative parts of the instruments. Whether the *loi de vigilance* or CSDDD would require companies in specific situations to put in place mechanisms as tangible and advanced as the Bangladesh Accord or open-book accounting is outside the scope of this chapter. For the mechanisms, see Salminen (n 32); Kajüter and Kulmala (n 14). Note that the first-ever complaint based on the German Supply Chain Act (*Lieferkettensorgfaltspflichtengesetz*) revolves around companies in the textile business sourcing from Bangladesh which refused to sign the Bangladesh Accord, see M Krajewski and S Dey, 'Effective Human Rights Due Diligence Ten Years After Rana Plaza?: Assessing the Complaint against IKEA and Amazon under the German Supply Chain Due Diligence Act' (VerfBlog, 5 October 2023), available at https://verfassungsblog.de/effective-human-rights-due-diligence-ten-years-after-rana-plaza/.

[91] For Lepora and Goodin's notion of global 'complicity' in EU sustainability regulation, eg, Scott, 'The Global Reach of EU Law' (n 45). This view can naturally be criticised. Concretely C Omari Lichuma, '(Laws) Made in the "First World": A TWAIL Critique of the Use of Domestic Legislation to Extraterritorially Regulate Global Value Chains' (2021) *81 Zeitschrift für ausländisches öffentliches Recht und Völkerrecht* 497–501; D Bose, 'Decentering Narratives around Business and Human Rights Instruments: An Example of the French Devoir de Vigilance Law' (2023) 8 *Business & Human Rights Law Journal* 18–42. From a more abstract conflict of law perspective, eg, Salminen and Rajavuori (n 28).

Embedded in the justifications of CMR are thus other interests, such as reliable and undistorted access to raw materials outside the EU. Sustainability and security seem effectively intertwined in the regulatory instrument.[92] In the end, the mechanisms for striving towards both goals are the same – the mapping and tighter contractual integration of value chains. This is also highlighted by instruments such as the CER Directive and the SMEI and CRM proposals which, while to some extent resembling the CMR in mechanisms deployed, focus solely on geosecurity.

D. Intensity and Modalities of Transnational Effects of GVC Regulations

This analysis of three types of transnational extension of regulation along value chains is not exhaustive, but it nonetheless points towards increasing contestation of transnational regulatory space along value chains. From the EU's perspective, a shift towards a transnational extension of EU law and the internal market is taking place under the explicit normative banners of sustainability and, increasingly, security interests. However, the EU's ambitions are enmeshed with other national and transnational regulators that have undertaken related initiatives, some in order to pursue substantive policies and others primarily with the aim of avoiding regulatory fragmentation. The latter is visible in EU law as well since the CSDDD seeks, according to its Explanatory Memorandum, to 'avoid fragmentation of due diligence requirements in the single market and create legal certainty for businesses and stakeholders as regards expected behaviour and liability'.[93]

When assessing the relative intensity of transnational effects generated by GVC regulations, the threefold typology proposed here would thus seem to express different degrees and modes of effect that regulations exert on third countries and on third-country companies.

The first type of regulation can already have profound effects outside the regulating jurisdiction. As with the example of the CBAM, it can also entail compilation of data related to production practices and processes outside the regulating jurisdiction when, for example, products enter the regulating jurisdiction. At the same time, it nonetheless fits existing Westphalian ideals of jurisdiction in that any extraterritorial effects are – or at least can be claimed to be – incidental.

The difference to the second and third types of regulation is how explicit both intentions and mechanisms are for extending the regulator's transnational reach. In the case of the second, mapping-style regulation, a regulator is not content with

[92] See, eg, E Cusato, 'Transnational Law and the Politics of Conflict Minerals Regulation: Construing the Extractive Industry as a "Partner" for Peace' (2021) 12 *Transnational Legal Theory* 269–93. Cusato notes that 'by framing the extractive industry as a "partner" for peace, these legal instruments contribute to the legitimizing of its continued operation in post-conflict countries, thereby stabilizing the prevailing global structures of power in natural resource governance'. Moreover, T Riofrancos, 'The Security–Sustainability Nexus: Lithium Onshoring in the Global North' (2022) *Global Environmental Politics* 1–22.

[93] CSDDD (n 64) 3.

knowing, for example, the carbon footprint of a product entering its jurisdiction. Instead, focus might be on knowing in detail where along the value chain this carbon footprint has accrued. The increase in transnational invasiveness is clear.

The second and third types of regulation are distinguished from one another by the level of acting required. While the second type requires lead firms to follow, map and track their value chains, the third type requires lead firms to act on this mapping, putting in place mechanisms that ensure compliance with the regulator's objectives. This may take place, for example, through explicit governance contracts that require lead firms to design and operationalise governance structures which ensure that value chain actors outside the lead firm's home state comply and align with the lead firm's interests, even if these are required by a foreign regulator. Established governance mechanisms such as open-book accounting[94] and the Accord on Fire and Building Safety in Bangladesh[95] provide good examples of how such governance might be structured, including building personal connections between key employees in different value-chain firms. Existing instruments also use explicit capability-building and burden-sharing obligations. The proposed CSDDD, for example, encourages EU lead firms to support third country operators in meeting the effects of the instrument's due diligence requirements.[96]

These three categories delineate the GVC approach on transnational sustainability regulation. In our view, the GVC-driven model that we call *transnational extension of EU law and the internal market along GVCs* enjoys several advantages over prior analytical schemes. The most obvious comparator, Joanne Scott's 'extraterritorial extension', for example, is focused on broader categories of transactions, companies and countries, and at the same time is more limited in its focus on *groups of actors* with a comparatively direct connection to the EU instead of a *network of actors* such as value chains.[97] In this sense, *transnational extension along GVCs* might express more accurately that the extension is not personal or territorial/jurisdictional, but functionally connected to the GVC and hence more emergent and dynamic than before. On the one hand, the GVC approach can be relatively intrusive, as regulation can follow the winding paths of GVCs to the other end of the world and back again. On the other hand, we have shown that transnational extension uses the medium of private governance to gain traction[98] and is hence exposed to the long debates on its inherent fallacies and biases.[99] Finally,

[94] Kajüter and Kulmala (n 14).

[95] Salminen (n 32).

[96] CSDDD (n 64), Preamble 47 and, more concretely, Article 7.

[97] Scott, 'The Global Reach of EU Law' (n 45).

[98] This is yet another parallel to the EU Digital Services Act which, despite its claim to depart from a self-regulatory paradigm, puts due diligence obligations on service providers that generate new forms of private governance, including structures of private enforcement. See I Buri and J van Hoboken, 'The DSA Proposal's Impact on Digital Dominance' in H Richter, M Straub and E Tuchtfeld (eds), *To Break Up or Regulate Big Tech? Avenues to Constrain Private Power in the DSA/DMA Package* (Max Planck Institute for Innovation and Competition Research Paper No 21–25 (2022)) 10.

[99] C Cutler and T Dietz, 'The Politics of Private Transnational Governance by Contract: Introduction and Analytical Framework', in C Cutler and T Dietz (eds), *The Politics of Private Transnational Governance by Contract* (London, Routledge, 2017) 1–36.

transnational extension can be seen to have more nuance in its driving regulatory techniques, which are not necessarily focused on 'ruling out' non-compliant actors but rather using EU lead firms to align global value chains to EU interests through private governance.

IV. EU REGULATION OF GVCS AND THE GLOBAL POLITICAL ECONOMY: 'EXTENSION THROUGH LAW'

As is evident from the discussion in section III, the EU currently deploys a large number of regulations and directives drawing on EU competences to shape the internal market (notably Articles 50(2)(g) and 114 Treaty on the Functioning of the European Union, but which also affect the conduct of third-country producers, traders and regulators. Access to the internal market serves as leverage and a key incentive for compliance.[100] Some EU instruments do so by conditioning the entry of products themselves, as the example of REACH demonstrates. This product-focused regulation which uses the spatial boundaries of the internal market is still prominent in the regulatory toolkit in the EU and beyond.[101] Starting in the 2010s, however, the EU has increasingly started experimenting with regulating more subtly the transnational *modes and processes of production*, acknowledging the complexity and the need to engage with the deeper layers of production. Following this approach, we propose that the transnational extension of EU law and the internal market along GVCs is embedded in this new modality of law, clearly visible in the EU's grasp at more transnational regulatory reach.

This development amounts to a new chapter in the development of EU law – and EU private law in particular. As is widely known, the European project and especially the internal market were brought into existence by way of 'Integration through Law'.[102] Specific legal mechanisms were instrumental in making and sustaining the European polity in light of diverging cultural and political traditions. This implied not only a certain substantive telos of the EU legal architecture, but also a certain modality of EU law that was instituted in the Four Freedoms, the rules and practices of EU competences and the foundational role of the European Court of Justice. For each stage in the genealogy of the unfinished and shifting European project, law offered a 'window of change',[103] innovating both its own legal form and the European polity. While 'Integration through Law' sought to overcome internal fragmentation into national cultural, political and economic units, many of the contemporary EU policies we have covered in this chapter adopt a broader, global lens and are concerned

[100] eg, Bradford (n 5).

[101] eg, US Uyghur Forced Labor Prevention Act, 23 December 2021, Public Law 117–78, 135 Stat. 1525.

[102] M Cappelletti, M Seccombe and JHH Weiler, 'Integration Through Law: Europe and the American Federal Experience. A General Introduction' in M Cappelletti, Mo Seccombe and JHH Weiler (eds), *Integration Through Law* (Berlin, De Gruyter, 1986) 3–70; recently L Azoulai, '"Integration through Law" and Us' (2016) 14 *International Journal of Constitutional Law* 449–63.

[103] N Walker, 'Legal Theory and the European Union: A 25th Anniversary Assay' (2005) 25 *OJLS* 581–601.

with the EU's external relations and even more the internal market's position in a global economy marked by geopolitical tensions.

Against this background, we hold that 'transnational extension' along GVCs can be read as a 'transnational extension through law', forming a new stage in the EU's global market-building project and requiring an attuned legal form of EU law. The legal medium for 'extension' differs from those used for 'integration' purposes. It is too early to attempt a more general conceptualisation, but we can highlight some initial characteristics of this new modality of (EU) law.

First, in terms of regulatory ambitions, 'extension through law' does not pursue a comprehensive polity-building – or even market-building – effort,[104] but uses a rather specific political substratum ('sustainability', 'human rights', 'security of supply') to move from a territorially defined vision of the internal market to a vision of global embeddedness through myriads of production networks.

Second, in terms of key legal instruments, the 'transnational extension through law' is not anchored in the four freedoms of the EU but relies more on what has been characterised as European (Regulatory) Private Law.[105] European Private Law is a layered and heterogenous legal order that serves particular regulatory functions, rather than core values such as individual autonomy as in the national architectures of private law.[106] The GVC turn consolidates this development by placing the logic of global trade above a systematisation of private law, partly to the dismay of traditional private lawyers. 'Transnational extension' utilises to its advantage the *private* mode of law instead of the public: The regulatory mode builds on the privately composed status quo of the governance of existing value chains, which it requires to satisfy additional normative requirements. In a sense, the EU's regulating along value chains can be seen as a more subtle alternative to the Chinese Belt and Road Initiative,[107] using private value-chain governance and its material and technological governance infrastructure to connect the global economy to European regulators. Selecting the channel of private governance allows those concerned to avoid, at least in formal terms, the touchy question of extraterritorial application. The lead firm's domicile serves as the connecting factor to the regulating jurisdiction.

Third, in terms of legitimacy, 'transnational extension' takes a similarly 'depoliticised' perspective on private law and private governance. This does, however, create different repercussions when compared to the earlier 'Integration through Law'. Under the latter, the distributive effects of European private law and the competing visions surrounding the field were insufficiently accounted for in the construction

[104] See M Bartl, 'Internal Market Rationality, Private Law and the Direction of the Union: Resuscitating the Market as the Object of the Political' (2015) 21 *European Law Journal* 572–98.

[105] G Comparato, 'What is European Regulatory Private Law? Stakes and Perspectives' (2018) *Revue Internationale de Droit Économique* 123–35.

[106] HW Micklitz, 'The Visible Hand of European Regulatory Private Law – The Transformation of European Private Law from Autonomy to Functionalism in Competition and Regulation' (2009) *Yearbook of European Law* 28, 3–59.

[107] J Chaisse and Jędrzej Górski (eds), *The Belt and Road Initiative: Law, Economics, and Politics* (Leiden, Brill, 2018).

of the EU polity.[108] In the new paradigm, the unacknowledged distributive effects are those of the 'green transition' which materialise outside of the EU, and predominantly in the Global South. The legitimacy of 'transnational extension' and the confident European political narrative around it are not only tempered by established criticisms of the accountability deficit and power asymmetries in private governance.[109] The risk also arises of 'sustainability' and 'security of supply' being unilaterally used to reshuffle the EU's role in select, critical value chains in new ways. Indeed, the GVC approach is grounded in development studies, focusing on why particular forms of global production benefit some while disadvantaging others.[110] Even as regulation along GVCs might appear as a surgical and moderate intervention, drawing on the seemingly neat and often invisible means of private governance, the regulatory interventions discussed in this chapter have robust effects on local producers, smallholders and communities beyond the EU. However, the centrality of private governance under 'transnational extension' has prevented the depth of conflicting interests to be fully elucidated. The way states are 'seeing'[111] the transnational through the lens of the 'green transition' is limited and open to capture and simplistic and often colonial discourses of development. For example, the EU's sustainability agenda, which enjoys a broad coalition of support from EU-internal labour, non-governmental organisation and corporate interests, has faced push-back from the Global South[112] and its diverse political, economic and legal effects on developing economies are rarely accounted for. One of these remote effects is to nourish a compliance industry building on a specific type of Western-modelled 'bureaucratic'[113] legality that will often prioritise audits and conformity assessment over capability building.

In other words, conflicting political and economic agendas in an era of 'geoeconomics'[114] need to be foregrounded in the debate. The creeping proliferation of regulation along value chains may lead us very soon to a veritable jungle of crisscrossing transnationally extended regulations piggybacking along the globally interconnected network of value chains.[115] In the absence of a plausible guiding

[108] Study Group on Social Justice in European Private Law, 'Social Justice in European Contract Law' (2004) 10 *European Law Journal* 653–74.

[109] Cutler and Dietz (n 99); T Sagy, 'What's So Private about Private Ordering?' (2011) 45 *Law & Society Review* 923–954.

[110] Gereffi (n 6); Milberg and Winkler (n 6).

[111] F Johns, 'From Planning to Prototypes: New Ways of Seeing Like a State' (2019) 82 *MLR* 833–863.

[112] Lichuma (n 91).

[113] On such forms of legality in modern public administration, C Vismann, *Files. Law and Media Technology* (Stanford, Stanford University Press, 2008); G Frug, 'The Ideology of Bureaucracy in American Law' (1984) 97 *Harvard Law Review* 1276–1388.

[114] M Babic, A Dixon and I Lio, 'Geoeconomics in a Changing Global Order' in M Babic, A Dixon, I Liu (eds), *The Political Economy of Geoeconomics: Europe in a Changing World* (London, Palgrave Macmillan, 2022) 1–27.

[115] To an extent this is already so. One example is provided by private regulation of factory safety in Bangladesh, where, depending on the choices of lead firms, individual factories would fall under the Accord on Fire and Building Safety in Bangladesh, the Alliance for Bangladesh Worker Safety, or both, see Salminen (n 32).

role from the World Trade Organisation, decentral co-ordination between competing claims, agendas and regulatory scopes will be necessary as GVCs emerge as the transnational locus for heated controversies around the future geoeconomic order.[116] The urgency of the ecological crisis has covered up some of the frictions in the EU's sustainability agenda, especially in its global reach. Like any other regulatory modality or strategy, regulating along GVCs has a range of impacts that materialise differently in different organisational and geographical parts of the value chain. The way these impacts are conceptualised and narrated matters for both the legitimacy and the outcomes of transnational extension. Historically, transnational space has been framed as depoliticised by means of private international law in the idea that private ordering would be the best infrastructure for international commerce.[117]

This is the fourth and final element by which we want to characterise the mode of legality of 'transnational extension'. Developing techniques of managing pluralism and incompatible visions of the 'green transition' between different regulators, communities and divergent local contexts of implementation will be a central point for the long-term viability of EU policies. In other words, rather than counting on its sheer global market power behind the 'Brussels effect', the EU should explore constructive ways to make its extensive experience in managing legal, political and cultural pluralism in its *internal* operation and market-building[118] available for 'transnational extension'. The EU law of 'transnational extension' needs to be equipped to find its place in a contested transnational regulatory space while remaining sensitive – in its diverse contexts of implementation along GVCs – to the local differences, ecologies and world-visions it encounters. A conflicts-of-law approach, broadly understood, appears as a promising legal form to *repoliticise* GVC regulations and mediate their diverse contexts.[119]

V. CONCLUSIONS: GVCS IN AN INCREASINGLY CONTESTED TRANSNATIONAL REGULATORY SPACE

The world economy operates on GVCs, which channel people, commodities, ideas and capital globally. At their heart, GVCs are utilised by private actors to control and govern global production for profit. But GVCs also channel regulation. This transnational regulatory space is increasingly relied on by national authorities that attempt to regulate the drivers, processes and outcomes of global production. A range of

[116] Roberts, Moraes and Ferguson (n 4); A Orford, 'Regional Orders, Geopolitics, and the Future of International Law' (2021) 74 *Current Legal Problems* 149–94.

[117] Bomhoff, Brandão de Oliveira and Biziková (n 22); Paul (n 22), as a reaction to the increased regulation of *national* markets following industrialisation, *cf* Atiyah (n 25).

[118] K Knop, R Michaels and A Riles, 'From Multiculturalism to Technique: Feminism, Culture, and the Conflict of Laws Style' (2012) 64 *Stanford Law Review* 589–656.

[119] C Joerges, PF Kjaer and T Ralli, 'A New Type of Conflicts Law as Constitutional Form in the Postnational Constellation' (2011) 2 *Transnational Legal Theory* 153–65.

novel regulatory instruments, spanning from sustainability to security, build on GVCs and craft increasingly intricate responses to their operation. The key lynchpin of GVCs – governance – is used to extend the regulator's reach along GVCs, employing lead firms and their governance efforts as a local proxy instead of trying to directly regulate the realities of extraterritorial economic activity.

Since the 2010s sustainability has been a key domain for increasing regulation along GVCs. While interest is growing in transnational sustainability laws in general and due diligence laws in particular, the transnational 'effectivity mechanisms' these instruments use have not been approached in analytical, integrated fashion. In this chapter, we have analysed the EU's sustainability regulation instruments, suggesting that the key to understanding the transnational reach of regulating along value chains consists in looking at the governance interventions undertaken by individual regulations.

In particular, following the private governance analytic of GVC theory and related disciplines, we have proposed an analytical scheme of regulating along GVCs. First, regulation can explicitly stop at jurisdictional boundaries, focusing within the traditional bounds of jurisdiction. Such regulation can nonetheless have a more or less intended effect outside the regulating jurisdiction. Second, regulation can prompt lead firms to start mapping and tracking their value chains outside the regulating jurisdiction. Here, regulators would explicitly require actors to extend their gaze along value chains instead of merely stopping at the border. Third, regulation can require lead firms to put in place specific governance mechanisms for not only mapping but also affecting how production takes place outside the regulating jurisdiction. Here, regulators explicitly require actors to act along their value chains.

While the first type fits in with current Westphalian models of jurisdiction, the second and third types move beyond by explicitly extending the regulator's reach transnationally. Even if this transnational extension is limited to follow select value chains, the increased invasiveness of such regulation may lead to growing contestation of transnational space, on the one hand between actors such as the USA, the EU and China as they grapple for control over transnational production, and, on the other hand, between these actors and the Global South jurisdictions in which production entities are often embedded. More research, particularly on different drivers and objectives of transnational extension, is needed to better understand this new reality of regulating along value chains and its theoretical and practical implications for global law.

Table 1 Typology of Transnational Effectivity Mechanisms in European Value Chain Regulations

	REACH (2006)	**CBAM (2023)**	**NFRD (2014)**	**CSRD (2023)**	**CMR (2017)**	**CSDDD Proposal**
Typology	**BOUNDARIES (MARKET ENTRY CONDITIONS THAT INFLUENCE VALUE CHAIN INDIRECTLY)**		**MAPPING (DISCLOSURE OBLIGATIONS THAT REQUIRE LEAD FIRMS TO MAP IMPACTS IN EXTRATERRITORIAL PARTS OF VALUE CHAINS)**		**ACTING (DUE DILIGENCE OBLIGATIONS THAT REQUIRE LEAD FIRMS TO ACT ON IMPACTS IN EXTRATERRITORIAL PARTS OF VALUE CHAIN)**	
Existing/ Future	**Existing**	**Future**	**Existing**	**Future**	**Existing**	**Future**
Type/Sector	Use and Import / Chemical safety	Import / Carbon Leakage	Reporting / Sustainability	Reporting / Sustainability	Due Diligence / Conflict Minerals	Due Diligence / Sustainability
Material Scope	Chemical substances.	Goods in certain sectors (cement, iron and steel, aluminium, fertilisers and electricity).	Environmental, social and employee matter, human rights, bribery and corruption.	Environmental, social and human rights and governance.	Conflict minerals (tin, tantalum, tungsten, gold).	Human rights, environmental and governance impacts; climate change.
Personal Scope	Manufacturers, importers and downstream users of chemical substances within EU. Obligations vary according to role in supply chain and substance (eg Art 37).	Declarants of goods.	Large public-interest companies with at least 500 employees.	Large companies; SMEs (with lighter obligations); third country companies with over 150 M€ EU turnover or an EU subsidiary.	Union importers of tin, tantalum, tungsten and gold originating from conflict-affected and high-risk areas whose imports exceed certain volume thresholds.	EU companies above certain thresholds (eg over 500 employees and EUR 150 million global turnover, lower thresholds for certain sectors); non-EU companies with EU-related turnover threshold.
Stated Primary Aim	Protection of human health and the environment, promotion of alternative methods for assessment of substance hazards, free circulation of substances on internal market, enhancing competitiveness and innovation.	Addressing greenhouse gas emissions embedded in goods in order to prevent the risk of carbon leakage.	Enhancing consistency and comparability of non-financial information relating to eg human rights, environment, and bribery; disclosure.	Ensuring adequate and comparable public information about corporate sustainability risks and impacts.	Curbing trade in conflict minerals.	Ensuring sustainability in global value chains stemming from the EU.

(continued)

Table 1 *(Continued)*

	REACH (2006)	CBAM (2023)	NFRD (2014)	CSRD (2023)	CMR (2017)	CSDDD Proposal
Typology	BOUNDARIES (MARKET ENTRY CONDITIONS THAT INFLUENCE VALUE CHAIN INDIRECTLY)		MAPPING (DISCLOSURE OBLIGATIONS THAT REQUIRE LEAD FIRMS TO MAP IMPACTS IN EXTRATERRITORIAL PARTS OF VALUE CHAINS)		ACTING (DUE DILIGENCE OBLIGATIONS THAT REQUIRE LEAD FIRMS TO ACT ON IMPACTS IN EXTRATERRITORIAL PARTS OF VALUE CHAIN)	
Existing/ Future	**Existing**	**Future**	**Existing**	**Future**	**Existing**	**Future**
Other Stated Aims	Sustainability and internal market cohesion.	Encouraging use of more emissions-efficient technologies by third-country producers.	Sustainability.	Intertwining of sustainability and effects on business of sustainability risks – thus, broadly understood, also a form of security of supply.	Security of supply.	Internal market cohesion.
Transnational Effectivity Mechanism	Import restrictions.	Import restrictions.	Mapping of value chains.	Mapping and tracking of value chains.	Mapping and governing value chains (eg through contractual partnerships).	Mapping and governing value chains (eg through contractual collaboration); liability for inadequate governance.
Value Chain Definition	Focus on all manufacturers and/or importers and/or downstream users in a supply chain (Art 3.17). However, *de facto* focus more expansive in practice as it covers all instances of substances, no matter what actor they originate from.	Expansive: Focus on emissions embedded directly in goods listed in Annex I. Also focus on developing methods of calculating embedded emissions based on environmental footprint, thus with a view to expanding scope to indirect emissions and other categories of goods.	Company's operations and, where relevant and proportionate, its business relationships.	Company's value chain, including its own operations, its products and services, its business relationships and its supply chain.	Covers both upstream and downstream supply chain.	Debate over scope; European Commission proposes classical 'value chain' covering production, use and end of life. European Council proposes more limited 'chain of activities', leaving out the use phase.

(continued)

Table 1 *(Continued)*

	REACH (2006)	CBAM (2023)	NFRD (2014)	CSRD (2023)	CMR (2017)	CSDDD Proposal
Typology	BOUNDARIES (MARKET ENTRY CONDITIONS THAT INFLUENCE VALUE CHAIN INDIRECTLY)		MAPPING (DISCLOSURE OBLIGATIONS THAT REQUIRE LEAD FIRMS TO MAP IMPACTS IN EXTRATERRITORIAL PARTS OF VALUE CHAINS)		ACTING (DUE DILIGENCE OBLIGATIONS THAT REQUIRE LEAD FIRMS TO ACT ON IMPACTS IN EXTRATERRITORIAL PARTS OF VALUE CHAIN)	
Existing/ Future	Existing	Future	Existing	Future	Existing	Future
Duty	Duty to ensure that substances manufactured, placed on the market or used do not adversely affect human health or the environment. General obligation to register substances, carry out safety assessments, and communicate information up and down the supply chain.	CBAM declaration; calculation of embedded emissions; verification; puchase of CBAM certificates.	Annual non-financial statement on human rights impacts and due diligence policies (comply-or-explain).	Annual report with information necessary to understand undertaking's sustainability impact and information necessary to understand sustainability effects on the undertaking's business.	Due diligence obligations including internal and external risk management systems, auditing and disclosure.	Duty to undertake due diligence procedure, with risk of liability. Different kinds of due diligence described for direct and indirect relations.
Due Diligence/ Risk Assessment	Risk management responsibility (precautionary principle, reasonably foreseeable conditions) on manufacturers, importers and downstream users.	Calculation and verification of embedded emissions.	Wide-ranging but light-touch reporting on sustainability.	Wide-ranging sustainability disclosures, including description of 'due diligence processes implemented with regard to sustainability matters'.	Extensive and precise due diligence obligations, including contract-based measures with suppliers.	Eg risk prevention action plans with stakeholder involvement, contractual assurances and cascading, investments in management or production processes and infrastructures, targeted and proportionate support, collaboration with other entities.

Index

www.ingramcontent.com/pod-product-compliance
Ingram Content Group UK Ltd.
Pitfield, Milton Keynes, MK11 3LW, UK
UKHW020230290926
15470UKWH00002B/456

9 781509 962921